Political Economy and International Economics

Political Economy and International Economics

Jagdish Bhagwati

edited by Douglas A. Irwin

The MIT Press
Cambridge, Massachusetts
London, England

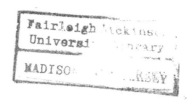
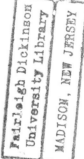
First MIT Press paperback edition, 1996

©1991 Massachusetts Institute of Technology

This book was set in Palatino by Asco Trade Typesetting, Ltd., Hong Kong
and printed and bound in the United States of America.

Library of Congress Cataloging-in-Publication Data

Bhagwati, Jagdish N., 1934–
  Political economy and international economics / Jagdish Bhagwati;
  edited by Douglas A. Irwin.
     p.   cm.
  Includes bibliographical references and index.
  ISBN 0-262-02322-9 (HB), 0-262-52218-7 (PB)
  1. Protectionism. 2. Free trade. 3. International trade.
4. Developing countries—Dependency on foreign countries.
I. Irwin, Douglas A., 1962–   . II. Title.
HF1713.B466   1991
337—dc20   90-13543
                                                 CIP

For Manmohan Singh, friend and kindred spirit

Contents

Editor's Preface

This is the fifth volume of Jagdish Bhagwati's collected writings on economics to be published by The MIT Press. The first two volumes, edited by Robert C. Feenstra and entitled *Essays in International Economic Theory*, appeared in 1983. They consist mainly of Bhagwati's theoretical work on international trade, commercial policy, factor mobility, and political economy. The second two volumes, edited by Gene M. Grossman and entitled *Essays in Development Economics*, appeared in 1985. The selections in these volumes concentrate on Bhagwati's theoretical and policy contributions to the economics of development, including foreign aid, international migration, and trade and development strategies.

The present collection (all of the essays were written after 1984) is somewhat more diverse than previous ones. New essays on theoretical topics featured in prior volumes appear in this one as well. Bhagwati's more recent interests, however, have been in the theory and political economy of economics and policy. (Indeed, he founded the new journal *Economics and Politics* to encourage further theoretical and empirical work on economic policy in the broader analytical framework provided by the theory of political economy.) Many of the papers herein touch on this relatively new but growing area of economic research. As a consequence of the mix of new and old and of the various approaches to economics taken in this book, the reader is treated both to Bhagwati's skill as an economic theorist, where we find the rigor and elegance that are his trademarks, and to his good sense as an analyst of the political economy of policy, where we find his penetrating insight delivered with clarity and grace.

I need to say little about Bhagwati's standing as an economic theorist. His seminal contributions to the theory of international trade, commercial policy, and economic development are well known. But Bhagwati has proved to be one of those rare economists who has moved easily from eminence as a theorist to prominence as a thoughtful and insightful observer dealing with broader questions of international economic policy. I would venture to say that his background as an original and penetrating theorist accounts in part for the soundness of his contributions to political economy. His success in this transition has, of course, been aided by his inimitable wit and lucid style, a sparkling combination that makes him a joy to read. Indeed, this combination of broad perspective and witty style accounts for the success of his book *Protectionism* (The MIT Press, 1988).

This volume has especially benefited from Bhagwati's eminence as an economist, which has marked him for numerous prestigious awards and distinguished lectures. These addresses, many of which have not been widely circulated, form the basis for a number of essays in this collection. As in *Protectionism* they provide an opportunity for Bhagwati to reveal his cogent argumentation, his enlightening perspective, and, of course, his mischievous wit. For those who have not had the pleasure of his company, the informal style of these lectures gives one a sense of the delight he takes in finding irony and sometimes even humor in ideas, history, and the English language.

Part I of this collection consists of essays on commercial policy where Bhagwati contends with new theories and policy developments in international trade. Of particular importance is the first chapter, which assesses and critiques these new developments and discusses their implications for the policy of free trade. Part II includes several contributions that build on his pioneering theoretical analysis of directly unproductive profit-seeking activities, such as the interaction between foreign investment and DUP activities. Also included is his study of a new instrument of commercial policy that has appeared on the scene—voluntary import expansions (VIEs). Part III contains further developments in another area that Bhagwati initiated, the theory of immiserizing growth.

Part IV discusses the economic and political aspects of international investment and migration. In this area Bhagwati shifted the focus of debate over factor mobility from the national gains and losses to the rights and obligations of nations and migrants (also see his *Income Taxation and International Mobility*, edited with J. D. Wilson, The MIT Press, 1989). Part V examines international trade in services, particularly in relation to the developing countries to which he applies his notion of splintering and disembodiment of services. Part VI looks at various problems facing developing countries, from the issue of poverty to the choices of trade policy. Of particular note is his Ernest Sturc Memorial Lecture on developing countries and the world economy.

Douglas A. Irwin

Author's Preface

This is the fifth volume of my collected works published by The MIT Press. The first two were on the theory of international trade and were edited by Robert Feenstra, who had been a student of mine at MIT and is now professor of economics at the University of California, Davis. The next two were on the theory and policy of development, copublished with Basil Blackwell, Oxford, and edited by Gene Grossman, another former MIT student and now professor of economics at Princeton University. Both Feenstra and Grossman have established themselves as among the most creative international economists of their generation, and they belong to a distinguished group of students, which includes Richard Brecher and Paul Krugman, whom I taught in Cambridge from 1968 before moving to Columbia in 1980.

Douglas Irwin, the editor of the present selection, belongs to the promising group of students whom I have taught at Columbia, among them Elias Dinopoulos and Kar-yiu Wong. His talents lie in a splendid sense of economic doctrine and in a deep interest in intellectual and economic history, as is evident from his fascinating work on Peel's conversion to the repeal of the Corn Laws, which brought free trade to England and indeed to the world for the first time since Adam Smith, and from his sensitive and scholarly introduction to a collection of Jacob Viner's essays (Princeton University Press, 1991).

These gifts make Irwin an apt editor for the present volume. For, here, there are many essays that synthesize, extend, and assess developments in economic theory and policy, not merely through analytical scrutiny but also by putting them firmly into historical and scholarly perspective. In addition, starting principally in the 1980s, there are essays—on political economy largely but not exclusively in relationship to international economics—that represent a major turning point in my intellectual efforts.

Within the theory of international trade, to which I have made the bulk of my theoretical contributions over the last thirty years, there have been two major developments in the last decade. Both are seminal and productive of new ferment.

One has been the extensive exploration of the effects of different market structures, other than perfect competition, resulting largely from the developments in the theory of industrial organization. The relevance of market structure to both the positive and normative doctrines of international economics is not altogether new of course. As the authors of the modern developments often note with exaggerated generosity, my 1965 paper on the equivalence of tariffs and quotas had explored theoretically the effects of monopoly in undermining such equivalence, which is traditionally asserted in competitive models. But the recent developments have filled out, with great insight and elegance, the large space between monopoly and perfect competition. These contributions constitute the "new" theory of international trade, to use Krugman's favorite description of these explorations of trade issues in the imperfectly competitive product-markets literature of recent years. (I might add, without detracting from the merits of these new contributions, that the exclusive recent focus on imperfect competition in product markets has led to unfortunate amnesia about the prevalence of imperfect competition in factor markets—a set of phenomena that may be of greater relevance in the developing countries and, if Lawrence Summers' empirical research is to be accepted, in the United States as well. The theoretical literature on commercial policy in the 1960s and 1970s, in which I participated actively with Harry Johnson, T. N. Srinivasan, and many others, extended to penetrating analysis of several such imperfections: sector-specific sticky wages, generalized sticky wages, wage differentials, factor immobility, monoposony, etc. If one believes that imperfect markets are worth introducing into trade theory, then it is somewhat odd to bring them into product markets and to drop from view the massive achievements in analyzing imperfect competition in factor markets.)

The other major development in the theory of international economics has come from the altogether different direction of political economy.* This

---

* While the imperfect-competition-in-product-markets developments are associated with the work of Avinash Dixit, Paul Krugman, Elhanan Helpman, Kelvin Lancaster, Gene Grossman, James Brander, and Barbara Spencer, to name many of the most visible economists in this school, the developments in the political-economy-theoretic analysis of international economics have come from an equally large group of theorists of repute: Robert Baldwin, Robert Feenstra, Anne Krueger, Ronald Findlay, T. N. Srinivasan, Steve Magee, Stanislaw Wellisz, Wolfgang Mayer, Raymond Riezman, Robert Staiger, Dani Rodrik, Arye Hillman, and John Riley, again to name many of the main writers in recent years.

is the area where my own interests have been in the 1980s, and many of the theoretical papers in this volume reflect this shift of interest in my research. As it happens, this interest has long been present in my thinking and teaching, though it has come to preoccupy my research interests only in the last decade.

Thus, in analyzing the Indian devaluation of 1966, as part of the major Bhagwati-Krueger-directed NBER project in the late 1960s on exchange control and liberalization in developing countries, I extensively explored the role of different groups within the Indian economy and polity in assessing the prospects of the devaluation's success. I must confess that my interest had been stimulated in these matters when, on being taken in to see Prime Minister Indira Gandhi just prior to the decision to devalue so as to convince her of the merits of the move, I had been asked by her precisely such questions, for which my formal economics training had not prepared me at all.

Again, I was interested, very early on, in explaining why certain industries were protected and others were not—a typical problem nowadays in the political-economy theory of protection. I came up with the idea that, the Kennedy Round having just been completed and having been based on across-the-board tariff cuts from which exemptions were granted on case-by-case lobbying, one had the near-equivalent of a unique "laboratory experiment" to examine the characteristics of the industries that had gotten these exemptions and then infer what types of industries got protection in the sense that they were spared the tariff liberalization. This problem was handed over to John Cheh, my MIT student, to analyze for his dissertation, and the results were published in the *Journal of International Economics* (1974) in a now-classic article. Short-run labor adjustment costs minimization was seen in the analysis to be the criterion that secured protection. This could then lead to a "supply-of-protection" inference—that the government's objective was to minimize such adjustment costs. Equally, or alternatively, one could make the "demand-for-protection" inference that labor adjustment costs enabled industries to press for protection more effectively by mobilizing labor and other groups. The problem therefore could be considered as one of inferring a "non-economic" objective instead of the pure goods-utilitarianism of conventional economic specifications of the objective function (philosophers are unaware that this idea has long been familiar to us trade theorists who have dealt with it formally in the theory of noneconomic objectives in the 1960s in the work of Corden, Johnson, Bhagwati, Srinivasan, and many others) *or* as one in the theory of political economy, where the ability of industries with labor adjustment problems to press for protection effectively is being inferred instead.

My own interest in political economy was further stimulated by the empirical-cum-analytical studies of the developing countries in the Bhagwati-Krueger project, where the pursuit of DUP (directly unproductive profit-seeking) activities as a major source of earning income became obvious to me. Evasion of tariffs and quotas, lobbying for industrial licenses handed out by the government and for rents on import entitlements, seemed to be so pervasive and of such great importance that its impact on resource utilization could not be dismissed as being of the second order of smalls. I began therefore with the analysis of tariff evasion or smuggling; Anne Krueger went ahead with the analysis of rent-seeking; Srinivasan and I extended her analysis to revenue-seeking; and the analysis took off in several directions, culminating in the series of theoretical papers on DUP activities and the theory of political economy more generally (as well as in areas as diverse as explaining tariff protection and explaining foreign investment) which are reprinted in Part II of this volume.

Evidently, in my view, this is an area of exceptional importance and is a key part of the broadening of economics to include also sociology, psychology, and philosophy that we have been witnessing in recent years. Economics and politics are natural bedfellows: How can we possibly explain what happens unless we bring in the political equations into our modeling at the same time? As the field has grown now, in the hands of international economists and other economists in different traditions, I have started the journal *Economics and Politics*, now in its second volume, published by Basil Blackwell, which provides an outlet for analytically strong work in this burgeoning field and should help shape its progress.

I fully expect the 1990s to continue being preoccupied with the theory of political economy, both in international economics and in economics generally, and ever more of my students at Columbia to turn to such questions for analysis. Certainly, volume 6 of my essays promises already to be in that mold!

I would be remiss if, in closing this preface, I did not mention my two student secretaries, James Benedict and Janet Roitman, who cheerfully assisted me in the task of putting these essays together. And I must recall with pleasure and gratitude the hospitality I enjoyed at many of the distinguished universities, among them the University of Lancaster in England and The Johns Hopkins School for Advanced International Studies, where the endowed Lectures reprinted here (in Chapters 17 and 23) were delivered.

Jagdish Bhagwati

I

**Commercial Policy:
Old and New**

1   Is Free Trade Passé After All?

1.1   Introduction

Let me express first my great pleasure at being awarded the Bernhard Harms Prize. In the field of international economics, it is now recognized as the profession's most notable award. I feel honored to join today the distinguished economists who have preceded me as recipients of this prestigious prize.

It would be logical for me to celebrate this occasion by addressing the great issue that led Adam Smith to give simultaneous birth to both economics and international economics. This is the issue of free trade, or what we now call the theory of commercial policy. This is undoubtedly the area to which I have given my reflection and research in the last three decades: here lie certainly my own comparative advantage and indeed the reason for today's ceremonial occasion.

But the subject deserves scrutiny also because the question of free trade has now returned to center stage. This is not simply because, since the 1970s, protectionist *demands* have increased—as certainly the beleagured executives and administrations of the European Community and the United States know. It is also because the resistance to the *supply* of protection by these executives may have been imperiled by careless and incomplete assessments of recent developments in the theory of commercial policy itself.

These developments, as I shall argue presently, are by no means one-sided in strengthening the analytical case for departures from free trade. One set of developments, addressed to the incorporation of imperfect competition systematically into the theory of international trade, does indeed augment the conventional case for such departures by focusing on market imperfections and failure. However, another set of developments, addressed to the more fundamental task of incorporating into the theory "political" processes such as rent-seeking and other unproductive (what I call directly unproductive profit-seeking, i.e., DUP) activities, generally weakens the case for such departures.

But the former set of developments has achieved greater currency recently. This is only partly because they are more conventional in scope and hence more appealing to the economist's taste. In replacing the perfectly competitive by the imperfectly competitive assumption in formal modeling, utilizing the new theoretical tools from the theory of industrial organization, they amount to fitting an old bicycle with new wheels, whereas the other, pro-free-trade set of developments, belonging to the new and unconventional field of political economy, constitutes a greater intellectual challenge: it amounts to taking the old bicycle down a different road.

But a key explanation also must be found in the fact that interests require the legitimacy that ideology provides. Protectionist forces, as they gathered strength in the 1970s, were looking precisely for the *coup de grâce* to free trade that a "new" and "more appropriate" theory of trade would provide. The trade-theoretic analysis incorporating imperfect competition in product markets seemed to provide exactly that since, as should be immediately obvious, such models of imperfect competition in repeated applications demonstrated the possibility of improving welfare by departing from free trade. And, if this fact itself could somehow be construed as a departure from what the theory of commercial policy taught, and hence as a "new" and radical development that made the "old" theory obsolete, the result could be electrifying. As it happens, reality has turned out to be not too far from this outlandish scenario.

It should suffice, for my purposes, to quote the latest, apparently the most meticulous and carefully crafted statement on this subject by Paul Krugman, my distinguished student at MIT who succeeded me in my chair there, and a leading proponent of these important developments. Writing in the new *Journal of Economic Perspectives* of the American Economic Association, where research findings are disseminated to the wider community of economists and policymakers, Krugman (1987, pp. 131–132) has this to say: "... the case for free trade is currently more in doubt than at any time since the 1817 publication of Ricardo's *Principles of Political Economy* ... In the last ten years the traditional constant returns, perfect competition models of international trade have been supplemented and to some extent supplanted by a new breed of models that emphasizes increasing returns and imperfect competition. These new models ... open the possibility that government intervention in trade via import restrictions, export subsidies, and so on may under some circumstances be in the national interest after all ... free trade is not passé, but it is an idea that has irretrievably lost its innocence. Its status has shifted from optimum to reasonable rule of thumb. There is still a case for free trade as a good policy, and as a useful target in the world of politics, but it can never again be asserted as the policy that economic theory tells us is always right."

This is surely puzzling. Not merely does the postwar theory of commercial policy, which I and others helped to shape during the 1960s and 1970s, show plainly that "import restrictions, export subsides, and so on, may under certain circumstances be in the national interest." It shows also, at great length, that one cannot assert that free trade is "the policy that economic theory tells us is always right": this is surely the core contribution of the postwar theory of distortions and welfare.[1] Moreover, the postwar theory of commercial policy goes beyond both these propositions to alert the analyst and the policymaker that, even when departures from free trade are justifiable, it is necessary to distinguish between policy interventions that are merely beneficial and those that are maximally useful: a prescription more often ignored than respected by some of the recent proponents of the theory of imperfect competition in international trade. For the sophisticated economist, who seeks to influence his nation's trade policy, some of the key questions to answer after these theoretical developments have been (i) what, in *theory*, is the nature of the appropriate intervention when departures from free trade (and domestic nonintervention) are justifiable, and (2) as a matter of *empirical judgment*, does your country's reality fits any of the numerous theoretically possible cases where such appropriate intervention is desirable?

Let me simply stress therefore that those who see the developments based on imperfect competition as "radical" and "new" in their implications for the scientific corpus of the theory of commercial policy are either unfamiliar with that theory or forgetful of its central tenets. Indeed, the recent models of imperfect competition are analytically seen best as augmenting the number of cases where the invisible hand falters and where therefore a benign government (in our conventional theory of economic policy where the government is simply and totally the puppet of the economist, speaking with his voice and acting to his command) can act to national advantage, through appropriate (domestic or trade) policy interventions. These added cases are perfectly compatible with, and indeed fit neatly and without surprise or paradox into, the impressive corpus of theoretical principles and framework that emerged as the theory of commercial policy during the postwar period.

Given then the misassessments and misconceptions that facilitate the protectionist capture of the theoretical developments based on imperfect competition,[2] and the comparative neglect of the important countervailing contributions made by the theoretical developments based on political economy, there is no task more compelling than to take a careful scholarly look at where we should now properly stand on the issue of free trade. This I propose to do now.

I shall consider the classical theory, the postwar contributions and the recent developments, in turn. At the outset, however, permit me to make an important, indeed a critical, distinction between free trade for one (section 1.2) and free trade for all (section 1.3), i.e., between *unilateral* and *universal* free trade, drawing essentially on the theory prior to the postwar period.

1.2   Free Trade for One

The distinction between unilateral and universal free trade is critical whether one is thinking of trade policy simply from the viewpoint of a single country's *national advantage* or whether one is considering the rather different question as to the nature of a *trade regime* for nations in the world economy. Thus, in the former case, one can ask: Should a country embrace free trade even if others do not? In the latter case, however, one may consider whether a regime, such as that provided by GATT, should involve free trade by all.

The question of regimes is a recent one. The question of a suitable trade policy for national advantage, by contrast, is a time-honored one since the days of Adam Smith. And the answer to the latter has, for nearly two centuries, been in favor of unilateral free trade. It is important to understand exactly why.

The precept of unilateral free trade should be seen as a blend of theory and empirical judgment about the relevance of that theory and the irrelevance of the exceptions to the theory's conclusions.

The Theory

Central to the theory is the notion that, given external trading opportunities, specialization and ensuing exchange would ensure gains from trade among nations engaged in voluntary transactions. It is easy enough to see this today. But when the early economists propagated this notion, it was in contradiction to the dominant doctrine of mercantilism.

The new science of economics focused on trade as an opportunity to specialize in production, undertake exchange of what one produced efficiently for what others produced efficiently, and wind up in consequence with more rather than less. A policy of free trade would guide the nation to an efficient utilization of this trade opportunity. In essence, as postwar theorists of international trade would clarify, free trade would maximize returns by efficiently utilizing two alternative ways of securing any good: (1) through specialized production of other goods then exchanged in trade for the goods desired, and (2) through domestic production of the desired goods oneself. Free trade would ensure that these two alternative techniques, trade and domestic production, were used efficiently, i.e., in such a mix as to produce equal returns at the margin.[3] Two critical assumptions underlie this neat conclusion—and the classical economists were cognizant of them in their own way.

First, free trade guided one to the efficient outcome only if the price mechanism worked well. Prices had to reflect true social costs. Thus, it was understood, particularly after the writings of List, that infant-industry protection could be justified. In modern language, if there were future returns that could not be captured by the infant industry but would dissipate to others in the country, this market failure justified protection.

Equally, if the country's trade in a sector was large enough to confer on it the ability to affect its prices, then John Stuart Mill warned that a tariff could enable the country to restrict its trade and gain more, exactly as a monopolist can increase profits by restricting his sales. Hence, this came to be known as the monopoly-power-in-trade argument for protection.

Second, the external trade opportunity had to be assumed to be independent of one's own trade policy. Suppose that, by imposing tariffs, you could pry open the protected markets of your trading partners. That could conceivably justify the use of tariffs. Unilateral free trade in that event would not be desirable. Even Adam Smith was aware of this possible qualification. Indeed, he considered[4] the question at some length:

The case in which it may sometimes be a matter of deliberation how far it is proper to continue the free importation of certain foreign goods, is, when some foreign nation restrains by high duties or prohibitions the importation of some of our manufactures into their country. Revenge in this case naturally dictates retaliation, and that we should impose the like duties and prohibitions upon the importation of some or all of their manufactures into ours. Nations accordingly seldom fail to retaliate in the manner.

There may be good policy in retaliations of this kind, when there is a probability that they will procure the repeal of the high duties of prohibitions complained of. The recovery of a great foreign market will generally more than compensate the transitory inconveniency of paying dearer during a short time for some sorts of goods. To judge whether such retaliations are likely to produce such an effect, does not, perhaps, belong so much to the science of the legislator, whose deliberations ought to be governed by general principles which are always the same, as to the skill of that insidious and crafty animal, vulgarly called a statesman or politician, whose councils are directed by the momentary fluctuations of affairs. When there is no probability that any such repeal can be procured, it seems a bad method of compensating the injury done to certain classes of our people, to do another injury to ourselves, not only to those classes, but to almost all the other classes of them.

His skepticism on this case for retaliatory protection would be shared later by Alfred Marshall and indeed many others at the end of the nineteenth century. They recognized the theoretical possibility but nonetheless propagated the wisdom of unilateral free trade in practice.

Empirical Judgment and the nineteenth Century British Debate

In the end, the intellectual case for free trade, and that too as a unilateral policy, had to rest on the empirical judgment that these exceptions were unimportant, if not theoretical *curiosa*, and further that, even if this were not so, protectionist policies based on them were likely to cause more harm than good.

This resort to empirical judgment is evident in the remarkable debate that ensued at the end of the nineteenth century when Britain, in relative decline as Germany and the United States rose in economic stature, found its longstanding unilateral free trade policy in serious jeopardy from "reciprocitarians" who sought to match foreign tariffs with their own as a way of prying open foreign markets. The arguments marshalled at the time against the reciprocitarians, by statesmen and economists wedded to unilateralism, consisted of the following:[5]

(1) The belief in the folly of protection was so complete that it was felt by many that the grievous losses on its practitioners would in themselves suffice to chastise and then induce them to embrace free trade in the end. (2) Others believed that the success of free trading Britain would set an example for other nations, ensuring diffusion of free trade policies. (3) Richard Cobden, the great crusader for repeal of the Corn Laws and adoption of free trade, went so far as to argue that insisting on reciprocal tariff reductions would only serve to make the task of free traders abroad more difficult by implying that free trade was really in the British interest rather than their own. (4) Equally, many felt that reciprocity was not an effective instrument for securing tariff reductions abroad simply because

Britain did not have the necessary economic power. (5) In addition, some feared that Britain itself was more vulnerable to retaliation than other countries. (6) Marshall even suggested that infant industry protection justified some of the foreign tariffs of Britain's new rivals, so that reciprocity aimed at opening foreign markets was inappropriate. (7) Finally, several economists at the time were convinced that however sound the rationale underlying the use of tariffs for reciprocity aimed at opening foreign markets, the policy would wind up being captured by protectionists and political interests. Thus Marshall, after observing the American experience with protection which reinforced his skepticism of rational tariff intervention, felt that "in becoming intricate it (i.e., protection) became corrupt, and tended to corrupt general politics."[6] This was undoubtedly an early manifestation of the recent developments in the theory of political economy and international trade which replace the orthodox view that governments are benign and omnipotent with the view that their policies may reflect lobbying by pressure groups. This may lead to defects in the visible hand that outweigh ones in the invisible hand for which remedy is sought—an issue that I will consider below.

1.3   Free Trade for All

But this prescription of free trade as a unilateral option, popular among economists, has had little appeal outside the nineteenth century British experience. In fact, mutual and symmetric access to each other's markets, i.e., universal rather than unilateral free trade, is the guiding principle in practice. It is also embodied, in essence, in GATT's functioning, for GATT is a contractarian institution, with symmetric rights and obligations for members.

Trade Regimes and Free Trade Everywhere

As it happens, the question of which rules a trade regime should have for member states has a distinct answer in the theory of trade in favor of universal free trade. It is to be found in the cosmopolitan (as distinct from the nationalist) theory of free trade. If we apply the logic of efficiency to the allocation of activity among all trading nations, and not merely within our own nation state, it is easy enough to see that it yields the prescription of free trade everywhere. That alone would ensure that goods and services were produced where it was cheapest to do so. The key to this conclusion then must be the notion that prices do reflect true social costs, just as it is to the case for free trade for one nation alone. If then any nation uses tariffs or subsidies, protection or promotion, to drive a wedge between market prices and social costs rather than to close one arising from market failure, then surely that is not consonant with an efficient world allocation of activity. The rule then emerges that free trade must apply to all.

Where therefore the nationalist theory of free trade glosses over the use of tariffs, quotas and subsidies by others, urging free trade for a nation regardless of what others do, the cosmopolitan theory requires adherence to free trade everywhere. The trade regime that we construct must then rule out artificial comparative advantage arising from interventions such as subsidies and protection. It must equally frown upon dumping insofar (and only insofar) as it is a technique used successfully for securing an otherwise untenable foothold in world markets.

National Advantage and Free Trade Everywhere:
Darwinism and "Fairness"

But, even within the perspective of national advantage, it is possible to contend that unilateral free trade is politically imprudent, likely to imperil the free trade policy itself, and hence must yield to symmetry of surrender by protectionists everywhere.

This is because the unilateralist prescription is at variance with the intuitive, Darwinian rationale for free trade. Think of the issue in the context of others using export subsidies while we keep our markets open, and you can see immediately what I mean to convey. It is hard enough to cope with the demise of an industry in pursuit of the gains from trade if the foreigner has a market-determined advantage. But if he is backed by artificial support from his government, that is likely to raise angry questions of "fairness." And it surely does.

While, therefore, an economist is right to claim that, if foreign governments subsidize their exports, this is simply marvelous as we get cheaper goods and we should unilaterally continue our free trade policy, he must equally recognize that the acceptance of this position will fuel demands for protection and imperil the possibility of maintaining the legitimacy, and hence the continuation, of free trade. A free trade regime that does not reign in, or seek to regulate, artificial subventions will likely help trigger its own demise. An analogy that I used to illustrate this unhappy "systemic" implication of the unilateralist position in conversing with Milton Friedman on his celebrated *Free to Choose* television series is imperfect but still apt.[7] Would one be wise to receive stolen property simply because it is cheaper, or would one rather vote to prohibit such transactions because of their systemic consequences?

We have here therefore a prudential argument for universal free trade even from the vantage point of *national* advantage. It buttresses the *cosmopolitan* argument for devising a world trading order that defines and seeks the principle of free trade for all, with provisions such as those permitting then the appropriate use of countervailing duty and antidumping actions to maintain fair, competitive trade.

In fact, it is notable that as nations have turned to freer trade, they have simultaneously tended to adopt and strengthen the provisions and processes for maintaining fair trade. Historically this happened in the 1930s in the United States as, in the aftermath of the disastrous Smoot-Hawley tariff, the country moved to what would turn out to be a half-century of trade liberalization. It is also true today in the developing countries such as Mexico which are shifting under IMF and World Bank prodding to a slow renunciation of their autarkic attitudes and policies. The important question, which I cannot consider adequately today, is how we can prevent these "fair trade" processes from turning, via capture by protectionist forces, into de facto instruments of protection as they have in recent times.[8]

1.4 The Postwar Theory of Commercial Policy

The major postwar developments in this theory of commercial policy were to appear principally from analysis addressed to two exceptions to the case for free trade for national advantage that I explained above: (1) market failure represented by the infant-industry argument, and (2) the presence of monopoly power in trade.

The former would lead to the influential theory of policy intervention for an open economy in the presence of distortions; the latter would pave the way for a systematic analysis of strategic trade-policy initiatives. In both cases, however, the developments can be argued as having strengthened the case for free trade, but in a subtle and sophisticated sense. Let me explain.

1. The new theoretical developments showed that the traditional case for protection when markets failed, as was the case for infant-industry protection, was weaker than had been thought. An appropriate tariff could improve welfare over free trade, but the more appropriate, optimal policy intervention was a domestic one targeted directly at the source of the

market failure. The first-best policy intervention in the case of domestic distortions (i.e., domestic market failure) was domestic; the tariff would only be a second-best policy. Tariffs were appropriate only when there was a foreign distortion: they were the first-best policy only when there was a monopoly power in external markets. Tariffs were thus demoted to a more limited role than in earlier theorizing.[9]

2. But even this monopoly-power-in-trade argument was called into question. It required the presence of nonnegligible market power in international markets. The scope for its application was therefore limited to cases where significant market shares obtain and entry is difficult.[10] But more seriously, the use of tariffs to exploit monopoly power opened up the distinct possiblity of retaliation—a possibility that had only been underscored by the interwar experience and the apparent reaction to the Smoot-Hawley tariff. Early theorists conjectured that, even though a country may reap a short-term advantage by exploiting with a tariff its market power, retaliation would leave all worse off. Later analysis, however, showed that an ultimate net gain, despite retaliation, could indeed be demonstrated as a possibility.[11] While therefore retaliation could not be demonstrated as definitely ruling out final gain to a country adopting a tariff to exploit its monopoly power in trade, that it could immiserize it and indeed others as well was also analytically established, calling into doubt the wisdom of even this time-honored exception to the argument that a free trade policy would maximize a nation's welfare.

I have interpreted both of these developments, the former already remarkable in its impact and the latter prescient in its introduction of later strategic analysis, as strengthening the pro-trade ideology. It is fair to say, however, that they, and especially the former, could well have been regarded in a different (but unsophisticated and wrongheaded) light as strengthening the protectionist hand instead. Indeed, if you were to read the massive literature that grew up on the theory of distortions and welfare during the 1960s and 1970s you would have found repeated analysis of market failures of one kind or another. Since some of the recent proponents of imperfect competition seem to suffer from amnesia even about matters only a decade old, it is necessary to recall the many contributions to the analysis of market failures arising from monopoly, factor market imperfections (e.g., monopsony, exogenous and endogenous wage differentials, and sticky wages), increasing returns, etc., that dominated the postwar analysis of commercial policy. If you then came away with the impression that market failure was all-pervasive, and that free trade made little sense, you could be excused. But you would also be betraying yourself as a careless economist who missed the central, overriding pro-free-trade message: that domestic market failures were best dealt with, not by trade policy interventions, but by choosing domestic policies tailor-made to assist and countervail the market failure at its source.[12]

1.5   Recent Developments: Political Economy and DUP Activities

But if the case for free trade was strengthened in this subtle fashion, it was to be assisted yet further by important developments in the theory, of commercial policy that came from the direction of political economy in the late 1970s.

You will recall that the postwar theory of commercial policy had shifted the focus away from protection for all market failures to domestic intervention (and hence continued free trade) for all failures of domestic origin (i.e., for domestic distortions). But this left intact the case for *appropriate* intervention in all cases of market failure. And underlying this case was the view of the conventional theory of economic policy, that the state was merely and exclusively an instrument for executing the policy recommendations of the economist, with no will or character of its own—what I have recently called (Bhagwati 1989) the *Puppet Government* assumption where the economist pulls all the strings according to instructions yielded by his policy analysis. Therefore, the case for free trade could be strengthened yet further if we could argue that:

1. Market failures were unimportant and/or self-correcting, hence needing no intervention at all.

2. The puppet-government view was an irrelevance and, when it was replaced by a more realistic view of the government as affected by pressure groups, the intervention was likely to be, not appropriate in keeping with the economist's recommendations, but perverse instead.

3. The cost of such perverse interventions was greater than conventional analysis suggested, once the costs of intervention-induced unproductive activities were also taken into consideration.

Let me address each of these arguments in turn.

First, the theorists of commercial policy have not generally been associated with the first line of defense of free trade above. Admittedly, some subscribe to the witticism that externalities, and hence promotion rather than *laissez faire* as the policy prescription, are the last refuge of the scoundrels, and others to its sequel that they are the *first* refuge instead. But many would be prepared to concede that externalities may well be important. Nor is it possible to find many adherents of the view that the Coase theorem's scope is sufficiently great to internalize all important externalities.

By contrast, the theorists of commercial policy have explored systematically the latter two lines of inquiry distinguished above, each relating to different aspects of political economy, and both leading to a possible new defense of the merits of free trade.

Second, many recent theoretical writings on trade policy have replaced the *Puppet Government* assumption by endogenizing policy. Thus, governments have been modeled as autonomous agents with objectives of their own—what I call the *Self-willed Government* assumption. Alternatively, at another extreme, they have been modeled as simply an arena where lobbies clash over policy—this is the *Clearinghouse Government* assumption. In either case, or combination thereof, the government is rescued from its fictitious and emasculated role as the economist's echo or sounding board.

When policy is so endogenized, the possibility arises that intervention, instead of being consonant with the economist's benign recommendations, is perverse. It obviously cannot be argued that this is necessarily, or over-whelmingly, so. But, in the case of tariff policy, a case may be made along the following lines (though I advance no formal proof here).

Thus, recall that there is, in the absence of retaliation and the presence of monopoly power in trade, a case for an optimal tariff for national advantage. Heuristically speaking, therefore, we would expect a benign, puppet government to levy higher tariffs on goods in inelastic world markets than on goods in elastic markets. But if pressure-group lobbying leads to tariff formation, and if the demand for tariff protection is greater in goods that are in highly elastic foreign supply (e.g., textiles) and hence highly competitive but less in goods with rising foreign supply price where therefore there is "natural" protection against substantial entry by foreign rivals, the endogenous tariff structure with a clearinghouse government may well be exactly the opposite of that which the conventional economist would like from a benign, puppet government.

Third, the endogenization of trade policy in recent theoretical work has played a substantially more dramatic role in the case for free trade than the foregoing possibility of perverse intervention would indicate.

This it has done by demonstrating that the cost of (erroneous, welfare-worsening) protection is greater, possibly significantly greater, than the conventional theory suggested. This demonstration is a direct consequence of what we now call the theory of directly unproductive profit-seeking (DUP) activities (Bhagwati 1982a). These are activities which constitute "unproductive" ways of making an income so that they use resources to produce income (or profit) but no socially valued output. Such DUP activities in trade policy, pertinent to my theme, can be distinguished into two major analytical groups, defining them relative to any given policy of import protection:

1. *downstream* activities, e.g., lobbying for the premium or windfall rents carried by import quotas (what Krueger 1974 has graphically called "rent-seeking") or its price counterpart for tariff revenues (what in our 1980 paper Srinivasan and I have called "revenue-seeking"). These downstream activities can arise whether the protection is exogenous or endogenous, of course; and

2. *upstream* activities, e.g., lobbying aimed at making (or opposing) protection, since its presence (or absence) will affect the income earned in productive activity: these are of course the activities that result in endogenizing trade policy.

It has thus become customary now to add to the conventional Harberger-Johnson-Meade "triangle" estimates of the deadweight cost of protection (which have been dismally low and singularly unfit as a weapon to fight protectionism on the ground that it is expensive) two further costs: from the upstream DUP-theoretic estimate of protection-seeking that precedes the protection and from the downstream DUP-theoretic estimate of rent- or revenue-seeking that follows the protection.

Of these two new arguments for augmenting the case against protection by adding to its cost, however, I should now stress that the downstream variety is the more robust, whereas the upstream variety raises serious conceptual difficulties which must make us pause. I will explain.

1. The *downstream* DUP-theoretic costs are certainly an important matter, as is evident even to the naked eye. In fact, they were suggested to Tullock (1967), Krueger (1974), and me (Bhagwati 1973), all of whom have theorized about them, during exposure to rent-seeking and revenue-seeking activities in developing countries. But I must also confess that the body of scientific literature that has now grown up on this theme suggests that the early presumptions in DUP theory that these added costs would be extremely large have given way to more modest expectations for at least two reasons.

First, the earliest estimates, particularly by Krueger (1974) in her seminal work, assumed that rent-seeking would lead to (market-value) losses as large as the rents being sought: an eye for an eye, a dollar lost for a dollar chased. This presupposes open competition among risk-neutral lobbyists. But, in reality, the Brother-in-Law theorem often applies: the brother-in-law usually has a better chance of getting the license and the rent it fetches, so it deters others from expending as many resources on rent-seeking as perfect competition would imply.[13]

Second, market losses are not necessarily social losses to society. If the import quotas have strongly distorted domestic allocation to begin with, the market price of a dollar's worth of resources diverted to rent-seeking aimed at the import quotas is not its true, social cost at all. In fact, in "highly distorted" economies, such resource-diversion, while directly unproductive, may paradoxically improve welfare indirectly.[14] In jargon, the shadow or social cost of factors of production withdrawn from productive use into unproductive DUP activity could be negative.[15] While there are countless such observations of "value subtraction" in productive activities, when social costs and values rather than market prices are used to make estimates, this is undoubtedly an extreme phenomenon. Suffice it to say that the social cost of rent-seeking is likely, in distorted economies, to be below its nominal, market cost.

But let me stress that, with both these *caveats* duly noted, this literature does strengthen the antiprotectionist hand.

2. The *upstream* DUP-theoretic costs would equally suggest an augmentation of the cost of protection. After all, if resources have been used in lobbying for protection, should we not add that cost also to the deadweight cost of protection?

This seems logical, at first sight. Thus, in figure 1.1, once resources have been used up in creating an endogenous tariff, the resources available for productive activity (producing goods X and Y) shrink, and so does the production possibility curve from $A'B'$ to AB. The given terms of trade, for this small country, define the free trade optimal production at P^*. The endogenous-tariff production is at $\hat{P}$. Now, the deadweight (production) cost of protection is measured in Hicksian equivalent-variational terms as CD, since the production at undistorted terms of trade (*and* with resources lost to lobbying for and against the tariff) would be at $\hat{P}^*$. But if these lobbying resources were also restored to productive use, the economy would operate at P^*. Therefore, the lobbying cost is DE. The total cost of protection is therefore:

$$CD \qquad\qquad + DE \qquad\qquad = CE.$$

(Deadweight loss)   (DUP-theoretic   (Total cost of protection)
lobbying cost)

The only question would then seem to be whether empirically DE is a substantial figure. But there is a problem, for, as soon as you endogenize policy upstream, you can lose the degree of freedom to vary policy as in conventional, puppet-government theory. The optimal, free-trade policy at P^* cannot meaningfully be compared with the tariff at $\hat{P}$ as in conventional analysis of rank-ordering of policies, for the augmented political-economic system yields the tariff at $\hat{P}$ as the policy that will emerge in this economy. To take free-trade policy at P^* as the reference point for measuring the cost of protection is then to impose back on the system a DUP-activity-free economy, wiping out the "political" part of the economy. This would make as much sense as saying: let us compare P^* with what would emerge as the equilibrium production if economic constraints were relaxed!

Upstream DUP-theoretic endogenization of policy then raises a fundamental difficulty. The theory of economic policy runs forthwith into what I have called the *determinacy paradox:* endogenizing (upstream) policy generally removes the degree of freedom to vary policy interventions (Bhagwati et al. 1984; Bhagwati 1987).

It is clear to me then that the impulse to add the *upstream-lobbying* costs to the conventional deadweight losses is conceptually treacherous. The implications of endogenous policy modeling of the upstream variety can be fruitfully found instead in other ways which can turn the theory of

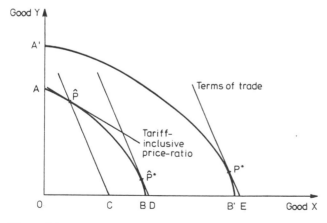

Figure 1.1

commercial policy in novel directions. Let me differentiate between two different such ways.

First, while one cannot now meaningfully vary economic policy and rank alternative policies, one can ask other *variational* questions—for example, how will welfare change (from $\hat{P}$ in figure 1.1) if a parametric change such as improved terms of trade occurs? Thus, whereas conventional puppet-government analysis would have rank-ordered different policies as efficient responses to the changed terms of trade, the new endogenous-policy approach would solve for the new policy that would emerge in response to the changed terms of trade and then would be able to evaluate whether welfare had improved or worsened (using the preferred welfare criterion). Prediction rather than prescription would then be the essence of this approach to economic policy.

Second, there still remains, however, one key way in which prescription can be rescued from total elimination by the determinacy paradox. Think of variational questions, not from the economic side of the economic model augmented by equations for the political process that endogenize (up-stream) policy but rather from the political side. Suppose, for instance, that the spread of ideas and ideology makes the cost of lobbying for a tariff greater: the government, converted to a free-trade bias, resists protectionist lobbying more strenuously. We could then analyze the welfare impact of this "regress" in the "production function" for a tariff. Alternatively, ima-gine that the institutional structure changes, in consequence of a cataclysm such as economic disaster or war, so that the cost of tariff-making changes. Once again, the consequence of this change on welfare could be analyzed within the specified model of the economic-cum-political process.

But as soon as you do this, the way opens to ask: If alternative institu-tional structures that bear on the final (endogenous) policy change could be specified, could we then not rank-order these institutional structures themselves?

There is, of course, the important question of how these institutional arrangements will be chosen in pluralistic societies. If we were to judge one such set to be more conducive to social welfare and hence preferable to another, the question still arises: How will we transit to the preferred set from the one we have as the initial condition? From this perspective, the notion that "constitutional amendments" should be undertaken to choose and freeze the optimal institutional choice for policymaking may often be only begging the question.[16]

But it remains useful nonetheless to ask: How would one institutional setup rank-order vis-à-vis another, if we had either in place and no lobbying resources were devoted to changing it (e.g., because the Constitution is framed in a way which makes such lobbying too expensive)? This may then be regarded as an exercise in the comparative dynamics of alternative institutions, with the question of the transition path from one steady state to another left out of the analysis.

Four examples of such comparatve institutional analysis by policy analysts in international trade should illustrate well this new set of developments. Each relates to the effect of alternative institutional arrangements on the degree of protection that will emerge in an economy.

1. The first example relates to the shift in tariff making authority from the U.S. Congress to the president following the cataclysm precipitated by the Smoot-Hawley tariff in 1930. Nearly half a century of trade liberalization followed. Among the causes cited is the fact that the Congress is necessarily more responsive to constituency pressure for tariffs whereas the president does not have to be. The institutional change to tariff-making by the president therefore shifts the "supply" curve of protection by the government to the left and given any demand for protection by protectionist lobbies, reduces (increases) the protection (liberalization) that will emerge.

2. The United States also shifted in 1934 from tariff-making in Congress to "administered protection" under which protection had to be sought by an industry or firm by going through "rule-oriented" administrative bodies such as the International Trade Commission which would determine whether, according to the rules defined, the party seeking protection should be granted protection. This meant that the net demand for protection again diminished for a subtle reason. Earlier, congressmen had yielded to constituency pressure to enact, as in Smoot-Hawley, made-to-order tariffs for constituents in a process of log-rolling where each congressman was permitted self-indulgence by the other in an atmosphere of what Schattschneider, the great historian of the Smoot-Hawley tariff, has called "reciprocal noninterference." Once, however, the protectionist lobby had to go by the rules, the lobbying had to seek changes in the rules themselves. But this then precipitated anti-tariff lobbying, since rule-change inevitably attracted much debate and competitive lobbying from mutually opposed pro-trade and anti-trade lobbies. Therefore, with the net demand for protection thus falling under the shift to a rule-oriented institutional structure for tariff-making, the amount of protection actually materializing could be expected to fall, ceteris paribus.[17]

3. Yet another example is provided by the comparison that Rodrik (1986) has undertaken of tariffs and subsidies as policy instruments for protecting

an industry. Now, tariffs are generally considered to be less desirable for this purpose in the conventional theory of commercial policy because they protect an industry by adding a gratuitous consumption cost in the process (Bhagwati and Ramaswami 1963; Johnson 1965). Suppose however that we were now to allow the protection to be determined endogenously. Suppose next that subsidies are tailor-made for each firm whereas tariffs cannot differentiate between firms and must be given to an industry generally. In that case, the free-rider problem will afflict the demand for tariff protection but not the demand for subsidy protection. The demand for protection therefore will be less in a regime where subsidies are granted than in a regime where tariffs are granted. Therefore, given the same resistance to protection by the government, the protection emerging will be less under a tariff regime than under a subsidies regime.

Of course, before anyone rushes in to act on this insight, it should be remembered that: (a) even if the protection with tariffs is less, its total cost may be greater because tariffs carry the consumption cost that subsidies do not; (b) the tariffs may be *supplied* more readily by governments (which see their effects on revenues as beneficial and the loss of revenue from subsidies as a problem instead); and (c) in reality, tariffs in many countries are adjusted to sufficient detail so as to be firm-specific as required whereas subsidies entirely specific to a firm (as in the case of "bailouts") are not very common. Nonetheless, the argument illustrates well the kind of question that theorists of commercial policy, as they grapple with the invigorating influx of political-economy-theoretic considerations, are now addressing.

4. Finally, it has now become manifest that the institutional structure of "administered protection" is designed in a fashion that does not balance the protectionist and anti-protectionist forces evenly but is in fact biased in favor of protection. Thus, for instance, the anti-dumping and counter-vailing subsidy mechanisms do not permit the weighing of consumer interests: these are typically left to the end of the process (in the United States, by the president) while the opening salvos in the game are left to be fired only by the industry or firm seeking protection. The failure to have impartial, multilateral panels to determine the outcomes of complaints of unfair trading practices such as dumping and foreign subsidies that often lead to protection also facilitates protectionist capture of these "fair trade" processes.

All of this translates into a greater effective demand for protection, and into more protection, ceteris paribus. Many international economists (Baldwin 1986; Finger 1982; Willet, 1984; Bhagwati 1988) have therefore called for a variety of institutional reforms so as to give pro-trade forces a fairer chance of success than they have had to date.

I have concentrated here on the theory-of-commercial-policy implications of the new developments in the political-economy analysis of international trade. But the prognosis, explanation and prediction components of these developments are equally exciting and can bring altogether new perspectives on old problems.[18]

This can be illustrated well by the recent theory of *quid pro quo* DFI or direct foreign investment (Bhagwati 1985, 1986). In this theory, DFI is undertaken in response to the threat of protection, *not* with a view to "jumping" the anticipated protection but with a view to *defusing* that threat. This reduction of the protectionist threat can follow because either the supply of protection by the host government is reduced due to the "goodwill effect" of the DFI *or* the demand for it is reduced because host-country firms and/or unions, the agents seeking protection, are co-opted by the DFI into not pushing for protection against foreign competition. For instance, consider the case where Toyota and General Motors have a joint venture in the United States. Toyota makes an otherwise unremunerative DFI which helps GM while the *quid pro quo* for Toyota is that GM breaks ranks with other U.S. carmakers later by opposing VERs renewal. First-period losses on DFI in the United States (compared to exporting more Toyotas to the United States) are then balanced against second-period gains that follow from the resulting reduction in the probability of renewal of U.S. VERs on Japanese cars.

This type of *quid pro quo* DFI has certainly been manifest in the U.S–Japan context recently and has been modeled in the competitive context in Bhagwati et al. (1987) and in the oligopolistic context by Dinopoulos (1989) and Wong (1989). It represents an altogether novel way in which political processes play an essential role in inducing profit-seeking DFI. It is an example of the power and originality that the new political-economy-theoretic approach has to offer to us.

1.4   Recent Developments: Increasing Returns, Market Structure, and Strategic Trade Policy

To return, however, to the theory of commercial policy, the recent developments also include progress from an altogether different direction. Inspired by the theory of industrial organization and new solution concepts in game-theoretic formulation, several trade theorists also turned their attention during the 1980s to models of imperfect competition in product markets, whose rationale lay in the phenomenon of economies of scale (internal to the firm).

Economies of scale, external to the firm but internal to the industry, are compatible with perfect competition. But they can result in loss of convexity with well-known consequences (e.g., Kemp 1964; Panagariya 1980) such as wrong specialization or suboptimality of free trade, depending on how precisely increasing returns operate. Such economies of scale therefore can justify an appropriate intervention to assist the invisible hand. Again, careful scholars have known that when multiple equilibria arise under increasing returns, identical economies can have trade, and indeed beneficial trade and reversed trade patterns are also demonstrable as possible multiple equilibria (e.g., Kemp 1964).

The recent developments, with similar results, assume, on the other hand, that increasing returns are internal to the firm. If such returns are large relative to the size of the market, evidently perfect competition will break down (as noted by Sraffa and Kaldor over four decades ago). The resulting imperfect competition can take the form of the large-group or the oligopolistic small-group case distinguished by Edward Chamberlin and Joan Robinson.

1. The *large-group* case is the less interesting one in terms of its implications for commercial policy. Since Chamberlin's analysis, we have known that the implication of monopolistic competition is that market failure characterizes *laissez faire*. Recent analytical developments—to be attributed most to Helpman and Krugman, drawing in turn on the pioneering work of Lancaster (1966, 1980), on the one hand, and Dixit and Stiglitz (1977), on the other—have enabled us to examine the issue more fully. In particular, as Lancaster's neo-Hotelling modeling of taste diversity underlines forcefully, the combination of increasing returns and taste diversity can lead to outcomes where the market leads to a suboptimal result: one where the exploitation of economies of scale in a limited range of products must be set against loss of product diversity, and the market outcome may therefore be improved upon.

But once again, the theory of commercial policy, as it evolved during the 1960s and 1970s, requires us to distinguish between different questions: Is free trade better than autarky, is trade policy intervention welfare-improving, and is trade policy intervention the ideal (first-best) intervention or is domestic policy intervention (or a mix of the two) yet better and more appropriate? The general answers here must be that, first, free trade is not necessarily better than autarky—this is simply a further instance of the proposition that free trade and autarky cannot be rank-ordered in the presence of distortions (Haberler 1950), one that is in turn explained also as an instance of the theory of immiserizing growth (Bhagwati 1971)—and that, second, trade policy intervention could improve welfare.[19]

But the question of *optimal* policy intervention remains more complex. Since, in an open economy, the variety-cum-increasing returns model of imperfect competition should generally imply both a domestic and a foreign distortion (Bhagwati 1971), it would follow that the optimal intervention would be a mix of trade and domestic policy interventions.[20]

But for all of the questions discussed above, it is important to remember that free trade may well have eliminated the problem of monopolistic competition by adding sufficiently to the size of the market in all sectors relative to increasing returns, and that trade restrictions may themselves be a source of the particular market failure for a country. My guess is therefore that few economists are likely to argue for the adoption of policy departures from free trade because of the large-group case.

2. The matter is somewhat different for the *small-group* case. In oligopolistic markets, where strategic interactions between firms are likely and firms can earn excess profits, free trade is evidently not optimal. As has been emphasized by Brander and Spencer (1981), in this situation, governmental intervention can shift production and therefore associated excess profits to one's own firms by altering the terms of competition among firms in different countries.

Theoretically, this case is sound. It is not surprising either. With oligopoly, prices do not generally reflect social costs: therefore, free trade cannot generally be better than autarky or be optimal.

Strategic interaction among firms must also arise: the analysis is more complex than, but nonetheless in the spirit of, the pioneering Johnson analysis of strategic interaction of governments. In the Johnson analysis, the firms are competitive but the two governments are in strategic interaction (though Johnson's analysis was entirely in terms of Cournot-Nash strategy), whereas now there are at least four actors who can engage in strategic interaction: the two governments and two firms (though the current analyses usually confine the strategic interaction only to the firms).

These analyses construct simple examples of strategic interaction between firms, with government policy undertaken often as a once-for-all intervention to influence the terms of interfirm competition, to show how free trade can be improved upon.[21]

There is no denying that, where perfect competition does not prevail, free trade will not be optimal—there is no new insight here, of course. The interesting policy question is rather: in this class of cases, where oligopoly is important and excess profits obtain, should governments intervene to increase national welfare?

The problem here, recognized by some of the more careful analysts of this class of cases, is that the precise intervention that will improve welfare depends critically on the nature of the strategic interaction between the oligopolistic firms. Thus, consider the highly simplified model[22] where two firms, one domestic and one foreign, produce a homogeneous product only for a third market where they may compete. Here, an export subsidy is socially optimal if the firms follow the (Cournot-Nash) strategy where each firm selects its optimal level of output taking the output of the rival as given. But if, in the very same model, we were to assume that, rather than choosing output levels and letting prices adjust correspondingly, the firms engage instead in the (Bertrand) strategy of setting prices and letting outputs adjust to the demands at those prices, the prescription for an intervention turns from an export subsidy into an export tax.[23]

This sensitivity, or lack of robustness, of the policy interventions to the assumptions on the nature of oligopolistic strategic interaction, creates information requirements for policy intervention that appear to many of the architects of this theoretical innovation to be sufficiently intimidating to suggest that policymakers had better leave it alone.[24] This viewpoint is further reinforced for them by doubts whether there are indeed (excess) profits to be shifted through such intervention. As Grossman (1986, p. 57) has put it cogently: "Often what appears to be an especially high rate of profit is just a return to some earlier, risky investment. Research and development expenses, for example, can be quite large, and many ventures end in failure. Firms will only undertake these large investments if they can reap the benefits in those instances where they succeed. Once the market is in operation, we will of course only observe those companies that have succeeded. We may then be tempted to conclude that profit rates are unusually high. But industry profits should be measured inclusive of the losses of those who never make it to the marketing stage." The practical application of the new and theoretically valid increasing-returns-based argument for policy intervention to shift profits toward oneself in oligopolistic industries is therefore beset with difficulties.

These are further compounded, as was the classical theoretical prescription for an optimal tariff, by the fact that the new case for export subsidization or import tariffs[25] is equally based on considerations of national advantage and presupposes that foreign governments do not retaliate.[26] As with the unilateral exercise of an optimal tariff to exploit monopoly power in trade, the asymmetric, unilateral use of export subsidies or import tariffs in oligopolistic industries to gain competitive edge and possibly shift profits to its advantage by a government is, however, likely to invite retaliation from aggrieved trading partners.

In fact, such retaliation is more likely in precisely the knowledge-intensive high-tech industries where economies of scale relative to world markets are presumed by the proponents of these new theories to be significant, for these industries are widely regarded as important in themselves. Their location behind one's own borders is supposed frequently to be a matter of securing broader political and economic benefits just as manufacturing generally was regarded by developing countries during the postwar years. Foreign governmental intervention, regardless of whether profit-sharing-related advantages exist or not, is generally seen therefore as an attempt to get a larger share of this important pie than is warranted by legitimate market forces. This is surely a major reason behind the sensitivity of the United States on this question as asymmetrical, predatory governmental interventions in such industries are alleged for Japan and retaliatory action sought concerning them.

If such retaliation occurs, then it is not beyond the ingenuity of economists to construct cases where it would still leave the country which initiated the profit-shifting game to remain better off. But, as with the earlier retaliation analysis of the optimal tariff for exploiting monopoly power, the competitive retaliatory policies provoked by attempts at profit-shifting are likely to leave each country worse off, especially if such actions spill over into other areas of trade policy or drag into the game other players simply because of the multilateral aspects of international trade.

To shift the perspective, however, should such retaliation be encouraged, or even embodied in one's national trade policy?

This has been recommended by some who build on Axelrod's (1981) celebrated advocacy of tit-for-tat strategy to induce nonpredatory cooperative behavior (after repeated games) by recalcitrant game players.[27] Under this strategy, the United States would play fair on the first move and then retaliate if Japan next makes a predatory move, matching whatever move Japan makes. The problems with applying such strategies to trade policy are legion and invalidate in my view the relevance of the Axelrod prescription. In particular, bilateral determination of the other player's fairness may be confidently expected to lean towards being self-serving: what is tit and what is tat becomes problematic and contentious. A tat, unfairly alleged, and retaliated against with a tit, will invite resentment and likely generate trade skirmishes rather than take you down the benign cooperative route that Axelrod conjures up for our acceptance. Indeed, in a protectionist climate such as today's, tats are likely to be found readily and charged against successful rivals and the Axelrod strategy likely to be captured by those who seek protectionism, as is evident from the efforts by U.S. semiconductor chips producers to gain guaranteed access to Japanese markets and to regulate competition in third markets too.[28]

For such reasons, I am strongly opposed to strategic trade policymaking, whether to shift profits to oneself or to retaliate against rivals allegedly doing this. To recapitulate (1) the case itself is limited to a few sectors where world markets are significantly small relative to economies of scale; (2) there are theoretical exceptions to it, as with earlier strategic-trade-policy analysis of governmental interventions, once governments can retaliate (i.e., act strategically among themselves); (3) the information requirements for suitable intervention, regardless of retaliation, are complex and outcomes are unusually sensitive to governments making the correct guesses and choices; and (4) the protectionist capture of this market is unusually easy in the high-tech, R&D-intensive industries to which it is allegedly applicable precisely because most governments want these industries because of an implicit belief in the economic and political advantages of having them at any cost, making the resistance to protectionist demands therefore less likely.

1.7 Concluding Observations

In conclusion, let me reiterate that certain developments make the case for free trade more robust whereas others make it less so. The former, however, are more interesting and compelling, and the latter are subject to many difficulties and dangers as one passes from the classroom to the corridors of policymaking and suggest strongly that common sense and wisdom should prevail in favor of free trade.

The case for free trade, as brought up to date from 1817 to 1987, is therefore alive and well. This is not to say that we have not learned its strengths and weaknesses, its nuances and subtleties, with greater understanding in light of the new developments. If we remain convinced of the virtues of free trade, it is then not in the spirit of Robert Frost's affirmation of the virtue of belief:

... why abandon a belief
merely because it ceases to be true.
Cling to it long enough, and not a doubt
It will turn true again, for so it goes.

Rather, it is in the spirit of T. S. Eliot:

We shall not cease from exploration
And the end of all our exploring
Will be to arrive where we started
And know the place for the first time.

Notes

Remark: This is the text of the acceptance speech on the occasion of the award of the Bernhard Harms Prize at the Kiel Institute, Germany, on June 25, 1988.

I should like to thank Martin Wolf for having long encouraged me to put the theory of commercial policy in perspective and to evaluate recent developments, focusing on all of them rather than only those related to imperfect competition. I have profited (if inadequately) from the comments received from Richard Brecher, Robert Feenstra, Douglas Irwin, Larry Summers, T. N. Srinivasan, Alasdair Smith, Martin Wolf and Aaron Tornell. I have retained, for publication, the informal lecturing style, keeping references down to a minimum. I seek therefore indulgence from many whose work I have profited from over the years but have not given explicit credit to here.

1. I have argued below, a careful grasp of even the classical theory of gains from trade would not lead one to conclude that "economic theory" makes free trade "always right." I might add also that it is historically inaccurate to think that there has been no loss of belief in free trade as a good policy in practice, i.e., that the premises leading to the case for free trade are not empirically valid. The most compelling such loss of belief occurred, as Hicks reminded us in the 1950s, during the years following the Great Depression, with Keynes among the many converts. Evidently, it made no sense to argue the virtues of a free trade policy in conditions of massive unemployment: market prices no longer reflected social costs.

2. The capture follows from the fact that if it is wrongly asserted that the theorists of commercial policy, who in fact wrote many volumes and over a hundred scientific papers during the postwar period on the appropriate nature of policy intervention and departure from free trade, were *doctrinaire* believers in free trade and that it took the "new" developments in the 1980s to save us from their unfortunate belief in the virtue of free trade derived from *inappropriate* scientific argumentation, then protectionists will happily reject that important body of scientific work and those theorists and proceed to assert that "new" and "more appropriate" theories have "finally" shown that protection can be scientifically sound and therefore should be pursued.

3. For a formal statement of these theoretical principles, most textual expositions should suffice. See, for example, Bhagwati and Srinivasan (1983, ch. 17).

4. Cf. Smith (1937, pp. 434–435). In principle, retaliation against exercise of one's monopoly power in trade also implies that the external trade opportunity is not independent of one's policy. But this question was not raised, to my knowledge, in

classical writings and I deal with it in Section IV where I consider it in the context of postwar developments in the theory of commercial policy since it did get considered then.

5. For more detailed discussion, see my 1987 Ohlin lectures (Bhagwati 1988).

6. Cited in Bhagwati (1988).

7. The analogy is imperfect because the systemic effects in the two cases arise from phenomena with altogether different ethical implications. It is apt because the parallel lies in the systemic consequences of the pursuit of immediate price advantage.

8. I have addressed this question at some length in the Ohlin lectures (Bhagwati 1988).

9. The postwar developments in the theory of commercial policy, as stated here, have been the work of many theorists, including Harry Johnson, T. N. Srinivasan, and Max Corden. But they originated in two independent contributions: the *Journal of Political Economy* article of Bhagwati and Ramaswami (1963) and Meade's (1955) volume on *Trade and Welfare*. For an excellent statement of the basic theory, see Johnson (1965), and for a synthesis and generalization, consult Bhagwati (1971).

10. I should emphasize that economists today would see the applicability of this exception as wider in scope than we believed in the 1950s, extending to industrial products and not just primary products such as jute and oil.

11. Scitovsky (1941) had conjectured the immiserization of all. Using a Cournot-Nash tariff-retaliation model, Johnson (1953) demonstrated the possibility of a final net gain nonetheless. Rodriguez (1974) showed that the Johnson analysis with quotas substituting for tariffs would restore Scitovsky's conjecture. For an excellent review of this literature, see McMillan (1986).

12. Of course, a trade policy can generally be decomposed into a sum of domestic policies. For example, a tariff on final goods is equivalent to a production tax-cum-subsidy plus a consumption tax-cum-subsidy, as noted in Johnson (1965) and elsewhere.

13. In turn, this presumption itself must be somewhat qualified since there could be resources spent on becoming the brother-in-law: an arduous exercise, I am sure. See also the recent analysis of Hillman and Riley (1989) which casts further light on the issue of how significant the rent-seeking losses may be in practice.

14. See Bhagwati and Srinivasan (1980), in particular.

15. Theoretically, this observation is of profound importance. For, it means that, contrary to the practice of Buchanan (1980) and many others in the public-choice school, it is not meaningful to *define* unproductive activities as necessarily welfare-worsening. I have therefore used the adjective "directly" to qualify these un-

productive profit-seeking activities: for, indirectly or in ultimate outcome, they may improve welfare. Hence I use the phrase DUP (directly unproductive profit-seeking) activities to describe the generic set of activities which use resources and produce income but zero output. On these questions which affect critically the untenable equation of direct and ultimate waste in *both* the public-choice school and the longstanding discussions since Adam Smith and Marx of the concept of unproductive labor and activities, see Bhagwati (1980, 1982a, 1983).

16. Assuming that the "original" constitution is devised according to one rule or the other is tantamount to assuming a puppet government. It makes approximate sense only in cases where, in a newly independent country, a constituent assembly is devising a constitution with which the country is to be endowed.

17. See Bhagwati (1988, p. 42). Nelson (1987) has developed these types of argumentation on administered protection.

18. There is now a growing body of literature, for instance, on models of tariff-making (Brock and Magee 1978; Findlay and Wellisz 1982; Feenstra and Bhagwati 1982; Mayer, 1984), on the endogenous choice between alternative policy responses to import competition (Bhagwati 1982b; Dinopoulos 1983; Sapir 1983), and on the endogenous choice between tariffs and subsidies (Mayer and Riezman 1987, 1989).

19. Since both foreign and domestic interventions are likely to be involved simultaneously in this case, it should not generally be possible to argue that trade policy intervention by itself would *necessarily* improve welfare. See Bhagwati et al. (1969, proposition 2).

20. A recent analysis of the nature of optimal intervention in imperfect competition is by Krishna and Thursby (1988).

21. The question of strategic interaction between an oligopolistic firm and its own government in the game of seeking and permitting protection may lead to pro-free-trade outcomes, however, cf. Tornell (1987).

22. This is originally due to Brander and Spencer (1981), pioneers in this area.

23. This is elegantly demonstrated in the context of conjectural-variation models by Eaton and Grossman (1986).

24. There are informational requirements to be sure, when conventional interventions for market failure are recommended. In this instance, however, we need information on behavioral assumptions which seem hard to track down. Attempts by Rodrik (1987) and others recently to provide guidelines or rules of thumb to make meaningful inferences of this kind are extremely interesting but not persuasive to me.

25. Import tariffs can also shift profits, while gaining for the protected industry economies of scale that give it competitive advantage vis-à-vis foreign firms that are then denied access to this segment of the world market; cf. Krugman (1984).

26. Strategic interaction is entirely confined to governments in conventional analysis because firms are competitive. It is both at the firm and the governmental level when firms are oligopolistic.

27. See, in particular, Goldstein and Krasner (1984).

28. For a useful analysis of other limitations of the Axelrod strategy in trade poiicymaking, see Brander (1986). I should emphasize, in particular, that the Axelrod strategy, as originally analyzed, works with two players who are as long-lived as the repeated games they play. By contrast, trade involves typically more than two players and, in democracies in particular, the players change with changes in governments and in bureaucracies.

References

Axelrod, Robert. 1981. The Emergence of Cooperation among Egoists. *American Political Science Review*, 75: 308–318.

Baldwin, Robert. 1986. *The Political Economy of U.S. Import Policy*. Cambridge: MIT Press.

Basevi, Giorgio. 1970. Domestic Demand and the Ability to Export. *Journal of Political Economy* 78: 330–337.

Bhagwati, Jagdish. 1971. The Generalized Theory of Distortions and Welfare. In Jagdish Bhagwati et al. (eds.), *Trade, Balance of Payments, and Growth*. Amsterdam. North Holland, pp. 69–90.

Bhagwati, Jagdish. 1973. *India in the International Economy: A Policy Framework for a Progressive Society*. Lal Bahadur Shastri Memorial Lectures. Hyderabad.

Bhagwati, Jagdish. 1980. Lobbying and Welfare. *Journal of Public Economics* 14: 355–363.

Bhagwati, Jagdish. 1982a. Directly-Unproductive, Profit-Seeking (DUP) Activities. *Journal of Political Economy* 90: 988–1002.

Bhagwati, Jagdish. (ed.). 1982b. *Import Competition and Response*. Chicago: University of Chicago Press.

Bhagwati, Jagdish. 1983. DUP Activities and Rent Seeking. *Kyklos* 36: 634–637.

Bhagwati, Jagdish. 1985. Protectionism: Old Wine in New Bottles. *Journal of Policy Modelling* 7: 23–33.

Bhagwati, Jagdish. 1986. *Investing Abroad*. Esmee Fairbairn Lecture. University of Lancaster.

Bhagwati, Jagdish. 1987. Directly-Unproductive Profit-Seeking Activities. In *The New Palgrave Dictionary of Economics*. New York: Stockton Press, pp. 845–847.

Bhagwati, Jagdish. 1988. *Protectionism*. Cambridge: MIT Press.

Bhagwati, Jagdish. 1989. The Theory of Political Economy, Economic Policy and Foreign Investment. In Deepak Lal and Maurice Fg. Scott (eds.), *Essays in Honor of I.M.D. Little*. Oxford: Oxford University Press.

Bhagwati, Jagdish, and V. K. Ramaswami. 1963. Domestic Distortions, Tariffs, and the Theory of Optimum Subsidy. *Journal of Political Economy* 71: 44–50.

Bhagwati, Jagdish, and T. N. Srinivasan. 1980. Revenue Seeking: A Generalization of the Theory of Tariffs. *Journal of Political Economy* 88: 1069–1087.

Bhagwati, Jagdish, and T. N. Srinivasan. 1983. *Lectures on International Trade*. Cambridge: MIT Press.

Bhagwati, Jagdish, Richard Brecher, and T. N. Srinivasan. 1984. DUP Activities and Economic Theory. In David Colander (ed.), *Neoclassical Political Economy: The Analysis of Rent-seeking and DUP Activities*. Cambridge, MA: Ballinger, pp. 17–32.

Bhagwati, Jagdish, V. K. Ramaswami, and T. N. Srinivasan. 1969. Domestic Distortions, Tariffs and the Theory of the Optimum Subsidy: Some Further Results. *Journal of Political Economy* 77: pp. 1005–1010.

Bhagwati, Jagdish, Richard Brecher, Elias Dinopoulos, and T. N. Srinivasan. 1987. Quid Pro Quo Investment and Policy Intervention: A Political-Economy-Theoretic Analysis. *Journal of Development Economics* 27: 127–138.

Brander, James. 1986. Rationales for Strategic Trade and Industrial Policy. In Paul Krugman (ed.), *Strategic Trade Policy and the New International Economics*. Cambridge: MIT Press, pp. 23–46.

Brander, James, and Barbara Spencer. 1981. Tariffs and the Extraction of Foreign Monopoly Rents under Potential Entry. *Canadian Journal of Economics* 14: 371–389.

Brock, William A., and Stephen Magee. 1978. The Economics of Special Interest Politics: The Case of the Tariff. *The American Economic Review, Papers and Proceedings*, 68: 246–250.

Buchanan, James. Rent Seeking and Profit Seeking. In James Buchanan, Robert D. Tollison, and Gordon Tullock (eds.), *Toward a Theory of the Rent-Seeking Society*. College Station: Texas A&M University, pp. 3–15.

Dinopoulos, Elias. 1983: Import Competition, International Factor Mobility and Lobbying Responses: The Schumpeterian Industry Case. *Journal of International Economics* 14: 395–410.

Dinopoulos, Elias. 1989. Quid Pro Quo Foreign Investment and Market Structure. *Economics and Politics* 1 (Spring).

Dixit, Avinash, and Joseph Stiglitz. 1977. Monopolistic Competition and Optimum Product Diversity. *The American Economic Review* 67: 297–308.

Eaton, Jonathan, and Gene Grossman. 1986. Optimal Trade and Industrial Policy under Oligopoly. *Quarterly Journal of Economics* 2: 383–406.

Feenstra, Robert, and Jagdish Bhagwati. 1982. Tariff-Seeking and the Efficient Tariff. In Jagdish Bhagwati (ed.), *Import Competition and Response*. Chicago: University of Chicago Press, pp. 245–258.

Findlay, Ronald, and Stanislaw Wellisz. 1982. Endogenous Tariffs: The Political Economy of Trade Restrictions and Welfare. In Jagdish Bhagwati (ed.), *Import Competition and Response*. Chicago: University of Chicago Press, pp. 223–234.

Finger, J. Michael. 1982. Incorporating the Gains from Trade into Policy. *The World Economy* 5: 367–377.

Goldstein, Judith, and Stephen Krasner. 1984. Unfair Trade Practices: The Case for a Differential Response. *The American Economic Review, Papers and Proceedings* 74: 282–287.

Grossman, Gene. 1986. Strategic Export Promotion: A Critique. In Paul Krugman (ed.), *Strategic Trade Policy and the New International Economics*. Cambridge: MIT Press.

Haberler, Gottfried. 1950. Some Problems in the Pure Theory of International Trade. *Economic Journal* 60: 223–240.

Hillman, Arye L., and John G. Riley. 1989. Politically Contestable Rents and Transfers. *Economics and Politics* 1: 17–39.

Johnson, Harry G. 1953. Optimum Tariffs and Retaliation. *The Review of Economic Studies* 21: 142–153.

Johnson, Harry G. 1966. Optimal Trade Intervention in the Presence of Domestic Distortions. In Richard Caves, Harry G. Johnson, and Peter B. Kenen (eds.), *Trade, Growth, and the Balance of Payments*. Chicago: University of Chicago Press, pp. 3–34.

Kemp, Murray. 1964. *The Pure Theory of International Trade*. Englewood Cliffs: Prentice Hall.

Krishna, Kala, and Marie Thursby. 1988. Optimal Policies with Strategic Distortions. NBER Working Paper 2527. Cambridge, MA.

Krueger, Anne O. 1974. The Political Economy of the Rent-Seeking Society. *The American Economic Review* 64: 291–303.

Krugman, Paul. 1979. Increasing Returns, Monopolistic Competition, and International Trade. *Journal of International Economics* 9: 469–479.

Krugman, Paul. 1989. Import Protection as Export Promotion. In H. Kierzkowski (ed.), *Monopolistic Competition and International Trade*. Oxford: Blackwell.

Krugman, Paul. 1986. *Strategic Trade Policy and the New International Economics*. Cambridge: MIT Press.

Krugman, Paul. 1987. Is Free Trade Passé? *Journal of Economic Perspectives* 1: 131–144.

Lancaster, Kelvin. 1966. A New Approach to Consumer Theory. *Journal of Political Economy* 74: 132–157.

Lancaster, Kelvin. 1980. Intra-industry Trade under Monopolistic Competition. *Journal of International Economics* 10: 151–175.

Mayer, Wolfgang. 1984. Endogenous Tariff Formation. *The American Economic Review* 74: 970–985.

Mayer, Wolfgang, and Raymond Riezman. 1987. Endogenous Choice of Trade Policy Instruments. *Journal of International Economics* 23: 377–381.

Mayer, Wolfgang, and Raymond Riezman. 1989. Tariff Formation in a Multidimensional Voting Model. *Economics and Politics* 1: 61–79.

McMillan, John. 1986. *Game Theory in International Economics.* New York: Harwood Academic.

Meade, James. 1955. *The Theory of International Economic Policy, Trade and Welfare,* vol. 2. London.

Nelson, Douglas. 1987. The Domestic Political Preconditions of U.S. Trade Policy: Liberal Structure and Protectionist Dynamics. Paper presented at the conference on Political Economy of Trade: Theory and Policy. World Bank, Washington.

Panagariya, Arvind. 1980. Variable Returns to Scale in General Equilibrium Theory Once Again. *Journal of International Economics* 10: 499–526.

Rodriguez, Carlos. 1974. The Non-equivalence of Tariffs and Quotas under Retaliation. *Journal of International Economics* 4: 295–298.

Rodrik, Dani. 1986. Tariffs, Subsidies and the Theory of the Optimum Subsidy. *Journal of International Economics* 21: 285–299.

Rodrik, Dani. 1987. Imperfect Competition and Trade Policy in Developing Countries. Harvard University Mimeo.

Sapir, Andre. 1983. Foreign Competition, Immigration, and Structural Adjustment. *Journal of International Economics* 14: 381–394.

Scitovsky, Tibor. 1941. A Reconsideration of the Theory of Tariffs. *Review of Economic Studies* 9: 89–110.

Smith, Adam. 1776. *The Wealth of Nations.* Cannan edition 1937, New York.

Tornell, Aaron. 1987. Time Inconsistency of Protectionist Programs. Columbia University Department of Economics Discussion Paper 386. New York.

Tullock, Gordon. 1967. The Welfare Costs of Tariffs, Monopolies and Theft. *Western Economic Journal* 5: 224–232.

Willet, Thomas. 1984. International Trade and Protectionism. *Contemporary Policy Issues* 4: 1–15.

Wong, Kar-yiu. 1989. Optimal Threat of Trade Restriction and Quid Pro Quo Foreign Investment. *Economics and Politics* 1 (July).

2   U.S. Trade Policy
at the Crossroads

The popular perception, and the objective reality, of U.S. trade policy is that it is in a state of flux; indeed, it may have taken a turn for the worse.[1]

It is not just that the administration of the United States has succumbed to mounting demands for protection against imports by negotiating a number of significant export restraints. Nor is it that the "unfair trade" provisions in American law for taking antidumping actions and levying subsidy-countervailing duties have been captured and misused by pro- tectionists[2]—even though less, perhaps, than in the European Community.

What is most disturbing is the weakened commitment of the United States to multilateralism, manifesting itself in a variety of new ways.[3] The evidence of a fundamental change in trade policy is the new interest in regional arrangements and the departure from the accepted way of "doing business" under the General Agreement on Tariffs and Trade (GATT) by asserting that demands can be made for unilateral trade concessions by others and enforced by threats of retaliation.

2.1 New Directions: Actual and Potential

The origins of some of the changes can be traced back to the Trade Act of 1974 (which reflected, inter alia, the trade concerns arising from the weak- ness of the American dollar before the collapse of the Bretton Woods system).[4] But the dramatic events that have marked a turning point in American trade policy are more recent. Two merit mention.

The U.S.–Canada Free Trade Agreement, finally approved by the two countries in 1988, was a significant event. It had been preceded by the free trade agreement with Israel, but the special relationship the United States has with Israel, given their constituencies, made that an event of little predictive value. The free trade agreement with Canada is a different matter altogether, representing a conscious reversal of policy not to exploit the

GATT's Article XXIV which provides for departures from the principle of nondiscrimination to form free trade areas or customs unions. It signaled that regionalism, or plurilateralism (as distinct from unconditional most-favored-nation, MFN, treatment). was now okay for the United States to pursue.[5] The coincidence with the move by the European Community to complete its internal market by the end of 1992 has led, in turn, to widespread fears that multilateralism is coming to an end—one symptom of which was Lester Thurow's celebrated Davos pronouncement, "GATT is dead."[6]

The other significant event was the passage by the U.S. Congress of the Omnibus Trade and Competitiveness Act of 1988—in the face of strenuous resistance by the administration to certain of its provisions. Better called the Ominous Act of 1988, this piece of legislation tightened, in various ways, the "unfair trade" laws of the United States with respect to antidumping actions and subsidy-countervailing duties.

What has attracted most attention, however, is the extension of Section 301 of the Trade Act of 1974 to create a blunt instrument of trade policy. Section 301 had been used, until then, mainly to remedy treaty-defined "unfair trade practices," determined as such under multilateral procedures when GATT obligations were in question. It has now been turned into a "crowbar" that could, with the aid of threatened tariff retaliation, pry open foreign markets determined by the United States to be closed to its exports and could be used also to remove foreign "unfair trade" practices, not defined as such by any treaty whatsoever but determined by the United States to be "unreasonable" and impacting adversely on its trade.[7]

Thus with one unhappy passage of legislation, the U.S. Congress has given legitimacy to *unilateralism* in defining America's trade rights, in determining their violation, and in meting out punishment to secure satisfaction. This marks a departure from key principles that the GATT reflects—in particular, that trade rights are defined by, and are available to, all GATT member countries and that all GATT member countries subject themselves to the same dispute-settlement procedures over alleged violations of those trade rights.

The 1988 act has also marked a departure from the conventional GATT approach of "first-difference" reciprocity in bargaining over "concessions" in multilateral trade negotiations. In place of "balanced" mutual reductions of barriers to trade, as in seven rounds of GATT negotiations since 1947, the U.S. Congress appears now to have embraced a novel method of moving to freer trade in particular situations: ask others to liberalize using not the inducement of one's own trade concession, but the threat to suspend one's trading obligations if the demands are not met.

This is the approach of the so-called Super-301 provisions of the 1988 act (actually set out in Section 310). It is an approach that has caused much consternation, both among domestic critics and foreign countries. It permits, at the end of a mandated course of actions, entire countries—not just individual industries, as under Section 301 of the 1974 act—to be castigated as unfair traders. Initially, the Super-301 provision requires the U.S. Trade Representative (USTR) to identify, in practice on the basis of a survey of 34 countries and two trading blocs, foreign trade practices whose elimination is likely to increase American exports significantly. The process thus results initially in the identification of "priority" practices and "priority" countries.

On May 25, 1989 the first stages of the process reached a climax when, following the USTR's report, President Bush named Brazil, India, and Japan as "priority countries" and specified five areas of "priority practices" that would be investigated further. The different stages will now face other mandatory deadlines. If, after 12 to 18 months of investigation and negotiation (where agreed by the named countries), the USTR finds the "priority practices" to be "unfair," the United States may take retaliatory action. The result of all of this has been an electrifying recognition of a definite shift in the trade policy of the United States.

What could be a final blow is threatened by the vociferous proponents of "managed trade." Their major policy initiative was a report submitted on February 10, 1989 by the President's Advisory Committee on Trade Policy and Negotiations. Focusing on Japan, the report asked for a "results-oriented" trade policy, opting for what I have called a "fix-quantity" regime, by contrast to the "fix-rules" regime that the GATT represents.

The popularity of the report on Capitol Hill and the fact that it represents the sentiments and policy views of an influential set of chief executives in the American business community are causes for concern. So were early reports of approbation by Carla Hills, the U.S. Trade Representative in President Bush's cabinet, which were subsequently denied and attributed to erroneous reporting. It is an open and disturbing question whether, in fact, "managed trade" will sneak its way into U.S. trade policy, past Ambassador Hills's emphatic rejection, by judging the "good behavior" of Japan and other targeted countries by "how much" they import—and how much of it is imported from the United States and from particular American industries.[8]

These changes in the trade policy of the United States coexist with the undoubted and considerable commitment of the administration to the success of multilateral efforts, in the Uruguay Round of multilateral trade negotiations in Geneva, to liberalize agricultural trade and trade in services as well as extend GATT rules to other "new areas."

American trade policy therefore presents two faces. But with governments that are not monolithic that is not a sign of schizophrenia. In the case of the United States, the multilateral initiatives are essentially those of the administration, while the shifts to unilateralism have been driven by the Congress. The latter reflect, in turn, a variety of forces, among them lobbying pressure from constituencies and the appeal of diverse arguments that seem to provide plausibility to the notion that America deserves unilateral trade concessions from her trading rivals, extracted if necessary by threats of tariff retaliation.

In the rest of this article, I therefore consider, in the next section, the general factors that have prompted the shifts in United States trade policy. In the third section, I consider the many arguments that are in currency, implicitly or explicitly, to justify the demands for unilateral reductions of trade barriers by others. Next I examine the appropriateness of the Section-301 and Super-301 methods used to extract those unilateral concessions. I conclude briefly with the questions of "managed trade" and regionalism.

2.2   Forces Underlying the Shifts in U.S. Trade Policy

In understanding the new embrace of regional initiatives and aggressive unilateralism in opening foreign markets, and in seeking the removal of foreign trade practices considered unilaterally to be unreasonable and hence unfair, it is important to appreciate the critical role played by the acceleration of import protectionism during the first term of the Reagan administration.[9]

The increased demands for import protection that surged in the U.S. Congress were not the run-of-the-mill kind that arise from time to time as random pressures on specific industries from imports and are translated in the political arena into demands for relief from foreign competition. They were over a much wider spectrum of industries. Their potency derived not merely from the pressure of constituents, reflecting *sectional* interests, but from the increasing sense in the Congress that the *social* good required support for troubled industries. Let me elaborate.

The Balance of Payments

1. The overvaluation of the American dollar put significant pressure for adjustment in the traded activities of the American economy—making

nontraded activities generally more profitable at the expense of the traded ones.

Mounting constituency pressure for relief from imports was an inevitable political outcome. It was handled inaptly by the administration during the first Reagan term. Until the Plaza Agreement, the appreciation of the dollar was regarded with indifference, seen simply as a consequence of the attractiveness of the American economy for foreign investable funds. The possibility that there could be, even in that case, serious adjustment problems imposed on the economy—as with the Dutch Disease problem—because of the magnitude of the resource reallocation required was not addressed.

The "high-track" export restraints that followed were thrown as crumbs to satisfy protectionist demands. But the crumbs turned into loaves, marring the free-trade image, and also the track record, that the Reagan administration wanted.[10]

2. But the "balance-of-payments" situation, in the shape of the trade deficit that persisted in spite of the significant post-Plaza realignment of the dollar, fostered a growing feeling that the trade deficit was unsustainable, had to be eliminated, and could not be tackled by exchange-rate realignment. The *broader* American interest required, therefore, that trade policy had to be deployed to address the trade deficit.

It is true that the unsustainability of the trade deficit and its elimination as a goal for the United States (whether in its own interest or that of countries "more in need of capital") are issues that are arguable, to say the least, and have been argued extensively. But the notion that exchange-rate changes cannot impact any more on the trade deficit has drawn somewhat greater strength from the empirical observation that the realignment of the dollar failed to reduce the trade deficit anywhere near as quickly and as much as many had hoped. It accordingly needs commenting upon. Two points should be made.

First, a cliché, but an important one. If excess spending continues, expenditure-switching policies, such as exchange-rate devaluations, will fail to produce more than ripple effects on the trade deficit.[11] If the budget deficit persisted, and no significant reduction in spending occurred in the private sector, the realignment of the dollar could not be expected to work.

Second, a novel consideration. If local prices do not rise, a devaluation cannot induce a switch of expenditure away from imports. Much was made, in the early years after the Plaza Agreement, of the failure of the "pass-through" effects of the currency realignment. Prices of imported goods did not rise by the amount of the dollar devaluation or, at least, not as much as "normal." A search for explanations started among macro-economists. The more interesting among them was the notion that invest-ments, once made, would lead to price-setting behavior to hold onto markets. Japanese firms, having invested for sales in American markets when the dollar was high, would tenaciously cut prices when the dollar fell, rather than close down and move out. This notion of "hysteresis," and lack of symmetry around a change back and forth, may have some merit insofar as the dollar was high for a long period and investors may not have foreseen the magnitude of the dollar's fall.[12]

But a natural and plausible explanation, pertinent to the discussion of trade policy, is one that the macroeconomists forgot to note, perhaps because their conventional thinking had not caught up with the way nontariff measures are used in developed countries generally and in the United States in particular to deal with "disruptive" imports.[13] This was simply that, as the dollar had long remained high, Japanese (and Far East-ern) exports had come to be heavily afflicted by export-restraint arrange-ments in various forms. This meant that there was often a substantial scarcity premium on Japanese goods. If the dollar was devalued, the deval-uation would first cut into this premium, with the final price to American consumers unaffected. Only after the devaluation had exceeded this pre-mium would an impact on final prices be seen. That is to say, the pass-through effects would be abnormally low at the outset, until the premia were absorbed.[14]

That this hypothesis has explanatory power is supported by the facts that Japanese goods were heavily restrained, that the dollar was devalued mainly against the yen, and that the pass-through effects improved after the dollar devaluation had become substantial. But it is additionally sup-ported by disaggregated industry studies undertaken in Japan.[15]

By ignoring the linkage between protection and exchange-rate inefficacy, analysts have encouraged the erroneous idea that protection is necessary *because* exchange-rate changes are ineffective. We are in danger, then, of experiencing a vicious circle: protection leads to the reduced efficacy of exchange-rate changes; in turn, the inefficacy of exchange-rate changes leads to protection.

But it is also necessary to remind politicians that if they think exchange-rate changes are inefficacious because "prices no longer matter," the same objection could apply to protection. Both are expenditure-switching policies (although they are not identical insofar as the exchange-rate change affects exports as well). In addition, neither policy can work unless it differentially affects domestic savings and investment, so as to produce an excess of the former over the latter at the margin.[16] Otherwise a lasting impact on the trade deficit is not possible.[17]

The Double Squeeze

The adjustment problem for the traded industries in the United States has been further accentuated by a "double squeeze."[18] The growth of exports from Japan and the Pacific "Gang of Four" (Hong Kong, Singapore, South Korea, and Taiwan) and the less spectacular but still impressive export performance of other newly industrializing countries, such as Brazil, and of the newly exporting countries, such as Malaysia and Thailand, have created problems for specific industries in the developed countries, obliging them to adjust to those changes.

A country that grows more rapidly than others will, on average, export at a volume and rate of growth that is hard for the other countries to accommodate without complaints from the domestic industries that must bear the brunt of the adjustment. Japan has been up against this phenomenon since the 1930s. Even then, when Japan was not yet dominant, Japanese diplomats were scurrying around negotiating "voluntary" export restraints—on pencils, electric lamps, safety matches, and other products —with the United States, Britain, Australia, and other trading partners, partners among whom a bilateral surplus in trade with Japan was common. The present surplus situation has compounded Japan's difficulties; but even if her surplus were to disappear, she would continue to attract the protectionist ire of disaffected competitors.[19]

De-industrialization and National Interest

The protectionist fallout, however, has come not merely from troubled industries seeking relief. There has been the national-interest concern that America is threatened with de-industrialization and that this, in turn, will damage the economic well-being of the United States.

The Democrats, in particular, fell easy prey to these views. For instance, in the 1984 presidential election campaign in the United States, the Democratic candidate Walter Mondale invoked images of Americans reduced to flipping hamburgers at McDonalds while the Japanese overwhelmed the country's industries. He might have invoked, with greater irony, a picture of American kids rolling rice cakes at sushi bars.

The fear of de-industrialization also agitated the leaders of trade unions in declining, protection-seeking industries. Sol Chaikin, for example, of the International Garment Workers' Union, protested in an article in *Foreign Affairs*: "Because there are relatively few well-paying jobs in the services sector, an economy devoid of manufacturing would also necessarily experience a general decline of living standards... Unrestricted trade and the investment practices of the multinationals ... can only lead to an America ultimately devoid of manufacturing."[20]

The effect was to make life easier for those seeking protection. These views made it less difficult for politicians to respond affirmatively to narrower interests seeking protection. Congressmen voting for protection could feel comfortable in their conviction that they were acting, not as politicians responding to the narrow sectional interests of their constituents, but as statesmen safeguarding the national interest.

From an objective point of view, however, the arguments advanced in support of the view that de-industrialization has deleterious consequences are sufficiently tenuous to make the recent "manufacturing matters" school of worriers in the United States as hard to side with as the members of the better-known and earlier school of de-industrialization in the United Kingdom, led by the late Nicholas Kaldor, the distinguished Cambridge economist and intellectual of the Labor party.[21] Let me address some of the principal arguments of the two schools.

Some contend that manufacturing plays an "integral role" in the American economy in the shape of "important linkages to the broader economy"[22] But linkages in the shape of input-output relationships reveal nothing about the desirability of policy intervention to correct market failure. It is commonplace among noneconomists to infer externalities from linkages. It is also a common non sequitur.[23]

It is often said that because American manufactures "constitute a significant source of demand for the output of other industries," an increase in manufacturing unemployment would create increased unemployment in other related industries[24] and, therefore, manufactures must be supported. But that is an argument that can be easily turned on its head. Would it not be sensible to reduce the size of an activity that can cause such sizable disruption? Besides, even accepting the form of the argument, one must build a plausible counterfactual to judge the matter. If manufactures go down, what goes up; and what then would be the new linkages?

Furthermore, the notion that services are *complementary* to manufactures has been used to argue that the promotion or defense, at a minimum, of manufactures is essential. The collapse of one would lead *not* to a "post-industrial" service economy but to something else (presumably more primitive, instead of progressive and pleasurable). Now let me quote from the chief proponents of this view (peculiar to the American school and, to my knowledge, foreign to the British school's way of thinking which saw manufactures as being a *substitute* to services):

There are ... linkages in the economy, such as those which tie the crop cluster to the cotton fields. the ketchup maker to the tomato patch, the wine press to the vineyards (to return our focus on agriculture). Here the linkages are tight and quite concrete... Beyond the limit of possible recommendations provided by the bounded space, the linkage is a bind, not a junction or substitution point. *Offshore the tomato farm and you close or offshore the ketchup plant. No two ways about it.* (emphasis added)[25]

When I first read this assertion, as I remarked in my Ohlin lectures, I was eating my favorite Crabtree & Evelyn marmalade and had not realized that England grew her own oranges![26]

Similar arguments have come from other proponents of manufactures. For instance:[27]

... many industries that feature prominently in visions of the "post-industrial" economy, such as education, banking and communications, are demanded in significant part by the manufacturing sector. The health of these progressive parts of the services sector is therefore tied to the performance of American manufacturing firms.

This statement confuses linkages with physical proximity or, at least, national production of producer services. But linkages in most modern services need not be either. Thanks to technical change, many modern services can now be delivered without the physical proximity of the supplier to the user: many are what are now called "disembodied" or, better still, "long-distance" services which can be delivered over the wire.[28] Technical change has greatly reduced the degree of local establishment necessary to deliver services to users even when efficient supply requires physical proximity. The assumption that there is a strong physical-proximity linkage that makes it impossible to supply producer services to manufacturing establishments elsewhere was never wholly true. Now it is almost fanciful. It derives almost certainly from an archaic haircuts-as-services conception of the services sector.

Turning, then, to more serious arguments for favoring the manufacturing sector, one must reckon with the different claims—implicit and explicit—of market failure. A particularly appealing one has resulted from the recent developments in the *theory of trade in imperfectly competitive product markets.* With sufficiently large economies internal to the firm, oligopolistic market structures can emerge. It follows that prices will generally not measure true costs, that excess profits will emerge, and that intervention in support of one's own industry can shift some excess profits away from foreign firms toward the domestic industry in question.[29]

These notions are scientifically interesting and have attracted well-deserved attention. But if they are used to support the promotion of manufactures, as has often been the case in Washington, it is necessary to note several compelling objections.

1. The profit-shifting argument has a predatory flavor. It can therefore lead to retaliation. Once that happens, everyone can be a loser. Certainly, the world trading regime would be a loser. Trade battles, even when settled, can leave scars, making it easier for protectionists to achieve their self-serving goals.

2. What is more, the argument presupposes that there are in fact significant rents to shift, but recent empirical analysis suggests that this is not so.[30]

3. The question of sizable increasing returns to scale to the firm can also be investigated empirically. Here again, the latest econometric findings for American and European industry indicate that there is very little evidence of internal economies even at the "two-digit" level of industries, leaving one to wonder whether they exist in a significant degree at the level of individual firms.[31]

4. Finally, if a special case is to be made for favoring manufactures because of the "strategic" profit-sharing theory, it is pertinent to note that some in developing countries currently cite that very theory to say that modern services are characterized by substantial economies of scale and hence freer trade in services should be rejected. Obviously, there is no shortage of pressure groups who want protection and no shortage, either, of theoretical "beneficial-protection" arguments that pressure groups will embrace (without detailed empirical justification) to further their cause. In any event, it is inconsistent for the makers of trade policy in the developed countries to use notions of "strategic" trade policy (based on economies-of-scale arguments) to pursue their own goals while denying them to the developing countries whom they castigate as "obstructionist" in negotiating an agreement on trade in services. Must economies-of-scale arguments be used only by those with scale (in terms of political power)?

Now for the overriding question of externalities. Do manufactures just have sex appeal to those who have never been close to a blast furnace, or do they have unusual externalities, giving differentially more to us than they take from the national pie?

Externalities are a phenomenon that many economists feel must exist and may even be important. Serendipity and the fact that its rewards are not generally appropriable by those who act as catalysts testify to the belief that we are talking about something tangible. But it is so hard to identify the differential significance of externalities within *specific* activities that many economists have tended to walk away from the concept for policy-making purposes, arguing that they are the last refuge of the scoundrel seeking special favors, perhaps even the first refuge.[32]

By contrast, politicians have little trouble deciding what sector or industry has unusual externalities and, as a result, is important to defend and even expand. Manufactures have been the beneficiaries of their attention in developing countries and from the members of the British and American de-industrialization schools. So have, of late, high-technology industries where politicians believe that having them must be important for the economy because they are at the forefront of modern technology.[33]

It is difficult to find sufficiently convincing evidence to support the case for promoting manufactures, or specific components thereof like high-technology industries, on grounds of unusual externalities. Something can be said, though.

1. The econometric studies cited as showing that internal economies of scale are not important in American (and European) industries also show that external economies are important. These external economies are further related to the overall size of the manufacturing sector.[34] But the authors could equally have used the overall size of the economy or the size of the manufacturing sector plus the modern financial sector and turned up the same result. (I have urged them to test the hypothesis in view of the significance of these distinctions for the current policy debate on the consequences of de-industrialization.)[35]

2. Does the fact that manufactures show a higher rate of increase in labor productivity than others indicate that they must be supported? This was the view implied in the so-called Verdoorn law that led Kaldor to recommend the "selective employment tax" in the United Kingdom to tax employment in services and thus make hiring cheaper for manufactures. Kaldor was careful to imply, however, that there was an externality here, that some sort of "learning by doing" operated in manufacturing.[36] The mere fact of a higher increase in productivity in a sector is in itself not an argument for policy intervention to support the sector. To my knowledge,

the British debate on Kaldor's thesis did not produce any compelling evidence that manufactures were characterized by a significant amount of such implied "learning by doing" or other externality and that the amount was sufficiently higher than in other sectors (such as modern services) to warrant differential support of manufactures.[37]

3. Yet another argument, used in the American debate, has been that the manufacturing sector accounts for over 90 percent of research-and-development (R&D) expenditures in the United States. This cannot be an argument, though, for supporting manufactures against a market-induced decline unless it is shown that the social rate of return on this R&D expenditure exceeds that on other capital spending. Again, one cannot really argue without further analysis that, no matter why and therefore where this sector shrinks in terms of industry-wise and firm-wise composition, R&D expenditures will shrink too. Maybe the shrinking will take place in firms that do not undertake research and development; it would in fact seem plausible that the R&D-intensive firms will be larger and, if import competition is causing the shrinkage, the firms that exit will be those that are smaller and not engaged in research and development. Thus even this version of the "productivity" argument for manufactures remains unproven.

4. Another argument is that for small ("infinitesimal") changes, a subsidy to manufactures will produce a negligible ("second-order") loss if manufactures do not have externalities but that, if they do, the gain will be nonnegligible ("first-order"). Given equal ignorance, one should then subsidize manufactures.[38] But there are problems with this argument. (1) Interventions are not infinitesimal. (2) The argument further presupposes that the world is efficient except for the possible externality in manufactures. (3) The argument may be equally applied to modern services, in which case the subsidizing of manufactures may do more harm than good. (4) Even within manufactures, it is highly unlikely that externalities obtain for all manufactures: even an infinitesimal across-the-board subsidy to all of them can then produce a net loss.

Finally, mention must be made of the interesting recent revival in the United States of the argument, originally considered relevant to developing countries, that manufactures have to pay excess wages for identical labor, these excess wages representing a distortion that requires appropriate intervention to support manufactures.[39] I find this personally satisfying since the argument was first developed by trade theorists in the 1960s and directly led to the major scientific developments in the theory of commercial policy during the postwar period.[40] It serves therefore an incidental but important purpose in refuting the claims sometimes made that, until the arrival in the 1980s of the theory of trade in imperfectly competitive product markets, free trade was regarded as the policy that "economic theory tells us is always right."[41] I nevertheless remain sceptical. Why?

1. It may well be that, even if all of the excess wage rates in an industry were treated as reflecting a distortion, it may not do more than dent the cost of existing trade restrictions on manufactured imports. Thus a recent study of the welfare and employment effects of U.S. import quotas on steel and automobiles concludes that the benefit of removing the quotas, in the presence of wage distortions, continues to be large, although diminished.[42] In short, for the United States, the degree of protection of key manufactures that may be justified as a second-best intervention to offset the maximal possible distortion from excess wage rates paid in these sectors appears to be well below what exists.

2. But the real problem, in my view, is that the interpretation of the wage differentials as distortionary is not yet robust enough, in spite of the enormous and systematic analysis of the issue. The degree of disaggregation for both industries and occupations is much too high—although large by conventional standards—to support the conclusions derived if the purpose is to provide actual policy support to industries and sectors with distortionary excess wages. Since the particular theory of wage distortions that Lawrence Summers et al. favor is that of efficiency wages needing to be paid to avoid shirking,[43] it would be useful if careful and extremely disaggregated microeconomic studies were produced, at least for an excess-wage-ranked pair of industries, showing that indeed shirking explains the wage differential. I am particularly concerned because, a priori, it would seem to me that shirking on the job should be a lot easier in service industries such as banking and insurance than in assembly-line manufacturing where shirking by an individual may show up immediately in disruption of the process. Yet the deviation of the wage from the all-industry average, adjusted for variables such as age, experience, and schooling, is +9.7 percent for manufactures and −13.2 percent for finance, insurance, and real estate.[44]

3. There is a puzzle in that the interindustry wage differentials are similar for different classes of occupations: "The industry wage structure also seems to be similar for different types of workers. In industries in which one occupation is highly paid, all occupations tend to be highly paid."[45] But it seems highly doubtful that technological differences between every

pair of industries would make everyone, whatever their level of occupation, shirk more in one industry than in the other. Can it not be that here we are catching something else altogether—possibly, the cost of living in different regions or the cost of labor migration to different regions and geographical specificity of different industries? For example, all Englishmen going to India in the nineteenth century, regardless of occupational level, would have had to be paid a "tropical" premium, a wage differential.

In short, it seems premature to make recommendations for sectoral-policy interventions on the basis of the empirical evidence available. If we are going to intervene selectively in favor of industries and sectors, especially when we know that selective interventions of this type cannot be insulated from capture and misuse, the standard of persuasion if not proof that we should expect greatly exceeds what we have before us. The jury is still out.

The "Diminished Giant" Syndrome

The payments difficulties and the "double jeopardy" phenomenon may have produced the conditions for increased demand by sectional interests lobbying for protection and for increased supply by influential Congressmen thinking that protection would also be in the national interest. But the overall ethos favorable to protectionism came from the national psychology produced by America's relative decline in the world economy. This might be called the "diminished giant" syndrome.

While the United States continues to be a dominant power, it has witnessed the erosion of its predominant status in the world economy as Japan has risen from the ashes and, too, as other Pacific countries have come to the fore.

The parallel with Britain at the end of the nineteenth century is dramatic. In both instances, the giant's diminution produced a protectionist backlash, sorely trying the pro-trade bias of the international regime.[46] Walter Lippmann characterized this as the American Century. In the same vein, the nineteenth century was Britain's. As the century ended, Britain was gradually losing her political and economic preeminence. The twentieth century is ending similarly for the United States. Staffan Burenstam Linder has already announced the arrival of the Pacific Century.[47]

The diminution in Britain's preeminence in the world economy led to a rise in protectionist sentiments and to demands for an end to Britain's unilateralist embrace of free-trade principles. And the United States has followed the same path. The present-day sentiments on trade policy in the

United States have been aimed pointedly at the newly successful rivals, just as their nineteenth-century British counterparts were. The United States and Germany were to Britain what the Pacific nations—Japan in particular—are to the United States today.

"Fair Trade" and "Level Playing Fields"

Aside, though, from aiding the rise of old-fashioned import protectionism, the diminished giant syndrome has prompted a significant shift in United States trade policy toward emphasis on "fair trade." One can argue cynically that words matter, as Orwell taught us, and it is easier to indulge protectionism if it is sold as a response to "unfair trade" rather than undisguised in its true form. The emergence, or reemergence, of the "fair trade" obsession in the United States grew as import competition grew with the rise of the dollar. And the growth of Far East trade can certainly be cited as a contributory factor.

But the diminished giant syndrome also helped. It is relatively easy, when one's premier status is in jeopardy, to think that the success of one's rivals must be due to perfidy. Panic produces petulance.[48] The persistent and pervasive belief that the countries in the Far East are "not playing by the rules," and that "level playing fields" must be established to compete with them, owes much to this syndrome.

In fact, "fair trade" and "reciprocity" emerged as issues in an equal degree in Britain when she faced her own relative decline at the end of the nineteenth century. The rise in Britain during the 1870s and 1880s of the National Fair Trade League, the National Society for the Defence of British Industry and the Reciprocity Free Trade Association are events that make the American sentiments and actions of the last decade more easy to comprehend.[49]

Growth of Export Interests

Apart from the emergence of concerns over unfair trade, the other dramatic change, and indeed a novelty in the political economy of trade policy generally, has been the growth of export interests in the United States.[50] This has given a special form, and a sharp edge, to the concerns over unfair trade and to the unilateralism that afflicts American trade policy today, while also explaining the embrace of regionalism and the thrust of positions adopted by the United States in the Uruguay Round negotiations.

Natural Forces—Interests and Ideology

The increasing globalization of economic activity, with the crisscrossing of investments among the major trading countries, has created a 'spider's web' phenomenon. The reaction of multinational enterprises (with global reach) to import pressures does not need to be the old-fashioned demand for import protection. This can, by spreading protection elsewhere and thereby affecting freer trade in the world economy, imperil the open trading system within which they can function best.

They now have another option. If they sell in other markets, as most do, they can also ease the pressure of competition on themselves by asking for, not higher import barriers against others, but lower import barriers by others. Aside from this providing an option that may equally relieve competitive pressures, it is also in keeping with the general multinational ethos and interests of achieving a freer world trading regime.

It has the added advantage that one might be able to fit it into the "unfair trade" framework, if applied at the level of products, firms and industries (as necessary to one's argument). If protection against American exports of automobiles in a particular country is greater than American protection against that country's exports of automobiles, that leads to a plausible claim of "unfair" competition.

Ideologically, this argument may also be shown to have support from trade theory on grounds of efficiency, not just fairness. International trade theorists have argued that, under large-enough scale economies to a firm, import protection can lead to the viability of one's firm at the expense of one's rivals, producing even the paradoxical phenomenon that import protection leads to export promotion.[51] In essence, it is easy to see that if firms are identical, economies of scale yield irreversible gains (as when learning occurs), and if one firm has access to two markets and the other has access to only one because its market is closed to imports and the other's is not, the firm in the protected market will gain a permanent advantage.[52] This may even be to social advantage (although this is not guaranteed).

The sudden popular awareness of this demonstration,[53] brought out from the closet by younger trade theorists and put into the political arena,[54] has lent critical ideological support to the export lobbies seeking outward reach in foreign markets and to congressmen who see in this a justification for aggressively "opening foreign markets".

The combination of export interests and ideology has been a heady brew, enough to provide the momentum for the "open foreign markets" thrust in United States trade policy. But export interests have profited equally from the payments difficulties discussed earlier. Just as the belief that import restrictions will cure the trade deficit refuses to die, rising ever again like Jaws in James Bond movies, so does its flip side: that lowering foreign trade barriers will cure the trade deficit. Those who make policy in Congress are doomed to believe it; and those who seek to export willy-nilly have not hesitated to exploit it.

Promoting the Lobbies
The growth of the export lobbies was encouraged by the administration. Faced with the outbreak of import protectionism in the country and on Capitol Hill, the administration back-tracked—with the Plaza Agreement —on its international macroeconomic position of benign neglect. The induced, and inevitable, realignment of the dollar was the safety valve that had to be opened.

Equally, the administration saw in the nascent export lobbies the opportunity to provide a political offset to the (import) protectionist lobbies. By nurturing them, and expanding trade through measures aimed at "opening markets," the administration would take the political momentum away from the protectionists who would "close markets."

In essence, the administration did this in two ways, one consonant with the tradition of multilateralism and the other not quite so. The former was to push energetically for a new GATT round of multilateral trade negotiations where barriers to trade in old and new sectors (agriculture and services) of *export* interest to the United States would be brought down. These efforts culminated in the current Uruguay Round negotiations. The other course was to embrace regionalism in the shape of the free trade agreement with Canada, a dramatic and visible "trade-expanding" move and one that also, in its inclusion of agreements on services, was supposed to provide a spur to the Uruguay Round negotiations in the deliberations on trade in services.

The preceding analysis focused on the many factors that have been driving the United States in the directions of unilateralism and regionalism even while it is an active participant in multilateral negotiations. The following analysis now offers an evaluation of these shifts, starting with unilateralism.

2.3   Arguments for Unilateral Concessions by Others

Unilateralism relates to three different issues: (1) seeking unilateral trade concessions from others; (2) refusing to submit oneself, as under the GATT, to the same dispute-settlement procedures in determining violations of one's trade rights that one uses against others; and (3) defining new "unfair trade" practices, and hence new trading rights and disciplines, through unilateral specification and threatened punishment for noncompliance rather than by negotiated treaty.

I shall have something to say (in the next section) about the use of threats by the United States, as embodied in the new 301 provisions, to establish new disciplines. Here, however, I address the pervasive view that America is entitled to something for nothing from others—especially from the Far East and Japan—by way of trade concessions. This view certainly lends the cutting edge to the forms of unilateralism distinguished above.

Economists have generally believed that unilateral trade liberalization by oneself is good. There are, indeed, well-known theoretical exceptions that are explained in the classroom that can cause the relation between the reduction of trade barriers and the increase in welfare to be nonmonotonic. But they are not of great policy consequence.[55]

The approach to trade liberalization, enshrined in the GATT, is to bargain concessions on trade. There is "first-difference" reciprocity: the reductions of barriers are generally mutual and "balanced." (Overall or full reciprocity—that is, balance of overall openness of one's markets—is presumably taken care of through setting an appropriate "price" to GATT membership.) Such reciprocity of trade concessions is often considered "mercantilist," it suggests that trade liberalization is a cost rather than a benefit. But it makes sense in two ways. (1) If I liberalize and get you also to liberalize reciprocally, I benefit twice: I reduce my own barriers while I also improve my trading gains through the reduction of your barriers.[56] (2) There is also a "second-best" argument when macroeconomics does not work well. In this event, trade liberalization by oneself may lead to short-run adjustment costs, whereas simultaneous trade liberalization by others will reduce these costs.[57]

But the current approach of the United States to trade liberalization is altogether novel. It appears to demand that *others* (such as Japan) liberalize unilaterally (or else the crowbar will be used). How is this to be justified? As one reads the occasional justifications in different sources, a number of rationales can be discerned in an emotionally charged debate.

Balance-of-Payments Arguments
A couple of arguments related to the payments situation can be distinguished:

1. Japan has an enormous surplus in her trade balance and therefore she should liberalize her trade barriers faster than others.

2. The United States has an enormous trade deficit and therefore it is appropriate to ask others, who do not have a similar affliction, to liberalize their trade unilaterally .

These two arguments are related but still distinct.[58] The latter, however, serves as the stepping stone to the former, which is the main driving force behind the pressures directed at Japan.

But this contention is not convincing because changes in trade barriers will not generally procure the sustained improvements in trade deficits which are desired unless a differential impact on the levels of savings and investment in the desired direction can be plausibly argued. In the absence of such impacts, the long-run effect of reduced foreign trade barriers will generally be to increase the trade-to-GNP ratio at which the United States deficit will persist.[59]

There is a further "systemic" objection to the argument. Suppose one wants to argue that freer world trade is a desirable goal, that it is (in the short run) easier for countries enjoying a large and persistent surplus to reduce trade barriers, and that, consequently, such countries ought to take unilateral actions to liberalize trade without matching, mutual, and reciprocal liberalization by others. If that is the case, one ought to work in the GATT, and in the IMF, to introduce such *rules* into the international institutions. Such rules could be built into revisions to the articles of the GATT that deal with balance-of-payments provisions (Article XII and Article XVIII).[60] But to use this notion selectively against Japan and other targeted countries, through the unilateral exercise of power and without the corresponding assumption of a similar obligation when one's own deficit will turn into a surplus (as it surely will), is to sanction the view that it is fine for the big dog on the block to bark at—and also bite—the little dogs. The GATT properly assigns instead a symmetry of obligations and rights, establishing the rule of law rather than the law of the jungle.

The "Japan-is-Cheating" Argument
What of the argument that Japan is cheating on the trade obligations that she assumed through the reduction of her trade barriers in successive GATT rounds during the postwar period? The negotiated cuts in Japan's trade barriers are not effective, it is said. Article XXIII, relating to impairment and nullification of obligations assumed by GATT members, is implicitly being invoked.

Japan, on this basis, can be asked to liberalize unilaterally. The demand, however, is not really for unilateral trade concessions. It is really a matter of returning to the true status quo as defined by obligations assumed earlier as part of the negotiated, reciprocal exchange of trade concessions.

The argument conjures up the image of the Japanese jackass refusing to move toward the carrot being offered. When you look behind him, you see the *samurai* holding him by the tail. One has to demonstrate, in short, that the effects of reduced trade barriers have been nullified and that this has been caused by governmental interventions aimed at securing such nullification.

The econometric studies directed at the problem of whether Japan imports "too little," either in aggregate or in manufactures, were motivated by this problem. If Japan is as open as she seems, how come her imports are so low? In particular, if Japan is significantly off the regression line on import shares, making her an outlier (in econometric jargon), then we can deduce that she is an out-and-out liar (in fulfilling her trade obligations). There are serious problems with this case against Japan.

1. As a recent paper by Koichi Hamada and T. N. Srinivasan argues, the econometric studies have been badly divided on the issue of Japan's import performance, but those which are better crafted and grounded in econometrically appropriate methodology[61] do *not* support the view that it is unduly disappointing.

2. But even had the econometrics gone the other way, the results would *not* reveal that the hand of the Ministry of International Trade and Industry (MITI) in Tokyo was responsible for those results or that the cause was instead a host of other factors, including buyer preferences and institutional features that are conventionally, and for good reasons, treated as part of a country's "givens" subject to which gains from trade are to be achieved in open markets.

The "Japan-Is-Different" Argument

In fact, it is interesting that Japan-bashing has now shifted increasingly away from the notion of the (malign) efficacy of the Japanese government's invisible hand as the culprit and toward, instead, the inefficacy of Adam Smith's invisible hand as the source of trouble! Let me explain.

Economists take one's tastes as one's own affair. Given your tastes and mine, each sovereign in this regard, we can still engage in profitable, voluntary exchange. Economists do not argue, quite properly, that you must change your tastes to suit my convenience.[62] That is the stuff of coercion and the politics of power. But that is precisely what some seem to want of Japan. They want her consumers and producers to change their tastes.

A recent *Newsweek* story typically reflected these sentiments when it reported on Japanese consumers.[63]

[Japanese] consumers [do not] seem about to shed their bias against foreign goods. At one of INBIX's NIC stores recently, a 50-year-old salaryman looked at a CD player made in South Korea. The price was less than half of what he would pay anywhere else in Tokyo. He shrugged, then put it back. "No," he said. "I'm afraid it might break."

The *Newsweek* reporters could have produced a more effective splash in the United States by repeating the story (no doubt apocryphal and born of the tensions produced by what is perceived as unfair Japan-bashing) where a Tokyo housewife walks into a Ginza store looking for a camera. Shown high-quality cameras, she asks: "Don't you have something cheaper?" The answer: "No. But just walk down the block. At the corner you will find a shop selling shoddy American stuff."

But not all tastes, for or against imported goods, are "irrational." They can be grounded in reality more than is conceded by those who point accusing fingers. I recall writing nearly three decades ago from New Delhi to Harry Johnson on Indian stationery, complaining like V. S. Naipaul about the "craze for foreign." He came back with what could have a lesson for the American–Japan debate: "If the quality of the paper you have written on is any indication, the craze seems quite sensible to me."

The question of buyer preferences among Japanese firms for one another's goods is an even more explosive issue. It has received support recently from Mordechai Kreinin's study, reported in *The World Economy*, of 62 subsidiaries in Australia of Japanese, European and American companies examining the comparative way they procure equipment from sources outside Australia.[64]

The issue is not whether such preferences exist. The issue is why. A large part of the buyer preference in Japanese businesses must relate to the value attached to customer relationships. That is an idea which is not merely sociological but is now incorporated as a possibly rational form of profit-maximizing behavior in the modern theory of industrial organization. Even casual empiricism, based on one's exposure to American firms and products, whether autos or suits, shows that the philosophy underlying the American approach to consumers is *caveat emptor*, buyer beware. Dissatisfied or duped consumers must take recourse to litigation, aided by the largest legal establishment in the world; they are also supposed to vote with their feet where repeat-buying is involved.

The Japanese way is different. Their legal establishment is also correspondingly of a piece, small and lean, not large and mean. Consumer loyalty follows. It then becomes hard for American-style competitors to lure customers away by simply offering discounts that carry no assurance of follow-through and commitment to consumer satisfaction. Large enough discounts could overcome this problem. Everything has its price. But complaints of collusive Japanese preference for their own fill the air when discounts that are within reason but below those necessary lead to failure to find Japanese customers. It is not surprising that American firms that have made the necessary effort to adapt to Japanese ways have done well and are not among the vociferous complainants against "autarkic" Japanese corporate buying preferences.

The buying preferences of Japanese consumers and firms are not grounds for demanding unilateral trade concessions from Japan. The appropriate attitude to the question of different Japanese preferences was conveyed by Paul Samuelson, who tells of encountering a charming old lady at a public lecture in Boston on trade policy. She went up to the Nobel Prize economist and said: "Professor Samuelson, I *would* like to help by buying American, but the Japanese goods are so much better. Am I wrong in buying them instead?" Professor Samuelson answered, "Madam, you should buy what you like. Leave it to us economists and the Congress to take care of the balance of payments."

In any event, buying preferences are not areas that can be significantly influenced by policy. Yasuhiro Nakasone's appeals to the Japanese, when he was their prime minister, to "buy American" are likely to have been as ineffective as, if more ludicrous than, those addressed by Americans to other Americans. Deterrent penalties and taxes by the government on those firms who do not buy American, or subsidies to those who do, are certainly policy instruments that could be deployed. But it is doubtful whether these can be seriously contemplated by a democratic government such as the Japanese any more than the U.S. Congress could enact a corresponding set of tax policies to penalize the consumption of American goods or subsidize the purchase of foreign ones.[65]

What, then, about the question of *access* to these buyers, no matter what their preferences? The retail distribution system in Japan, with its 1.6 million mom-and-pop-style stores dotting the country and protected against large stores (recently by the passage in the Diet of the Large-Scale Retail Store Law), militates against the distribution of foreign goods.[66]

This question is tricky. It needs careful handling at the level of general principles rather than immediate expediency. In particular, we need to ask here (and, indeed, similarly for other institutional issues) the following questions:

1. Are these institutions designed to discriminate in favor of domestic goods and against foreign rivals?

2. If their unintended fallout is to affect trade directly, can we think of "next-best" ways in which such effects can be minimized?

3. In seeking such relief, can we think not just of others accommodating to our needs but of establishing general disciplines, and neutral procedures to settle disputes relating thereto, to which we subject ourselves as much as we seek to subject others?

In the case of the Japanese distribution system, the answer to question 1 is surely, no. The answer to question 2 is that it does inhibit, although it does not prevent, access for firms that prefer marketing products through large outlets, but that these firms could adapt their sales techniques with possibilities such as mail-order selling, which has begun and offers a possible way out. As for question 3, if national distribution systems are to be considered legitimate grounds for foreign scrutiny, the United States should propose procedures under which it becomes possible for other trading countries generally to challenge its own distributive institutions and methods as well.[67] An advantage of such general procedures, applying symmetrically, is that it would slow down the one-way demands for others to "reform" which are otherwise readily generated by lobbies in the United States. The argument by the administration that one's excesses can come home to roost has traditionally helped to contain such excesses. There is no reason to expect that it would fail to do so in this area.

It is necessary to observe that the path down which the United States is currently going in its negotiations with Japan under the rubric of the Structural Impediments Initiative, where matters such as Japan's retail distribution system and even her "high" savings rate are being discussed as obstacles to trade, is the path of folly. This is so not merely because it proceeds on a one-on-one basis without the benefit of general procedures uniformly applying to all. It is also because, once one starts bringing into the trade arena issues such as rates of savings, one is essentially arguing that everything affects trade, that policy (or absence thereof) on virtually everything will affect trade, and, accordingly, every policy can be put on the line in discussing what is "fair trade" and a prerequisite for legitimate free trade.

Thus, if Bangladesh currently has a comparative advantage in textiles, due to lower wages, we no longer need to worry about being scolded as protectionists when we reject imports of Bangladeshi textiles as unfair trade caused by her "pauper labor." After all, the low Bangladeshi wages are a result of inadequate population-control *policies* and, too, of inefficient economic policies that inhibit investment and growth and thus a rise in real wages. Or, if the United States continues to produce textiles that rely heavily on immigrant labor, often illegal, this is unfair trade because American immigration *policy* encourages this outcome and, therefore, a demand for changes in immigration policy needs to be made against the United States simply to ensure a level playing field.

In going down this unwise trade route, the American makers of trade policy have put the world trading system at great risk. If *everything* becomes a question of fair trade, the only outcome will be to remove altogether the possibility of ever agreeing to a rule-based trading system. "Managed trade" would then be the outcome, with bureaucrats allocating trade according to what domestic lobbying pressures and foreign political muscle dictate.

Unfortunately, this danger is not seen by many in the United States who, in the current psychology attending the "diminished giant" syndrome, fail to look at the long-run and systemic implications of what they propose as short-term policy options for the United States.

The Divergence between Ex ante and Ex post Outcomes
Yet another reason for making demands for unilateral trade concessions by others can be detected. It is based on the notions of Japan's anti-foreign-goods biases, "natural" and institutional, but uses them in an altogether different way.

The argument is that when Japan's cuts in trade barriers were accepted during earlier GATT rounds as "equivalent," "matching," or "balanced" relative to American cuts, the negotiators for the United States overestimated the extent to which Japanese imports would rise—given Japan's buying preferences and institutions. But, as we *now* know, these forces are of such importance that what Japan gave was far below what America gave. The ex post realities show that the trade in concessions was unbalanced, thus giving the United States the moral, perhaps even the legal, right to "reopen the issue" and ask for unilateral concessions from Japan.

This notion that "first-difference" reciprocity be negotiated (inevitably) on ex ante perceptions of mutual advantages while it can be *renegotiated* on the basis of ex post outcomes is certainly present in some of the sentiments for unilateralism in American demands for others to move toward new trade concessions without reciprocal concessions by the United States. Edmund Dell, secretary of state for trade in the British government in 1976–78, writes cogently on the subject:

There has been a feeling in the United States that in many cases, whatever the intention or skill of American negotiators, reciprocity has not been achieved. Some of its trading partners have been found to have had the better of the bargain. This is particularly seen to be the case in the trade relations of the United States with Japan... Robert Dole, now majority leader in the United States Senate, [has argued] that "reciprocity should be assessed not by what agreements promise but by actual results—by changes in the balance of trade and investment between ourselves and our major economic partners." There is pressure, therefore, to the effect that the United States should withdraw something of what it has conceded—especially, although not entirely, in its relations with Japan.[68]

More important, the sentiment and the pressure translate into unilateral demands for unmatched concessions by Japan, in particular. But there are several things to be said about this sentiment.

1. In terms of GATT law, is the "reopening" of negotiated concessions in this fashion permissible? Article XXIII relates to impairment and nullification of negotiated GATT agreements. Whether this would extend to alleged ex post outcomes that depart from expected outcomes is highly dubious. There certainly do not seem to be any precedents in dispute settlements under Article XXIII that would provide ammunition to the General Counsel to the U.S. Trade Representative, should the latter take up the matter for an authoritative ruling on the subject.

2. The reopening of contractual commitments is generally considered destructive of orderly trade and intercourse, with exceptions permitted only when the contract was signed under duress or when the doctrine of "intervening impossibility" can be invoked—both exemptions usually requiring a heavy burden of proof by those who seek relief. If the United States were to argue for nullification of its trade obligations toward Japan, it seems improbable that it could win, with legitimacy, on either of the two grounds mentioned.

3. Moreover, just imagine what would happen to the trading system if ex post outcomes, themselves reflecting a host of factors that cannot possibly be isolated and quantified persuasively, were to be used to renege on trade concessions or to demand more from others after deals had been struck at trade negotiations.

The "Imbalance-from-Shift-in-Comparative-Advantage" Argument

A different argument for unilateral liberalization because of ex post realities diverging from ex ante expectations can be traced to the feeling that shifts in comparative advantage have created an imbalance of mutual advantages from earlier trade concessions.

American policymakers, persuaded by lobbies and by independent evidence, feel that American comparative advantage has shifted in favor of agriculture and services. These are the sectors that are subjected to high trade barriers and to the failure of GATT disciplines.[69] In consequence, the same structure of trade barriers produces now, in the American view, a lower average barrier in the markets of the United States for others than for the United States in the markets of others.

Therefore, although the initial reductions of barriers were balanced, they cannot be regarded as such anymore. The United States is accordingly justified in asking for changes in trade barriers in these sectors simply to restore the balance of negotiated advantages. While, of course, the United States is willing to have mutual reductions in trade barriers in these new sectors, the fact that they are of principal export benefit to itself means that they amount to an unbalanced trade concession going its way.

The "Coming-of-Age" Argument

An argument that applies not to Japan but to other countries of the Far East (and potentially to other newly industrializing countries that are successful exporters) is that they have had a free lunch so far, having been afforded special-and-differential treatment in GATT negotiations, thanks to which they could use tariffs and other trade barriers but profited from the general reductions in the trade barriers of developed countries in the postwar period because of unconditional MFN treatment. In terms of "first-difference" reciprocity, these countries secured unbalanced trade concessions in their favor, making overall access to their markets significantly less than their access to the markets of the developed countries. For those countries, such as South Korea and Taiwan, which have come of age in terms of both exports and per capita incomes, this "affirmative action" is no longer justified. They must now assume their full obligations as GATT members, as the developed countries do. This means that they must unilaterally lower trade barriers or, what is the same thing, provide greater concessions in future negotiations than they get.

Within the logic of reciprocity, the argument is well taken. Special-and-differential treatment for the developing countries was never granted by other GATT members as a permanent "benefit," simply because the GATT is premised on the assumption of symmetric rights and obligations and on "first-difference" reciprocity as a method of negotiation to reduce barriers, and for that reason, any exemption from the symmetric obligations has to be legitimated. For developing countries, this legitimacy was provided by infant-industry and balance-of-payments arguments (as reflected in Article XVIII). But the developmental status of some developing countries has changed, and the theoretical support for exempting any of them from the obligations of open market access on grounds such as balance-of-payments difficulties has also waned.[70] On both grounds, the "coming-of-age" argument for seeking unilateral concessions from South Korea and Taiwan has acquired cogency.

The "I-Am-More-Open-Than-Thou" Argument

Finally, there is in many quarters the firm belief that the United States is more open than other countries, not just the developing ones. This also helps to fuel demands for unilateral trade concessions by others, especially when combined with another belief that immediately after World War II and in the 1950s and 1960s the United States was altruistic in trade policy but, in its age of relative decline, must now rejoin the human race and "look after its own interests."

But evidence on the trade barriers of the United States, particularly after the proliferation of high-track as well as low-track protection in the 1980s, certainly does not provide support for the view that it is now significantly more open than other developed countries.[71]

This is hard to believe because the United States, formed by immigration, is far more "open" in its cultural attitudes and willingness to experiment with foreign ideas, foreign influences, and foreign goods than most other countries, most of all Japan. But culture does not necessarily translate into corresponding trade policy. The latter reflects equally the play of politics and economic forces. There is in consequence nothing inconsistent, although much that is incongruous, about a culturally open society having access to its markets as restricted by trade policy as a country (such as Japan) which is more inward looking in its citizens' attitudes.

Again, the culturalists find it difficult to believe that protectionism can coexist with a deficit in the balance of trade. Thus James Fallows has recently written: "Japanese and Korean politicians now complain about American 'protectionism,' but how protectionist can a country with a $10 billion monthly trade deficit really be?"[72] Fallows, whose initial wisdom on America's "Japan fixation" has unfortunately yielded to exaggerated pessimism and folly in later writings, is remiss here. Any given degree of protectionism is generally compatible with any level of trade surplus or deficit.

Perhaps the only countervailing argument in support of the presumption that the United States is more open is that it is most open in regard to receiving foreign investment and that this can give foreign suppliers in some cases more effective access to the American market.[73] This asymmetry certainly applies to Japan and is an argument for pressing Japan for greater mutuality of openness in the matter of foreign investment.

As for the view that the United States acted altruistically—that is, as a unilateral free trader of sorts—during the postwar period, this too can be exaggerated. It is useful to remember that, unlike Britain through most of the nineteenth century, the United States has never been a unilateral free trader, generally insisting on reciprocity in trade concessions—as signified by the Reciprocal Trade Agreements Act of 1934 and later by the contractarian conception of the GATT. Do not forget either that the first agricultural waiver from GATT discipline was secured by the United States in 1955, effectively leading to the chaotic situation in agriculture today. The United States was also among the earliest countries to start restricting textile imports, initiating the descent down the road to the Multi-fiber Arrangement (MFA) that restricts and regulates exports of textiles and clothing from developing to developed countries.

These matters need a reminder, not to deny the justly celebrated leadership of the United States (as distinct from altruism) in the conduct of trade policy and in promoting the concerted reduction of tariff barriers through successive GATT rounds, but simply to prevent exaggerated notions of past altruism leading to current policies of system-destroying selfishness.

It is perhaps worth remarking that the theme of America's greater openness can be used selectively and has not deterred similar pressures being exercised against countries for trade concessions even when they are unambiguously more open than the United States. While America's greater openness vis-à-vis Japan is open to doubt, Hong Kong's greater openness vis-à-vis America is not. In fact, Hong Kong, aside from nineteenth-century Britain, is a textbook example of (substantially) free trade. Yet the highhandedness of the United States in dealing with its legal services industry was a matter of public dispute in early 1989 as the legal profession of Hong Kong was threatened by punitive tariff retaliation for the colony unless it opened up Hong Kong to American lawyers.[74] In short, the assumed greater openness of the United States has served as a way of demanding unilateral trade concessions from others, used where it can be made without obvious implausibility and discarded when it plays the wrong way.

2.4 The Crowbar: Section 301 and Super 301

These arguments for unilateral trade concessions by others, many of them not compelling on detailed scrutiny, but all of political potency, together with the growth of interests that were sketched earlier, made it inevitable that the trade policy of the United States would move in the direction of Section 301 and Super 301 with the Trade Act of 1988. Such one-way demands cannot be satisfied with the conventional techniques and within the framework of the GATT. In the GATT framework, trade concessions can be found only by offering one's own. By contrast, unilateral concessions must be extracted, not by gentle negotiations but by threat.

Moreover, export interests are evidently at a disadvantage in the GATT framework where trade concessions by others are available on a non-discriminatory basis to all GATT members and hence give one no privileged access in the new markets, whereas trade concessions can be captured to one's preferential advantage through "voluntary import expansions" (VIEs) and trade diversions toward themselves when the concessions are obtained instead in a one-on-one bilateral framework.[75] Section 301, originally enacted in 1974, but suitably endowed with sharper claws in the 1988 act, is a policy instrument that can serve these ends, amounting therefore to what can be fairly described as "export protectionism."[76]

But there are two other, partly interrelated, factors that must also be cited as having led to the rise of Section 301 to its prominent role in policymaking.

First, the panic identified earlier over the trade deficit and over possible de-industrialization certainly produced a sense of crisis which created, in turn, the sense that urgent action was needed to prevent America's continuing ruination. Even if the many arguments for extracting something for nothing in trade had not been seen to be legitimate, the impatience for quick results on the trade front would have imperiled the commitment to multilateralism under the GATT. Given the indisputable (even if diminished) strength of the United States and new willingness to wield a crowbar and thus use its muscle, it could certainly go *faster*, even in getting others to make balanced and mutual (rather than unilateral) concessions in matters that it considered essential to its trade interests, if it used one-on-one techniques. In place of the GATT, sometimes (naively) denounced as the General Agreement to Talk and Talk, the Section-301 procedures could guarantee the quicker attention and response that was considered urgently necessary.

Second, there was also the more benign view that one-on-one techniques were complementary to, rather than substitutes for, GATT-centered multilateralism. They would, by ruffling feathers and demonstrating American resolve, bring other countries to the bargaining table at the GATT on agricultural trade and on the "new issues" of trade in services, trade-related investment measures (TRIMs) and trade aspects of the protection of intellectual property rights (TRIPs)[77] when others had been dragging their feet.

For both these arguments the underlying common denominator is the sense of urgency and consequent impatience. But the payments deficit driving the impatience has little demonstrated relationship to results on trade policy. It is a non sequitur to translate urgency on the trade deficit into urgency on getting results in the conduct of trade policy.

Nor can it be seriously maintained that the type of unilateralism characterized by Section 301 was necessary to get the Uruguay Round negotiations going. Admittedly, the European Community's refusal to support the launch of multilateral trade negotiations, as desired by the United States, at the special GATT ministerial meeting of November 1982 was a major blow to American efforts to get new disciplines negotiated multilaterally. But three factors, other than the new Super-301 provisions (enacted less than two years *after* the Uruguay Round negotiations were launched), were responsible for the Community's turning around:

1. There was a growing realization by the Community, not present in 1982, that on the new issues of trade in services, TRIMs, and TRIPs, its member countries would benefit as well as the United States so that they also had much to gain from a new GATT round.

2. The free trade proposal with Canada suggested that the United States would embrace regionalism more extensively as a substitute for GATT-wide multilateralism, extending this approach also to the new issues, if the other trading countries did not agree to a new GATT round.

3. And the mood in the U.S. Congress, as often before earlier GATT rounds, was protectionist and ugly enough to make it seem necessary for other countries to begin multilateral trade negotiations to help the U.S. administration resist protectionist pressures.[78]

There is very little to suggest that Section 301 was necessary or was instrumental in any way in getting the Uruguay Round negotiations launched.

Unfortunately, the Section-301 instrument has many difficulties inherent in it and corresponding possibilities of damage to the world trading system. Some difficulties are bad enough. Others are serious.

When the United States confronts the strong, such as the European Community, with Section-301 actions, it is likely to provoke strongly spirited reactions—as in fact happened with the Section-301 action that led to the dispute over trade in hormone-fed beef. While such disputes will settle, with cataclysms such as generalized "trade wars" highly improbable, the battle still leaves scars. The ethos spreads that the trading system is unfair. Xenophobia can strengthen. Protectionists can only find this to their advantage as they continually seek to manoeuvre the legislative and administrative processes to obtain protection.

When the United States confronts the weak, the latter are likely to buckle under, as South Korea did on insurance earlier and on the Super-301 threats she escaped on May 25, 1989. But the danger now is that the smaller countries that the United States confronts in trade will view the Super-301 actions as the way of the bully, reviving the image of the "ugly American," leading gratuitously to anti-Americanism.

But, even if American policymakers were unmindful of these consequences, there is a strong likelihood that the targets of their Section-301 actions will satisfy American demands by diverting trade from other countries (with smaller political clout) to the United States, satisfying the strong at the expense of the weak.[79] America does not open markets efficiently this way. She diverts trade. While this serves the interests of the United States and its exporters, it replaces economic efficiency with political clout as the determinant of trade.

This danger has been recognized by the U.S. Trade Representative. Ambassador Hills now repeatedly stresses how she will ensure that markets are opened under Super 301 in a nondiscriminatory fashion. But ex ante intentions can diverge from ex post outcomes. The lobbies in the United States that influence the USTR do not really care whether markets open generally. Their objective is to secure market access for themselves, and their general thrust is to judge openness in terms of their own success. Equally the countries targeted for action know that the American pressures are therefore more likely to ease if the United States gets a good share than if it does not. The game is set up in terms of implicit pro-trade–diversion-bias rules that all parties recognize as political realities.

Then again there is the problem with the actual use of the crowbar. It is not merely unwise. It has also been occasionally GATT illegal.

The GATT has the legal force of a treaty in the United States.[80] GATT illegality therefore violates a treaty commitment. The feeling that the GATT can be disregarded ("Who cares about the GATT?") because "we never ratified it" is widespread but unjustified. Consequently the United States is not free to retaliate at will by raising tariffs on goods. It has nonetheless done so in the cases of Brazilian informatics, beef from the European Community, and arguably Japanese semiconductors. In this regard, it was not surprising that at the GATT Council meeting in January 1989, 51 member countries joined in invoking Article XXIII in protest against the American violation of GATT obligations; and the Super-301 actions of May 25, 1989 (which offer the prospect of ultimate GATT-illegal retaliation if they are to be effective) have drawn virtually unanimous condemnation from other trading countries.

The United States therefore stands in the dock accused of violating (or threatening to violate) GATT rules. This brings into disrepute the administration's efforts in the Uruguay Round negotiations to strengthen the GATT trading system by putting the United States in what foreign countries see as an inconsistent position via-à-vis the GATT.

Even if one were to disregard GATT illegality, on the (not persuasive) ground that some "creative illegality" was necessary to get GATT member countries to agree to a new GATT round, the essential drawback to Super 301, as currently designed, is that it does not impose on the United States the same disciplines, and the same procedures to establish them and settle disputes under them, as it imposes by threat on others. It is thus built on the asymmetry of power that serves the United States interests because it is the more powerful vis-à-vis most targets. But this is not the way of a properly functioning international trade order in which rights and obligations are symmetrical. The GATT was correctly built on the conception of the rule of law where obligations apply reasonably uniformly to all.[81]

In view of the serious drawbacks of the Super-301 instrument, how does one cope with it? The Super-301 actions on May 25, 1989, suggest that, given the strength of congressional sentiments, the Bush administration is unwilling to expend political goodwill to stop the folly of its use when "push comes to shove."[82] It cannot be eliminated by new legislation: the U.S. Congress is the problem, not the solution. The only way out is to defang the monster. Bearing in mind that Super 301 cannot work unless the threat of retaliation is credible, and that such retaliation would be almost certainly GATT illegal, the targeted countries should raise the matter formally in the GATT whenever retaliation is undertaken).[83] A finding that Super-301 retaliatory actions would be GATT illegal would then put the matter squarely into President Bush's lap. He must either violate the treaty obligations of the GATT or exercise the discretion built into the 1988 Act and say "no" to the protagonists of Super-301 actions. I imagine he would choose the latter option.[84]

2.5 Fix-Quantity Trading Regimes or Managed Trade

While the analysis of the demerits of the Super-301 approach to prying open foreign markets, and of its intimate relationship with export interests and the ethos legitimizing the seeking of unilateral trade concessions by others, requires sophisticated reasoning, the demerits of managed trade are more egregious and obvious to economists.

The proponents of managed trade seek to define targets of "appropriate" exports in specific industries to foreign countries with commitments by those countries to fulfil the targets.[85] While these targets can relate to total imports, or to total imports from the United States, they are typically more narrowly defined as specific quantitative targets for specific imports from the United States. An example is the American pact with Japan on trade in semiconductors, recording the demand for a 20 percent American share in the Japanese market.

The 1980s have seen a proliferation of such "fix-quantity" trade arrangements in regard to one's imports: "voluntary" export restraints (VERs) on autos and steel are a typical example. If the managed-trade proponents had their way, there would be "voluntary import expansions" for one's exports to match these VERs for one's imports.

These demands derive from some of the same conceptions about Japan that drive the demands for unilateral trade concessions by her: in particular, that her policies, preferences, and institutions make Japan hard to penetrate. Therefore, quantitative commitments by Japan to import specific quantities of particular goods from the United States, in whatever way the Japanese do so, are deemed necessary.

This would mean the replacement of the fix-rule approach to trade, as built into the GATT, by a fix-quantity trade regime. We would be replacing the rule of law that the GATT embodies, where trading countries compete subject to common rules, by a system where politics and bureaucrats would essentially determine trade quantities. Before this retrograde step is taken, the case for it must be examined, for it is exceptionally flawed.

For one thing, the notion that Japan's policies, preferences and institutions make it hard, even impossible, to sell to her people is unsupported by the facts. Not merely is it impossible to support econometrically, with any confidence, the contention that Japan imports too little. But, at the margin as well, there is enough evidence to show that Japan's imports respond to price changes, such as the rise of the yen and the fall of the dollar, much the way other countries' imports do.[86] Despite their many cultural differences, known to anyone who has read the great novelist Junichiro Tanizaki's beautiful essay *In Praise of Shadows*, the Japanese belong to the same human race that Adam Smith wrote about.

It is not meaningful to ask countries to ensure target quantities of specific imports. They can restrain exports by enforcement. But how are they to ensure imports by their consumers unless the state is the buyer? Subsidies by the United States could be an instrument to encourage more purchases, but how would the United States reconcile this with its general position in the GATT and in national practice against subsidization? Indeed, the United States imposes countervailing duties against subsidies by foreign rivals.

There is also the oft-repeated claim that the targets to be set and enforced for imports of specific items from the United States by Japan will reflect the "fair" and "appropriate" share of the Americans in the Japanese market. But this is not sensible.

There is no sufficiently unambiguous and plausible way in which such fair shares can be estimated in general. Third-market shares of the United States and Japan are often cited by some to argue that Americans ought to enjoy similar shares in Japan herself. These third-market shares, however, will reflect relative expenditures by Americans and Japanese in cultivating these markets, the differential incidence of protection against Japanese exports in third markets (for example, the European Community has conducted a "Fortress Europe" policy against Japan throughout the 1980s), the value attached by these markets to different product characteristics and a host of other factors that do not carry over mechanically into the Japanese market.[87] Besides, if Americans were to apply this approach to estimating how much they deny a fair share of their market for each traded product to other trading countries, they would be unpleasantly surprised, I am sure, at the "findings" of their own hidden barriers against imports of specific items from specific countries.

These objections apply also to the less restrictive versions of managed trade. The demand that Japan import specific quantities without specifying sources is better. But it is no more feasible and desirable than the demand for source-specific increases in imports by Japan. Nor is the version that Japan increase her total imports, or total imports of manufactures, by a target figure or be penalized.[88]

To proceed down the road to managed trade, despite its popularity with the export lobbies, its appeal on Capitol Hill and its advocacy by some, would just be another act of folly.[89]

2.6 Regionalism

While, then, the turn to unilateralism and the pressures to embrace managed trade are matters which economists can reasonably agree to consider detrimental, and even perilous, to the world trading system, the issue of regionalism is a matter where they can reasonably disagree.

In theory, economists have long known that preferential trading arrangements can always be devised between any group of countries so that they are welfare improving for those who undertake them and do not harm those who are outside.[90] By the conventional criteria for evaluating policies, such preferential arrangements would be considered desirable.

The relevant question is whether the specific arrangements, such as the European Community or the U.S.–Canada Free Trade Agreement, meet these conditions. This question was seriously discussed in the 1960s when the Community was formed and when all kinds of regional arrangements such as EFTA, LAFTA, PAFTA, and NAFTA[91] were being pursued or contemplated in different regions around the world in an early "play" of what many think ahistorically is a novel trend today, two decades later (after the first trend died despite a similar show of apparent strength).

Interestingly, this kind of question has hardly been posed in recent discussions of the U.S.–Israel Free Trade Agreement and the U.S.–Canada one, at least at the time of the intense political debate that surrounded the latter. In short, one cannot find any parallel degree of scepticism and interest in the U.S. Congress or in academic analyses concerning the question whether the U.S.–Canada Free Trade Agreement would lead to trade diversion and, if so, sufficiently to reduce rather than increase welfare for the United States, its partners, and the world.[92]

The reason lies, it seems, in the virtue seen in the mere fact that the Canadian–American agreement represented, to the public eye, a dramatic pro-trade measure that would take the political momentum, away from the protectionists. Trade diversion was no more a worry for policymakers here than it would be for those who ignored the likelihood of producing VIEs rather than multilaterally open foreign markets when undertaking Super-301 actions.

Virtue was also found in the fact that, as part of the Canadian–American agreement, progress was made in negotiating trade in services. This, too, was seen as imparting momentum, not merely by example but also by implied threat (that the United States, if necessary, would move ahead with "like-minded" countries on services if the GATT talks failed), to the progress of the talks on trade in services in the Uruguay Round negotiations.

An undisputed merit of the U.S.–Canada Free Trade Agreement has again been the inclusion, on Canadian initiative and insistence, of a bi-national procedure for reviewing national "unfair trade" adjudications. In a world where countries increasingly make charges of unfair trade at one another, the old-fashioned ways of doing business in these matters are getting rapidly obsolete. The traditional way, where (say) Americans complain, and American institutions judge, much like Judge Dee of medieval China who acted as the prosecutor and the judge, makes little sense in today's world. Increasingly, we need to settle such complaints by neutral, impartial procedures, like those of the GATT. The Canadian–American agreement made a real contribution in that direction, paving the way for future models of institutional change designed to handle better and contain the damage from the increased obsessions with unfair trade.

The problem, however, is that these benefits must be balanced against the costs. The major cost comes from an unanticipated fallout of the U.S.–Canada Free Trade Agreement. The *coincidence* of the Canadian–American agreement and "Europe 1992" was fortuitous. Europe 1992 was prompted by the wholly different goal of making the common market commoner, taking the last, difficult, almost insuperable, steps toward the political and economic unification that the Treaty of Rome had adopted as its objective. But the coincidence of these two dramatic events, plus the jaundiced view of the GATT on Capitol Hill and the indifference to the GATT illegality of the actions contemplated under the Super-301 provisions of the Trade Act of 1988, suggested to many abroad that, despite professions to the contrary from the administration and its efforts at the Uruguay Round negotiations, the American commitment to multilateralism had ended. Regionalism had arrived. The world was fragmenting into trading blocs.

Unfortunately, this inference of a trend from two observations can be self-fulfilling. It has tended to produce a sense in the Far East, for instance, that a Japan-centered regional bloc in the Asian–Pacific region may be necessary in a bloc-infested world. The effect would surely be to undermine the energies spent on making the Uruguay Round negotiations successful, with its vast and difficult agenda of remaking the GATT to suit the needs of the modern world.

In my view, it is absolutely imperative for the United States to reject the temptation therefore to move towards further such regional arrangements, eschewing the suggestions to strike special deals with Mexico and others, so as to convey a clear message that the Canadian–American free trade area was a special event, much like European unification, with Europe 1992 as its culmination.[93] Here lies the greater wisdom, if less immediate profit.[94]

2.7 Concluding Observations

United States trade policy presents a confusing picture today, even a disturbing one. It is conceivable that the trends toward unilateralism and regionalism will fade away. Nothing in economics is predictable with certainty. But if the analysis presented here is accurate, many of the under-lying causes of these trends are fundamental and, therefore, they are unlikely to vanish in the immediate future.

The pessimistic scenario is that the United States will find itself unable to play the role of an energetic supporter of GATT-based multilateralism, being constrained by the powerful forces working through the Congress. One may fear equally that, unless the administration manages to persuade the Congress that the extension of multilateral disciplines to complex new areas such as trade in services has necessarily to be a continuous and slow process, not to be judged in terms of immediate quick-fixes and "results," the congressional embrace of unilateralism and regionalism will intensify after the Uruguay Round negotiations are concluded at the end of 1990 and weaken further the capacity of the administration to strengthen and revitalize a GATT-focused multilateral trading regime.

At the same time, the newly emerging power, Japan, will not be able to play a major role either in that direction, much as it is also in her own interest, simply because she has never played the role before, having only recently acquired her economic sinews. There may then be a leadership vacuum, with the GATT and multilateralism falling through the cracks during this transition.

The optimistic scenario, on the other hand, is that a clear delineation of these dangers, sharply sketched, will alert the U.S. administration to the impending dangers and spur it into making the effort, both in Washington and in Geneva, to save the multilateral trading system that has served the United States and the world economy so well in the post-World War II period.

Notes

1. This article is based on a paper delivered at a conference on United States Trade Policy at Columbia University, New York, on September 8, 1989, sponsored by the Department of Economics and the Program on Journalism and International Economics, financed by the Sloan and Ford foundations respectively. In writing the paper. I have profited from the human capital of many. The writings of Michael Aho, Robert Baldwin, Michael Finger, Robert Hudec, Douglas Irwin, Robert Lawrence, Gary Saxonhouse, and Martin Wolf have been particularly helpful. Thanks are due to Claude Barfield, Jr., Richard Clarida, Paul Samuelson, T. N. Srinivasan, and Lawrence Summers for helpful comments.

2. For a detailed discussion of these developments, see Jagdish Bhagwati, *Protectionism* (Cambridge, Massachusetts: MIT Press. 1988) ch. 4. Also, see the excellent review article by David Palmeter, The Capture of the Antidumping Law, *Yale Journal of International Law*, New Haven, no. 14, 1989, pp. 182–198.

3. The verbal commitment to multilateralism remains high in Washington. But the actual developments are not so sanguine.

4. See Robert E. Baldwin, United States Trade Policy, 1945–1988: From Foreign Policy to Domestic Policy, mimeograph, Department of Economics, University of Wisconsin, Madison, 1989, for an insightful analysis documenting this.

5. (1) The Caribbean Initiative and recent bilateral arrangements with Mexico are other, relatively minor, examples of the new willingness in United States trade policy to work with less-than-multilateral (that is, less than GATT-membership-wide) trade arrangements. (2) On a related front, the United States has also adhered to the view that the GATT codes negotiated in the Tokyo Round deliberations established conditional, rather than unconditional, MFN rights for signatory countries. (3) Again, the U.S. negotiating position in the Uruguay Round negotiations on services has been reported to involve going, if necessary, with "like-minded" countries and not extending the benefits on an unconditional MFN basis to the nonsignatory developing countries.

6. Cf. Lester C. Thurow, GATT Is Dead, speech to the Davos symposium, World Economic Forum, January 1989, mimeograph, obtainable from the Sloan School of Management, Massachusetts Institute of Technology.

7. For a lucid and authoritative clarification of the relationship of Section 301 under earlier legislation and the 1988 Trade Act, see Judith Bello and Alan Holmer, The Heart of the 1988 Trade Act: a Legislative History of the Amendments to Section 301, *Stanford Journal of International Law*, Fall 1988, pp. 1–44; and Unilateral Action to Open Foreign Markets: the Mechanics of Retaliation Exercises, *The International Lawyer*, Chicago, Winter 1988, pp. 1197–1206.

8. The semiconductor pact fitted the bill precisely in this way: 20 percent of the Japanese market to be set aside for U.S. semiconductors. While there was ambiguity about whether 20 percent was a target or a "guideline," the United States

showed no hesitation in treating it as a target when undertaking retaliation for noncompliance.

9. I insert the adjective "import" not because of unfamiliarity with the rule of redundancy, but deliberately. Later I argue that pressures for "export protectionism" have appeared on the U.S. scene, accounting for some of the disturbing shifts in U.S. trade policy.

10. Adjusting for the vastly increased demands for protection, the Reagan administration may be defended as having "supplied" no more protection than its predecessor under President Carter. But the increased "demands" for protection were partly a consequence of the administration's own macroeconomic policies.

11. Michael Gavin has alerted me to remind the reader that devaluations may affect excess spending as when they successfully switch expenditure toward home goods in a situation of Keynesian unemployment or, second, as when the rise in import prices increases real saving due to the wealth effect, as in the celebrated Laursen-Metzler-Harberger analysis. The former model is not valid currently; the latter effect could not be important. Also see notes 16 and 19 below.

12. The chief proponents have been Richard Baldwin, Hysteresis in Import Prices: the Beachhead Effect, *American Economic Review*, no. 4, 1988, pp. 773–885; and Richard Baldwin and Paul Krugman, *Persistent Trade Effects of Large Exchange Rate Shocks*, NBER Working Paper No. 2017 (Cambridge, MA: National Bureau of Economic Research, 1986).

13. This is evident from a report by Robert Kuttner (of a conference of the leading figures in international macroeconomics in late 1987), The Theory Gap on the Trade Gap, *New York Times*, 17 January 1988, Section 3, p. 1, where the presence of trade barriers as an explanation of the failure of the pass-through effect is not mentioned. This omission is also in the early studies, including Catherine Mann, Prices, Profits, Margins and Exchange Rates, *Federal Reserve Bulletin*. Washington, June 1986, pp. 366–379, and Paul Krugman, *Exchange Rate Instability* (Cambridge: MIT Press, 1989).

14. This hypothesis is discussed at length in Bhagwati, The Pass-through Puzzle: The Missing Prince from Hamlet, Department of Economics, Columbia University, New York, December 1988. The paper was summarized in an Economics Focus column, "Passing the Buck," *The Economist*, London, February 11, 1989, p. 63, and is reprinted in this volume (chapter 5).

15. In particular, the experience of the automobile industry bears out this hypothesis. See Kiyohiko Shibayama, Michiko Kiji, Toshihiro Horiuchi, and Kazuharu Kiyono, *Market Structure and Export Prices*, Discussion Paper No. 88-DF-1 (Tokyo: Research Institute of International Trade and Industry, Ministry of International Trade and Industry, 1988). The impact of the trigger-price mechanism on U.S. steel imports on the pass-through effect is also borne out. As Dr Shibayama communicated to me: "On the aggregate level, pass-through ratios for Japanese exports have been lower during this post-1985 period than during the 1977–78 period of

the high yen. More than half of this decline may be attributed to a decrease in the pass-through ratios for Japanese steel and automobiles, two of our country's principal exports." (Letter dated February 14, 1989.)

16. For careful analysis of this question, see W. M. Corden. Trade Policy and Macroeconomic Balance in the World Economy, in Charles Pearson and James Riedel (eds.), *Essays in Honor of Isaiah Frank* (Baltimore: Johns Hopkins Press, 1990). Also see Richard H. Clarida, The Trade Deficit, Protectionism and Policy Co-ordination, *The World Economy*, vol. 12, no. 4, 1989.

17. Some economic studies show that U.S. protection will improve the trade deficit. But these results come from peculiar assumptions—for instance, that the revenues from the tariffs are saved. The implied notion that the United States has become sufficiently underdeveloped to need revenues from tariffs, as many poor countries used to do, would be amusing if it were not so damaging to sensible policymaking. See Rudiger Dornbusch, External Balance Correction: Depreciation or Protection?, *Brookings Papers on Economic Activity*, Washington, no. 1, 1987, pp. 249–269.

18. See Bhagwati, *Protectionism*, op. cit.

19. Cf. Bhagwati, A Giant among Lilliputians: Japan's Long-run Trade Problem, in Ryuzo Sato and Julianne Nelson (eds.), *Beyond Trade Friction: Japan–United States Economic Relations* (Cambridge: Cambridge University Press. 1989).

20. Sol Chaikin, Trade, Investment and Deindustrialization: Myth and Reality, *Foreign Affairs*, New York, Spring 1982. p. 848. Other telling examples are quoted in Bhagwati, *Protectionism*, op. cit., pp. 99–101.

21. The foremost members of the de-industrialization school in the United States are Stephen Cohen and John Zysman, Manufacturing Matters: *The Myth of the Post-industrial Economy* (New York: Basic Books, 1987). While the British school has virtually become defunct, after an initial splash and having had a temporary impact on British legislation in the form of a selective employment tax designed to create differential incentives tor employment in manufacturing at the expense of services (see Bhagwati, *Protectionism*, op. cit., ch. 5), the American school has recently gained a few academic converts.

Whether and how soon the American school will atrophy like the British school should depend on the different interactions between the manufacturing sector and academics in the two countries. While the Labor party and generally left-wing British economists who led the de-industrialization school had little to do with the manufacturing corporations who would profit from a promanufacturing policy, this is not so for the academic converts to the de-industrialization school among the new Democrats in the United States. This contrast offers an interesting subject for analysis.

22. Cf. Dornbusch, James Poterba, and Lawrence Summers. *The Case for Manufacturing in America's Future* (Rochester: Eastman Kodak Company, 1988). Since there is yet another Kodak study by Dornbusch, but now with Paul Krugman and Yung Chul Park, *Meeting World Challenges: United States Manufacturing in the 1990s* (1989), I refer to these hereafter as Kodak I and Kodak II.

23. I return later to the question whether there *are* such externalities to manufactures.

24. Cf. Kodak I, op. cit., p. 10.

25. Cohen and Zysman, op. cit., p. 16.

26. Bhagwati, *Protectionism*, op. cit., p. 114.

27. Cf. Kodak I, op. cit., p. 10.

28. See the extended analysis and introduction of these concepts in Bhagwati, Splintering and Disembodiment of Services and Developing Nations, *The World Economy*, June 1984, pp. 133–143. Their implications for the Uruguay Round negotiations are considered in Bhagwati, Trade in Services and the Multilateral Trade Negotiations, *World Bank Economic Review*, Washington, No. 4, 1987, pp. 549–569. An excellent analysis of the conceptual issues is also contained in Gary Sampson and Richard Snape, Identifying the Issues in Trade in Services, *The World Economy*, June 1985, pp. 171–182.

29. Pioneered originally by James Brander and Barbara Spencer, the theory has been elegantly developed by Avinash Dixit, Gene Grossman, and Jonathan Eaton, among others. Such intervention is called "strategic" because it involves taking the reactions of oligopolistic foreign firms to one's decisions into account. The "large-group" case, distinct from the small-group oligopoly case, has also been developed as part of the general interest in market structure and was pioneered by Kelvin Lancaster, Dixit and Joseph Stiglitz, and Elhanan Helpman and Paul Krugman. The earliest formal treatments of market structure in international trade began with consideration of pure monopoly: with my analysis of the nonequivalence of tariffs and quotas in the presence of monopoly and with Peter Svedberg and Homi Katrak analyzing the optimal policy for a country faced with a monopolistic supplier. Cf. Bhagwati, On the Equivalence of Tariffs and Quotas, in Robert E. Baldwin et al. (eds.), *Trade, Balance of Payments and Growth: Essays in Honor of Gottfried Haberler* (Amsterdam: North Holland, 1965), and Peter Svedberg, Optimal Tariff Policy on Imports from Multinationals, *Economic Record*, Melbourne, March 1979, pp. 64–67.

30. This is the conclusion of Lawrence Katz and Summers, Industry Rents: Evidence and Implications, *Brookings Papers: Microeconomics*, No. 2, 1989, pp. 209–275. The paper looks at evidence for 74 manufacturing industries in the United States for 1984.

31. See Ricardo J. Caballero and Richard Lyons, *The Role of External Economies in United States Manufacturing*, mimeograph, Department of Economics, Columbia University, New York, April 1989, and *Internal versus External Economies in European Industry*, Columbia Discussion Paper No. 426 (New York: Columbia University, 1989). The European countries covered are the Federal Republic of Germany, France, Belgium, and the United Kingdom. A similar conclusion is drawn by Dale Jorgenson, Frank Gollop, and Barbara Fraumeni, *Productivity and United States Economic Growth* (Cambridge: Harvard University Press, 1987) p. 210.

32. This dilemma, where one believes a phenomenon is important but cannot plausibly substantiate it with evidence, recurs often in economics as in other social sciences. Roy Harrod, in his biography of Keynes, recalls how he worked with Lord Cherwell, Prime Minister Churchill's adviser, during the war but resigned and returned to Oxford. He could not tolerate a situation where the physicist wanted to know the dimensions of anything that Harrod would argue to be important. Harrod, like most of us, felt strongly that something was significant, but had no way of measuring and proving it to be so.

33. In my view, the belief that these industries have critical economic externalities, as also the "noneconomic" desire to have a "modern" economy, is what drives politicians to battles designed to get an appropriate share of these industries. The weapons used are whatever come to hand, including charges of "unfair trade" practices by successful rivals and an occasional invoking of 'strategic' trade policy.

34. Cf. Caballero and Lyons, op. cit.

35. Adding the total economy as another explanatory variable for output did not improve the explanation over what total manufacturing did. But that suggests that total size of the economy might have worked as well as the size of the manufacturing sector as an explanatory variable signifying externalities.

36. Of course, the theory of noneconomic objectives and policy intervention, as developed in the 1960s by W. M. Corden, Harry G. Johnson, Bhagwati and T. N. Srinivasan, Adolf Vandendorpe and others, shows that the optimal subsidy, in case of learning related to manufacturing output, would be to production, not to employment.

37. See, in particular, Robert Rowthorn, What Remains of Kaldor's Law?, *Economic Journal*, Cambridge, March 1975, pp. 10–19; Nicholas Kaldor, Economic Growth and the Verdoorn Law—A Comment on Mr Rowthorn's Article, *Economic Journal*, December 1975, pp. 891–896; Rowthorn, A Reply to Lord Kaldor's Comment, *Economic Journal*, December 1975, pp. 897–901; and Rowthorn, A Note on Verdoorn's Law, *Economic Journal*, March 1979, pp. 131–133.

The empirical evidence on "learning by doing" is summarized and extended in Marvin Lieberman, The Learning Curve and Pricing in the Chemical Processing Industries, *Rand Journal of Economics*, Santa Monica, California, No. 2, 1984, pp. 213–228. This article, which is the most careful to date, is, however, based on price rather than cost data and, more important, does not distinguish between learning by doing related to the output of the firm (which should not produce any market failure unless it is so large relative to market expansion as to make perfect competition unsustainable) and learning by doing related to industry output which it measures (and which may include what I have called "learning by others doing" which constitutes an externality leading to market failure in the absence of appropriability).

On the other hand, there is some systematic evidence from the analysis of patent data in the United States that R&D spillovers exist across firms, in different industries but in technological space defining "technological neighbors," and that they will result in higher profits to the beneficiaries of such spillovers, indicating lack of full appropriability. See Adam Jaffee, Technological Opportunity and Spillovers of R&D: Evidence from Firms' Patents, Profits, and Market Value, *American Economic Review*, no. 5, 1986, pp. 984–1001. If market failure obtains, with mutual lack of appropriability being unequal among competitive firms undertaking R&D, there would be a case for subsidizing R&D by the firms that lose on balance from the lack of full appropriability.

38. This argument has been made by Lawrence Summers.

39. This revival is due to Lawrence Summers who, in papers with Katz, op. cit., and Alan Krueger, Efficiency Wages and the Inter-industry Wage Structure, mimeograph, Department of Economics, Harvard University, February 1986, has developed this argument empirically with tenacity and ingenuity.

40. Originating with Mihail Manötesco, the argument was developed in a classic paper by Everett Hagen, An Economic Justification of Protectionism, *Quarterly Journal of Economics*, November 1958, pp. 496–514. It was then generalized to the theory of domestic distortions and welfare by Bhagwati and V. K. Ramaswami, Domestic Distortions. Tariffs and the Theory of Optimum Subsidy, *Journal of Political Economy*, Chicago, no. 1. 1963, pp. 44–50, culminating in the postwar theory of commercial policy.

41. Quoted from Krugman, Is Free Trade Passé?, *Journal of Economic Perspectives*, no. 1, 1987, pp. 131–144. These claims are regrettably without foundation in ignoring the numerous arguments for appropriate trade and domestic interventions that were developed in the postwar theory of commercial policy. They are also dangerous in suggesting to the protectionists that all earlier theoretical arguments were falsely premised: this encourages the populist and congressional dismissal of the scientific corpus of thought on commercial *policy* which the new work by no means supplants but only adds to. See Bhagwati, Is Free Trade Passé After All?, Bernhard Harms Prize Speech, *Weltwirtschaftliches Archiv*, Kiel, no. 1, 1989, pp. 3–30, reprinted in this volume (chapter 1).

42. See David G. Tarr. *A General Equilibrium Analysis of the Welfare and Employment Effects of United States Quotas in Textiles, Autos and Steel*, Bureau of Economics Staff Report to the Federal Trade Commission (Washington: U.S. Government Printing Office, 1989) ch. 8, pp. 6 and 7.

43. Richard Brecher, An Efficiency-wage Model of Unemployment in an Open Economy, mimeograph, Department of Economics, Carleton University, Ottawa, March 1989, has examined trade policy when shirking obtains in an otherwise conventional general-equilibrium model. Brecher's theoretical analysis correctly emphasizes that shirking will lead both to higher wage rates to make the penalty of job loss greater if caught *and* to monitoring costs as well. The higher wage differential is therefore only one consequence; the empirical work must simultaneously look for monitoring costs (which would not show up in this way) if the shirking inference is to be made.

44. Cf. Krueger and Summers, op. cit.

45. Katz and Summers, op. cit., p. 226.

46. See, for detailed analysis, Bhagwati and Dougas A. Irwin, The Return of the Reciprocitarians: US Trade Policy Today, *The World Economy*, June 1987, pp. 109–130.

47. Staffan Burenstam Linder, *The Pacific Century* (Stanford: Stanford University Press, 1986).

48. In some instances, contempt has yielded to fear. Who cannot recall President de Gaulle's disdainful remark about the Japanese prime minister: "Who is this transistor salesman?" The European Community's frenetic use of antidumping actions to hold Japanese imports down suggests an altogether changed attitude to the subject matter, as splendidly documented by Brian Hindley, Dumping and the Far East Trade of the European Community, *The World Economy*, December 1988, and Patrick Messerlin, The EC Anti-dumping Regulations: A First Economic Appraisal, 1980–85, *Weltwirtschaftliches Archiv*, no. 3, 1989, and GATT-inconsistent Outcomes of GATT-Consistent Laws: the Long-Term Evolution of the EC Anti-dumping Law, paper for the Trade Policy Research Centre as part of its programme of studies on Regulatory Trade Measures and the Concept of Unfair Trade.

49. There are other parallels and contrasts, too, which are analyzed in Bhagwati and Irwin, op. cit.

50. The growth of the export interests in the United States has been noted and analyzed in three independent contributions: Bhagwati, *Protectionism*, op. cit.; Helen Milner, *Resisting Protectionism: Global Industries and the Politics of International Trade* (Princeton: Princeton University Press, 1988); and I. M. Destler and John Odell, *The Politics of Anti-protection* (Washington: Institute for International Economics, 1987). While all authors consider the benign role of these interests in shifting trade policy away from import protectionism to exports and "opening markets," the first considers also the down side of the phenomenon—that these export interests may capture trade policy to foster "export protectionism," as discussed below.

51. For early analyses, see Georgio Basevi, Domestic Demand and Ability to Export, *Journal of Political Economy*, no. 2, 1970, pp. 330–340, and, in particular, Richard Pomfret, Some Interrelationships between Import Substitution and Export Promotion in a Small Open Economy, *Weltwirtschaftlichies Archiv*, no. 4, 1975, pp. 714–727.

52. The *permanent* advantage results only in the classroom model. In the real world, countless factors are altering the relative fortunes of firms over time, of course. To go from this classroom demonstration of permanent and irreversible advantage to a policy prescription of protection is therefore to make a leap that is not sensible.

53. The scale argument was beautifully formalized in the Brander-Spencer framework by Krugman, Import Protection as Export Promotion, in Henryk Kierzkowski (ed.), *Monopolistic Competition and International Trade* (Oxford: Oxford University Press, 1984).

54. See, in particular, Krugman (ed.), *Strategic Trade Policy and the New International Economics* (Cambridge: MIT Press, 1986).

55. History has few recorded cases of unilateral free traders or unilateral trade liberalizations. More common are unilateral trade liberalizations *imposed* on developing countries as part of conditionality packages attached to IMF and World Bank assistance.

56. Again, there are classroom exceptions leading to paradoxical outcomes.

57. The bargaining of trade concessions has the well-known downside effect that it may induce countries that want to liberalize unilaterally to "hold back" until they can bargain the trade liberalization instead of "throwing the chips away." Also, it may induce countries to impose tariffs in order to acquire chips.

58. Thus Japan could be asked to reduce her trade barriers, because of the latter arguments, even if she did not have a big surplus.

59. There are numerous ways in which one's trade regime can affect investment and savings, in principle. Empirical analysis of many countries' trade and payments policies also suggests many such possibilities, but it also shows that these effects can go in several different directions. Cf. Bhagwati, *The Anatomy and Consequences of Exchange Control Regimes* (Cambridge, MA: Ballinger, for the National Bureau of Economic Research. 1978) ch. 6. which reviews the theoretical and empirical findings on the relationship of trade policy to domestic savings. Also see Clarida, op. cit., for other theoretical arguments. And also recall Note 16.

60. The "scarce-currency" clause at the IMF is a useful precedent of sorts in this regard.

61. These are by Edward Learner and Gary Saxonhouse. See T. N. Srinivasan and Koichi Hamada, *The United States Japan Problem*, paper presented to the Conference on United States Trade Policy, Columbia University, New York, September 8, 1989. Surprisingly, the report of the Advisory Committee on Trade Policy and Negotiations, mentioned at the start, ignores these studies and concentrates instead on the findings of Robert Lawrence, of the Brookings Institution, which are favourable to their recommendations for managed trade with Japan.

62. Of course, economists familiar with ethics allow for meta-preferences—that is, preferences about preferences. If you are a racist, I certainly will not take a "value-free" position, allowing you free play. But to imagine that the Japanese housewife's preference for Japanese goods falls into this class of meta-preferences is to invite ridicule.
   Again, if one recognizes that tastes can be partly endogenous due to advertising and other forms of diffusion of information, one might argue that Japanese housewives have less access to information about foreign goods than the American housewife. But this would be implausible indeed for postwar Japan and for a period when American cultural hegemony has been a source of worldwide concern.

63. *Newsweek*, New York, February 13, 1989, p. 50.

64. Mordechai E. Kreinin, How Closed is Japan's Market? Additional Evidence, *The World Economy*, December 1988, pp. 529–542.

65. The closest that anyone came to trying to do this was the German government in regard to aid-tying. When the United States and the United Kingdom imposed source-tying restrictions on their aid, during their payments-deficit years, the German Finance Ministry tried to avoid similar aid-tying because of the German surplus. In the end, however, it could not because German exporters were out-raged by the fact that this meant that they were unable to tender for American-aid financed contracts while American exporers could tender for German-aid-financed contracts. See the discussion in Bhagwati, The Tying of Aid, study prepared for UNCTAD, reprinted in Bhagwati, *Dependence and Interdependence: Essays in Development Economics*, vol 2, edited by Gene Grossman (Oxford: Basil Blackwell, 1985; and Cambridge: MIT Press, 1985).

66. See, for instance, Paul Blustein, Finding a Retirement Home for Japan's "Papa-Mama" Stores, *The Washington Post National Weekly*, August 21–27, 1989, p. 19. There is disagreement, however, over how restrictive really is the Japanese retail distribution system. See *The Economist*, August 26, 1989.

67. For example, some countries, and economists, believe that retail price main-tenance is a good thing (because, for instance, consumers do not have to shop around). For foreign firms used to the "orderly" distribution system that also attends such retail price maintenance, the American distribution system may ap-pear too chaotic and difficult to adapt to. Again, within the European Community, the retail distribution systems of member countries exhibit substantial variations, reflecting different cultural, historical, and economic factors.

68. Edmund Dell, Of Free Trade and Reciprocity, *The World Economy*, June 1986, p. 134.

69. Ironically, the original 1955 waiver granted to agriculture by the GATT was to the United States. Equally, the question of trade in services was first raised internationally at UNCTAD rather than at the GATT. How the world changes!

70. On these questions, see the splendid analysis by Martin Wolf, Differential and More Favourable Treatment of Developing Countries and the International Trad-ing System, and also Shailendra Anjaria, Balance of Payments and Related Issues in the Uruguay Round of Trade Negotiations, *World Bank Economic Review*, Sep-tember 1987. This issue contains a symposium on The MTN and Developing Country Interests.
   Also see the excellent articles by Isaiah Frank, Import Quotas, the Balance of Payments and the GATT, *The World Economy*, September 1987, pp. 307–318, and Richard Eglin, Surveillance of Balance-of-Payments Measures in the GATT, *The World Economy*, March 1987, pp. 1–26.

71. A review of 40 measures by the United States that impede the European Community's exports was released, for instance, in May 1989. See *EC News*, Washington, No. 13/89, May 1989. The IBRD-UNCTAD index of nontariff bar-

riers also suggests the same conclusion, although the index has well-known conceptual problems.

72. James Fallows, Containing Japan, *Atlantic Monthly*, May 1989. In his earlier book, *More Like Us* (Boston: Houghton Mifflin, 1987), Fallows takes the position that the American response to the Japanese challenge should be to improve and strengthen its own institutions along lines more consonant with its flexible and open traditions.

73. This argument has been made by Isaiah Frank.

74. See the report in *South China Morning Post*, Hong Kong, February 21, 1989, p. 1. In particular: "There was clear evidence of threats of retaliation by American law firms that Hong Kong would suffer trade restrictions unless the Government allowed foreign lawyers entry."

75. The concept of VIEs where the importing countries are asked to increase imports of specific items from particular countries by given amounts is the counterpart of the familiar concept of VERs ('voluntary' export restrictions) where exports by these countries are restrained thus. The concept and terminology of VIEs were introduced in Bhagwati, VERs, Quid Pro Quo DFI and VIEs: Political-Economy-Theoretic Analyses, *International Economic Journal*, Seoul, Spring 1987, pp. 1–12, and are further discussed in Bhagwati, *Protectionism*, op. cit., pp. 82–84.

76. The fact that, thanks to economists' efforts at education, the office of the U.S. Trade Representative now is explicit in saying that it will call for nondiscriminatory trade concessions under Section-301 and Super-301 procedures does not invalidate the argument in the text as to why Section 301 came to acquire its appeal at the outset. Nor does it assuage the worry that, despite the USTR's present policy, the Section-301 and Super-301 actions will not anyway result in VIEs and trade diversion rather than in trade creation, as discussed later.

77. TRIMs and TRIPs are both acronyms happily suggesting good health and gratification to the harried negotiators in the Uruguay Round talks.

78. The Jenkins Bill on textiles was defeated. But the launching of the Uruguay Round negotiations did not work to stop the passage of the 1988 Trade Act.

79. For a story on how South Korea planned to do precisely this with her agricultural imports, see *Financial Times*, April 27, 1987. Also see Bhagwati, *Protectionism*, op. cit., pp. 82–84, for analysis of the issue, and the recent story in *Fortune* (February 27, 1989, pp. 88–89, story by Rahul Jacob) recording these concerns as well.

80. This was demonstrated in John H. Jackson. The General Agreement on Tariffs and Trade in the United States Domestic Law, *Michigan Law Review*, Ann Arbor, December 1967, pp. 249–332.

81. For an illuminating analysis of Section-301 provisions along these lines, see Robert E. Hudec, Thinking About the New Section 301: Beyond Good and Evil, mimeograph, School of Law, University of Minnesota, Minneapolis, June 15, 1989.

82. Claude Barfield, Jr., has remarked that the presidential discretion not to take action was built in by the Reagan administration as a necessary precaution, with the administration understanding that it would indeed be exercised. On the other hand, the congressional activists pushing Super 301 believed that presidential discretion would not be allowed to come in the way of Super-301 actions. The change of administration, and the greater willingness of President Bush to work in harmony with the Congress, seems to have tilted the balance in favour of the latter presumption, favoring Super-301 actions.

83. Bhagwati, Super 301's Big Bite Flouts the Rules, *New York Times*, June 4, 1989, and Taking the Teeth out of Super 301, *World Link*, World Economic Forum, July—August 1989, no. 7/8, p. 7.

84. The fact that Super 301 is an altogether inappropriate instrument for trade liberalization does not mean that the United States or, for that matter, any significant country in world trade should not exercise pressure in *appropriate* ways for liberalizing trade. The USTR practice of compiling estimates of trade barriers facing the United States, and the European Community's response thereto, is most welcome. So are the annual trade policy reviews of specific countries, starting this year at the GATT. The notion that those opposed to America's unilateral one-on-one tactics are for laissez faire toward foreign trade barriers is based on a non sequitur.

85. See *Analysis of the United States-Japan Trade Problem*, Report of the Advisory Committee on Trade Policy and Negotiations (Washington: USTR, 1989).

86. This is documented by Robert Z. Lawrence, Imports in Japan: Closed Markets or Closed Minds? *Brookings Papers on Economic Activity*, no. 2, 1987, pp. 523—524. Also see the forceful argumentation in the response to the ACTN Report by the Japan—U.S. Business Council, Can a "Results-Oriented" Trade Strategy Work?, 26th Conference, San Francisco, June 30, 1989.

87. Even for the more homogeneous case of semiconductors, the accusations against the Japanese are not overwhelmingly persuasive.

88. For example, how is the target to be set, how is it to be achieved by Japan which is not a centrally planned economy, how are penalizing tariffs invoked at high levels against Japan (for failure to meet the target increases in imports) to be reconciled with the GATT, and what would be the reaction of Japan finally to such ham-fisted and authoritarian indulgence of Japan-bashing? None of these considerations has crossed the mind of Rudiger Dornbusch (*New York Times*, Sunday Business, September 24, 1989) who has recently proposed this form of managed trade. See the devastating critique offered by the economics columnist, Hobart Rowen, in the *Washington Post*, September 24, 1989.

89. Clyde Prestowitz has even argued that Japan's cultural differences, and the resulting impenetrability of the Japanese market, make Japan surplus-prone (*Newsweek*, Japan, June 1, 1989). In response (*Newsweek*, Japan, ibid., and *Wall Street Journal*, July 28, 1989), I have noted that, in that case, it is astonishing that it took

so long since Commodore Perry opened Japan in the nineteenth century for this inevitable surplus to emerge. Sarcasm aside, Japan has run deficits over sustained periods in this century. Nor can anyone ignore the fact that Japan's recent surplus has been great at a time when Japan's cultural differences were being reduced rather than increased. The "culturalists" who go from culture to surpluses to managed trade need to take a basic course in macroeconomics and another in economic history.

90. See the classic article by Murray Kemp and Henry Wan, Jr., An Elementary Proposition Concerning the Formation of Customs Unions (1976), reprinted in Bhagwati (ed.), *International Trade: Selected Readings* (Cambridge: MIT Press, 1981).

91. The European Free Trade Association (EFTA), formed almost concurrently with the European Community, was followed by the formation of the Latin American Free Trade Association, which soon came to grief, and in the last half of the 1960s proposals were made for a Pacific free trade area and a North Atlantic one.

92. The issue of trade diversion is not as flimsy as might be imagined just because there were few tariffs between Canada and the United States before the free trade agreement. As David Palmeter has shown, the rules of origin have been drastically changed by the free trade agreement to make protectionist trade diversion easier through arbitrary misuse of the new rules. Cf. Palmeter, The FTA Rules of Origin: Boon or Boondogle?, paper presented to the Canadian Centre for Trade Law and Policy, Ottawa, May 5, 1989.

93. I reject therefore not merely the economic logic but also the policy wisdom of the Kodak II recommendations to promote regional and bilateral arrangements because preferential access over other exporting countries (whether efficient suppliers or not) is one of the "benefits" of such arrangements! By contrast, see the excellent essay on the subject by Michael Aho, More Bilateral Trade Agreements Would Be a Blunder: What the Next President Should Do, *Cornell International Law Journal*, Ithaca, November 1989.

94. The key point is the important, antimultilateralist signal conveyed by the American conversion to regionalism in the shape of Article XXIV. Regional arrangements of one kind or another, in a *wider* sense, have always been around and have generally not aroused similar expectations as has the free trade agreement. Thus as J. H. Jackson, *World Trade and the Law of GATT* (Charlottesville: Michie, 1969), has remarked, "It has been pointed out that today [1965] more than two thirds of the membership of the GATT are nations that belong to one or another regional arrangement" (p. 588).

3

The Return of
the Reciprocitarians:
U.S. Trade Policy Today

with Douglas A. Irwin

We are always willing to be trade partners, but never trade patsies
—President Ronald Reagan.
State of the Union Message, 1987

Walter Lippmann characterized the 1900s as the American Century. In the same vein, the nineteenth century was Britain's. But if the nineteenth century ended in Britain's gradual loss of preeminence, politically and economically, the twentieth century is ending similarly for the United States. Staffan Burenstam Linder has already announced the arrival of the Pacific Century.[1]

This parallel suggests that the response of the two countries, both suffering from a "diminished giant" syndrome, would exhibit similarities. As it happens, this is, indeed, the case with respect to trade policy. As each country lost hegemony, faced foreign competition, and suffered domestic distress, the commitment to free trade that characterized the hegemonic period would be challenged. Demands for "fair trade," or equivalently for reciprocity, would surface. The reciprocitarians, rampant in diminished Britain, would return in the diminishing United States.

We address here these parallels, while also noting the contrasts between the British and the American situations. We thus gain insight into the current American predicament enabling us to conclude with observations pertinent to the trade policy of the United States as it moves increasingly toward fair trade.

3.1 The Giant Diminishes

In strikingly similar fashion, Britain toward the end of the nineteenth century and the United States toward the end of the twentieth century faced a shrinking position in the world economy and confronted domestic macroeconomic problems.

Both countries emerged from a war as the dominant political and economic power in the world. The end of the Napoleonic Wars, together with the Industrial Revolution, saw Britain emerge as the unchallenged world leader. The end of World War II, with the destruction of industrial capacity in Europe and Japan, saw the United States attain a similar position.

Neither country could seriously hope to maintain its status once other countries industrialized or regained their industrial potential. One difference is that while American policy in the early postwar period encouraged and promoted economic recovery in Western Europe and Japan, Britain did not actively court the industrialization of continental Europe and America.

The inevitable relative decline of Britain and the United States would manifest itself in two ways: the smaller relative size of their economies in the world economy and the rise of domestic economic difficulties.

From 1870 to 1913, Britain's share of world industrial production fell from 31.8 percent to 14.0 percent. At the same time, Germany's share rose partially and the United States expanded its share of the world total from 23.3 to 35.8 percent.[2]

Similarly, the United States has seen its share of world output decline since the war. In 1950, the United States accounted for 40.3 percent of total world gross domestic product (GDP); by 1980 this fraction was down to 21.8 percent. Over the same period, Western Europe's and Japan's share of world GDP increased from 21.1 to 29.8 percent and from 1.6 to 8.8 percent, respectively. In addition, the developing countries boosted their share from 12.7 to 17.9 percent over the same period.[3]

Both countries saw their share of world trade decline as well. From 1880 to 1913, Britain's share of world manufactured exports fell from 41.4 to 29.9 percent. Over the same period, the United States expanded its share from 2.8 to 12.6 percent and Germany increased her share from 19.3 to 26.5 percent.[4]

In 1950, exports of the United States accounted for 16.7 percent of the value of total world exports: by 1980 this share was 11.0 percent. During this period, Western Europe increased its share from 33.4 to 40.2 percent as did Japan, from 1.4 to 6.5 percent.[5]

At the same time, the structure of British and American imports changed. As the first major country to industrialize, Britain had a near monopoly in many export markets and was left unchallenged at home. For example, in 1860 manufactured goods comprised only 6 percent of British imports. As industry spread to other countries, British manufacturers faced competitive pressure in home markets from foreign manufacturers for the first time . By 1880, manufactured goods accounted for 17 percent of imports, the share rising to 25 percent by 1900. This remarkable change prompted concern among British industrialists and politicians about the wisdom of the country's free trade policy.[6]

The manufactured goods component of American imports has fluctuated widely in the postwar era, showing no particular trend. From 1981 to 1985, however, when protectionist pressures increased greatly, that share rose from 54.6 to 71.5 percent.[7]

Merchandise trade deficits increased for both countries. The political impact of this was clear, as the deficits were cited as prima facie evidence of "unequal market access" and the need for fair trade and reciprocity. The British trade deficit increased during the last quarter of the nineteenth century, from an average £97 million over the 1880s to £133 million over the 1890s. The deficit peaked at £181.3 million in 1903—precisely the time when Joseph Chamberlain's famous campaign for tariff reform flourished.[8]

The United States, too, has experienced merchandise trade deficits during the period when protectionist and fair trade sentiment is running high. The United States had trade surpluses for every year in the immediate postwar period, until 1971 when they yielded to a deficit. The trade account has been in deficit for every year since 1976, and the deficit expanded tremendously in the 1980s, growing from $28 billion in 1981 to $148 billion in 1986.[9]

In addition to changes in the world economy, both Britain and the United States faced several domestic pressures that sparked a questioning of the country's trade policy. Macroeconomic difficulties stand out. Both countries experienced slower growth and higher unemployment compared with earlier years, consequently spurring protectionist sentiments.

In Britain, growth slowed in both industrial production and national income. Feinstein's index of Britain's industrial output shows an average annual growth rate of 3.2 percent from 1855 to 1872 and a growth rate of 2.2 percent from 1872 to 1900. Unemployment rates in Britain varied greatly from year to year. There was a rise in unemployment during the "great depression" of prices during the 1880s, when the unemployment rate rose from 2.3 percent in 1882 to 10.2 percent in 1886 (although by 1889 it was 2.1 percent). Among the engineering, metals, and shipbuilding workers, hit particularly by foreign competition, unemployment rose from 2.3 percent in 1882 to an average of 11.9 percent from 1881 to 1887.[10]

For the United States, real gross national product (GNP) grew at an average rate of about 4.0 percent during the 1950s and 1960s, but slowed to 2.8 percent during the 1970s, then to 1.9 percent from 1980 to 1985.

The unemployment rate was an average 4.5 percent during the 1950s and 1960s, 6.1 percent during the 1970s, then 8.0 percent from 1980 to 1985.

3.2   Rise of the Reciprocitarians: Britain

The combination of the "diminished giant" status and the domestic distress in Britain (and now in the United States) fueled opposition to free trade. "Fair trade," not free trade, became the slogan of many politicians and industrialists who felt adversely affected by the changed circumstances.

Thus during the 1870s and 1880s, the rise of fair trade organizations such as the National Fair Trade League, the National Society for the Defence of British Industry, and the Reciprocity Free Trade Association marked the beginning of a campaign to change Britain's trade policy. The fair traders, businessmen, and politicians alike, suggested that retaliatory threats, tariff changes, and countervailing duties would protect home industries and open foreign markets and, in addition, would be a superior and more flexible approach than a pure free trade policy.

Arguments for Reciprocity and Fair Trade

A frequent complaint was of simple equity. Regardless of whether one was hurt economically, playing by asymmetric rules was plainly "unfair". If Britain renounced tariffs, but her competitors embraced them, Britain was unfairly handicapped. Naturally, this view prevailed among those who, in the mercantilist mould, believed that protection helped rather than hurt competitiveness and efficiency.

The frustration, reflecting the impatience with the inequity of asymmetric rules, was expressed well by Joseph Chamberlain: "We are losing our foreign markets, because whenever we begin to do a trade, the door is slammed in our faces with a whacking tariff ... as if that was not enough, these same foreigners who shut us out, invade our markets and take the work out of the hands of our working people and leave us doubly injured." This was, he said, "unfair and one-sided."[11] The *Foreign Times* equally decried Britain's "one-sided free trade" policy and found the Bismarck tariff of 1879 in Germany and the McKinley tariff of 1890 in the United States as galling then as today the United States finds the European Community's protection and Japan's alleged resort to inscrutable protection.[12]

Others were less concerned with the equity of the trade situation than with its efficiency. They thought that a British trade policy that tolerated both large trade deficits and excessive import penetration inflicted damage on the British economy. The competition suffered by British industry would prove to be harmful to the economy in the long run, they claimed. Again, Chamberlain expressed the fear of many in declaring: "We are to lose the great industries for which this country has been celebrated, which have made it prosperous in the past. We are to deal with inferior and subsidiary industries. Sugar is gone. Let us not weep for it, jam and pickles remain! Now, all of these workmen, these intelligent artisans, who were engaged tending and making the machinery for sugar refining in this country, I would like to know how many have found a resting-place, have found equivalent wages and comfort, in stirring up jam-pots and bottling pickles." [13]

Interestingly, a change in the British policy of unilateral free trade toward requiring reciprocity of access was also considered desirable since it would enable Britain to open foreign markets and thereby increase the gains from trade beyond what unilateralism would procure. British tariffs could be used to destroy foreign tariffs, in a tit-for-tat strategy. Tariffs would thus be a mere instrumentality with which to arrive at multilateral and therefore wider-ranging than unilateral, free trade. Lord Randolph Churchill, for example, was a leading advocate of using tariff policy as an instrument to pry open foreign markets. Foreign markets, like oysters. he said, needed to be opened with a "strong clasp knife, instead of being tickled with a feather." [4]

Arguments against Reciprocity and Fair Trade

The unilateral free traders, whose ranks included many of Britain's leading economists as well as numerous politicians, mobilized their wits and their pens against these arguments.

As prime minister, William Gladstone, in particular, was convinced that reciprocity and fair trade were simply euphemisms that masked old-fashioned protectionism. In a speech after the formation of the Fair Trade League, he remarked: "I must say it bears a suspicious likeness to our old friend Protection (cheers and laughter). Protection was dead and buried 30 years ago, but he has come out of the grave and is walking in the broad light of day, but after long experience underground he endeavours to look somewhat more attractive than he used to appear ... and in consequence he found it convenient to assume a new name (laughter)." [15] With his own brand of sarcasm, Gladstone loved to rip into those who opposed free trade: "There is a quack remedy which is called Reciprocity. And this quack remedy is under the special protection of quack doctors. And among the quack doctors I am sorry to say there appear to be some in very high station indeed."[16]

But political rhetoric aside, there were serious rebuttals of the contentions of the reciprocitarians.

The staunch supporters of Britain's (unilateral) free trade policy rejected the notion that reciprocity was necessary to pry open foreign markets. The belief in the virtues of free trade was so complete that it was felt that the folly of protectionism would cause grievous losses on its practitioners, inducing them to embrace free trade in the end. *The Times* argued that protectionist policies were self-destructive: "Protection, as we well know, brings its own punishment. We are safe, therefore, in leaving its, adherents to the stern teaching of facts. Nature will retaliate upon France whether we do so or not."[17]

If some were convinced that the consequences of their folly would make the foreign protectionists change their ways, others believed that the success of free-trading Britain set an example for other countries. As Robert Peel had argued in Parliament, in defence of unilateral free trade policy: "If other countries choose to buy in the dearest market, such an option on their part constitutes no reason why we should not be permitted to buy in the cheapest. I trust the Government ... will not resume the policy which they and we have found most inconvenient, namely the haggling with foreign countries about reciprocal concessions, instead of taking that independent course which we believe to be conducive to our own interests," the prime minister said. "Let us trust to the influence of public opinion in other countries—let us trust that our example, with the proof of practical benefits we derive from it, will at no remote period insure the adoption of the principles on which we have acted."[18]

Richard Cobden, the great crusader for the repeal of the Corn Laws and the adoption of free trade, went so far as to argue that insisting on reciprocal tariff reductions abroad would only serve to make the task of free traders abroad more difficult by implying that free trade was really in the British interest rather than their own. Thus the Anti-Corn Law League emphasized the British gain from a free trade policy, but "expressly refrained from appealing to any foreign sentiment in favour of the [free trade] cause. For they rightly judged that such appeals were certain to be misrepresented by the interests which stood behind protective tariffs and would play into the hands of their enemies."[19] Cobden put it thus: "We came to the conclusion that the less we attempted to persuade foreigners to adopt our trade principles, the better; for we discovered so much suspicion of the motives of England that it was lending an argument to the protectionists abroad to incite the popular feeling against free-traders by enabling them to say, 'See what these men are wanting to do; they are partisans of England and they are seeking to prostitute our industries at the feet of that perfidious nation ...' To take away this pretense, we avowed our total indifference whether other nations became free-traders or not; but we should abolish Protection for our own selves and leave other countries to take whatever course they like best." [20]

Equally, many felt that reciprocity was not an effective instrument for securing tariff reductions abroad simply because Britain did not have the necessary economic power. The economist Alfred Marshall suggested that England "is not in a strong position for reprisals against hostile tariffs, because there are no important exports of hers, which other countries need so urgently as to be willing to take them from her at considerably increased cost; and because none of her rivals would permanently suffer serious injury through the partial exclusion of any products of theirs with which England can afford to dispense." [21]

In addition, some feared that Britain herself was more vulnerable to retaliation than other countries. Gladstone explained: "Can you strike the foreigners hard by retaliatory tariffs? What manufactures do you import from abroad? In all £45 million. What manufactures do you export? Nearer £200 million ... If you are to make the foreigners feel, you must make him feel by striking him in his largest industrial interests; but the interests which he has in sending manufactures to you is one of his smallest interests and you are invited to inflict wounds upon yourself in the field measured by £45 million, while he has got exactly the same power of inflicting wounds upon you on a field measured by more than £200 million." [22]

Marshall even suggested that infant-industry protection justified some of the foreign tariffs of Britain's new rivals, so that reciprocity was inappropriate. He wrote that "it would have been foolish for nations with immature industries to adopt England's [free trade] system pure and simple." [23]

Finally, several economists at the time were convinced that, however sound the rationale underlying the use of tariffs for reciprocity, the policy would wind up being captured by protectionists and political interests. Thus Marshall, after observing the American experience with protection that reinforced his scepticism of rational tariff intervention, felt that "in becoming intricate, [protection] became corrupt and tended to corrupt general politics." [24] He was not alone in this view. A manifesto signed by a number of distinguished British economists warned that "protection brings in its train the loss of purity in politics, the unfair advantage given to those who wield the powers of jobbery and corruption, unjust distribution of wealth and the growth of sinister interests."[25] This was undoubtedly an early manifestation of the recent developments in the theory of political economy and international trade which replace the orthodox view that governments are benign and omnipotent with the view that their policies may reflect lobbying by pressure groups. This may lead to defects in the visible hand that outweigh ones in the invisible hand for which remedy is sought.

Reciprocity Vanquished

The fair trade movement gained ground by finding favor with members of the Conservative party. Whenever protectionist mutterings were heard, they inevitably came from the Conservatives, who remained suspicious of Cobdenite orthodoxy. *The Economist* commented in 1881 that, "unless some authoritative declaration to the contrary is speedily made, the country will be bound to assume that reciprocity has been formally adopted as part of the new Conservative platform."[26]

While the Conservative leadership, the Marquess of Salisbury in particular, hinted at experimenting with changes in the tariff, it was constrained from a full and ringing endorsement of fair trade because of the political costs of the food issue. As prime minister, Arthur Balfour explained to Chamberlain that "the prejudice against a small tax on food is not the fad of a few imperfectly informed theorists. It is a deep-rooted prejudice affecting a large mass of voters, especially the poorest classes, which it will be a matter of extreme difficulty to overcome."[27]

This hesitancy among the leadership did not prevent Conservative associations in Yorkshire, the Midlands, Scotland, and, in 1887, the Conservative associations in England as a whole from passing, by great majorities, statements calling for "speedy reforms" in tariff policy.[28] Other Conservatives such as Lord Randolph Churchill were outspoken in blaming Britain's economic ills on free trade. Yet while the Conservative party actively flirted with the fair traders, it ultimately kept them subdued. While the backbenchers remained susceptible to the reciprocitarians, the leadership was cautious and avoided making common cause with them.

As the fair trade movement faltered, with lack of support from labor, consumers and other groups, it sought to make allies. In panicular, the fair traders looked for links with the imperialists who favored closer economic ties with the colonies.

This alliance was predicated on the appreciation that the imperialist sentiment was a substantial force which could be harnessed to advantage.[29] Equally, it reflected the perception that imperial preference in trade policy offered a mutual-gain bargain to both movements. The preference would cement colonial ties and, by cushioning the impact of reciprocity-based tariffs on nonimperial competitors, would also weaken the arguments of critics who felt that Britain would pay dearly for such protection.

The alliance, however, was an uneasy one, for the imperialists occasionally worried that their movement was in danger of being infiltrated by closet protectionists. "The [Imperial Federation] League was never quite able to overcome the impression that many of its members were merely stowaways on the good ship Empire because their own protectionist ship had little prospect of making port," wrote the historian Benjamin Brown.[30]

But the alliance nevertheless was welcome to many insofar as it also reflected the desire to trade with friends rather than with rivals. Chamberlain explained that he believed in "a British Empire ... which ... should yet, even if alone, be self-sustaining and self-sufficient, able to maintain itself against the competition of all its rivals ... Do you think it better to cultivate the trade with your own people or to let that go in order that you may keep the trade of those who, rightly enough, are your competitors and rivals?"[31]

In the end, however, both the fair trade movement and the imperial preference campaign failed to gain adequate political standing. Rudyard Kipling would lament the failure of Chamberlain to promote both causes in his 1904 poem "Things and the Man."[32] Written "In Memoriam, Joseph Chamberlain," it was a dirge for the demise, not of Chamberlain, but of his movement.

The arguments against a change in policy may have been more persuasive than those in favor, but the central factor in the survival of Britain's free trade policy appears to have been the politically divisive nature of the protectionist stance. Labor, in particular, remained opposed to reciprocity: cheap food continued to require cheap imports, providing the same "pressure group" reinforcement of the free trade ideology that had paved the way for the original embrace of free trade by Peel. A leading industry, cotton textiles, also abstained because it required imports of raw materials. And the fortunes of the reciprocitarians rose and fell with the business cycle, preventing the gathering of momentum in the political arena. After the landslide victory of the free trade Liberals in the general election of 1906, the fair trade movement dwindled into the background until after World War I.[33]

3.3   Return of the Reciprocitarians: The United States

But if the reciprocitarians failed in Britain, they have returned to the United States today, under the parallel circumstances sketched earlier. Congressmen, businessmen, editorialists, and the media have repeatedly emphasized fairness in trade, "level playing fields," and reciprocity of access as a precondition for a trade regime to be acceptable to the United States.

New Variants of Full Reciprocity

But there are new twists to reciprocity now which the British in the nineteenth century did not envisage. Reciprocity of access was then viewed as an adoption by foreign countries of British-style free trade. Hence Britain would enact unspecified tariffs if trading rivals did not abolish theirs. The policy debate was mainly at the esoteric level of the general principle of reciprocity. The questions of which specific tariffs would be deployed and on what criteria were not generally elevated, during the heyday of the movement, to the realm of discourse and debate.[34]

In the current debate in the United States, however, reciprocity has rapidly moved to this level of concreteness, with the consequence that it has been advocated in curious forms that the British reciprocitarians had not contemplated.

To see this clearly, distinguish first between the *first-difference* reciprocity, sanctioned by the General Agreement on Tariffs and Trade (GATT), and *full* reciprocity. Under the GATT, negotiations for trade liberalization generally focus on matching concessions from the initial conditions. Thus reciprocity is sought at the margin, with reciprocity of changes and reductions; that is, first-difference reciprocity. By contrast, the nineteenth-century reciprocitarians, and those today, would seek full reciprocity; this is, reciprocity of access, reciprocity of trade restrictions, "level playing fields."[35]

But the full reciprocity envisaged today is not simply at the level of broadly matching mutual restrictions or openness of trade regions. It has sprouted two specific variants which are particularly bothersome: first, that the reciprocity of access must be met by individual sectors, which is to say at micro and not just the overall macro level; and second, that the reciprocity of access must further be assessed by bilateral trade balances such that if a rival enjoys a trade surplus, it is ipso facto evidence that it is not granting equal reciprocal access.[36]

The former variant has been at the centre of many complaints, especially directed at the Far Eastern countries such as Japan, the Republic of Korea, and Taiwan. For example, that Japanese construction companies successfully compete in the United States, while the American companies have been unable to tender for the construction of Kansai airport in Japan, has galled fair traders. Construction firms in the United States have not won a major contract in Japan since 1965 while the Japanese did $1.8 billion in construction business in the United States in 1985 alone. One senator has reportedly been planning to petition the U.S. Trade Representative (USTR) in President Reagan's cabinet to press the government of Japan to open up the Kansai bidding process.[37]

The latter variant, on the other hand, has been evident in the repeated demands that protection should be directed against countries running trade surpluses with the United States. For example, the proposed legislation (HR 4800), which passed the House of Representatives by a margin of 3 to 1 in May 1986, hoped to put a spotlight on countries that registered "excessive" trade surpluses with the United States. Country-specific reciprocity, focusing like the mercantilists on trade balances, was embodied in protectionist measures aimed at reducing the deficits by a certain amount each year. The former Democratic governor of Arizona, Bruce Babbitt, who has announced his presidential candidacy, has proposed yet more draconian solutions. Countries with persistent trade surpluses with the United States would be slapped with punitive, across-the-board tariffs rising to 100 percent.[38]

Reciprocity: Old Arguments Resurrected

Not surprisingly, there are also many parallels with the nineteenth century in the kinds of concerns that feed the demands for full reciprocity.

Thus, matching Joseph Chamberlain's concerns, Walter Mondale has argued: "We've been running up the white flag when we should be running up the American flag ... What do we want our kids to do? Sweep up around the Japanese computers?"[39] His speechwriter during the unsuccessful presidential campaign invoked images of Americans reduced to flipping hamburgers at McDonalds while the Japanese captured American industries. He might have invoked, with greater irony, the image of American kids rolling rice cakes at sushi bars! The latest imagery in the American political lexicon is that of the United States becoming a "Taco Bell" economy, implying double jeopardy by compounding the "de-industrialization" complex with the fears of a Hispanic destiny.

The fear of de-industrialization has gone beyond politicians to its exploitation by labor unions in declining, protection-seeking industries and by the media. Sol Chaikin, the leader of the International Ladies' Garment Workers' Union, has protested: "Because there are relatively few well-paying jobs in the service sector, an economy devoid of manufacturing would also necessarily experience a general decline in living standards ... Unrestricted trade and the investment practices of the multinationals ... can only lead to an America ultimately devoid of manufacturing" and hence manifestly robbed of her riches![40] But his lament pales beside Theodore White's exclamation that "the Japanese are on the move again in one of history's most brilliant commercial offensives, as they go about dismantling American industry."[41] This is reminiscent of the warnings by British reciprocitarians about the "deliberate and deadly [economic] rivalry" provoked by Germany and the United States, as the book *American Invaders* published in 1902 suggests.[42]

The sense of inequity, that the United States has been had by rivals playing by different rules, also matches the complaints of British fair traders about the injustice of others' tariffs while Britain plays by the rules of free trade. Lloyd Bentsen, Chairman of the Senate Finance Committee, has complained that, while foreigners can sell in an open American market, "we are not being able to sell them but a pittance. I don't think those things are fair and I don't think we need to roll over and play dead."[43]

The notion, paralleling Lord Randolph Churchill's sentiment that one's tariffs can be deployed to destroy others' tariffs or that the United States should threaten to close its markets—and even follow through—to pressure its rivals into lowering their trade barriers, has also been evident on the current American scene. In fact, it underlies the energetic use of Section 301 which is one of the principal tools of American tit-for-tat policy aimed at leveling the playing field for specific industries. Section 301 of the Trade Act of 1974 is one of the few American trade laws that focuses on American exports, not imports. Unfair and unreasonable foreign practices and policies that burden American commerce are attacked under threat of retaliation. It authorizes the president to take action against foreign trade practices that either violate international trade agreements or burden or restrict American commerce in an "unjustifiable, unreasonable or discriminatory fashion."[44] Although these provisions make this a unilateral and essentially arbitrary tool, presidential prudence has been evident in exercise of this authority. Jeanne Archibald, former chairperson of the Section 301 Committee in the office of the U.S. Trade Representative, has written: "Since the President is unrestricted as to what he may consider unreasonable, the practitioner may assume that any foreign government behavior is actionable under this provision. However, USTR and the President have exercised great caution in the use of this standard, reflecting their concern that precedents of too broad a scope not be established."[45] But congressional pressure to put even more teeth into Section 301, undercutting this caution, is increasingly evident.

Reciprocitarians Now versus Then: Asymmetries

If the reciprocitarians failed in nineteenth-century Britain, they are more potent in their return to the present-day United States. The reasons for this basic asymmetry are important to ponder.

First, while the British reciprocitarians were engaged in overturning nearly half a century of British commitment to unilateral free trade, today's reciprocitarians are well within the American tradition of trade policy which never embraced unilateralism. This compelling contrast invites analysis.

As it happens, Britain had in fact followed a policy of reciprocity for many years prior to free trade in the nineteenth century. From 1823 until the repeal of the Corn Laws, Britain "offered reciprocity treaties to any countries who were willing to enter into negotiations."[46] "Once a Treaty had been negotiated, it was up to the British trader to look after his own interests in fair and equal competition with rival foreign traders, and the Foreign Office would intervene only to protect him against injustice or against evasion of the terms of the Treaty itself."[47] Thus the British government would attempt to reduce barriers to trade in other countries on the basis of reciprocal concessions, but it would not intervene thereafter to promote British export interests.

As many have noted, however, Britain's efforts at procuring reciprocal treaties did not succeed. "In dealing with her equals, Britain failed to make headway."[48] "Between 1831 and 1841, for example, [Britain] failed to reach agreement through four sets of commercial negotiations with France"[49] It appeared that Britain's rivals were just not prepared to reduce their barriers to trade. Gladstone, who was vice president, then president, of the Board of Trade in the first half of the 1840s, observed: "The task was supplied on our side with sufficient zeal, but in every case we failed; I am sorry to add that in my opinion we did more than fail. The whole operation seemed to place us in a false position. Its tendency was to lead countries to regard with jealousy and suspicion, as boons to foreigners, those alterations in their laws, which though doubtless of advantage to foreigners would have been of far greater advantage to their own inhabitants."[50]

Free traders in Britain concluded that reciprocity had failed and that the intransigence of other countries in lowering their tariffs should no longer block Britain from unilaterally lowering tariffs to capture some gains from trade expansion. As Adam Smith pointed out, "there may be good policy in retaliations ... when there is a probability that they will procure the repeal of the high duties or prohibitions complained of ... When there is no probability that any such repeal can be procured, it seems a bad method of compensating the injury done to certain classes of our people, to do another injury to ourselves, not only to those classes, but to almost all other classes of them."[51] Thus it became British policy to assume that the trade policy of other countries was a "given," not alterable by British negotiations and actions. For example, a majority of the members on the Royal Commission on the depression of industry and trade, set up in 1885, argued that foreign tariffs, although a major cause of British ills, were largely independent of Britain's control. This attitude stands in marked contrast to the recent American view that barriers to trade in other countries can be beaten down under threat of retaliation.

Thus after the removal of the Corn Laws in 1846, unilateralism in free trade became a critical feature of British free trade doctrine. As the economist Thomas Tooke described it, the policy was "not to render our own commercial reforms in any way dependent on the fears, the wishes or the diplomacy of other states," but "to act at once upon the principle that every reduction of duties which admits a larger quantity of the produce of foreign countries must at least be paid for by commodities which it is profitable for this country to export, whatever may be the degree of folly or wisdom displayed in the tariffs of the foreign countries to which they are sent."[52] It held so strong that even when the French proposed mutual tariff reductions, Cobden "objected that a treaty was opposed to the principles on which the great English tariff reform of 1846 had been based."[53] In 1859 Cobden wrote to Michel Chevalier: "It would of course be agreeable to me to see your Ministers of State. But I attach very little importance to such interviews; for there is always a latent suspicion that I, as an Englishman, in recommending other governments to adopt free trade principles am merely pursuing a selfish British policy. Thus my advice is deprived of all weight and even my facts are doubted ... But on totally different grounds I should be glad to see a removal of the impediments our foolish legislation interposes on the intercourse between the two countries."[54]

Cobden's reluctance, shared initially by Gladstone, to enter into a reciprocal treaty with France (subsequently known as the Cobden-Chevalier
Treaty of 1860) soon gave way to support for such negotiations. But the
striking point is the intellectual pull the unilateral free trade policy had on
members of the British government. Die-hard free traders opposed the
commercial treaty as violating Britain's previous unilateral tariff policy.[55]
"The conclusion of a commercial treaty," said *The Times*, "is nothing less
than a solemn declaration against those doctrines of political economy
which have regulated the practice of this country since 1846."[56] Britain's
unilateral free trade policy would come into question once again when
France terminated the treaty in 1872 and began to return to protection. In
a memorandum to the Foreign Office on negotiating commercial treaties,
Gladstone wrote: "In sum, we made in the case of the Treaty of 1860 a
great and marked exception to a well established rule for what we thought
well defined and very strong reasons. We seem by this means to have
given considerable force to the Free Trade movement on the continent of
Europe. When these powerful considerations are removed, and not only
removed but reversed, is not our safest course to fall back upon our old
basis, namely that the cause of freedom in commerce will, as a rule, be most
effectively advanced by leaving each nation to consider the subject in light
of its own interests alone?"[57] Thus when a new French administration
proposed to revamp the 1860 treaty, the British told them that Britain "had
had enough of commercial treaties and that she believed in the freedom of
each country to set its own tariffs subject only to security for British trade
and navigation against any special disfavour."[58]

Hence, when the reciprocitarians sought to turn Britain's trade policy
from unilateralism to reciprocity, from free trade to fair trade, they were up
against a powerful diplomatic tradition and economic ideology.[59] It is not
surprising that they failed.

By contrast, the United States, a latecomer to industrialization, had never
embraced the ideology of unilateral free trade. Protection had, without
shame, long been part of American trade policy and commanded intellectual respectability ever since Alexander Hamilton's *Report on Manufactures*
of 1791. At the same time, and in consequence thereof, the United States
has regarded reciprocity as the only appropriate way to proceed. Most
commercial treaties therefore included conditional most-favored-nation
(MFN) clauses, requiring tariff cuts to be reciprocated.

Indeed, from the Reciprocal Trade Agreements Act of 1934, down to
Bretton Woods at the end of World War II, the United States consistently
stuck to reciprocitarian ideas on tariff policy. The absence of unilateralism

in free trade as a policy basis is evident also in the GATT, which the United States largely shaped. The GATT, whose conventional modus operandi of tariff negotiations reflects only first-difference reciprocity, is itself a contract. The United States expected each contracting party to the GATT to accept symmetric obligations and enjoy identical rights. Moreover, first-difference reciprocity was a procedural device; the implicit goal was free trade, more or less, which would imply full reciprocity of market access.[60]

As it happened, however, actual postwar American trade policy was by no means characterized by unbending reciprocity. The United States, the undisputed *force majeure*, looked the other way when it came to requiring GATT members to accept symmetric obligations. In the political interest of building a New Europe, for example, the United States allowed asymmetry of access during the long period when Western Europe was shifting to convertability in current-account transactions. It also tolerated the incorporation in the GATT of Article XXIV permining the formation of customs unions and free trade areas even though it negated the full acceptance of MFN obligations toward GATT members outside a customs union or free trade area. It was under Article XXIV that the European Community was formed. Equally, the United States acquiesced in the enactment of Part IV of the GATT and the special-and-differential treatment of developing countries. This granted that developing countries were handicapped and hence permitted them exemption from symmetric GATT obligations which their under-developed status seemed to justify—much along the lines today of "affirmative action" in domestic programs.

It is possible to view this postwar period from two different, stylized perspectives. Either one can argue with the American economist Charles Kindleberger that the United States played a leadership role in supplying the "public good" of a GATT regime oriented toward freer trade, while letting "free riders," such as Western Europe in the immediate postwar period and the developing countries, escape the "burden" of accepting symmetric market-access obligations.[61] Or one can draw the inference that the United States was acting as the leader in the different sense of sustaining the GATT by permitting justifiable asymmetries of obligations for those countries on a *temporary* basis.

The latter seems to be the appropriate interpretation, more consonant with the events. It also suggests that the return of the reciprocitarians in the United States was inevitable. As these temporary circumstances ended, with the recovery of Western Europe and more recently the dramatic growth of the newly industrializing countries, the United States would surely return to its original conception of the GATT as a contract and begin to look for reciprocity of market access.

But the return to reciprocity, and its surprisingly greater strength and success now, owe equally much to the different circumstances of political economy today. These changes in political economy have made the proponents of freer trade, and an open trading system as envisaged under the GATT, responsive to reciprocitarian ideas for three mutually reinforcing reasons: one of political accommodation, one of political psychology, and the last of political alliance.

The "diminished giant" syndrome and the "overvalued" dollar, combined with the historical appeal of reciprocitarian ideas, have made fairness in trade a politically potent force on the American scene. Much as the proponents of freer trade would like to reject reciprocity on grounds such as those advanced by the British antireciprocitarians of the nineteenth century, they must come to terms with the powerful appeal of the fairness-in-trade doctrine. Without reciprocity, free trade itself could be overwhelmed politically. Political accommodation with the reciprocitarians is therefore viewed as a sine qua non for maintaining the open trading system.

This accommodation is manifest in the shift of the Reagan administration, from its first-term advocacy of freer trade and its muted indifference to the rhetoric of fair trade, to its second-term espousal of the need to ensure reverse market access. The continued pressure from Democrats, who have moved from overt protectionist demands to reciprocitarian planks favoring fair trade, and the continued trade deficit have forced increasing numbers of Republicans to consider reciprocity, not as the slippery path to protectionism but in a more benign light. There is no more dramatic evidence of this than in the sight of the U.S. Trade Representative, Clayton Yeutter, on television, being repeatedly mauled early in his tenure by irate senators demanding "results" on access to foreign markets, and the later crispness exhibited by Ambassador Yeutter on similar questions. The emerging consensus by both parties on fair trade as a component of "competitiveness," the buzz word of 1987, is evident.

But this consensus is not merely a matter of accommodation by the free traders, despite their fears. It is also a matter of psychology. The aggressive stance of reciprocity should particularly seduce those Republicans who insist that America is tall but stands diminished simply because she does not insist on her rights. Thus it is not surprising to find the former U.S. ambassador to the United Nations, Jeanne Kirkpatrick, the latest reciprocitarian, arguing that "[focusing on reducing the dollar's value to cure the payments deficit] takes no account of an array of discriminatory practices imposed by other nations to keep U.S. products out of their markets ... Shielding industries from competition is one thing, insisting that they be permitted to compete is another. The issue today is less protecting American industries than gaining access to foreign markets ... New thinking is required ... It should begin by acknowledging that Americans are producers as well as consumers. We therefore need access and competitiveness." [62]

In fact, there may well be an affinity at a different but related psychological level between free traders and reciprocitarians in the United States today. To see this, it is necessary to recall the frequent argument that, in politics, free trade comes as one's ideological preference only when one is strong: the Darwinian process appeals to those who expect to emerge the winners. It is therefore the preferred doctrine of those who possess actual or perceived competitiveness. There is undoubtedly an element of truth in this, as witnessed by the reluctance of many latecomers to forgo the use of protection for their industrialization in the nineteenth and twentieth centuries.

Interestingly, however, the British conversion to free trade in 1846 remains, on further scrutiny, an exception to this hypothesis in spite of appearances to the contrary. Thus as prime minister, Robert Peel, by his own proclamation, was converted to free trade by the principles of political economy and repealed the Corn Laws in 1846 to usher in free trade at the cost of his political career (since he betrayed his own protectionist party in this matter). [63] Peel's embrace of free trade had an ideological, cerebral basis (although one may still wonder cynically whether his conversion would have survived a counterfactual scenario where Britain was not ahead of the pack during the Industrial Revolution).

By contrast, President Ronald Reagan's commitment to free trade appears to be instinctual. Although he was an economics major at Eureka College, it is doubtful that he was animated by the theory of comparative advantage or that he now sits in his study reflecting on the wisdom of Adam Smith and David Ricardo. Rather, his attachment to free trade seems to reflect an intuitive sense of the Darwinian process and America's ability to come out as Number One. In fact, his remarkable appeal to the American public comes from his evident faith in America's strength after the reverses of Vietnam and the sense of American impotence thereafter. His confidence in America speaks to a deep-seated and widespread yearning to regain America's central influence in world affairs.

This confidence in America also surely implies that President Reagan can contemplate America's struggle in a world of free trade with equanimity, secure in the view that America can only win and prosper. But if the free trade ideology is instinctual in the Darwinian sense, rather than cerebral in the Adam Smith mold, it is more susceptible to the demands of reciprocitarians for "level playing fields" since it is not anchored in the economic notion that unilateral free trade is good for a country even if others do not follow that practice.

In fact, the more-open-than-thou assertions of reciprocitarians can become particularly seductive to these instinctual-Darwinian free traders. Free traders with faith in the ability of American industries to compete are more likely to conclude that if the United States does in fact do badly in the Darwinian struggle, despite assumed superiority, there must surely be underhanded unfairness by foreign competitors which should not be tolerated—a conclusion and an attitude that Japan, in particular. has increasingly faced in the United States. Then the reciprocity approach acquires legitimacy to these free traders.

Reciprocitarians have also prospered in the United States because some free traders have seen them as possible allies in fighting protection rather than as closet protectionists. The political economy of protection has always been stacked against free trade because consumers, who are hurt by protection, are often too numerous to unite, while producers, who profit from protection, are small in number and can organize effectively.[64] Export interests, which are hurt by the bias against exports resulting from import protection,[65] are also unable to see this connection—which escapes even large numbers of economists! Besieged by protectionists, the U.S. administration, which seeks freer trade, has actively looked for political allies who would be interested in freer trade rather than in protection. By promising the opening of foreign markets, the administration can mobilize the export interests as countervailing lobbies to be pitted against the protectionist interests that seek to close markets instead. The theme of opening foreign markets, which is the key feature of the fair trade proponents, is seen then as a strategic device to manipulate the political economy environment and to harness it in the war against protectionist forces.

3.4   Perils of Reciprocity: Voluntary Import Expansions and So On

But if fair trade has come to stay, and the return of the reciprocitarians in the United States seems more enduring and crowned with success, it is not without the perils which had been voiced in Britain when the reciprocitarians had first surfaced. The specific focal points at which fair trade is particularly in danger of turning into either novel violations of the open trading system or overt protectionism in the current context may be briefly noted. The former relate primarily to American exports; the latter, to American imports. The exports of the United States are open to abuse via voluntary import expansions; the imports of the United States, via misuse of subsidy-countervailing and antidumping actions.

While opening foreign markets is certainly better than closing one's own, the actual outcome in the fair trade atmosphere is likely to degenerate into replacing VERs (voluntary export restraints) on one's imports by VIEs (voluntary import expansions) on one's exports. Both are departures from the principles of an open trading system where rules matter and quantity outcomes do not. Whereas VERs restrict imports of specific goods from specific countries by getting these countries to adopt either export quotas or (as in the recent Canadian lumber case) export duties, VIEs require imports of specific goods by specific countries by whatever means possible.[66]

Opening up Japan degenerates, in a reciprocitarian climate, into assessing this openness by reference to results, rather than by reference to rules.[67] If quantities do not show up as desired, then there must be inscrutable, unfair protection! But the exercise occasionally degenerates further by asking: how much is the United States, not just the world, exporting to Japan in specific sectors? When VIEs (explicit or implicit) surface, the country being bashed is pressured to ensure the expansion of its imports of the specific items in question from the country doing the bashing. This is tantamount to "export protectionism."

There is evidence of the United States sometimes falling into this trap, given the intense pressure for reciprocity and the lobbying by export sectors nurtured as countervailing pressure groups against protectionists wanting to close American markets. In the case of semiconductor chips, the United States reportedly wanted to include in its pact with Japan an assurance that 20 percent of the Japanese market would be supplied by American producers by a target date. While the formal agreement is reported not to include this provision, interviews confirm that it will remain on the table as a way of measuring Japan's fulfilment of her commitment to open her market.[68] Similarly, American pressure put on Japan to open her beef market was aimed at getting Japan to increase her imports of American beef by increasing the quota for the United States, rather than getting Japan to liberalize her import regime, the most likely consequence of which would be Australia outcompeting both Japan and the United States!

Again, in relation to cases involving Section 301, an official statement on the case against Japan on leather and leather footwear quotas contains the following pertinent statement: "On leather, Japan has responded to the GATT panel decision by offering to replace the leather quota with tariffs, but the US has rejected that offer because it would not improve access to the Japanese leather market and in fact could even further reduce our negligible share of the market," suggesting that the United States might lose to more competitive suppliers if market access was provided by replacing a quota with a nondiscriminatory tariff.[69]

The other, better understood peril in the rise of fair trade notions is that it can easily turn the twin measures of subsidy-countervailing and antidumping duties, designed to maintain "fair competition," into de facto "soft core" protection.

In a climate of prosperity and relaxed attitudes towards an open trading system, subsidy-countervailing and antidumping duties may be operated perhaps without being converted into instruments of harassment of foreign exporters. But there is strong likelihood that these instruments will, indeed, be used by protectionists to "go after" successful foreign competitors, when protectionist sentiments are high and the notion of fair trade is riding yet higher. In fact, not merely in the United States (where subsidy-countervailing duties are more fashionable) but also in the European Community (where antidumping duties are favoured), a trend towards rapid escalation of such actions, often as a prelude to VERs and even VIEs, has been observed.[70]

Given procedures where these actions are almost entirely decided on by national bodies, rather than impartial arbitrators, and no costs are levied against unsuccessful petitioners, the possibility of petitions designed to harass successful foreign competitors is always a very real one. And the probability of this perverse outcome increases as protectionist and fair trade sentiments gather strength, as in recent years.

As ideas of reciprocity gain force, for reasons outlined earlier, it is important to keep these perils in clear view. Otherwise, reciprocity turns rapidly into a negation of an open trading system, making fair trade an enemy of free trade, not its ally.

Notes

1. Staffan Burenstam Linder, *The Pacific Century* (Stanford: Stanford University Press, 1986).

2. François Crouzet, *The Victorian Economy* (London: Methuen, 1982), p. 378.

3. *Handbook of International Trade and Development Statistics 1983*, UNCTAD Secretariat, Geneva, pp. 446–447.

4. S. B. Saul, The Export Economy: 1870–1914, *Yorkshire Bulletin of Economic and Social Research*, Leeds, May 1965, p. 12.

5. *Handbook of International Trade and Development Statistics 1984*, UNCTAD Secretariat, Geneva, p. 2.

6. Crouzet, op. cit., p. 351.

7. *Economic Report of the President* (Washington: U.S. Government Printing Office, 1987), p. 362.

8. B. R. Mitchell, *Abstract of British Historical Statistics* (Cambndge: Cambridge University Press, 1962), p. 334.

9. One important difference between the two cases should be noted here. Britain always had current-account surpluses during these years because overseas investment earnings and invisibles more than compensated for the trade deficit. The United States had a mixture of current-account surpluses and deficits during the trade-deficit years, until 1983 when the current account fell sharply into deficit.

10. Mitchell, op. cit., pp. 64–65.

11. Charles W. Boyd (ed.), *Mr Chamberlain's Speeches* (Boston: Houghton Mifflin, 1914), vol. II, pp. 169–170.

12. Quoted in Benjamin H. Brown, *The Tariff Reform Movement in Great Britain 1881–1895* (New York: Columbia University Press, 1943), p. 8.

13. Quoted in A. W. Coats, Political Economy and the Tariff Reform Campaign of 1903, *Journal of Law and Economics*, Chicago, April 1968, p. 215.

14. Quoted in B. H. Brown, op. cit., p. 61.

15. *The Times*, London, October 8, 1881.

16. W. E. Gladstone, *Midlothian Speeches 1879* (New York: Humanities Press, 1971), p. 106.

17. *The Times*, September 2, 1881.

18. *Parliamentary Debates*, House of Commons, London, June 29, 1846.

19. J. A. Hobson, *Richard Cobden: The International Man* (New York: Henry Holt, 1919), p. 40.

20. Quoted in ibid., p. 41. The fact that many thought Britain would gain from unilateral free trade does not, of course, imply that she actually gained from such a policy. For instance, Donald McCloskey has argued that free trade harmed Britain through worsened terms of trade, meaning that an optimal tariff was necessary. See Magnanimous Albion, in Donald N. McCloskey, *Enterprise and Trade in Victorian Britain* (London: Allen & Unwin, 1981).

21. Memorandum on Fiscal Policy of International Trade (1903), in J. M. Keynes (ed.), *Official Papers of Alfred Marshall* (London: Macmillan, 1926), p. 408.

22. *The Times*, October 8, 1881.

23. Memorandum, op. cit., p. 392.

24. Ibid., p. 394.

25. *The Times*, August 15, 1903. The list of signatories included F. Y. Edgeworth, Sir Arthur Bowley and Edwin Cannan.

26. *The Economist*, London, September 3, 1881.

27. Quoted in Robert Blake, *The Conservative Party from Peel to Thatcher* (London: Methuen, 1985), p. 171.

28. B. H. Brown, op. cit., pp. 67–69.

29. In fact, the imperialist movement's impressive growth was itself a result of the "diminished giant" syndrome that spawned the fair trade movement. As *The Times* put it on June 18, 1891: "With the colonies massed around us, we can hold our own in the ranks of the world powers ... Without them we must sink to the position of a merely European kingdom—a position which for England entails a slow but sure decay."

30. B. H. Brown, op. cit., p. 41.

31. *The Times*, May 16, 1903.

32. *Rudyard Kipling's Verse: Inclusive Edition 1885–1926* (New York: Doubleday Doran, 1931) pp. 240–241. The poem began by citing Genesis: "And Joseph dreamed a dream, and he told it his brethren and they hated him yet the more."

33. As Martin Wolf has pointed out to us, Britain did succumb to the attractions of protectionism and imperial preferences in the interwar period, notably under Joseph Chamberlain's son Neville. Furthermore, in the period since World War II, Britain has fully absorbed the reciprocitarian ideology for trade in goods. It is interesting that this shift has done little to reverse the country's relative decline in manufacturing industry. At the same time, the performance of the one sector in which Britain has continued with her traditional unilateral liberalism, namely, financial services, remains impressive.

34. Only by 1903 Chamberlain would propose an across-the-board tariff of 10 percent on manufactures on grounds of fair trade and reciprocity.

35. On the relationship between reciprocity and the most-favored-nation (MFN) principle in the GATT, see Martin Wolf, An Unholy Alliance: The European Community and Developing Countries in the International Trading System, *Aussenwirtschaft*, Zurich, March 1987.

36. William R. Cline, in his pamphlet, *"Reciprocity": A New Approach to World Trade Policy?* (Washington: Institute for International Economics, 1982), has noted that

"US reciprocity objectives in the past meant seeking reciprocal *changes* in protection in trade negotiations; the new approach seeks reciprocity in the *level* of protection *bilaterally* and over a certain *range of goods*" (p. 7). As noted in the text, however, a key shift seems to be in the way reciprocity of access is *assessed* (that is, in judging it by reference to bilateral trade balance) and not just in whether it is *demanded* bilaterally, the latter being inevitable under full reciprocity.

37. *International Trade Reporter*, Bureau of National Affairs, Washington, January 21, 1987, pp. 62–63.

38. *Washington Post*, December 6, 1986.

39. *New York Times*, October 13, 1982, p. A31.

40. Sol C. Chaikin, Trade, Investment and Deindustrailization: Myth and Reality, *Foreign Affairs*, New York, Spring 1982, p. 848.

41. *New York Times Magazine*, July 28, 1985, p. 23.

42. F. A. McKenzie, *American Invaders* (London: Longman, 1902). See also E. E. Williams, *Made in Germany* (London: Heinemann, 1896).

43. *Washington Post*, December 21, 1986.

44. *White House Press Release*, Executive Office of the President, Washington, September 7, 1985, p. 1.

45. Jeanne Archibald, Section 301 of the Trade Act of 1974, mimeograph, Office of the U.S. Trade Representative, Washington, 1984.

46. Lucy Brown, *The Board of Trade and the Free Trade Movement 1830–1842* (Oxford: Clarendon Press, 1958), p. 116.

47. D. C. M. Platt, *Finance, Trade and Politics in British Foreign Policy 1815–1914* (Oxford: Clarendon Press, 1968), p. 85.

48. A. A. Iliasu, The Cobden-Chevalier Commercial Treaty of 1860, *Historical Journal*, Cambridge, March 1971, p. 69, cited in Arthur Stein, The Hegemon's Dilemma: Great Britain, the United States and the International Economic Order, *International Organization*, Philadelphia, Spring 1984, p. 361.

49. Stein, op. cit., pp. 361–362.

50. Quoted in Francis Edwin Hyde, *Mr Gladstone at the Board of Trade* (London: Cobden-Sanderson, 1934), p. 126.

51. Adam Smith, *The Wealth of Nations*, edited by Edwin Cannan (London: Methuen, 1961), vol. I, bk IV, ch. ii, p. 490.

52. Quoted in Hyde, op. cit., p. 126.

53. Arthur Louis Dunham, *The Anglo–French Treaty of Commerce of 1860 and the Progress of the Industrial Revolution in France* (Ann Arbor: University of Michigan Press, 1930) p. 50. See also Platt, op. cit., pp. 86–87.

54. Quoted in Dunham, op. cit., pp. 51–52.

55. See John Morley, *The Life of Richard Cobden* (London: Macmillan, 1908), pp. 326–331.

56. *The Times*, January 23, 1860, quoted in Dunham, op. cit., p. 106.

57. Quoted in Dunham, op. cit., p. 303.

58. Platt, op. cit., p. 89.

59. Two qualifications to the thesis that Britain had adopted unilateral free trade should be noted, although they do not detract from the substance of the thesis. First, when it came to trade with unequals, Britain did not maintain a stance of unilateralism. Reciprocal market access, even market access not balanced by full reverse market access, was forced on colonies such as India. Second, Britain continued to rely on import duties for a sizable fraction of her revenue, up to as much as one fifth during the 1860s and nearly twice as much during the 1850s. See Stein, op. cit., p. 363. Therefore, Britain never quite had free trade because revenue tariffs have protective effects, but the intent was not to protect and the commodities taxed were not great in number.

60. Think of the analogy with armament negotiations where first-difference reciprocity involving mutual balanced arms reductions may be the path to eventual disarmament which constitutes full reciprocity.

61. Charles P. Kindleberger, Dominance and Leadership in the International Economy: Exploitation, Public Goods and Free Riders, *International Studies Quarterly*, Columbia, South Carolina, June 1981, pp. 242–254.

62. *Washington Post*, January 25, 1987. The article takes for granted, of course, that the United States is open and foreign markets are not. It also makes the remarkable claim that the European Community is preferential arrangement that harms the United States so much that the United States must seek such arrangements with Latin America! That the Community is sanctioned by GATT Article XXIV, and that the United States itself has established a free trade area with Israel and is undertaking negotiations for such an arrangement with Canada (without the attributes of political integration and freedom of factor mobility, etc.), is ignored in the article.

63. This ideological conversion, of course, would not have taken place without the lobbying by Cobden's Anti-Corn Law League which drew much of its support from the fact that cheap imports of corn were seen as profitable for consumers and for industry, thus providing ample "sectional interest," pressure group, lobbying support for Cobden's social-interest-inspired drive for repeal. The lobbying therefore simply provided the necessary stimulus and information. Peel was persuaded, not purchased; batized, not bought. Norman Gash, *Robert Peel* (Totowa, NJ: Rowman and Littlefield, 1972), pp. 567–568.

64. This argument has been developed systematically by Mancur Olson, *The Logic of Collective Action* (Cambridge, Harvard University Press, 1965), and has been

stated earlier in a neglected passage by Vilfredo Pareto in his *Manual of Political Economy* (London: Macmillan, 1971), p. 379, translated from the French edition of 1927: "A protectionist measure provides large benefits to a small number of people and causes a very great number of consumers a slight loss. This circumstance makes it easier to put a protectionist measure into practice."

65. For a recent discussion, see Kenneth W. Clements and Larry A. Sjaastad, *How Protection Taxes Exporters*, Thames Essay No. 39 (London: Trade Policy Research Centre, 1984).

66. The term VIEs was introduced in Jagdish N. Bhagwati, VERs, Quid Pro Quo DFI and VIEs: Political-Economy-Theoretic Analyses, *International Economic Journal*, Seoul, Spring 1987, pp. 1–12, reprinted in this volume (chapter 9).

67. Cross-country regression analysis is also deployed now to deem Japan an offender. Thus even a sophisticated economist such as Bela Balassa has run such a regression on the share of imports in gross national product (GNP) to argue that Japan "imports too little" and therefore has invisible but effective trade restraints. But, except for recent years of substantial surplus, regressing the share of exports in GNP on the same explanatory variables should show Japan off the regression as "exporting too little" and hence the *outside world* as too protectionist. Moreover, the Balassa regression can be interpreted differently to mean that Japan is allowed to export too little and therefore has too little to spend on imports! See Bela Balassa, Japan's Trade Policies, paper presented at a Conference on Free Trade in the World Economy: Towards an Opening of Markets, convened by the Institut für Weltwirtschaft, Kiel, June 24–26, 1986.

68. The formal agreement was concluded *ad referendum* in July 1986, with Japan agreeing to provide, among other things, "fair and equitable access to its domestic market for foreign semiconductor products." It was formally signed on September 3, 1986.

69. *White House Press Release*, September 7, 1985, p. 2.

70. See the important studies by Patrick Messerlin, Public Subsidies to Industry and Agriculture and Countervailing Duties, paper presented to a European meeting on the Position of the European Community in the New GATT Round, jointly convened by the Spanish Ministry of Economy and Finance and the Trade Policy Research Centre, Villalba, October 2–4, 1986; Chong-Hyun Nam, Export Promoting Policies under Countervailing Threats: GATT Rules and Practice, Development Policy Issues Series, World Bank, Washington, December 1986; and J. Michael Finger and Julio Nogués, International Control of Subsidies and Countervailing Duties, paper presented at a Conference on the Role and Interests of the Developing Countries in the Multilateral Trade Negotiations, jointly convened by the World Bank and the Thailand Development Research Institute, October 30, to November 1, 1986.

4   Export-Promoting Protection: Endogenous Monopoly and Price Disparity

That an industry, once protected, may slide up the scale of comparative advantage and become eventually an exporter is not a novelty. This sequence, when it occurs, is likely to reflect a successful maturing of an infant industry, though anyone familiar with the scope of interventions in the form of direct and indirect export subsidies in certain countries may be forgiven for not immediately jumping to the conclusion that this sequence, described by the Japanese economist Akamatsu as the "flying geese pattern," is a result simply of the operation of market forces reflecting the industry's having attained to successful adulthood.

But can protection improve export performance even if we were to rule out learning and other dynamic externalities that may turn an import-substitute into an export activity eventually? The answer is in the affirmative if we deploy a model in which protection, invoked in the presence of domestic monopoly, permits price discrimination between domestic and foreign markets. This is demonstrated in section 4.1, where it is shown that the protection-induced export promotion will be characterized by a "price disparity": the domestic price will exceed the export price. Such price disparity is indeed observed in several developing countries which use prohibitive or nearly prohibitive tariffs or QRs on imports of items that are exported.

Section 4.2 then shows that if a protective duty, explicit or implicit, is matched by an export subsidy (as is roughly done in countries that practise the export-promoting EP trade strategy),[1] the price disparity will be accompanied by a yet further expansion of exports.

Section 4.3 offers concluding observations.

4.1

Conventional Thesis

The conventional wisdom, critical of the impact of protection on exports, is reflected in figure 4.1. The model in it is of the familiar partial-equilibrium variety. $S_F (AR_F = MR_F)$ represents the infinitely elastic foreign-supply curve with constant average and marginal revenues. AR_D and MR_D are the domestic average- and marginal-revenue curves. The domestic monopolist's marginal-cost curve is MC.

If there is free trade, the monopolist's monopoly is eliminated by foreign competition. In this case, the monopolist produces AB while BD is the level of free-trade imports, M_f.

Now let a tariff be imposed at rate t, so that $OE = OA(1 + t)$. The domestic monopolist can then charge domestic price OE while producing AC (at C, his marginal cost equals marginal revenue in domestic sale) for domestic consumption.

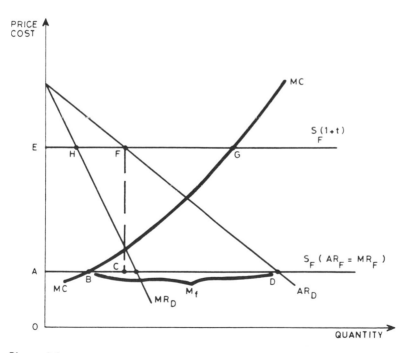

Figure 4.1

Thus, relative to free trade, protection increases domestic production (from *AB* to *AC*), raises domestic price (from *OA* to *OE*), and diminishes imports (from *BD* to zero).

This configuration is probably what is widely understood to be the effect of protection in the presence of domestic monopolies which, while exogenous in origin, are endogenous to the trade policy itself. It is not surprising, therefore, for economists to believe that, even in the presence of monopoly, protection will have an adverse impact on trade, exactly as it does in conventional competitive arguments.

Alternative Thesis

Consider, however, the different configuration of prices and costs in figure 4.2.[2]

In free trade, the domestic monopolist loses his monopoly and produces *AC* (at *C*, his marginal cost equals marginal revenue), domestic price is *OA*, and domestic demand is *AD*. *CD* represents, therefore, the attendant imports under free trade, M_f.

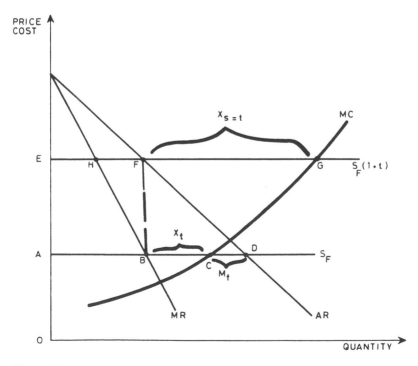

Figure 4.2

Replace free trade now by a tariff at rate t. The domestic price then will be OE, with the import supply curve, S_F, now turning into $S_F(1 + t)$. At price OE, the domestic monopolist can successfully maximize his profits by producing AB for the domestic market and charging OE for it, selling BC for export at price OA instead, and using the import tariff at rate t to prevent arbitrage and to facilitate the market segmentation that permits this price discrimination between the home market and the foreign market.

Thus, protection-induced exports, X_t, contrast with free-trade-induced imports, M_f. Evidently, by facilitating price discrimination, protection has led to export promotion.

It is important to note that this remarkable result has nothing to do with economies of scale (the marginal-cost curve is upward sloping), externalities, or export subsidies. It is an elementary result of protection interacting with domestic monopoly to create price discrimination.

However, where figure 4.1 produces the orthodox result, figure 4.2 produces the *protection-induced export-enhancement* paradox. The reason is manifest in the behavior of marginal cost. In the former case, the marginal costs being high relative to foreign price, protection simply shuts off imports. In the latter case, where the marginal costs are more favorable relative to foreign price, protection permits the domestic monopolist to exploit price discrimination between foreign and domestic markets and opens up the possibility of protection carrying import substitution over into export performance![3]

4.2

Suppose next that the country, having protected the domestic monopolist, gives a matching export subsidy so that the relative incentives (effective exchange rates, in the trade-and-developments literature) between exporting and import-substitution are equal rather than biased against exports.

In this event, in figure 4.2, the export incentive at rate $s = t$ is also reflected by $S_F(1 + t)$ rather than by S_F. Then, equilibrium production by the domestic monopolist shifts to EG, with EF produced for the home market and FG sold as export $(X_{s=t})$.[4] Protection helps export performance; matching subsidization helps it yet further.

4.3

But while these results are interesting and match the observed reality in several cases, the reader must be warned that they do *not* imply that protection is good. Indeed, by sustaining domestic monopoly, such protection will be contributing more losses to the usual deadweight loss from protection.

Moreover, note that the case analyzed in the text is likely to apply particularly to countries (such as India) where the creation of domestic monopoly is buttressed by restrictions on domestic entry through investment licensing. By contrast, in countries of the Far East, it appears that domestic entry is much easier, and hence domestic monopoly is often not a suitable assumption to make.

Finally, the presence of price disparity *in itself* need not be explained in terms of the price-discrimination model. Thus, for instance, an observed price disparity, such that the export price is below the domestic price, may simply reflect the phenomenon of underinvoiced exports. Such underinvoicing can be a consequence of high export duties that exceed the black-market premium on foreign exchange (Bhagwati, 1964).

Notes

The substance of this note, though perhaps understood intuitively by many analysts of trade regimes in the developing countries, does not appear to have been developed rigorously anywhere. The immediate motivation for writing the note was provided by the author's learning from Syed Nawab Haider Naqvi, on a visit to the Pakistan Institute of Development Economics in 1985, that a survey of export industries had found that export prices were often below domestic prices in several activities which were protected by the trade regime from import protection at the same time. Comments by Sam Laird, Patrick Messerlin, and Richard Pomfret have been helpful.

The views expressed herein are those of the author and should not be attributed to the World Bank or its affiliated organizations.

1. See Bhagwati (1978, 1986, ch. 8) for a definition and analysis of the EP strategy.

2. Ignore s, the export subsidy in figure 4.2 until the next section, i.e., ignore $X_{s=t}$, H, and G.

3. I should note that the analysis in figure 4.2 of price discrimination is in itself not original. in fact, standard textbooks on international economics have often incorporated it, to illustrate price discrimination in international trade by a monopolist, wholly following Joan Robinson's classic analysis of the problem and simply and implicitly assuming that *somehow* the domestic and foreign markets can be delinked. What is new is twofold: (1) linking protection to imports as the key policy that enables the monopolist to preserve his monopoly and simultaneously to delink the foreign and domestic markets so that price discrimination becomes possible, and (2) demonstrating that, *compared with the free-trade case*, the protection-inducedprice discrimination leads to export promotion. Richard Pomfret has pointed

out to me that point (1) has been made earlier by Basevi (1970), though in the context of exploitation of scale economies. See also the important early article by Pomfret (1975), which also anticipates the later, interesting article by Paul Krugman (1984) in demonstrating that scale economies can make a tariff lead to export promotion.

4. Any domestic sale less than *EF* would mean that the domestic price would exceed *OE*, which is impossible under the stated assumptions.

References

Basevi, Giorgio. 1970. Domestic Demand and Ability to Export. *Journal of Political Economy* 78: 330–337.

Bhagwati, Jagdish. 1964. On the Underinvoicing of Imports. *Bulletin of the Oxford University Institute of Economics and Statistics* 26: 389–397.

Bhagwati, Jagdish. 1978. *The Anatomy and Consequences of Exchange Control Regimes*. Cambridge, MA: NBER, Ballinger.

Bhagwati, Jagdish. 1986. *Export Promoting Trade Strategy: Issues and Evidence*. World Bank, VPERS Working Papers (Mimeographed). Forthcoming in *World Bank Research Observer*. January 1988.

Krugman, Paul. 1984. Import Protection as Export Promotion. In Henryk Kierzkowski (ed.), *Monopolistic Competition and International Trade*. Oxford: Oxford University Press.

Pomfret, Richard. 1975. Some Interrelationships between Import Substitution and Export Promotion in a Small Economy. *Weltwirtschaftliches Archiv*. 3(4): 714–727.

Rieber, William J. 1981. Tariffs as a Means of Altering Trade Patterns. *American Economic Review* 71 (December): 1098–1099.

5

The Pass-Through Puzzle: The Missing Prince from Hamlet

Much has been made of the "puzzle" that the past appreciation and recent depreciation of the dollar have not resulted in an equal pass-through in dollar prices of imports within the United States as in earlier periods.[1] The media (e.g., Robert Kuttner 1988 in the *New York Times* a year ago, reporting on a 1987 Brandeis Conference of local experts on international macroeconomics) have presented this with some fanfare and, presumably encouraged by economists in the field, as a major crisis in international economic theory. And it has led to a search for explanations, including a revival of the Samuelson-Kemp-Wan type of hysteresis theories by Richard Baldwin (1988) and by Baldwin and Krugman (1986).

But a major and indeed obvious explanation has simply been missed. It lies, of course, in the fact that the early 1980s (when the U.S. dollar was overvalued) saw a significant rise in nontariff barriers in the form of high-track protection such as voluntary export restrictions (VERs). In lieu of depreciation to correct for the overvaluation, imports were therefore restricted, leading to substantial premia in a number of sectors such as autos and steel.[2]

It is well known to those such as myself who worked on exchange rate and trade policies for developing countries in the 1960s and 1970s that a devaluation with such import restraints will not result in a comparable pass-through as a devaluation without such restraints. The devaluation will generally cut into the premium, which will "absorb" the devaluation's impact.

In Bhagwati (1962), therefore, I argued in India, while working on the economics of the forthcoming June 1966 devaluation, that it was inappropriate to assume that a devaluation would necessarily increase domestic prices as commonly assumed: import restrictions already had led to import premia in the range of 50 to 70 percent on many imports. (I also argued that given the excess of imports over exports, reflecting substantial aid-absorption, a devaluation would be deflationary—again, contrary to traditional presumptions—and that this implied, ceteris paribus, that the price level could even fall, following the devaluation.[3])

Moreover, I advanced at the time the distinction between "gross" and "net" devaluation: the latter, on the import side, was the parity change *minus* the tariffs that were removed once devaluation was undertaken. This distinction has become commonplace for nearly two decades to international theorists who are familiar with developing countries where nontariff barriers (NTBs) and exchange controls are the name of the game.[4] It is time for it to be finally recognized by conventional macroeconomists.

5.1 The Main Facts and Proposed Explanation

The principal facts that have created the puzzle are best seen through the important work of Catherine Mann (1986). She used the weighted average exchange value of the U.S. dollar to calculate the "estimated" unit value of U.S. non-oil imports, assuming a conventional 60 percent pass-through based on pre-1980 experience.

Plotted against the actual behavior of the unit value of non-oil imports, based on the trade-weighted consumer price index, the estimated series naturally mimics beautifully the actual until 1980. But thereafter, there is a remarkable divergence (figure 5.1).

Why? Let me then propose that the main explanation is to be found in the fact that the 1980s showed a progressive increase in the share of U.S. imports covered by VERs and other nontariff barriers (NTBs). Thus, table 5.1 shows a significant increase in NTBs to U.S. imports over the early 1980s. Their index shows a 23 percent increase from 1981 to 1986. Nogues, Olechowski, and Winters (1986) document that by 1983 over 40 percent of U.S. imports were covered by some sort of explicit NTB or monitoring measure. Table 5.2 shows a similar increase in a subset of hard-core NTBs in the United States. Laird (1988) finds that VERs constituted the single most important category of NTBs (excluding the Multi-fiber Arrangement, MFA) in the United States and that between 1981 and 1986 the percentage of trade affected by VERs nearly doubled. In 1986, 14.5 percent of all U.S. trade was affected by VERs (including MFA). In that same year, according to Laird, 37 percent of imports from Japan were affected by VERs (not including other types of barriers), over 20 percent of trade with Greece and Spain, and nearly 17 percent of imports from Korea.

We are, therefore, evidently dealing with a significant phenomenon whose presence and consequences for the "pass-through" puzzle cannot be

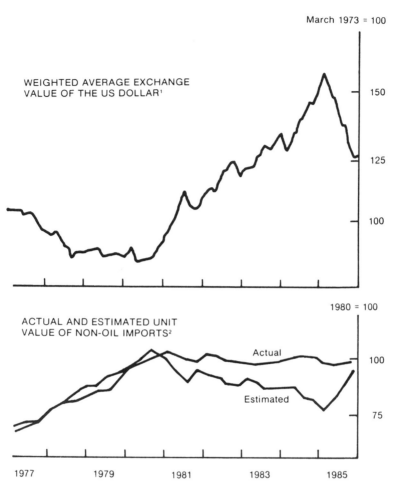

Figure 5.1
Above: Weighted average exchange value of the U.S. dollar against total trade shares of foreign G10 countries, using 1972–76 averages. *Below*: Actual and estimated unit value of non-oil imports, using the multilateral trade-weighted consumer price index and a contemporaneous 60 percent pass-through of exchange rate changes. Source: Mann (1986, p. 366).

Table 5.1
Import coverage index of a subgroup of NTBs applied by selected industrial market economies, 1981–86 (1981 = 100)

	NTBs				
Importer	1982	1983	1984	1985	1986
Austria	100.0	100.0	100.0	100.0	99.3
Canada	108.6	106.0	108.4	112.1	121.3
EC[a]	105.7	110.9	113.9	120.8	118.3
Finland	102.5	102.5	102.5	101.0	101.0
Japan	99.2	99.2	99.2	99.2	98.6
New Zealand	100.0	100.0	100.0	92.6	86.1
Norway	101.1	96.4	94.4	86.6	85.3
Switzerland	100.4	100.4	100.8	100.8	100.8
United States	105.5	105.6	112.1	119.2	123.0
All	104.6	107.1	110.2	115.3	115.8

Source: UNCTAD, *World Development Report* (1987, table 8.5).
Note: The figures in the table are to be regarded as preliminary and subject to revision. The data cover all products other than fuels.
a. Excluding Portugal and Spain.

Table 5.2
Industrial countries' imports subject to hard-core NTBs, 1981 and 1986 (%)

	Industrial countries' imports		Developing countries' imports	
Importer	1981	1986	1981	1986
EC	10	13	22	23
Japan	29	29	22	22
United States	9	15	14	17
All industrial countries	13	16	19	21

Source: *World Development Report* (1987, table 8.3).
Note: "Hard-core" NTBs represent a subgroup of all possible NTBs. They are the ones most likely to have significant restrictive effects. Hard-core NTBs include import prohibitions, quantitative restrictions, voluntary export restraints, variable levies, MFA restrictions, and nonautomatic licensing. Examples of other NTBs not included are technical barriers (health and safety restrictions and standards, etc.), minimum pricing regulations, and the use of price investigations (for countervailing and antidumping purposes, etc). and price surveillance. Percentage of imports subject to NTBs measures the sum of the value of a country's import group affected by NTBs, divided by the total value of its imports of that group. Data on imports affected in 1986 are based on 1981 trade weights. Variations between 1981 and 1986 can therefore occur only if NTBs affect a different set of products or trading partners.

ignored.[5] The pass-through therefore should have been dampened: the fall in domestic U.S. prices, ceteris paribus, that would pass through should have been offset by the scarcity premium the NTBs would impose, leaving the actual price level more or less unaffected if the size of the two opposing forces was evenly matched. But when the dollar began to fall from 1985, the NTBs were in place: the devaluation would, therefore, have first cut into the scarcity premium on imports. The facts of the vanished pass-through are therefore in conformity with the view that, even with our conventional view of competitive supplies and demands,[6] the mere recognition of the new phenomenon of NTBs may well explain a great deal of the pass-through puzzle.[7]

If this is so, it may well be hysterical to turn to hysteresis, inter alia, for an explanation of the facts at hand. Though, it would not be the first time that a failure to understand the true cause of a phenomenon would have led to theoretical developments of interest in themselves. Let me now state carefully the theoretical argument and then explain precisely the pass-through phenomenon behavior in the 1980s.

5.2   Some Theory

Figure 5.2 shows the phenomenon of an incomplete pass-through in a perfectly competitive model, using the conventional Marshall-Lerner diagrammatic technique. With the dollar price of Japanese exports in the U.S. market and the quantity of Japanese exports in the U.S. market on the two axes, DD is the U.S. demand curve for Japanese exports and SS is the Japanese supply curve. With an appreciation of the dollar, the supply curve shifts to $S'S'$. The dollar price of Japanese exports in the United States then falls from A to F. But while AB therefore is the price change or "price-through," AC is the appreciation so that AB/AC is the 60 percent pass-through estimated for the pre-1980 period in the United States.

Figure 5.3 then shows how this analysis must be modified in the presence of NTBs. Figure 5.3 illustrates a combination of dollar appreciation with simultaneous imposition of NTBs by the United States (i.e., import restrictions). Basically, I reproduce figure 5.2, with one important difference. Assume now that along with the dollar appreciation, an import quota of OQ is imposed. Then, the domestic consumer price in the United States will be back up to A: the effect of the appreciation will have been fully offset by the NTB. The *actual* U.S. price will then not have changed; the pass-through from the appreciation will have been zero. If the quantity

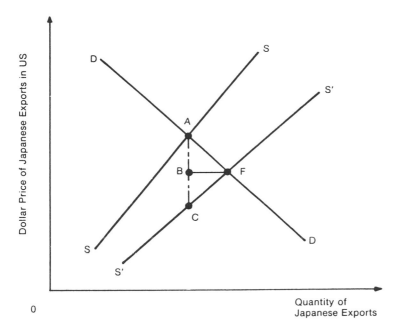

Figure 5.2
Appreciation of dollar and pass-through under perfect competition (the pass-through is
AB, and failure of it is *BC*).

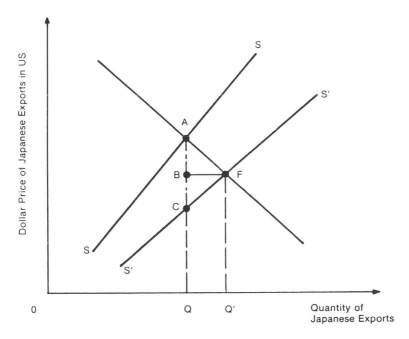

Figure 5.3
Dollar appreciation with simultaneous imposition of NTBs on Japan (with imposition of
NTBs restraining imports to *OQ*, the pass-through is zero).

restraint is varied up from OQ to OQ', the pass-through will also rise correspondingly.[8]

If, instead of import restraints, we had export restraints by Japan—through VERs, OMAs, and so on—then figure 5.3 must be reinterpreted a little. The import premium AC in the zero-pass-through case will now accrue to the Japanese; the pass-through will of course remain unchanged.[9]

5.3   Explaining the Pass-through in the 1980s: A Recapitulation

Consider anew the unfolding scenario in the 1980s. The dollar appreciates through the 1980s, but NTBs are imposed on an increasing basis to offset the import effects of the appreciation. The actual price is more or less left unchanged: the historical pass-through relationship is broken, and the divergence of the estimated conventional-pass-through-based price level from the actual price level increases with increasing dollar appreciation. With the Plaza Agreement, the dollar begins to fall sharply, with the conventional-pass-through-based estimated price level moving up rapidly toward the actual price level, but with the premium on scarce imports absorbing the dollar devaluation, there would be little impact on the actual price level itself. A cursory look at Catherine Mann's (1986) chart, figure 5.1, confirms this broad scenario.

5.4   Further Observations

If my explanation of the pass-through failure is reasonable, then important implications follow.

First, the view is occasionally advanced that exchange rates no longer work: the evidence cited is precisely for the exchange rates in the 1980s. Thus, for instance, Paul Krugman (1989, p. 40) has recently argued that exchange rates "seem to matter so little" since import prices no longer quickly adjust to them, while altogether forgetting from his brief excursion into empirics the fact of trade barriers. If exchange rates did not matter much during the dollar's appreciation, and they mattered as little during the dollar's depreciation, a major (possibly the critical) reason was surely the growth of trade barriers (as explained in this note). In consequence, exchange rate changes could not be expected to have the desired impact: if prices faced by the economic agents are not allowed to change, the expenditure-switching that must occur for a favorable impact on the balance of trade will simply not follow.

Second, we can then wind up in a catch-22 situation: trade barriers will make the exchange rate changes ineffective, and the inefficacy of exchange rate changes will prompt the imposition of more trade barriers. Failure to diagnose the key role of trade barriers in the pass-through phenomenon may then have costly consequences even though it may be good for the development of economic science!

Notes

I briefly state a hypothesis to explain the "pass-through" puzzle that macroeconomists have been concerned with recently. I have advanced orally this explanation over the last two years to many macroeconomists, past students, and present colleagues among them, after reading Mann (1986) and especially after noting Paul Krugman's omission of the explanation in a talk on the pass-through problem in early 1987 at the World Bank. I felt that the explanation needed to be written down for a wider audience since the main body of macroeconomists continues to be puzzled by the pass-through phenomenon. The hypothesis advanced here fits the broad facts on an eye-scan. Thanks are due to Mike Gavin and Paul de Grauwe, whose favorable response to the proposed explanation encouraged me to explore it systematically here. I am also grateful to Catherine Mann for pointing out her more recent work where the role of trade barriers is noted in the context of examining the influences on import prices. Douglas Irwin has been enormously helpful with insightful comments, as usual. Guillermo Calvo and Avinash Dixit also provided useful suggestions.

1. The phrase "pass-through," to my knowledge, was first used by my former student, Steve Magee (1973), in a classic article on the subject. It is not clear to me that the pass-through is, or should be, particularly stable, anyway. Mann (1986, pp. 369–370) herself notes several studies of pre-1980 experience that show pass-through varying from 50 to 80 percent! But this problem is ignored in the present note.

2. For an estimate of the rents transfered from VERs on textiles, see Hamilton (1986).

3. Richard Cooper (1971) subsequently developed the same idea independently. A later article by Krugman and Taylor (1978) also has examined more intensively the possibility of a deflationary depreciation.

4. It was, for example, used in some of the Bhagwati-Krueger NBER studies on exchange control and the trade regimes of developing countries published in the 1970s. It was used extensively in the Bhagwati and Srinivasan (1975, ch. 6) study of Indian policies for this project. Thus the presence of tariffs, subsidies, and NTBs should be taken systematically into account is evident also from the fact that effective exchange rates, inclusive of incentives implied by such measures, are commonly used since the 1970s in studying the trade-and-payments regimes of

developing countries but are still not part of the tool kit of conventional macro-economic specialists.

5. VERs and "fair value" cases amounting to "administered protection," of course, are discriminatory between countries (and even firms) and therefore can be a form of "porous" protection, as discussed in Bhagwati (1987, 1988). In that case, they would be less restrictive than comparable, nondiscriminatory import protection so that the dampening effect of the pass-through would be less than in the latter case. It is unlikely, however, that the effect would be rendered negligible.

6. I stress the fact that the competitive assumption is compatible with the facts because there is a growing tendency to regard all kinds of empirical phenomena, capable of being explained within the framework of perfect competition, as if they justified our necessarily having to work with imperfect-competition models—a good example being the phenomenon of intraindustry trade. Just as Casanova saw sex everywhere, the recent practioners of imperfect-competition-in-product-markets see imperfect competition everywhere.

7. The argument is carefully stated in section 5.3.

8. I should add the caveat that the analysis here is in partial equilibrium, like the small-group imperfect-competition-in-product-markets analysis of trade today. The pass-through can vary, even given the supply and demand curves. But it can vary also if these curves shift over time, as may be relevant if they are embodied in general-equilibrium models where the consequences of exchange rate changes with and without trade barriers are compared.

9. On the other hand, because VERs are in practice discriminatory, there will be differential effects arising from the porosity of such protection, as noted earlier.

References

Baldwin, Richard. 1988. Hysteresis in Import Prices: The Beachhead Effect. *American Economic Review* 78(4): 773–785.

Baldwin, Richard, and Paul Krugman. 1986. Persistent Trade Effects of Large Exchange Rate Shocks. NBER Working Paper No. 2017, September.

Bhagwati, Jagdish. 1962. The Case for Devaluation. *The Economic Weekly* (India). August 4. Reprinted in J. Bhagwati, *Essays in Development Economics (Vol. 2): Dependence and Interdependence* (ed. by Gene Grossman). Cambridge: MIT Press, 1985, ch. 10.

Bhagwati, Jagdish. 1987. VERs, *Quid Pro Quo* DFI and VIEs: Political-Economy Theoretic Analyses. *International Economic Journal* 1(1): 1–12.

Bhagwati, Jagdish. 1988. *Protectionism*. Cambridge: MIT Press.

Bhagwati, Jagdish, and T. N. Srinivasan. 1975. *India*. New York: Columbia University Press.

Cooper, Richard. 1971. *Currency Devaluation in Developing Countries.* Essays in International Finance No. 86, International Finance Section, Princeton University.

Hamilton, Carl. 1986. An Assessment of Voluntary Restraints on Hong Kong Exports to Europe and the U.S.A. *Economica* 53 (August): 339– 350.

Hooper, Peter, and Catherine Mann. 1987. The U.S. External Deficit: Its Causes and Persistence. International Finance Discussion Paper No. 316. Washington, DC: Federal Reserve System. November.

Hooper, Peter, and Catherine Mann. 1989. The Emergence and Persistence of the U.S. External Imbalance: 1980–87. *Princeton Studies in International Finance.*

Krugman, Paul, 1989. *Exchange Rate Instability.* Cambridge: MIT Press.

Krugman, Paul, and Lance Taylor. 1978. Contractionary Effects of Devaluation. *Journal of International Economics* 8(3): 445–456.

Kuttner, Robert. 1988. The Theory Gap on the Trade Gap. *New York Times.* January 17, sec. 3, p. 1.

Laird, Sam, 1988. VERs—Recent Developments. World Bank mimeo. Prepared for conference on Political Economy of Export-Restraint Agreements, Washington, DC, September.

Magee, Steve. 1973. Currency Contracts, Pass-through and Devaluation. *Brookings Papers on Economic Activity* 1: 303–323.

Mann, Catherine. 1986. Prices, Profits, Margins and Exchange Rates. *Federal Reserve Bulletin* (June): 366–379.

Nogues, Julio J., Andrzej Olechowski, and L. Alan Winters. 1986. The Extent of Nontariff Barriers to Imports of Industrial Countries. World Bank Staff Working Paper No. 789. February.

World Development Report. 1987. Washington, DC: International Bank for Reconstruction and Development.

II   DUP Activities and Political Economy

6   Directly Unproductive Profit-Seeking (DUP) Activities

Directly unproductive profit-seeking (DUP) activities are defined (Bhagwati, 1982) as ways of making a profit (i.e., income) by undertaking activities that are directly (i.e., immediately, in their primary impact) unproductive, in the sense that they produce pecuniary returns but do not produce goods or services that enter a conventional utility function or inputs into such goods and services.

Typical examples of such DUP (pronounced appropriately as "dupe") activities are (1) tariff-seeking lobbying that is aimed at earning pecuniary income by changing the tariff and therefore factor incomes, (2) revenue-seeking lobbying that seeks to divert government revenues towards oneself as recipient, (3) monopoly-seeking lobbying whose objective is to create an artificial monopoly that generates rents, and (4) tariff-evasion or smuggling that de facto reduces or eliminates the tariff (or quota) and generates returns by exploiting thereby the price differential between the tariff-inclusive legal and the tariff-free illegal imports.

While these are evidently profitable activities, their *output* is zero. Hence, they are wasteful in their primary impact, recalling Pareto's distinction between production and predation: they use real resources to produce profits but no output.

DUP activities of one kind or another have been analyzed by several economic theorists, among them (1) the public-choice school's leading practitioners, their major work having been brought together in Buchanan, Tullock and Tollison (1980), (2) Lindbeck (1976) who has worked on 'endogenous politicians', and (3) the Chicago "regulation" school, led by Stigler, Peltzman, Posner and recently Becker (1983).

However, a central theoretical breakthrough has come from the work of trade theorists who have systematically incorporated the analysis of DUP activities in the main corpus of general equilibrium theory.

The early papers that defined this general-equilibrium-theoretic approach, and that were set in the context of the theory of trade and welfare, were Bhagwati and Hansen (1973) which analyzed the question of illegal trade (i.e., tariff-evasion), Krueger (1974) which analyzed the question of rent-seeking for rents associated with import quotas specifically and quotas more generally, and Bhagwati and Srinivasan (1980) who analyzed the phenomenon of revenue-seeking, the "price" counterpart of Krueger's rent-seeking, where a tariff resulted in revenues which were then sought by lobbies.

The synthesis and generalization of these and other apparently unrelated contributions, showing that they all related to diversion of resources to zero-output activities, was provided in Bhagwati (1982a), where they were called DUP activities. The following significant aspects of the theoretical analysis of DUP activities are noteworthy.

First, they are generally related to policy interventions (but they need not be: plunder, for instance, predates the organization of governments). In so far as policy interventions induce DUP activities, they are analytically divided into two appropriate categories (Bhagwati and Srinivasan, 1982):

1. *Policy-triggered DUP activities.* One class consists of *lobbying* activities. Examples include rent-seeking analysis of the cost of protection *via* import licences (Krueger, 1974) and revenue-seeking analysis of the cost of tariffs (Bhagwati and Srinivasan, 1980), of shadow prices in cost-benefit analysis (Foster, 1981), of price *versus* quantity interventions (Bhagwati and Srini-alternative distorting policies such as tariffs, production, and consumption taxes (Bhagwati, Brecher and Srinivasan, 1984), of the optimal tariff (Dinopoulos, 1984), of the transfer problem (Bhagwati, Brecher and Hatta, 1985), and of voluntary export restrictions relative to import tariffs (Brecher and Bhagwati, 1987).

Another class consists of *policy-evading* activities. Examples include analysis of smuggling (Bhagwati and Hansen, 1973), its implication for optimal tariffs (Johnson, 1974; Bhagwati and Srinivasan, 1973), and alternative modeling by Kemp (1976), Sheikh (1974), Pitt (1981), and Martin and Panagariya (1984).

2. *Policy-influencing DUP activities.* The other generic class of DUP activities is not triggered by policies in place but is rather aimed at influencing the formulation of the policy itself. The most prominent DUP-theoretic contributions in this area relate to the analysis of tariff-seeking. Although Brock and Magee (1978, 1980) pioneered here, the general-equilibrium

analyses of endogeneous tariffs began with Findlay and Wellisz (1982) and Feenstra and Bhagwati (1982), the two sets of authors modeling the government and the lobbying activities in contrasting ways. Notable among the later contributions are Mayer (1984), who extends the analysis formally to include factor income-distribution and therewith voting behavior, and Wellisz and Wilson (1984). Magee (1984) has an excellent review of many of these contributions. The implication of endogenizing the tariff for conventional measurement of the cost of protection has been analyzed in Bhagwati (1980) and Tullock (1981).

The *choice* between alternative policy instruments when modeling the response of lobbies and governments to import competition has also been extensively analyzed. The issue was raised by Bhagwati (1982b) and analyzed further by Dinopoulos (1983) and Sapir (1983) in terms of how different agents (e.g., "capitalists" and "labor") would profit from different policy responses such as increased immigration of cheap labor and tariffs when import competition intensified. It has subsequently been explored more fully by Rodrik (1986) who compares tariffs with production subsidies.

Second, Bhagwati (1982a) has noted, generalizing a result in Bhagwati and Srinivasan (1980), that DUP activities, while defined to be those that waste resources in their direct impact, cannot be taken as *ultimately* wasteful, i.e., immiserizing, since they may be triggered by a suboptimal policy intervention. For, in that event, throwing away or wasting resources may be beneficial. The shadow price of a productive factor in such "highly distorted" economies may be negative. This is the obverse of the possibility of immiserizing growth (Bhagwati, 1980). Thus, Buchanan (1980), who has addressed the issue of DUP activities and *defined* them as activities that (ultimately) cause waste, has been corrected in Bhagwati (1983): the definition of DUP activities cannot properly exclude the possibility that DUP activities are ultimately beneficial rather than wasteful. This central distinction between the direct and the ultimate welfare impacts of DUP activities is now universally accepted. DUP activities are therefore defined now, as in Bhagwati (1982b) and subsequent contributions, as wasteful only in the direct sense.

Third, Bhagwati, Brecher, and Srinivasan (1984) have raised yet another fundamental issue concerning DUP activities. Thus, where DUP activities belong to category 2 distinguished above, full endogeneity of policy can follow. If so, the conventional rank-ordering of policies is no longer possible. We have the *Determinacy Paradox*: policy is chosen in the solution to the full "political-economy," DUP-theoretic solution and cannot be varied at will. These authors have therefore suggested that, where full endo-geneity obtains, the appropriate way to theorize about policy is to take variations around the observed DUP-theoretic equilibrium. Thus, tradi-tional economic parameters such as factor supply could be varied; similarly now the DUP-activity parameters such as, say, the cost of lobbying could be varied. The impact on actual welfare resulting from such variations can then be a proper focus of analysis, implying a wholly different way of looking at policy questions from that which economists have employed to date.

Finally, DUP activities are related to Krueger's (1974) important cate-gory of rent-seeking activities. The latter are a subset of the former, in so far as they relate to lobbying for quota-determined scarcity rents and are therefore part of DUP activities of category 2 distinguished above (Bhag-wati, 1983).

Bibliography

Anam, M. 1982. Distortion-Triggered Lobbying and Welfare: A Contribution to the Theory of Directly-Unproductive Profit-Seeking Activities. *Journal of International Economics* 13 (August): 15–32.

Becker, G. S. 1983. A Theory of Competition among Pressure Groups for Political Influence. *Quarterly Journal of Economics* 93 (August): 371–400.

Bhagwati, J. 1980. Lobbying and Welfare. *Journal of Public Economics* 14 (December): 355–363.

Bhawati, J. 1982a. Directly-Unproductive Profit-Seeking (DUP) Activities. *Journal of Political Economy* 90 (October): 988–1002.

Bhagwati, J. 1982b. Shifting Comparative Advantage, Protectionist Demands, and Policy Response. In *Import Competition and Response*. Jagdish Bhagwati (ed.), Chicago: University of Chicago Press.

Bhagwati, J. 1983, DUP Activities and Rent Seeking. *Kyklos* 36, 634–637.

Bhagwati, J., and Hansen, B. 1973. A Theoretical Analysis of Smuggling. *Quarterly Journal of Economics* 87: 172–187.

Bhagwati, J., and Srinivasan, T. N. 1973. Smuggling and Trade Policy. *Journal of Public Economics* 2: 377–389.

Bhagwati, J. and Srinivasan, T. N. 1980. Revenue-Seeking: A Generalization of the Theory of Tariffs. *Journal of Political Economy* 88 (December): 1069–1087.

Bhagwati, J., and Srinivasan, T. N. 1982. The Welfare Consequences of Directly-Unproductive Profit-Seeking (DUP) Lobbying Activities: Price *versus* Quantity Distortions. *Journal of International Economics* 13: 33–44.

Bhagwati, J., Brecher, R., and Hatta, T. 1985. The Generalized Theory of Transfers and Welfare: Exogenous (Policy-Imposed) and Endogenous (Transfer-Induced) Distortions. *Quarterly Journal of Economics* 100(3): 697–714.

Bhagwati, J., Brecher, R., and Srinivasan T. N. 1984. DUP Activities and Economic Theory. In David Colander (ed.), *Neoclassical Political Economy: The Analysis of Rent-Seeking and DUP Activities*. Cambridge, MA: Ballinger.

Brecher, R., and Bhagwati, J. 1987. Voluntary Export Restrictions and Import Restrictions: A Welfare-Theoretic Comparison. In Henryk Kierzkowski (ed.), *Essays in Honour of W. M. Corden*. Oxford: Basil Blackwell.

Brock, W., and Magee, S. 1978. The Economics of Special Interest Politics: The Case of the Tariff. *American Economic Review* 68 (May): 246–250.

Brock, W., and Magee, S. 1980. Tariff Formation in a Democracy. In John Black and Brian Hindley (ed.), *Current Issue in International Commercial Policy and Diplomacy*. New York: Macmillan.

Buchanan, J. 1980. Rent Seeking and Profit Seeking. In James Buchanan, Gordon Tullock, and R. Tollison (eds.), *Towards a General Theory of the Rent-Seeking Society*. College Station: Texas A & M University Press.

Buchanan, J., Tullock, G. and Tollison, R. (eds). 1980. *Towards a General Theory of the Rent-Seeking Society*. College Station: Texas A & M University Press.

Dinopoulos, E. 1983. Import Competition, International Factor Mobility and Lobbying Responses: The Schumpeterian Industry Cases. *Journal of International Economics* 14 (May): 395–410.

Dinopoulos, E. 1984. The Optimal Tariff with Revenue-Seeking: A Contribution to the Theory of DUP Activities. In David Colander (ed.), *The Neoclassical Political Economy: The Analysis of Rent-Seeking and DUP Activities*. Cambridge, MA: Ballinger.

Feenstra, R., and Bhagwati, J. 1982. Tariff Seeking and the Efficient Tariff. In Jagdish Bhagwati (ed.), *Import Competition and Response*. Chicago: University of Chicago Press.

Findlay, R., and Wellisz, S. 1982. Endogenous Tariffs, the Political Economy of Trade Restrictions, and Welfare. In Jagdish Bhagwati (ed.), *Import Competition and Response*. Chicago: University of Chicago Press.

Foster, E. 1981. The Treatment of Rents in Cost-Benefit Analysis. *American Economic Review* 71 (March): 171–178.

Johnson, H. G. 1974. Notes on the Economic Theory of Smuggling. In Jagdish Bhagwati (ed.), *Illegal Transactions in International Trade*. Series in International Economics, Amsterdam: North Holland.

Kemp, M. 1976, Smuggling and Optimal Commercial Policy. *Journal of Public Economics* 5: 381–384.

Krueger, A. 1974. The Political Economy of the Rent-Seeking Society. *American Economic Review* 64 (June): 291–303.

Lindbeck, A. 1976. Stabilization Politicies in Open Economies with Endogenous Politicians. Richard Ely Lecture. *American Economic Review* 66 (May): 1–19.

Magee, S. 1984. Endogenous Tariff Theory: A Survey. In David Colander (ed.), *Neoclassical Political Economy: The Analysis of Rent-Seeking and DUP Activities*, Cambridge, MA: Ballinger.

Martin, L., and Panagariya, A. 1984. Smuggling, Trade, and Price Disparity: A Crime-Theoretic Approach. *Journal of International Economics* 17 (November): 201–218.

Mayer, W. 1984. Endogenous Tariff Formation. *American Economic Review* 74 (December): 970–985.

Pitt, M. 1981. Smuggling and Price Disparity. *Journal of International Economics* 11: 447–458.

Rodrik, D. 1986. Tariffs, Subsidies and Welfare with Endogenous Policy. *Journal of International Economics* (November): 285–299.

Sapir, A. 1983. Foreign Competition, Immigration and Structural Adjustment. *Journal of International Economics* 14 (May): 381–394.

Sheikh, M. 1974. Smuggling, Production and Welfare. *Journal of International Economics* 4: 355–364.

Tullock, G. 1981. Lobbying and Welfare: A Comment. *Journal of Public Economics* 16: 391–394.

Wellisz, S., and Wilson, J. D. 1984. Public Sector Inefficiency, a General Equilibrium Analysis. Columbia University International Economics Research Center Discussion Paper Series No. 254.

7   DUP Activities and Economic Theory

with Richard A. Brecher
and T. N. Srinivasan

Recently, several economists have directed their talents to examining the impact of what have been termed *directly unproductive profit-seeking* (DUP) activities (Bhagwati 1982c). Among the more prominent such contributors, distinguished by different schools of thought, are (1) Buchanan, Tullock, and other important members of the public choice school, with their major work now conveniently collected in Buchanan, Tollison, and Tullock (1980) and reviewed well in Tollison (1982): (2) Bhagwati, Findlay, Hansen, Krueger, Magee, Srinivasan, Wellisz, and other international economists, whose work is reviewed and systematized in Bhagwati (1982c) and Magee (1984); (3) Becker (1983), Peltzman, Posner, Stigler, and other members of the Chicago school, whose notable work is variously available; and (4) Lindbeck (1976), whose influential work on "endogenous politicians" is widely known.

The quantity and variety of this work suggest its importance but, to date, no one has examined just how important it is. Thus, this chapter examines the ambitious question: How serious for economic theory, as conventionally practiced, is the systematic integration of DUP phenomena into our analysis?

The first section defines DUP activities and offers a taxonomy of DUP categories or types that will serve our later analysis. The subsequent sections consider the implications of different DUP categories for positive analysis and address welfare or normative implications.

7.1   DUP Activities: Concept and Taxonomy

The phenomena addressed in this book share one essential characteristic. They all represent ways of seeking profits (income) by undertaking directly unproductive activities. That is, they yield pecuniary returns but produce no goods or services that enter a conventional utility function directly or indirectly. Insofar as such activities use real resources, they result in a contraction of the availability set open to the economy. Tariff-seeking lobbying, tariff evasion, and premium seeking for given import licenses, for example, are all privately profitable activities. However, their direct output is zero in terms of the flow of goods and services entering a conventional utility function. Tariff seeking yields pecuniary income by changing the tariff and hence factor rewards; evasion of a tariff yields pecuniary income by exploiting the differential price between legal (tariff-bearing) imports and illegal (tariff-evading) imports; and premium seeking yields pecuniary income from the premiums on import licenses. (Krueger's 1974 analysis of what she termed *rent-seeking* activities relates to a subset of the broad class of these DUP activities; she is concerned with the lobbying activities triggered by different licensing practices of governments.[1])

From the viewpoint of the analysis presented below, DUP activities call be categorized as endogenous or exogenous.[2] Endogenous DUP activity results from the interplay of the DUP acitvity with the otherwise orthodox economic specification of the "pure" economic system. Exogenous DUP activity is embodied in a model where the policy can be *exogenously* specified while the DUP activity is endogenous to that policy. Examples of the former, using tariff theory, are models where the tariff is endogenously determined; examples of the latter are models where a tariff, exogenously specified to be in place, leads to seeking for the revenues resulting from the tariff, and models where the tariff is evaded. The former class of DUP activities raise deeper questions for economic analysis than the latter, as we will contend.

7.2   DUP Activities and Positive Analysis

Exogenous Policy

When the policy that induces DUP activity is exogenously specified, the implications of such DUP activity for positive analysis are tantamount to introducing an essentially nontraded sector with zero output but positive inputs into the formal model. Depending on the problem and the model, such a specification alters the analytical conclusions and the policy intuitions derived therefrom. We illustrate this by briefly considering two recent DUP-theoretic analyses in tariff and transfer theory: one on revenue seeking, by Bhagwati and Srinivasan (1980), and one on transfer seeking, by Bhagwati, Brecher, and Hatta (1982).

Revenue Seeking and the Metzler Paradox

Conventional trade theory tells us that, provided that suitable convexity assumptions are satisfied, a small country will find that a tariff necessarily increases the domestic price and output of the protected good. The Metzler paradox is that, for a large country (one that can influence its terms of trade), the tariff leads to such an improvement in the international terms of trade that the tariff-inclusive domestic price of the importable good falls and hence the importable good is paradoxically deprotected. We thus have the Metzler *price* paradox and hence what we can call, the Metzler *production* paradox, in the conventional 2 × 2 model of trade theory.

The introduction of revenue seeking, as Bhagwati and Srinivasan (1980) have shown, allows us to obtain the Metzler production paradox, even if the Metzler price paradox is eliminated by assuming a small country. To see why, consider figure 7.1. $F_y F_x$ is the production possibility curve, and

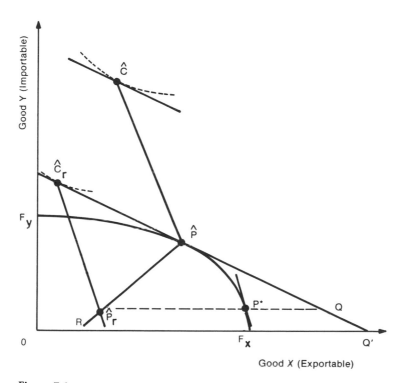

Figure 7.1
Revenue-seeking and the Metzler production paradox.

the world price is determined by the slope of the-line through P^*. With free trade, this small economy would produce at P^*. With a tariff, production shifts to $\hat{P}$, implying that production of the importable good Y has increased, and consumption shifts to $\hat{C}$. However, if the tariff leads to DUP lobbying for the tariff revenues, then the production of one or both goods must decline as resources are diverted toward revenue seeking. If we make the one-for-one assumption—that competitive revenue seeking leads to diversion of one dollar's worth of resources for every dollar's worth of revenue—then the equilibrium will shift such that consumption is at $\hat{C}_r$ on the national-income-at-market-price budget line $\hat{P}\hat{C}_r$, and production is at $\hat{P}_r$ where the world price line $\hat{C}_r\hat{P}_r$ intersects the generalized Rybczynski line $\hat{P}R$ (which reflects successive withdrawals of resources for revenue seeking, at the given tariff-inclusive prices). Trade is defined by $\hat{C}_r$ and $\hat{P}_r$; tariff revenue therefore is equal to the dashed distance $\hat{P}_rQ$, which in turn exactly equals (given the one-for-one assumption) the value of resources diverted to revenue seeking because it is equal to the value of reduced output of goods as measured by the difference between $\hat{P}$ and $\hat{P}_r$ at domestic prices. Revenue seeking, in this depiction, takes the form analytically of a non-traded activity that pays market-determined wages and rentals to factors (equal to those in goods production) and whose output is simply the revenue that is sought by the lobby.

An alternative analytical approach is to assume that tariff collection involves the use of real resources (for building customs sheds, paying customs inspectors, etc.). In the one-for-one case, each dollar of revenue collected involves a dollar's worth of real resources in its collection. With either depiction, while the value of goods production reduces, thanks to real resource diversion, it is fully offset by the *revenue* in equilibrium, and hence national income/expenditure on goods at domestic market prices is determinate as $\hat{P}\hat{C}_r$, with factor income in goods production being determined at $\hat{P}_r$ and factor income in revenue seeking being equal to the revenue and both adding up to OQ' as the national expenditure or budget line.

Note then that figure 7.1 shows the production of the imported good Y at $\hat{P}_r$ as less than at P^*; the Metzler production paradox obtains. The conventional substitution effect of the tariff does protect, taking production from P^* to $\hat{P}$; but this is more than offset by the *income* effect of the induced revenue seeking, which shifts production again, to $\hat{P}_r$. That the (generalized) Rybczynski line is positively sloped, as in the present example, is a necessary but not a sufficient condition for this outcome.

Transfer Seeking and the Terms-of-Trade-Change Criterion
An application of this analysis to the transfer problem can again be shown
to change dramatically the conventional criterion for change in the terms
of trade—as in the article by Bhagwati, Brecher, and Hatta (1982).

Thus, consider the case where the transfer, instead of being received
directly by consumers or given to them as a lump-sum gift as in conventional analysis, goes into the governmental budget and then leads to
transfer-seeking lobbying. (In principle, we could also assume symmetrically that the donor country experiences reduced lobbying when it makes
the transfer, a case we discuss later.) Also consider again the one-for-one
assumption such that the transfer-seeking lobbying uses up a value of
domestic primary factors *equal* in total to the amount of the transfer. This
situation is analyzed in figure 7.2.

Initially, the recipient country produces on its production-possibility
frontier $F_y F_x$ at point P, consumes on its social indifference curve $V_y V_x$ at
point C, and trades with the donor country (the rest of the world) along
price line PC from point P to point C. Let us now consider the case where
the terms of trade cannot change.

In the small-country case, the transfer has of course no impact on the
goods—price ratio. The transfer-seeking activity of lobbyists, however,
causes output in the recipient to move down the generalized Rybczynski
line PR until production reaches point $\hat{P}$, where the value of national output
has fallen by the amount of the transfer to the level represented by the
price line (parallel to PC) through point $\hat{P}$. Since this value of output plus
the transfer equals national expenditure, consumption remains at point C.
Thus, the transfer has paradoxically failed to enrich the recipient.

In the case of a large country, the recipient's welfare could actually
decline, if the marginal propensity to consume good X (along the income-
consumption curve) in the donor is less than the (analogous) marginal
propensity to produce this good along the (generalized) Rybczynski line
PR in the recipient. In this case, the transfer at initial prices would create an
excess world demand for good X, and (given stability) the relative price of
this commodity would rise to clear world markets. As the equilibrium price
line steepens from the initial position PC, the recipient must reach a lower
indifference curve, provided that the relative price of X does not rise above
the autarkic level (where an indifference curve would touch curve $F_y F_x$). By
similar reasoning, the opposite ranking of marginal propensities would lead
to a fall in the world price of good X, and hence enrichment of the
recipient.

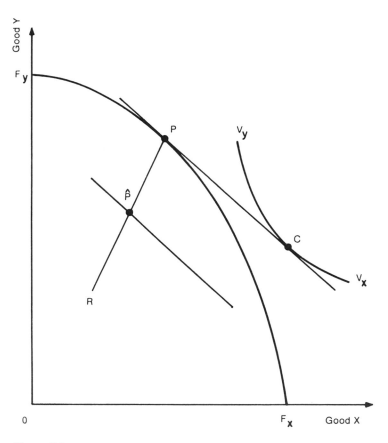

Figure 7.2
Transfer-seeking equilibrium.

In the *symmetric case* analyzed in the article by Bhagwati, Brecher, and Hatta (1982), the transfer-seeking DUP activity in the recipient country is matched by identical effects of DUP activity in the donor. To make the symmetry complete, the analysis assumes (1) that the donor was initially disbursing a given amount of revenue domestically, resulting in equivalent utilization of resources in competitive subsidy-seeking lobbying and (2) that the subsequent international transfer payment reduces by an equivalent amount the subsidies subject to domestic lobbying and hence also reduces the resource use on such lobbying equivalently. As they then show, given market stability and the aforementioned proviso about the autarkic level of relative prices, national welfare will then improve (worsen) for the donor and worsen (improve) for the recipient *if and only if* the recipient's marginal propensity to produce its own importable is greater (less) than the donor's marginal propensity to produce this good.

Endogenous Policy

The endogenization of policy *via* DUP activity is also subversive of traditional intuitions. Traditionally, economists are trained to think of governments as neutral in positive analysis and of economic agents who compete, perfectly or imperfectly, in alternative types of market enviromnents. Once policy is endogenized, this approach is undermined. With endogenous policy, economic agents attempt to influence policy in their favor; thus, there is a noneconomic marketplace, in which economic agents can simultaneously conduct their profit-making activities.[3] We thus have *two* components of the overall model: the orthodox *economic* specification and the *political* specification. Profit motivation may equally extend to both, but the economic returns accrue through induced-policy changes influencing economic returns in the traditionally economic sphere of the model.

As with the exogenous-policy DUP activities analyzed earlier, the results in positive analysis are extremely sensitive to the change in the way the total economic system is modeled. For example, the customary view is that, given an exogenously specified tariff, an improvement in the terms of trade will reduce the domestic production of the importable good in an economy with given resources, well-behaved technology, and perfect markets. But this conclusion need not follow, or may be seriously weakened, if the effect of the terms of trade change is to trigger tariff-seeking lobbying successfully.

While there is a vast and growing literature on political economy models that endogenize policy through DUP-activity specification in a variety of contexts, several efforts of a general-equilibrium type have emerged recently in trade-theoretic literature in particular.[4] We will give an indication here of the nature of these models by drawing on two of the early papers on tariff seeking: Findlay and Wellisz (1982) and Feenstra and Bhagwati (1982). These papers may be characterized in the following way:

1. Economic *agents* that engage in lobbying are defined. Findlay and Wellisz include two specific factors in two activities in the specific factors model. Their interests are in conflict since goods price changes affect them in an opposite manner. In Feenstra-Bhagwati (1982), there is only one economic agent (that hurt by import competition) who engages in lobbying, in the 2 × 2 Heckscher-Ohlin-Samuelson model.

2. The agents lobby to have a *policy* adopted or to oppose it. If the model is interpreted as a steady state rather than a static one, agents have to continue lobbying in a steady state to retain a policy once it is adopted or to preclude its adoption at any time. In both the Findlay-Wellisz paper and Feenstra-Bhagwati, that policy is uniquely defined to be a tariff, but the model can be generalized to other forms of trade restrictions.

3. The "government," as an economic agent, is not explicit in Findlay-Wellisz. The cost-of-lobbying functions that postulate the tariff as a function of the lobbying resources spent in proposing and opposing a tariff are *implicitly* assuming a government that is subject to these opposing lobbying efforts. In Feenstra-Bhagwati, by contrast, there is a *two-layer* government: the lobbying process interacts with one branch of government (e.g., the legislature) to enact a *lobbying tariff*. Another branch of the government (e.g., the president in the United States) then uses the subsequent tariff revenues to bribe the lobby into accepting a different, welfare-superior *efficient tariff*. The revenue bribe *plus* the earned income from the marketplace at the efficient tariff yields the same income for the lobby as does the lobbying tariff.[5]

These papers nicely define how the theoretical analysis of endogenous policymaking can be approached in the conventional manner of economic theory. By taking a simple set of political-cum-economic assumptions they manage to get a neat, simple model working. Through a combination of elements from the Findlay-Wellisz and Feenstra-Bhagwati models, this work will eventually lead to the extension of the traditional 2 × 2 × 2 model of the Heckscher-Ohlin-Samuelson (HOS) type to an augmented 2 × 2 × 2 × 2 model, in which two lobbies and capitalists and workers engage in tariff-seeking lobbying.

These models can also be enriched in different directions. One way is to develop further the role of the government. Recall that the Feenstra-Bhagwati model postulates a two-layer view of the government. It combines the view (taken exclusively in Findlay-Wellisz) that the government is "acted upon" by political lobbies causing the tariff to become a function of the resources expended (presumably in financing reelection) by the respective lobbies, with the view that the government acts so as to maximize a conventional social welfare function. Instead, one could develop the sometimes-propounded view that the government acts to maximize its revenue, since doing so maximizes its patronage. If so, Harry Johnson's (1950–51) classic analysis of maximum-revenue tariff in a conventional world where other economic agents are not engaged in lobbying yields the politically endogenous tariff.

The analysis can also be extended to include a larger set of *policy instruments* for which the economic agents can lobby in response to import competition. Thus, as a supplement to tariffs, one can consider policy instruments in regard to international factor and technological flows. Without formally incorporating them into a model that endogenously yields the equilibrium choice or policy mix of instruments in response to import competition, Bhagwati (1982b, c), Sapir (1983), and Dinopoulos (1984) have analyzed the *preferences* that different economic agents could have between these instruments when faced by import competition (i.e., improved terms of trade). Such analyses throw light on the incentives for lobbying for different policy adoptions by the government and hence yield the necessary insights into why certain policy options rather than others emerge as actual responses to import competition.

7.3   DUP Activities and Welfare Analysis

Exogenous Policies

The welfare effects of specific policies, and of parametric changes in the presence of exogenously specified policies, can be extremely sensitive to whether induced DUP activities are built into the model or not. We will consider two cases.

Shadow Prices in a Tariff-Distorted Small Economy in Cost-Benefit Analysis
Bhagwati and Srinivasan (1982), following on Foster's (1981) work, have shown that shadow prices for primary factors in a small tariff-distorted open economy are different, depending on whether the tariff has resulted

in revenue seeking. In fact, the shadow prices can be shown to be the market prices when revenue seeking obtains.

The shadow factor prices for a small tariff-distorted economy are known from the cost-benefit literature to be derivable from the world goods prices given the distorted techniques. On the other hand, it is obvious from the fact that if revenue seeking is present, as in figure 7.1, the economy operates on the national expenditure, social budget line defined at the market, tariff-inclusive prices. Therefore, a marginal withdrawal of factors from the distorted DUP equilibrium will evidently imply an opportunity cost reflecting the market prices.[6] To put it another way, with the entire revenue sought away, the consumer expenditure on goods equals income at market prices for factors. And these factor prices do not change (as long as incomplete specialization continues), as we vary factor endowments, thanks to the tariff. As such, the value of change in the labor (capital) endowment by a unit is its market reward. Hence, the shadow factor prices in this DUP-activity-inclusive model are the market prices.[7] The invisible hand strikes again!

Policy Rankings with Revenue Seeking

Recall that, for a small economy, a consumption tax on the importable (production tax on the exportable) is welfare superior to a tariff at the same ad valorem rate since it avoids the additional production (consumption) loss associated with the tariff. Once full revenue seeking à la Bhagwati and Srinivasan (1980) is consistently taken into account, however, this welfare ranking is reversed. This is seen as follows.

With a tariff at ad valorem rate t, let the output vector of the economy be (X^t, Y^t) under no revenue seeking. Let the free-trade (i.e., zero-tariff) output vector be (X^0, Y^0). With full revenue seeking under the tariff, consumers maximize utility given a relative price of $(1 + t)$ of the importable good Y (with the world relative price normalized at unity) and income y equal to $[X^t + (1 + t)Y^t]$. They thus derive utility $v(1 + t, X^t + (1 + t)Y^t)$ expressed in terms of their indirect utility function $v(p, y)$. On the other hand, with a consumption tax at an ad valorem rate t and full revenue seeking, they face the same price $(1 + t)$ but an income of $(X^0 + Y^0)$, thus obtaining utility: $v(1 + t, X^0 + Y^0)$. From the fact that (X^t, Y^t) maximizes the value of output given the tariff t, we get

$$\{X^t + (1 + t)Y^t\} \geqslant \{X^0 + (1 + t)Y^0\} \geqslant \{X^0 + Y^0\}.$$

Hence,

$$v(1 + t, X^t + (1 + t)Y^t) > v(1 + t, X^0 + Y^0);$$

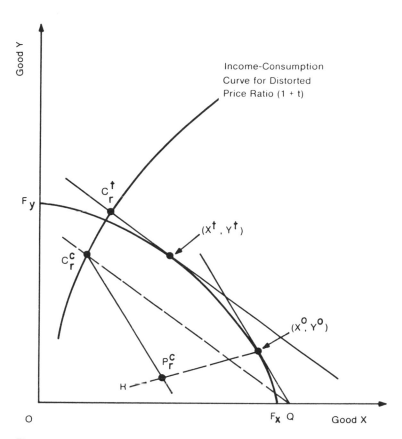

Figure 7.3
Tariff versus consumption tax, both with full revenue seeking.

that is, a tariff with full revenue seeking is superior to a consumption tax with full revenue seeking.

The foregoing argument is illustrated in figure 7.3.[8] Without any revenue seeking and free trade, equilibrium production is at (X^0, Y^0). With a tariff, production shifts at relative price ratio $(1 + t)$ to (X^t, Y^t). With tariff-revenue seeking, consumption is at C_r^t, as shown in figure 7.1 also. Shift, however, to a consumption tax on good Y with attendant revenue seeking. Production then remains at (X^0, Y^0) and the income, measured in terms of good X, is OQ, and is spent at the consumption-tax-inclusive price ratio $(1 + t)$ along line QC_r^c, taking consumption to C_r^c. Figure 7.3 also shows production in the consumption-tax-cum-seeking equilibrium. It is given at P_r^c by the intersection of the world price line from C_r^c and the R-line, which is the Rybczynski line for the world price ratio (unity) at (X^0, Y^0). Evid-

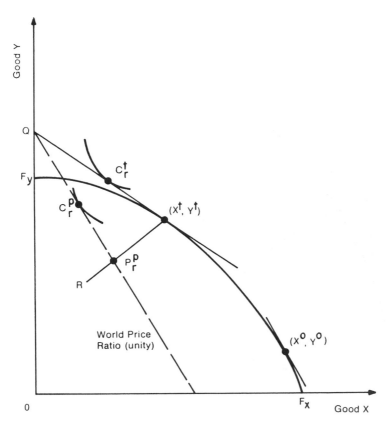

Figure 7.4
Tariff versus production tax, both with full revenue seeking.

ently, welfare at C_r^t dominates that at C_r^c: the tariff is superior to the consumption tax.

Consider now the comparison between a production tax on good X and a tariff, both yielding identical domestic producer price ratio and with attendant full revenue seeking. Under the tariff, equilibrium consumption is then at C_r^t in figure 7.4. But shift now to the production tax. Income, in terms of good Y, will then be OQ as with the tariff, but consumers will face the world price ratio (unity) and consumption will be at C_r^p. The production equilibrium will then be at P_r^p, the intersection between the expenditure line QC_r^p and the R-line from (X^t, Y^t) at the tax-distorted price $(1 + t)$. Evidently, C_r^t dominates C_r^p: welfare under the tariff exceeds that under an identical production tax, when full revenue seeking obtains in each case.

The intuitive explanation of these results is that, with no revenue seeking, a consumption (production) tax generates more revenue than a tariff at the same rate,[9] the reason being that the offsetting production (consumption) subsidy effect of a tariff is absent. In effect, what we are getting into is a situation where there are two distortions, rather than one, associated with each of the policies being ranked: the direct distortion implied by the policy itself and the indirect distortion implied by the (induced) DUP activity. What is interesting in the specific policy-rankings considered here is that these rankings are still possible, and in fact get reversed, when the indirect DUP effect is considered.

From a welfare-theoretic viewpoint, therefore (policy-induced) DUP activities can play a possibly critical role in determining desirable policy intervention. This conclusion is also dramatically supported by the welfare-theoretic analysis of transfers. Recall from our discussion of the DUP-theoretic transfer problem and from figure 7.2 that, in the traditional 2×2 (non-DUP) framework, exacting a reparation payment will always be enriching for the recipient of the resulting transfer in a Walras-stable market. Once, however, full transfer seeking is permitted, this is no longer so! Thus, take the case of a "large" recipient country, as illustrated in figure 7.2. Deterioration in the terms of trade is *sufficient* to immiserize the recipient in a Walras-stable market, whereas such deterioration in the terms of trade cannot ever be large enough to offset the primary gain from the transfer in a Walras-stable market in the orthodox non-DUP-activity 2×2 model.

We therefore need to reexamine a number of policy intuitions if policies do induce DUP activities in the real world, as they indeed do. The world lies somewhere along the continuum defined by two end points: one where no DUP activity is induced and the other where DUP activity is induced fully (on a one-for-one basis).[10] But whereas we have charted reasonably in depth the former end, we are only beginning to understand and sketch the latter end. An agenda for research to map the latter landscape clearly awaits a new generation of researchers in all branches of economic theory.

Endogenous Policy

A far more critical question is raised, however, once you fully endogenize policy in DUP-theoretic models. Take a tariff-seeking model of any species that you prefer. The endogenous tariff that emerges then in such a model may be illustrated in figure 7.5. $F^{ex}F^{ex}$ is the production possibility curve when all resources are deployed for producing X and Y and an *exogenous* tariff leads this small economy from P^* at given world prices to $\hat{P}^{ex}$ under protection. But now the model is augmented to endogenize the tariff; in equilibrium, resources are used up in tariff-seeking DUP activity, and the tariff-inclusive equilibrium is at $\hat{P}^{en}$. The hypothetical production possibility

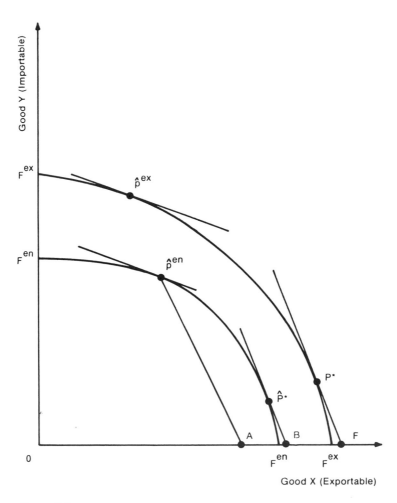

Figure 7.5
Welfare costs of endogenous and exogenous tariffs.

curve $F^{en}F^{en}$ takes the endowment of factors as *net* of those used up in tariff-seeking *equilibrium*: the tariff-inclusive goods price ratio must therefore be tangent to it at P^{en}. It is assumed, of course, that revenue-seeking-induced DUP activity is not simultaneously present here.[11]

As Bhagwati (1980) has shown, if we wish to measure the cost of protection in this endogenous-tariff model, the appropriate way to do it would be to put the world price ratio tangent to $F^{en}F^{en}$ at $\hat{P}^*$ and, using the Hicksian equivalent-variational measure, to take the move from $\hat{P}^{en}$ to $\hat{P}^*$ as the standard production cost of protection, reflecting the distortion of prices faced by producers) and the further move from $\hat{P}^*$ to P^* as the added cost of tariff-seeking lobbying (reflecting the loss due to resource diversion to lobbying). Hence the *total* cost of protection in an endogenous-tariff model would be AF, reflecting the comparison between the free-trade-equilibrium position at P^* and the endogenous-tariff-equilibrium position at $\hat{P}^{en}$. In turn, it is decomposed then into AB, the conventional "cost of protection," and BF, the "lobbying cost." It might be appropriate perhaps to speak of the total cost as the cost of the "protectionist process," to avoid confusion between AF and AB.[12]

While this analytical innovation to extend the traditional cost-of-protection analysis to the case where the tariff is endogenous may be applauded, it raises the deeper question that we now wish to address.

Once the tariff is endogenized, it will generally be determined uniquely as at $\hat{P}^{en}$ (though, of course, multiple equilibriums can be introduced as readily as in conventional "strictly economic" models). To compare this outcome with a hypothetical free-trade policy leading to P^* is to compare a policy choice that is made as a solution to the entire, augmented economic-cum-policy-choice system with a wholly hypothetical policy that descends like manna from heaven! Such a comparison makes obvious sense, of course, when we take policies as exogenous: we are then simply varying them, given the conventional economic system, and reading off their welfare consequences. But, with only one policy outcome determined endogenously, the comparison between it and another hypothetical policy arrived at by exogenous specification, while of course possible, is not compelling. It is virtually as if we had wiped out one side of our model (the political side) for our point of reference!

It would appear therefore that we need to *change* the way we pose welfare-theoretic questions once policies are endogenized critically, as in the foregoing analysis. Thus, it is not particularly meaningful to rank-order policies as in traditional analysis, once policies are endogenous. Nor is it appropriate to compare them vis-à-vis a reference point (such as P^* in figure 7.5) that reflects an exogenously specified policy.

Rather, it would appear that the analysis must now shift focus and concentrate on *variations around the endogenous equilibrium* itself (i.e., around $\hat{P}^{en}$ in figure 7.5). Thus, it is customary to ask, given a policy, what happens to welfare when accumulation comes about, or when technical know-how changes, etc. We can rephrase those questions as follows, keeping in mind that there are now two parts of the overall economic system, the economic and the political: What will happen to welfare if, on the economic side of the model, changes such as accumulation and technical progress occur; and what happens if changes occur instead on the political side such as an increased cost of lobbying for a tariff if there is an exogenous shift in attitudes against protection?[13] In short, the overall system must be solved for endogenous policy change and for final welfare impact for parametric changes that can occur now *either* in the economic *or* equally in the political side of the overall, augmented system. An interesting way to decompose the overall welfare impact of such parametric changes on either the economic or the political side of the system could be to assume first that policy does remain exogenous and then, in the next stage, to allow it to change to its endogenous value. The first stage might capture the essence of what we have come to think of as the customary impact of a parametric change in the system; the second stage may be taken to correspond to the fact that policy is endogenous.

7.4   Concluding Remarks

Evidently, therefore, the integration of DUP activities into theoretic analysis is a serious business. We hope that we have raised the issues sharply enough to stimulate the response of our fellow economists in the shape of future research on what promises to be an extremely important innovation in economic theorizing.

Notes

1. Her focus is on licensing or quantity restrictions and the rents thereon, and her generic set of rent-seeking activities excludes from its scope other DUP activities such as price-distortion-triggered DUP activities or distortion-triggering DUP activities. For a fuller analysis of the relationship, analytical and terminological, between DUP and rent-seeking activities, see Bhagwati (1983).

2. Other classifications, addressed better to other purposes, are also possible, as in the synthesis of the welfare effects of DUP activities in Bhagwati (1982c).

3. Of course, this is also true of DUP lobbying and policy-evading models. We considered in the case where the policy *causing* the DUP activity was specified exogenously.

4. The earliest, pioneering work is that of Brock and Magee (1978, 1980).

5. Feenstra and Bhagwati note that the efficient tariff may paradoxically exceed the lobbying tariff if the shadow price of lobbying activity is negative.

We might add that some critics have expressed concern that any model should have a multilayered or multipolar government, that this amounts to viewing government as "schizophrenic." However, the view that governments must be monolithic seems inconsistent with a reading of even the *New York Times*, not to mention political-science literature. Dinopoulos (chapter 9 of this book) also considers a two-layer government where the revenue-seeking lobby acts on the legislature and the executive determines the optimal tariff taking this lobbying into account.

6. Thus, as Anam (1982) has shown, Johnson's (1967) type of immiserizing growth in the presence of a tariff is impossible when all tariff revenues are sought.

7. If not all of tariff revenues are subject to seeking, the shadow prices would be differently defined, as noted by Anam (1982).

8. For an important diagrammatic analysis of a consumption tax with revenue seeking, see Anam (1982). Anam showed that such a tax might be welfare-inferior to a tariff in achieving a given level of consumption for one good.

9. See also Anam (1982) on this point.

10. The latter end point may even be more drastic if, as Tullock (1980) has suggested, seeking leads to more resources being spent on chasing a prize than the value of the prize itself, depending on how you model the terms and conditions of such a chase.

11. Tullock (1980) and Bhagwati (1982b) analyze the case where this DUP activity is simultaneously present.

12. Bhagwati (1980) also shows that it is incorrect to argue that the cost of an endogenous tariff at t percent always exceeds the cost of an exogenous tariff at t percent. This proposition involves comparing $\hat{P}^{ex}$ with $\hat{P}^{en}$, and since this is a second-best comparison, the endogenous tariff can be less harmful than the exogenous one. This is also at the heart of the problem with the Buchanan-Tollison definition of DUP activities, as discussed in Bhagwati (1983).

13. On this point, see Brecher (1982).

References

Anam, Mahmudul. 1982. Distortion-Triggered Lobbying and Welfare: A Contribution to the Theory of Directly-Unproductive Profit-Seeking Activities. *Journal of International Economics* 13: 15–32.

Bhagwati, Jagdish. 1980. Lobbying and Welfare. *Journal of Public Economics* 17.

Bhagwati, Jagdish. 1982. Lobbying, DUP Activities, and Welfare: A Response to Tullock. *Journal of Public Economics* 19: 335–341.

Bhagwati, Jagdish. 1983. DUP Activities and Rent Seeking. *Kyklos* 36: 634–637.

Bhagwati, Jagdish, and T. N. Srinivasan. 1980. Revenue Seeking: A Generalization of the Theory of Tariffs. *Journal of Political Economy* 88: 1069–1087.

Bhagwati, Jagdish, and T. N. Srinivasan. 1982. The Welfare Consequences of Directly Unproductive Profit Seeking (DUP) Lobbying Activities. *Journal of International Economics* 13: 33–44.

Brecher, Richard. 1982. Endogenous Tariffs, the Political Economy of Trade Restrictions, and Welfare: Comment. In J. Bhagwati (ed.), *Import Competition and Response*. Chicago: University of Chicago Press for NBER.

Brock, William, and Stephen Magee. 1978. The Economics of Special Interest Politics: The Case of the Tariff. *American Economic Review* 68: 241–250.

Brock, William, and Stephen Magee. 1980. Tariff Formation in a Democracy. In J. Black and B. Hindley (eds.), *Current Issues in Commercial Policy and Diplomacy*. New York: St. Martin's.

Buchanan, James M., Robert D. Tollison, and Gordon Tullock (eds.). 1980. Toward a Theory of the Rent-Seeking Society. College Station: Texas A&M University Press.

Dinopolous, Elias. 1984. The Optimal Tariff with Revenue Seeking: A Contribution to the Theory of DUP Activities. In D. Colander, *Neoclassical Political Economy*. Cambridge, MA: Ballinger.

Feenstra, Robert C., and Jagdish Bhagwati. 1982. Tariff Seeking and the Efficient Tariff. In J. Bhagwati (ed.), *Import Competition and Response*. Chicago: University of Chicago Press for NBER.

Findlay, Ronald E., and Stanislav H. Wellisz. 1982. Endogenous Tariffs, the Political Economy of Trade Restrictions, and Welfare. In J. Bhagwati (ed.), *Import Competition and Response*. Chicago: University of Chicago Press.

Johnson, Harry G. 1950–51. Optimum Welfare and Maximum Revenue Tariffs. *Review of Economic Studies* 19: 28–35.

Johnson, Harry G. 1967. The Possibility of Income Losses with Increases in Efficiency or Factor Accumulation in the Presence of Tariffs. *Economic Journal* 77: 151–154.

Krueger, Anne O. 1974. The Political Economy of the Rent-Seeking Society. *The American Economic Review* 64: 291–303.

Sapir, André. 1983. Foreign Competition, Immigration and Structural Adjustment. *Journal of International Economics* 14: 381–394.

Tullock, Gordon. 1980. Rent Seeking as a Negative Sum Game. In J. Buchanan et al. (eds.), *Towards a Theory of the Rent Seeking Society*. College Station: Texas A&M University Press.

8

The Theory of
Political Economy,
Economic Policy, and
Foreign Investment

In this chapter I consider recent developments in the analysis of foreign investment that reflect the new thinking in economic theory along the lines of political economy. Section 8.1 provides an overview of the developments in the theory of political economy generally, focusing equally on its profound implications for the theory of economic policy. Section 8.2 turns then to the analysis of foreign investment in light of this overview, discussing how analysis of foreign investment changes in light of political economy-theoretic considerations, drawing particularly on the new theory of quid pro quo foreign investment.

8.1   The Theory of Political Economy: An Overview

The new theory of political economy is distinguished chiefly by its explicit consideration of political action by economic agents in the simultaneous determination of economic policy and economic phenomena.

Puppet Government: Echoing the Economist

Conventional economic theory typically postulates a government whose role is to echo the policy that the economist, presented with the technocratic information on the economy and choosing an appropriate objective function, proposes as the optimal one from a set of policy instruments. The government is therefore in essence a fictitious device. It simply represents a surrogate for the economist, impervious to any identity of its own as a participating agent in the economic process and equally to any activities by other economic agents to influence policy outcome in their preferred direction. I therefore call this manner of modeling government in conventional (and indeed dominant) economic theory the *puppet government* view of how government functions. The economist is the puppeteer: the government is only, and exclusively, his voice.

The new theoretical developments in political economy essentially depart from this approach by endowing the government with autonomy from the economist. But they vary in the way in which the government then interacts with the conventionally defined economic system (e.g., the Walrasian value-theory model of general equilibrium) to define both economic policy and outcome. Two approaches to endowing an explicit role to the government can be distinguished.

Self-willed Government: Full Autonomy

One approach has been to endow the government with its own objective function and the power to determine policy, with the rest of the economic system providing simply the playground for the government to maximize its own welfare. The government is fully autonomous: it neither echoes the economist nor is it responsive to the forces of pluralist politics. This is essentially the approach underlying modeling in the spirit of Niskanen (1968) whose government bureaucrats maximize revenues for their own benefit, the Leviathan writings of Brennen and Buchanan (1977), and the purely predatory views of government espoused by others. There is no active feedback from the economic system to the government in such models: it is just that the government, now autonomous of the economist, has its own preference function and corresponding agenda.

The welfare-theoretic analysis of policymaking in such analysis cannot consist in devising optimal policy and ranking alternative policy instruments in a hierarchy of welfare outcomes. Instead, it must turn to asking what the welfare effect of a government setting its own agenda will be on the rest of us.

To see this contrast sharply, consider the conventional argument for trade policy for a large open economy. Under the orthodox *puppet government* approach, we choose the *optimal* tariff (Johnson, 1950–51; Graaff, 1949) as the first-best among available policy instruments, whereas domestic interventions appear as second-best improvements (Bhagwati and Ramaswami, 1963) over laissez-faire. On the other hand, a Niskanen government will choose the *maximum-revenue* tariff (Johnson, 1950–51). The welfare consequence of the maximum-revenue tariff for society can then be calculated as the loss relative to what the optimal tariff would yield.

Clearinghouse Government: Primacy of Pluralist Politics

An altogether contrasting approach, on the other hand, has been to make the government again lose its autonomy, not to the economist, but now to the economic system whose agents within a pluralistic political regime play the policy-influencing game that determines the policy outcome.[1] The lobbies compete for policy outcomes; the government is de facto a play-ground where this competition or conflict results in policy outcome. The government has no ego, no identity, in this approach. It is best described as the *clearinghouse government* approach to political economy modeling.

Thus, in recent models of tariff-seeking that endogenize tariff formation, the traditional general-equilibrium models of the open economy are aug-mented by a set of political equations that reflect the lobbying activities aimed at influencing the policy choice. Essentially, political markets are introduced as methods of affecting policy and hence one's income: these augment the conventional economic ways of earning income.

To take a specific example, in the Findlay-Wellisz (1982) model of tariff-seeking, the specific-factors 3×2 model of general equilibrium is augmented by lobbying functions for the specific factors in each of the two sectors. The specific factor in the import-competing sector gains from a tariff; that in the other sector loses from it. The model is solved for the endogenous tariff that equates the return from lobbying to its cost, both at the margin.

As I observed, the government here is captive to the economic system whose agents essentially operate in political markets to equate returns from them with the returns to activity in the conventional economic markets.[2] (The Niskanen-Brennan-Buchanan type of approach, on the other hand, has the economic system captive to the government which plays, or perhaps preys, on it to pursue its own ends.)

I should add that, in an implicit fashion, the role of the government as an autonomous agent can be imagined none the less in this approach. For, the effectiveness of lobbying for a tariff in these models for instance can be considered to be a function, not merely of the expenses incurred by oneself and by the opposing lobby, but also of "ideology" or the objective func-tion of the government. But just as weather shapes the production function in agriculture but plays no role in microeconomic analysis, this view of the government's ideology plays no analytical role in the pluralistic, lobbying models of *clearinghouse government*.

Once again, however, the analysis of economic policy undergoes a shift. With policy endogenously determined, it becomes impossible to seek to rank policies by their welfare impact as in conventional, *puppet government* analysis. The degree of freedom to do this is not available, in general, any longer. This is what is now known as the *determinacy paradox* (Bhagwati et al., 1984; Bhagwati, 1986). The role of policy analysis and welfare economics is not lost, however. It just shifts to *variational* questions around the observed, political economy equilibrium. Thus, if any parametric shift occurs, either in the economic or in the political part of the model, we can ask: how will policy change, and how will the associated welfare change?

While the preceding two classes of modeled departures from the *puppet government* approach are polar cases, a realistic analysis of political economy must often draw on *both*. The government typically has objectives, and different branches of governments often have different objectives as well, so it is often necessary to disaggregate.[3] By setting policy defined over the economy, the government can and does pursue these objectives. At the same time, economic agents within the economy typically seek to influence policy to their advantage in light of their own preference functions.[4] The interaction of these two sets of agents, the government and others, whether strategic or not, leads to the policy and associated economic outcome.

8.2   Foreign Investment: Quid pro quo DFI etc.

The underlying core of the theory of political economy, as just outlined, provides a necessary introduction to the recent political economy-theoretic analysis of foreign investment.

The conventional analysis of international capital and labor flows and of direct foreign investment (DFI) typically analyzed *either* the consequences of exogenously imposed policies (e.g., tariffs) on variables such as the international flows of productive factors[5] or the optimal policy intervention when countries trading with one another also had international factor mobility between them.[6] But political economy-theoretic considerations have recently emerged in the theoretical analysis of international factor flows, and new ideas have been modeled in consequence in the theory of foreign investment.

These ideas have surfaced mainly in the context of response to import competition. Thus, the conventional economic analysis simply argues that, if import competition intensifies (i.e., the terms of trade improve), then a country will be better off (under the potential welfare-improvement Pareto criterion).[7] A benign "puppet" government will continue its free trade policy; or, if there is monopoly power in trade, it will suitably adjust its optimal monopoly-power-in-trade tariff to the new situation.[8]

But suppose now that the response to import competition is to trigger lobbying by the adversely affected economic agents to change economic policy so as to cushion this impact. Then, government policy becomes a function of this lobbying among factors.

The conventional modeling in trade theory of such endogenized policy-making focused on *one* policy instrument, i.e., tariffs (or, their quantity counterpart, import quotas). However, starting in the early 1980s, the question of the *choice of instruments* was raised, in the context of response to import competition, in Bhagwati (1982). There, I considered in different models the differential incentive of different economic agents to seek one of several possible policy interventions.[9] In particular, I distinguished between "capital" and "labor." I also explicitly considered policy instruments that went beyond trade policy to international factor mobility. Thus, I considered the following possibilities in response to import competition in Schumpeterian industries:

1. Seek protection (tariffs or quotas) or promotion (subsidies).

2. Seek relaxed immigration quotas (as in the *gastarbeiter* system of Western Europe) to import more cheap labor to compete better.

3. Go abroad (the Atari option) where labor is cheaper, thus undertaking DFI abroad.

4. Use the threat of protection to get successful foreign rivals to invest here, thus getting their DFI into the home country.

This last option, a novelty in recent years, implies foreign firms investing in the home country to defuse the threat of protection in a variety of ways. Thus, for instance, Toyota undertakes a joint venture in the United States with General Motors, essentially giving General Motors an apparently gratuitous share in profits from Toyota's superior know-how on small cars. In exchange, however, General Motors breaks ranks on VER (voluntary export restraint) renewal. The quid pro quo for Toyota from an otherwise uneconomical DFI in the United States is then the reduced threat of protection that follows. Hence, I have christened this political economy-theoretic phenomenon as "quid pro quo" foreign investment (Bhagwati, 1984, 1985).

Such quid pro quo investment by foreign firms can also appeal to domestic labor threatened by foreign competition. For it can help maintain jobs. Thus, UAW's interest in auto-protection would be inversely related to Japanese willingness to invest in the United States, though the threat of protection must be created and sustained to induce this investment.

Therefore, domestic agents, both firms and unions, can be expected to create a protectionist threat to induce investment in one's country by successful foreign rivals in joint ventures à la GM-Toyota in the former case and more generally to placate labor in the latter case. This argument therefore is explicitly political economy theoretic. It says that Japanese DFI is undertaken to affect U.S. trade policy: by "rewarding" U.S. firms and/or labor, it co-opts them into reducing the protectionist effort that they would otherwise undertake. Hence I also call this the *tariff-threat-reducing* DFI, to distinguish it from the traditional *tariff-jumping* DFI where the tariff is both realized and exogenously specified in the manner of conventional analysis.

1. The arguments above suggest that the foreign (e.g., Japanese) *firms* would seek DFI in order to defuse the threat of protection in their external market (e.g., in the United States). This requires, of course, that the firm be large enough, and the counterpart (U.S.) firm and/or union be significant enough, for this political quid pro quo to be a significant factor in the firm's decision making. If these conditions are met, then a natural way to formulate the resulting DFI is to consider a foreign, say Japanese, firm in a two-period setting, with two alternatives: producing in Japan and selling in the United States and producing (at higher cost) in the United States and selling in the United States. In period 1, given the quid pro quo phenomenon, the firm would gravitate toward the latter option to the extent that it equates the marginal cost in period 1 from higher-cost production in the United States with the discounted expected marginal benefit in period 2 from reduced probability of the U.S. market being closed by protection. In essence, this is the underlying structure of the early formulation in Dinopoulos and Bhagwati (1986) and the later, more complete analysis in Dinopoulos (1987), my former Columbia student.

2. But suppose that the Japanese firms are not in a position to seek such quid pro quos. Even then, there may be a *generic* case for Japan, seeking national advantage, to increase the size of Japan's DFI in the United States to reduce anti-Japanese, protectionist sentiment in the U.S. Congress. In this case, the quid pro quo angle arises, not necessarily through co-opting of the economic agents who lobby Congress, but by reducing the willingness of congressmen to respond to domestic protectionist pressures by these economic agents. Japan Inc. can reap the quid pro quo of reduced protectionism by encouraging Japanese DFI abroad. The simplest, economical way to model this generic argument for quid pro quo investment then would be to introduce, in a competitive model, a protectionist threat function which has first-period investment as one argument, with the partial derivative less than zero. This is, in essence, the type of analysis that we have recently undertaken (Bhagwati et al., 1986).

3. But these analyses, whether oligopolistic and at firm level in Dino-poulos et al. or perfectly competitive and at national level in Bhagwati et. al., consider the threat to protect in period 2 as *exogenously* specified. The firm, or the government, then chooses an optimal DFI level in period 1 so as to maximize an intertemporal profit or welfare function. Let me elaborate.

Thus, consider the following agents:

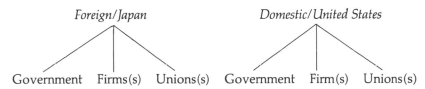

The Dinopoulos analysis assumes that the Japanese firm undertakes DFI in period 1, to influence the probability of the U.S. government imposing a tariff in period 2.[10] The threat is exogenously specified but a function of Japanese DFI; no intermediation of protectionist lobbying by co-opted domestic agents is explicitly modeled. The analysis, like that in recent work on the small-group analysis of strategic trade policy, is partial equilibrium and basically shows how, even in the absence of Japanese government action, firms in imperfectly competitive small-group situations will change the level of trade and investment when their investment can serve to defuse protectionist threats.

In the Bhagwati-Brecher-Dinopoulos-Srinivasan analysis, the protection-defusing action belongs to the Japanese government instead. In a perfectly competitive world, the nongovernmental agents in both countries are not modeled as influencing U.S. policy. Rather, the Japanese government inter-venes to influence U.S. trade policy by influencing Japanese investment in period 1 since that influences the exogenously specified protectionist threat in period 2. The analysis is then an extension of the analysis of optimal policy intervention (Bhagwati and Srinivasan, 1976) when a country finds that its exports in period 1 can (adversely) affect the prospects of a market-disruption-related quota being invoked by the importing country in period 2.[11] The analysis is in general equilibrium and focuses on optimal inter-vention by the Japanese government and associated impact on foreign investment.

4. A recent analysis by Kar-yiu Wong (1987), another of my Columbia students, has however addressed the modeling of quid pro quo investment in a manner that is, in some respects, more satisfactory. He endogenizes the threat by explicitly modeling a U.S. union whose lobbying activities reflect

the unemployment resulting (in a fixed-wage context) from imports sent by a monopolist Japanese firm. The quid pro quo investment then reflects the fact that, by reducing unemployment in the United States, the Japanese firm is able to reduce the lobbying by the U.S. union and hence act towards defusing the protectionist threat in the United States. The analysis is in partial equilibrium but extended to the welfare impact of quid pro quo investment on either country.

The three ways of modeling quid pro quo investment, sketched above, are not exhaustive. By looking at the possible set of agents that I set out earlier, we can see that a variety of other models is possible.

Thus, in an imperfectly competitive setting, the explicit modeling could reflect the Toyota-GM variety of quid pro quo investment where a Japanese firm undertakes joint production with a U.S. firm, at a first-period loss to itself and gain to the U.S. firm, and the lobbying effort of the U.S. firm to get protection is then influenced favorably. This analysis would endogenize the protectionist threat, as in Wong's U.S.-union-centered analysis, and generate quid pro quo investment equally. Doubtless, other models, with different mixes of the foreign and domestic agents, can and will be built to analyze quid pro quo investment.

Evidence

While the analysis of such political economy-theoretic quid pro quo investment is proceeding rapidly since I started writing about it in the early 1980s, the question arises: Is there systematic evidence for such investment?

That quid pro quo investment was a phenomenon from Japan to the United States in the early 1980s is not to be doubted. I developed the hypothesis, and the subsequent theoretical analysis, on the basis of casual empiricism, the classic route to new theorizing. In particular, I had been impressed by a luncheon conversation with Mr. Toyoda at Columbia University early in 1980, when he was expressing great hesitation about investing in the United States but suggesting that the political pressure on him, to avert the U.S. protectionist threat through investment and hence expression of goodwill by Japan to the United States, was considerable. He really wanted to know, not whether his and other Japanese investments would create goodwill in the United States and hence moderate the protectionist threat, but whether that threat was really serious. I assured him that it was.

That Mr. Toyoda was under pressure from the Japanese government to invest in the United States, because the Japanese government was conscious of the protectionist threat in the early 1980s, and encouraged

Japanese investment in the United States on quid pro quo grounds, was evident. In fact, in a recent article, Professor Toshio Shishido (1986) of the International University of Japan recalls a conversation with Mr. Toyoda as follows:

In 1978, I had a talk with Mr. Eigi Toyoda, the President of Toyota Motors ... At that time, Mr. Toyoda stated that Toyota had no intention to practice local production in America. I then said to him, "Judging from the tense relationship between Japan and the United States, why don't you think about an expansion of car production in America, in the form of cooperation [with] the government policy [in] national interest?" He said. "Toyota is not making an automobile for the nation." He clearly defined the standpoints of private enterprise. He clearly ... was not able to do the direct investment [in] America, thinking [only] about the profit of Toyota. (p. 15)

The interesting question of course is whether, independently of Japanese governmental pressure, the big Japanese firms thought of foreign investment *themselves* on quid pro quo grounds. For example, did Mr. Toyoda finally invest in a joint venture with General Motors simply because it would be doing a good turn to Japan generally by helping to moderate Japan-bashing outbreaks of U.S. protectionism or because he saw the quid pro quo more directly in terms of gains to Toyota in consequent increase in the probability of auto VER termination? The fact that he teamed up finally with General Motors, the most important U.S. firm with the biggest political clout, and that General Motors broke ranks and successfully opposed VER renewal subsequently, suggests that Mr. Toyoda may finally have seen some substantial quid pro quo for himself and not just for Japan.

In any event, I should mention that Shishido reports on a MITI survey on motivations for Japanese investments in developed countries abroad after 1980, reproduced here in table 8.1. While there is not sufficient information on the category "avoiding trade friction," which is the major reason advanced by the interviewees, it is certainly consistent with the hypothesis that quid pro quo considerations were important in motivating Japan's direct investments abroad.

The correspondents were not saying that, because they expected trade friction to result in trade protection, they were investing abroad in markets that they expected to close. Rather, they were saying that they expected to avoid trade friction and hence presumably trade protection by investing in the United States. What is not clear from Shishido's all-too-brief summary report is whether this expectation, if it reflected industry-level quid pro quo considerations, was because the foreign investment would (1) produce goodwill in the U.S. Congress and hence resistance to any given demand for "high-track" (VER-style) administered protection in the industry, and/

Table 8.1
Motivations for direct investments abroad (to advanced countries after 1980) (%)

	Avoiding trade friction	Market expansion	Following clients	Superiority on cost	Others
Business machines	96.7	3.3	—	—	—
Machine tools	77.1	14.3	—	—	8.6
Consumer electric machines	53.6	13.6	10.7	14.3	7.8
Electronics	30.0	32.1	11.3	10.8	15.6
Automobiles	66.0	24.0	—	—	10.0

Source: MITI, "Research on Foreign Local Production of Japanese Enterprises" (cited in Shishido, 1986, p. 25).

or (2) co-opt the economic agents and hence reduce the demand for protection itself by these agents, and/or (3) simply make "low-track" administered protection related to market disruption and safeguards action under Section 201 more difficult to sustain beacuse it must relate to import levels. The *exact* modeling of quid pro quo investment, from among the possibilities I discussed, and others, should reflect the choice among these alternative routes through which the Japanese investors expect the quid pro quo to operate.

Motivational studies, however, are not sufficient, for obvious reasons. It should be possible to test for the quid pro quo investment by examining Japanese investment in the United States for 1980–85 before the dollar–yen exchange rate began to adjust and made quid pro quo reasoning obsolete by making Japanese DFI in the U.S. profitable on straightforward, conventional economic grounds.

A key problem, of course, is in distinguishing between tariff-threat-defusing and tariff-jumping investment. If one takes the firm-level decision making as leading to quid pro quo foreign investment, how is one to decide, from cold data, whether a Japanese direct investor came into the United States because he expected his export market to close or because he expected that his investment would help to moderate that threat for any of several quid pro quo-type arguments considered here? One approach, suggested by Robert Lawrence of Brookings, is to see if the large Japanese firms (which could reasonably expect to have such quid pro quo influence) came first into the United States in the sequence of Japanese firms entering an industry. Another approach, since the model applies to the Japanese against whom protectionism is typically threatened, would be to see if

Japanese preceded European investment in the United States in specific protection-threatening industries. Dinopoulos and others are engaged in this empirical investigation currently.[12]

8.3   Concluding Remarks

The political economy-theoretic analysis of foreign investment, and indeed of other economic phenomena, thus offers a rich agenda for novel and important theoretical and empirical analysis.

By endogenizing the government and policy in an essential fashion, this type of analysis opens up a significantly different way of analyzing both economic policy and economic phenomena, raising in turn (as noted in section 8.2) some fundamental questions as well.

Hence, of the two recent developments since the early 1970s in international trade theory—the development of imperfectly competitive analysis (Brander, Dixit, Eaton, Grossman, Helpman, Krugman, Lancaster, Spencer, etc.) and of political-economy DUP-theoretic analysis (Anam, Baldwin, Bhagwati, Brecher, Findlay, Hillman, Krueger, Mayer, Srinivasan, Wellisz, Wilson, etc.)—the latter would appear to be the more interesting and significant. The former consists in fitting the old bicycle (competitive trade theory) with a new motor (imperfectly competitive markets), whereas the latter consists in taking the old bicycle (puppet-government trade theory) down a new road (explicit government trade theory). Surely one does not need to say which is more fundamental.

Notes

In discussing recent developments in both the theory of economic policy and the theory of foreign investment, I hope that this chapter provides an appropriate tribute to Ian Little in view of his seminal theoretical contributions to the former and his insightful policy writings on the latter. An early draft of the paper on which this chapter is based was presented to the American Economic Association meeting in Chicago, December 1987, and has profited from the comments of David Colander and Mancur Olson.

1. Mancur Olson's (1965) classic work on the free-rider problem and the logic of collective action is a pioneering contribution to this approach.

2. The recent literature on activities by economic agents to secure profits or income (1) by influencing policy—e.g., tariff-seeking (Tullock, 1969)—or (2) by earning rent from existing policy—e.g., rent-seeking (Krueger, 1974)—by chasing import quotas already in place, or revenue-seeking (Bhagwati and Srinivasan, 1980) to secure tariff revenues resulting from tariffs imposed endogenously or exogenously, or (3) by evading policy—e.g., smuggling (Bhagwati and Hansen,

1973), (Johnson, 1974), (Kemp, 1975), (Pitt, 1980), (Panagariya and Martin, 1981)—
now describes them as DUP (directly unproductive profit-seeking) activities
(Bhagwati, 1982), They are undertaken by using resources to produce profit or
income but not (socially valued) goods or output. On immediate impact, or *directly*,
therefore, they are unproductive. But *indirectly*, in terms of final impact on welfare,
they may be beneficial (owing to second-best considerations). Krueger's (1974)
quota-rents-generated rent-seeking lobbying activities are an important *subset* of
such DUP activities and should not be confused as being identical with them. Cf.
Bhagwati (1982, 1983).

DUP activities of type 1 above, which endogenize policymaking. lead to important analytical consequences such as the determinacy paradox noted in the text.
Not so, DUP activities of types 2 and 3 if the policy that triggers them is still left
exogenous. Cf, Bhagwati et al. (1984).

3. A two branch model of government is developed in Feenstra and Bhagwati's
(1982) analysis of the efficient tariff.

4. Sometimes, the theory of political economy is supposed to embrace the extension of economic analysis to preference functions that go beyond goods-
orientated utilitarianism. But this is simply confusing. Such extension, which
international economists have considered and analyzed under the theory of noneconomic ojectives since the late 1950s long before it became fashionable for
others to consider nonutilitarian objectives, is fully compatible with the conventional *puppet government* approach.

5. This is exemplified by the celebrated Mundell (1957) analysis of how factor-
price equalization can lead to commodity-price equalization when an exogenously
specified tariff is combined with international factor mobility in a Heckscher-Ohlin
world.

6. This is exemplified by the analysis of Kemp (1966) and Jones (1967) which
considered the optimal structure of taxes and subsidies on trade and capital flows
from the viewpoint of one country's advantage, in a world economy characterized
by two countries and international capital mobility. In principle this analysis carries
over to labor mobility as well. However, there is an overwhelmingly critical
difference. For, when labor moves across horders, the important question arises:
Should such labor he excluded then from the set over which one defines the
welfare function to he maximized for national advantage? Cf. Bhagwati (1972) and
Bhagwati and Wilson (1989).

7. This intutive proposition needs some careful and extended argumentation: cf.
Krueger and Sonnenschein (1967).

8. If a suboptimal trade policy is in place when import competition intensifies, the
theory of immiserizing growth (Bhagwati, 1968) tells one immediately that the
result may be paradoxically to worsen, rather than improve, one's welfare. Cf.
Batra and Pattanaik (1970).

9. The analysis of differential incentives for different agents in Bhagwati (1982)
was followed up by Dinopoulos (1983) and Sapir (1983). Subsequently, Rodik

(1986) and Mayer and Riezman (1987a, b) have also considered the choice between tariffs and production subsidies as possible instruments of protection in more complete models.

10. Two models are used: one where there is a Japanese firm and a U.S. firm, another where there are two Japanese firms.

11. Whereas therefore Bhagwati and Srinivasan (1976) define the threat as a function only of first-period exports, Bhagwati et al. (1980) define it also as a function of first-period capital outflow.

12. Kar-yiu Wong has drawn my attention to the remarkable fact that, during each year of the period 1982–86, Japanese direct investments in manufacturing in the United States made losses, although there were good profits for foreign investments as a whole in this sector. This would seem to provide prima facie evidence in support of the quid pro quo hypothesis for Japanese investment in the United States, although other explanations are possible.

References

Bhagwati, J. 1986. Investing Abroad. Esmée Fairbairn Lecture. University of Lancaster.

Bhagwati, J. 1985. Protectionism: Old Wine in New Bottles. *Journal of Policy Modeling* 7: 23–34.

Bhagwati, J. 1983. DUP Activities and Rent Seeking, *Kyklos*, 36, pp. 634–637.

Bhagwati, J. 1982. Shifting Comparative Advantage, Protectionist Demands and Policy Response. In J. Bhagwati (ed.), *Import Competition and Response*. Chicago: University of Chicago Press.

Bhagwati, J. 1982. Directly-Unproductive Profit-Seeking (DUP) Activities. *Journal of Political Economy* 90: 988–1002.

Bhagwati, J., and Hansen, B. 1973. A Theoretical Analysis of Smuggling. *Quarterly Journal of Economics* 87 (May).

Bhagwati, J., and Ramaswami, V. K. 1963. Domestic Distortions, Tariffs and the Theory of Optimum Subsidy. *Journal of Political Economy* 71 (February).

Bhagwati, J., and Srinivasan, T. N. 1976. Optimal Trade Policy and Compensation under Endogenous Uncertainty: The Phenomenon of Market Disruption. *Journal of International Economics* 88: 1069– 1087.

Bhagwati, J., and Wilson, J. (eds.). 1989. *Income Taxation and International Mobility*. Cambridge: MIT Press.

Bhagwati, J., Brecher, R., and Srinivasan, T. N. 1984. DUP Activities and Economic Theory. In D. Colander (ed.), *Neoclassical Political Economy*. Cambridge, MA: Ballinger, pp. 17–32.

Bhagwati, J., Dinopoulos, E., and Srinivasan, T. N. 1988. Quid Pro Quo Foreign Investment and Welfare: A Political-Economy-Theoretic Model. *Journal of Development Economics* (1988).

Brecher, R., and Díaz-Alejandro, C. 1977. Tariffs, Foreign Capital and Immiserizing Growth. *Journal of International Economics* 7: 317–322.

Brander, J. A., and Spencer, B. J. 1986. Foreign Direct Investment with Unemployment and Endogenous Taxes and Tariffs. Mimeo.

Brennan, G., and Buchanan, J. 1977. Towards a Tax Constitution for Leviathan. *Journal of Public Economics* 8: 255–273.

Brock, W., and Magee, S. 1978. The Economics of Special Interest Politics: The Case of the Tariff. *American Economic Review* 68: 246– 250.

Buck, J. 1986. Direct Foreign Investment as a Game between Home and Host Country Firms and the Host Country Government. Madison: University of Wisconsin. Mimeo.

Dinopoulos, E. 1983. Import Competition, International Factor Mobility and Lobbying Responses: The Schumpeterian Industry Case. *Journal of International Economics* 14: 395–410.

Dinopoulos, E. 1987. Quid Pro Quo Foreign Investment. Paper presented at the World Bank Conference on Political Economy (June). Forthcoming in *Economics and Politics* 1(2), Summer 1989.

Dinopoulos, E., and Bhagwati, J. 1986. Quid Pro Quo Foreign Investment and Market Structure. Presented at the 61st Annual Western Economic Association International Conference in San Francisco (July).

Feenstra, R., and Bhagwati, J. 1982. Tariff Seeking and the Efficient Tariff. In Bhagwati (1982a), pp. 245–258.

Findlay, R., and Wellisz, S. 1982. Endogenous Tariffs, the Political Economy of Trade Restrictions, and Welfare. In Bhagwati (1982a), pp. 223–234.

Graaff, Jan. 1949–50. On Optimum Tariff Structures. *Review of Economic Studies* 17/42.

Johnson, Harry G. 1950–51. Optimum Welfare and Maximum Revenue Tariffs. *Review of Economic Studies* 19: 28–35.

Johnson, Harry G. 1974. Notes on the Economic Theory of Smuggling. *Malayan Economic Review* (May 1972). Reprinted in J. Bhagwati (ed.), *Illegal Transactions in International Trade* Series in International Economics. Amsterdam: North Holland.

Jones, R. 1967. International Capital Movements and the Theory of Tariffs and Trade. *Quarterly Journal of Economics* 81: 1–38.

Kemp, M. 1966. The Gain from International Trade and Investment: A Neo-Heckscher-Ohlin Approach. *American Economic Review* 56: 788–809.

Kemp, M. 1967. Notes on the Theory of Optimal Tariffs. *Economic Record* 43/103: 395–404.

Krueger, Anne 1974. The Political Economy of the Rent-Seeking Society. *American Economic Review* 66 (May): 1–19.

Krueger, Anne, and Sonnenschein, H. 1967. The Terms of Trade, the Gains from Trade and Price Divergence. *International Economic Review* 8: 121–127.

Mayer, W. 1984. Endogenous Tariff Formation. *American Economic Review* 74 (December): 970–985.

Mayer, W., and Riezman, R. 1987. Endogenous Choice of Tariff Instruments. *Journal of International Economics*, 23 (November).

Mayer, W. 1987. Endogenous Choice of Trade Policy Instruments. Paper presented to World Bank Conference on Political Economy: Theory and Policy (June), forthcoming in *Economics and Politics*.

Mundell, R. A. 1957. International Trade and Factor Mobility. *American Economic Review* 47: 321–335.

Niskanen, W. 1968. The Peculiar Economics of Bureaucracy. *American Economic Review* 58: 293–305.

Olson, M. 1965. *The Logic of Collective Action*. Cambridge: Harvard University Press.

Pitt, M. 1981. Smuggling and Price Disparity. *Journal of International Economics* 11 (November): 447–458.

Rodrik, D. 1987. Tariffs, Subsidies and the Theory of Optimum Subsidy. *Journal of International Economics* 21: 285–299.

Sapir, A. 1983. Foreign Competition, Immigration and Structural Adjustment. *Journal of International Economics* 14: 381–394.

Shishido, T. 1986. Capital transfer from Japan to U.S. for Avoiding Trade Friction. In *Beyond Trade Friction*, Japan–U.S. Symposium (September 1–2, 1986), Tokyo. Center for Japan–U.S. Business and Economic Studies, New York University.

Tullock, G. 1967. The Welfare Cost of Tariffs, Monopolies and Theft. *Western Economic Journal* 5: 24–32.

Wong, K. Y. 1986. Are International Trade and Factor Mobility Substitutes?' *Journal of International Economics* 21: 25–43.

Wong, K. Y. 1987. Optimal Threat of Trade Restriction and Quid Pro Quo Foreign Investment. (Seattle: University of Washington. Mimeo. Forthcoming in *Economics and Politics* 1(3), Winter 1989.

9

VERs, Quid pro quo DFI, and VIEs: Political-Economy-Theoretic Analyses

This paper mainly examines VERs (voluntary export restrictions). It addresses their causes and consequences in sections 9.1 and 9.2, respectively. Section 9.3 goes beyond trade issues to consider the effects of VERs (and protection generally) on direct foreign investment. Section 9.4 offers concluding observations on the prospective new growth of VIEs (voluntary import expansions), addressed to the partner-trading-country's imports rather than exports.

A principal feature of the analysis is that it reflects the influence of the new developments in the theory of political economy in general equilibrium that constitute a major revolution in the theory of international trade and which help focus our attention on questions and insights that offer a better hold on the real world and hence on policy as well.[1]

9.1 VERs: Causes

VERs as a form of protection have grown in recent years. They are today an important part of the NTBs (nontariff barriers) on trade and are widely regarded as constituting a major component of the "new protectionism." Measurement of the incidence of these and other NTBs has preoccupied UNCTAD and the World Bank research bureaucracies for some time now.[2]

How did VERs emerge? Who should be assigned the blame or the credit for this innovation on the trade-restrictions scene? There are two ways to approach question. One is to ask how VERs arose historically; the other is to ask what purpose they have served and why therefore they may have endured. The former is primarily a historical question, the latter a "structure-and-function" type question familiar to social anthropologists. Thus, if you observe manna on earth, you can ask where it came from and get the answer that it came from heaven. But you can also say that it has endured because of the specific role it has played in human society and hence seek to define and discuss that role.

VERs appear to me to have their historical origin in Japan, though this is little more than a hypothesis still awaiting further research. I find it very suggestive that, when California was enacting the exclusion acts against Oriental immigration roughly two decades prior to the enactment of national immigration legislation in 1921, the Chinese were covered by these exclusion acts, whereas the Japanese preferred to accept Gentlemen's Agreements under which they regulated emigration of their nationals themselves! Again, it is known that Japanese used VERs extensively during the 1930s when their exports gave rise to protectionist demands abroad. The Japanese preference for "voluntary" restraints when such restraint is inevitable seems to lie deep perhaps in Japanese culture which prefers greyness and lack of frontal explicitness, as is beautifully set forth in the great novelist Junichiro Tanizaki's famous essay, *In Praise of Shadows*. They would rather do an unpleasant act themselves (as with *harakiri*) than have it done explicitly to them by the other party. Consonant with this psychocultural thesis is the witticism that the foreign residents in Japan offer to new visitors: in Japan, never take "yes" for an answer.

But this does not explain why VERs have been found to be so useful and enduring an instrument in the world trading system. Let me therefore turn to this question next. In answering it, admittedly in a "stylistic" fashion, I shall develop two alternative political-economy-theoretic arguments or models: one is familiar, but the other, I believe, is novel. The former may be called the "rent-transfer" model; the latter is appropriately christened the *porous-protection* model.

In appreciating each of these two alternative models, it is necessary to distinguish among two wholly separate aspects of VERs. The first, and in my view inessential, feature of VERs is that they are *quantity* rather than *price* restrictions on trade. I call this aspect inessential because it is easy to envisage the exporting country "voluntarily" restraining its exports through an export tariff (which is a price instrument) rather than by an export quota. Nonetheless, since VERs have often been invoked as quota rather than tariff restrictions on trade, this quantity-*versus*-price aspect can be distinguished and indeed has been in the theoretical literature that has recently emerged on the effects of VERs. Indeed, this literature would suggest (although this inference has not yet been drawn) that, if we wish to have the exporting country do the trade restricting, we might do better by asking it to do it by using VERs in the form of export tariffs instead of export quotas.

But the other aspect of a VER, i.e., that it is a trade restraint imposed by the *exporting* country instead of by the importing country, is absolutely essential.[3] Indeed, that also defines the principal reasons why VERs have proliferated vis-à-vis importing country trade restraints (as under Article XIX of the GATT). Let me therefore turn to the key role played by this contrast in analyzing the question at hand and explore two essential ways in which exporting-country trade restraints generate incentives for *both* exporting and importing countries to prefer them to importing-country trade restraints.

Rent-Transfer Model

In a partial-equilibrium competitive setting, we know that an import tariff generates revenues which, under an alternative import quota set instead at the tariff-restricted level, will accrue as import premia to the recipients of the quotas.[4]

Richard Brecher of Carleton University and I (Brecher and Bhagwati 1985) have recently shown that this rent-transfer proposition breaks down if we bring in general-equilibrium considerations which essentially imply that the supply and demand curves of partial-equilibrium analysis are not independent of the policy instrument deployed (as assumed in the equivalence analysis). When equivalence breaks down, we also know that we can change the usual equivalence question and ask: Subject to some target value for a variable (e.g, the domestic price-ratio or the quantity of imports), which policy instrument can be used at lower welfare cost? Therefore, in the Brecher-Bhagwati (1985) analysis, VERs and importing country restrictions are compared subject to two alternative targets: that the importing country's domestic import-competing *production* be held constant, and that the quantity of *imports* be fixed instead. It turns out that the rent-transfer proposition holds for the latter but not for the former objective as a general outcome. Their analysis also extends to the possibility that the revenues from the VER and importing-country tariffs trigger revenue-seeking lobbying à la Bhagwati and Srinivasan (1980). In this event, the rent (or revenue) transfer to the exporting country under the VERs is a mixed blessing: it triggers primary waste of resources into revenue-seeking DUP activity. Needless to say, the rent-transfer presumption is even weaker in that event, and VERs need not dominate importing-country trade restrictions from the viewpoint of the exporting country's advantage.

But these recent theoretical refinements need not detract from the notion that VERs are *believed* to transfer rents to the exporting country. For

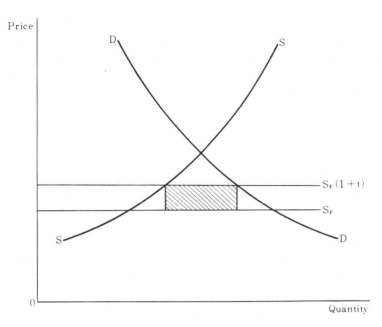

Figure 9.1
DD and *SS* are the domestic demand and supply curves. S_F is the foreign supply curve in absence of VERs. With an import tariff at rate t, the striped rectangular area accrues as revenue to the importing country's government. Under an import quota, it is the premium on import licenses. Under export-quota VERs, the premium accrues to foreign exporters. Under export-tariff VERs, it is the revenue earned by the exporting country's government.

motivating the exporting countries into accepting them, it is the perception, not the objective reality, that matters.[5]

Therefore, when protection is inevitable, the rent-transfer model indicates that the exporting country will prefer VERs to importing-country trade restraints. But to deduce that this will lead to the spread of VERs, and the disuse of Article XIX, for instance, we also have to indicate why the importing country prefers VER's despite the rent-transfer. Here, economists have fallen back on a series of ad hoc arguments:

1. VERs may be quicker to impose, and therefore possibly easier to remove, than importing-country tariffs and quotas.

2. The nontransparency of the VERs as a restrictive device makes it easier to maintain the mythology of, and hence the momentum for, freer trade than enactment of more visible importing-country tariffs and quotas.[6]

3. Compensation for importing-country trade restrictions, in the wake of politically unmanageable "market-disruption"-related pressure for protec-

tion, is easier to manage domestically through VERs—where it is non-transparent and therefore little understood—than with outright subsidies which would draw obvious flak; it is also less disruptive than under Article XIX where the compensation takes the form of reversing tariff concessions to the importing country in turn.[7]

"Porous-Protection" Model

But if this "rent-transfer" model has applicability to industries such as autos, there is yet another model which would appear to provide a better fit to VERs in industries, such as footwear and textiles, where two key characteristics seem to hold:

1. Undifferentiated products (e.g., cheaper varieties of garments and footwear) make it easy to "transship," i.e., to cheat on rules of origin, passing off one's products restricted by VERs as products of countries not covered by VERs.

2. Low start-up cost, and therefore small recoupment horizons, apply in shifting investment and production to adjacent third countries that are not covered by VERs, and hence one can get around (admittedly at some cost) the VERs on one's source by "investment-shunting" to these VER-unafflicted sources, recovering investment costs by the time the VERs get around to covering that alternative source or are eliminated as the political pressure subsides (as happened with U.S. footwear VERs).[8]

In both ways, therefore, VERs in these types of industries can yield a "close-to-free-trade" solution for the exporting countries that are afflicted by the VERs. They can continue to profit from their comparative advantage by effectively exploiting, legally (through investment-shunting) and illegally (through transshipments), the fact that VERs leave out "third countries," whereas importing-country tariffs and quotas do not.

But the question then arises: Why would the protecting importing countries prefer this "porous protection"? Does it not imply that the market-disrupted industry fails to be protected as it would under a corresponding import trade-restraint? Indeed it does. But that is precisely its attractiveness.

If executives want free trade in the "national interest," whereas legislatures respond to the "sectional interests"—the stylized description of the "two-headed" democracies in the United States and the United Kingdom, for sure—then one can produce the argument that executives will prefer to use a porous form of protection that, while assuring market access closer to free-trade levels, will nonetheless manage to appear as a concession to the political demands for protection from the legislature or, in turn, from the constituencies. Doubtless, these protectionist groups, or their congressional spokesmen, will complain in due course about continuing imports. But then the executive can always cite its VER actions, promise to look into them and perhaps bring other countries into the VER net, and continue to obfuscate and buy time without effectively protecting.

This two-headed version of governments, of course, is what Robert Feenstra and I (1980) formally built into a model of what we called the *efficient tariff*, where we postulated that one ("special-interest") branch of government would interact with a protectionist lobby to enact a political-economy tarif while the other ("national-interest") would use the resulting tariff revenues to bribe the lobby into accepting a less-socially-harmful tariff. At the time, many trade theorists reacted by calling this a strange "schizophrenic-government" model since trade theory generally works with a monolithic government. But modeling the government as a multi-headed phenomenon is obviously an advantage and illuminates what the traditional monolithic assumption hides.

Does this "porous-protection" model really contribute to the explanation of why VERs have proliferated as a preferred form of protection? I cannot say that the model has been tested yet, since I have only just formulated it. But let me state the suggestive evidence that led me to think of it in the first place.

1. A number of papers, starting with the pioneering work of Hughes and Krueger (1984), have suggested that, *despite protectionism*, the exports from developing countries continued at a rapid pace right up to 1983. Evidently, protectionism was barking, even biting (with VERs proliferation) but not with great efficiency if these findings were correct. This was a puzzle: Why was protection apparently ineffective?

2. In this context, the brilliant recent papers of Robert Baldwin (1982) (1985) on the "inefficacy" of trade restraints *generally* were most suggestive too. Baldwin did not distinguish between different forms of protection and compare them for their respective degrees of porousness. However, he was a pioneer in drawing our attention to this aspect of the problem. Thus, among the many factors that he discussed are the following:

Consider the response of exporting firms to the imposition of tighter foreign restrictions on imports of a particular product. One immediate response will be to try to ship the product in a form which is not covered by the restriction ... One case involves coats with removable sleeves. By importing sleeves unattached, the rest of the coat comes in as a vest, thereby qualifying for more favourable tariff treatment.

The use of substitute components is another common way of getting around import restrictions. The quotas on imports of sugar into United States only apply to pure sugar, defined as 100 percent sucrose. Foreign exporters are avoiding the quotas by shipping sugar products consisting mainly of sucrose, but also containing a sugar substitute, for example, dextrose ... At one time, exporters of running shoes to the United States avoided the high tariff on rubber footwear by using leather for most of the upper portion of the shoes, thereby qualifying for duty treatment as leather shoes.

Evidently, Baldwin's general discussion enables us to throw light on the Hughes-Krueger findings by underlining the various ways in which developing countries can get around protection in *any* form. What is suggestive, however, and what Baldwin does not himself note, is that VERs may well be more porous than importing-country trade restrictions and that this itself may be an important source of the spread of VERs and of the continuing growth of trade despite their proliferation (or rather, if I am right, *because* of them vis-à-vis alternative forms of protectionism).

3. Yet another important clue to my hypothesis concerning VERs is provided by the oft-repeated contention that the U.S. VERs are "GATTable" in the sense that the United States could have taken them the route of GATT Article XIX and gotten relief but that United States chose instead the VERs route. This contention is not directly verifiable. But, if the contention is correct, then one possible interpretation of it is that the U.S. executive found VERs closer to the free-trade solution than relief under Article XIX: i.e., my hypothesis in this paper would have added support. The question is indeed open; but it remains interestingly suggestive.

4. Then again, it has long been contended by Kiyoshi Kojima (1970, 1978) of Hitotsubashi University in Japan that Japan's DFI (direct foreign investment) is virtuous whereas the Western DFI is not, because Japanese DFI is in labor-intensive industries and hence in line with the host countries' comparative advantage since these are developing countries, whereas Western DFI is in capital-intensive industries. Kojima has developed ingenious arguments to explain this contrast. But evidently, since Japan has been hit hardest by VERs, the compeling explanation might simply be the investment-shunting that I explained earlier![9]

5. Finally, on the importing-country side, the recent book by David Yoffie (1983), entitled *Power and Protectionism*, provides a detailed analysis by an insightful political scientist of the textiles and footwear VERs. Among the

many splendid nuggets lying around in this book, which an economist can pick up and put into his framework, are suggestions that the U.S. executive was indeed often interested in keeping market access to the United States open in the teeth of legislative pressures, and that the exporting countries seemed to prefer VERs also because they perceived the instruments as consistent with aggressive pursuit of export earnings.

If then my hypothesis is correct, the porous-protection model provides an alternative model for the popularity and proliferation of VERs. I would regard it as relevant to industries which have the two characteristics that I distinguished at the outset, whereas the rent-transfer model seems appropriate to highly differentiated, high-start-up-cost industries such as autos. Between them, the two political-economy models provide perhaps the chief explanations for the growth of VERs in recent years. And my porous-protection model also provides simultaneously a model of DFI (i.e., investment shunting).

9.2 VERs: Consequences

VERs, of course, have many consequences other than promoting DFI of the investment-shunting variety (which, in turn, encourages the use of VERs as protective devices if the preceding argument is correct).

Recall that one can distinguish two broad areas of difference between VERs and importing-country restrictions. The first and essential difference relates, of course, to the fact that VERs are exporting-country restrictions: a difference that has already been highlighted and explored in section 9.1. But the other difference which has been focused upon in recent theoretical analysis is that VERs are generally *quantity* rather than *price* instruments.[10] In this event, the consequences of VERs, as opposed to importing-country trade restrictions, can be considered to be the following:

1. *Quality upgrading.* That quotas will lead to quality upgrading was noted in classic articles by Rodriguez (1979) and Falvey (1979). Basically, the argument is that the quota will clear at a market premium. Insofar as higher quality has a higher market price, the use of the quota to export higher-quality products means that the implied ad valorem tariff is lower than that for the lower-quality and hence lower-priced products. Therefore, ceteris paribus, the quota will cause exporters to shift to higher-quality exports compared to what a uniform ad valorem tariff would.

As it happens, several empirical studies have corroborated the upgrading of quality with VERs and quota restraints. The classic work is by Feenstra

(1985) (1986a) on auto VERs by the United States. But estimates have been made of upgrading in steel by Randi Boorstein (1986) at Columbia, and in footwear by Chang (1984) at Wisconsin and by Ben Aw and Mark Roberts (1986).

While therefore these analytical and empirical studies provide support for the notion that quantity restraints on trade will promote upgrading, it is worth noting that the upgrading that has been analyzed to result could well have been the result instead of quality-upgrading incentives provided by the VER-afflicted governments because they wished to increase foreign exchange earnings. Thus, it is interesting that Yoffie remarks that South Korea and Taiwan provided such incentives in order to increase export earnings in the teeth of quantity constraints. Further research therefore needs to be done on this subject, to see whether the upgrading has occurred because of Rodriguez-Falvey type of reasons or simply because of upgrading-incentives artificially created by the exporting countries in reaction to VERs or because of both sets of reasons in varying degrees.[11]

2. *Market structure and nonequivalence.* In the 1960s, I had noted (Bhagwati 1965) that the removal of the assumption of perfect competition could imperil the equivalence of tariffs and import quotas. Thus, for example, if there were a domestic monopolist, a tariff would lead to a lower price and greater output than if instead a quota were set at the import level generated by the tariff.

As it happens, Brian Hindley (1985) has a fascinating application of this so-called Bhagwati proposition where he shows how the EEC's VERs on VCRs were modeled after the competitive model when in fact the merger of Grundig and Philipps led to the creation of a monopolist in the EEC which required the use of the monopoly model and hence totally different rules for fixing quotas. Thus, the rule used was to tighten quotas if domestic output fell: this would reflect the competitive model since reduced output implies that the protection was not enough. But a domestic monopolist would restrict output with a quota, in which case the EEC rule would tighten the quota leading to increased incentive to reduce domestic output! Thus, the extremely simple, pure monopoly model illuminated a real-life case very well.

The recent application of industrial-organization market-structure theory has redemonstrated elegantly the asymmetric effects of quotas and tariffs, implying nonequivalence, in more complex market structures such as duopoly as in Kala Krishna's (1983) interesting work on VERs as "facilitating practices."

3. *Endogenous market structure.* Whereas the nonequivalence literature treats the market structure as exogenously specified as policy instruments are varied, it must be recognized that the market structure itself may reflect, and be adapted by, the policy instrument.

Thus, VERs (when used as quantity instruments) require that the exporting country allocate the quotas. When this is done by invoking a cartel of the industry in question, the result could well be the creation of a cartel where there was none.[12] The result in turn could be the exercise by this cartel of now-perceived and exercisable monopoly power where there was no such perception and exercise before. The VERs would then turn into truly "voluntary" restraints even if they were formally terminated. This is an interesting theoretical possiblity; but, to my knowledge, no empirical case has been demonstrated in support of it.[13]

Again, it would appear that a direct implication of this possibility is that economists may be better off asking the exporting countries to use export tariffs rather than export quotas. The former do *not* require direct allocations. Besides, there is also the added advantage that the rents (revenues) accrue to the government rather than to the industry. Where they accrue to the industry, they can be viewed as a subsidy to the industry which the choice of the trade-restricting device provides to it; and the effect can be viewed as counterproductive to improving one's competitiveness vis-à-vis the exporting-country's industry.

9.3   VERs and Quid pro quo Foreign Investment

Next, I may turn to a wholly new way in which protectionism, whether VERs or importing-country trade restraints, can affect DFI and is indeed doing already. Here I refer, not to the actual enactment of protectionist trade barriers, but rather to the *threat* of imposing or continuing them, often with a view extracting DFI from countries that are the source of the import competition.

This has indeed become a common form of DFI where the foreign firm invests in period 1, at a present loss in the opportunity-cost myopic sense, with a view to influencing favorably the threat of protection in period 2 later and thereby making more profits by keeping markets open. Thus, the aim of such DFI is to *defuse* the protectionist threat; hence I have christened it, in recent writings, as *Quid pro quo* DFI, the quid pro quo to the DFI being the defusing of protectionist threat in period 2 (Bhagwati (1982, 1985, 1986).[14]

How does DFI defuse the protectionist threat? Chiefly, this can occur because DFI is regarded, and can be exploited by lobbies in behalf of the exporting country, as a helpful phenomenon that "saves jobs" in the importing country, whereas the imports are "costing jobs" instead. Such "image building" can influence Congress to withstand the protectionist pressures from the import-competing industry. But it also can reduce that pressure itself by co-opting the protectionist lobbies themselves. An excellent example is provided by "the GM-Toyota deal in the United States apparently prompted by the threat of domestic-content protection ... The *quid pro quo* for Toyota in this deal, which benefits GM and creates jobs for the United Auto Workers (UAW) Union, is evidently the conversion of GM to a free trader stance in local U.S. politics: this is manifest from the fact that GM alone among the U.S. automakers has been arguing against the extension of the auto VERs" (Bhagwati 1985, p. 31). Again, unions are increasingly seeing DFI by the foreign exporter as a preferable job-saving alternative to protection.

The novel phenomenon of quid pro quo DFI—or what might equally be described as "tariff-threat-defusing" DFI to contrast with the "tariff-jumping" DFI—may thus be a generic phenomenon, as when all Japanese DFI is seen as defusing the *overall* threat of protection against Japan. But it can also be an industry-specific phenomenon as when DFI in a specific industry, as in autos, for example, helps to defuse the overall threat of VERs on autos. In either case, the optimal policy of the exporting country will be influenced, raising the question as to what it might be.

Bhagwati, Brecher, Dinopoulos, and Srinivasan (1986) have recently analyzed precisely such quid pro quo DFI and, using a perfectly competitive model, in an extension of the Bhagwati-Srinivasan (1976) market-disruption analysis, developed the anatomy of policy interventions that would be called for in this case where period-2 effects on the probability of protectionism from period-1 DFI levels are taken into account by the exporting country. Dinopoulos and Bhagwati (1986), on the other hand, take a market-structure approach where the necessary interventions are taken by the investing-cum-exporting firms themselves in a simplified partial-equilibrium framework instead.

Evidently, this is a new form of DFI, which has its roots in the new theory of political economy as much as the porous-protection model has. In each case, the interaction between governments and lobbying agents is central to the argument. An interesting question that remains for the analysis of quid pro quo DFI, aside from further modeling that is obviously necessary, is how it contrasts with the *tariff-jumping* DFI with which we are all familiar.

9.4   VIEs: The Latest Innovation

In conclusion, it is interesting to note a new development that has graced the scene of trade policy, albeit in low key to present date. Again, we owe it, as I suspect with VERs, to the problem of Japan in the world economy.

This new phenomenon can be christened "voluntary import expansions" (VIEs): the counterpart on the import side of VERs on the export side of the country against whom these instruments are exercised. Thus, in contrast to the 1930s when Japan was faced only with discriminatory duties and VERs on a variety of her exports such as pencils, electric lamps, watches, and textiles, present-day Japan is faced with an interesting and better demand: to open its markets. Since Japanese markets are assumed by many to be closed beyond what is apparent from their visible trade barriers, the demand for opening Japanese markets has tended to become a demand for "results." Hence there is pressure to accept, as criterion of Japanese good faith, quantity targets for increased imports into Japan from specific countries by specific sectors.

But such quantity targets (e.g., that 20 percent of the Japanese market for semiconductor chips must be supplied by U.S. exporters by a target date: a demand that was successfully resisted by the Japanese as impractical but that still hangs as a sword which could fall if the U.S. suppliers failed to reach that "reasonable" figure) of voluntary import expansions do imply, as do VERs, a departure from the GATT approach which insists on "rules" rather than "outcomes" or "quantities."

While therefore a case can be made in defense of the policy of putting pressure on Japan to assume reciprocal obligations to open import markets rather than to force the closure of Japan's export markets, VIEs hardly seem to be the way to do this. In fact, VIEs not merely violate the GATT approach of going by rules: they are also likely to be explicitly protectionist in reality.

A good example of this danger is provided by the U.S. desire to increase exports of beef to Japan. The United States, in putting pressure for VIEs on Japan, is reported to have wanted a larger quota for U.S. beef rather than genuine trade liberalization where both Japanese and U.S. producers would have lost shares to Australia in the Japanese beef market.

Unless therefore the major trading countries such as the United States keep in view the distinction between VIEs and genuine trade liberalization through forcing down protection elsewhere, we will be simply trading in one kind of departure from the rules of free trade (VERs) for another (VIEs). That certainly would not serve the cause of the principles of free trade.

Notes

An earlier draft of this paper was prepared for presentation at the Western Economic Association Meetings in San Francisco, July 1986. Some of the ideas here have been presented also in a lecture at the World Bank. Helpful comments were received from Elias Dinopoulos, Sunil Gulati, Brian Hindley, Arye Hillman. T. N. Srinivasan, Kar-yiu Wong, and David Yoffie.

1. Among the principal contributions to the new theory of political economy, see in particular Bhagwati (1980), Krueger (1974) and Bhagwati, and Brecher and Srinivasan (1984) on the theory of DUP (directly unproductive profit-seeking) and rent-seeking activities in general equilibrium. An insightful review of one important segment of the new political-economy-theoretic developments, i.e., the DUP-theoretic tariff-seeking literature, by the political scientist Douglas Nelson (1986) is also noteworthy.

2. An important paper embodying the findings of such research is by Nogues, Olechowski, and Winters (1986).

3. I refer here simply to which country enacts the restraint and operates it. That a VER is actually "involuntary" and is forced by the importing country is not relevant to the argument in the text. Again, importing-country quotas could well be de facto turned into VER export quotas if they were assigned directly to exporters rather than to importers.

4. This is the "equivalence" of tariffs and import quotas proposition that I analyzed in the 1960s, showing how it broke down in the presence of market structures other than perfect competition; cf. Bhagwati (1965, 1969).

5. In my judgment, the rent transfers do exist empirically, and the Brecher-Bhagwati analysis may be interpreted as suggesting that these rent transfers are not as large, in a social cost-and-gain sense, as generally believed by looking at premia on VERs.

6. President Reagan did indeed announce the auto VERs on Japan as if he had managed to avoid protection!

7. Also see a fine article by Kent Jones (1984) for further discussion, especially of the interests of third countries.

8. The investment-shunting need only occur insofar as is necessary to meet "value-added" rules on origin, of course, making its cost even less than otherwise.

9. David Yoffie has drawn my attention to the fact that Lou Wells (1983) has looked at the foreign investment decisions by companies in Hong Kong and elsewhere and found that in many cases the investment was to circumvent VERs through foreign assembly.

10. This difference is not essential, as argued already, since VERs could well be levied as exporting-country tariffs rather than as exporting-country QRs. But since they have been QRs in practice, it has become customary to regard them as quantity instruments.

11. I should also add that in contrast to the Rodriguez-Falvey argumentation, another *theoretical* route can lead to quality downgrading rather than upgrading Thus, Feenstra (1986b) has recently noted, "... consider the case where consumers are choosing over a continuum of products indexed by quality ... In a free trade equilibrium, there may be either a positive or negative correlation between quality purchased and surplus received by consumers. That is, consumers purchasing the highest-quality products may receive the largest surplus, or the lowest (zero) surplus, depending on the utility function assumed. Now suppose a quota is imposed, raising the price for any quality product by the same specific amount (as in Falvey). Then the change in *average* quality will depend on which consumers drop out of the market. If consumers purchasing the lower quality products receive the smallest surplus, then they will drop out and average quality will rise. But if consumers purchasing the highest quality products drop out then average quality will instead fall."

12. That this in fact may have happened during the growth of VERs on Japan in the 1930s suggested by Teijiro Uyeda (1936).

13. That restraint has sometimes continued even when VERs have been terminated may merely mean that the restraint, while voluntary, may be simply prudential to avoid new disruption-related complaints and demand for renewed VERs.

14. At a recent conference in Tokyo, Professor Shishido of the International University of Japan related how a 1986 MITI survey suggested that a substantial fraction of the new Japanese DFI in the OECD countries is of this "political," i.e., quid pro quo, variety.

References

Aw, Bee Yan and Roberts, Mark J. 1986. Measuring Quality Change in Quota-Constrained Import Markets: The Case of U.S. Footwear. *Journal of International Economics* 21: 45–60.

Baldwin, Robert. 1982. *The Inefficiency of Trade Policy.* Princeton University, Department of Economics, Frank D. Graham Memorial Lecture, Essays in International Finance no. 150.

Baldwin, Robert. 1985. Ineffectiveness of Protection in Promoting Social Goals. *The World Economy* 8: 109–118.

Bhagwati, Jagdish. 1965. On the Equivalence of Tariffs and Quotas. In Richard Caves et al. (eds.). *Trade, Balance of Payments and Growth.* Amsterdam: North Holland.

Bhagwati, Jagdish. 1969. On the Equivalence of Tariffs and Quotas. In *Trade, Tariffs and Growth*. London: Weidenfed and Nicolson.

Bhagwati, Jagdish. 1980. Lobbying and Welfare. *Journal of Public Economics* 14: 355–363.

Bhagwati, Jagdish. 1982. Shifting Comparative Advantage, Protectionist Demands, and Policy Response. In Jagdish Bhagwati (ed.), *Import Competition and Response*, Chicago: University of Chicago Press.

Bhagwati, Jagdish. 1985. Protectionism: Old Wine in New Bottles. *Journal of Policy Modelling* (Spring): 23–33.

Bhagwati, Jagdish. 1986. *Investing Abroad*, Esmee Fairbairn Lecture, University of Lancaster, England.

Bhagwati, Jagdish, Brecher, Richard, and Srinivasan, T. N. 1984. DUP Activities and Economic Theory. *European Economic Review* (April): 291–307.

Bhagwati, Jagdish, Brecher, Richard, Dinopoulos, Elias, and Srinivasan, T. N. 1986. *Quid pro quo* Investment and Policy Intervention: A Political-Economy-Theoretic Analysis. *Journal of Development Economics*, forthcoming.

Bhagwati, Jagdish, and Srinivasan, T. N. 1976. Optimal Trade Policy and Compensation under Endogenous Uncertainty: The Phenomena of Market Disruption. *Journal of International Economics* 6: 317–336.

Bhagwati, Jagdish, and Srinivasan, T. N. 1980. Revenue Seeking: A Generalization of the Theory of Tariffs. *Journal of Political Economy* 88: 1069–1087.

Boorstein, Randi. 1986. Quality Upgrading in the Steel Industry: The Case of the 1968–74 VRA. Columbia University. Unpublished manuscript.

Chang, E. T. 1984. The Effects of Quantitative Controls on Imports of Footwear from Korea and Taiwan. University of Wisconsin. Unpublished manuscript.

Dinopoulos, Elias, and Bhagwati, Jagdish. 1986. *Quid pro quo* Investment and Market Structure. Paper presented to the Western Economic Association Conference, San Francisco, July 1986.

Falvey, Rodney E. 1979. The Comparison of Trade within Import-Restricted Product Categories. *Journal of Political Economy* 88: 1142–1165.

Feenstra, Robert C. 1980. Monopsony Distortions in an Open Economy: A Theoretical Analysis. *Journal of International Economics* 10: 213–235.

Feenstra, Robert C. 1985. Automobile Prices and Protection: The U.S.–Japan Trade Restraint. *Journal of Policy Modelling* (Spring): 49–68.

Feenstra, Robert. 1986a. Quality Change under Trade Restraints: Theory and Evidence from Japanese Autos. University of California-Davis. Unpublished manuscript.

Feenstra, Robert. 1986b. Addendum to "Quality Change in U.S. Autos, 1980–81: Quality, Employment and Welfare Effects." In R. Baldwin and A. O. Krueger, (eds.), Chicago: University of Chicago Press, 1984. Written for, and appearing in J. Bhagwati (ed.), *International Trade: Selected Readings*, 2d ed. Cambridge: MIT Press.

Feenstra, Robert and Bhagwati, Jagdish. 1982. The Efficient Tariff. In Jagdish Bhagwati (ed.), *Import Competition and Response*. Chicago: Chicago University Press.

Hindley, Brian. 1986. European Community Imports of VCRs from Japan. *Journal of World Trade Law* (March/April): 168–84.

Hughes, Helen, and Krueger, Anne. 1984. Effects of Protection in Developed Countries on Developing Countries. In Robert Baldwin and Anne Krueger (eds.), *The Structure and Evolution of Recent US Trade Policy*. Chicago University Press for NBER.

Jones, Kent. 1984. The Political Economy of Voluntary Export Restraint Agreements. *Kyklos* 37: 82–101.

Kojima, Kiyoshi. 1970. Towards a Theory of Agreed Specialization: The Economics of Integration. In W. A. Eltis (ed.), *Essays in Honour of Sir Roy Harrod*. Oxford: Oxford University Press.

Kojima, Kiyoshi. 1978. *Direct Foreign Investment: A Japanese Model of Multinational Business Operations*. London: Croom Helm.

Krishna, Kala. 1983. Trade Restrictions as Facilitating Practices. Princeton University, Unpublished manuscript.

Kruger, Anne. 1974. The Political Economy of the Rent-Seeking Society. *American Economic Review* (June): 291–303.

Nelson, Douglas. 1986. Economic Theory as Political Theory: The Case of Endogenous Tariff Theory. World Bank, Report DRD-1E. Washington, DC: World Bank.

Nogues, Julio J., Olechowski, Andrzej, and Winters, L. Alan. 1986. *The Extent of Nontariff Barriers to Imports of Industrial Countries*. World Bank Staff Working Papers, No. 789. Washington, DC: World Bank.

Rodriguez, Carlos Alfredo. 1979. The Quality of Imports and the Differential Welfare Effects of Tariffs, Quotas, and Quality Controls as Protective Devices. *Canadian Journal of Economics*, 12(3): 439–449.

Uyeda, Teijero. 1936. *The Recent Development of Japanese Foreign Trade*. Institute of Pacific Relations, Japanese Council, Paper No. 3.

Wells, Louis T., Jr. 1983. *Third World Multinationals: The Rise of Foreign Investment from Developing Countries*, Cambridge: MIT Press.

Yoffie, David. 1983. *Power and Protectionism*. New York: Columbia University Press.

10

Voluntary Export Restrictions versus Import Restrictions: A Welfare-Theoretic Comparison

with Richard A. Brecher

The theoretical analysis of voluntary export restrictions (VERs) is notable for its paucity. In partial equilibrium, Takacs (1978) has compared with them alternative trade restrictions from the viewpoint of "equivalence" as defined and considered by Bhagwati (1965, 1968, 1969, ch. 9) and later writers. Subsequent to theoretical work of Falvey (1979) and Rodriguez (1979), Feenstra (1984) has demonstrated elegantly that Japanese VERs on auto exports to the United States have induced a shift toward higher-quality exports, and has calculated the magnitude as well as analyzed the implications of this shift.

As a long-standing part of the conventional wisdom, moreover, there is also the following principal proposition on VERs: VERs, relative to import restrictions, would be beneficial for the exporting country and detrimental to the importing country in a two-country framework, since they would appropriate[1] to the former the restriction-induced rents that would otherwise accrue to the latter. In fact, in the policy-oriented discussions, as in the analysis of market disruption and proposed changes to GATT Article XIX, it is generally assumed that VERs build into themselves automatic compensation to the exporting countries whose markets are being restricted, and that therefore no explicit compensation needs to be paid when VERs are imposed.[2]

It is the purpose of this paper to subject this conventional wisdom to analytical examination. Our results, in general equilibrium analysis, are startling: they demonstrate that the question is more complex than has been assumed to date.

Section 10.1 briefly outlines the conventional wisdom and its customary theoretical foundation in partial equilibrium analysis. Section 10.2 then introduces general equilibrium analysis of the problem, demonstrating the need for, and analyzing the differential consequences of, the following two alternative assumptions: (1) the policy objective of the two alternative restrictions being compared is to fix the volume of home imports; (2) the objective is instead to fix the home price ratio. For analytic convenience only, we assume that the VERs and the import restrictions are "price" (rather than "command") instruments: that is, we compare export duties abroad with import duties at home.[3] Since either policy therefore generates revenue, the former abroad and the latter at home, we extend our analysis in section 10.3 to the case where the policies lead to "revenue-seeking," as in Bhagwati and Srinivasan (1980); the revenue in this analysis is not assumed to be redistributed in a lump-sum fashion to consumers but instead is assumed to be dissipated to the clients of revenue-seeking lobbyists. Thus, our analysis in section 10.3 is yet another application of what Bhagwati (1982) has termed the theory of "directly unproductive profit-seeking" (DUP) activities, and indeed is a further demonstration of how the introduction of DUP activities has a critical impact on theoretical analysis.

10.1 The Conventional Argument

The proposition that VERs, relative to import restrictions, benefit the foreign country while hurting the home country is demonstrated readily with well-known partial equilibrium reasoning.

In figure 10.1, DD' and SS' are the home import demand and foreign export supply curves. With an import tariff at ad valorem rate FG/GQ, the demand curve shifts to D_tD_t', the international price falls to HO, the domestic price in the home country becomes $HO + EH = EO$, imports are reduced to OQ, and the area of rectangle $EFGH$ represents the revenue accruing to the home government. Now shift the policy to a VER, i.e., an export duty at rate FG/FQ by the foreign government. In this event, the supply curve shifts to S_tS_t' (whereas the demand curve returns to DD'); the domestic price in the foreign country remains HO; the international price rises to EO, which now becomes also the domestic price in the home country; and the revenue represented by rectangle $EFGH$ now is clearly earned by the foreign government. Since the real equilibrium at home and abroad is otherwise undisturbed, the conventional proposition readily follows: VERs, relative to import restrictions, benefit the foreign country and harm the domestic country.

Figure 10.1 clearly assumes perfect competition. To ensure consistency of comparison, the rest of this paper will therefore continue to focus on the perfectly competitive case.

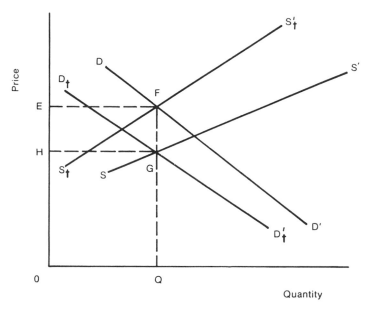

Figure 10.1
The area of rectangle *EFGH*, accruing originally as revenue to the home country,
subsequently accrues instead as revenue to the foreign country when the policy is shifted
from a home import duty at ad valorem rate *FG/GQ* to a foreign VER at rate *FG/FQ*.

10.2   General Equilibrium Analysis

Once we shift to general equilibrium analysis, however, the implicit partial
equilibrium assumption—that the underlying supply and demand curves
are independent of the policies being compared—is no longer valid. In
analyzing the switch from one policy to the other, we must now take into
account the general equilibrium effects of the international purchasing-
power transfer represented by rectangle *EFGH* in figure 10.1. Once these
effects are considered, VERs and import restrictions are no longer "equivalent" policies in Bhagwati's (1965) well-known sense; in other words, the
replacement of one policy instrument by the other does not yield an
identical real equilibrium. It equally follows that we must now distinguish
between alternative objectives (or constraints) subject to which foreign
VERs are compared with home import tariffs, as we do immediately
below.[4]

    It would appear that there are two important reasons for restricting
trade. There may be either a quantity objective, in the sense of a maximum

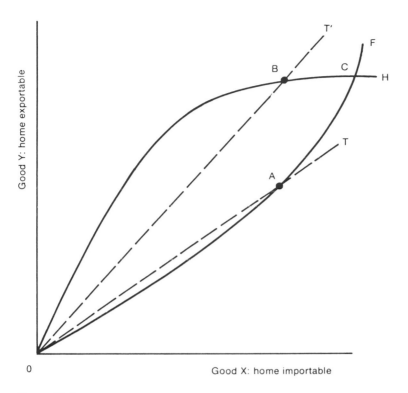

Figure 10.2

acceptable level of home imports, or a price objective, in the sense of a minimum acceptable level for the relative price of the importable within the home country. We consider these objectives now, in turn, comparing a home-country import tariff with an alternative foreign-country VER export tariff in each instance.[5] The revenue generated in either case is assumed in this section to be redistributed to consumers in a Meade-like lump-sum fashion as in conventional general equilibrium tariff theory.

Case 1: Fixed Volume of Home Imports

In figure 10.2, *OH* and *OF* are the free trade offer curves of the home and foreign countries, which export goods Y and X, respectively. As usual, we assume that all offer curves are well behaved, in the sense of never bending back towards the origin. Also, for simplicity of exposition only, all offer curves are assumed to be elastic.

To restrict its imports below the free trade level at point C, the home country can use an import tax to shift curve OH inwards to pass through, say, point A. Alternatively, to achieve the same reduction in trade of good X, the foreign country can impose an export tax which shifts curve OF inwards to pass through point B (vertically above A). By drawing in the usual trade indifference curves, we could readily see that the move from A to B unambiguously raises foreign and lowers home welfare, since the foreign (home) country gets increased (constant) imports for constant (increased) exports. Thus, in this particular case, the welfare effects of switching from home to foreign taxation accord with the conventional wisdom.

It is easy to see intuitively why the conventional wisdom holds here. Home welfare must necessarily decline on shifting from A to B by changing from the import to the export tax, since the terms of trade worsen (from OT to OT') without any mitigating improvement as the volume of imports does not increase. Foreign welfare, on the other hand, must necessarily improve since the terms of trade improve with no offsetting deterioration as the volume of exports does not diminish.

Case 2: Fixed Home Price Ratio

In figure 10.3, where OH is the free-trade offer curve of the home country, an import tax of this country leads to (say) point A, at which the ratio of international (and foreign) prices is given by the slope of ray OT, while the home price ratio is given by the necessarily greater slope of line DD'. Foreign welfare is represented by the trade indifference curve FF', tangent to ray OT at point A, whereas home welfare is given by the trade indifference curve (not shown) tangent to line DD' at A.

When the home country's import tax is replaced by a foreign tax on exports, the equilibrium shifts to point B, where the ray OT' (parallel to DD') intersects OH, so that the home price ratio remains unchanged. By requiring a foreign export tax (rather than subsidy) to keep the home price ratio constant, we are implicitly assuming no Metzler paradox for the home country. Also, without this assumption the home country would have paradoxically used an import $subsidy$ (rather than tax) to achieve the price objective in the first place.

The move from A to B clearly lowers home welfare because home expenditure declines, at constant prices, by OD units of good X. In the case illustrated, however, foreign welfare remains unchanged at the level defined by curve FF'. For this constant-welfare result to occur, we must have point B lying south-west of A, thereby implying that good Y is

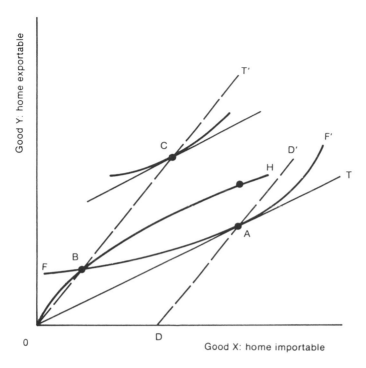

Figure 10.3

inferior in home consumption.[6] (Note that, as at point A, the home country has an undrawn trade indifference curve tangent to the home-price line through point B.) If the home country had a smaller (larger) marginal propensity to consume good Y, ceteris paribus, foreign welfare would fall (rise). Thus, in the event of shifting to the export from the import tax, a rise in foreign welfare would be ensured by normality in home consumption.[7]

Again, the intuition behind this result is readily spelled out. The home country is necessarily hurt by the shift to VERs because, with the domestic price ratio fixed, this shift must imply worsened international terms of trade with no offsetting production and consumption gain. On the other hand, for the foreign country the corresponding improvement in the international terms of trade, and hence welfare can be offset by diminished gains from a reduced volume of exports (which may be a sufficiently large reduction if the home country's exportable good Y is inferior in consumption and therefore the home country's demand for imports falls sharply as its real income falls).

The move from A to B can be decomposed, as follows, into two conceptual stages that provide further insight into our analysis. In the first stage, the home import tax is replaced by a foreign export tax that leaves the domestic price ratios of both countries constant, with the following consequences: the home country goes to B; the foreign country moves to point C, where its (unlabeled) trade indifference curve cutting the new international terms-of-trade ray OT' has a tangent parallel to OT; and (in the example illustrated) the world develops an excess supply of good X (and demand for Y), which is represented by line segment BC. This market imbalance is eliminated in the second stage, by raising the export tax of the foreign country until this country reaches B. The first-stage impact on welfare is negative for the home but positive for the foreign country (as in the partial equilibrium analysis), since we essentially have the primary (constant-price) effect of a purchasing power transfer of OD units (evaluated at the new international terms of trade) from the former to the latter country. The second-stage impact on welfare, however, is zero for the home country, but (in the present illustration) sufficiently negative for the foreign country to offset exactly the first-stage gain of this country. Thus, this case can be interpreted as another example of a transfer payment that paradoxically fails to enrich a recipient whose tax-affected importable is inferior in the donor's consumption, in consonance with results reported by Brecher and Bhagwati (1982) and Bhagwati, Brecher, and Hatta (1985).[8]

As demonstrated by the foregoing treatments of cases 1 and 2, our general equilibrium analysis depends importantly on the importing country's underlying objective, namely, quantity or price. Which of these two objectives is the more realistic? At first glance it may appear that the quantity objective is the appropriate one, since exporting countries and industries are often forced to agree to specific export levels. However, this view is probably naive, since the quantities fixed thus, as with the well-known VERs on autos from Japan, are only an instrumentality through which the government of the importing country seeks to maintain the import-competing industry's price (and hence output): quantities are, in fact, continually renegotiated to ensure such an outcome. If anything, therefore, we would argue that the price objective, distinguished in our formal analysis, is quite possibly the more appropriate one.

10.3   Introducing Revenue-Seeking

We now extend our analysis to incorporate revenue-seeking activity, which draws scarce primary inputs away from the production of goods X and Y, assumed (as usual) to be the only arguments in the national utility functions. Since the burden of DUP activity is shifted from the home to the foreign country when the former's import tax is replaced by the latter's export tax, we would intuitively expect that home welfare may increase at the expense of foreign welfare. This outcome is indeed possible under certain specific conditions, as shown by the following analysis.

Case 3: Revenue-Seeking with Home Imports Fixed[9]

Consider now figure 10.4, where the production possibility frontier for the home country is QQ' drawn for the fixed endowments of capital and labor under constant returns to scale. Initially, with the home country taxing imports, the home price ratio is given by the slope of line AC, which touches curve QQ' at point A. Now, as Bhagwati and Srinivasan (1980) have shown, consumption must then take place on a community indifference curve at point C, where national welfare is maximized subject to expenditure equalling income at factor cost, if (as we assume) revenue-seeking occurs and

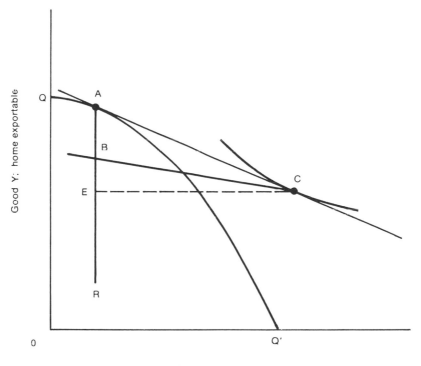

Good X: home importable

Figure 10.4

results in a wastage of resources worth the fully dissipated proceeds of the import tax. Moreover, as they establish, production takes place at B, which is the point of intersection for the following two lines: the international price line BC, drawn through C; and the (generalized) Rybczynski line AR, drawn through A, for the withdrawal of productive factors into revenue-seeking activity.[10]

The Rybczynski line is drawn vertical in figure 10.4, to illustrate the break-even case where a shift from the import to the export tax will have no impact on home welfare. (As we shall subsequently show, moreover, this case readily suggests the alternative conditions under which such a policy shift will instead improve or worsen welfare.) To see the logic of the break-even case, replace the import tax by an export tax such that the international price line facing the home country worsens to AC, which therefore continues to be the domestic price line at home (now that the import tax has been eliminated). Under these circumstances, production remains at point A, consumption stays at point C, and home country's imports of good X remain fixed at CE, as required under the quantity objective. In this case, since consumption is at point C under both the import tax and the export tax, we clearly have the same level of home welfare under either policy.

By similar reasoning, if the Rybczynski line through point A passed instead to the left or right of vertical line AR, replacement of the import tax by the export tax would cause home welfare to rise or fall, respectively. In the former case, for example, the Rybczynski line would intersect the international price line BC to the left of point B, and hence the initial level of home imports would exceed CE. To keep imports fixed at the initial level as required, the home price line would have to flatten (from AC) when the import tax was replaced by the export tax. Thus, the home country would clearly reach a higher indifference curve under this tax replacement scheme. The change in foreign welfare can be evaluated symmetrically to show a gain or loss, respectively, as the foreign Rybczynski line passes to the left or right of a vertical line through the initial production point.

Case 4: Revenue-Seeking with Home Price Ratio Fixed

Since the home price ratio is fixed by assumption, national income at factor cost remains unchanged when the home tax is replaced by the foreign one. Thus welfare of the home country is correspondingly constant, unambiguously. The situation could be described again by figure 10.4 without modification.

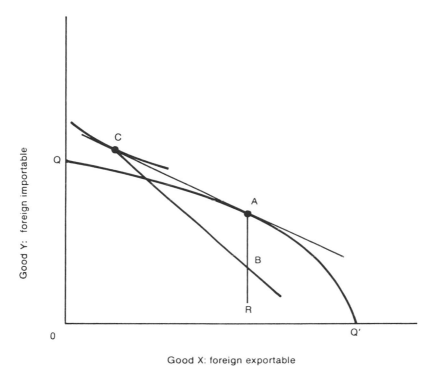

Figure 10.5

To analyze the change in foreign welfare, however, introduce figure 10.5, where QQ' is the production possibility frontier for the foreign factor endowments under constant returns to scale. Initially, given the home country's tax on imports, production is at point A and consumption is at point C, with the slope of line AC giving the ratio of international prices. After the shift to the foreign country's tax on exports, the ratio of international prices is given by the slope of the necessarily steeper line BC (parallel to AC of figure 10.4). If the Rybczynski line AR has the same slope as its home-country counterpart, foreign consumption would remain at point C while production shifted to point B, since the trade triangle constructible from line segment BC of figure 10.5 is then equal to the analogous triangle corresponding to line segment AC of figure 10.4. (This result does *not* require that the Rybczynski lines be vertical, but only that they be equally sloped.) Thus, in this case foreign welfare too is unchanged when the import tax is replaced by the export tax.

Suppose instead that the foreign Rybczynski line passed to the right of the vertical line AR, while the home Rybczynski line was still vertical.

Then, the foreign tax needed to keep consumption at point C in figure 10.5 would raise foreign exports (and hence home imports) above the level consistent with the fixed home price ratio in figure 10.4. Thus, the foreign country would have to raise its tax somewhat more, thereby increasing its domestic relative price of good Y, to keep the international price ratio (now equal to the fixed home price ratio) constant. Therefore foreign welfare would be diminished in figure 10.5, as the foreign price line flattens relative to AC. (Again, what matters is the comparative slopes of the Rybczynski lines, not the absolute slope of either one.) By similar reasoning, a Rybczynski line passing to the left of BC in figure 10.5 (given figure 10.4 as drawn) would imply a rise in foreign welfare.[11]

10.4   Concluding Remarks

Our analysis casts doubts on the conventional wisdom, according to which the home country loses while the foreign country gains if responsibility for trade restriction passes from the former to the latter. In fact, the actual welfare outcomes depend importantly on the objective of trade restriction and on the method of disbursing the resulting (tariff) revenues or (quota) rents.

We have been asked, how important are these analytical complexities *in practice*? Should we not continue believing that, for all practical purposes, VERs replacing import restrictions harm the importing country and enrich the exporting country?

The honest answer has to be that it depends on the case at hand. Evidently, the received doctrine relies on restrictive assumptions, although this reliance has not been appreciated to date. Are these assumptions, such as the absence of lobbying generated by the restrictions, sensible to make most of the time? Apparently not. Reverting to the revenue-seeking analysis, for example, we find that few analysts today would reject out of hand the argument that *some* fractional revenue-seeking activity must be allowed for. In fact, let us take its more intuitive quantity counterpart, premium-seeking: Can there be any doubt that firms will tend to compete for a share of the trade-restricting, premium-fetching licenses? We would argue that this competition is generally an important consideration in the case of quantity-constraining VERs[12] such as those set through the Multifiber Arrangement (MFA) on textiles. Lobbying for licenses occurs not only among firms within each MFA country, but also among the MFA countries themselves, and indeed between these countries and new entrants (as was doubtless the case when China was recently negotiating its textiles share with the United States and therefore impacting on the older exporters' market shares).

Notes

For helpful comments and suggestions, thanks are due to Robert Feenstra, Gene Grossman, Rachel McCulloch, Makoto Yano, and the participants at the Third Annual Conference on International Trade Theory at the University of Western Ontario. Bhagwati's research has been partially supported by the National Science Foundation.

1. Diagrammatic partial equilibrium discussions of this appropriation may be found in a variety of places; see, for example, Bergsten (1975) and Caves and Jones (1973, p. 289). Concern over the international distribution of rents from trade restriction appears also in Meade (1951, ch. 21), who paid careful attention to whether the importing or exporting country enjoys "the margin between the buying and selling price."

2. See Bhagwati (1977) for an analysis of the question of market disruption in the context of GATT Article XIX, and Bhagwati and Srinivasan (1976) for a theoretical analysis of the issue. The former accepts the conventional wisdom on VERs which is reexamined in the present paper.

3. Given the assumptions specified below, our results would hold equivalently for a comparison between export quotas abroad and import quotas at home. Thus, our analysis should be viewed generally as comparing trade-restricting actions by exporters versus importers, regardless of whether the restrictions are imposed by taxes or quotas. Also see note 12.

4. This has been done also in the "equivalence" literature on tariffs versus quotas, as in the important papers by McCulloch and Johnson (1973), Pelcovits (1976), and others. See Bhagwati (1978) for a detailed review and synthesis.

5. As shown by Lizondo (1984), a home import restriction and foreign VER that give rise to the same volume of trade may lead to different domestic price ratios for the home country in a general equilibrium context.

6. This implication is evident from a comparison of points A and B. At A, where home welfare is higher, exports of good Y are greater. Thus, with home production unchanged because of a constant domestic price ratio at A and B, home consumption of good Y at A must be less than at B, implying that Y is an inferior good in the home country.

7. If foreign welfare remains constant, as in figure 10.3, the domestic relative price of good X within the foreign country falls, since curve FF' is flatter at point B than at A. A fall in this price would still occur if the foreign country instead suffered a deterioration in welfare, given that FF' belongs to a family of nonintersecting trade indifference curves. Thus, foreign welfare would rise if the domestic relative price of good X in the foreign country remained unchanged (as in the partial equilibrium

case of figure 10.1) or became larger, although a rise in foreign welfare might occur even with a fall in the domestic relative price of good X within the foreign country.

8. An alternative two-stage decomposition, along the following lines, is also worth considering. In the first stage, the home import tax is replaced by a foreign export tax that leaves constant the volume of international trade in good X, thereby leading both countries to move (as in case 1) vertically from point A to curve OH in figure 10.3, and (in the situation illustrated) causing the home price line to flatten. Therefore, to restore the home price ratio to its original level, the second stage requires raising the foreign export tax until the world reaches final equilibrium at point B. (Ceteris paribus, the magnitude of this tax rise depends positively on the home offer curve's elasticity, which in turn depends negatively on the marginal propensity to consume good Y.) Whereas the first-stage impact on elfare is (as in case 1) unambiguously beneficial to the foreign but detrimental to the home country, the second-stage impact happens (in the present illustration) to be harmful for both countries. Home welfare must thus undergo an overall decrease, while foreign welfare remains (in the example depicted here) unchanged on balance.

9. The following analysis can be readily translated into offer-curve diagrammatics, but is more intuitively understood as developed below.

10. To obtain the equivalence mentioned in note 3, we would clearly have to assume the same technology for rent-seeking with quotas as for revenue-seeking with taxes.

11. If the Rybczynski line in figure 10.4 is not vertical, home output of good X will change. Thus, we must now distinguish between the possible aims of fixing the domestic output of this good and fixing the internal product price ratio, exactly as Bhagwati and Srinivasan (1980) were forced to distinguish between the Metzler output paradox and the Metzler price paradox. Our analysis can be extended readily to handle an output constraint, subject to which the foreign country might still fail to gain at the home country's expense.

12. Note also that the use of VERs, which evidently are an *instrument* constraining quantities, is not to be regarded as automatically implying import restraint as the *objective*. As emphasized by our discussion in section 10.2, a quantity instrument such as a VER may be deployed to achieve a price objective. Failure to make this important distinction could seriously flaw the analysis and interpretation of VERs.

References

Bergsten, C. Fred. 1975. On the Non-equivalence of Import Quotas and "Voluntary" Export Restrictions. In C. Fred Bergsten (ed.), *Towards a New World Trade Policy: The Maidenhead Papers*. Lexington, MA: Lexington Books.

Bhagwati, Jagdish N. 1965. On the Equivalence of Tariffs and Quotas. In Robert E. Baldwin et al. (eds), *Trade, Growth and the Balance of Payments: Essays in Honor of Gottfried Haberler*. Chicago: Rand McNally.

Bhagwati, Jagdish N. 1968. More on the Equivalence of Tariffs and Quotas. *American Economic Review* 58: 142–147.

Bhagwati, Jagdish N. 1969. *Trade, Tariffs and Growth: Essays in International Economics*. Cambridge: MIT Press.

Bhagwati, Jagdish N. 1977. Market Disruption, Export Market Disruption, Compensation, and GATT Reform. In Jagdish N. Bhagwati (ed.), *The New International Economic Order: The North–South Debate*. Cambridge: MIT Press.

Bhagwati, Jagdish N. 1978. *Anatomy and Consequences of Exchange Control Regimes*. Cambridge, MA: Ballinger.

Bhagwati, Jagdish N. 1982. Directly Unproductive Profit-Seeking (DUP) Activities. *Journal of Political Economy* 90: 988–1002.

Bhagwati, Jagdish N., Brecher, Richard A. and Hatta, Tatsuo. 1985. The Generalized Theory of Transfers and Welfare: Exogenous (Policy-Imposed) and Endogenous (Transfer-Induced) Distortions. *Quarterly Journal of Economics* 100: 697–714.

Bhagwati, Jagdish N., and Srinivasan, T. N. 1976. Optimal Trade Policy and Compensation under Endogenous Uncertainty: The Phenomenon of Market Disruption. *Journal of International Economics* 6: 317–336.

Bhagwati, Jagdish N., and Srinivasan, T. N. 1980. Revenue Seeking: A Generalization of the Theory of Tariffs. *Journal of Political Economy* 88: 1069–1087.

Brecher, Richard A., and Bhagwati, Jagdish, N. 1982. Immiserizing Transfers from Abroad. *Journal of International Economics* 13: 353–364.

Caves, Richard E., and Jones, Ronald W. 1973. *World Trade and Payments: An Introduction*. Boston: Little, Brown.

Falvey, Rodney E. 1979. The Composition of Trade within Import-Restricted Product Categories. *Journal of Political Economy* 87: 1105–1114.

Feenstra, Robert C. 1984. Voluntary Export Restraints in US Autos, 1980–81: Quality, Employment and Welfare Effects. In Robert E. Baldwin and Anne O. Krueger (eds.), *The Structure and Evolution of Recent US Trade Policy*. Chicago: University of Chicago Press for NBER.

Lizondo, Jose Saul. 1984. A Note on the Nonequivalence of Import Barriers and Voluntary Export Restraints. *Journal of International Economics* 16: 183–187.

McCulloch, Rachel, and Johnson, Harry G. 1973. A Note on Proportionally Distributed Quotas. *American Economic Review* 63: 726–732.

Meade, J. E. 1951. *The Balance of Payments*. Oxford: Oxford University Press.

Pelcovits, Michael D. 1976. Quotas versus Tariffs. *Journal of International Economics* 6: 363–370.

Rodriguez, Carlos Alfredo. 1979. The Quality of Imports and the Differential Welfare Effects of Tariffs, Quotas, and Quality Controls as Protective Devices. *Canadian Journal of Economics* 12: 439–449.

Takacs, Wendy E. 1978. The Nonequivalence of Tariffs, Import Quotas, and Voluntary Export Restraints. *Journal of International Economics* 8: 565–573.

11

Religion as DUP activity

with T. N. Srinivasan

Can religion be rescued from the dark recesses of our souls and brought into the intellectual folds of the dismal discipline of economics?

Along with mortal suicide and divorce, divine Providence should be readily vulnerable to the desiccated diagnosis of conventional economics. At the same time, a quiet contemplation of the social scene on Sundays in Christian countries, if not a pleasurable afternoon spent with G. K. Chesterson's entertaining Father Brown, immediately suggests that organized religion, where man must stand on the shoulders of other men to reach out to the heavens above, may be yet another DUP (directly unproductive, profit-seeking) activity whose implications can be analyzed in the spirit of the unconventional public-choice-theoretic approach to economics.

Below, therefore, we proceed to center our analysis on organized religion as indeed a DUP-theoretic phenomenon, revealing to our readers the Truth for their Enlightenment. In an appendix, we then consider the heresies of Dixit and Grossman (1984) who, in a contribution laced with frivolity and wit (which we seek to preserve here), have preceded us with an analysis of organized religion which they christened with characteristic inspiration as directly unproductive prophet-seeking activity.

11.1 Three States of Nature: Organized Religion and Counterfactuals

1. To analyze organized religion (OR) and its consequences, we must construct an appropriate counterfactual.[1] There are really two counterfactual states of nature which we could create. We have first simply the economists' conventional, godless world where religion is known not to rear its head at all. Then again, we can have a state of nature where religion does appear but *not* in an organized fashion: i.e., man communes with God but

there are no intermediaries, simply the Lutheran directness or the quiet Hindu contemplation of the Infinite without the instrumentality of the Maharishi's Transcendental-Meditation mantra. The latter, we shall christen the "unorganized religion" (*UR*) state of nature; the former, the "godless" (*G*) state of nature.

Both these counterfactuals are interesting. The *UR* state of nature evidently implies, relative to *G*, that religion "diverts" resources from worldly welfare. But, to suggest therefore that *UR* is a second-best situation and hence *UR* < *G*, we should *impose* the social planner's (and indeed the Marxist) view that the social weight to be assigned to heavenly welfare is zero. If one does not, and instead prefers individual valuation, then *UR* and *G* are simply characterized by different utility functions for the members of the population; and they are each a noncomparable first-best, Pareto-optimal situation. In what follows later, we plan to take both points of view successively, to analyze the impact of the organized religion (*OR*) state of nature: for, each viewpoint leads to a different judgement on organized religion.

Next, we must consider the problem of an appropriate design of the *OR* state of nature. Organized religion does indeed pose intermediaries between man and God. In so doing, it turns religion into a DUP activity. But it simultaneously can affect the relative valuation of worldly and heavenly welfare (formally, a change in the utility function) and the perceived efficacy of prayer (formally, a change in the production function for brownie points in securing heavenly access). The earthly intermediaries of the God in heaven propagate doctrines which vary from a holistic rejection of worldly welfare to a wholesome Calvinistic compatibility of worldly and heavenly welfare; they also determine how many spins of the prayer wheel or rounds of rosary are necessary to secure access to heaven.[2] These two elements must surely be considered necessary and intrinsic attributes of organized religion as we generally know it.

11.2   Organized Religion: Consequences

An appropriate formalization of organized religion and its consequences should then contrast *OR* with *UR* and *G*, allowing the model specification to include the role of prayer, its perceived efficacy, and the relative valuation of worldly and heavenly welfare. We should distinguish between two contrasting approaches to religion: where the supplicant is sovereign and heavenly welfare cannot be disregarded from policy evaluation, and where heavenly welfare is regarded as illusion (like the māyā of Hindu meta-physical speculations) or equally as an opiate,[3] and hence assigned a social valuation of zero such that the three states of nature are ranked only on the scale of worldly welfare.

Case 1: Sovereign Supplicants: The High Road

In this case, we have already remarked that UR cannot generally be rank-ordered vis-à-vis G, since one state of nature introduces heavenly welfare whereas the other does not.

However, UR can indeed, under appropriate conditions, be rank-ordered vis-à-vis OR. The diversion of resources to the intermediaries that engage in DUP activity is evidently a loss since the resource-loss occurs from a first-best situation (Bhagwati, 1982). On the other hand, these very in-termediaries may increase the "efficiency" of prayer, as would epicureans or churchmen who indulge in indulgences, such that one spin of the prayer wheel suffices where two were needed before.[4] If so, this is the equivalent of costless technical progress, albeit in producing the passes to heaven; and this is a welfare-improving effect. The net result could evidently be to give OR the edge over UR.[5] We thus draw the moral: UR and G are non-comparable; where comparable, $UR \gtrless OR$.

Case 2: Valuing Only Worldly Welfare: The Low Road

But if heavenly welfare is wholly disregarded, the rules change and so can the outcome. UR now offends clearly vis-à-vis G: the use of any resources to pray is simply a wasteful, zero-output activity that must necessarily immiserize.

On the other hand, OR cannot be ranked uniquely vis-à-vis UR even if the intermediaries (as in Dixit and Grossman, 1984; see appendix) *merely* regulate heavenly access to their DUP-theoretic advantage. For, the DUP activity will divert resources from production of worldly goods and heavenly passes; but this diversion may, à la Rybczynski "ultrabiased" effects, increase the production of worldly goods and reduce that of heavenly passes, so that worldly welfare rises and paradoxically results in $OR > UR$! The introduction of changes in the rates of substitution between worldly and heavenly welfare, and in the productivity of prayer, can again produce results in either direction. Generally, therefore, $OR \gtrless UR < G$.

11.3   A Mathematical Offering and a Prayer

While these results are evident on slight reflection, we need not appeal to the faith of the faithful for their acceptance. We have developed them, in the conventional manner of our august discipline, in the form of a mathematical offering which is available from us for all those who seek complete knowledge. While the sacred scriptures of the Hindus assert that prayers to all gods must reach the same Supreme Being just as all raindrops reach the same ocean,[6] all models need not yield the same answer. We have therefore two models, each yielding the lessons we have drawn above.[7] In lighting two candles, we also urge the Almighty to count one toward Dixit and Grossman's welfare, and pray that they be rewarded with heavenly access for their sparkling wit and their meritorious first steps without which our own would not have been possible.

Appendix: A Discourse on Dixit and Grossman

Dixit and Grossman (1984), hereafter DG, model organized religion differently from us, as a direct and immediate application of the Bhagwati-Srinivasan (1980) model of revenue-seeking.

In building their necessary counterfactual, DG assume that there is then no religious activity at all, that the production possibility set can therefore be defined properly and exclusively on worldly goods, and that "places in heaven" (the rewards normally reserved for religious activity) are nonetheless present but are simply awarded randomly by an inscrutable omniscient Being with no perceived relationship to exertions and exhortations by the pious.[8] This bleak and brutal world of total determinism is christened, with dark humor, as Nirvana by DG.

Organized religion then intrudes on the scene as a DUP activity. It is assumed that there are only a limited number of places in heaven. The assumption of limited places is invoked by DG simply to generate a scarcity price or rent for heavenly access which then equals in worldly opportunity cost the value of worldly output that the average aspirant is willing to forgo in achieving heavenly access. Once this scarcity price ($\mathring{P}$) of heaven here and now is so determined, organized religion leads to the Church cornering access to these preassigned heavenly slots ($\mathring{N}$), such that the value of the resulting artificially constructed market rents on heavenly access is $\mathring{P}\mathring{N}$. With ministers and cathedrals, like Dennis Robertson's man and spade, moving into this lucrative market till they earn "normal" profits in this DUP activity rather than in gainful employment elsewhere, the result is inevitable social waste. Organized religion has immiserized the population: Marx has triumphed, and the rejoicing of his flock must be sweeter still since the conquest is with neoclassical weapons! DG backtrack a trifle here, arguing that other *unrelated* imperfections may, apropos of Bhagwati and Srinivasan's (1980) discovery of the paradox of negative shadow factor prices, make the diversion of resources to profiting from paradise-seeking of the population socially profitable nonetheless. But that religion, modeled as a DUP activity, creates primary waste and ultimate social loss remains the central message.[9]

In contrast to our analysis in the text, the DG model has two central features that are rather inappropriate: that there are limited places in heaven and further that these are randomly awarded to the population without any religious activity on their past. DG have a heaven but no prayer! The exclusion of prayer distances the model from nearly all religious societies as we know them: for, there are few societies where, even in the presence of fatalism and determinism, prayer, and supplication aimed at earthly reward and heavenly access are absent.[10]

Equally unnatural is the assumption of limited places in heaven. Do not all modern religions assure every convert a place in heaven? Undoubtedly you have to be twice-born to do this in certain religions; and, in this respect, the Christians do it more efficiently than the Hindus since the Hindus generally must (and are indeed fated to) go through death to be reborn, whereas the Christian can do so instantaneously in this very life! But the notion that every soul cannot transcend to heaven, as long as certain necessary and sufficient conditions are fulfilled, appears to contradict the belief propagated by most religions. Religions simply do not seem to pattern their heavenly constructs after the game of musical chairs![11]

Notes

The knowledge embodied in this note was revealed to us, as were the Vedas to the ancient Hindus; no research support therefore needs to be acknowledged.

1. The economist is paralyzed into inaction if a counterfactual is unavailable. As the story goes, an economist, on being asked how his wife was, replies: "Compared to what?" The counterpart of this for psychiatrists is the story where one runs into another and says: "You are fine, how am I?"

2. Organized religion may also serve to reduce, through assurance by the intermediaries, the uncertainty that may haunt the pious in the *UR* state of nature about their prospects for heavenly access. We leave this interesting aspect of organized religion to be modeled by those who doubtless will follow in our footsteps.

3. The reader may want to ponder over the deep implications of the apocryphal Socratic exhange after China's conversion to communism, where the question, "What is the opium of the Chinese masses," has the answer: "opium."

4. A classic example of such "technological innovation" by the Church is provided by Jacques Le Goff's (1984) fascinating intellectual analysis of the birth of Purgatory in the twelveth and thirteenth centuries. By creating a triad where the Purgatory was interjected between Heaven and Hell, and in tying the progress of the souls in the Purgatory to prayers of the living *provided* they were offered through the intermediation of the Church, the Church could be interpreted as innovating to its DUP-theoretic advantage. To quote from Goff (1984, pp. 11–12): "Purgatory is an intermediary other world in which the trial to be endured by the dead may be abridged by the intercessory prayers, the 'suffrages,'of the living... And for the Church, what a marvelous instrument of power! The souls in Purgatory were considered to be members of the Church militant. Hence, the Church argued, it ought to have (partial) jurisdiction over them, even though God was nominally the sovereign judge in the other world. Purgatory brought to the Church not only new spiritual power but also, to put it bluntly, considerable profit, as we shall see. Much of this profit went to the mendicant orders, ardent propagandists of the new doctrine. And finally, the 'infernal' system of indulgences found powerful support in the idea of Purgatory." Again, it is interesting to note that the idea that the Church play this critical intermediating role appears to have been supported and canvassed by none other than St. Augustine. Goff (1984, p. 67) writes: "Augustine is also explicit about who may offer up efficacious prayer for these souls capable of being saved: those affiliated in an institutional capacity with the Church, either the Church itself or 'a few pious men.'" Lest the readers consider St. Augustine's views to be wholly devoid of self-interest, they should heed Gordon Tullock's reminder that he was Bishop of Hippo.

5. If the intermediaries were also to shift the relative weights between worldly and heavenly welfare, then we face again the dilemma that utility functions have changed, and the yardstick for making meaningful comparisons across different states of nature disappears.

6. These syncretic and inclusive sentiments are repeatedly expressed in the Mahābhārata, the Indian epic, especially in the Vishnusahasranāmam and the Celestial Song, the Bhagwat Gītā.

7. Since we must consider the case where only worldly welfare is valued, this is done with simplicity and rigour by assuming in both models a social welfare function which is separable in worldly and heavenly welfare. The models differ however on their "technological" dimensions: in particular, the DUP-theoretic diversion of resources to organized intermediaries is modelled in the "tithes" model as a certain fraction of national income.

8. To quote them, "the important point here is that the mechanism of awarding these places in heaven cannot be influenced by the population, and no resources need be spent in seeking activities" (1984, 1087).

9. In Bhagwati and Srinivasan (1980), and in Bhagwati (1982), the demonstration that DUP activities may be paradoxically welfare-improving is stricter: the second-best considerations are critically related to the DUP activities themselves, as when a distorting tariff itself triggers the revenue-seeking DUP activity.

10. As discussed in the text, moreover, OR can influence the "productivity" of prayer and thereby open up the paradoxical possibility of a welfare-improving organized religion.

11. Alas, there are always exceptions to the most compelling generalizations. Jehova's Witnesses leap to our attention as being faithfully in the DG mold when they interpret, as some of them do, the sealing of the 144,000 members of the 12 Israeli tribes, in the Book of Revelations in the New Testament, as providing an upper bound to heavenly access. We are assured by our pastors, however, that even then it may be sensible to interpret this position as compatible with more places in heaven, with the elite places assigned to the 144,000 and the more proletarian ones open to all others. Evidently, the dual-markets characterization of heaven becomes then an intriguing research agenda!

Secular Works Cited

Bhagwati, J. N. 1982. Directly-Unproductive Profit-Seeking Activities. *Journal of Political Economy* 90 (October): 988–1002.

Bhagwati, J. N., and Srinivasan, T. N. 1980. Revenue-Seeking: A Generalization of the Theory of Tariffs. *Journal of Political Economy* 88 (December): 1069–1087.

Dixit, A., and Grossman, G. 1984. Directly-Unproductive Prophet-Seeking Activities. *American Economic Review* 74 (December): 1087–1088.

Goff, Jacques Le. 1984. *The Birth of Purgatory*. Translated by Arthur Goldhammer from the original *La naissance du Purgatoire* (1981, Editions Gallimard).Chicago: University of Chicago Press.

Scriptures Mentioned

The Book of Revelations, The New Testament.
The Mahābhārata.

Patron Saints Invoked

Karl Marx, T. M. Rybczynski.

III

Immiserizing Growth and Transfers

12   Immiserizing Growth

The theory of immiserizing growth has been developed by theorists of international trade, though it has recently been the focal point of research also by mathematical economists. It is central to understanding several important paradoxes in economic theory and has significant policy implications.

That growth in a country could immiserize it is a paradox that was first noted by trade theorists such as Bhagwati (1958) and Johnson (1955) in the context of the postwar discussions of dollar shortage. They established conditions under which, in a two-country, two-traded-goods framework of conventional theory, the growth-induced deterioration in the terms of trade would outweigh the primary gain from growth. It was shown that this paradox, unlike the paradox of donor-enriching and recipient-immiserizing transfers, was compatible with Walras-stability.

The phrase "immiserizing growth" was invented by Bhagwati (1958) and has now been widely accepted (including by literary editors who have long ceased to insist on changing it to the correct English versions such as "immiserating"), the theory itself being generally attributed (e.g., Johnson, 1967) to this 1958 article. Interestingly, as often in economics, Bhagwati happened to chance upon an early contribution by Edgeworth (1894), where Edgeworth developed an example of what he called "indamnifying" growth; and the controversy surrounding this result at the time and its relationship to the Bhagwati–Johnson analyses of the 1950s was reviewed in Bhagwati and Johnson (1960).

Later, Johnson (1967) demonstrated another paradox of immiserizing growth. If a small country had a distortionary tariff in place, and then exogenously it experienced growth, the result again could be to immiserize the country. Later, Bertrand and Flatters (1971) and Martin (1977) established formally the conditions under which this new paradox of immiserizing growth could arise.

Bhagwati (1968) got to the bottom of these paradoxes and produced the central insight that explains why these, and other immiserizing-growth paradoxes, can readily arise. He showed that, if an economy was sub-optimally organized, the primary gain from growth, measured hypothetically as if the economy had an optimal policy in place before and after the growth, could be outweighed by accentuation of the loss from the distortion-induced suboptimality when growth occurred. In the original Bhagwati (1958) example, since the terms of trade could deteriorate, the economy had monopoly power in trade but was following free trade policy which is evidently suboptimal. In the Johnson (1967) example, the tariff was being used by a small country with given terms of trade and was therefore also a suboptimal policy. In both cases the suboptimal policy produced losses which were accentuated by the growth and then managed to outweigh the primary gains from growth that would have occurred if optimal policies were in place. The result was a powerful generalization that placed the theory of immiserizing growth squarely into the central theory of distortions and policy intervention (Srinivasan, 1987) that lies at the core of the modern theory of trade and welfare. Evidently, immiserizing-growth paradoxes could arise only if there was a distortion present.

This central result has immediate implications. If an economy has a suboptimal money supply, growth could be immiserizing. If trade policy is highly distorted, growth could be immiserizing. The well-known results of trade theory, which show that free trade need not be welfare-improving relative to autarky (e.g., Haberler, 1950) under distortions, are also seen as instances of immiserizing-growth theory; free trade augments the availability set relative to autarky, implying "as-if" growth, and if distortions are present, then there is no surprise to the immiseration that free trade brings. Again, if a country uses tariffs to induce foreign investment (the so-called tariff-jumping investment that developing countries often used in the postwar period), such investment could immiserize the host country: this being a simple extension of the Johnson (1967) demonstration, argued to be relevant to analysis of developing countries in Bhagwati (1978), and analyzed extensively in Bhagwati (1973), Brecher and Alejandro (1977), Hamada (1974), Minabe (1974), Uzawa (1969), and Brecher and Findlay (1983). Yet another important insight from the immiserizing-growth theory is that, in the new and growing theory of DUP (directly unproductive profit-seeking) activities, which incorporates several quasi-political activities essentially into the corpus of economic theory, a DUP activity that wastes resources directly need not cause ultimate loss of welfare. This is because the waste may occur from a suboptimal situation, thus resulting in welfare-improvement paradoxically. This is the obverse of immiserizing growth: in one case, growth immiserizes; in the other, throwing away or wasting resources enriches. This is at the heart of the contention in Bhagwati (1980) that an exogenous tariff at t percent may be welfare-superior to an endogenous tariff, procured by tariff-seeking lobbies that have diverted uses to such DUP activity, also at t percent. Several such implications of the theory of immiserizing growth are discussed in Bhagwati and Srinivasan (1983, ch. 25).

Two further developments need to be cited. First, the dual of immiserizing growth, when such growth is due to factor accumulation, clearly yields negative shadow factor prices. This aspect is relevant to certain formulations in cost—benefit analysis; see, in particular, Findlay and Wellisz (1976), Diamond and Mirrlees (1976), Srinivasan and Bhagwati (1978), Bhagwati, Srinivasan, and Wan (1978), and Mussa (1979).

Next, mathematical economists such as Aumann and Peleg (1974), and then Mas-Colell (1976) and Mantel (1984), among others, have rediscovered the original immiserizing-growth paradox, illustrating how economists working apart or in different traditions may rediscover one another's findings, often decades apart. A synthesis of the two literature has been provided in Bhagwati, Brecher and Hatta (1984). A complete and formal reconciliation of the conditions established in Bhagwati (1958) and in Mas-Colell (1976) and Mantel (1984) for the original immiserizing-growth paradox is provided by Hatta (1984).

Bibliography

Aumann, R. J., and Peleg, B. 1974. A note on Gale's Example. *Journal of Mathematical Economics* 1: 209–211.

Bertrand, T., and Flatters, F. 1971. Tariffs, Capital Accumulation and Immiserizing Growth. *Journal of International Economics* 1(4): 453– 460.

Bhagwati, J. 1958. Immiserizing Growth: A Geometrical Note. *Review of Economic Studies* 25 (June): 201–205. Reprinted in *International Trade: Selected Readings*, ed. J. Bhagwati, Cambridge: MIT Press, 1981.

Bhagwati, J. 1968. Distortions and Immiserizing Growth: A Generalization. *Review of Economic Studies* 35 (October) Reprinted in J. Bhagwati, *The Theory of Commercial Policy*, vol. 1. Cambridge: MIT Press, 1983.

Bhagwati, J. 1973. The Theory of Immiserizing Growth: Further Applications. In *International Trade and Money*, eds. M. Connolly and A. Swoboda. Toronto: University of Toronto Press.

Bhagwati, J. 1978. *Foreign Trade Regimes and Economic Development: The Anatomy and Consequences of Exchange Control*. Cambridge, MA: Ballinger.

Bhagwati, J. 1980. Lobbying and Welfare. *Journal of Public Economics* 14 (December): 355–363.

Bhagwati, J. Brecher, R., and Hatta, T. 1984. The Paradoxes of Immiserizing Growth and Donor-Enriching "Recipient-Immiserizing" Transfers: A Tale of Two Literatures. *Weltwirtschaftliches Archiv* 120(4): 228–243.

Bhagwati, J., and Johnson, H. G. 1960. Notes on Some Controversies in the Theory of International Trade. *Economic Journal* 60: 74–93.

Bhagwati, J., and Srinivasan, T. N. 1983. *Lectures on International Trade*. Cambridge: MIT Press.

Bhagwati, J., Srinivasan, T. N., and Wan, H., Jr. 1978. Value Subtracted, Negative Shadow Prices of Factors in Project Evaluation, and Immiserizing Growth: Three Paradoxes in the Presence of Trade Distortions. *Economic Journal* 88: 121–125.

Brecher, R., and Díaz-Alejandro, C. 1977. Tariffs, Foreign Capital and Immiserizing Growth. *Journal of International Economics* 7: 317–322. Reprinted in *International Trade: Selected Readings*, ed. J. Bhagwati. Cambridge: MIT Press, 1981.

Brecher, R., and Findlay, R. 1983. Tariffs, Foreign Capital and National Welfare with Sector-specific Factors. *Journal of International Economics* 14: 277–288.

Diamond, P., and Mirrlees, J. 1976. Private Constant Returns and Public Shadow Prices. *Review of Economic Studies* 43: 41–48.

Edgeworth, F. Y. 1894. The Theory of International Values. *Economic Journal* 4: 35–50, 424–443, 606–638.

Findlay, R., and Wellisz, S. 1976. Project Evaluation, Shadow Prices and Trade Policy. *Journal of Political Economy* 84(3): 543–552.

Haberler, G. 1950. Some Problems in the Pure Theory of International Trade. *Economic Journal* 60: 223–240.

Hamada, K. 1974. An Economic Analysis of the Duty-Free Zone. *Journal of International Economics* 4(3): 225–241.

Hatta, T. 1984. Immiserizing Growth in a Many-Economy Setting. *Journal of International Economics* 17: 335–345.

Johnson, H. G. 1955. Economic Expansion and International Trade. *Manchester School of Economic and Social Studies* 23(2): 95–112.

Johnson, H. G. 1967. The Possibility of Income Losses from Increased Efficiency or Factor Accumulation in the Presence of Tariffs. *Economic Journal* 77: 151–154. Reprinted in *International Trade: Selected Readings*, ed. J. Bhagwati. Cambridge: MIT Press, 1981.

Mantel, R. 1984. Substitutability and the Welfare Effects of Endowment Increases. *Journal of International Economics* 17: 325–334.

Martin, R. 1977. Immiserizing Growth for a Tariff-Distorted, Small Economy. *Journal of International Economics* 3(4), 323–326.

Mas-Colell, A. 1976. En torno a una propiedad poco atractiva del equilibrio competitivo. *Moneda y Crédito* 136: 11–27.

Minabe, N. 1974. Capital and Technology Movements and Economic Welfare. *American Economic Review* 64: 1088–1100.

Mussa, M. 1979. The Two-Sector Model in Terms of Its Dual: A Geometric Exposition. *Journal of International Economics* 9(4): 513–526. Reprinted in *International Trade: Selected Readings*, ed. J. Bhagwati. Cambridge: MIT Press, 1981.

Srinivasan, T. N., and Bhagwati, J. 1978. Shadow Prices for Project Selection in the Presence of Distortions: Effective Rates of Protection and Domestic Resource Costs. *Journal of Political Economy* 86(1). Reprinted in *International Trade: Selected Readings*, ed. J. Bhagwati. Cambridge: MIT Press, 1981.

Uzawa, H. 1969. Shinon jiyutato kokumin keizai (Liberalization of foreign investments and the national economy). *Ekonomisuto* 23 (December): 106–122.

13

The Paradoxes of Immiserizing Growth and Donor-Enriching "Recipient-Immiserizing" Transfers: A Tale of Two Literatures

with Richard A. Brecher and Tatsuo Hatta

Two phenomena have received considerable attention (since Gale 1974 and Aumann and Peleg 1975) in mathematical economics literature, and (since Leontief 1936 and Bhagwati 1958) in trade-theoretic literature over a substantially longer period:

1. the paradoxical possibility of immiserizing growth, to use Bhagwati's (1958) phrase now in general currency, such that an agent is worse off after growth of its endowment[1], or its "dual" counterpart of negative shadow prices of factors as in Srinivasan and Bhagwati (1978), or what Aumann and Peleg (1975) discussed as the "advantageous destruction of endowments" by an agent, and

2. the paradoxical possibility of an immiserized recipient, or of an enriched donor, or both simultaneously, when a donor makes a transfer to a recipient[2].

It is not at all surprising that the theorists on these two sides of the street have not noticed one another: this is a common scientific phenomenon. As it happens, the neglect can be assigned to either side. Bhagwati (1958, 1968a) was missed by Aumann and Peleg (1975) in the case of the paradox of immiserizing growth, and Gale (1974) was missed by Brecher and Bhagwati (1981) in the case of the transfer paradoxes, to focus only on the initiating writings in the two massive, recent literatures on these paradoxes in trade (and public-finance) theory and in mathematical economics.[3]

The present paper is designed to build a bridge between these two literatures on each of the two sets of paradoxes. The precise questions addressed by the two sets of theorists have reflected their respective traditions. The central theorems derived by them, therefore, appear at first blush to have little relationship with one another. Even the conditions established for the paradoxes to obtain, in what appear to be identical models, seem at times to be different and contradictory. In view of the central importance of these phenomena and their analysis, for several critical areas of theory and policy, the objective of the present paper hardly needs to be justified. Section 13.1 deals with immiserizing growth. Section 13.2 considers the transfer paradoxes.

13.1   Immiserizing Growth

Trade-Theoretic Analysis

We begin with Bhagwati's (1958) analysis of immiserizing growth, prompted by the concern over the postwar dollar shortage. Consider an economy with endowed primary factors producing two traded goods entering a conventional social utility function, $U(C_1, C_2)$, where C_1 and C_2 are the consumption levels of the two goods, 1 and 2. Let the growing country be I, the outside country being II. Then, following well-known analysis, we can write the effect of endogenous growth on country I's welfare as

$$\frac{dU^I}{dD_e^I} = \frac{\partial U^I}{\partial C_1^I} \cdot \left[\frac{\gamma^I + \varepsilon'^I + (\varepsilon^{II} - 1)}{(\varepsilon^I + \varepsilon^{II} - 1)} \right], \tag{1}$$

where D_e^I is the national expenditure of I, γ^I is the change in the production of I's importable good at constant pregrowth goods prices, ε^I and ε^{II} are the import demand elasticities of countries I and II, respectively, and $\varepsilon'^I = (\varepsilon^I - m^I)$ and $\varepsilon'^{II} = (\varepsilon^{II} - m^{II})$ are the compensated import-demand elasticities of I and II, respectively, whereas m^I and m^{II} are the marginal propensities to import.

Now immiserizing growth implies that $dU^I/dD_e^I < 0$. Bhagwati (1958), therefore, deduced that (1) if Walras-stability (or its equivalent, the Marshall-Lerner condition) obtains, i.e., $\varepsilon^I + \varepsilon^{II} - 1 > 0$, and (2) because $\varepsilon'^I > 0$ since it is the compensated elasticity, then immiserizing growth requires that *either* $(\varepsilon^{II} - 1) < 0$ *or* $\gamma^I < 0$.

Now, by a well-known relationship, $(\varepsilon^{II} - 1) = n^{II}$ is the foreign country II's offer-curve elasticity of supply of exports with respect to price. If $n^{II} < 0$, it means that the growing country I operates on country II's offer curve in the inelastic range QR in figure 13.1.

On the other hand, $\gamma^I < 0$ means that the "output effect" on the supply of the importable good, at the pregrowth goods price-ratio, is negative: i.e., at constant goods prices, the importable good's production falls *absolutely*

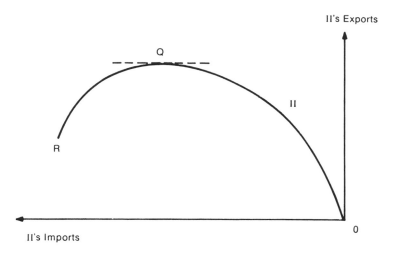

Figure 13.1

with the productivity change or factor supply augmentation that causes growth. Drawing on Rybczynski (1955) for the case of factor accumulation and on Johnson (1967) and Findlay and Grubert (1959) for the case of productivity change, trade theorists have long recognized that $\gamma^I < 0$ can indeed arise.[4]

We also make now, from the viewpoint of the mathematical economics (abbreviated hereafter to "math-econ") literature, the following three observations.

1. If one deals with changes in endowments of the traded *goods* directly, as the math-econ literature does in using exchange models with given endowments of goods rather than primary factors that interact with technology to produce the goods, the condition $\gamma^I < 0$ has an important consequence. This condition implies that the growth consists of an initial endowment change such that the value of national income or expenditure at initial goods prices indeed increases (i.e., $dD_e^I > 0$), reflecting the postulated growth, but that some *component* of the change in goods endowment is negative. Specifically, the endowment increase, *in goods*, is such that the total value of the endowments increases at initial goods prices but the endowment of one component, the importable good, is diminished.

Suppose, therefore, that one is interested in the math-econ theorists' following question: can we rule out the possibility of immiserizing growth for *any* conceivable type of endowment increase, by putting restrictions only on demand? The clear implication of the Bhagwati (1958) analysis is that such an Impossibility Theorem could not be proven, since $\gamma^I < 0$ is compatible with any *demand* restrictions one may well choose to impose for the proposed theorem. To put it another way, such an Impossibility Theorem could be shown *only if* the possibility of $\gamma^I < 0$ were implicitly or explicitly excluded. In the exchange model of the math-econ theorists, this means assuming that the goods endowment increases, or strictly does not fall, for *every* good. We will say more on this below, when we directly discuss the math-econ literature.

2. Next, note that the trade-theorist does not "go behind" the demand elasticities to specification of the underlying demand assumptions with respect to whether goods are net or gross substitutes, or complements. Suppose that we were to do this, while continuing to assume that Walrasian (*tâtonnement*) stability obtains. Then it is immediately evident that, since the growing country I has both goods as necessarily net substitutes, the compensated elasticity $\varepsilon'^I > 0,$[5] whereas if the foreign country II has both goods as gross substitutes, the uncompensated elasticity $n^{II} > 0$ and hence $(\varepsilon^{II} - 1) > 0$. If $\gamma^I \geq 0$, i.e., diminution in the production of the importable good (or equivalently its endowment in the exchange model) at constant prices is ruled out, and if Walrasian stability is assumed, then it is evident that we must have $dU^I/dD_e^I > 0$ in eq. (1).

Therefore, with Walras-stable markets, and with endowment changes necessarily nonnegative, the demand assumptions that goods are net substitutes in the growing country (an assumption necessarily satisfied in a 2-good world) and gross substitutes in the foreign country should suffice to rule out the paradox of immiserizing growth.

3. But suppose now that we do not wish to assume that markets are Walras-stable. Then, we cannot assume that the denominator in eq. (1) is necessarily positive, i.e., that $(\varepsilon^I + \varepsilon^{II} - 1) > 0$. Therefore, we need an added restriction on demand in the growing country if we wish to rule out immiserizing growth. To see this, rewrite the denominator as $[(\varepsilon'^I + m^I) + (\varepsilon^{II} - 1)]$. Now, $(\varepsilon^{II} - 1) > 0$, since demand in country II is characterized by gross substitutability. With demand in the growing country I characterized by net substitutability, $\varepsilon'^I > 0$. However, $m^I < 0$ is possible and the importable good may be sufficiently inferior to make $(\varepsilon^I + \varepsilon^{II} - 1) < 0$ and hence $dU^I/dD_e^I < 0$, ushering in the paradox which we seek to rule out! Therefore, $m^I \geq 0$ must be assumed as well: i.e., if we assume that the *growing* country does not have inferior goods, that assumption along with the other demand restrictions (and the restriction that $\gamma^I \geq 0$) will then guarantee the absence of immiserizing growth.

Math-Econ-Theoretic Analysis

Our preceding three remarks are, in fact, designed precisely with a view to the math-econ-theoretic literature on immiserizing growth. While Aumann and Peleg (1975) simply constructed an example, in an exchange economy, of such a phenomenon (formulating the question rather as one of enriching destruction of endowments), the next important contribution is by Mas-Colell (1976).

Mas-Colell, who assumed that changes in the endowment (in his exchange economy) were nonnegative for every component (i.e., $\gamma^I \geqslant 0$), showed that the paradox at issue could be ruled out in the 2-good model if goods were normal for the agent in question (i.e., country I above) and if the aggregate excess demand function of all other consumers (i.e., the foreign country II above) exhibited the property of gross substitution.[6] Our remarks above demonstrate exactly, in terms of the trade-theoretic algebra, why the Mas-Colell result is correct and how it relates to the conditions for immiserizing growth as derived by Bhagwati (1958) from eq. (1).

Mantel (1982) basically shows the invalidity of the Mas-Colell conjecture that, *even in the many-good case*, it would be sufficient to assume such normalcy and gross substitutability to rule out immiserizing growth. The assumption of net substitutability characterizing the agent's (I's) excess demand function needs to be explicitly added. This need follows intuitively from the fact that net substitutability does not continue to hold automatically when we proceed to more than two commodities. Hatta (1982) has formally extended the results of both Bhagwati and Mantel to an *n*-commodity economy with variable production.

We have thus established fully the correspondences between the theorems and the insights developed in the trade-theoretic and the math-econ-theoretic literatures on immiserizing growth. One other important insight on the trade-theoretic side, however, has no parallel on the math-econ-theoretic side and needs to be mentioned.

Trade theorists have argued that the phenomenon of immiserizing growth, while discovered in the context of a country/agent sufffering a growth-induced deterioration in its terms of trade in a competitive world in both Bhagwati (1958) and Aumann and Peleg (1975), reflects an underlying rationale that is perfectly general. This rationale has been developed as the generalized theory of immiserizing growth in Bhagwati (1968a). It is shown there that growth *in the presence of a distortion* can be immiserizing. For, the loss imposed by a distortion may be accentuated in the postgrowth situation. In the Bhagwati (1958) example, and the subsequent Aumann and Peleg (1975) example, the distortion is simply the failure to exercise the economic agent's monopoly power: free trade is not an optimal policy when the terms of trade are not fixed[1]. The "dual" counterpart of immiserizing growth is the concept of "negative shadow factor prices", developed in Srinivasan and Bhagwati (1978), and Bhagwati, Srinivasan and Wan (1978). This concept has been widely used in trade-theoretic and public-finance-theoretic literature and applies to "highly distorted" situations where the withdrawal of resources (as in Aumann and Peleg) from "productive" use leads to welfare improvement rather than to welfare loss.

It is not really surprising that this particular insight has not emerged independently from the general-equilibrium analysis of the math-econ theorists but has originated on the trade-theoretic side. The latter set of theorists typically examines positive and normative aspects of a problem from the viewpoint of single agents: the nation state. Failure to exercise monopoly power is therefore a foreign distortion from that perspective, as argued in Bhagwati (1971). However, from the viewpoint of the former group of theorists, who typically take a worldwide or total-system efficiency view, the situation of an economy with all agents and institutions characterized by perfect competition is not a distortionary one. Since the immiserizing growth phenomenon involves a distortion from a single agent's perspective, it is only natural that the math-econ literature has not independently chanced upon the generalized theory of immiserizing growth.

13.2 Transfer Paradoxes: Immiserized Recipient, Enriched Donor, and Double Perversity

Having synthesized the two literatures on immiserizing growth, we now turn to a bridge-building exercise on the transfer paradoxes.

While the transfer problem looks superficially like the growth case, there is in fact a critical difference that leads to important asymmetries of outcomes. In the immiserizing growth case, there is postulated growth of endowments for *one* agent. In the transfer case, the endowments must change for (at least) *two* agents. Trade theorists have been explicit about the resulting differences. However, the early math-econ-theoretic literature on the transfer paradoxes—starting with the transfer paradox in Gale (1974), which prompted in turn the immiserizing growth analysis of Aumann and Peleg (1975)—may have left in consequence an impression of ambiguity in this regard.[8]

Trade-Theoretic Analysis

We start again from the trade-theoretic side since, as with immiserizing growth, the central contributions on the math-econ side quickly and intuitively fall into place in light thereof.

The trade-theoretic analysis begins with Leontief's (1936) classic demonstration that, for a 2-agent transfer model, an immiserizing transfer is possible. Samuelson (1947) subsequently observed that this early Leontief paradox was incompatible with Walras-stable markets.[9] This observation set the stage for a long neglect of the paradoxical possibility until Johnson (1960) and Komiya and Shizuki (1967), on the one hand, and Brecher and Bhagwati (1981), on the other hand, independently reopened the question of the transfer paradoxes in the context of Walras-stable markets in the framework of 3-agent analysis.[10]

Here, we draw on Bhagwati, Brecher and Hatta's (1982a) analysis—rather than the initiating Brecher and Bhagwati (1981) treatment—since it lends itself more readily to the desired bridge-building with the math-econ-theoretic analysis.

Bhagwati, Brecher and Hatta consider a duality formulation, allowing for full substitution in production and consumption, writing their model for three countries/agents: α the donor, β the nonparticipant (as far as the transfer process is concerned), and γ the recipient. (Of course, this γ is not related to the γ^1 used in the previous section.) Adopting their notation, let q denote the relative price of good X, T the value of the transfer in terms of good Y, u^i the welfare of country $i (=\alpha, \beta, \gamma)$, and $x^i(q, u^i)$ the *compensated* import-demand function—as introduced originally by Hatta and Fukushima (1979) and Hatta (1977)—for country i. The Bhagwati-Brecher-Hatta analysis then establishes the following propositions (assuming, without loss of generality, that the marginal utility of good Y in the pre-transfer equilibrium equals unity for every country):

$$\frac{du^\alpha}{dT} = \frac{x_q - x^\beta(x_u^\beta - x_u^\gamma)}{\Delta}, \tag{2}$$

$$\frac{du^\gamma}{dt} = -\frac{x^q - x^\beta(x_u^\beta - x_u^\alpha)}{\Delta}, \tag{3}$$

where $\Delta \equiv x^\alpha x_u^\alpha + x^\beta x_u^\beta + x^\gamma x_u^\gamma - x_q$, $x_q \equiv x_q^\alpha + x_q^\beta + x_q^\gamma$, and subscripts always indicate partial differentiation with respect to a particular variable (e.g., $x_u^i \equiv \partial x^i / \partial u^i$ and $x_q^i \equiv \partial x^i / \partial q$). In the case of Walras-stable markets, moreover, $\Delta > 0$.

Next, concentrating on the donor's welfare, apply the Slutsky equation to (2) to get

$$\frac{du^{\alpha}}{dT} = \frac{x_q^{\alpha} + x_q^{\gamma} + \overline{x}_q^{\beta} + x^{\beta}x_u^{\gamma}}{\Delta},$$ (4)

where $\overline{x}^{\beta}(q)$ is the uncompensated import-demand function for the non-participant country β. With $\Delta > 0$ for Walras-stable markets, and assuming without loss of generality that $\overline{x}^{\beta} < 0$ (i.e., country β exports X), we see that the paradox of donor enrichment will arise only if *either* $x_q^{\gamma} < 0$, *or* $\overline{x}_q^{\beta} > 0$ or both: i.e., *either* X must be an inferior good to the recipient *or* the offer curve of the nonparticipant country must be inelastic. Similarly, for immiserization of the recipient (with $du^{\gamma}/dT < 0$), *either* $x_u^{\alpha} < 0$ *or* $\overline{x}_q^{\beta} < 0$, or both.

Now, two remarks are in order. First, the remarkable thing about the results stated above is not that they demonstrate the possibility of Walras-stability-consistent transfer paradoxes or, better still, that they establish the necessary conditions for such paradoxes to arise. Rather, it is that Bhagwati, Brecher, and Hatta go on to demonstrate that their results depend critically, just as the immiserizing growth results do, on the presence of a distortion. Thus, if the donor and the recipient set an optimal, common external tariff against β, the paradoxes cannot arise. Needless to say, this trade-theoretic insight is not to be found on the math-econ-theoretic side, presumably for much the same reason, as stated above, why the generalized theory of immiserizing growth came from the trade-theoretic side instead.

Second, suppose that one wants to ask the question: Given any arbitrary parametric specification of the donor (α) and the recipient (γ), can we *always* embed them in a world economy, i.e., choose a suitable nonparticipant (β), such that the paradoxes in question could arise? Our answer then would be rather intuitively in the affirmative. Since we know from (4) that x_q^{β} can be chosen to be sufficiently positive (i.e., β's offer curve can be chosen to be sufficiently inelastic) to produce the donor-enrichment paradox, it is immediately evident that β's characteristics can be chosen always such that either or both paradoxes will arise. This, in fact, is the main result of the Guesnerie-Laffont (1978) paper in the math-econ-theoretic literature on the transfer problem, which we discuss immediately now.

Math-Econ-Theoretic Literature

The classic note of Gale (1974) simply and beautifully produced an example where the donor, in a 3-agent exchange model, was enriched along with the recipient. However, in this contribution, the Walras-stability-consistency of this donor paradox was not explicitly investigated, though it is possible to verify that the example does indeed satisfy such stability. While, moreover, Gale did not examine the paradoxical possibility of immiserization of the recipient, it is immediately intuitive that, if the donor paradox can be shown, so can the recipient paradox: simply have γ repay the transfer, thereby immiserizing α!

Gale's (1974, p. 64) real problem, however, was the he could not introduce substitution in consumption into his example: "I should point out, however, that my example is one with nonsmooth preferences, and several attempts to construct examples involving smooth preferences have been unsuccessful, so that for the present the question of existence of smooth examples of this phenomenon remains open."[11] As it happens, if the reader looks at eq. (2) above from Bhagwati, Brecher and Hatta (1982a),[12] it is immediately evident that substitution *dampens* the possibility of the donor paradox arising, and, from eq. (3), we can see that the same conclusion applies to the recipient's immiserization paradox. Gale's puzzlement is thus resolved by the trade-theoretic analysis, in an illuminating fashion.

Presented with Gale's striking example, Guesnerie and Laffont (1978, p. 840) in one of the important contributions on the math-econ side, raised the question: "Considering *a group of agents* with given characteristics, can they belong *to an economy* in which they could *find profitable to reallocate their initial endowments?*" Their answer was unambiguous: "'Nearly' any group of agents may be imbedded in an economy (and even in infinities of economies) in which it will find (infinities of) possibilities of advantageous 'cheating' on initial endowments" (i.e., transfer paradoxes). Our analysis in the preceding subsection makes the Guesnerie-Laffont result fully intuitive. Their theorem is tantamount to arguing that a nonparticipant β, and indeed an infinity of β's, can be suitably chosen, for any pre-chosen α and γ, such that a transfer between α and γ will yield the paradoxes at issue.

But we can go beyond this Guesnerie-Laffont result, utilizing eqs. (2) and (3) above, to argue the following Impossibility Theorem, stating it in math-econ terms for the 2-good, 3-agent Bhagwati, Brecher, and Hatta model:

Theorem 1   If all goods are normal for the recipient ($x_u^\gamma > 0$, therefore) and the donor ($x_u^\alpha > 0$, therefore), and the excess demand functions for the non-participant country are characterized by gross substitutability ($\bar{x}_q^\beta < 0$, therefore), the paradoxes of donor enrichment and recipient immiserization can be ruled out in the presence of Walras-stable markets.

In conclusion, we must mention the interesting math-econ-theoretic contribution of Balasko (1978), who utilizes differential methods to analyze the question of transfer paradoxes between Walras-stable equilibria in the older 2-good, 2-agent context of Leontief and Samuelson. Balasko apparently builds on the fact—noted by Marshall—that unstable equilibria are surrounded by stable ones in a 2-good model. Hence, a transfer may shift the world from a stable equilibrium on one side of the unstable point to another stable equilibrium on the other side. Therefore, while a transfer paradox cannot obtain locally in the neighborhood of each stable equilbrium, such a paradox appears to be obtainable globally in the sense just indicated.

All this is readily understood in terms of the familiar trade-theoretic technique of transfer-shifted offer curves, which permit production to be variable of course. Thus, turn to figure 13.2, where *OD* and *OR* are the pre-transfer offer curves of the donor and recipient, respectively, while the

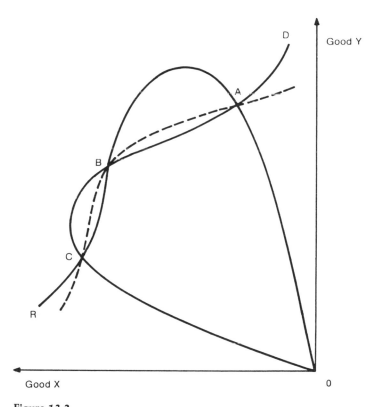

Figure 13.2

dashed curve *ABC* is the world's efficiency locus formed from the common tangencies of trade-indifference curves (not drawn) for the two agents.[13] As may be readily verified, the contract curve *ABC* must everywhere lie between the two offer curves *OD* and *OR*.[14] Points *A* and *C* are stable equilibria, whereas the equilibrium at point *B* is unstable. As the world moves continuously along the contract curve from point *A* through point *B* to point *C*, the recipient's welfare successively increases at the expense of the donor's

Figure 13.3 reproduces (from figure 13.2) the recipient's offer curve and the world's contract curve, but omits the donor's offer curve to avoid clutter. As a result of the transfer equal, say, to the length *OO'* in terms of good *X*, curve *OR* shifts to *O'R'*.[15] (These two curves cannot intersect at any point, since the unique indifference curve through such a point of intersection would—impossibly—have to touch both rays joining the point to origins *O* and *O'*.) Similarly, the donor's offer curve shifts to *O'D'* (not drawn), which must intersect curves *O'R'* and *ABC* at points *A'*, *B'*,

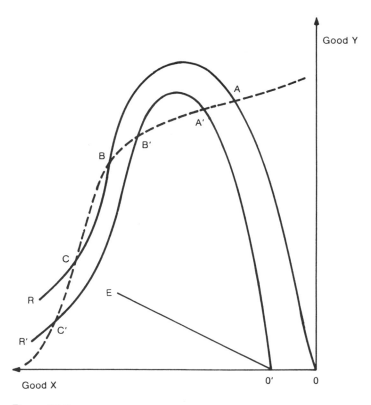

Figure 13.3

and C'. As before, there is one unstable equilibrium (B') flanked by two stable ones (A' and C').

If the world begins at point A before the transfer, the post-transfer equilibrium is at either A' or C'. Therefore, in either case, the recipient's welfare must increase at the donor's expense.

Alternatively, the world could be initially at point C. Then, the transfer would again immiserize the donor and enrich the recipient if the resulting equilibrium is at point C', but would paradoxically have the opposite effects on welfare if instead point A' were the post-transfer equilibrium.[16]

As Balasko notes, no paradox could arise if equilibrium were unique either before or after the transfer. If curve OR in our figure 13.3 were redrawn to eliminate all but one of the pre-transfer equilibria, the only remaining equilibrium before the transfer would be at point A, from which paradoxical movements are impossible as shown above. Similarly, no paradox could arise if instead curve $O'R'$ were redrawn to eliminate exactly two post-transfer equilibria, since point C' would be the only remaining equilibrium after the transfer.[17] In this way, we can readily understand Balasko's theorem 2, which may be rephrased as follows:

Theorem 2   Within the 2-good, 2-agent model, transfer paradoxes are possible if and only if multiple equilibria are present in both (pre-transfer and post-transfer) situations and the initial equilibrium is neither the donor's best nor (equivalently) the recipient's worst.

But, before leaving Balasko, we must still consider the following important question. Under Walrasian *tâtonnement*, could the world ever adjust to the post-transfer equilibrium A' after starting at point C before the transfer? The answer to this question is unambiguously negative, as demonstrated in the next paragraph. Consequently, the possibility of transfer paradoxes is more apparent than real under the postulated mechanism of adjustment.[18]

In figure 13.3, let the initial equilibrium be at point C. Thus, before the transfer, the world's product–price ratio is given by the slope of ray OC (not drawn), parallel to ray $O'E'$, which is the price line immediately after the transfer but before Walrasian *tâtonnement* commences to clear world markets. (By well-known reasoning, ray $O'E$ passes above or below point C' as the recipient's and donor's marginal propensities to import sum to less or more than unity, respectively.) Since ray $O'E$ necessarily passes below point C and hence below point B' (the unstable equilibrium in the post-transfer situation), the world must eventually reach point C'. (By familiar reasoning, the adjustment process would lead instead to point A' if and only if ray $O'E$ passed—impossibly—above point B'). Thus, the transfer unambiguously enriches the recipient and immiserizes the donor.[19]

This welfare result genealizes readily, as follows, to any (odd) number of equilibria:

Theorem 3   Within the 2-good, 2-agent model, a transfer always moves the world along the contract curve, from one stable equilibrium to another, in the direction that involves increasing the recipient's welfare at the donor's expense.

Of course, this proposition need no longer hold if Walrasian *tâtonnement* is abandoned in favor of some other adjustment rule (perhaps a political one), in which case the transfer might lead the world paradoxically from point C to point A'. Under these circumstances, however, a move from point C to point A without any transfer might be equally possible, thereby casting doubt on the significance of a transfer per se as an explanation of the welfare paradox. In any case, for any initial equilibrium, there always exists one or more recipient-enriching (donor-immiserizing) post-transfer equilibria satisfying the Marshall-Lerner condition, as made clear by figure 13.3. This last result is perhaps not surprising in view of the insight provided by the trade-theoretic analysis of multiple equilibria in the presence of tariffs. As shown by the analysis of Bhagwati (1968b), Kemp (1968), and Vanek (1965), raising an existing tariff may paradoxically enrich a small atomistic economy in the presence of multiple equilibria, but then an immiserizing equilibrium must also exist in the higher-tariff situation.

Notes

The original stimulus for writing this paper came when, having completed our (1982a, 1982b) two-part study, we came across Guesnerie and Laffont (1978) on the transfer paradoxes, and when Avinash Dixit referred us to Mantel (1982) and Mas-Colell (1976) on immiserizing growth and sent us unpublished notes on Mantel's (1982) paper. Our thanks are due to Avinash Dixit, Robert Feenstra and Elhanan Helpman for helpful conversations on the substance of the present paper. Partial financial support for this research was provided to Bhagwati by the National Science Foundation.

1. Edgeworth (1894, 1899), in an early contribution discovered and discussed in Bhagwati and Johnson (1960), used the phrase "indamnifying growth".

2. The terminology of an "immiserized recipient" and "enriched donor" is from Bhagwati, Brecher, and Hatta (1982a, 1982b). The phrase "immiserizing transfers from abroad" was used in Brecher and Bhagwati (1982).

3. Gale, and Brecher and Bhagwati, in turn, were preceded by Johnson (1960) and Komiya and Shizuki (1967) in important contributions that have only recently been rediscovered.

4. Therefore, the inelasticity of the foreign offer curve (i.e., $n^{II} < 0$) is not a *necessary* condition for immiserizing growth—although this point has not always been clearly recognized. If we were to assume, however, complete specialization on the exportable good, we would have $\gamma^I = 0$; hence $n^{II} < 0$ would indeed become a necessary condition for immiserizing growth.

5. For a 2-good model, the net substitutability assumption is necessarily satisfied. $\varepsilon'^I > 0$ follows when we also assume that production responses to price change are normal.

6. He also considers an alternative assumption to the 2-good model, namely that the agent (I) has a log-linear utility function. As Mantel (1982) shows, either implies that the agent's demand function exhibits the property of net substution.

7. Trade theorists have considered many other examples of immiserizing growth: e.g., Johnson (1967) has shown how growth may be immiserizing for a "small" country with fixed terms of trade but a "distortionary" tariff in place.

8. However, the important papers of Mas-Colell (1976), Mantel (1982), and Guesnerie and Laffont (1978) are entirely clear on this point.

9. In terms of the notation underlying eq. (1) above for immiserizing growth, and defining T as the transfer from country I to country II, we can derive

$$dU^{II}/dT = (\varepsilon'^I + \varepsilon'^{II})/(\varepsilon^I + \varepsilon^{II} - 1).$$

With Walras-stable markets, $(\varepsilon^I + \varepsilon^{II} - 1) > 0$. And with the compensated elasticities in the numerator necessarily positive, dU^{II}/dT is necessarily positive, thus ruling out immiserization of the recipient. Symmetrically, dU^I/dT is necessarily negative, ruling out the enrichment of the donor.

10. The possibility of such transfer paradoxes arising despite Walrasian stability has been shown also in the presence of price distortions (such as tariffs, production and consumption taxes) by Brecher and Bhagwati (1982) and Bhagwati, Brecher and Hatta (1982b) in the international context, and in the context of internal redistribution by Hatta (1973). Here, we ignore this alternative resurrection of the transfer paradoxes consistent with Walrasian stability.

11. In his footnote 1 on page 64, Gale mentions other nonsmooth examples by McFadden and by Drèze and Gabszewicz. Subsequent discussion also with a fixed-coefficients model of exchange (in a "North–South" context within the literature of development economics) can be found in Chichilnisky's (1980) paper; see, however, Srinivasan and Bhagwati's (1983) comments on this paper.

12. Brecher and Bhagwati (1981)—and Yano (1983) written independently in 1981 at Cornell University as a mimeographed paper and proceeding from Gale's (1974) work—also focus on the role of substitution effects in consumption and in

production. We are grateful to Murray Kemp for drawing our attention to an earlier version of Léonard and Manning (1983), who provide a smooth example of Gale's (1974) phenomenon in an exchange economy with fixed endowments of goods.

13. Readers interested only in the exchange model, as analyzed by Balasko, may interpret our point O to be the endowment bundle of an Edgeworth box, and our curve ABC to be the efficiency locus of the same box.

14. The results below would not be qualitatively affected by either of the following possible complications stemming from sufficiently strong inferiority in consumption: curves OD and OR could eventually (but only temporarily) bend back toward the origin; and curve ABC could be positively sloped in part.

15. Without qualitatively affecting the results below, the transfer could be respecified in either of the following two ways: in terms of good Y; or in terms of a combination of both goods, not necessarily both in positive amounts, provided that the sum of these amounts is positive at initial equilibrium prices.

16. Incidentally, figure 13.3 also illustrates neatly the Leontief-Samuelson possibility of welfare paradoxes between Walras-unstable equilibria, with a transfer-induced movement from point B to point B'.

17. A fortiori, no paradox could arise if curves OR and $O'R'$ both yield unique equilibria, even if an in-between position of the recipient's offer curve (for an intermediate transfer smaller than the length OO') gives rise to multiple equilibria. This situation corresponds to Balasko's figure 1.

18. On this point—but confined to an exchange economy without any mention of Balasko—see also the independent discuss of Postlewaite and Webb (undated, pp. 5, 6). For drawing our attention to their unpublished manuscript, we are grateful to John Chipman.

19. The reader may wonder whether the same conclusion would hold if the pre-transfer equilibrium were at point B, an unstable equilibrium, rather than C. The answer is yes. We have demonstrated this, and established general results on global stability, in Bhagwati, Brecher, and Hatta (1983).

References

Aumann, Robert J., and Bezalel Peleg. 1975. A Note on Gale's Example. *Journal of Mathematical Economics* 2: 209–211.

Balasko, Yves. 1978. The Transfer Problem and the Theory of Regular Economies. *International Economic Review* 19: 687–694.

Bhagwati, Jagdish N. 1958. Immiserizing Growth: A Geometrical Note. *Review of Economic Studies* 25: 201–205.

Bhagwati, Jagdish N. 1968a. Distortions and Immiserizing Growth: A Generalization. *Review of Economic Studies* 35: 481–485.

Bhagwati, Jagdish N. 1968b. Gains from Trade Once Again. *Oxford Economic Papers*, N.S., 20: 137–148.

Bhagwati, Jagdish N. 1971. The Generalized Theory of Distortions and Welfare. In Jagdish N. Bhagwati et al. (eds.), *Trade, Balance of Payments and Growth*. Amsterdam: North Holland pp. 69–90.

Bhagwati, Jagdish N., and Harry G. Johnson. 1960. Notes on Some Controversies in the Theory of International Trade. *Economic Journal* 70: 74–93.

Bhagwati, Jagdish N., Richard A. Brecher, and Tatsuo Hatta. 1982a. The Generalized Theory of Transfers and Welfare (I): Bilateral Transfers in a Multilateral World. Mimeo. *American Economic Review* 73 (1983): 606–618.

Bhagwati, Jagdish N., Richard A. Brecher, and Tatsuo Hatta. 1982b. The Generalized Theory of Transfers and Welfare (II): Exogenous (Policy-Imposed) and Endogenous (Transfer-induced) Distortions. Mimeo. Forth-coming in *Quarterly Journal of Economics*.

Bhagwati, Jagdish N., Richard A. Brecher, and Tatsuo Hatta. 1983. Comparative Statics in the Theory of International Trade Revisited: A Global Analysis. Unpublished Manuscript.

Bhagwati, Jagdish N., Thirukodikavai N. Srinivasan, and Henry Wan, Jr. 1978. Value Subtracted, Negative Shadow Prices of Factors in Project Evaluation, and Immiserizing Growth: Three Paradoxes in the Presence of Trade Distortions. *Economic Journal* 88: 121–125.

Brecher, Richard A., and Jagdish N. Bhagwati. 1981. Foreign Ownership and the Theory of Trade and Welfare. *Journal of Political Economy* 89: 497–511.

Brecher, Richard A., and Jagdish N. Bhagwati. 1982. Immiserizing Transfers from Abroad. *Journal of International Economics* 13: 353–364.

Chichilnisky, Graciela. 1980. Basic Goods, the Effects of Commodity Transfers and the International Economic Order. *Journal of Development Economics* 7: 505–519.

Edgeworth, Francis Y. 1894. The Theory of International Values. *Economic Journal* 4; part I: 35–50; part II: 424–443; part III: 606–638.

Edgeworth, Francis Y. 1899. On a Point in the Theory of International Trade. *Economic Journal* 9: 125–128.

Findlay, Ronald, and Harry Grubert. 1959. Factor Intensities, Technological Progress and the Terms of Trade. *Oxford Economic Papers*, N.S., 11: 111–121.

Gale, David. 1974. Exchange Equilibrium and Coalitions: An Example. *Journal of Mathematical Economics* 1: 63–66.

Guesnerie, Roger, and Jean-Jacques Laffont. 1978. Advantageous Reallocations of Initial Resources. *Econometrica* 46: 835–841.

Hatta, Tatsuo. 1973. Compensation Rules in Multiple-Consumer Economics. Johns Hopkins University, Baltimore. Mimeo.

Hatta, Tatsuo. 1977. A Recommendation for a Better Tariff Structure. *Econometrica* 45: 1859–1869.

Hatta, Tatsuo. 1982. Immiserizing Growth in a Many-Commodity Setting: A Generalization of Bhagwati, Mascolell, and Mantel. John Hopkins University, Baltimore. Mimeo. Forthcoming in *Journal of International Economics*.

Hatta, Tatsuo, and Takashi Fukushima. 1979. The Welfare Effect of Tariff Rate Reductions in a Many Country World. *Journal of International Economics* 9: 503–511.

Johnson, Harry G. 1960. Income Distribution, the Offer Curve, and the Effects of Tariffs. *Manchester School of Economics and Social Studies* 28: 215–242.

Johnson, Harry G. 1967. The Possibility of Income Losses from Increased Efficiency or Factor Accumulation in the Presence of Tariffs. *Economic Journal* 77: 307–309.

Kemp, Murray C. 1968. Some Issues in the Analysis of Trade Gains. *Oxford Economic Papers*, N.S., 20: 149–161.

Komiya, Ryutaro, and T. Shizuki. 1967. Transfer Payments and Income Distribution. *Manchester School of Economics and Social Studies* 35: 245–255.

Léonard, Daniel, and Richard Manning. 1983. Advantageous Reallocations: A Constructive Example. *Journal of International Economics* 15: 291–295.

Leontief, Wassily. 1936. Note on the Pure Theory of Capital Transfer. In *Explorations in Economics: Notes and Essays Contributed in Honor of F. W. Taussig*. New York, pp. 84–91.

Mantel, Rolf. 1982. Substitutability and the Welfare Effects of Endowment Increases. Paper presented to Econometric Society Meetings in Mexico, February. Forthcoming in *Journal of International Economics*.

Mas-Colell, Andreu. 1976. En torno a una propiedad poco atractiva del equilibrio competitivo. *Moneda y Crédito*, no. 136: 11–27.

Postlewaite, Andrew, and Michael Webb. n.d. *The Effects of International Commodity Transfers: The Possibility of Transferor-Benefitting, Transferee-Harming Transfers*. University of Pennsylvania and University of Kentucky. Mimeo.

Rybczynski, Tadeus M. 1955. Factor Endowment and Relative Commodity Prices. *Economica* 22: 336–341.

Samuelson, Paul A. 1947. *Foundations of Economic Analysis*. Cambridge, MA.

Srinivasan, Thirukodikavai N., and Jagdish N. Bhagwati. 1978. Shadow Prices for Peoject Selection in the Presence of Distortions: Effective Rates of Protection and Domestic Resource Costs. *Journal of Political Economy* 86: 97–116.

Srinivasan, Thirukodikavai N., and Jagdish N. Bhagwati. 1983. On Transfer Paradoxes and Immiserizing Growth: Part I. *Journal of Development Economic* 13: 217–222.

Vanek, Jaroskav. 1965. *General Equilibrium of International Discrimination: The Case of Customs Unions.* Cambridge, MA.

Yano, Makoto. Welfare Aspects of the Transfer Problem. *Journal of International Economics* 15: 277–289.

IV

Trade in Services

14 International Trade in Services and Its Relevance for Economic Development

Economics, as we all know to our regret if we are wedded to conventional wisdom and to our reward if we wish to write our next *magnum opus*, has a habit of being overtaken by reality. This is nowhere more true than in the area of services.

Until only a decade ago, economists tended to equate services with "nontraded goods." Doubtless, they were aware that occasionally a country's nationals bought foreign insurance policies or shipped goods in foreign bottoms. Indeed, if nothing else, their increased jetsetting to exotic lands to attend conferences and deliver lectures would have seemed to remind them of the possible tradability of skilled services. A sophisticated economist should certainly have therefore noticed that the wholesale equating of services with nontraded goods was not quite consistent with reality.

But the weight of tradition continued to favor the older perception which might be best described as the "haircuts view" of services. Haircuts, universally considered as a service, typically cannot be had long distance, at least as of now. They have therefore been a classic example of how and why services are nontraded. Though, having procrastinated on getting a haircut this summer and gotten a cheaper one in consequence in India, I must say that even this example frays a little at the margin. But what this mainly proves is that few rules are totally unimpregnable. I must recall the embarrassing moment for Noam Chomsky, the celebrated linguist, who asserted in a public lecture that, in every human language, two negatives make a positive but two positives do not make a negative only to have my good friend, the philosopher Sidney Morgenbesser, shout from the back of the room in rich Yiddish: "Yeah, yeah?"

Of course, today services are increasingly traded. International rules and regimes for overseeing and facilitating such trade have become increasingly the focal point of concern in international negotiations. Continuing equation of services with nontraded goods would appear therefore to be a travesty.

Nonetheless, it is useful, as a point of departure for my main theme today, to reflect more closely on why services have been traditionally regarded as synonymous with nontraded goods. Such an exercise serves to throw light on the reasons why trade in services, as distinct from goods, poses new and difficult problems. I shall take this opportunity also to digress at the outset on the empirical and theoretical puzzles and problems that preoccupied economists when they thought of services as nontraded goods, turning later to the shifting concerns that arise now that services are considered tradable instead.

14.1 Characteristics of Services

In our classrooms, we typically write traditional utility functions as defined on the availability of "goods and services" conveying to the students that there is a difference between the two while, of course, proceeding to analyze the problems at hand as if there was none. The attempt at distinguishing between the two, along the lines of the classical economists, who sought correspondingly to contrast "productive" and "unproductive" labor, has long disappeared from the modern scene. It has survived only in the national accounts of the socialist countries, which persist in excluding from national income the component of what we would call today "final demand" services.

On the other hand, our national income accounts, both in their sectoral composition of value added as also in the sectoral breakdown of final expenditures in GDP, continue to draw upon the distinction between goods and services. The latter total, in focusing only on final expenditure, excludes the producer or intermediate services that enter the production process. Again, the IMF balance of payments procedures distinguish services as invisibles in the current account and proceed to differentiate factor service from nonfactor services, and the former in turn from remittances that are instead categorized as transfers. The latter practice is in consonance with James Meade's prescription in his classic work on *The Balance of Payments*, based on the theory that what people (as distinct from foreign investment) produce abroad is part of the *foreign* national income and hence a remittance therefrom is a transfer, an assumption that sits wholly ill at ease with much modern international migration that consists simply of relocation without change in nationality.[1]

How do services, so defined and measured in accounts that economists devise and constantly use, differ conceptually from goods? A glance at the sectors that are categorized as services is suggestive. Hotels and restaurants, education, medical services, communication, insurance, government, barber and beauty shops: these are among the common listings under the umbrella of services. What do they have in common that would legitimate the practice of setting them apart from "goods"?

Several attempts at defining the unique characteristics of services have been made. Among the least appealing is the criterion that services have a relatively low value of commodities embodied in them as intermediate inputs. Aside from the fact that this fails to provide an endogenous cutoff point in the continuum of goods and services, it is also a criterion that would exclude sectors such as retailing from categorization as services since the goods retailed must surely be treated as intermediates and are often a high proportion of retail sales.

I believe that Professor Hill, who has addressed the question splendidly in a classic paper 1977, offers interesting observations on the matter. Thus, he remarks:

The production of a service cannot generally be distinguished from that of a good by means of the technology used but by the fact that the producer unit operates directly on goods which already belong to the consumer of the service. (1977, p. 319)

Services are consumed as they are produced in the sense that the change in the condition of the consumer unit must occur simultaneously with the production of that change by the producer: they are one, and the same change ... the fact that services must be acquired by consumers as they are produced means that they cannot be put into stock *by producers*. (1977, p. 337; italics added).

These descriptions or criteria immediately suggest exceptions. Thus, Peking duck cooked, served and eaten in a Chinese restaurant is not altogether nonstorable by producers: many of us have suffered from being served leftovers from the freezer at restaurants we do not care to visit again. Yet, by and large, it is true that restaurants do service us in the sense that Professor Hill describes: our use of the service occurs practically simultaneously with its provision by the producer of the service. Again, messages are now storable and indeed stored by "answering services," thus violating the letter again of the definition that suggests that services are nonstorable because they are used as they are provided.

But I would say that the equation of services with nonstorability, resulting from the simultaneity of provision and use thereof, is a useful and generally sensible criterion. Its utility consists in the fact that, as I shall argue presently, this characteristic bears critically on the issues that the question of tradability of services raises for theory and for trade policy.

The *other* characteristic of services that Professor Hill's discussion pin-points is the fact that services occur *between* different economic agents. This, of course, immediately implies that the definition of services reflects economic organization or "market structure." The simple act of having Mr. Smith paint your goods in the assembly line by hiring him from another firm rather than by employing him directly will shift his contribution to national value added from being a good to being a service. This leads to the familiar "in-house out-house" connundrum that has plagued all analysts of questions such as the share of services in national income by sector of origin.

The popular conception that services are nontraded derives critically from the first of these two characteristics. If services must be used as they are produced, then a pertinent observation follows: there must be necessary *interaction* between the user and the provider of the service. A producer of goods, by contrast, can produce but store and generally transact with users at any subsequent time.

But this interaction, in turn, implies that we can contemplate two essential categories of services: *first*, those that necessarily require the physical proximity of user and the provider; and *second*, those that do not, though such physical proximity may indeed be useful. I drew this important distinction sharply in my recent article in *The World Economy* (1984, p. 101):

Basically one has to draw a distinction between services as embodied in the supplier of the services and requiring their physical presence where the user happens to be and services which can be disembodied from the supplier and provided without physical presence being necessary.[2]

Physical Proximity Essential

The class of services where physical proximity is essential is again usefully thought of as consisting of three categories:

Category 1: Mobile-Provider, Immobile-User
There is an extraordinarily important class of services that *requires* that the provider go to the user, where the reverse mobility is simply impossible. When the M-6 was being built, and an Indian or South Korean construction firm was bidding for the contract, the designs and skilled inputs could perhaps be provided from home base. But the labor services simply could not have been provided except by moving Indian or South Korean labor to

England where the motorway was to be built. Supplies of brute, Ricardian-style, basic labor services must be relocated where the user is, exactly as we have seen in the Middle-East during the 1970s and indeed the way your ancestors took mine to East Africa to build the railways many years ago.

Category 2: Mobile-User, Immobile-Provider
Next, there is another important class of services where the user must move to the provider because there is really no way to do it the other way around. Thus, open-heart surgery simply cannot be done in Zaire because, even though Dr. Cooley can go from Houston to Kinshasa, there is no way the necessary support and hospital care can be duplicated or even approximated. Again, President Houphouët-Boigny cannot enjoy French cuisine in the elegance of Maxim's in Abidjan but must travel to Paris to so indulge himself. And I cannot shop in the English ambience of Harrods except when I am in London. In this class of services, the location-specificity of the provider arises from the fact that the service provided is a vector of characteristics where some key elements are simply not transferable geographically to the user's location, whereas in the preceding category this location-specificity applied instead to the user of the service.

Category 3: Mobile-User and Mobile-Provider
Finally, there is a range of services where mobility is symmetrically possible. Haircuts, tailored suits, lectures, etc., are in principle transmittable between user and provider in either's location, the only difference being the cost of so doing.

Physical Proximity Inessential: The "Long-Distance" Services

But then there is also the second broad class of services where, while physical proximity between providers and users may be useful, it is not strictly speaking necessary.

There are basically what we should christen "long-distance" services, in the sense that transactions do not require the immediacy of geographical proximity. Traditional banking and insurance services fall into this category, I should imagine, because loans could be secured by mail or telephonic transactions, and insurance policies are indeed often so purchased. Again, retailing of the Sears-Roebuck stores variety, where one orders by catalog, is an example which fits the "long-distance" pattern, whereas retailing in my Harrods example is not.

I shall return to these distinctions below. But it is immediately evident, from reflecting on them, why services have tended to be internationally nontraded to date.

For the predominant class of services that require physical proximity, it is evident that the cost of the necessary mobility has often made it prohibitive for trade to occur, thus shifting such services into the ranks of nontraded activities internationally. And, in cases where such costs may not have been prohibitive, restrictions on the mobility of labor across countries have served to inhibit service transactions that required the provider to get to the user of the services. These restrictions have traditionally tended to apply to unskilled labor services rather more stringently than to skilled services. However, regulatory provisions by professional guilds, often indulging in what we call today directly unproductive profit-seeking (DUP) behavior aimed at earning rents from resulting protection, have also served to curtail such mobility by professionals from other nations, restricting therefore the provision of such services to the vastly narrower scale necessitated by the movement of the user to the producer instead.

I shall argue below that technical change, construed in a broad sense, is now changing this situation in ways that have tended to bring ever more services into the tradable category, as when the need for physical proximity between user and producer is eliminated and the service can be rendered "long-distance." Immediately, however, let me turn to the issues that economists have addressed as they equated services by and large with nontraded goods.

14.2   Empirical Regularities and Service Characteristics

The revival of interest in services can be traced back at least to Friedrich List, who was interested in the evolution of growing economies through three stages culminating in the "commerce"-inclusive stage characterized by a significant share of the service sector in production and in consumption.[3] However, for the Anglo-Saxon economists in the mainstream of economic science, the economists who are commonly associated with the notion of stages are Allan Fisher and Colin Clark.

Writing from the 1930s through 1940s, these two pioneers proposed that it was fruitful to distinguish among the primary, secondary, and tertiary sectors in the economy. But they did not agree on the precise definition of the tertiary sector, though Clark manifestly included with it what we would today call services. Colin Clark's practice was to include in this omnibus category "all forms of economic activity not included under primary and secondary,"[4] thus defining the sector to include transport and communication, commerce and finance, professional workers, and those engaged in public administration, entertainment and sport, personal and domestic service. (Construction was added to the group in some instances.[5]).

From these and subsequent writings, economists have inherited an interest in analyzing several "stylized" facts and predictions concerning services as they interact with economic development. Principal among these have been two relationships: first, the real (or relative) price of services as economies get richer and, second, the share of services in national income, by sector-of-origin and by final expenditure. Let me treat each, in turn, drawing on the analysis of the two key characteristics of services that I have discussed already.

The Real Price of Services

Colin Clark had already argued in *The Conditions of Economic Progress* that his trend data showed a secular rise in the price of services relative to manufactures.

Since *per capita* incomes tend to rise with time, it would be natural to infer that growth of *per capita* income would also show, in cross-section data, that services were cheaper in the poor countries. I suspect that, if adjustment for quality was systematically made, the Colin Clark result would be only reinforced. For, manufactures have continually improved in quality: a fact which, when ignored, contributed to the erroneous inference at one time that the terms of trade of the primary-product-exporting developing countries had secularly declined. At the same time, the quality of many services has tended to decline over time. How many of you are aware that, in nineteenth-century London, there were twelve mail deliveries per day, including Saturday, and one delivery on Sunday? If you had the misfortune to live in New York, you would also have been witness to a decline in the mail service to the point where the regular 22 cents letter can take anywhere up to a week to reach Wall Street downtown from Columbia University uptown, the Special Delivery charge of $2.95 simply assures you that as and when your letter reaches downtown it will be promptly delivered, and an ovemight Express Mail rate of $9.95 is now necessary to resurrect the next-day delivery that was routinely the practice at the lowest rate only a few years ago.

You may legitimately wonder that this is all casual empiricism and anecdotal economics. Though, let me remind you that the Law of Gravity and arguably also Relativity theory were born of casual empiricism. And, as for the value of anecdotal economics, I must recall the Oxford seminar run by the late Lord Balogh, my teacher, colleague, and friend, where Professor Charles Kindleberger of MIT was lecturing only to have Balogh reject each of his empirical propositions by saying that it was not true for Algeria where he was advising President Ben Bella or for India where he had just been visiting Prime Minister Nehru. Frustrated, Kindleberger declared: no more anecdotal economics. Balogh sat quietly, biding his time until Kindleberger told a story. When Balogh jumped to his feet, expostulating that the story was anecdotal economics and hence inadmissable, Kindleberger swiftly retorted: "But Tommy, I read it in a book, that makes it scholarship!"

As it happens, careful and painstaking research, for which our profession is greatly indebted to Professors Irving Kravis, Alan Heston, and Robert Summers, has provided systematic cross-sectional evidence supporting their proposition that increasing *per capita* income is associated with a rising real price of services. The source of this KHS finding is their monumental work on comparative price structures and their implications for international comparisons of national incomes. Extending to 34 countries, for 1975, and aggregated by six *per capita* GNP groups, their data show that the price of services, relative either to the GDP deflator or to commodity price, generally rises with *per capita* GDP, as indicated in figure 14.1.

This phenomenon has attracted the theorists among us, who have focused on the nontradedness of services, to produce a variety of alternative explanations, all of which probably are pertinent simultaneously in varying degrees in explaining the empirical regularity at hand. I should like to distinguish among three principal explanations, all drawing on rather different ways of exploiting the theory of general equilibrium but each resting squarely on the fact that services are nontraded so that their prices do not tend to be equalized across countries through trade.

Explanation 1: International Productivity Differentials
One explanation, originally developed systematically by Professors Bela Balassa (1964) and Paul Samuelson (1964), and subsequently advocated by KHS (Kravis, Heston, and Summers), relies on the contention that wages reflect productivity in the traded goods sector; that rich countries have comparatively greater productivity in the traded sectors; that the traded goods prices being by and large equalized through trade the wages would be higher in the rich countries due to the higher productivity; and hence, with nontraded goods and services being characterized by much smaller

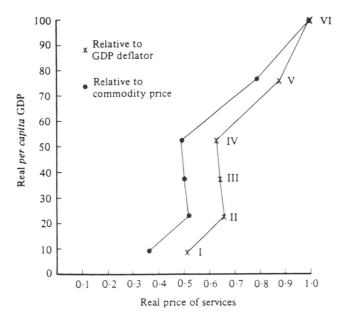

Figure 14.1
Relative price of services and per capita GDP for six country groups, 1975.

productivity differentials if any, the unit cost of supplying services would be higher in the rich countries.

Although these distinguished economists worked essentially with single-factor Ricardian models to advance this explanation, it is easy to extend the argument to a less restrictive general-equilibrium model. Thus, consider figure 14.2a where I illustrate the argument for a standard model with the following structure: a tradables, 2 primary factors—capital (K) and labor (L)—and one service sector that is nontraded. (The argument I presently advance is immediately extended to the case where the 2×2 tradable-cum-primary-factors structure is replaced by an $n \times n$ structure, and where the number of services is multiplied at will.) The suffixes R and P refer to the rich and poor countries, respectively. With customary restrictions on constant-returns-to-scale production functions in all activities, the wage-rental price-line, ω, can be put tangent in figure 14.2 to the corresponding isoquants in the usual Lerner fashion, showing then in turn the associated goods price-ratio. With prices of the traded goods X and Y equalized fully through trade, the factor price-ratio ω will imply then in figure 14.2a a traded goods price-ratio that exchanges $\bar{X}_P$ for $\bar{Y}_P$ in the poor country, each exchanging in turn for $\bar{S}_P$.

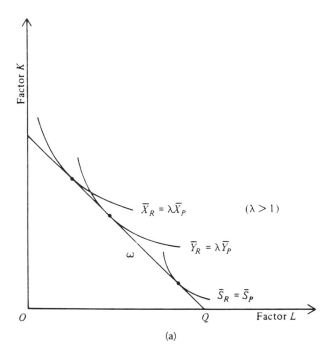

(a)

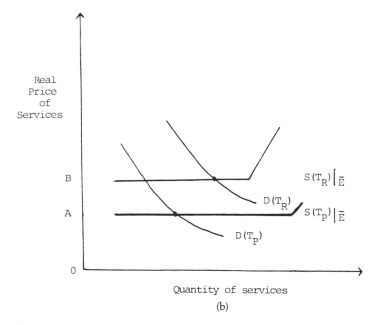

(b)

Figure 14.2
International productivity differentials explanation developed by Balassa, Samuelson, and Kravis-Heston-Summers.

If then the rich country is uniformly more productive in the two traded sector, this advantage being measured by scale factor $\lambda(> 1)$, the same argument will imply that λX_P will exchange for $\lambda \overline{Y}_P$ in the rich country, each exchanging in turn for $\overline{S}_P$ ($= \overline{S}_R$ since there is no productivity differential between the rich and the poor countries in the service sector). It immediately follows that services will be λ-times more expensive in the rich country.

Figure 14.2b retells you, in the more familiar Marshallian diagram in general equilibrium, focusing on the service sector equilibrium, what is happening. The supply curve for services $S(T_P)|_{\overline{E}}$ is for the poor country, with its tradable-goods technology (T) and endowments (E). It is perfectly elastic (as long as we remain within the diversification cone, defined by ω). When we shift to the rich country, the supply curve remains flat but moves up to $S(T_R)|_{\overline{E}}$: tradables are more productive but endowment is unchanged. The real *price* of services moves up from OA to OB. The *quantity* of services produced and transacted is all that demand determines. Figure 14.2b shows the demand curve shifting upward as income *per capita* rises. It also shows the quantity transacted in the rich country increasing, but the quantity could well have fallen (absolutely) despite the increase in demand.

The Balassa-Samuelson-KHS explanation relies on two critical assumptions: first, that productivity rises less rapidly in services (and nontraded goods), and second, that it does not diffuse rapidly across countries. Both assumptions have something to be said for them. In regard to the postulate of stagnant productivity growth in the service industry, the recent evidence corroborates the casual impression that, while most services are characterized by stagnation, some are highly innovative. Thus, analyzing data for the U.S. economy for 1947–76 (table 14.1), Professors Baumol, Blackman, and Wolff (1985) have reported that, by various alternative measures, services indeed are generally unprogressive, a strong exception being communications and broadcasting and somewhat weaker ones being trade and (surprisingly) real estate.

Explanation 2: Factor Endowments
I have recently advanced (1984), however, an alternative explanation that altogether eschews productivity differential across countries and instead builds rigorously on the notion that factor endowments make labor cheaper in the poor country and that this makes services cheaper in turn since they are labor intensive.

One advantage of this explanation is that it also can be shown to explain several other phenomena such as the Kuznets-Chenery-Syrquin finding for

Table 14.1
Average Annual Rate of Productivity Growth by Sector, 1947–76

Industry	Measure			
	GPO/L (1)	GDO/L (2)	ρ (3)	λ (4)
1. Agriculture	3.59	4.47	1.56	3.95
2. Mining	2.70	2.76	0.08	1.38
3. Construction	1.66	1.19	−0.34	1.49
4. Manufacturing-durables	2.52	2.80	0.58	3.08
5. Manufacturing-nondurables	3.21	3.23	0.41	2.56
6. Transportation and warehousing	1.74	2.74	0.68	2.42
7. Communication and broadcasting	5.42	5.50	3.99	5.21
8. Utilities	4.96	4.77	1.53	2.96
9. Trade		2.17	1.09	2.19
a. Wholesale trade	2.37			
b. Retail trade	1.99			
10. Finance and insurance	0.50	0.31	−0.27	0.57
11. Real estate	2.72	3.10	1.21	4.86
12. General services	0.93			
a. Hotels, personal and repair (except auto)		1.37	−0.31	1.35
b. Business and professional services		1.70	0.83	2.30
c. Auto repair and services		1.45	−0.84	1.04
d. Movies and amusements		0.99	−0.56	0.64
e. Medical, educational and nonprofit		−0.46	−1.14	−0.19
f. Household workers		−0.21	−0.21	−0.21
13. Government enterprises	−0.51	1.10	−0.52	0.99
14. Government industry	0.31	−0.18	0.08	−0.18
Overall: GDP	2.16			
GNP		2.18	1.17	2.18

Source: W. J. Baumol, S. A. B. Blackman, and E. N. Wolff, "Unbalanced Growth Revisited: Asymptotic Stagnancy and New Evidence," *American Economic Review*, September 1985, pp. 806–817, table 1.
Notes: Measures (1), (2), and (4) are alternative measures of labor productivity change, involving calculations of annual (compounded) rates. GPO is gross product originating in the corresponding sector, with L representing persons employed; GDO is gross domestic output in constant dollars, an input-output concept, equaling the gross value of a sector's output or sales deflated by the sector's price deflator. λ is also a labor productivity measure but takes both direct and indirect labor inputs into account. ρ is the closest to a proper measure of productivity, being a *total*-factor-productivity measure. For details, see Baumol, Blackman, and Wolff (1985).

the period 1950–70 that the (labor) productivity of the service sector relative to the goods sector tends to be inversely related to the *per capita* income level of the country. It also has the advantage of symmetrically explaining why *some* services may, in fact, be more expensive in the poor countries: this may be simply because they are capital intensive rather than labor intensive. Thus, capital intensity rather than nonprogressivity can explain why telephone communications are expensive in poor compared to rich countries. Indeed, if one adjusts for the quality of the service, they are wildly more expensive as a visit to Cairo or New Delhi from London or New York will underscore. In fact, I tell my students that one excellent way to tell apart the underdeveloped from the developed countries is by looking at their phone systems: in the underdeveloped countries, you go crazy making phone calls; in the developed countries, receiving them!

How does this explanation proceed analytically? Consider the same basic model as in figure 14.2a. But now assume, as in figure 14.3a, that the rich and poor countries have identical production functions in each sector: productivity differences are thus assumed to be nonexistent. Let ω_R be the wage-rental ratio obtaining in the rich country, implying that $\bar{X}_R$ exchanges for $\bar{Y}_R$ for $\bar{S}_R$.

If, however, the poor country were to have this wage-rental ratio, its overall endowment ratio $(\bar{K}/\bar{L})_P$ for all employment would have to spanned by OA and OC, with AOC (not drawn) constituting the McKenzie-Chipman diversification cone. But if, as in figure 14.3a, $(\bar{K}/\bar{L})_P$ lies outside this diversification cone, ω_R is not feasible and the poor country, being so abundantly endowed with labor, would have to have a *lower* wage-rental ratio such as ω_P. The consequence is that production of X is no longer possible at the goods price ratio $\bar{X}_R = \bar{Y}_R$ given from the rich country, whereas $\bar{Y}_P$ ($= \bar{Y}_R$) will now exchange, *not* for $\bar{S}_p$ but for $\bar{S}_p$, the choice of K/L ratios being OE and OD, respectively, in the poor country. The new diversification cone defined by EOD, of course, spans $(\bar{K}/\bar{L})_P$. This immediately means that the relative price of services is cheaper in the poor country, since $\bar{S}_p > \bar{S}_p$.

Again, the factor-endowments explanation can be illuminated in the Marshallian diagram in figure 14.3b. The supply curves are again totally elastic but move up vertically for the rich country with higher per capita income due to higher capital relative to labor (E), while the productivity or technology (T) is commonly shared. Further, this upward shift implies that the real price of services is higher, though the quantity produced and transacted will reflect the demand factor exactly as in the differential-productivity explanation.

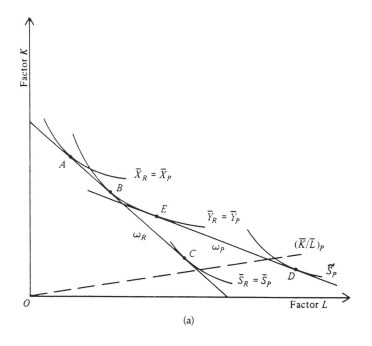

(a)

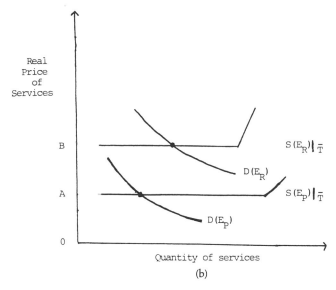

(b)

Figure 14.3
Factor endowments explanation of Bhagwati and Kravis-Lipsey.

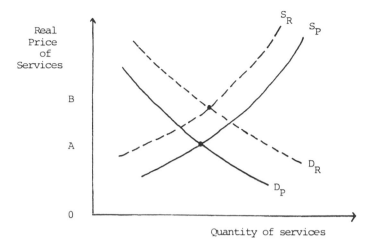

Figure 14.4
Rising supply price according to Clague and Panagariya.

Explanation 3
An alternative argumentation has been presented recently by Professors Christopher Clague (1985) and Aravind Panagariya (1985), building on the specific-factors model. Let me present here just the essence of it. If the two traded sectors are modeled to use mobile labor but specific capitals, and the service sector is assumed to use only labor, it is immediately obvious that, for any given technology and endowments, the supply curve of services will be upward-sloping, unlike in the previous two models I just presented. Thus increased services can be produced only by drawing more labor away from the traded activities and, given diminishing returns due to the specific capitals there, release of labor for services can only take place at increasing marginal cost. If the rich country then has more income *per capita* because it has more specific capital in the traded sectors or has neutral technical advantage there, the supply curve of the rich country will be to the left of that for the poor country. On the other hand, the rich country should have, for normal goods, its demand curve for services shift to the right of that for the poor country. As the dotted curves show, the rich country will then have a higher real price for services.[6]

Service Share in National Income

All these formal explanations build, among other postulates. on the assumed basic property of services: that they tend to be nontraded. In turn, this conceptualization has a bearing on the other question of the shares of different sectors in national income that I distinguished earlier.

For, if services are largely nontraded, their income share would tend to be dominated by demand factors: the demand for nontraded items cannot, ipso facto, be satisfied by producing traded goods and exchanging them for the nontraded services that you wish to use. It follows that the thinking on shares has heavily reflected presuppositions concerning income elasticities of demand. More specifically, the service sector would tend to increase since the income elasticity of demand for services would exceed unity. Thus, equating prediction with prescription, as do some modern students of development and its impact on economic structure, Allan Fisher (1933, pp. 380–381) argued that "when certain standards of efficiency in primary and secondary production have been reached, it is desirable that Adam Smith's "unproductive" services should occupy a rapidly increasing proportion of the time of the community. It is the growing importance of these services which characterizes the tertiary stage." Colin Clark even went so far as to suggest to Fisher, in private correspondence, that "a precise line of demarcation [between goods and services] might be based upon the measurement of income elasticity of demand suggested in Allen and Bowley's *Family Expenditure*. Any commodity for which income elasticity, so measured, exceeded unity could be *defined* as a tertiary product!" (Fisher, 1939, p. 34; italics added). Indeed, it is safe to conclude that the income elasticity of demand for services was generally regarded as high.

Implicitly, however, this line of argument ignored the possibility that development could raise the real cost of supplying nontraded services, and thus reduce the output of services or at least their relative share in value added despite high income elasticities of demand for them. Thus, in all the three models I presented above the rising real price of nontraded services implies that, *ceteris paribus*, quantities transacted would fall if the demand curve was normally downward-sloping. As it happens, the economists who have followed Fisher and Clark have noted extreme intances of this effect: where specific services have been priced out by rising real prices thereof. Domestic servants are a prime example of this phenomenon; and I have often thought that the complaints of housewives that servants are getting harder to find and expensive to hire are one of the surest indexes of successful development! I might also add that life is further complicated for the Fisher-Clark thesis because it is not evident that all final-demand services would have high income elasticities of demand.

But the fact that there are also many *producer* services, which serve as intermediates, immediately suggests that the final-demand income elasticites are in any event an inadequate guide to what can happen to the sector-of-origin share of services in national income as distinct from their final-demand shares in national expenditure. Except for unpredictable compositional effects, one might expect that the sector-of-origin shares might be more stable because of possible Leontief-type fixed-requirement relationships between intermediates and outputs, whereas the final demand composition at best might reflect more any possible Fisher-Clark effects.

Even this presupposition. however, is belied, and indeed turned on its head, by the statistics at hand. Professor Kravis has noted that rather his data suggest that, whereas there is no significant difference between the rich and the poor countries in their share of services in final expenditure, there is a significantly greater share of services by sector-of-origin in the rich than in the poor counries. Why?

The clue seems to be provided by the second key characteristic of sevices I distinguished earlier: namely, that they presuppose outhouse transactions between users and producers of the service. Imagine that, as development proceeds, services performed previously on an in-house basis, and hence treated in goods production as part of value added in goods, increasingly became provided instead by specialized firms on an out-house basis and hence were now classified as services. This in itself would mean that a simple reorganization of the production process results in a greater share of services by sector-of-origin as development proceeds: an explanation that has not missed Professor Kravis' attention.

As it happens, this is precisely the kind of objection that Professors Peter Bauer and Basil Yamey, both now at our host institution, had raised in 1951 when they argued that Fisher, Clark et al. had been misled into thinking that the poor countries had fewer people in the service sector because much of the service sector activity that occurred out-house in the rich countries was conducted in-house by producers and hence not accounted for as services. Focusing on the proposition in both Clark and Fisher that higher *per capita* income was associated with relatively greater number in the tertiary sector, they wrote (1951, p. 753):

Over a considerable period of deveiopment many activities, especially trading, porterage and domestic service, would not be regarded as separate occupations either by official enumerators or by the subjects themselves ... As specialization becomes more definite and pronounced and as these activities are carried out by specialists, the performers and their performance are more easily identified and recognised and their quantitative extent looms larger, possibly much larger in occupational statistics, even though in total the volume of these activities may be unchanged or even reduced.

The *caveat* that changing shares in services may reflect largely organizational changes rather than objective shifts in occupational and production structure needs to be reinforced by reminding ourselves that service data are bedeviled by several other factors that may bear differentially on countries at different stages of development. Three deserve attention.

1. A difficult and deeper issue is raised if we reflect on the Bauer-Yamey observation that economic development, or secular economic change more generally, can itself shift specific services in and out of the household. Thus, if electrical repairs get expensive, households will tend to allocate their own time to in-household repairs on a do-it-yourself basis. And if a service gets cheaper to buy, as when influx of cheaper foreign labor occurs legally or illegally, housewives would have an added incentive to work outside rather than on household chores inside. What happens then is that unless the corresponding household work is computed as part of national income you get, not a shift in given value added between goods and services as you go from in-*household* to out-*household* mode of production but instead, a shift in the computed value added itself. Questions raised since the earliest days of national income accounting, concerning imputdtion procedures for nonmarket transactions, and debated recently in connection with feminist demands to include women's contribution in the household in national accounts,[7] thus bear directly also on the question of the share of services in national income.

2. Next, the illegal, underground. "black," "second,' or "parallel" economy may well be more important in the developing countries where controls tend to proliferate so that the invisible hand is hardly ever seen. Insofar as such activities tend to belong disproportionately to the service sector— construction, repairmen, and domestic servants typically come to mind— and are not picked up in the official statistics. the data on service-sector share in the developing countries would be downward biased.

3. Again, the developing countries typically have a relatively larger share of what is now formally described as the "informal" sector but has, in my judgment, no formal definition that is satisfactory analytically. This is generally the urban sector where small-scale entrepreneurship flourishes, with self-employed artisans and repair shops, teastalls, car-washing services, and numerous such activities characterized therefore by job and employment characteristics that approximate in some fashion the "secondary" labor sector in Professor Michael Piore's celebrated dual-labor markets thesis. Insofar again as this sector escapes systematic documentation by the statistical organizations of the developing countries *and* is dispropor-

tionately intensive in services, as seems to be the case from recent studies, the service share in national income of the poor countries would be understated.

All this only underscores the fact that services are an omnibus category, subsumed under one umbrella by principles that I outlined earlier. These principles still permit enormous diversity in the relationship of different services to direct final demand, intermediate demand, accounting conventions, evasion proneness, and other characteristics that bear on questions such as their observed share in national income. It seems useful therefore to depart from a highly-aggregated approach and to consider *subsets* of services that are grouped by criteria that are more consonant with the question being addressed and with the empirical regularity being searched and then sought to be explained. More robust structural regularities, reflecting the share of these narrower groups of services in national income, could certainly emerge; and it is conceivable that the aggregate tendency of services to show a positive relationship between per capita GDP and service share in GDP by sector-of-origin may conceal important segments of services where the relationship is the opposite or nonexistent.

14.3   The Splintering Process

This kaleidoscope of services and goods is in fact a shifting one as technical change, in a broad sense embracing organizational innovations as well, occurs. Technical change leads to what I have christened recently as the "splintering process" where goods splinter from services and services, in turn, from goods.

Then again, technical change has also served increasingly to transform services, as part of what I have described (1984) as a "disembodiment" phenomenon, from the category where physical proximity between users and providers was necessary to the "long-distance" category I distinguished above: with direct implications of course for the tradability of services. Again, services, even where physical proximity remains essential, have increasingly shifted into the tradable category by making essential but hitherto de faco impossible provider-mobility a distinct economic possibility thanks to organizational innovations resulting from fortuitous changes in the world economy.

I shall presently return to these implications for the increased tradability of services and their consequences in turn for the question as to how we ought to approach the current question of the appropriate framework for governing trade in services. First, however, let me turn to the shifting-kaleidoscope argument, for it helps also to illuminate, in my view, why many services are stagnant and some are not.

Services splinter off from goods, as I have already noted, mainly through being shifted from the in-house to the out-house mode. This often happens as economies-of-scale make it advantageous, as enough demand develops with development, to set up specialized firms supplying these services. I would hypothesize that, *properly measured*, services that materialize this way would tend to show more progressivity: as indeed the Baumol-Blackman-Wolff calculations suggest for the broad category entitled *Business and Professional Services*. There has been recent evidence of reversion in some instances in the United States to in-house professional services. But I suspect that a fraction of it must reflect the need to have in-house professionals, much like terminals, to receive and process the out-house inputs.

It also occurs to me that the process of "service-destruction"—as against service-splintering, which arises when stagnant services get increasingly expensive à la the Balassa-Samuelson-KHS argumentation and then retreat into the household as unrecorded do-it-yourself amateur activities—will tend to take out of reckoning the stagnant components in services and thus "bias" upward the measured progressivity of these service sectors.

But when we contemplate the reverse splintering process where goods spring from services, the effect is likely to be exactly the opposite: and for an interestingly exotic reason. In many services where technical change is rapid, I would contend that the change itself often proceeds to splinter off new goods to supply (in a Lancastrian vector-of-characteristics sense) similar needs. In the process, the service sector in question is left behind, in statistical records, as an unprogressive sector, with the technical progressivity being subsumed instead under the goods sector where the new goods are statistically assigned.

I can do no better than quote from my 1984 essay to illustrate what I have in mind:

When the gramophone was invented, there was in fact a tremendously sharp technical change in the service activity called "musical service." But what happened in the classification of goods and services? Gramophones and records are "goods" and the technical change simply resulted in a new industry that goes into the goods sector. Thus we have been left with the ex post observation that the "musical services" industry is technically unprogressive and also highly labor intensive in general. If technical progress in traditional services industries, such as music, lecturing, etc. (mostly final-use services), indeed takes the form where the service is "disembodied" from the physical presence of the provider and embodies those services in goods that can then be bought in the marketplace, then we have a splintering process where technical change simply creates new goods that tend to displace the services from which they grew and where technical change therefore leaves behind, in the services sector, the labor-intensive and "unprogressive" component of the pre-technical-change sector.

The disembodiment effect that characterizes technical change creating goods from services is accordingly responsible for a class of services where progressivity is generally considered to be low. We then have this paradox: that technical progress in these sectors itself creates the outcome that, given the way these sectors are defined, they wind up technically stagnant!"

While, appropriately measured, progressivity in the service sectors that experience such goods-creating technical change will indeed show stagnation, I might warn that the crude and wholly inappropriate *labor*-productivity measures, all too often used to infer progressivity or lack thereof, could in principle go either way in these service sectors. You can convince yourself of this "paradoxical" possibility by simply constructing an outcome where the wage-rental ratio rises with the technical-change-led emergence of the new good, the (old) service sector is labor intensive, its capital-labor ratio and hence labor productivity as well rise in consequence, and may do so even differentially relative to other sectors.

14.4   Increased Tradability of Services: Long-Distancing Phenomenon and Innovations in Provider-Mobility

1. The "disembodiment" phenomenon I have discussed above in the form of services splintering into goods extends alternatively to services becoming, not goods, but *long-distance* services so that the physical presence of the provider of the services is no longer necessary for the transaction with the user.[8] Two consequences then follow: first, the technical progressivity *will* then continue to be recorded in the service sector, unlike in the case where the disembodiment led to embodiment instead in goods, and, second, the nontradability resulting from artificial or natural barriers to bringing the provider in physical proximity to the user will yield to tradability and may indeed lead to trade.

The enormous speed with which technological change has progressed in the communications and information sectors, commonly grouped under the "telematics" rubric, has shifted an ever-increasing number of activities to the long-distance category where they may be executed "over the wire" and hence become more readily tradable and traded in consequence. Banking transactions from computer terminals at home, engineering services communicated by satellite, and medical diagnoses by video transmission are evident examples. My favorite illustration has been President Reagan's bringing Dresser Industries Paris branch to a halt over President Mitterrand's recalcitrance over the Soviet gas pipeline affair by simply turning off the transmission of critical engineering and related   information flows from Dresser Industries headquarters in Dallas. But this will not hold a candle to the story I read recently which carried pictures of a young lady standing in her lingerie in front of a mirror and trying on dresses over the wire in a fashion store hundreds of miles away!

2. But if tradability of services has increased through "long-distancing" trends in provision of services, it has also increased for the very different reasons that, where physical proximity continues to be necessary but has been traditionally difficult or impossible to achieve across countries, "organizational" innovations have appeared recently that have made such proximity feasible and even economical.

Thus, in the class of services where, as with my M–6 example, the provider of services had to travel to where the motorway had to be built, it has been rare in modern times for unskilled labor services to be so provided. Both lack of *supply* by organized construction firms and of demand due to restrictions ill-adapted to accommodating such supply in any event have generally prevented such services from being internationally transacted.

However, this is no longer true as numerous construction firms have materialized in the post-OPEC 1970s to take not just skilled but also entire teams of unskilled labor to the labor-scarce Middle East economies feverishly engaged in spending oil revenues. This "innovation" in organization, fortuitously resulting from the OPEC-led change in the world economy, has made it possible now for us to contemplate a transition of unskilled labor services, and hence of the category of services where the provider must necessarily move to the user, from its hitherto nontraded status to the tradable category.

Several instances, such as when entire medical facilities, were provided inclusive of nonimmigrant doctors and administrators who would come into Saudi Arabia and Kuwait on fixed-term contracts, underscore the vastly increased opening up of this form of relocation of the provider of services to where the user is in the *skilled*-labor categories as well.

3. Paradoxically, however, the major thrust toward negotiations for a framework governing trade in services has come not from the beneficiaries of the two phenomena I just outlined as increasing tradability of services.

Rather, it has come from sectors such as banking where traditional long-distancing practices and reasonable ongoing tradability are considered to be no longer adequate because of technical change that, in revolutionizing the nature of banking services, has made extremely profitable the possibility of physical proximity by the provider where the user is. Demands for the "right to establish" or its euphemistic equivalent, the "right of presence," reminiscent of Commodore Parry's demand on the Tokugawa Japan and Secretary Connolly's demands on today's Japan, have thus appeared from potential beneficiaries such as the American Express Company.

The contrast with the preceding case of unskilled and several skilled labor services is interesting. These latter have always required provider-mobility—either as a physical necessity as with unskilled services or as a virtual necessity with skilled services that require complementary facilities simply impossible to duplicate in the user's location. Organizational innovations have rendered such provider-mobility internationally increasingly feasible and therefore restrictions on it, as I shall contend below, must be viewed as *necessarily* restrictive of trade in services. On the other hand, the same degree of necessity does not, in my judgment, characterize the services that seek the "right to establish" presently.

This asymmetry of need, on the one hand, and desirability, on the other hand, between these two classes of services seeking provider-mobility should suggest that the beneficiaries in the *former* than in the latter class should have taken the center stage. Ironically, the articulate lobbies have emerged for the *latter* group instead while there are no matching spokesmen for the *former*! This irony also has an added twist since the latter group is overwhelmingly in the developed, and the former is preponderantly in the developing countries.

Developed and Developing Country Interests: Conflict or Convergence?

There are several reasons in fact why the United States has played the catalytic role in the ongoing exploration for an international framework to regulate and facilitate trade in services. These also explain why the focus of the U.S. role has tended to be on certain kinds of services and why the developing countries have found themselves in an adversary role on this.

The U.S. focus, given its pluralistic politics, has naturally reflected the lobbying pressures from those service sectors in the United States that seek greater access, and right to establish, in other countries. This was evident from the considerable pressures that were brought to bear on the participants at the November 1982 GATT Inter-Ministerial where, as Sir Roy

Denman has remarked, the hardsell from the U.S. multinational banks in particular was manifest and almost counterproductive.

But it is not just the lobbying pressure. There is also a substantial element of economic philosophy or ideology, reflecting the conviction that the liberal trading order is desirable, which drives the U.S. leadership toward the extension of the rule of law in trade to the service sectors. The U.S. efforts can therefore be interpreted, quite properly in my judgment, as part of its leadership role that Professor Charles Kindleberger believes is central to providing the "collective good" that an international trade regime represents. If you are skeptical of this benign interpretation, I would remind you that Peel's repeal of the Corn Laws, which constituted the first triumph of the free traders, was not just a result of the relative strength of Cobden over his opposing lobby. In the end, Peel confessed, he was simply convinced of the virtues of free trade. As Disraeli accused him, when he crucified him in Parliament, Peel had unscrupulously let political economy triumph over loyalty to his party!

There has also been an acute sense in the United States that *national* interest, and not just the narrow interest of the lobbies or the general interest of the world at large, dictates that services be brought into the trading order. This is a result of the increasing perception that the U.S. comparative advantage has shifted to service transactions. And that it is simply "unfair" to have U.S. markets open to goods while foreign markets are closed to U.S. services. Given the rise of the doctrine of "aggressive reciprocity," and of the increased demands for "a level playing field" unmindful of the fact that some live up on the mountain and others down in the valley, this has translated into an aggressive posture by the United States on the question of trade in services and has also shaped the central thrust of these demands in terms of the concepts embraced for legitimacy and the sectors chosen for emphasis.

The lack of enthusiasm of the developing countries in general for these initiatives and pressures—though there are notable exceptions such as Singapore whose outward orientation extends also to offshore banking, giving them a greater stake in the extension of the trade regime to services—has stayed fairly robust since 1982. Their latest willingness at Geneva to play along can only be put down to circumspection prompted by the sense that, compared to 1982, more developed countries had joined U.S. ranks, notably the United Kingdom where the pro-manufactures and anti-services views of Professor Nicholas Kaldor and his Cambridge pupils seem less fashionable now than some years ago.[9] Again, the protectionist threat in the United States has grown extremely acute, after years of neglect of the budget and trade deficits, so that the choice has seemed increasingly to narrow down politically to having the United States open up new markets abroad or closing old ones at home, and hence also to talking about services or having the U.S. door closed to goods.

What have been the worries of the developing countries? And what do we need to bring them more fairly and enthusiastically into the regime-making game on services? I would group their concerns into three broad categories: first, that comparative advantage in services belongs to the developed countries and therefore the returns to extension of orderly trade rules to services enabling service transactions to expand will accrue to the developed rather that to the developing countries, second, that focusing on services will turn attention away from making progress on keeping trade in goods reasonably free, thus harming the developing countries whose comparative advantage lies in goods trade instead, and third, that the services that will expand under such a new regime will be in areas where infrastructure buildup, externalities, and political sensitivity are important—the rule-oriented GATT-type regime, where quantlties may come out where they will, is inapplicable in consequence.

Let me address these issues in turn.

1. The fear that comparative advantage in services belongs to the developed countries, and implied rejection therefore of the initiatives to open up trade in them, are understandable but misplaced.

Economists will immediately assert that, by and large, dismantling of trade barriers should be welfare-improving mutually. Of course one knows, thanks to the theory of second-best which was conceived at LSE (London School of Economics) itself, that perverse effects can always follow for both parties to trade if barriers are dismantled only partially. But, unless one is clever but not wise, or (in Sir Dennis Robertson's classic description of a younger and brilliant colleague) is "silly-clever," these are exceptions that are best confined to the classroom in the present instance.

Thus, in the context of services, it has been customary for economists, as also negotiators from the developed countries, to emphasize the virtues of freer trade in services and its advantage to the developing countries even if they are importers of services. In particular, the argument has been advanced that giving their own producers and exporters greater access to cheaper and more efficient banking and insurance services from the developed countries will imply better export and economic performance for the developing countries. And that they are only hurting themselves hy protecting their banking and insurance sectors, much as protecting intermediates such as imported steel would hurt the export of tractors and diesel engines and hence the economy in turn.

Unfortunately, in the game of trade, these arguments are rarely compelling. Where economists see mutual gain, politics tends often to see zero-sum outcomes. Typically, the other's gain is seen as possibly one's loss. If therefore service liberalization will expand others' exports, the gains accrue to *them*, not to oneself.

Again, the developing countries tend to see the economic arguments advanced by developed-country spokesmen in favor of service trade as self-serving when for decades these very service sectors were heavily regulated domestically and protected against external competition (and, in the case of the United States, even against interstate competition down to this day). While one may not buy the imperial theory of free trade in the nineteenth century, it would be naive to ignore the fact that many countries have tended to embrace free trade only when they felt they were strong and ahead.

All of this suggests that, to bring the developing countries into the service negotiations, it will be necessary to encourage them, as indeed one can, to see that they too have advantage in *some* services: that this particular extension of trading rules, complex as it is, has something for everyone in this political-economy sense. In order to do this, we also have to move away from the biased focus that has been provided in the discussions to date on those services where the developed countries have substantial advantage, and to bring into the agenda those services where the developing countries have something to export.

2. Before I utilize my earlier themes to elaborate on how this can be done, let me turn to the fear that the focus on services would reduce the energies spent on goods. The recent GATT Expert-Group Report (1985, p. 46) addresses this concern by stating:

... we are also convinced that there will be no progress on services without substantial progress on trade in goods. There is no future for an effort to involve GATT in services while neglecting its central and essential responsibilities. An attempt to extend a rule-based approach to new areas of economic relations while permitting the rules for trade in goods to continue to decay would lack credibility.

But it is precisely lack of faith in this built-in safeguard against neglect of goods if services are let in past the door that worries the developing countries, and the GATT experts offer no convincing reason to them to do otherwise.

A variant on this services-*versus*-goods theme is that the developed countries will want to swap concessions on services (where they will benefit) against concessions on goods (where the developing countries will benefit). And that the concessions offered on goods will mostly consist of rolling back the de facto violations of GATT such as voluntary export restrictions against them, including the MFA (multifibers greement) which while arranged under GATT auspices is widely regarded by developing countries as, at best, a bastard progeny that should never have been delivered. In short, since services are a new area not contemplated as subject to GATT protocol, the developing countries will get a raw bargain: an unrequited concession masquerading as a quid pro quo trade agreement.

This contention of the developing countries, in my view, has merit. On the other hand, it runs into the contrary viewpoint, advanced by some developed-country proponents, that the developing countries have been hiding behind Part IV and have undertaken few GATT obligations on goods in consequence,[10] and that it is time now for them to "begin paying" through graduated suspension of Part IV provisions and also through other areas, especially services. In short, the "free lunch" is over, and the ongoing, GATT-sanctioned unrequited transfer to the developing countries must stop!

To recapitulate these two conflicting perceptions in terms of table 14.2, the developing countries' viewpoint is that current protection under item 3 is quasi-illegal, and item 4 has no merit since Part IV, like Article XXIV, is a well-recognized exception to corresponding GATT obligations so that the developed-countries' demand for item 2 is simply gratuitous and unfair, whereas the developed countries see item 3 as the quid pro quo for developing countries granting item 2 and agreeing to item 4.

It is evident that little multilateral progress on services can be made if they are caught in the middle of these irreconcilable overall-bargaining perspectives. My view therefore is that we broaden the scope of 2, and as I argue below in a manner that appropriate conceptualization of the question requires in any event, so that it goes on *both* sides of table 14.2,

Table 14.2
Benefit-perceptions on different trade-negotiating proposals

Proposals perceived as resulting in:	
Benefit to developing countries	Benefit to developed countries
Add Agriculture (1) to GATT (or similar action): (1)	*Add* services to GATT (or similar agency): (2)
Standstills and (3) rollbacks on existing protection (including MFA): (3)	*Remove* Part IV benefits (on graduated basis): (4)

generating a quid pro quo, no matter how unequal, *within the service sector itself*.

3. This need is further compounded by the fact that the lobbies-led focus has inevitably been on service sectors where the developed countries, ipso facto, appear to have advantage. Besides, these particular sectors happen to raise acutely rather difficult questions concerning infrastructure, externalities, and hence also political control of sensitive areas of economic activity.

While, as many have recently noted,[11] there is a tendency to exaggerate the untoward effects, the problem remains that perceptions are not easily changed by analysis and logic. In my judgment, it is not inconceivable that substantial progress can be made in both banking and insurance, for example, toward permitting foreign companies to operate under rules of "national treatment," without compromising infrastructure control. However, the political obstacles may still be insurmountable when the developing countries want to have only state-owned firms in these sectors and therefore entry by foreign firms is off-bounds, similar to the situation in the defense sector in many countries. In that event, political preferences become dominant, as when the United States denies "national treatment" even to foreign residents in regard to ownership in its media sector.

This question has arisen even more sharply in the area of telematics which is seen, as in France, as critical to the evolution of society at several levels in view of the importance of the Information Revolution. For India and Brazil, among the more influential developing countries, domestic control over this key broad sector does not appear to be an item that should be brought under a GATT-type "rule of law" regime. "Who gets what," rather than "what rules do you play by," becomes the relevant question, much as in the question of disarmament negotiations.

Compounding yet further the difficulties that some developing countries envisage is the question of the "right to establish" that some of these sectors have raised, as I noted earlier. This question raises in turn questions relating to direct foreign investment, and, in many developing countries, that is a politically more sensitive area than trade.

If then the developing countries are to be brought on board as willing and energetic participants instead of being dragged screaming into the service-trade negotiations, we need to recognize frontally these problems. A two-front assault is necessary.

First, the comparative advantage of the developing countries in service trade itself must be explored and the negotiations must clearly embrace the areas where such comparative advantage lies and not just those where the developed countries have advantage. Second, the negotiating forums and modalities must reflect the constraints imposed by the special characteristics of such services, rather than constituting a simple extension of existing frameworks and institutions such as the GATT which have evolved primarily in relation to trade in goods.

Comparative Advantage of Developing Countries in Services
It is probably true that the developing countries will not have comparative advantage in services such as banking and insurance. Even here, however, I am not entirely sure since, as with trade in similar goods, there may well be opportunities for trade in similar services. Indeed services are even more likely to depart from the identical-product mold and to lead therefore to the possibility of mutual trade between developed and developing countries. Thus, for example, it is not uncommon to find travelers who prefer to fly Singapore or Japan Airlines because they offer more effusive onboard treatment than on Pan Am or TWA, each reflecting the personal-service culture of the country of the airline! The developing countries may therefore well be too pessimistic about such trade being *all* one-way to them rather than from them.

Again, I think that some of the developing countries ought to develop considerable comparative advantage in the newly emerging "long-distance" services as time passes by. If I may quote from my recent paper (1984) again:

... it is possible to argue that the more advanced developing countries, the newly industrialising countries, which are abundantly endowed with skills, may well find a new comparative advantage opening up in the over-the-wire transmission of their skilled services! This has already happened with respect to software. It could happen, à la Dresser engineering services,with data being transmitted to users in overseas locations for engineering, medical, and a host of other skilled services. Thus the newly industrializing countries may well find that there is something for them, too, in the GATT being extended to trade in services—provided that the extension is truly to services of all kinds.

But, for a really substantial class of services where a number of developing countries can confidently expect to have comparative advantage, we must turn to the category of provider-mobility where labor is relocated for the purpose of providing services to users abroad. South Korea, India, the Philippines, Egypt. Bangladesh, Pakistan, and a growing number of developing countries are already waiting to redo in the developed countries what they have been allowed to do in the Middle East. Indeed, I am informed that South Korea has already applied to the European Economic

Community for formal permission to enable its firms to enter the EEC in this fashion. More will certainly follow suit. With numerous qualified professionals also available in some of these developing countries, and unable to get past the immigration controls for permanent residence in the developed countries, there is also increasing prospect of such demands for provision of medical facilities, legal firms, etc., where the professionals may enter, not as permanent residents, but to execute specific medium-term jobs and assignments in the developed countries.[12]

I believe that it is inappropriate to reject such "temporary relocation of factors to execute service transactions" as inadmissible simply because it is a "factor-service" transaction in current conceptualization. What I have argued above is that such factor relocation is *necessary* to permit the service transaction in these cases, so that the very nature of these services requires that restrictions on such temporary relocation of the provider must be removed if we are examining the question of service trade with an appropriate conceptual framework. We need to discard the notion that, for *the purpose at hand*, the distinction between factor-services and nonfactor services is meaningful. Rather, we need to take what I would christen as the *provider-relocation-requiring* services out of the factor-service category and put them squarely into the net and treat them as on a par with nonfactor service trade for the question of analyzing the framework of rules for trade in services.

If we do not do that, we are not merely ignoring the essential nature of certain services and rendering therefore transactions or trade in them infeasible. We are also doing that in a manner that systematically stacks against the developing countries the emerging discussion of the rules to be designed for service trade!

Negotiations: Where and How?
The agenda that emerges from this analysis then forcefully indicates the difficulties that attend the question of expanding the goods-trade GATT-type framework to services.

Goods trade, by and large, does not get us entangled into questions of externalities, infrastructure, and especially the need to allow for provider-relocation across borders, with its own attendant difficulties which are so evident that I have not thought it necessary to spell them out explicitly. On the other hand, services, by and large, do raise these questions. Besides, different services raise each of these questions in differing degree. Moreover, they benefit the developing and the developed countries, in the narrow but politically relevant sense, differently.

All of this immediately suggests that first, the negotiations on services ought to be comprehensive in scope, with simultaneity in these negotiations on several services ensuring that trade-offs can occur between different sectors and hence progress assured on the entire subject matter; second, seeking common rules extending to all international service transactions is doomed to failure—however, such rules can indeed be sought within each service sector, while we must recognize that the rule-led GATT-type approach will have to be compromised to permit negotiated quantity-outcomes, at least for developing countries, in many sectors; and third, the GATT experience with negotiating NTB (nontariff barrier) codes in the Tokyo Round provides one key component of the requisite expertise in providing the umbrella for service transactions negotiations—for, in case of NTBs, commonality of rules was again unobtainable between different NTB practices concerning goods trade, but nonetheless progress was made on rules within broad groups of NTB instruments.

I would therefore urge the developing countries to join the developed countries in service negotiations under GATT auspices, ensure that the negotiations are comprehensive in scope and extend to services of interest to themselves and that adequate quantity-outcome safeguards are negotiated where, after careful analysis, they are deemed necessary and reasonable in specific sectors.[13] Equally, I should stress that the developed countries must recognize the interests of the developing countries and broaden the scope of the proposed negotiations away from near-exclusive focus on services of interest largely to themselves.[14]

Otherwise, there is real danger, as the GATT Expert-Group Report correctly emphasises, of bilateral and regional fragmentation of the trading world in the area of service trade. Such an outcome would surely be tragic when it is evident that we must move to bring services systematically and increasingly into the discipline of the world trading order.

Notes

Tenth Annual Lecture of the Geneva Association at the London School of Economics and at the Graduate Institute of International Studies, Geneva. This revised text of the lecture has benefited from comments by the invited discussants, Professors Henryk Kierzkowski, Viktor Norman, Andre Sapir, and Jean Waelbroeck, as also from suggestions made by Brian Hindley, Ronald Findlay, Sunil Gulati, and Manuel Sebastiao.

1. Cf. Meade (1963): "... the clue to the logical and formal consistency of what we have done is to be found in the definition of the national income. Is the interest on A's capital invested in B part of A's or B's national income? And are the emigrants

remittances from B to A part of A's or of B's national income? There must be international consistency on this point. These items must be treated as either A's or B's income; they must not be treated as the income of both or of neither. We have treated the interest payment to A as an invisible export by A, because we shall treat the interest on this capital as part of A's national income and not as part of B's national income. If this is done, the receipt of a larger interest on A's foreign investment in B will represent an increase in A's national income; and the payment to A must be treated as a return for an export from A, since A's net visible and invisible exports to B are meant to represent all those payments by residents of B to residents of A which directly generate national income in A.

Emigrants' remittances from B to A we have, on the other hand, treated as part of B's national income and not as part of A's national income. That is to say, when an individual in B transfers $100 m. to an individual in A we have not represented that as a fall in B's and a rise in A's national income, but as a transfer out of a given national income in B to supplement the purchasing power obtained from a given national income in A. For this reason the transaction must be treated as a transfer and not an item of invisible trade; it does not directly generate income in A."

2. In my 1984 paper, I then proceeded to discuss the *latter* class of services which I had distinguished, discussing how the "disembodiment" effect can, in effect, frustrate the intention of immigration restrictions on skilled labor and also what implication followed for the comparative advantage of the developing countries in services. (Later in this lecture, I christen this class of services as "long-distance" services.) On the other hand, Dr. Gary Sampson and Professor Richard Snape (1985), have drawn on this twofold distinction in my 1984 article to explore further the *former* class of services, where physical proximity of the provider and the user is involved, with an important taxonomy aimed at trade negotiations. By contrast, I offer here a simplified taxonomy where I focus more sharply on the aspect of the physical proximity being *required* for service transactions and, more important, therefore, also on the conceptual implication concerning the traditional distinction betweeen "factor-services" and "nonfactor services." The latter, in turn, implies that we must model trade and factor relocation across countries in critically related ways that are different from traditional trade-theoretic models: a task that my Columbia students, Sunil Gulati and Manuel Sebastiao, have already embarked upon.

3. See the interesting historical discussion in Professor Henryk Kierzkowski's (1984) insightful, recent paper.

4. This is cited in Allan G. B. Fisher (1939. p. 36); it is in turn extracted from Clark's 1938 Joseph Fisher Lecture.

5. By contrast, Fisher seems exceptionally confusing in his approach to the definition of the tertiary sector. Thus, he states in a remarkable passage (1939, p. 32) that "... tertiary production is concerned with every new or relatively new type of consumers' demand. the production and distribution of which is made possible by improvements in technical efficiency, which release resources hitherto required for primary or secondary production!" Then he adds, in a footnote, that "The production of radio sets, which was clearly a tertiary activity in, say, 1924, should perhaps

today be regarded as secondary"! Then again, later (p. 33) he argues that services for final demand clearly belong to the tertiary sector but then wants to withdraw that epithet from services which are "merely ancillary to primary or secondary production," possibly excluding therefore "transport and retail trading!"

6. Panagariya (1985) adds an interesting wrinkle to this model by allowing for economies of scale to operate in one of the traded sectors in this sector-specific model. In consequence, even if the rich country is simply a *blown-up* version of the poor country in its endowments (i.e., proportionately more of every factor) and has identical know-how so that under constant-returns-to-scale and homothetic tastes, it could not have a higher *per capita* income, Panagariya can generate a higher service price plus a higher *per capita* income for the rich country.

7. See Professor Padma Desai's (1975) useful analysis of this question for the first International Women's Year Conference by the United Nation in Mexico, and the early references cited therein on questions pertaining to imputation in national income accounting.

8. Thus, instead of Pavarotti singing on the gramaphone record, he sings over statellite TV. The former is disembodiment *via* embodiment into goods, the latter is disembodiment *via* long-distance service. In both cases, the physical presence of the provider in proximity to the user is eliminated.

9. See my commentary (1984) on the Kaldor views. There is also a splendid critique by Lady Hall (1968).

10. I include here the entire question of discriminatory, special and preferential treatment of developing countries (including the NICs).

11. Of particular interest and importance is the recent article by Professors Brian Hindley and Alasdair Smith (1984) which analyzes in depth the contentions concerning infant-industry type externalities, problems arising from need to regulate, etc., and generally concludes that these worries are unduly exaggerated.

12. Progress is already being made in some cases, such as the legal profession. On the general question of trade in professional services, and the problems and prospects therein, see the contributions by Barton, Bhagwati, Feketekuty, Cone, and Rossi in *The Legal Forum*, a new journal of the University of Chicago Law School, forthcoming in fall 1986.

13. This was the main theme of my *Op. Ed.* piece in *The Economic Times*, addressed to Indian policymakers and public opinion; cf. Bhagwati (1985c).

14. This, on the other hand, was the main contention of my *Op. Ed.* articles in *The New York Times* (1985a) and *The Financial Times* (1985b).

References

Balassa, B. 1964. The Purchasing-Power Parity Doctrine: A Reappraisal. *Journal of Political Economy*, 72 (December): 584–596.

Baumol, William, Blackman, Sue, and Edward Wolff. 1985. Unbalanced Growth Revisited: Asymptotic Stagnancy and New Evidence. *American Economic Review*, 75: 806–817.

Bauer, Peter, and Basil Yamey. 1951. Economic Progress and Occupational Distribution. *Economic Journal* (December).

Bhagwati, Jagdish N. 1984. Splintering and Disembodiment of Services and Developing Nations. *The World Economy* (June).

Bhagwati, Jagdish N. 1984. Why Are Services Cheaper in the Poor Countries? *Economic Journal* (June).

Bhagwati, Jagdish N. 1985a. Opening up Trade in Services: US Should Heed Third World Demands. *The New York Times*, November 10.

Bhagwati, Jagdish N. 1985b. GATT and Trade in Services: How We Can Resolve the North–South Debate. *The Financial Times* (London), November 27.

Bhagwati, Jagdish N. 1985c. Trade in Services: How to Change Indian Strategy. *The Economic Times* (India), December 2.

Clague, Christopher. 1985. A Model of Real National Price Levels. *Southern Economic Journal* 51.

Clark, Colin. 1951. *The Conditions of Economic Progress*. 2d. ed. London: Macmillan.

Desai, Padma. 1975. Participation of Women in the Economies of Developing and Developed Countries, Ways of Recognizing their Contribution to National Income, and Strategies for Ensuring their Economic Independence in Developing Countries. Paper prepared for the International Women's Year Conference, United Nations, Mexico, June. Mimeo.

Fisher, Allan G. B. 1939. Production, Primary, Secondary and Tertiary. *Economic Record* (June).

GATT. 1985. *Trade Policies for a Better Future: Proposals for Action*. GATT, Geneva, Switzerland. March.

Hall, Margaret. 1968. Are Goods and Services Different? *Westminster Bank Review* (August).

Hill, T. P. 1977. On Goods and Services. *Review of Income and Wealth* (December).

Kierzkowski, Henryk. 1984. Services in the Development Process and Theory of Trade. Discussion Papers in International Economics No. 8405, The Graduate Institute of International Studies. October.

Kravis, Irving. 1983. Services in the Domestic Economy and in World Transactions. Working Paper No. 1124. Cambridge, MA: National Bureau of Economic Research.

Kravis, Irving, Alan Heston, and Robert Summers. 1978. *International Comparisons of Real Product and Purchasing Power.* Baltimore: Johns Hopkins Press, for the World Bank.

Hindley, Brian, and Alasdair, Smith. 1984. Comparative Advantage and Trade in Services. *The World Economy* (December).

Meade, James E. 1951. *The Balance of Payments.* Oxford: Oxford University Press.

Panagariya, Aravind. 1985. Economies of Scale as an Explanation of International Differences in Service Prices and Some Associated Phenomena. University of Maryland. Mimeo.

Sampson, Gary, and Richard Snape. 1985. Identifying the Issues in Trade in Services. *The World Economy* 8(2): 171–182.

Samuelson, P. A. 1964. Theoretical Notes on Trade Problems. *The Review of Economics and Statistics* 46 (May): 145–154.

Sapir, Andre, and Ernst Lutz. 1981. *Trade in Services: Economic Determinants and Development-Related Issues.* IBRD Staff Working Paper No. 480. Washington, DC. August.

UNCTAD. 1984. *Services and the Development Process.* TD/B/1008. UNCTAD, Geneva Switzerland. August 2.

Weiss, Frank D. 1984. Scope for Trade in Services. Trade Policy Research Center, Mimeo. May.

15   Economic Perspectives on Trade in Professional Services

This paper will bring an economist's perspective to bear on three questions raised at this conference by some of the other important contributions:

1. How are services different from goods?

2. What implications do these differences have for the rules we seek to negotiate to free trade in services?

3. How can we induce the key developing countries, such as Brazil, Egypt, and India which have generally opposed liberalization of trade in services, to support it?

Answers to these questions will naturally bear critically on the narrower question of international trade in professional, and especially legal, services, since recommendations and decisions on a component of the service sector cannot properly be made until the broader perspectives and principles are addressed and understood.

15.1   The Distinction between Goods and Services

As Geza Feketekuty has made abundantly clear,[1] the interest in service trade is very recent. One by-product of this is that the relevant data are both unreliable and far too limited. The limitations on data now available are a function not only of logistical problems in data collection but also of unresolved conceptual questions which impair our present ability to generate meaningful and adequate statistics on the matter at hand. It is still not clear, for example, how services are to be defined, or how they are different from goods.

Nonstorability

Perhaps the earliest useful attempt to define the distinction between services and goods was made by T. P. Hill only one decade ago.[2] Hill focused on the nonstorability of services, stressing that services must be consumed as they are produced and cannot be put into stock by producers. This key characteristic does not cover all items which we customarily report as services; "answering services," for example, do store messages nowadays. Such exceptions, however, do not detract from the usefulness of a definition of services that characterizes them as nonstorable because they require simultaneous provision and use.

User-Producer Interaction

If services must be used as they are produced, there must be *interaction* between the user and the provider of the service. A producer of goods, by contrast, can generally store the finished product and transact with users at any subsequent time. This interaction, in turn, implies that we can contemplate two essential categories of services: those that necessarily require the physical proximity of the user and the provider, and those that do not, though such physical proximity may indeed be useful even in the second category.[3] "Basically one has to draw a distinction between services as embodied in the supplier of the services and requiring [the supplier's] physical presence where the user happens to be and services which can be disembodied from the supplier and provided without a physical presence being necessary."[4]

Physical Proximity Essential
The class of services where physical proximity between provider and user is essential is usefully thought of as consisting of three categories.

Category A: Immobile-User, Mobile-Provider. There is an important class of services which *requires* that the provider go to the user, where the reverse mobility is simply impossible. For example, when the Connecticut Turnpike was being built, an Indian or South Korean construction firm bidding for the contract could perhaps have provided the designs and skilled inputs from home base. But such a firm simply could not have supplied the labor services, except by moving Indian or South Korean labor to Connecticut where the turnpike was to be built. Services of this sort are aptly referred to as "temporary-factor-relocation-requiring" services.

Category B: Mobile-User, Immobile-Provider. There is another important class of services where the user really must move to the provider rather than the provider to the user. This location-specificity of the provider arises from the fact that the service provided is a vector of characteristics, some key elements of which are simply not transferable geographically to the user's location. Complex neurosurgery, for example, simply cannot be done in Gabon because, even though the Massachusetts General Hospital can fly their surgeons over there, there is no way the necessary support services and hospital care can be duplicated or even approximated.

Category C: Mobile-User, Mobile-Provider. Finally, there is a range of services where mobility is symmetrically possible. For example, haircuts and lectures are in principle transmittable between user and provider in the location of either, the only difference being the cost of providing the service in one location rather than the other.

Physical Proximity Inessential: The "Long-Distance" Services
In the second broad class of services, physical proximity between providers and users may be useful, but it is not, strictly speaking, necessary. These are basically "long-distance" services, in the sense that the transactions do not require the immediacy of geographical proximity. Traditional banking and insurance services would fall into this category, because loans and insurance policies can be secured by mail or phone. The type of legal services here discussed, however, presumably require continual contact with the client. Because an attorney serving a corporation may have to interact face-to-face with many of the corporation's employees, legal services could be provided long-distance only in an extremely inefficient and hence expensive fashion. This applies equally to a large class of other professional services such as accounting or management consulting.

15.2   The Implications of This Taxonomy for
Service Trade Negotiations

The above taxonomy of the service sector has significant implications for the optimal structure of international negotiations in service trade. I will focus here on the special considerations relevant to trade in temporary-factor-relocation-requiring services, which require the provider to move to the user.

First, because it requires factor relocation, trade in such services simultaneously implies *either* direct foreign investment *or* labor migration *or* both. Permitting trade in services, therefore, is tantamount to permitting such factor flows. It is thus inappropriate to think of such service trade in the customary category of trade as distinguished from the category of factor flows: the two are inextricably tied together. For this reason, it is preferable to think of service *transactions* rather than of service *trade*.

Second, the opening up of such service transactions between nations creates immediate difficulties stemming from the differences between what has traditionally been considered acceptable with regard to factor flows as against trade, differences which often reflect political sensitivities as well as economic considerations. Thus, Frank Rossi, in his excellent contribution regarding the restraints on the operations of international accounting organizations, cites as one obstacle possible restrictions on the repatriation of earnings encountered in several developing countries.[5] Yet these are precisely the kind of restraints that apply to all direct foreign investment in these countries. Moreover, domestic enterprises in the same service sectors are subjected to the very same restrictions arising from exchange control.

Yet analyzed as a trade issue, rather than as a transactional issue, such restraints look totally unreasonable: the trade access is not meaningful unless profits can be repatriated. The lobbies favoring increased facilitation of transactions in services will have to keep this aspect of the problem very much in mind and pursue their objectives slowly and delicately so as not to pressure hesitant countries to the point where they opt out of negotiations that seem to make impossible demands. Perhaps it is not for nothing that Geza Feketekuty, who deserves much of the credit for opening up the important subject of trade in services, keeps stressing the trade, rather than the factor-movement, aspects of service transactions.

The third implication of this two-sided nature of service transactions is that attention must be paid to factor-mobility restrictions. Because they are in essence factor flows, service transactions can be readily impeded simply by preventing the requisite factor flows, rather than by establishing trade tariffs or prohibitions. This critical issue is abundantly highlighted in several of the papers presented today.[6]

Restraints on factor mobility can arise simply from visa restrictions, or, as with legal services, from the restrictions imposed by regulatory bodies such as the Bar or the Bench on the foreign nationals desiring to provide such services.[7] In the case of the United States, complications also arise from the difficulty of getting all states to adopt uniform policies, thus making the question of reciprocity as a way of opening access even more intractable than it is otherwise.[8]

Fourth, it is important to understand why I keep emphasizing the *temporary* aspect of "factor-relocation-requiring" services. What John Barton calls

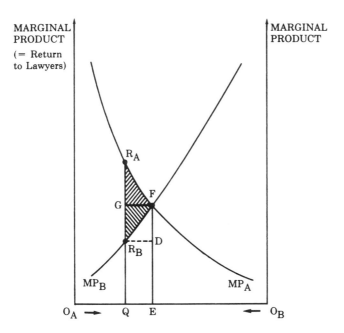

Figure 15.1

"migratory" (or permanent) as distinct from "transient" (or temporary) labor flows[9] raise a different, and more difficult, set of issues which, if brought into the discussion, would compromise the possibility of making significant progress on the issue. Two critical reasons underlie this judgment.[10]

One reason is best seen through, figure 15,1, a highly simplified model which teaches an important lesson. Imagine a world populated only by lawyers.

$O_A O_B$ is the total number of lawyers in countries A and B together. $O_A Q$ is the pre-migration number of lawyers in country A, $O_B Q$ in country B, with O_A as the origin for country A and O_B for country B. Given other factors and know-how in each country, the marginal product of more lawyers is assumed to decline in each country: MP_A and MP_B being the marginal-product curves for countries A and B, respectively.

Now, before migration, $R_A Q$ is the marginal product, and hence the return (assuming that factors are paid their marginal product) to lawyers in A. Similarly, $R_B Q$ is the return to lawyers in B. Since $R_A Q$ exceeds $R_B Q$, lawyers will migrate from B to A until their returns become equalized and further movement is not attractive. This will happen when EQ number of lawyers have moved to A, equalizing the return in both countries at FE.

What is the impact of this migration on economic welfare? The answer can depend upon whether the migration is considered "permanent" or "transient". This is because, while the nonmigrants in A and the migrants from B are both better off, the nonmigrants in B are worse off. If the migration is permanent, the country of emigration B may well consider this to be an undesirable phenomenon by excluding these migrants' welfare improvements from its calculus. On the other hand, if the migration is temporary, the sociological and political basis for including their gains in the overall calculus of national benefits from migration is clear.

Remembering that the *entire* area under the marginal product curve represents the *total* increment in product as the number of lawyers increases, the total gains and losses in this model are as follows:

B:

Gain of migrants
from B

: $GFDR_B$

Loss of nonmigrants
in B

: FDR_B

Total gain of migrants
and nonmigrants in B

: $GFR_B (= GFDR_B - FDR_B)$

A:

Total gain of
nonmigrants in A

: $R_A FG$

A + B:

World gain
(including all three groups)

: $R_A FR_B (= GFR_B + R_A FG)$

Evidently, migration improves world welfare, as well as the welfare of nonmigrant nationals in the country of immigration A. Welfare improves for the country of emigration B, however, only if the welfare of the migrants is counted. If migrant welfare is not counted, total welfare in country B diminishes.[11]

These income-distributional conflicts between migrants and nonmigrants could be moderated if only fiscal policy instruments could be devised to effect income redistribution. The exit tax, abused by the Soviet Union, may be thought of as an approximate exercise of such a policy option. The preferred alternative is the exercise of income tax jurisdiction on nationals abroad, following, in effect, the practice of global taxation based on the citizenship nexus. The United States and the Philippines are the only countries currently practicing this precept, however; and, despite many discussions at the United Nations Conference on Trade and Development and in several academic fora, it does not seem probable that the elites of the developing countries which could profit from changing their tax systems will follow the egalitarian U.S. model and begin to extend their income tax jurisdiction to their prosperous citizens abroad.[12]

The second reason for distinguishing temporary from permanent immigration is that permanent immigration is generally judged by moral-philosophical principles very different from the utilitarian calculus that underlies the economic case for free trade and free investment flows. The "right to exclude" is simply not consistent, in general, with the efficient allocation of world resources, because it prevents some labor inputs from being put to their highest valued use. Instead, a country's exclusion of immigrants is often defended on the basis of "communitarian" ideas such as those developed by philosophers such as Michael Walzer.[13] Such communitarian arguments flatly reject efficiency as the standard against which government policy is to be judged; they are based instead on other moral judgments.

An added reason for concern is that the professional groups that fear substantial loss of earnings are exceptionally well organized, and can often adduce attractive arguments to support their protectionist goals. The American Medical Association, for example, can invoke the possibility of deleterious impact on public health to reject an open-ended services compact permitting free and permanent immigration. It is important therefore that the *temporary* nature of factor relocation, designed to permit service transactions to transpire, be made explicit in negotiations on service trade regulation. If it is not, the possibility of negotiating anything worthwhile will be lost.

15.3   Bringing Developing Countries into the Negotiations

I turn finally to the question of how to convince developing countries that it is in their best interest to negotiate an international compact on service transactions. The central cause of their hesitation to support negotiations on service trade is the fear that comparative (i.e., export) advantage in service transactions belongs entirely to the developed countries. Lobbying for a GATT-type compact on services has indeed come from sectors in the United States, such as insurance and banking, which see themselves as expanding rapidly in world markets and thus seek the global reach that such a services compact would make feasible. In addition, the proposed service compacts have tended to exclude the temporary-factor-relocation-requiring services in which the developing countries are strong, especially services such as construction, defined so as to include the use of unskilled foreign workers.

Such developing countries as India and Egypt, which are most reluctant to enter international service trade agreements, will see a clearer comparative advantage for themselves if the compact permits increased transactions involving temporary relocation of factors such as skilled and unskilled labor.[14] Interestingly, South Korea has already tried to get into both the European Economic Community and Canada with offers to undertake construction projects using Korean workers on a *temporary* basis, exactly as in the Middle East. These attempts have not been successful, but they are totally consonant with the objective of expanding service transactions in theory and in practice. Excluding labor service transfers because they involve unskilled workers is conceptually untenable, because such services clearly belong to the category of "immobile-user, mobile-provider" described above. Such exclusion could also be self-serving on the part of developed countries, which should seek rules that are informed by basic principles, as with GATT on goods, rather than crippled by self-interest.

Even if a services trade compact were initially limited to the professional service sectors, it should still interest the developing countries that presently oppose the U.S. initiatives. The expansion of transactions in professional services will result in a mutual, rather than one-sided, export advantage. The developing countries must not be misled into thinking otherwise simply because the initiative to include such trade in a services compact comes almost wholly from multinational firms in the developed countries.

The mutual export advantage stems from the fact that professional services are not uniform. It is best to think of "dualistic" structures here: within a service sector such as law or accounting there are both more sophisticated, high-quality services and less sophisticated, bread-and-butter services. The advantage in tendering services at the "upper" multinational level is certainly likely to inhere in developed countries: multinational service providers are following their multinational clients in other sectors as the clients begin operations abroad. But even here, as the developing countries expand their own multinationals in non-service sectors, as they are only just beginning to do, they will begin to piggy-back their own professional-services multinationals on their multinational producers of goods. Developing country providers of more sophisticated services will therefore stand to benefit from liberalization of service trade.

Moreover, at the "lower" end of the spectrum, the advantage surely must belong to lawyers, doctors, accountants, etc. in the developing countries, simply because they are not only bright, accessible and agreeable, but they can also work more cheaply. If they are allowed to come in under "temporary-factor-relocation" visas to facilitate service transactions, there seems to be no reason why they cannot increasingly take a sizeable fraction of the market at that level.

Such a "dualistic" view is consonant with the modern view of trade in goods in which international economists have increasingly come to terms with mutual trade in "similar products."[15] A product has numerous characteristics and different countries may well have an advantage in some characteristics but not in others. This view is all the more relevant to service transactions where physical proximity accentuates such differential elements and can lead to mutual comparative advantages within a sector for suppliers from different countries.

Although developing countries could find export possibilities in professional services alone, negotiations between the developing and the developed countries should certainly proceed, either simultaneously or sequentially, in both the professional and the unskilled-labor sectors. Once the agenda on services is explicitly broadened to include all varieties of temporary-factor-relocation-requiring services, more developing countries should see the *mutuality* of interests and benefits for themselves in including services in the forthcoming trade talks. Broadening the agenda, so that the developing countries see a clear prospect of gaining their own export advantage within the service sector, would also provide a salutary lesson to the negotiators of the service compact in the developed countries. For, driven by the momentum of domestic lobbying, the developed countries tend to overlook the legitimate concerns of countries that hesitate to open up this new area to GATT-type rules. The "role reversal" created by requiring developed countries to face up to concerns about competitive disadvantage in service sectors where *they* would face successful import entry would be most helpful in making the negotiations fair, equitable and genuinely two-sided.

In particular, this would lead to the realization that we should be prepared to move only gradually toward stablishing a comprehensive service trade accord. As in GATT, we should aim at general principles, especially such things as most favored nation status, bindings and national treatment. Yet we should not forget that we are dealing with areas in which countries have traditionally behaved as if the GATT-type "rule-of-law" could not be allowed to decide "who gets what" in world commerce. Banking and insurance raise specters of loss of fiduciary and monetary control as well as loss of effective regulation over vital infrastructure; transborder flows of information create worries about loss of political sovereignty;[16] and temporary entry of foreign professionals generates fears of dilution of service quality and possible hazard to national efficiency and health. It is not by chance that services have remained out of the bounds of a GATT-type compact to date. Imagine what would happen if a humorless economist were to propose that the international location of armaments production should be determined by comparative advantage!

The ideal way to handle the problem of gradualism may well be to seek a compact that is based on a set of general principles and rules as GATT is, but which simultaneously allows for appropriate Article XIX-type safeguards to hedge against the "quantity-outcomes" of such rules.[17] The reverse route of beginning with quantity-swaps (e.g., India admits ten U.S. banks in exchange for the U.S. allowing in ten Indian ones), in the hope that general rules will ultimately emerge, is unlikely to succeed.

Notes

This paper is based on comments made at the University of Chicago Legal Forum symposium on "Barriers to International Trade in Professional Services," February 8, 1986.

1. Geza Feketekuty, Trade in Professional Services: An Overview, 1986 U. Chi. Legal F. 1.

2. See T. P. Hill, On Goods and Services, Review of Income and Wealth 315–338 (1977). There is, however, no dearth of earlier discussion, beginning with Adam Smith and John Stuart Mill. See Adam Smith, The Wealth of Nations, Book I, ch. 3 (1776); John Stuart Mill, Essays on Some Unsettled Questions of Political Economy, Essay III (1844).

3. If the interaction of economic agents were omitted from the definition of services, all activity and value added would fall within the service sector; yet this is far from the meaning normally attributed to the word "services." Because services can exist only when economic agents interact, every definition of services assumes the existence of an economic organization or "market structure." This has what appears to be the arbitrary result that if a worker paints a car on the assembly line inside an auto plant as an employee, his or her wages are part of goods production and value added. But if the same person does the same job from his or her own establishment, the resulting wages or income are part of service production and value added. For a detailed discussion of this question, see Jagdish N. Bhagwati, International Trade in Services and Its Relevance for Economic Development, Xth Annual Lecture of the Geneva Association, delivered at the London

School of Economics and the Graduate Institute of International Studies, Geneva, Services World Forum, Geneva (November 1985) (drawing upon earlier commentary by several distinguished economists including Irving Kravis, Peter Bauer, and Basil Yamey); Jagdish N. Bhagwati, Splintering and Disembodiment of Services and Developing Nations, 7 World Econ. 133 (1984).

4. Bhagwati, 7 World Econ. at 141 (cited in note 3). In that article, I discuss the *latter* class of services (here called "long-distance" services). I evaluate how the "disembodiment" effect can frustrate immigration restrictions on skilled labor, and discuss the implications of this effect for the developing countries' comparative advantage in services. Gary Sampson and Richard Snape have drawn on this twofold distinction to explore instead the *former* class of services, where physical proximity of the provider and the user is required, articulating a useful taxonomy for such services which I draw upon in the text below. Gary Sampson and Richard Snape, Identifying the Issues in Trade in Services, 8 World Econ. 171–182 (1985).

5. Frank A. Rossi, Government Impediments and Professional Constraints on the Operations of International Accounting Organizations, 1986 U. Chi. Legal F. 135.

6. See particularly Sydney M. Cone, III, Government Trade Policy and the Professional Regulation of Foreign Lawyers, 1986 U. Chi. Legal F. 169; John H. Barton, Negotiation Patterns for Liberalizing International Trade in Professional Services, 1986 U. Chi. Legal F. 97.

7. See Cone, 1986 U. Chi. Legal F. at 169–173 (cited in note 6).

8. Id.

9. See Barton, 1986 U. Chi. Legal F. at 100–102 (cited in note 6).

10. There is substantial literature on the subject of international migration which develops the important differences between "transient" (or "to-and-fro") and "permanent" migration. See in particular, Jagdish N. Bhagwati, International Factor Mobility, in Robert Feenstra, 2 Int'l Econ. Theory, chs. 42–45 (1983); Jagdish N. Bhagwati, Dependence and Interdependence, in Gene Grossman, ed., 2 Essays in Development Economics (1985); Koichi Hamada, Taxing the Brain Drain: A Global Point of View, reprinted in Jagdish N. Bhagwati, ed., The New International Economic Order: The North-South Debate, ch. 5 (1978).

11. It should be stressed that this model sharply illustrates the consequences of the distinction between temporary and permanent migrants through migration's differential impact on the welfare of migrants and non-migrants. The model is not intended to provide a complete analysis of the welfare consequences of migration *in practice*.

12. Considerable literature now exists on this subject. See in particular Oliver Oldman and Richard D. Pomp, The Brain Drain: A Tax Analysis of the Bhagwati Proposal, 3 World Dev. 754 (1975); Richard D. Pomp, The Experience of the Philippines in Taxing its Nonresident Citizens, 17 N.Y.U.J. Int'l L. & Pol. 245 (1985); Jagdish N. Bhagwati and Martin Partington, eds., Taxing the Brain Drain:

A Proposal (1976); Jagdish N. Bhagwati and John Wilson, eds., Income Taxation and International Personal Mobility (1989).

13. Michael Walzer, Spheres of Justice: A Defense of Pluralism and Equality (1983).

14. See generally Bhagwati, Dependence and Interdependence (cited in note 4); Jagdish N. Bhagwati, Opening Up Trade in Services: U.S. Should Heed Third World Demands, N.Y. Times, Section III, col. 1, p. 3 (November 10, 1985); Jagdish N. Bhagwati, GATT and Trade in Services: How Can We Resolve the North–South Debate, Financial Times, p. 27, col. 6 (November 27, 1985); and Trade in Services: How to Change India Strategy, Economic Times (Bombay), Editorial Page (Dec. 2, 1985).

15. See, e.g., Kelvin Lancaster, Variety, Equity and Efficiency (1979); Elhanan Helpman and Paul Krugman, Market Structure and Foreign Trade (1985).

16. See, for example, the acute concerns expressed by Deepak Nayyar, a former official in the Indian Ministry of Commerce, in International Trade in Services: Implications for Developing Countries, ExIm Bank of India Annual Lecture (1986).

17. Article XIX of GATT permits the adoption of trade restraints when market-disruption-related difficulties emerge in industries facing import competition. It therefore builds into the GATT an explicit safeguard against unmanageable consequences of adherence to GATT rules on binding trade commitments.

16 Trade in Services and the Multilateral Trade Negotiations

The question of inclusion of services in the Uruguay Round was a principal source of discord between the Group of Ten (G10), led by Brazil and India, and the developed countries, led by the United States in the negotiations prior to the Punta del Este meeting.[1] In between these two "hard-line" groups[2] were doubtless other developing countries who shared G10-type concerns. Nonetheless, they felt sufficiently pressured by the ballooning protectionist threat in the United States and the energetic and relentless diplomacy of its negotiators, to become with the European Community (EEC) the "moderate" brokers of a compromise solution at Punta del Este.

But the compromise merely clears the way for the trade talks to be launched despite the discordant views on services. The compromise relates to procedures on which the contending parties fought because, as I shall explain below, they symbolized substantive differences. These differences are serious and they raise both broad conceptual questions and narrow negotiating issues. This article seeks to address these issues and to define the possible agenda that the developing countries may seek in the service negotiations that are now to begin.

16.1 The Question of Tracks: Form and Substance

The procedural issues that divided the United States from the G10, if we may confine ourselves to the principals, related to two questions:

1. Would the General Agreement on Tariffs and Trade (GATT) be augmented to handle a service compact, or would there be a separate institution or agreement to oversee and regulate world commerce in services?

2. Would the negotiations for arriving at such a compact be conducted under GATT auspices or independently; by contracting parties or by a

different group; land parallel to the next round of talks on goods or disjoint therefrom?

The U.S. position at the outset was to augment the GATT to include services, leaving the form of such an augmentation to the negotiations themselves. That form may, as a witticism went, be simply to add to the GATT Articles the two words "and services" wherever the word "goods" appeared, or alternatively, taking the cue from the conventional Oxford English Dictionary where "man" embraces "woman," to declare that "goods" imply "services" in the Agreement. But, as often, good wit is bad economics; and services raise issues that go well beyond the scope of the GATT as it currently stands.

It followed equally that the United States wanted the new round of trade talks to include the negotiation of the services compact. The so-called single track was therefore the preferred U.S. option.

By contrast, Brazil and India, and the G10 as a whole, wished to delink the GATT from a potential services agreement and derive comfort rather than suffering embarrassment from the fact that the acronym for the General Agreement on Services would be GAS. In turn, therefore it was reasonable for them to seek a neat separation in the negotiating procedures for goods and for services: this was the dual-track procedure proposed by Brazil in June 1985.

The negotiations, according to this formula, would be distinct for services, would be undertaken by governments rather than GATT contracting parties, need not be parallel to those in goods, would not be under GATT auspices, and would lead to a services compact outside the GATT.

What transpired at Punta del Este was a compromise between these two opposed procedural designs. The dual track was preserved in that the "contracting parties" would negotiate on goods but would change their hats to "governments" when they negotiated on services. But the G10 yielded to the extent that both groups would operate under the aegis of the Trade Negotiating Committee, to which they would take their recommendations; and the question of whether the GATT would be augmented or bypassed via a separate services compact was deliberately avoided.

Why all this fuss? Was it really a "farce," as U.S. ambassador Yeutter is reported to have remarked? As it happens, it was not. Underlying these procedural issues is a key, substantive source of discord. The United States, and lately the EC, have given the impression that they would trade concessions on their imports of goods, for concessions on their exports of services. Recent U.S. Section 301 actions (which are trade actions directed largely at what are deemed unfair practices affecting U.S. exports) have even explicitly followed this type of linkage with a degree of energy that leaves little doubt of U.S. earnestness in the matter. The linkage has been formulated not merely in terms of "rollbacks" of barriers against developing countries' exports of goods in exchange for access to developing-country markets in services. More seriously, the linkage has been made in terms of denying "standstills" and hence *added* protection being threatened, for developing-country exports of goods if they did not offer "reverse" market access on services.

Opposed to this approach has been the position of the G10 that most "rollbacks" and "standstills" on goods merely call for the contracting parties to conform to explicit GATT rules. The demands of the developed countries such as the United States that goods and services should be linked are seen as offering conformity to GATT rules on goods as an exchange for developing countries opening up new areas such as services to market access. This is considered to be unfair and wrong. In short, the U.S. position is construed as a demand for an *unrequited* concession by developing countries on services masquerading as a quid pro quo trade of concessions by developing and developed countries.

The single-track and dual-track modalities are therefore not superficial phenomena but reflect the desires of their respective proponents to choose bargaining procedures that reflect and hence enhance these substantive positions. Single-track negotiations do underline linkage; dual-track negotiations do not.

16.2   Services versus Goods: Concepts and Consequences

It is important, at the outset, to recall the conceptual advances that international economists, following as usual in the footsteps of activist policy-makers, have now made in the matter of defining services. This conceptualization should provide the underpinnings for the positions that governments must consider in formulating the general principles of a services compact, just as the theory of trade and welfare provides the underpinnings for the general principles that underlie GATT and for the impulse to trade liberalization that informs current World Bank conditionality.

How, then, are services to be defined? Or how are they different from goods? Adam Smith, John Stuart Mill, and many others raised these questions, but perhaps the earliest answer to them was attempted by T. P. Hill (1977) only recently. Hill focused on the fact that producers cannot accumulate a stock or inventory of services, stressing that services must be consumed as they are produced. This key element will not characterize all items which we customarily define as services: for example, "answering services" do store messages. But such exceptions do not detract from the usefulness of a definition of services that characterizes them as nonstorable because they require the simultaneity of provision and use.[3]

Services Requiring Physical Proximity versus "Long-Distance" Services

If services must be used as they are produced, then there must of necessity be *interaction* between the user and the provider of the service. A producer of goods, by contrast, can produce but store, and generally transact with users at any subsequent time. But this interaction, in turn, implies that we can contemplate two essential categories of services: first, those that necessarily require the physical proximity of the user and the provider; and second, those that do not, though such physical proximity may be useful. I noted this important distinction sharply in a recent article (1984):

Basically one has to draw a distinction between services as embodied in the supplier of the services and requiring their physical presence where the user happens to be and services which can be disembodied from the supplier and provided without a physical presence being necessary."[4]

Physical Proximity Essential
The class of services where physical proximity is essential is usefully thought of as consisting of three categories based on the mobility of the provider and user of the services.

The first category is *mobile-provider, immobile-user*. This class of services requires that the provider go to the user, while the reverse mobility is physically infeasible. If an Indian or Korean firm had won the bid for construction of the Connecticut Turnpike, unskilled Indian or Korean labor services could have been provided only by moving them to Connecticut. Supplies of brute, Ricardian-style labor services must be relocated to the user's locale, as we have seen in the Middle East since the 1970s.

The second category is *mobile-user, immobile-provider*. This is another important class of services in which the user must move to the provider. Open-heart surgery cannot currently be done in Zaire because, even though Dr. Cooley can go from Houston to Kinshasa, there is no way the necessary support services and hospital care can be duplicated there. In this class of services, some key elements are simply not transferable geographically to the user's location.

The third category is *mobile-user, mobile-provider*. For this range of services, mobility is symmetrically possible. Haircuts, tailored suits, and lectures are the type of services which are in principle transmittable between user and provider in either's location, the only difference being the cost of so doing.

The generic class of services, where the provider must move to the user, as a sheer physical necessity (as in the first category above) or because of overwhelming economic advantage in so doing relative to alternative means of effecting the service transaction at long distance (as discussed immediately below), I call "temporary-factor-relocation-requiring" services.

Physical Proximity Inessential: The "Long-Distance" Services
In the second broad class, which I call "long-distance" services, physical proximity between providers and users may be useful, but it is not necessary. Live music concerts and data transmission "over the wire" are obvious examples. Traditional banking and insurance services fall into this category, in principle, since loans could be secured by mail or phone, and insurance policies are often so purchased. The scope for long-distance service transactions will increase with the advance of technology (see Bhagwati 1984). This has important implications for broader issues such as the trend effect of immigration restrictions on the relative wages of skilled and unskilled labor since skilled services may increasingly be transacted "long-distance" whereas the latter cannot.

Physical proximity between provider and user in many services (especially in banking) does involve substantially greater efficiency, however, and at times may allow a wider range of possible transactions even when long-distance or arm's length transaction is feasible. Technical change which has opened up product diversification in banking, for instance, has reinforced this aspect. In legal services, continuous interaction between local client and overseas lawyers is deemed essential for efficient service and has fueled lobbying efforts by multinational legal firms to secure ways of establishing physical proximity to their clients abroad.

The vast majority of service providers are likely to require and therefore press for physical proximity. The question of devising a service compact, whether as part of an augmented GATT or outside the GATT, is thus inextricably bound up with the question of provider-mobility across national borders.

The negotiations on services must therefore come to terms somehow with the implications of this essential connection, in many services, between international factor mobility and international trade. While we have accepted the distinction between these two phenomena since the founding of both economics and the GATT, it vanishes for these, indeed the preponderant class of, services. Factor mobility and trade are simply two integral aspects of the service transaction. For this reason, I prefer to talk of service *transactions* rather than service *trade*, so that we do not lose sight of this dual nature of the services that do not fall into the "long distance" mold.

This essential connection of services with international factor mobility has critical implications for government restrictions on service transactions. If services require factor mobility, then the ability of governments to exclude or impede service transactions does not depend altogether on restrictive border measures on trade. Restrictions on factor inflow can suffice for this purpose.

Hence arises the immediate and compelling need to go beyond the conventional focus on border trade measures such as tariffs or nontariff barriers (NTBs) for services. This fuels the demands for the "right to establish" domestic outlets.[5]

But the phrase "right to establish" conceals a continuum of factor-mobility phenomena which embrace both capital and labor mobility. It can cover the right of an American bank to establish a branch in Bombay, implying foreign investment, and the right to employ foreign personnel locally, implying skilled and semiskilled importation of labor. It can extend to a Korean firm's right to construct a road or a harbor by importing skilled and unskilled labor, *both* constituting (according to sound economic theory as spelled out above) an integral component of the service transaction in that sector.

Equally, it can extend to an English multinational legal firm setting up an office in Tokyo, with local personnel but with English barristers or American lawyers who fly in and out to work with multinational Tokyo-based and other local clients. It could include hospital management contracts with short-term inflows of managerial personnel.

In short, factor mobility can be complex, not fitting into any particular mold. What *is* certain however is that the concept of the "right to establish" cannot meaningfully or justifiably be circumscribed to exclude the inward mobility of foreign labor and its services. And the problem that this raises cannot be dismissed simply by saying, "Oh, we cannot dismantle immigration restrictions and have free mobility of labor across national borders." For, as I have argued earlier (Bhagwati 1987a), the concept that we can work with is that of *"temporary-factor-relocation-requiring"* services and hence of temporary residence by foreign labor to execute service transactions. For example, Korean construction firms would bring in workers to build a turnpike; when the task was completed, the workers would return to Seoul. Or an Indian legal firm would have lawyers come from New Delhi for specific assignments or predetermined periods, the firm then rotating the personnel as necessary to avoid permanent residence (for example, immigration) of specific individuals.

Conceptual clarification of the nature of service transactions therefore has led to a keen awareness that freeing trade in services and the associated "right to establish" question, will raise serious questions relating to labor relocation as well. As long as the "right to establish" was regarded as simply a question of U.S. banks, insurance companies, and multinational professional firms setting up branches in Bangkok, Dar-es-Salaam, and Tokyo, there was at times a certain sense of patronizing disdain for the hesitations of the countries that found the factor-mobility aspects worrisome.

As Hindley (1987) shrewdly remarks, however, a certain ambivalence has apparently crept into the U.S. negotiating attitudes, now that the labor-mobility issue suggests that openness to foreign services may create immigration problems for the United States. On the one hand, the impression has been given by U.S. officials at times that the overall services compact should confine itself to long-distance and arm's-length transactions, ruling out "right-to-establish" questions and hence the corresponding enormous range of services that require such establishment.

On the other hand, since the powerful U.S. lobbies from the service sector continue to clamor for the "right to establish," some official spokesmen have instead tended to opt in favor of an emasculated (and conveniently self-serving) notion of the "right of presence" or "right of market access," euphemisms which are designed to ensure artfully that the labor-mobility aspects of the "right to establish" questions will be soft-pedaled.[6]

Exclusion of services that require significant temporary relocation of labor, however, would rule out of the compact a range of services in which some of the principal developing countries that have been skeptical about or opposed to negotiating services happen to have sufficient skills and endowments to consider developing exports of such services.[7] Except for a handful of developing countries such as Singapore and Hong Kong, which entertain offshore banking and insurance establishments without hesitation, "such a definition of 'services' ... excludes any substantial export interest on the part of developing countries" (Hindley 1987, p. 4). It would also necessarily reinforce the position of those developed countries which seek concessions on services from developing countries in exchange for their (real or apparent) concessions on goods to the developing countries. The question therefore is pertinent to the issues that divide the G10 and the United States.

Regulation

Another aspect of the difference between services and goods is the much more pervasive application of regulation to services than to goods, and the rare harmonization of regulatory provisions across national boundaries.

The *critical* difference, however, arises from the fact that these regulations often apply to the *provider* of the services while their intent is to protect the user of the services, whereas with goods the regulations apply to the *product itself.* Thus, with trade in goods, it is possible for foreign suppliers to meet national regulations by manufacturing to necessary standards. While it is not uncommon to hear complaints about how different health, safety, and human rights traditions and standards result in "unfair" competition, it is conventional with goods not to be bothered by the behind-the-trade-scene regulations as they differentially affect rival *producers* in competing countries. With services, this detachment is often impossible. The regulations imposed on the provider can critically affect the service transaction, as for instance with reserve requirements that an insurance company has to meet before it is allowed to even begin to attract any customers.

This regulatory difference between services and goods implies that, while local establishment by a foreign provider to supply a service will permit the fulfillment of local regulatory criteria, sale of such services from a base abroad where the regulatory criteria are less strict, will not. This difficulty with regulation arises with "long-distance" or arm's-length transactions, whereas the difficulty (identified earlier) with service transactions requiring physical proximity between provider and user arose where such long-distance transactions were infeasible or significantly inefficient.

The nonharmonization of regulatory systems has led to major difficulties with service trade liberalization in the EEC (Hindley 1986a). The EEC does not lack for the "right to establish." But the incapacity to sell services from a base abroad, where the regulatory regimes are dissimilar, has been a major obstacle to liberalization and accounts for the miniscule progress observed to date.

A gung-ho reaction to this issue would be to permit regulatory systems to "compete through their outputs." A less demanding or restrictive system would then prosper at the expense of ones that restrict or regulate more. In their present deregulatory mood, U.S. officials may then see a triumph of the more efficient resulting over the less efficient. It is unlikely that others will see the matter this way, however, any more than the United States would if the shoe were on the other foot. Within the EEC freer service trade has not been permitted to transpire; and successful efforts have not been made to harmonize the service trade regimes. It is unlikely that the developing countries, where regulation sometimes tends to be stiffer, will be enthusiastic about these matters either.

Between the hesitations over the "right to establish" and the desire to emasculate it to developed-country advantage, on the one hand, and the hesitations over the indirect competition between unharmonized regulatory regimes that the developing countries with greater attention to the role of the state must fear when services are transacted without the benefit of local establishment, on the other hand, it seems as if progress toward the general principles underlying a service compact is likely to be slow.

Infrastructure, National Security, and Other Constraints on Liberalization

Overlaying these difficulties is the fact that some of the service sectors (for example, banking) are regarded by the hesitant developing countries to be part of their infrastructure which they feel they must control for political reasons much as, say, the U.S. restricts ownership by foreign nationals in its media (services) sector. Again, transborder data flows and the information sector are regarded as sensitive areas that raise issues bordering closely on "national security" for the "middle powers" such as Argentina, Brazil, and India.

In these areas it is therefore difficult to urge the developing countries to discard such notions altogether, especially when these types of asymmetrical views about some services and many goods are held by many influential citizens within the developed countries themselves. (As I argue later, however, their fears and concerns are greatly exaggerated and need to be carefully evaluated in their own interest.) Consider the following impassioned pronouncement:

We ought to be exporting computers, not shares of IBM. We should seek to sell more, not sell out.

To accept the de-industrialization of [our nation] while exulting in the growth of foreign ownership and influence in our domestic institutions could be an unwitting prescription for slowly becoming an economic colony again.

It came, not from Prime Minister Rajiv Gandhi or from President Alfonsin. The author was U.S. Representative Jim Wright, majority whip in the U.S. Congress, writing in the *Wall Street Journal* (October 3, 1985).

16.3   Comparative Advantage in Services, Cost of Protection, and Policy-Mix Solutions

The foregoing analysis highlights the difficulties that emerge for the impending service negotiations, especially as they reflect the special characteristics that serve to set services apart from goods. But before I turn to the prospects for different solutions to these difficulties, it is necessary to speculate on where the comparative advantage in service transactions may lie, especially between the developing and the developed countries. Several observations on that issue are in order.

First, while the trade data for services are extremely unreliable, Sapir's (1985) careful analysis of what is available underlines strongly what common sense would suggest: many traded services tend to be intensive in the use of technology and of capital, whether human or physical. This should give the developed countries the competitive edge since they are abundant in the endowment of human and physical capital. It is suggestive that, when Sapir (p. 37) looks at the balance of trade in services, it is the advanced newly industrializing economies such as the Republic of Korea, Singapore, and Taiwan that come out with small positive or negative balances rather than the large deficit of many developing countries.[8]

However, it would be totally wrong to infer that developing countries simply cannot find traded services that they can export successfully. Table 16.1, compiled by Sapir, gives an aggregated and very rough picture of service trade among the two groups of industrialized and developing countries for 1980. The data can be read two ways. On the one hand, they show that the service exports of developing countries are a substantially smaller fraction of their total exports than is the case with industrialized countries' share of service to total exports. On the other hand, the developing countries' service exports are by no means negligible, as recorded, and seem to reflect earnings not only from tourism and transport but also from "other private services" (which include professional, design, construction, and related services).

Second, detailed studies further underline the export possibilities that the energetic, outward-oriented newly industrializing economies have in services. Thus, for example, table 16.2 suggests that the earlier U.S. domination of the world market for international *construction* may have

Table 16.1
Trade between the industrialized and developing countries, 1980 (billions of dollars[a])

Category of merchandise and services	Industrialized-country exports to developing countries	Developing-country exports to industrialized countries
Merchandise trade, of which:	277	385
Fuels	6	258
Other primary products	44	67
Manufactures	227	60
Service trade, of which:	72	30
Transport	35	10
Travel	14	12
Other private services	23	8

a. Billion is 1,000 million.
Source: Sapir (1985, table 2); data for merchandise trade are based on GATT (1983); and for service trade, on own estimates.

Table 16.2
Market share of international construction measured by new contracts awarded to the top two-hundred fifty international contractors, 1980–84 (billions of dollars)

Country	1980	1981	1982	1983	1984
United States	48.3	48.8	44.9	29.4	30.1
	(45%)	(36%)	(36%)	(31%)	(38%)
France	8.1	12.1	11.4	10.0	5.4
	(7%)	(9%)	(9%)	(11%)	(7%)
Germany, Fed. Rep.	8.6	9.9	9.5	5.4	4.8
	(8%)	(7%)	(8%)	(6%)	(6%)
Italy	6.2	9.3	7.8	7.2	7.8
	(6%)	(7%)	(6%)	(8%)	(8%)
United Kingdom	4.9	8.7	7.5	6.4	5.7
	(5%)	(6%)	(6%)	(7%)	(7%)
Other European	9.2	12.6	10.3	9.1	7.2
	(8%)	(9%)	(8%)	(10%)	(9%)
Japan	4.1	8.6	9.3	8.7	7.3
	(4%)	(6%)	(8%)	(9%)	(9%)
Korea, Rep.	9.5	13.9	13.8	10.4	6.8
	(9%)	(10%)	(11%)	(11%)	(8%)
All other	9.4	10.5	8.6	7.0	5.9
	(9%)	(8%)	(7%)	(7%)	(7%)
Total	108.3	134.4	123.1	93.6	80.5

Source: Various issues of *Engineering News Record*; from ongoing studies by U.S. Office of Technology Assessment.

diminished with the medium-level developed countries and a newly industrializing economy such as Korea taking significant shares in the 1980s. A nonnegligible share of the developing countries is evident from table 16.3. In the more complex field of international design contracts, again the data show a sizable share of contracts being awarded to firms from Brazil, India, Korea, Lebanon, and Taiwan (Sapir 1986, table 3).

Third, there is little doubt that the broader group of newly industrializing economies, not just the super exporting economies like Korea but also the traditionally inward-looking ones like India, have the skills to develop export advantages, not merely in computer software (a good, not a service) and in an increasing range of "on-the-wire" services that new technologies make possible, but also in the services that imply temporary relocation of skilled labor. I would expect that legal and professional services, with right of establishment, exhibit a *mutual* rather than one-sided export advantage for developing and developed countries. The developing countries must not be misled into thinking otherwise simply because the initiative to include such trade in a services compact comes almost wholly from multinational firms in the developed countries. Why?

The reason is that such services are not homogeneous. It is necessary to think of "dualistic" structures here (Bhagwati 1986d). The advantage in tendering services at the multinational level is likely to inhere in developed countries: in fact, these multinationals are piggybacking on their multinational clients in other sectors that have operations abroad. Only as the developing countries expand their own multinationals in nonservice sectors, as is beginning to happen, will they begin to develop some "linked" advantage in professional services.

At the other end of the spectrum, however, the advantage must belong to lawyers, doctors, and accountants in the developing countries, because, while they are equally competent, they can work more cheaply and offer a range of services where price competition is decisive.[9] If they are allowed to enter under "temporary-factor-relocation" visas to make service transactions possible, I see no reason why they cannot increasingly take a sizable fraction of the market at that level.[10]

Such a "dualistic" view is quite consonant with mutual trade in "similar products." A product is a vector of characteristics, and different countries can have advantage in some and not in others. In service transactions, physical proximity accentuates such differential elements and can lead to mutual comparative advantages within a sector for suppliers from different countries.

Table 16.3
Cumulative foreign awards of top international contractors by economy, 1978–83 (billions of dollars)

Economy	Awards
All countries, of which:	566.6
All developing countries, of which:	99.2
Korea Republic	56.2
Turkey	10.0
Yugoslavia	7.4
Brazil	5.8
India	3.9
Taiwan	3.4
Philippines	3.2
Argentina	3.0
Lebanon	1.4
Pakistan	1.3
Kuwait	0.7
Singapore	0.6
Malaysia	0.5
Panama	0.4
Mexico	0.2
Thailand	0.2
United Arab Emirates	0.2
Colombia	0.1
Indonesia	0.1

Source: Compiled by Sapir (1986, table 2) from *Engineering News*, various issues.
Note: Countries are ranked according to the foreign contract values of their top firms. Until 1980, the top 200 firms were surveyed; since then, this number was raised to 250.

Fourth, the export possibilities become even more compelling for developing countries if the issue of unskilled labor mobility in the execution of specific short-term contracts (as in the Middle East), is resolved in favor of its inclusion in the "right to establish." It is already within the realm of probability, thanks to the widespread use of such unskilled labor, including that by U.S. international contracting firms, during the 1970s and 1980s. It also has legitimacy in the practice of Western Europe in its postwar "guest-worker" systems and in the latest U.S. legislation which permits over 300,000 workers to be imported for specific types of short-term work (that is, in U.S. agriculture).[11]

Fifth, it is important for developing countries to recognize that a great number of traded services are intermediates. Protecting banking and insurance sectors for example, increases domestic prices of these services. As they are inputs into other goods, this can raise prices of export goods and undermine export prospects.

The effects of protecting intermediate services are similar to those that result from increasing the cost of intermediate goods such as steel.[12] But the adverse effects on exports of goods are more serious in the present instance because, in denying the domestic exporters of goods access to efficient banking services, the protective policies succeed in denying access to more than cheaper credit. More important, exporters are denied access to the entire vector of services that modern international banks can provide to facilitate international commerce. The protection of intermediate services, in the interest of goals such as political control, therefore has costs that are not negligible and have presumably not been properly assessed by the developing countries.

Finally, it is important to recognize that policies such as the protection of locally produced computer hardware in the telematics and information sectors may represent an unnecessarily expensive way of securing one's objectives. If the objective is to build up national technological know-how through "learning by doing" (rather than to develop the industry itself), then the cost of such a policy is to spread computer illiteracy in the population and high costs to producers who must make do without lower-cost access to modern information technology in the production process.[13]

A country such as India (and possibly Argentina and Brazil as well) has the possibility of using an alternative policy instrument to achieve the desired mastery of know-how without these costs. Remember that the know-how is embodied in one's citizens. If one then looks at the national-origin composition of scientists in only the artificial intelligence, robotics, and computer science labs and institutes in the United States, it is possible to find numerous Indian mathematicians and scientists, even in leadership positions. These Indians embody know-how in these fields at the very cutting edge of technology.

Since the sociology of international migration of professional classes increasingly permits immigrants to retain ethnic ties to their countries of origin, and therefore the "diaspora" model has increasingly come into its own, the Indian government has the option of utilizing this U.S.-based resource any time it wishes to do so.[14] Going the protectionist route will yield a lower level of embodied technology in resident nationals (who may also leave anyway) *and* will sacrifice computer literacy and efficiency in production. Permitting cheap imports at world prices avoids these costs, and utilizing the superior know-how embodied in one's nationals abroad also secures know-how at its best and cheapest.[15]

To put it differently, the *two objectives* of (1) spreading computer literacy and encouraging adoption of efficient production processes, and (2) building up technical know-how among one's nationals are impossible to achieve with one policy instrument, namely, protection. They are achievable, and are in effect Pareto-dominated in outcome, by the use of *two policy instruments*: (1) world-price imports of computers and related technology, and (2) an open-door policy on emigration combined with a policy to utilize the know-how embodied in one's nationals abroad.

Such a policy mix breaks from the protectionist mold and requires an imaginative and simultaneous use of policies from what are generally considered to be unrelated areas of governmental intervention. But they do offer the prospect of a superior approach for those countries such as India which have the talents and the skills in the field of information to make such an approach feasible.

16.4 Developing Countries: Bargaining Options and Strategies

What positive approaches emerge that the developing countries may take in the forthcoming negotiations on services?

Developing countries cannot be expected to opt en bloc for any one approach on services any more than we can expect them to have identical positions on agricultural liberalization or the developed countries to agree on the optimal redesign of safeguard procedures. Thus, Hong Kong and Singapore can be expected to be agreeable to the more "hard-line" developed-country positions on services. Brazil and India can be expected to oppose them. They, and also the developing countries that initiated the

Uruguay Round under the G48 umbrella, will have to decide what kind of game they want to play now that the players are coming onto the field.

The options that they must consider are best determined by the demands that the developed countries, especially the United States, have been making.[16] These options will have to be defined in terms of the *responses* that the developing countries make to these demands or negotiating positions, as they have been indicated so far. Let me begin with what are generally understood to be the broad outlines of the current U.S. positions, however negotiable they may turn out to be in the course of the Uruguay Round itself.

Generally Perceived U.S. Positions

Inclusion of services in the Uruguay Round, and indeed of other "new" sectors and areas such as intellectual property and trade-related investment rules, is considered to be part of a 'grand trade-off" where these new areas benefit the United States. *In return*, the United States is willing to consider rollbacks and standstills (consistent with the exercise of trade-affecting, GATT-compatible actions such as countervailing duties, antidumping, and Section 301 actions) on goods (see also, however, the discussion below).

The "grand trade-off" is seen in terms of both cosmopolitan interest (that is, what international economists describe as "world welfare") as well as U.S. interest (that is, what international economists describe as "national welfare"). The former position emphasizes that an efficient world allocation of resources requires that "everything be put on the table": the outmoded GATT must be redesigned, augmented in scope, and brought up to date to embrace new realities. The latter position is developed in terms of U.S. comparative advantage having shifted to the new areas so that, if United States is to yield on goods, it is fair for it to ask others to yield on services and new issues. A brief tabular arrangement of United States—perceived losses and gains in relation to those of the developing countries in terms of the mercantilist logic of trade-barriers-bargaining is presented in table 16.4.

A third argument in the United States in favor of this grand trade-off is that the current presidential administration is too beleaguered to hold protectionists at bay in Congress unless the advanced developing countries (and, of course, Japan and the EEC) open up their markets to U.S. exports of services as a quid pro quo.[17] These countries are faced with what could be construed as a rather difficult situation: trade concessions appear to be demanded of them as a way of ensuring that market access for their exports is continued.

Table 16.4
Perceived U.S. benefits and losses in relation to those of developing countries from the prospective liberalization of trade in the Uruguay Round

U.S. "benefits"	U.S. "losses"
1. Services	1. Rollback of the Multifiber Arrangement (MFA) and other voluntary export restraints (VERs) and orderly marketing agreements
2. Intellectual property	
3. Trade-related investments	
4. Reverse market access to developing countries	2. Standstill on VERs, OMAs on goods
5. Agriculture[a]	3. More stringent use of safeguards and tighter rules to prevent abuse of countervailing-duty and antidumping actions
	4. Improved structural adjustment

a. Agriculture is included as a benefit because agricultural liberalization in cereals is expected to favor U.S. exports, mostly at the expense of the EEC and Japan but, depending on the final package, even at the expense of some developing countries.

But this, in turn, reflects a substantial shift in U.S. positions in trade negotiations from what I have called GATT-style "first-difference" reciprocity to "full" reciprocity.[18] The United States has increasingly looked at, not the balance of advantages from *changes* in trade barriers, but the balance of advantages from the trading system in toto.

Doubtless this attitude stems from the macroeconomic difficulties that the overvalued U.S. dollar entails and the resulting substantial adjustments forced on the traded sector. It also stems from the "diminished giant syndrome" that has affected the United States as its effortless postwar hegemony in the world economy has been threatened by the relentless advent of the Pacific Century.[19] But overlaying these two factors has been the fundamental fact that the GATT's basic conception, and indeed that of the United States as its leading founder, was always based on contractual and (fully) reciprocal rights, with member states enjoying symmetrical rights and obligations. The United States, which emerged as the *force majeure* in the 1940s, permitted Western Europe effectively to get away with nonreciprocity while it worked through the 1950s to achieve current account convertibility, and agreed to special and differential treatment for developing countries until now.

The current U.S. insistence on full reciprocity can then be seen as an inevitable return to the original symmetrical conception of the world trading order. Hence, it is *not* a position that the developing countries (or Japan, which is alleged, rightly or wrongly, to offer less-than-symmetrical access to its own markets) are likely to be able to challenge with success, much as they consider it to be unfair from the perspective of first-difference reciprocity. My judgment therefore is that the developing countries must proceed from the unhappy premise that the United States, especially its Congress, cannot be expected to trade access to its markets any longer without significant elements of reciprocity from the developing countries, even if the balance-of-trade deficits are somehow eliminated.

The Developing-Country Options

From the viewpoint of the hesitant developing countries, the U.S. position presents one major difficulty even if they are prepared to accept the reality of full reciprocity and yield on their sense hitherto that the so-called bargain being offered to them simply is not one. It is unclear what the United States and the EEC can offer by way of standstills and rollbacks on goods if these developing countries offer concessions on services. I quote one influential commentator, who was a member of the U.S. administration:

The issue for the United States is whether a meaningful standstill and rollback commitment would apply to existing U.S. restrictions in sugar, meat imports, textiles, steel, automobiles, etc. as well as the use of future 301 actions in both goods and services trade. Ideally, the United States would like this commitment to apply only to new measures, not existing restrictions or extensions of existing programs (such as another VRA [voluntary restraint agreement] in steel or tightening sugar quotas under the existing programs). According to U.S. interests, it would not apply at all to trade legislation consistent with GATT (201, CVD [counter-vailing duty], and AD [antidumping] provisions and national security), and it would mean submitting 301 cases to GATT but only in goods. In new areas—services, etc.—the United States would remain free to retaliate under 301, including retaliation in goods areas, without submitting to GATT rules. (Nau 1986, pp. 22–23)

This has been the sense of the remarks reported in the U.S. press by Ambassador Yeutter on his return from Punta del Este. This is also consonant with the substance of Martin Wolf's "Europessimistic" argumentation on special and differential treatment presented in this volume: few meaningful concessions on rollbacks and standstills on goods can really be expected and the developing countries ought to yield on reverse market access largely because it is good for them to liberalize as suggested by the export-promoting strategy.[20] Doubtless, as I have already emphasized in section 16.3, even unilateral trade liberalization in intermediate services should have big payoffs for the developing countries. But if only we could persuade trading nations to accept such compelling arguments, we would not have to worry about rollbacks and standstills either. The developing countries cannot realistically be expected to be less mercantilist than those who preach free trade but practice mercantilism themselves. This is a pity, but a reality too.

This reinforces, in my judgment, a suggestion I had made earlier (Bhagwati 1985c), that the developing countries ought to participate actively in the service negotiations instead of rejecting them on grounds of first-difference-reciprocity unfairness. They should then seek quid pro quo (in terms of export possibilities) within the service sector itself.

Not merely is it risky to establish linkage between goods and services when the goods "benefit" is less likely than the services "loss." It is also silly to let the developed countries define the service compact all by themselves in a way that can then be fully expected to serve their own narrower, export interests rather than reflecting more fairly and adequately the general principles as set out in recent analyses and recapitulated in section 16.2.[21] The latter would also serve the interests of developing-country exporters.

As I argued in section 16.3, quid pro quo within the service sector certainly exists for the skill-abundant, newly industrializing countries, and especially so if the temporary-factor-relocation-requiring labor-intensive and skilled-labor-intensive services are not omitted in the formulation of a services agreement.[22]

The difficulties that I detailed in section 16.2 that plague rapid progress in service liberalization also imply that the Uruguay round is unlikely to yield anything more concrete than a code or an agreement of principles. It is improbable that actual service liberalization under the code will emerge during the course of the Round itself.

This prospect also underlines the wisdom of a strategy in which the developing countries offer to discuss services, thus assuaging the desire to begin bringing them under trade discipline and hence helping to head off protectionist pressures on goods trade. At the same time, they can use the opportunity to ensure that their export prospects are adequately reflected in the service code.

My suspicion is that, while this multilateral "constitution making" on the principles of a services agreement will go on, the United States will continue to use bilateral approaches with the aid of Section 301 to pry open selected service sectors in selected countries. This is probably unavoidable, given the immense Congressional and lobbying pressures to produce quick results.

To some extent, the U.S. Trade Representative (USTR) can be expected to ensure that these bilateral approaches are adopted to "set useful precedents" for the wider, multilateral code. At the same time, there is some cause for apprehension that the sectoral lobbying pressures to produce results may lead to "quantity" rather than "rule" outcomes (as strongly suggested in an insightful study by Cho (1986) of the United States–Korea 301 episode on the opening of the Korean insurance market).[23] This tendency to substitute "quantity" outcomes in favor of U.S. export sectors rather than to secure rule-oriented liberalization abroad is a peril that has not been easy to avoid. This was evident in the case of beef quotas in Japan in which the United States reportedly wanted a larger quota rather than genuine Japanese liberalization which would have allowed Australian beef to triumph over that both from the United States and Japan. Similarly, in negotiations on trade in semiconductor chips, an assured market share in Japan for U.S. firms was actively urged and, while not finally in the pact, is still the basis by which Japanese "performance" on the pact has been judged to be inadequate and hence to require the retaliatory tariffs imposed by President Reagan in April 1987. This is such an interesting innovation in trade policy that I have recently (Bhagwati 1987b) christened it as VIEs (voluntary import expansions).[24]

There is little that the developing countries targeted for bilateral negotiations will be able to do since it is evidently a case where the strong prevail over the weak. This is the oldest argument in the book for resort to multilateralism, which has been regarded as the only shield of the weak. Evidently, as such bilateral targeting and quantity targets multiply, the wisdom of the developing countries joining in devising a multilateral compact will become increasingly evident.[25]

Yet another compelling reason for the developing countries to join in writing the multilateral rules is that rules written between "equals" will tend to underplay the problems that "unequals" face in service liberalization. One would have to be deranged to imagine the largest American banks taking over wholly from the largest five British banks in the United Kingdom if banking were fully liberalized. Yet such fears are routine in New Delhi and Dar-es-Salaam. The "political control" issues take an added significance in the context of such fears. I spend a fair amount of time arguing with the risk-averse that such scenarios do not make much sense for New Delhi either, that it would be an act of insanity for a large American bank to open branches in India's vast hinterland, that its clientele and operations would most likely be in international transactions.

But it is evident that the unequals have fear; and, as the Russian proverb goes, fear has big eyes. So, we will need to incorporate, at least for developing countries, some quantity-safeguards, just as we have GATT Article XIX as a safeguard on goods. These would have to be more generous for the developing countries, subject to eventual and negotiated erosion with "graduation," perhaps even slower-paced than as now discussed for goods. In essence, therefore, we should contemplate freer, not free, trade in services, and, contrary to the conventional rules of the strange English language where "freer" should mean more free than "free," the developing countries should remember that it is just the other way around. But these explicit safeguards to assuage their fears will not arrive like manna from heaven. The developing countries will have to argue for this; they cannot do it if they do not actively participate in the rulemaking.

Everything therefore points to one simple piece of advice for the hesitant developing countries: get into the negotiations on the code and exercise a voice; to exit is certainly the inferior alternative.

Notes

Thanks are due to Brain Hindley, Ambassadors Shukla and Batista at the GATT, and Ambassador Muchkund Dubey for helpful conversations. The comments of Harvey Bale, Narongchai Akrasanee, David Lee, Tony Lane, Paul Leuten, Martin Wolf, and others at the Bangkok conference where the paper was presented, have also led to necessary revisions.

1. The G10 was the group of developing countries consisting of Argentina, Brazil, Cuba, the Arabic Republic of Egypt, India, Nigeria, Peru, Tanzania, Vietnam and Yugoslavia.

2. It has become customary in some sections of the press to describe the G10 as "hard-line" developing countries and the G48 as being led by "moderate" developing countries and "medium-sized" developed countries, when equally accurately the latter could be described as the "medium-sized" developing countries and the "moderate" developed countries. The dialogue between the two sides with opposed view-points is hard enough to manage without the addition of such pejorative characterizations of the principals.

3. Another characteristic of services which is necessary is that services occur *between* different economic agents or otherwise all activities and value added would collapse into the service sector. An implication of this characteristic is that the definition of services reflects economic organization or "market structure." If Mr. Smith paints a car on the assembly line inside your auto plant as your worker, then his wages are part of goods production and value added. But if he does the same job from his own establishment, his wages or income are part of service

production and value added. For a detailed discussion of this question, see Bhagwati (1987a, 1984).

4. In my 1984 paper, I focus on the latter class of services (which I now call "long-distance" services) discussing how the "disembodiment" effect can frustrate the intention of immigration restrictions on skilled labor. Conversely, Gary Sampson and Richard Snape (1985) have drawn on this twofold distinction in my 1984 article to explore further the *former* class of services, where physical proximity of the provider and the user is involved, with a valuable classification of such services which I use, with some simplification, below.

5. At the time of U.S. treasury secretary Connolly's efforts to "open up Japan," the "right to establish" question applied to *goods* trade. It was then believed that, unless Japan permitted U.S. goods exporters to set up their own retail outlets, market access to Japan could not be effective. The economic implications of this issue have been discussed and modeled in Bhagwati (1982a).

6. Compare with Hindley's (1986a) penetrating discussion of this issue.

7. This implication was noted earlier in Bhagwati (1987a, 1985a, 1985b) and has been further discussed by Hindley (1987), among others.

8. In itself, however, the trade balance would be, of course, an inconclusive piece of evidence on the issue.

9. The question of whether they would be allowed to indulge in price competition is critical. Attempts by professional associations to regulate minimum prices would then be in restraint of trade.

10. It is important not to confuse the "brain drain" question with the issue of temporary relocation of labor. I have discussed the contrasts in Bhagwati (1985c).

11. In the spirit of the U.S. service sectors' demands, the developing countries may well ask for equal access to these jobs instead of having them de facto assigned to applicants south of the Rio Grande.

12. The successful outward-oriented regimes have managed to ensure that internationally traded intermediate goods are available to domestic producers at world prices. Similar logic should apply to internationally traded intermediate services as well.

13. In India, import-substitution in computer hardware has led to higher costs, unavailability, and enormous lags in the use of computers in tourism, the judiciary and the schools. The import-substitution policy manages to distance greatly even a highly educated population and skills-endowed economy such as India from the modern world outside. It also inhibits the rapid adoption of modern information-technology-based processes that are essential to absorbing high-productivity economically efficient advances in the manufacturing sector.

14. When a people are geographically dispersed but ethnically linked, this new reality has several important implications for a variety of other policy issues such

as the appropriate exercise of income tax jurisdiction on one's nationals when they are internationally mobile. See Bhagwati (1982a) and Bhagwati and Wilson (1987).

15. Although I talk of "nationals," there is little doubt that even those who change nationalities today often have attachment to their countries of origin. Nonetheless, this distinction in turn raises the issue whether developing countries ought not to consider permitting their nationals to hold dual nationality as part of the policy option that I advocate above.

16. While the discussion below focuses on the United States, it is clear that, unlike in the 1982 GATT Ministerial meeting, the EEC also perceives export competitiveness for itself in services and hence is closer to the U.S. positions on it than before. See, for example, the recent statements of Willy de Clercq (1986) to this effect. Table 16.4 on the United States (below) therefore could be readily modified to one for the EEC, with agriculture being considered as a "loss" instead of a "gain." Japan, with its enormous surplus, also sees clear comparative advantage in the financial services area.

17. The U.S. government has encouraged such export-seeking lobbies as a political countervailing force to the trade-threatening protectionist lobbies.

18. I note with pleasure that Brian Hindley, in his article in this volume, has embraced this terminology. The use of the phrase "aggressive reciprocity" to denote full reciprocity is inappropriate: full reciprocity could equally be pursued in a tranquil way.

19. On this, see Bhagwati and Irwin (1986) on the parallels between late nineteenth-century Britain and the present-day United States in the rise of "fair trade" movements.

20. On the merits of this strategy, see the extended review in Bhagwati (forthcoming).

21. It seems probable that the failure of the developing countries to be actively involved in the Tokyo Round negotiations on the subsidies code, for example, until fairly late may have caused the code to be written against their interests (for example, in the blanket restrictions on export subsidies) and hence have led to widespread refusal by the developing countries to sign it.

22. Feketekuty's (1986) extended analysis and documentation of U.S. visa practices in regard to domestic entry for *temporary* business purposes needs to be read by the skeptical among the developing countries. Evidently, there is far more room for active diplomacy and negotiations here than is commonly believed. Also, the reader should consult the entire issue of the *Chicago Legal Forum* (1986, vol. 1, no. 1), which deals with the question of trade in legal services across nation states and which contains the Feketekuty (1986) and Bhagwati (1986c) papers, especially the papers by Barton, Cone, Noyelle, and Rossi. Needless to say, the negotiators will have to address complex issues which get even worse in dealing with unskilled labor mobility. For example, while firms can bring in professionals of different

nationalities under the temporary visas, could a U.S. firm bring in Bangladeshi construction labor to Düsseldorf?

23. Thus, one of Cho's central conclusions is that "both governments approached the case with the perception that the main issue of negotiation is the *sharing of profit* [rents] in Korea's insurance market. In the process of negotiation, both governments (especially U.S.) basically represented the interests of their insurance industries. The effect of the results of the negotiation on other sectors and efficiency of the economy as a whole has not been an important consideration." (1986, p. 17).

24. See also the discussion of this issue in Bhagwati and Irwin (1987) in the context of recent U.S. trade policy.

25. For those in the United States who believe therefore that such bilateralism, or "plurilateralism"—what a lovely euphemism for "regionalism" and other non-multilateral arrangement—is only a tactical device to get rapidly towards multi-lateralism, it would be wise to remember that such arrangements create vested interests *against* new entry, no matter what you write into the rules!

References

Bhagwati, Jagdish. 1982a. Structural Adjustment and International Factor Mobility: Some Issues. In Karl Jungenfelt (ed.), *Structural Adjustment in the World Economy*. London: Macmillan.

Bhagwati, Jagdish. 1982b. Taxation and International Migration. In Barry Chiswick (ed.), *The Gateway: U.S. Immigration Issues and Policies*. Washington, D.C.: American Enterprise Institute.

Bhagwati, Jagdish. 1984. Splintering and Disembodiment of Services and Developing Nations. *World Economy* 7, 2 (June): 133–143.

Bhagwati, Jagdish. 1985a. GATT and Trade in Services: How We Can Resolve the North–South Debate. *Financial Times*, November 27.

Bhagwati, Jagdish. 1985b. Opening Up Trade in Services: U.S. Should Heed Third World Demands. *New York Times*, November 10.

Bhagwati, Jagdish. 1985c. Trade in Services: How to Change Indian Strategy. *Economic Times* (India), December 2.

Bhagwati, Jagdish. 1986. Economic Perspectives on Trade in Professional Services. *Chicago Legal Forum* 1, 1 (March): 45–56.

Bhagwati, Jagdish. 1987a. International Trade in Services and Its Relevance for Economic Development. In Orio Giarini (ed.), *The Emerging Service Economy*. Services World Economy Series 1. New York: Pergamon Press.

Bhagwati, Jagdish. 1987b. VERs, Quid pro quo DFI and VIEs: Political-Economy-Theoretic Analyses. *International Economic Journal* (Seoul) 1, 1 (Spring). 1–15.

Bhagwati, Jagdish. 1987c. Export Promoting Trade Strategy: Issues and Evidence. *World Bank Research Observer*, Forthcoming.

Bhagwati, Jagdish, and Douglas Irwin. 1986. Lessons from Nineteenth Century Britain: Fair Trade Could Trap the Democrats. *New York Times*, June 22.

Bhagwati, Jagdish, and Douglas Irwin. 1987. The Return of the Reciprocitarians: U.S. Trade Policy Today. *The World Economy* 10, 2 (June): 109–130.

Bhagwati, Jagdish, and John Wilson (eds.). 1987. *Income Taxation and International Personal Mobility*. Amsterdam: North Holland.

Cho, Yoon Je. 1986. U.S.-Korea Disputes on the Opening of Korean Insurance Market: Some Implications. Washington, DC: World Bank: Development Research Department. Processed.

de Clercq, Willy. 1986. The European Community and GATT Negotiations on Trade in Services. Speech at Lugano Economic and Financial Symposium, May 27.

Feketekuty, Geza. 1986. Trade in Professional Services: An Overview. *Chicago Legal Forum* 1, 1 (March).

GATT. 1983. *International Trade 1982–83*. Geneva: GATT Secretariat.

Hill, T. P. 1977. On Goods and Services. *Review of Income and Wealth* 23, 4 (December).

Hindley, Brian. 1986a. Introducing Services into GATT. Paper prepared for the European meeting on the position of the European Community in the New GATT Round convened by the Spanish Ministry of Finance and the Economy and the Trade Policy Research Centre, Residencia Fuente Pizarro, Collado-Villalba, Spain, October 2–4.

Hindley, Brian. 1986b. Liberalization of Service Transactions. Washington DC: World Bank Development Research Department. Processed.

Hindley, Brian. 1987. A Comment on Jagdish Bhagwati's Geneva Association Lecture. In *The Emerging Service Economy*, Services World Economy Series 1. Orio Giarini (ed.), New York: Pergamon Press.

Nau, Henry. 1986. Bargaining in the New Round: The NICS and the United States. Georgetown University Paper for the Quadrangular Forum Meeting, Vermont, July 18–20.

Sampson, Gary, and Richard Snape. 1985. Identifying the Issues in Trade in Services. *The World Economy* 8, 2 (June): 171–182.

Sapir, André. 1985. North-South Issues in Trade in Services. *The World Economy* 8, 1 (March): 27–41.

Sapir, André. 1986. Trade in Investment-Related Technological Services. *World Development* 14, 5: 605–622.

V

International Investment and Migration

Investing Abroad

Direct foreign investment, or DFI as I shall call it today, has grown energetically in the postwar period. The net direct investment outflow from the OECD countries rose fourfold to over $13 billion annually between 1965 and 1980. The stock of DFI abroad, on the other hand, had increased nearly threefold within a decade to over $300 billion by 1980.

DFI has also diversified in its sectoral composition over this period, away from the historical preponderance of raw materials and extractive industries, to manufactures and then again, in recent years, to services. The sectoral shifts are manifest particularly in the estimates of the stock of U.S. DFI in the developing countries: in 1976, only 18 percent of this total was in extractive industries, whereas the share of services had risen to 43 percent.

The flows have further diversified into a veritable web. Developed countries invest in developing countries and into each other, while developing countries also seek global outreach in other countries. Even the socialist countries have turned increasingly to DFI from the capitalist West, with the Coke-Pepsi market wars played out vicariously in Sino-Soviet rivalries as Mr. Brezhnev embraced Pepsi and Mr. Deng naturally then turned to Coke!

The resulting "globalization" of economic activity has emerged as an important new reality. It reflects the interplay of "natural" market forces with policy changes, both in developing and developed countries, during the postwar period. Recently, new forces have emerged that serve to invigorate and strengthen these trends toward more DFI and globalisation. Important consequences for economic analysis and policymaking are also becoming manifest. These causes and consequences of DFI, in their major outline, are what I propose to address today.

17.1   The Postwar Interplay of Market Forces and Policies

Market Forces

The market forces that have fueled the postwar growth of DFI have attracted the intellectual attention of both conventional economists and, quite naturally, the Marxists among us as well.

Hymer, Vernon, et. al.
The mainstream history of DFI analysis is now universally regarded as the handiwork of the late Stephen Hymer, with whom I was privileged to study at MIT during the mid-1950s. As always, there are antecedents. But the credit inevitably will go, not to those who had insights and no system, but to those who design the architecture. Here, Hymer broke through the unproductive equation of DFI with international capital flow analysis and its emphasis therefore on interest rate differentials and arbitrage as the explanatory variables. In its place, he emphasized the rents that a firm could earn from setting up its own production elsewhere, using special advantages such as know-how in its possession. Today, we distinguish between firm-specific and country-specific advantages. And the question of "appropriability" of these rents through DFI as against simply sale of technology at arm's length has been fruitfully analyzed. But the central Hymer insight has remained at the core of these important analytical developments.[1]

The most popular and justifiably celebrated progeny of the Hymer revolution was the *product cycle* theory of Professor Raymond Vernon. Starting with home-based R&D and innovation generating a new product, the firm would produce at home and then extend sales abroad. Next, however, as the production process got simplified, de-bugged and transplantable to where factor costs were lower, the foreign sales would yield to DFI and production elsewhere. As such shift in production to foreign locales via DFI occurred, reverse sales to the home market would also follow in the last stage, closing the circle. The story could have been told by simply substituting DFI with sale of the simplified technology at arm's length to foreign producers instead. DFI, however, comes in, bringing in Hymer critically since it generates greater returns to the firm's specific advantages than arm's-length sale of know-how would.

Many DFIs fit this mold, of course. But you will have noticed that the product cycle story essentially involves the shift of investment location in response to factor proportions advantage, without involving the question of competition and market structure in any essential way. The DFI could be, for instance, by a single secure monopolist. But a great number of DFIs are undertaken essentially in the context of *import competition*, where DFI is a *response* to a situation of intensifying competitive threat from foreign producers of similar products. A shift in location, admittedly still founded on Hymer-type specific advantages, so as to reduce costs by exploiting foreign factor costs and thus increase survivability in a competitive struggle, is the scenario that better fits many DFIs. Not exploiting the factor costs that give your competitors abroad a competitive edge is to look at the Darwinian process from the vantage point of a loser.

But if you recycle the Hymer-Vernon theory thus, it becomes evident that DFI may be inhibited by other, alternative responses to such intensification of competition, or that DFIs of other variety may appear if the source of the international competitive pressure is other than simply factor costs. Let me elaborate.

Alternative Responses: Labor Importation
Perhaps the most interesting alternative response in the postwar period has been the importation of foreign labor, as under the *gastarbeiter* program of the European countries such as Germany and Switzerland, until the early 1970s when the policy fell victim to the economic slowdown in the aftermath of the OPEC successes.

The irony is that the "big thinkers" such as Marx and Lenin failed to predict this response, assuming that the capitalists would reach out for the proletariat but not that the proletariat would move to the capitalists. The irony is even more compelling when you think of the asymmetry in their thoughts between the *internal* process where the proletariat indeed moved to the capitalists (as when the rural enclosures were argued to create and supply to the urban areas the necessary proletariat) and the *external* process where the movement was supposed to to be exactly the other way around.

If then DFI takes the firm out to cheap labor, whereas the *gastarbeiter* policy brings the cheap labor to the firm, the two phenomena could be regarded as *substitutes* in the economist's sense. But are they necessarily so? I suspect that the importation of labor did dampen the outflow of DFI from Western Europe during the 1960s. Perhaps the outflow of DFI might even have accelerated during the 1970s, as the *gastarbeiter* programs were abruptly frozen, had it not been for the slowdown of investment generally as part of the depressed world economy which had triggered the termination of the *gastarbeiter* program in the first place.

But I should add that DFI and labor importation across nation states may also turn out to be complements in a different sense and context. Thus, in the recent policy discussions concerning how the country of immigration may reduce the numbers seeking to come in and hence, given the enforcement expenditures, diminish in turn those who immigrate illegally, it has been assumed that DFI (and indeed foreign aid too) can stem the tide by creating more jobs in the countries of emigration and by reducing the wage gap that must influence the decision to seek illegal entry. Thus, the U.S.– Mexico problem of illegal immigration is widely regarded as amenable to a partial solution along these lines. In this sense, DFI and illegal immigration are again seen as substitutes: one impacts negatively on the other.

But it is not evident that the argument is valid, even if plausible. For, ceteris paribus, any reduction in wage differentials and in expected income improvements from migration ought to reduce the incentive to migrate. However, as always, paradoxes can surface: (1) Immigrants may be those who can afford to migrate, in the face of imperfect capital markets. If so, the capacity to migrate may be the constraint on migration rather than the incentive to do so. Foreign investment or aid, in raising incomes of the proletariat, may then bring more migrants over the border, rather than less. (2) Again, the networking aspect of migration means that multinational corporations (MNCs) may serve to provide conduits whereby migration may increase. Thus, the Mexican employees of Coca-Cola in Mexico City may establish contacts with their U.S. fellow-managers and workers, get these U.S. friends to procure jobs and labor certification required for immigration, and manage to get further down the road on to immigration into the United States than they otherwise would have done. (3) Then, again, in an interesting recent contribution, the sociologist Sassen-Koob (1984) has argued that foreign investment and immigration are complementary rather than substitutes because DFI itself creates a proletariat in the host countries, leading in turn to outmigration eventually.

Among the arguments advanced by Sassen-Koob in support of this contention are the following: (1) export-oriented MNCs use female labor which, in turn, creates a female proletariat that is itself integrated ideologically into a nontraditional set of values that are a precondition to outmigration to the capitalist center; (2) often, the female workers experience rapid turnover, creating female unemployment that also fuels outmigration; (3) the spread of the proletarian ideology goes beyond the female workers to their families and other work force members so that outmigration of others also is encouraged; and (4) the city centers such as New York, in turn, are now the source of low-level jobs even in high-tech modern industries where this emerging proletariat can find jobs. These arguments are imaginative, but the evidence in support of them is not compelling, I am afraid.

I might add that the possibility of complementarity between immigration and investment can arise also because the former leads to the latter instead. Thus, German firms may get used to working with Turkish labor in Germany, and this itself may encourage them to take up profitable opportunities to invest in Anatolia. Again, the returning Turkish *gastarbeiter* may have spread seeds of modernization and proletarian values that serve to accelerate the formation of the type of labor that German MNCs would like to employ, thus facilitating their investment in Turkey. Again, networking may imply that the immigrant groups in a developed host country may serve as conduits for facilitating the perception of investment opportunities, may promote joint ventures between themselves and MNCs in their countries of origin, and so on. Thus, even if one were to observe that, at least at first glance, DFI and immigration were positively rather than inversely related, the relationship could go from immigration to DFI rather than the other way.

I might finally observe that, from the "grand" Marxist perspective, the theme that outward DFI from the capitalist center may itself prompt inward immigration of the (DFI-created) proletariat from the periphery with abundant labor is most satisfying (even though the evidence for it is unconvincing). For, it represents an intriguing new twist, a novel and fitting finale, to the evolutionary, historic stages through which capitalism evolves as a "world system" in the Immanuel Wallerstein sense.[2] It restores therefore the phenomenon of immigration of the proletariat abroad, as against the taking of DFI to this proletariat, from its contrapuntal position vis-à-vis Marxist prediction to a more organic, consistent position within the unfolding drama of the world capitalist system.

Alternative DFIs: Cross-investments à la MPI

Let me then turn to the issue, not of responses to import competition that constitute an alternative to DFI, but rather of DFI responses other than outward DFI to exploit lower factor costs.

I have long argued that, where the source of import competition is technical change in progressive Schumpeterian industries, causing competition among similar products, the response of the producers of import-competing similar products (none dominant) cannot logically be outward DFI since lower factor costs abroad are not what is driving the foreign competition. Rather, it may be the *mutual penetration of investment* (MPI) response, yielding mutual DFI by international competitors into one another. Thus, in 1972, reviewing Professor Vernon's (1971) important volume on *Sovereignty at Bay*, I wrote:

There is also at least one more dramatic form of international investment which neither Vernon nor other researchers in the MNC field has noted but which may well be the pattern to emerge as a dominant form. In contrast to the case where the MNCs, having developed new products *via* R&D, export them and then transit to producing them abroad, there is an alternative "model" where MNCs in different countries have R&D-induced advantages in producing different types of subproducts (e.g., one MNC in Japan is excellent with small cars and one MNC in United States has an edge on large cars, or tire firms in different countries have acquired edge in producing and competing effectively in different types of tires). In competing in each other's home countries or in third markets in both types of subproducts, it is natural that each MNC would find it difficult to compete effectively with the other in subproducts where it does not have the edge. I would expect that, in this situation, there is likelihood of these MNCs deciding that mutual equity interpenetration, with productionwise accommodation in subproduct specialization according to the advantage possessed, is profitable. Thus, the MNC in United States (say, GM) that finds it difficult to compete with the MNC in the small-car field, with the MNC in Japan (say, Toyota) that finds it difficult to compete with the MNC in United States in the large-car field, would each decide that the best strategy if you cannot compete with comfort is to follow the policy: "if you cannot beat them, buy them." Thus GM would want to buy equity in Toyota for the small-car production and Toyota in GM for the large-car production; and GM in United States would go off spending resources in producing and improving its own small car, while Toyota in Japan would similarly hold back on its own large-car efforts. One thus gets mutually interpenetrating MNCs within industries, with accompanying division of labour and a novel form of "cartelization" which goes by subproducts. Linder has made us familiar with trade in commodities between similar countries as consisting of subproduct exchanges, and Hymer and Rowthorn have noted that MNCs from different countries penetrate into each other's countries. My "model" essentially combines these two and predicts that MNCs with R&D induced specialization in different types of subproducts within an industry in different countries will interpenetrate.

This model is almost ideally illustrated by the following example which Martin Zimmerman has unearthed for me. *Forbes* of November 15, 1970 (p. 22), notes the following "international marriage":

Long the friendliest of competitors, Dunlop and Pirelli neatly complement each other. Dunlop is primarily a manufacturer of conventional cross-ply tires, Pirelli concentrates on radials. In Europe, Dunlop has perhaps 18% of the market, Pirelli 12%, as against 12% for Michelin, the next largest competitor. In Europe, Pirelli crosses Dunlop's path only in West Germany: Elsewhere, where Dunlop is active, Pirelli stays out; where Pirelli is active, Dunlop stays out. Outside of Europe, Pirelli is active, Dunlop stays out. Outside of Europe, Pirelli is active mostly in Latin America, Dunlop in the Commonwealth and North America.

The two companies have even diversified into different areas—Dunlop into sporting goods and precision engineering products, Pirelli into paper, electronics and cables.

Eventually, of course, both marketing organizations will work as one, with Dunlop pushing Pirelli products where Dunlop is strong, and Pirelli pushing Dunlop products elsewhere. "The greatest benefits should come from a pooling of R&D, however," explains J. Campell Fraser, a Dunlop director: "In the seventies and eighties, competition will be more and more in terms of innovations. In the UK we have a home base of about 55 million people—that isn't big enough for the kind of R&D we'll need. Pirelli has an even smaller home base, about 45 million. By merging, we'll have a home base of 100 million, enough for the kind of R&D we'll need around the world ... There will not even be any exchange of public shares. Instead each will acquire an interest in the other's operating subsidiaries. The British and Italian companies will operate on their own.

The report goes on to note (p. 23) that there will be four companies: Dunlop Home (United Kingdom and Europe) with Dunlop owning 51 percent and Pirelli 49 percent; Dunlop International (rest of the world) with Dunlop holding 60 percent and Pirelli, Milan and Switzerland, 20 percent each; Pirelli Milan (Common Market) with Pirelli Milan holding 51 and 49 percent and Pirelli Switzerland (all other Pirelli operations) with Dunlop holding 40 percent, Pirelli Milan 20 percent, and Pirelli Switzerland 40 percent.

I must yield to the temptation to quote the further remark, in view of its anticipation of my theme of quid pro quo DFI later tonight:

But interpenetration among MNCs with competing R&D-induced specialization in different subproducts may not be the only important new form of international MNC investments to emerge. Alternative possibilities are one-way penetrations by MNCs. Thus, it is entirely possible for GM to expect to buy its way into profitable Japanese small-car production, for example, by merely offering its distributive outlets, access to funds and/or R&D facilities, and perhaps the political offer of not clamouring for quota protection. Indeed, the recent political pressures on MITI in Japan to open up Japan to U.S. investment in several areas has been so considerable that it seems entirely probable that the model of one-way penetration is about as relevant as the model of interpenetration.

I should warn you, however, that despite my prescient resort to the hypothetical General Motors—Toyota DFI outcomes, you should not lay the fact of their later realization at my door but rather attribute it to the importance of the forces whose consequences for novel DFI outcomes I was noting.[3]

The MPI variety of DFI, in fact, can be regarded also as a fascinating subspecies of the phenomenon of "cross-investment" that Hymer and Rowthorn (1970) had noted in response to Servan Schreiber's hysterical alarm over the American DFI invasion of Europe. They were concerned with noting that the investments into each other's country were a growing reality. But what they addressed were principally mutual DFI in wholly different industries: e.g., German DFI in U.S. automobiles and American DFI in Germany in tractors. But it is easy to see that cross-investments may occur in a more interesting form, within the same industry: as when MNCs invest in each other's country in office equipment manufacture, a phenomenon that Hymer was no stranger to. But the MPI variety of cross-investment is far the most dramatic: it occurs across and mutually within the firms in the industry. Hence the three varieties of cross-investments I have distinguished may be christened: national-level, industry-level and firm-level cross-investments.

While the formal modeling of the national-level cross-investments can readily reflect the product-cycle scenario, and can be therefore placed in the context of conventional competitive models,[4] the latter two require resort to the new theories of competition and hence of trade in similar products. My former student, Professor Elias Dinopoulos (1985b), has done precisely this: modeling the MPI theory of DFI in the context of the Lancaster-Helpman theory of trade in similar products, but in a major variant thereof that reflects a formalization in turn of the taste-difference-generated "biological" model of trade in similar products that I have proposed recently (Bhagwati, 1982; Dinopoulos, 1985a).

Policy Factors

While therefore these *market* forces have propelled DFIs into a growing role in the world economy, the role of *policy* measures, in the broadest sense, has also been significant.

(1) The factor-proportions variety of DFI, seeking lower costs of production abroad, has been attracted by developing countries following the export-promoting (EP) strategy, with export-processing zones, tax concessions, etc. In turn, the developed countries have occasionally enacted tariff concessions on offshore assembly, again encouraging assembly-type DFI abroad. (2) By contrast, the majority of the developing countries, following the import-substituting (IS) strategy, have used tariffs and quota restrictions to protect domestic markets and therewith to induce "tariff-jumping" DFI. (3) Again, in a significant and growing variant on this strategy, recently the *threat* of protection has been used to induce foreign firms, who are crowding out domestic production through exports, into undertaking DFI so as to defuse that threat. (4) Finally, the governments of the devel-

oped countries, and their multinationals, have increasingly accommodated to the notion, somewhat inflammatory at the outset of the postwar period, that the host country regulations and "performance requirements" have come to stay, thus creating the adaptive and consensual ethos that has permitted DFI to grow in the postwar period to date. Let me address these diverse pro-DFI factors, in turn.

EP-Oriented Interventions
The host country incentives, such as tax holidays, to attract DFI of the EP variety are commonplace enough. Among the EP-strategy countries, however, the major incentive has been simply the conjunction of cheaper costs and the EP orientation.

The interesting phenomenon is rather the emergence of duty free zones in many of the IS-oriented economies, designed to attract EP-type DFI. This flirtation with free trade, in arm's-length *enclaves*, while continuing the policy of protection on the mainland, reminds me of the remark of Professor Paul Rosenstein-Rodan, the great pioneer of development economics who never gave up his Austrian ways: "promiscuity is easier than marriage." But if such zones are easier to embrace than the EP-strategy, DFI attracted by them may equally be counterproductive in terms of your welfare. Here we have yet another example of the *caveat* that Professor Jacob Viner made us familiar with by drawing attention to the possibility of trade-diverting customs unions: that a move *toward* free trade is not the same as a move *to* free trade; the former may immiserize you, even though the latter will generally be beneficial.[5]

But if EP-oriented DFIs have been attracted thus by host-country policies, a contribution has also been made by policies of the countries from which DFI originates. Principal among these policies have been the "offshore assembly" incentives that have been enacted by several developed countries. Thus, for example, Joseph Grunwald and Kenneth Flam (1985) at the Brookings Institution, who have recently produced an important work on this subject, note that the United States under tariff items 806.30 and 807.00 permits the duty-free entry of U.S. components sent abroad for processing or assembly, whereas the countries of the European Economic Community also have similar "outward processing" provisions: all encouraging foreign assembly, often via DFI in adjacent countries with cheap labor. Thus, more than half of U.S. sales of certain products in textiles and electronics are assembled abroad now, whereas the imports of such products constitute presently a sixth of total U.S. imports of manufactures. No estimates are offered by these authors of how much offshore-assembly DFI would have occurred, through market forces alone, and how much there-fore should be attributed to these tariff-concession incentives. But there is little doubt that the incentives have played a contributory role.

IS-Oriented Interventions

In the end, however, the market forces have basically driven the EP-type DFI, with the policy factors playing a modest role. By contrast, the IS-type DFI has been almost wholly policy driven. The IS strategy, on both domes-tic investments and DFI, has been cut from the same cloth: "Protect your market and attract home-based investments to serve that market." Popu-larly, this is also known as the strategy for attracting "tariff-jumping" DFI, though the developing countries pursuing this strategy often resorted to quota restrictions rather than tariffs as their policy instruments.

Two major questions have been raised concerning the IS-oriented DFI. The major object of attention has been the issue of the benefits that such DFI confers on the host country. The most dramatic analytical insight has been provided by several international trade theorists who have considered the serious possibility that such DFI may actually be harmful, not just less productive than it appears to the naked eye. The complicating factor, producing the paradox, is of course that the influx of DFI is being induced by a distorting protectionist policy. It is then evident, as the theory of immiserising growth implies and I noted (Bhagwati, 1973), that the returns to DFI *may* exceed its social marginal product. Professor Hirofumi Uzawa, and subsequently other Japanese economists such as Professors Noburo Minabe and Koichi Hamada, arrived at the stronger proposition that, in a conventional neoclassical 2 × 2 model with the importable good capital-intensive, protection-induced capital inflow would *necessarily* immiserize. Independently, and insightfully, this proposition was developed and inte-grated into both the theory of capital mobility and the theory of immi-serising growth by Professors Richard Brecher and Carlos Díaz-Alejandro (1977). I have argued (Bhagwati, 1978) that this analytical finding may well be a significant element in the explanation of the observed failure of IS-addicted countries to perform as well as the EP-oriented countries.[6]

I have also suggested (Bhagwati, 1978, ch. 8) that, over the long haul, the magnitude of IS-oriented DFI cannot be as striking as with EP-oriented DFI, for the simple reason that it is limited by the host-country market which induces it in the first place. Professor Balasubramanyam (1984), who is distinguished for his work on DFI in the developing countries, has examined this hypothesis and his preliminary analysis has led him to conclude:

The lack of detailed time series data on inflows of FDI into LDCs with different types of foreign trade regimes prevents a full scale statistical test of this hypothesis. However, the data that could be readily assembled lend some support to the first facet of the hypothesis concerning the relative magnitude of FDI under the IS and EP strategies of development (Table 2). In order to take account of the differences in market size, data on the total stock of FDI for selected LDCs are expressed as a proportion of their population and GNP. These indicators relate to the years 1967 and 1978.

For the year 1978 FDI as a percentage of GNP was high in countries pursuing the EP strategy (Singapore, Hong Kong, Taiwan, Malaysia and Kenya) compared to that in countries pursuing the IS strategy in the recent past (India, Brazil, Ghana, Argentina). Much more significant is the fact that in the case of most countries pursuing the EP strategy the stock of FDI as a percentage of GNP increased substantially over the period 1967–1978. In a majority of the countries pursuing the IS strategy, however, this ratio of FDI to GNP declined appreciably. (Balasubramanyam, 1984, pp. 125–126).[7]

Quid pro quo (or Protection-Threat-Induced) DFI
Let me now turn your attention to a novel class of policy-induced DFI, arising presently among the developed countries, which I like to call Quid pro quo DFI (Bhagwati 1985a). Increasingly, the *threat* of protection has been used to stimulate DFI from foreign competitors in an industry. The quid pro quo for the investing firms is in the reduced threat of protection that follows from such DFI (as I explain below) and hence in less impaired access to the market of the host country.

Of course, the use of protection to attract DFI was a well-known tactic of the import-substituting developing countries, as I have already discussed, and it led to "protection-induced" (or, in common parlance, "tariff-jumping") DFI. By contrast, the quid pro quo investments that are emerging are "protection-threat-induced" DFI.

Why does the threat of protection attract DFI? I do not have in mind a trivial variation on the theme of tariff-jumping investment: i.e., that DFI occurs in anticipation of a closing market. Rather, the argument is that DFI may be aimed at *defusing* the protectionist threat which, in fact, may have been designed precisely with a view to stimulating such DFI in the first place. I will presently discuss why such a "defusing effect" may follow. But, assuming that it does operate, the rationale of the quid pro quo DFI can be readily spelled out. Essentially, from the viewpoint of the exporting country, if DFI can help it to reduce the potential threat of protection, the losses (or reduced profits) from producing partially in the host country via DFI rather than at home are offset by the profits gained through keeping access to host-country markets open. Individual firms making the DFI will of course undertake such DFI perceiving this effect on their own profitability. But there would also be an incentive for governments to encourage such DFI if the effect of such DFI is to defuse the protectionist threat more generally, constituting an externality to the individval firm.[8]

DFI can reduce the probability of the host countrys' invoking protection by influencing favorably the Congresses and the Parliaments where the protectionist lobbies operate; it can also co-opt these lobbies themselves into softening their protectionist efforts. Let me address each route, in turn.

DFI from the exporting country is often seen as a thoughtful gesture that contributes to employment in and the well-being of the importing country. It can thus help defuse protectionist threats quite generally in the legislatures where the lobbyists of the exporting country can cite the benefits accruing from such investments to soften the hostile attitudes and threats directed at the exporting country. The most dramatic example of such a linkage is in the case of Japanese DFI in the United States.

There are, indeed, as everywhere, alarmist voices raised by American politicians at the social implications of DFI. My favorite examples includes Governor Lamm of Colorado, worried about "economic colonialism," declaring: "It seems so clear that, when the Japanese are buying our pro-ductive resources, it has serious long-term implications. The United States invented the video recorder and now they'll be made by the Japanese. The long-term implication is that our children will be working for the Japanese." (*New York Times*, September 16, 1985). Then again, Representative Jim Wright, majority whip in the U.S. Congress, wrote recently in the *Wall Street Journal*:

We ought to be exporting computers, not shares of IBM. We should seek to sell more, not sell out.

To accept the de-industrialization of America while exulting in the growth of foreign ownership and influence in our domestic institutions could be an unwitting prescription for slowly becoming an economic colony again. (October 3, 1985)

But these viewpoints are very much a fringe phenomenon. There is little doubt that Japanese DFI in the United States is viewed as a positive contribution, as "a way to keep American factories open and workers employed" (*New York Times*, July 26, 1985).

The protection-threat-defusing effect can equally operate through the co-opting of the agents, firms, and unions that agitate for protection. By offering technology and profits through joint ventures, the firms can be converted to freer trade; by offering jobs, DFI can turn unions equally away from protection. In fact, I might venture to suggest that whether quid pro quo DFI, so inspired, will be in the form of wholly owned subsidiaries or joint ventures with host-country producers may reflect factors such as the relative lobbying strength of labor and capitalists in the industry. Toyota teamed up with General Motors, to produce a small car under the umbrella of New United Motor Manufacturing, presumably reflecting the clout that General Motors carries with the administration. Quite appropriately, it was rewarded when the automobile voluntary export restraints (VERs) came up for renewal last year: of all the carmakers, General Motors was the one that broke ranks and lobbied against new VERs. But wholly owned subsidiaries, where the foreign investor continues competing with local firms instead of joining them, may also make sense if the labor unions are strong and also the more effective protection-threatening lobby. By offering contracts and jobs to these unions, the incoming DFI can coopt these unions into accepting continuing imports.

How significant is quid pro quo DFI today? Qualitatively, it is easy to recognize its importance on the U.S.–Japan scene. In fact, quite aside from Japanese firms' own statements, it is manifest that the Japanese government is acutely aware that DFI generates positive externalities for Japan and that it therefore encourages such DFI and seeks to profit from it through lobbying in the United States.

Thus, the Japanese Economic Institute, which is associated with the Japanese government, issues regular bulletins from its Washington headquarters on Japan's expanding DFI in the United States. Arguing that "Japanese-affiliated manufacturing companies have become an important source of jobs for American workers, both directly and indirectly through their purchases of goods and services" (*JEI Report* No. 15A, p. 4), these handouts explicitly describe DFI from Japan as being protectionism-related. A recent report observes:

Although Japanese exporters have always regarded onshore manufacturing as a way to bolster their sales in the United States, many companies with a significant stake in the US market did not decide to invest here until they were faced with actual or potential import restrictions.

In what has become the best known example of the correlation, Mitsuibishi Electric Corp., Sharp Corp., Toshiba Corp., and Hitachi, Ltd., began to supply the US colour television market primarily from domestic production facilities after an orderly marketing agreement with Japan went into effect in 1977, thereby joining Sony Corp., Matsushita Electric Industrial Co., Ltd., and Sanyo Electric Co., Ltd., which already has US color television plants. Japan's top bearing makers— Nippon Seiko K.K., NTN Toyo Bearing Co., Ltd., NachiFujikoshi Corp. and Nippon Miniature Bearing Co., Ltd.—also built or acquired plants in the United States to avoid trade barriers.

For other Japanese manufacturers, the threat of US trade restrictions tipped the scales in favor of US production. Microwave ovens, which were the subject of an antidumping investigation, are made in the United States by four Japanese producers—Mitsushita Electric, Sanyo Electric, Sharp and Toshiba. Japan's leading semiconductor manufacturer—Fujitsu, Ltd., Nippon Electric Co. Ltd., Hitachi and Toshiba—also invested in American production facilities in the late 1970s, prompted in part by mounting complaints about their market inroads from domestic producers. (*JEI*, 1982, p. 2)

I should warn you, of course, that some of this Japanese DFI may simply be protection induced as with the conventional tariff-jumping investments. That, however, a fair fraction of it is undertaken to *defuse*, rather than *circumvent*, protection and hence qualifies as quid pro quo DFI is evident from the GM-Toyota and other examples. Sorting out the relative role of these two model-types is a task awaiting further research.

I might add that the beneficial quid pro quo linkage applies to DFI and not really to portfolio investments. In fact, it is arguable that the enormous increase in Japanese portfolio investments in the United States has produced, not goodwill but rather illwill toward Japan. By raising the price of the U.S. dollar, such inflows have created the Dutch Disease phenomenon: creating the current-account deficit as its counterpart, bringing enormous pressure on the export industries of the United States, and fueling greatly the demands for protection against Japan. Forgotten in the arithmetic are the jobs that are created by the inflow of the portfolio capital in the first place! This remarkable asymmetry in the linkage effects of portfolio capital inflow and DFI is somewhat reminiscent of the contrast that developmental economists have long noted between project aid and general-purpose or program aid. The former has always been preferred by donors who correctly observe that projects are visible and readily create goodwill for the donors, whereas program aid is invariably lost into oblivion since no one can readily identify its often considerable benefits.

I should also observe that, whatever mechanisms by which the quid pro quo of reduced protection threat is obtained—whether through goodwill in the legislatures or through reduced protectionist lobbying by consequently co-opted capitalists or labor unions in the host country—this type of DFI reflects artificial pressures, rather than market forces. It thus shares with protection-induced DFI the demerits of being fundamentally inefficient: it distorts the allocation of economic activity among nations. But the parallel terminates there, for the protection is actually *in place*, and it serves to create the artificial profits that crystallize the DFI in the *protection*-induced latter case. However, with the *threat*-induced former case, the objective of the DFI is precisely to reduce, and possibly eliminate, the probability of protection being enacted at all! Again, the implications for the lobbying positions of the foreign investors are dramatically different under the two DFIs. In the latter case, since the protection serves to make the host-country's market profitable for the DFI in the first place, the DFI is likely to become party to the lobbies seeking to keep the protection intact. However, the DFI that responds to the threat of protection, seeking therewith to moderate that threat, will join in lobbying against protection instead.

Adaptive Attitudes and Policies

I should be remiss if I did not also note the steady accommodation in the attitudes of the developed-country multinationals undertaking DFI and their governments toward the control-oriented policy shifts by the developing countries in the postwar period, progressively reducing the early tensions that Professor Raymond Vernon (1977) described as "storm over multinationals" and facilitating the growth of DFI that I have sketched.

The political scientists Professors Charles Lipson (1985) and Stephen Krasner (1978, 1985, ch. 7), in brilliant studies of the evolution of the international regime pertaining to DFI, have noted how multinationals have accommodated to the domestic-control-oriented aspirations and policies of host countries. Lacking co-operation for tougher postures from the allies in Europe and Japan, and faced by internal "corporate fractionalization and divergent self-interest" that equally undermine the feasibility of hard-line positions, even the hegemonic U.S. government has had no option except to take up "adaptive strategies" that work generally within the guidelines set by the host developing countries themselves. Greater tolerance for host-country policies, such as those analyzed well by Professor Charles kindleberger (1973), including insistence on joint ventures and performance requirements relating to the hiring of indigenous labor and exporting a target fraction of output, has become commonplace.[9] Even expropriation, steadily diminishing as a phenomenon, has been sought to be handled by investment guarantees rather than by gunboat diplomacy, with the occasional flexing of muscle in the Congress tantamount to little more than ritualistic reflex action.

As Professor Isaiah Frank (1980) has documented persuasively through extensive interviews recently, the multinationals have come to accept this new implicit regime, cooling the "high noon" atmospherics of conflict between national sovereignty and multinationals "beyond control" that seemed at one time certain to afflict foreign investment in the developing countries.[10]

The growing sophistication of several developing countries in dealing with DFI, by policy rather than by inflammatory rhetoric, has also assisted in the process, pulling DFI back into the mutual-gain arena of commerce and economics and away from the zero-sum presumptions of politics.

17.2 New "Systemic" Factors Favoring DFI

As it happens, this mutually adaptive process has been reinforced by new "systemic" factors that have recently emerged, favoring the growth of DFI. Among these, three are notable.

Shifting Ideological Attitudes: China and India

First, there is a shift of ideological attitudes in some important developing countries that returns DFI to a warm embrace by them today.

China under Mr. Deng is a supreme example, of course. It is interesting to recall Lenin's window to the capitalist West under the New Economic Policy (NEP) from 1921. Lenin then sought, and secured, Western trade and credits extensively. But the ideological rationalization then was that this was the way to build communism by exploiting capitalist greed, the faster then to destroy the very capitalist systems abroad eventually. As Kamenev put it pointedly in 1921, justifying the Anglo-Soviet Trade Agreement:

the foreign capitalists, who will be obliged to work on the terms that we offer them, will dig their own grave ... Foreign capital will fulfill the role Marx predicted of it. (quoted by Kennan, 1962, p. 178)

George Kennan's imagined Politburo proclamation captures this cynical ideological affirmation, even as the capitalists are embraced, beautifully:

We despise you. We consider that you should be swept from the earth as governments and physically destroyed as individuals ... But since we are not strong enough to destroy you today—since an interval must unfortunately elapse before we can give you the *coup de grace*—we want you during this interval to trade with us, we want you to finance us ...

An outrageous demand perhaps. But you will accept it nonetheless. You will accept it because you are not free agents, because you are slaves to your own capitalist appetites, because when profit is involved, you have no pride, no principle, no honor. (Kennan, 1962, p. 176)

Little of this ideological militancy can be detected in Mr. Deng's China. The "open door" policy toward capital, techniques, and know-how from the capitalist West is not simply a tactical manoeuvre: It is very much part of an end of communist ideology and the rise of the capitalist mentality.[11] The external policy changes in support of DFI, etc., have been firmly embedded in a policy shift that exhibits cascading reforms aimed at dismantling the Maoist legacy in internal economic organization as well.

I find it fascinating, and an intellectual puzzle, that these external and internal policy changes have been accompanied by astonishing Chinese claims as to their anticipated impact on China's economic performance. Growth rates up to AD 2000 of nearly 10 percent annually have been projected. Even sophisticated visitors such as Leonard Silk (1985b) of the *New York Times* have written of growth rates during the last few years of nearly 11 percent and lately of 18 percent. These claims must sound utterly implausible to development economists who know that, with 80 percent of its labor force in agriculture where long-sustained growth rates of output of even 4 percent are a supreme achievement, you would need a Confucian miracle for such manna to fall from the capitalist skies. It would appear as if the Chinese leaders have moved from one Great Leap Forward to another. Chairman Mao's was to be taken by Marx's altruistic, complete man; Mr. Deng's is to be taken by Adam Smith's selfish, economic man! One can only hope that, when ex post realities fall well below ex ante promises, Adam Smith's wisdom will not fall by the wayside, returning China to its old ways.

As of now, however, Mr. Deng's China is actively embracing DFI in its four *special Economic Zones*, all located along the coast of South China. Aimed initially at overseas Chinese, these zones have been made increasingly attractive to all others with the usual enticements: tax holidays, guarantees on repatriation, increased access to the mainland markets and tax-free imports. In April 1984, China went further and announced the creation of 14 "open cities" along its long coastline where DFI would enjoy somewhat similar privileges (Sit 1985).

India, the other "sleeping giant" of Asia, has also witnessed a similar, if more measured and less frenetic, shift toward more welcoming role for DFI. The Indian shift has also resulted from a change in regime, from Mrs. Gandhi's to Mr. Rajiv Gandhi's stewardship. Fabian socialism has given way to pragmatism and a willingness to shift the economy out of a constricting bureaucratic stranglehold and an excessively inward-oriented posture. The young prime minister's desire to absorb high-tech know-how rapidly has, in turn, accelerated a more tolerant attitude toward DFI recently.

Debts and Conditionality: South America

While the new warmth of China and India toward DFI is to be attributed largely to the decline of ideology, the door to DFI is being slowly opened also in the countries of South America because of sheer economic necessity. The acute economic difficulties in these debt-ridden countries, and their hopelessly precarious foreign exchange situation, have shifted the margin in favor of accommodating to the inflow of DFI when its costs and benefits are being assessed. The door to DFI is being slowly opened wider, under these economic compulsions, almost as predicted by the leftwing critics of debt-led growth in the 1970s who claimed that such a strategy of financial integration into the capitalist center would inevitably pave the way to facilitated entry, into the periphery, of monopoly capital—i.e., in bourgeois language, of DFI.

This aspect of the current situation makes the impatient attitude of the more ideologically inclined members of the U.S. administration rather dangerous and counterproductive. It is not uncommon to encounter declarations of resentment at the continuing host country's regulations on DFI when foreign exchange is so evidently scarce and relief is desired on debts. The itch to kick open the slowly opening door to DFI has thus been very much evident in the United States in recent years. But, in kicking the door open, one may well swing it back shut, for the leaders of these developing countries walk on a political tight-rope where they must protect their left flanks even as they turn to capitalist DFI.

The ideological compulsions and the special-interest lobbying from DFI-seekers have even found their way into the Baker Plan, unveiled in October 1985 at the Seoul meeting of the International Monetary Fund (IMF) and the World Bank, for meeting the deteriorating debt situation. After years of focusing on the IMF, hard conditionality, and deflation as a way of restoring the creditworthiness of the debtor developing countries, the U.S. government saw its IMF-centered strategy imperilled by the threatened spread of de facto defaults and unilateral actions such as President Garcia's announcement that repayments would not exceed 10 percent of Peruvian exchange earnings annually. The fact that little new *net* lending was forthcoming despite great austerity à la IMF programs meant that the intended return of the debtor countries via trial and tribulation to creditworthiness had been simply too optimistic.

Increasingly, therefore, the debtor countries saw the choice facing them to be between, on the one hand, the IMF program solution of the pre-Baker Plan variety, which produced deflation and distress but no net funds, and alternatively saying: "we will go alone, at our own pace," in which case there would be no conditionalities, and the fund-inflow situation would be *no worse* since the Western banks simply would have to lend involuntarily the accruing amortization and interest liabilities or face a de jure default, which would force a major crisis engulfing them as well. Thus seen, the IMF–U.S. programme to deal with the debt crisis was in evident peril. A few weeks before the Seoul meeting, President de la Madrid of Mexico virtually stated that unless the scales were tipped by international measures to increase the net inflow of funds, his and other debtor governments would be sorely tempted to move in favor of the latter option, following in Peruvian footsteps.

In consequence, the Baker Plan, put together to forestall these untoward possibilities, has shifted focus from the IMF to the World Bank, with emphasis on generating new net inflows, and on growth rather than deflation in the debtor countries. Ideas that only three years ago were ideologically reprehensible have thus been embraced as the second Reagan administration has shifted, from the first administration's view that a strong dose of necessary deflation would be followed by the market forces generating new flows, to necessary intervention to generate the necessary flows through multilateral measures.

But the quick step is still in ideological shoes, for the World Bank funds, in turn, are predicated on conditionality that includes micro-incentives reflecting market forces *and*, pertinent to my theme today, warming moves toward DFI. Mr. Baker may himself be an ideologue, or he may be simply sugarcoating for Senator Jesse Helms and his friends the compelling shift to the World-Bank-centered, liberal-sounding strategy. Either way, the desire to push DFI heavy-handedly past the governments of the debtor counties, as they seek the funds under the Baker Plan, is manifest and will have to be prudently restrained lest, in the volatile political climate of the debtor countries, it proves destabilizing and hence counterproductive.

Multilateral Trade Concerns

Finally, there is a set of interesting trade-related powerful recent factors that has emerged, forcing DFI onto our multilateral concerns and certainly promising to favor its future growth. Two related arguments may be distinguished.

DFI-Requiring, Effective Access to Markets
First, trade itself may be inhibited, and hence the promised access to foreign markets may be compromised, if critically related DFI is not permitted. This concern surfaced during the term of the U.S. Treasury Secretary Connolly who felt that the access to Japanese markets was de facto reduced for U.S. exporters of goods because Japanese distributors raised the effective cost of handling U.S. goods through a variety of practices that could be interpreted as implying an invisible tariff surchage. Presumably, such implicitly collusive Japanese behavior could raise the "true" tariff facing U.S. (and other foreign) exporters over and above the much-touted, low visible tariff of Japan. The way to circumvent this phenomenon therefore was via DFI that would, by establishing local distributive outlets, acquire access to Japanese consumers at the visible tariff. Such "tariff-reducing" DFI, of course, poses an interesting analytical possibility: an otherwise harmful DFI by an exporting country may become beneficial because of the gains from trade accruing from the reduction in the invisible tariff.[12] Whether, in fact, Japan's import performance can indeed be correctly regarded thus as an act of inscrutable Oriental tariff making by implicit social consensus that requires the antidote of Occidental DFI is another matter. On that, my view is sceptical, based on the econometric work of the Japanologist Gary Saxonhouse which suggests that, by disaggregated Standard International Trade Classification (SITC) categories, Japan's import shares are well within the range predicted by several explanatory variables on cross-country data, leaving no room for an inadequacy to be explained by invisible tariff making. But this would not be the first time that an interesting theory has no empirical basis but has impacted on policy nonetheless.

Trade in Services and DFI
The other interesting but realistic argument for DFI has emerged in the context of the recent focus on trade in services. Services are to be distinguished from goods by the characteristic that they are generally nonstorable, being provided to the user as they are produced. As a result, interaction between provider and user is essential. Such interaction, however, may be possible at long distance, as when services are provided on the wire: as might have been the case if, in the event of an unforeseen emergency preventing me from making this pleasurable journey to Lancaster today, you had decided to hear me anyway from New York. But haircuts cannot still be had at long distance. User-provider *physical proximity* is thus a key characteristic of many service transactions even though

technical change may be turning more of them into long-distance services where such proximity becomes unnecessary.

The argument has been forcefully advanced by the banking and telematics sectors recently that proximity to their users has become increasingly necessary for their services to be transacted efficiently.[13] They, and increasingly other service-sectors such as insurance companies, accounting and legal firms and providers of other business services such as advertising, have therefore, lobbied to have the "right to establish," i.e., the right of making DFI, granted and embodied in an international compact on service trade that would complement the General Agreement on Tariffs and Trade (GATT) which, by original protocol and subsequent practice, governs only trade in goods.

DFI, in the shape of the right to establish, is thus seen by many as an essential component of the *trade* compact that would have to be negotiated to bring services, now estimated at over a quarter of world commerce, into the discipline of a facilitating international framework. Indeed, it is presently an important component of the negotiating strategy at the forthcoming trade talks by the United States, the leading proponent of a services compact. That DFI is also a key ingredient, as I have argued, of the current U.S. administration's economic ideology only serves to accentuate the U.S. trade negotiators' position on this issue. Both factors in turn combine to constitute a significant DFI-supporting role by the United States, still the *force majeure* in the world economy.

17.3   Policy and Analytical Consequences of Growing DFI

As these systemic forces foster DFI, and the world economy gets more globalized and intergrated in consequence, both in manufactures and increasingly in services, there follow serious consequences for economic policy and analysis which we must recognize if we are to continue being relevant. I should like, in conclusion, to focus on three such consequences which I find particularly compelling.

Tariff Making at Bay

A remarkable implication of the DFI process has been that the world economy now has fairly influential actors who have a commitment to free trade.

A fairly common complaint on the part of analysts of political economy has been the asymmetry of pressure groups in the tariff-making process:

the beneficiaries of protection are often concentrated, whereas its victims tend to be either diffused as are final consumers or are unable to see the losses to themselves as when protection indirectly affects exports and hence those engaged in producing exportables adversely.

DFI, and the growing maze of globalized production, have changed this equation perceptibly. When DFI is undertaken, not for tariff-jumping locally selected markets, but for exports to home country or to third markets, as is increasingly the case, protectionism threatens clearly the investments so made and tends to galvanize these influential multinationals into lobbying to keep markets open.

Thus, for example, it was noticeable that when the U.S. semiconductor suppliers recently gathered to discuss antidumping legal action against Japanese producers of memory microchips known as EPROMs (or erasable programmable read-only memories), noticeably absent were Motorola Inc. and Texas Instruments Inc. who produce semiconductors in Japan and expect to be shipping some back to United States.[14]

In fact, I should imagine that a main reason why U.S. protectionism has not translated into a disastrous Smoot-Hawley scenario, despite high unemployment levels and the seriously "overvalued" dollar (in the Dutch Disease sense), is that few congressmen have constituencies where DFI has not created such pro-trade, antiprotectionist presence, muddying waters where otherwise protectionists would have sailed with great ease. The "spider's web" or "spaghetti-bowl" phenomenon resulting from DFI that criss crosses the world economy has thus been a stabilizing force in favor of holding the protectionists at bay.

While I have detailed here the consequences of DFI already *in place*,[15] I should remind you that the *possibility* of undertaking DFI when faced with import competition *also* provides an alternative to a protectionist response. Since this is the capitalist response, rather than that of labor which would "lose jobs abroad," the defusion of protectionist threat that is implied here works by breaking and hence weakening the customary alliance between both pressure groups within an industry in their protectionist lobbying with which Professor Steve Magee has made us long familiar.

Interestingly, if you will recall the quid pro quo DFI that I discussed earlier, labor unions can themselves use DFI as an altenative response to protection, by using the protectionist threat to induce the foreign competitive firms to invest rather than export, to "create" rather than "destroy" jobs.

In short, both actual DFI (through "spaghetti-bowl" effect) and potential DFI (outward by domestic capital and quid pro quo inward by foreign capital) are powerful forces that are influencing the political economy of tariff-making in favor of an open economy.

Inferring Competitive Efficiency, etc.

Yet another significant consequence of DFI expansion has been the growing irrelevance of concepts such as competitive efficiency and comparative productivity growth when applied, as traditionally, to domestically situated activities alone.

If many industries today are establishing DFI abroad, producing and exporting from these "offshore" facilities, how can it make sense to focus wholly on "mainland" activity and its characteristics to make inferences about the competitive position of a country or its industries? Indeed, since DFI is undertaken by the more progressive Schumpeterian industries which respond to import competition by going abroad, there would be a systematic downside bias in confining one's attention to progressivity in the mainland activities! And yet prominent economists, including Professor Lester Thurow recently, have been doing precisely this, and drawing alarmist conclusions about the decline of American industry and its competitiveness![16]

While I drew your attention earlier to the importance of DFI and hence of offshore production and exports in overall sales and exports of multinationals, permit me to underline this phenomenon in the present context. Professor Silvio Borner (1985) of Basle, in his recent work entitled appropriately *Die sechste Schweiz*, Switzerland's sixth canton constituted by Swiss production abroad, has focused our minds clearly on the issue that I am raising here. His analysis of 15 largest Swiss industrial multinationals showed, for instance, that they have expanded their foreign employment dramatically until in 1980 only 25 percent of their employees were located in Switzerland. The share of investment also has declined on mainland to 32.4 percent, and production to 25.6 percent. Even 38 percent of R&D expenditures are now incurred abroad.

As for the United States, the conclusions are equally startling in magnitude. Professors Magnus Blomstrom and Robert Lipsey, who are currently engaged on an extensive statistical analysis of Swedish and American DFI abroad, have preliminary findings that show that the proportion of manufacturing exports by U.S. affiliates abroad (excluding sales to United States) to the total exports by U.S. multinationals and their affiliates in manufactures is as high as 52 percent, and that this share has steadily grown between 1965 and 1978. Again, the commonly cited figure that the U.S. share of world exports of manufactures has fallen steadily in two decades from 21.3 percent in 1957 to 12.3 percent in 1977 turns out to be wholly midleading. When the exports of U.S. affiliates offshore are added, the 1977 share of the United States in world exports of manufactures climbs again well over 20 percent! I hardly need to say more to alert you to the perils of drawing inferences in disregard of these remarkable facts.

Policy Effects

Finally, the interdependence that the growth in DFI represents has affected policymaking in critical ways. Professor Richard Cooper, the pioneer in exploring such effects, has noted how such effects can include the erosion of policy effectiveness and also the reversal of the expected consequences of traditional policy instruments.

On the *policy-erosion* phenomenon, let Professor Cooper (1985) speak for himself:

... structural changes in the world economy [i.e., greater openness and inter-nationalization of markets] ... [are leading] to an erosion of our government's capacity to do things the way it used to. The United States occasionally responds to this erosion by lashing out and extending its jurisdiction to the rest of the world, leading to international friction. I see extraterritoriality, as it is called, as a natural, although not necessarily a desirable, response to the erosion of our capacity to control our own environment. So when we find Canadian securities traded in the US over-the-counter market, the Securities and Exchange Commission (SEC), which is charged with protecting the American public from securities fraud, sends letters to Canadian companies instructing them to comply with SEC regulations. Well, the Canadians are outraged; the SEC does not have any jurisdiction over them, according to them. But the SEC is doing its job the only way it considers workable. When the US government embargoes trade to Cuba or to Vietnam, as it did many years ago, and the US firms operating out of France, Belgium, Spain or Canada sell US-designed products made by US owned firms to Cuba or Vietnam, the US Treasury responds by imposing asset controls on US firms operating abroad. The Belgians are outraged. They argue that while the company is owned by an American firm, it is legally a Belgain entity, subject to Belgian, not US, law. In 1982 the Reagan administration felt very strongly about preventing a new gas pipeline from the Soviet Union to Europe. In its frustration with its inability to persuade foreigners to its view, the US government simply slapped both export and asset controls on the US and foreign firms that had the technology for the pipeline (and it thereby gave the Soviet Union a foreign policy coup in Europe that in its wildest imagination Moscow could not have gotten on its own). Even Britain, our firmest ally, was most outraged by the extension of American jurisdiction of British firms.

The *policy-altering* effect of DFI is evident, on the other hand, in the recent theoretical analyses of Professor Richard Brecher and myself[17] where we have explored how traditional conclusions such as the optimality of free trade may be reversed if foreign factors of production are present in the economy. The distribution of income implied by a policy, otherwise optimal, may lead to a welfare loss that outweighs the gains traditionally calculated for economies without DFI in their midst. Heuristically, shifting from autarchy to free trade will yield gains from trade, as Adam Smith and Paul Samuelson have shown, but these gains may be outweighed by a redistribution of income away from domestic to foreign-owned factors in your midst. While I would not consider these particular reversals of our traditional policy conclusions important enough to worry about, in general, they do alert us to possibilities that may well be important in specific parametric cases as when the proportion of DFI in total investment may be sizable.

It is evident therefore that economists and policymakers alike have to be increasingly alert to the significant consequences that the increased globalization of the world economy through DFI entails. Stephen Hymer was wrong when he predicted that the multinational corporation, or DFI, would overwhelm the nation state and render it impotent or obsolete. But his instincts were uncannily correct: DFI would grow into a phenomenon that we simply could not ignore.

Notes

1. See in particular, Magee (1977) and the recent modelling by Markusen (1984) and Helpman (1984). See also Dunning (1981) and Caves (1982) for fine, recent reviews of many contributions to DFI analysis.

2. For an illuminating and comprehensive review of Marxist, dependency and world-system views on the development process and hence tangentially on the role of DFI therein, see Blomstrom and Hettne (1984).

3. I have discussed the MPI and related DFI scenarios further in Bhagwati (1982a, ch. 6). I am indebted to Professor Vernon for reminding me that the MPI type of cross-investment *may* be fragile, perhaps more so than the product-cycle variety and others, and that the Dunlop-Pirelli MPIs did not survive long. We have too little experience to date, however, to offer informed guesses on the issue of fragility or stability of the different types of DFI.

4. See the recent model by Jones, Neary, and Ruane (1983), which generates such cross-investment by using the sector-specific factor model.

5. See the analysis by Hamada (1974), Hamilton and Svennson (1982), and Wong (1986) of duty free zones and their welfare effects.

6. Frobel, Heinrichs, and Kreye (1980), writing from a Marxist perspective, and focusing implicitly on EP-oriented DFI's have argued for the ill-effects of such investments as well. Considering them to be part of "worldwide" economic inter-penetration" (p. 8), they are led to argue that such DFIs contribute to "the economic dependency of the developing countries on the industrialised countries." Again, "after decades and centuries of the underdevelopment of the so-called developing countries the recent export-oriented industrialisation of these countries offers but faint hope that [sic] living standards and conditions of the mass of their populations will undergo any substantial improvements in the foreseeable future" (p. 7). I am afraid I find neither of these contentions to be persuasive, and the latter is certainly inconsistent with the facts of the EP-strategy's results.

7. He is currently engaged in the necessary statistical tests, which, at the present date, suggest that this conclusion is robust.

8. Bhagwati, Brecher, Dinopoulos, and Srinivasan (1986) have recently modeled quid pro quo DFI in a competitive framework, where capital flows occur in a world with atomistic firms, utilizing and augmenting the analytical framework in the earlier analysis of Bhagwati and Srinivasan (1978) which had shown that, if the first-period export level can affect the probability of market-disruption-induced quotas being invoked in the second period, an optimal tariff argument exists for restraining exports in the first period below the myopic one-period-maximization level. Dinopoulos and Bhagwati (1986) models quid pro quo DFI, on the other hand, in a market-structure context where individual firms undertake DFI in a two-period context, taking into account the nonmyopic interaction between DFI and protection.

9. See, for instance, the article by Robert Gibson (1985) in the *Los Angeles Times*, documenting the increasing willingness of U.S. multinationals to entertain joint ventures abroad. Export performance requirements have, however, come under critical scrutiny from the U.S. government recently as part of its increasing pre-occupation with the question of "fair trade."

10. Lipson has analyzed beautifully how the interplay of "corporate preferences" and "state interests" has brought this about, as also the role played by the efforts at legitimation of the new regime by developing countries on the international stage.

    Krasner (1985, p. 195) is also perceptive and worth quoting on the remarkable nature of this outcome, compared to other issues dividing the developing and the developed countries:

Developing countries have altered principles, norms, rules, and decision-making procedures related to direct foreign investment. National regulations are increasing. The sanctity of contracts can no longer be adequately defended. The proposition that under the old regime MNCs possessed unfair bargaining power has been widely accepted. Particularly in raw-material exploitation there has been a fundamental shift in effective control in favour of host countries. Multinationals have been compelled to alter their behaviour. Simply by being sovereign states, by utilising the constitutive principle of the international system, develop-ing countries have been able to change the rules of the game for direct foreign investment.

In other issue areas, where domestic action alone has more limited impact, the Third World has had a more difficult time.

11. The internal war against Maoist remnants is not entirely over yet, however. See, for example, Leonard Silk's (1985a) recent report on China's infighting on ideology, filed from Canton. Inevitably, the revisionist supporters of Mr. Deng's new ways invoke tactically the numerous writings of Lenin during NEP in support of supping with the capitalist devil even if one was ideologically a committed Marxist. See, for example, Li Huajie and Zhang Hanyang (1982).

12. I have analyzed this possibility further in my 1982 Yxtaholm IEA conference paper (1985b).

13. See the extended conceptual analysis, as also the discussion of its consequences for the forthcoming trade talks, in my 10th Annual Lecture of the Geneva Association recently (Bhagwati, 1985c).

14. See the report by Miller (1985) in the *Wall Street Journal*.

15. These are well known, in fact, from the important work of Professor Gerald Helleiner (1977) and others. These authors have shown that MNCs have become active agents exercising political pressure in favor of free trade, especially in products that they produce. See also the interesting econometric analysis of U.S. MNCs, and their effect on the structure of U.S. trade barriers, by Lavergne and Helleiner (1985). Their work, however, does not extend to the *potential* DFI effects in favor of freer trade which I discuss above.

16. See my review of Thurow's *The Zero-Sum Solution*, in *The New Leader* (Bhagwati 1985d) where I raise some of these questions.

17. See Bhagwati and Brecher (1980) and Brecher and Bhagwati (1981), and also the earlier analysis by Bhagwati and Tironi (1980).

References

Balasubramanyam, V. N. 1984. Incentives and Disincentives for Foreign Direct Investment in Less Developed Countries. *Weltwirtschaftliches Archiv* 120, 720–735.

Bhagwati, Jagdish. 1972. Review of Vernon: Sovereignty at Bay. *Journal of International Economics* 2: 455–462.

Bhagwati, Jagdish. 1973. The Theory of Immiserizing Growth—Further Applications. In Michael Connolly and Amexander Swoboda (eds.), *International Trade and Money*. London: Allen & Unwin, pp. 45–54.

Bhagwati, Jagdish. 1977a. Review of Hymer. *Journal of Development Economics* 4: 391–395.

Bhagwati, Jagdish (ed). 1977b. *The New International Economic Order: The North–South Debate*. Cambridge: MIT Press.

Bhagwati, Jagdish. 1978. *Anatomy and Consequences of Exchange Control Regimes.* Cambridge, MA: Ballinger.

Bhagwati, Jagdish. 1979. International Factor Movements and National Advantage. *Indian Economic Review* 14(2): 73–100; 9th V. K. Ramaswami Memorial Lecture. Reprinted in Bhagwati (1983), ch. 42.

Bhagwati, Jagdish N. (ed.). 1982a. *Import Competition and Response.* Chicago: Chicago University Press.

Bhagwati, Jagdish. 1982b. Shifting Comparative Advantage, Protectionist Demands and Policy Responses. In Bhagwati (1982a), pp. 153–184.

Bhagwati, Jagdish. 1983. *Essays in International Economic Theory*, vols. 1 and 2. edited by Robert Feestra. Cambridge: MIT Press.

Bhagwati, Jagdish. 1984. Incentives and Disincentives: International Migration. *Weltwirtschaftliches Archiv* 120(4): 678–701.

Bhagwati, Jagdish. 1985a. Protectionism: Old Wine in New Bottles. *Journal of Policy Modelling* 7(1): 23–33.

Bhagwati, Jagdish. 1985b. Structural Adjustment and International Factor Mobility: Some Issues. In Karl Jungenfelt and Douglas Hague (ed.) *Structural Adjustment in Developed Open Economics.* Proceedings of a Conference of the International Economic Association held at Yxtaholm, Sweden London: Macmillan.

Bhagwati, Jagdish. 1985c. *Trade in Services and Developing Countries.* 10th Annual Lecture of the Geneva Association. Delivered at London School of Economics, November 28, forthcoming.

Bhagwati, Jagdish. 1985d. "Pull-up" Not "Trickle-Down" *The New Leader*, December 16–30. New York.

Bhagwati, Jagdish, and Richard Brecher. 1980. National Welfare in an Open Economy in the Presence of Foreign Owned Factors of Production. *Journal of International Economics* 10 (February): 103–115.

Bhagwati, Jagdish, and T. N. Srinivasan. 1978. Shadow Prices for Project Selection in the Presence of Distortions: Effective Rates of Protection and Domestic Resource Costs. *Journal of Political Economy* 16: 97–116.

Bhagwati, Jagdish, and Ernesto Tironi. 1980. Tariff Change, Foreign Capital and Immiserization: A Theoretical Analysis. *Journal of Development Economics* 7 (March): 71–83.

Bhagwati, Jagdish, and John Ruggie (eds.). 1984. *Power, Passions and Purpose. Prospects for North–South Negotiations.* Cambridge: MIT Press.

Bhagwati, Jagdish, Richard Brecher, Elias Dinopoulos, and T. N. Srinivasan. 1986. *Quid pro quo* Foreign Investment and Optimal Policy Intervention (revised). Columbia University. February. Mimeo.

Blomstrom, Magnus, and Bjorne Hettne. 1984. *Development Theory in Transition.* London: Zed Books.

Borner, Silvo. 1985. Global Structural Change and International Competition among Industrial Firms: The Case of Switzerland. *Kyklos* 38: 77–103.

Brecher, Richard, and Jagdish Bhagwati. 1981. Foreign Ownership and the Theory of Trade and Welfare. *Journal of Political Economy* 89(3): 497–511.

Brecher, Richard, and Carlos Díaz-Alejandro. 1977. Tariffs, Foreign Capital and Immiserizing Growth. *Journal of International Economics* 7: 317–322.

Caves, R. E. 1982. *Multinational Enterprise and Economic Analysis.* Cambridge: Cambridge University Press.

Cooper, Richard. 1985. International Economic Cooperation: Is It Desirable? Is It Likely? *Bulletin of the American Academy of Arts and Sciences* 39(2): 11–35.

Dinopoulos, Elias. 1985a. A Formulation of the 'Biological' Model of Trade in Similar Products. Columbia University International Economics Research Center Working Paper No. 60. January. Forthcoming in *Journal of International Economics,* 1986.

Dinopoulos, Elias. 1985b. Mutually-Penetrating, Intra-industry Cross-investment: A Theoretical Analysis (revised). Michigan State University. October. Mimeo.

Dinopoulos, Elias, and Jagdish Bhagwati. 1986. *Quid pro quo* DFI and Market Structure. Columbia University. February. Mimeo.

Dunning, John. 1981. *International Production and the Multinational Enterprise.* London: Allen & Unwin.

Frank, Isiah. 1980. *Foreign Enterprise in Developing Countries.* Baltimore.

Frobel, Folker, Heinrichs, Jurgen, and Kreye, Otto. 1980. *The New International Division of Labour.* Cambridge: Cambridge University Press.

Gibson, Robert W. 1985. Firms Warming to Joint Ventures Abroad. *Los Angeles Times,* June 9.

Grunwald, Joseph, and Kenneth Flamm. 1985. *The Global Factory: Foreign Assembly in International Trade.* Washington, DC: Brookings Institution.

Hamada, Koichi. 1974. An Economic Analysis of Duty-Free Zones. *Journal of International Economics* 4: 225–241.

Hamilton, Carl, and Lars Svennson. 1982. On the Welfare Effects of a Duty-Free Zone. *Journal of International Economics* 12: 45–64.

Helleiner, G. 1977. Transnational Enterprises and the New Political Economy pf United States Trade Policy. *Oxford Economic Papers.* March.

Helpman, Elhanan. 1984. A Simple Theory of International Trade with Multinational Corporations. *Journal of Political Economy* 92: 451–471.

Hymer, Stephen. 1960. *The International Operations of National Firms*. Ph.D. dissertation. Massachusetts Institute of Technology.

Hymer, Stephen, and Robert Rowthorn. 1970. In C. P. Kindleberger (ed.), *The International Corporation*. Cambridge: MIT Press.

Japan Economic Institute. 1982. *Report No. 15A*. Washington, DC.

Jones, R. W., J. P. Neary, and F. Ruane. 1983. Two-Way Capital Flows: Crosshauling in a Model of Foreign Investment. *Journal of International Economics* 13: 357–366.

Kennan, George F. 1960. *Russia and the West*. New York: Mentor Books.

Kindleberger, Charles P. (ed.). 1970. *The International Corporation*. Cambridge: MIT Press.

Kindleberger, Charles. 1973. Restrictions on Direct Foreign Investment in LDCs. In J. Bhagwati and R. S. Eckaus (eds.), *Development and Planning*. Cambridge: MIT Press.

Krasner, Stephen. 1978. *Defending the National Interest: Raw Material Investments and US Foreign Policy*. Princeton: Princeton University Press.

Krasner, Stephen. 1985. *Structural Conflict: The Third World Against Global Liberalism*. Berkeley: University of California Press.

Lavergne, Real, and G. Helleiner. 1985. United States Transnational Corporations and the Structure of Unites States Trade Barriers: An Empirical Investigation. Mimeo.

Li Huajie and Zhang Hanyang. 1982. Xue xi Liening guanyu zurangzhi de lilun (Learn from Lenin's Theory Regarding the Leasing System). *Gang-Au jingji* (Guangdong), 4.

Lipson, Charles. 1985. *Standing Guard*. Berkeley: University of California Press.

Magee, Steve. 1977. Information and the Multinational Corporation: An Appropriability Theory of Direct Foreign Investment. In Bhagwati (1977).

Markusen, James. 1984. Multinationals, Multi-plant Economies, and the Gains from Trade. *Journal of International Economics* 16: 205–226.

Miller, Michael. 1985. Big US Semiconductor Markers Expected to Sue over "Dumping" of Japanese Chips. *Wall Street Journal*, October 1.

New York Times. 1985. Foreign Investment in US Up Sharply. September 16.

Sassen-Koob, Saskia. 1984. *The Foreign Investment Connection: Rethinking Migration*. Cambridge: Cambridge University Press.

Silk, Leonard. 1985a. China's Fight over Ideology. *The New York Times*, October 2.

Silk, Leonard. 1985b. China Hits Its Stride. *The New York Times*, October 27.

Sit, Victor S. F. 1985. The Special Economic Zones of China. *The Developing Economies* 23(1): 69–87.

Vernon, Raymond. 1966. International Investment and International Trade in the Product Cycle. *Quarterly Journal of Economics* 80 (May): 190–207.

Vernon, Raymond. 1971. *Sovereignty at Bay*. New York: Basic Books.

Vernon, Raymond. 1977. *Storm over the Multinationals: The Real Issues*. London.

Wong, Kar-yiu. 1986. International Factor Movements, Repatriation and Welfare. *Journal of International Economics*, forthcoming.

Wright, James. 1985. Letter to the Editor. *Wall Street Journal*, October 3.

18   Incentives and Disincentives: International Migration

The phenomenon of international migration is one characterized by dis-incentives rather than incentives. The twentieth century witnessed the rise of immigration quotas, sanctioned by national legislations as in 1905 in Great Britain and in 1921 in the United States.[1] It is probably true to say that today, except for international personal mobility assured in arrange-ments such as the European Economic Community, international migration is influenced and inhibited primarily by legislation.

Emigration, as distinct from immigration, is substantially less restricted, of course. In fact, it is generally confined to the socialist countries which, for well-known reasons, do not permit outmigration of their nationals. It is probably pertinent to remark that, were these countries to permit freer outmigration, the effective constraint on the numbers migrating would soon become the immigration legislations of the destination countries. The Chinese Prime Minister is supposed to have retorted cynically to human-rights complaints about emigration restrictions: tell us how many million Chinese you want and we will be happy to supply them. The effective, binding constraint on the present outmigration levels from these countries, however, does continue to be their own restrictions on emigration. The only counterpart to such restrictions in other countries is the occasional, often ineffectual, attempt by some developing countries to create disincen-tives for outmigration of nationals with high skills, in particular doctors.

The focus of this paper therefore must be on immigration restrictions, especially their anatomy and consequences. In fact, I should add at the outset that the most compelling contrast between internal and international migrations is provided by the fact that the former is generally free, whereas the latter is constrained by controls.

Of course, this contrast is not total. Socialist countries inhibit mobility within their boundaries: the civil rights of their populations do not extend to uninhibited freedom to move where one wishes.[2] And, in countries such as India, while movement cannot be constitutionally restricted, there are several instances of job—and college—admission reservations in favor of local people that serve to inhibit the immigration of certain classes of people from other states, as has been extensively studied by Weiner and Katzenstein (1981). Again, international migrations also occasionally exhibit elements of substantially unimpeded entry: as in the case of the virtually uncontrollable illegal Mexican immigration to the United States, or the legal migration of *gastarbeiters* in the postwar period into Europe until the early 1970s, a migration which was under immigration regimes that implied a sort of quasi-open-door policy of immigration. Nonetheless, the fact remains that international migration is significantly affected by the nature of immigration controls, whereas (except for the socialist countries) internal migration is generally not.

I might also add that the contrast that I have just drawn between internal and international migrations immediately impacts on the way one wants to model and analyze the causes and consequences of such migrations. For one thing, one cannot begin to analyze international immigration unless one first understands the immigration control system pertinent to any given parametric situation. For another, the internal-migration models, for the same reason, are not readily transferable to analyzing international migrations. I like to illustrate this latter contention by reference to the well-known Harris-Todaro (1970) model of rural-urban, internal migration. In this model, the actual rural wage is equated in equilibrium to the *expected* (higher sticky) urban wage, with the underemployed or unemployed subsisting in the urban areas. In fact, the Harris-Todaro model is aimed at explaining urban unemployment as much as urban immigration. But consider the same mechanism operating in the international context. Here, again the higher wage in New York, multiplied by the probability of getting past the immigration controls into the United States and hence earning that American wage, may be held to be equal to the actual lower Filipino wage. However, the *physical location* of the unemployed cannot be in New York because of the immigration restrictions, whereas in the internal version of the same model the unemployed reside in the urban cities. The economic and political consequences of this international immigration restriction, even when one applies a similar argumentation, therefore are likely to be different in the end.

With these general remarks, I can now turn to analyzing the causes and consequences of immigration restrictions: section 18.1 considers the causes briefly and section 18.2 the consequences at greater length.

18.1 The Causes of Immigration Restrictions

A somewhat remarkable hierarchy obtains in terms of the extent to which the operation of liberalism in the economic sphere is considered to be acceptable in modern nation states. In the postwar period, *trade in goods* has come to be regarded fairly generally as governable by economic rules such as the GATT embodies, though we all know that politics (broadly construed) enters into this realm as well, e.g., with concerns about "failure to get your share of high-tech without which a modern society cannot function" infesting the most advanced countries in a disconcerting reminder that such concerns are not an exclusive attribute of the developing countries who had similar concerns about industrialization per se during the period leading up to the enactment of Part IV at the GATT. When it comes to *trade in services*, such concerns become even more pervasive, as the United States has discovered in its attempt to extend GATT to services, with several countries apparently worried about whether they would be able to maintain national control of their "infrastructure". The problems get much worse, however, with "noneconomic" considerations in the forefront, when *direct investment* is considered: worries about "dependence," "loss of sovereignty," etc., are not just a Canadian fetish or a Latin American intellectual's favorite pastime but can be found to surface over a much wider arena and to translate into policies as well. But there is practically universal agreement, among modern states, that free *flows of human beings*, no matter how efficacious for world efficiency, should not be permitted. Today, immigration restrictions are virtually everywhere, making immigration the most compelling exception to liberalism in the operation of the world economy.

Why? This question can be addressed at different levels. In moral-philosophical terms the question translates into why nation states feel they can exclude others from their borders. Consider first the arguments for universal freedom to move: (1) If one treats the human race as one, it may seem from this *single-planetary-rights* viewpoint that there should be freedom to move into, and out of, societies and that this freedom should be part of human rights or what Dworkin likes to describe as a set of "Plato principles" of decent human behavior. Evidently, however, this principle is not acceptable to modern sensibility: human societies, as constituted, simply do not seem to accept such absence of exclusivity. (2) The freedom to locate wherever one wishes to on this planet earth may also follow from a *cosmopolitan-utilitarian* approach: such freedom may be established to yield the maximum of world efficiency. Again, however, societies, even if compensation were undertaken for actual losses from the income-distributional impact of such a Pareto-best policy, do not appear to accept this approach. (3) The theory of *imperial conquest* at the time of the opening of the Americas shows a yet further moral-philosophical justification in the Spanish writings at the time. Thus, Francisco de Vittoria asserted what he termed the "right of Natural Society and Communication" and sought to provide the ethical rationale for the Spaniards proceeding to the Indies to settle there by arguing that "it has been the custom from the beginning of the world for anyone to go into whatever country he chooses and prohibition of entrance is a violent measure not removed from war." Needless to say, this particular doctrine of "natural rights" provided a rationale for conquest; it is unlikely that it would have been propounded with equal conviction if the movement of people, settlements, and conquest was in the reverse direction!

The revealed ethical preference of societies is rather for the assertion of the right to exclude, a right which is widely described in recent discussions of immigration reform to establish better control of immigration inflows in the United States as being a natural attribute of national "sovereignty." I might add that many Western societies have moved in the recent century however to consider the parallel right to hold back, i.e., to prevent someone from emigrating, as not acceptable. This asymmetry does not make sense if one adopts the single-planetary approach to rights, giving everyone the right to locate where he wishes to, or the cosmopolitan-utilitarian approach. The asymmetry therefore gives us an important insight into the psychological mainsprings of why the manifest ethical viewpoints are what they are: (1) Although socio-biological and similar "deterministic" models of human behavior are, in my judgment, inappropriate, it is nonetheless suggestive that "territoriality" is a widespread (though not universal) behavioral pattern among animals, suggesting that similar territoriality, and unwillingness to permit entry into one's space at will to strangers outside the pack, appears to many as a "natural" right, compatible with basic human decency in a civilized society.[3] (2) Parallel to this position is the notion that the central values and ethos that characterize one's society could be diluted by the entry of individuals and groups who do not share them and that the right to assign entry selectively is simply a matter of being "true to oneself," and hence a "natural" right. This position translates practically into ethnic preferences on entry, going from racially explicit quotas (as in the early legislation in the United States which excluded Orientals) to less explicitly racist hemispheric quotas that de facto favored white immigration from Western Europe into the United States, to refugee selection procedures that effectively tend to favor entrants belonging to specific ethnic groups in many countries.

High principles and low prejudice thus combine uneasily in the restrictive immigration practices of most countries: in fact, they blend together.[4] Does economics then have little to offer here? Not quite. Even if construed narrowly as the analysis of the consequences of the profit motive, economics certainly can be utilized to throw light on why the immigration rules are what they are, and indeed to discuss the question as to why the immigration legislations arose at the turn of the century, and not just to analyze the consequences of immigration restrictions resulting from "noneconomic" factors.

While I later indicate how some aspects of immigration systems can be understood as resulting from economic motivation, I should like to refer here to the interesting study by Williamson (1982) of the U.S. economy at the time of the enactment of the 1921 Act restricting immigration into the United States. He argues that, by the turn of the century, the absorptive capacity of the U.S. economy, in regard to continuing influx of unskilled labor, had become substantially less, so that the income-distributional impact of further immigration on real wages would have been quite adverse and dramatic. He attributes the changes in absorptive capacity to demand-side changes such as sectoral patterns of technical change militating against demand for unskilled labor, higher supply price of new lands, etc. What this argument does, of course, is to provide an economic rationale as to why labor groups might have opposed continued, free immigration.[5] But it must be connected up with actual lobbying in this regard by labor, and must reckon with the fact that this would equally create a pressure group on the part of one or more of the other factors to encourage continued immigration.[6] But, nonetheless, the argument is interesting and suggests how the growth of immigration regimes can be analyzed within the framework of modern political economy, utilizing tools and insights provided by the recent theorists who have addressed this area of what I have called directly unproductive profit seeking (DUP) activities (see Bhagwati, 1982a).

18.2   The Consequences of Immigration Restrictions

Illegal or "Undocumented" Migration

Since immigration systems are control systems, the first question that they raise is: How effective are they? Even a casual acquaintance with reality underlines the important fact that they lead to evasion, and hence inevitably to unanticipated effects on both economic and social dimensions, as I will argue presently.

Factors Impacting on the Illegal Inflow
How much illegal migration actually occurs is a subject inevitably surrounded by controversy, with the U.S. figures ranging for example from 2–3 million to 10 million, depending on the sources; not surprisingly, the Mexican estimates tend to be generally lower than the U.S. estimates. The magnitudes have to be a function of the ease with which illegal immigration can occur: long, open, uncontrollable borders with potential pools of migrants, loopholes, and the presence of already-migrated nationals from the potential source countries, all contribute to large migration levels of "undocumented" migrants.

1. The long border of the United States with Mexico is as uncontrollable as the long border that Bangladesh has with India's State of Assam. In both instances, the government of the country of immigration is virtually helpless: millions have simply crossed over and, in the case of the United States, they come back almost as soon as they are deported. At a seminar on U.S. immigration, a racetrack owner from Chicago told us the story of how the Immigration and Naturalization Service (INS) had rounded up several illegal Mexicans working on his racetrack, and he had taken a bet that they would all be back from Mexico within a fortnight. Well, he lost because one came back three weeks later. Asked why, the Mexican said: Since I was home, I thought I would stay a little longer and have a proper vacation! But neither India nor the United States can officially acknowledge that the border is uncontrollable: that would be political suicide and each must attempt measures that, while simply ineffective, at least give the appearance of a government that is "taking action." The Simpson-Mazzoli immigration bill, presently pending before the Congress, plans to impose sanctions on employers of illegal immigrants; and yet official studies show how this will probably work with as little efficacy as sanctions have worked in European countries, while simply becoming a nuisance to Hispanic immigrants already legally in the U.S.[7] Again, the Indian government, in desperate reaction to the unmanageable and explosive reaction in Assam to the influx of illegal Bangladeshi migrants, recently started constructing a fence on the long border, and we were deprived of the pleasure of observing how long it would take before the fence would start being sold in the black markets of Dacca, inch by inch, simply because the Indian government stopped the construction when Bangladesh protested!

2. The specific features of the control system can also be utilized to avoid and effectively evade immigration restrictions by exploiting loopholes. A splendid example of this is provided by the U.S. immigration system where immigration of professionals is often undertaken by *first* acquiring student status (which is on the face of it legitimate) under J, F, and H visas and *then* "staying on" with conversion of that status to an immigrant status, a process that is easier obviously than one of "direct" migration under the third and sixth preference category visas for Professional, Technical, and Kindred (PTK) immigrants. Table 18.1 shows how the ratio of these student "stay-ons" to the direct migrants has been remarkably high. Several consequences have followed. First, U.S. education (for some foreign students at least) has become an instrument of migration! Much like the educational theory of fairness-in-hiring with education as an instrument of job competition which I and Srinivasan (1977) propounded some time ago, education cannot then be perceived in human-capital-theoretic terms à la Becker or in screening terms à la Spence. It simply yields private returns to the student by enabling him to stay on in the United States, since he cannot

Table 18.1
Student "stay-ons" vis-à-vis direct PTK immigrants in the United States

Year	"Stay-ons"[a] (1)	Direct PTKs[b] (2)	(1)/(2) × 100 (3)
1965	5,723	6,961	82.2
1966	11,548	16,349	70.6
1967	9,614	18,687	51.4
1968	9,085	24,620	36.9
1969	12,616	27,058	46.6
1970	16,993	26,522	64.1
1971	20,390	24,668	82.7
1972	16,247	21,681	74.9
1973	14,785	22,224	66.5
1974	12,664	22,899	55.3
1975	13,738	20,492	67.0
1976	15,314	17,823	85.9
1977	23,732	21,635	109.7
1978	19,363	28,200	68.7

Source: Immigration and Naturalization Service (INS), *Annual Reports*, cited in Agarwal and Winkler (1983).
a. F, H, and J visa conversions to immigrant status.
b. Third and sixth preference PTK immigrants.

migrate directly. Second, this undoubtedly encourages widespread evasion of immigration restrictions by encouraging students, much like overaged football players with brawn and no brains, to remain on student rolls simply so that they can continue residing in the United States. Third, we then get here a splendid example of that well-known phenomenon: controls inherently have loopholes that lead to more controls to plug them, and then you get new loopholes, and then new controls, and so controls proliferate with efficiency and equity implications inevitably following. It has thus become evident now that, because of the problem with stay-ons, which is not really manageable, U.S. consuls have taken to rejecting legitimate student visa applications in considerable numbers. More disturbingly, the procedures now require the applicant to produce a sponsor in the United States who has a bank balance in the range of $20,000, etc., a procedure that would tend to crowd out those students who have merit but no connections. Besides, U.S. consuls, who are not formally required to justify their decisions, are reputed now to reject applications from the poorer students on the alleged and unproven theory that the poor are the more likely to stay on! All this is not merely inequitable; it is also in violation of the egalitarian spirit of the immigration that the United States was built on and still characterizes U.S. approaches to public policy.

Yet another example of these unintended consequences of immigration restrictions is provided by the well-known fact that the post-OPEC tightening of the immigration systems in the Western European countries led to increased attempts at getting political asylum as a way of getting past the immigration quotas! This, in turn, led to a situation where the asylum system itself was clogged, and, for some time, it became difficult even to get information on the number of asylum applicants in certain countries because the grant of legitimate requests for asylum in Western countries is an important tradition and attempts to curb its abuse by potential immigrants creates serious public-relations problems.[8]

3. The illegal immigration, as indeed legal immigration, is also fed by the presence of one's own ethnic group in the countries of immigration. To get around control systems, you need to have local knowledge. Indeed, for this reason, MNCs in highly controlled countries employ host-country nationals in their firms even if not compelled to do so by indigenization rules. Networking plays therefore an important role in legal immigrants learning how to get past the restrictions. But illegal immigrants are also helped, somewhat differently. They are *protected* to some extent, and hence encouraged, by the fact their "compatriots" provide the necessary "protective

coloring": Mexican illegals can blend into the legal Hispanic community. The local, legal-immigrant community can also provide the moral support, the lobbying for their "human right," etc., all of which reduces the cost of the illegal status which they suffer from.

4. In addition, the influx of illegal immigrants is naturally a function of the restrictiveness of the quotas. It has been widely remarked that the low incidence of illegal immigrants into Western Europe until the mid-1970s was a function of the fact that substantial immigration of foreign workers was legally permitted as under the *gastarbeiter* system in West Germany and Switzerland, thereby reducing the "pull" factor's impact on illegal immigration.

Consequences of the Illegal Inflow

In addition to the consequences I have already noted, the illegal inflows have led to several interesting *equity* problems. Thus, in the case of the United States there is little doubt that the large influx from Mexico has increased the determination of the Reagan administration to stop the influx, however more compelling on human-rights grounds, from other sources: to be seen able to control your border, even if you do that at the wrong border simply because that is feasible, becomes a virtue when you face an open sieve elsewhere and there is a political hot potato on your hands. I see the extraordinarily rough treatment of the "boat people" from Haiti, wholly inconsistent with U.S. traditions, as reflecting partly this factor, and only partly the fear that, if treated "normally," the new stream would swell into another major influx in the future. The presence of the illegal immigrants has also created tough moral-philosophical issues, such as the rights of the children born unto them: can children born to people who have no legal status in a country enjoy rights given to native children of that country or should they, like in traditional Japan, be deprived along with their parents? The U.S. courts have recently taken a prudential view on the subject, in a celebrated 1980 Texas judgment,[9] extending to these children the right to public education using I believe the consequentialist argument that it would not pay society to have children grow up without these benefits. In themselves also, the class of undocumented workers is seen as an exploited underclass, deprived and anguished, bereft of many of the rights that native workers automatically enjoy, and hence possessed of a discriminatorily less favored status. The Simpson-Mazzoli proposal to grant legal immigrant status to large numbers of such illegal immigrants has also raised the question: Is it fair to grant permanent entry to illegal migrants, however exploited, when entry has been denied to those who were good enough to take the high road and get onto the long waiting list for legal entry?

Foreign Investment and Foreign Aid
An interesting consequence of illegal immigration has been that the countries of immigration have been exploring alternative ways of stemming the influx. Among these has been the possibility of using greater outflow of aid funds to, and direct foreign investment in, the countries from which the influx is occurring. Two alternative rationales can be detected here.

First, there is no doubt that aid is conceived partly as a way of "bribing" countries of outflux into cooperation on controlling the illegal flow. U.S. aid to Haiti can be certainly seen in this light. Second, if the aid is used wisely and leads to greater economic prosperity, it is expected that it would create more employment and/or higher wages, thus reducing the "push" factors that fuel the illegal flows. Direct foreign investment is also expected to play this latter role. The U.S.–Mexico problem is widely regarded as amenable to a partial solution along these lines.

Is the latter argument valid? It certainly seems plausible. Any reduction in wage differentials and in expected income improvements from migration ought to reduce, ceteris paribus, the incentive to migrate. However, as always, paradoxes can surface: (1) Immigrants may be those who can afford to migrate, in the face of imperfect capital markets. If so, the capacity to migrate may be the constraint on migration rather than the incentive to do so. Foreign investment or aid, in raising incomes of the proletariat, may then bring more migrants over the border, rather less. (2) Again, the networking aspect of migration means that MNCs may serve to provide conduits whereby migration may increase. Thus, the Egyptian employees of Coca-Cola in Cairo may establish contacts with their U.S. fellow-managers and workers, get these U.S. friends to procure jobs and labor certification required for immigration, and manage to get further down the road on to immigration into the U.S. than they otherwise would have done. (3) Then, again, in an interesting recent contribution, the sociologist Sasson-Koob (1984) has argued that foreign investment and immigration are complementary rather than substitutes because direct foreign investment itself creates a proletariat in the host countries, leading in turn to outmigration eventually.

Among the arguments advanced by Sasson-Koob in support of this contention are the following (1) export-oriented MNCs use female labor which, in turn, creates a female proletariat that is itself integrated ideologically into a nontraditional set of values that are a precondition to out-migration to the capitalist centers; (2) often, the female workers experience rapid turnover, creating female unemployment that also fuels outmigration; (3) the spread of the proletarian ideology goes beyond the female workers to their families and other workforce members so that outmigration of others also is encouraged; and (4) the city centers such as New York, in turn, are now the source of low-level jobs even in high-tech modern industries where this emerging proletariat can find jobs. These arguments are imaginative but the evidence in support of them is not compelling, I am afraid.

I might add that the possibility of complementarity between immigration and investment can arise also because the former leads to the latter instead. Thus, German firms may get used to working with Turkish labor in Germany, and this itself may encourage them to take up profitable opportunities to invest in Anatolia. Again, the returning Turkish *gastarbeiter* may have spread seeds of modernization and proletarian values which serve to accelerate the formation of the type of labor that German MNCs would like to employ, thus facilitating their investment in Turkey. Again, networking may imply that the immigrant groups in a developed host country may serve as conduits for facilitating the perception of investment opportunities, may promote joint ventures between themselves and MNCs in their countries of origin, and so on. Thus, even if one were to observe that, at least at first glance, investment and immigration were positively rather than inversely related, the relationship could go from immigration to investment rather than the other way.

Quite aside from these arguments, it is interesting then to ask whether there are any patterns of complementarity or substitution that the data suggest for major countries of immigration in the postwar period. For example, did West Germany direct its foreign investments abroad to Turkey, Yugoslavia, Spain, Portugal, Greece, and Italy before the labor inflows from these countries grew to phenomenal levels during the 1950s and 1960s under the *gastarbeiter* system? I should doubt this, though my distinguished discussant Dr. Klaus-Werner Schatz probably can come up with the data to address this question at the Conference. I would instead hazard the guess that it was the unwillingness of German firms, or their inability, to invest abroad where the cheap labor was that led to greater reliance on labor importation, subverting partially the predictions of Marx and Lenin that monopoly capitalism would seek investments abroad in its later phase. And, in fact, it may be that the general post-1973 tightening of labor immigration in European countries has, in turn, led to a greater

outflow of European MNCs to the erstwhile countries of *gastarbeiter* supply: a hypothesis that is worth checking out.

Consequences of Restrictions: Some Conceptual Issues

While therefore reality intrudes in the shape of illegal inflows of labor
around the existing immigration control regimes, and one may safely
predict that over time these inflows will increase, there is no prospect that
they can altogether eliminate the effects of the quotas. What are these
effects?

We need to distinguish, as always, between positive and normative
aspects. The latter, in particular, raise somewhat new questions since our
habit of discussing "national" welfare must be carefully qualified in the
context of international migration. For example, when Turks migrate to
West Germany as *gastarbeiters*, is their welfare to be subsumed under
"Turkish" welfare or "German" welfare or both or neither? As I have
argued in Bhagwati (1979b), depending on the sociological, political and
other factors impacting on the immigration flows, each answer may have
relevance. The consequences of this complexity, not afflicting the analysis
of financial capital flows, are somewhat drastic. For example, since the
labor-intensive textile industry in the U.S. intensively uses LDC-immigrant
labor, protecting it raises LDC-emigrant labor incomes but hurts LDC-
nonmigrant welfare. If only the nonmigrant LDC labor enters the LDC
social welfare function, the DC protection is unambiguously harmful in
general to LDC welfare; if both migrant and nonmigrant labor do so, then
paradoxes of welfare-improving protection can arise.[10] In much of the
positive debate on *skilled* migration from the LDCs to the DCs, the implicit
assumption has been to define LDC welfare only over the so-called TLBs
("those left behind": a properly evocative phrase in the context of immigration restrictions!), whereas (as in the Hamilton-Whalley exercise described below) the opposite migrant-inclusive assumption is made in the
context of unskilled or general migration, and both are utilized in recent
analyses of the public-finance-theoretic question as to which country ought
to exercise income tax jurisdiction, and how, when there is international
personal mobility: a novel question opened up recently and analyzed at
length by Bhagwati and Hamada (1982), Mirrlees (1982), Baumol (1982)
and Wilson (1982) in a recent symposium in the *Journal of Public Economics*.

In my judgment, there are numerous equity issues, cutting across different groups, that impact critically on immigration questions: on their causes
and on their consequences. Emigrants versus TLBs; immigrants versus

hostcountry natives and residents; immigrants from alternative sources vis-à-vis one another; specific groups within these categories vis-à-vis one another (e.g., unskilled immigrants versus unionized labor in low-wage occupations or labor versus employers in the country of immigration): these are all different types of "horizontal equity" issues that impact on immigration issues fairly critically. In judging welfare questions realistically, therefore, we have to keep these distributional aspects close in view.

What If Restrictions Were All Abolished?

There are two kinds of economic questions which one may ask, in regard to immigration restrictions: (1) What would happen if the world could be reorganized such that people could move freely around the world? (2) Given the restrictions, what can one say about their structure and proximate consequences vis-à-vis alternative forms of such restrictions? Both questions, of course, involve a counterfactual as indeed all economic questions must; the former postulates a counterfactual where all restrictions go whereas the latter assumes a counterfactual where the form of restrictions is changed but not their existence.

The former question is utopian but intriguing. The only authors who have had the courage to attempt an answer to it are Hamilton and Whalley (1984), who examine the consequences of such a scenario in a 179-country model, using 1977 data, and a simple methodology which I must describe and assess shortly, to conclude that (1) enormous gains in efficiency, and (2) improvement in the distribution of world income among nation states would follow from the dismantling of immigration restrictions. The former gains are recorded in table 18.2, which gives the "unadjusted" estimates, with gains amounting anywhere from U.S. $4.7 trillion to U.S. $16 trillion! The latter effect is seen from the Lorenz curve in figure 18.1. In under-

Table 18.2
Estimates of annual worldwide efficiency gains from free labor mobility ($ trillion 1977)

Removal of controls on labor mobility between	Elasticities of substitution in production in all regions				
	1.5	1.25	1.0	0.75	0.25
All countries	16.02	14.46	12.28	9.26	5.80
The "rich" and "poor" Regions	7.02	6.81	6.49	5.92	4.74

Source: Adapted from table 4 in Hamilton and Whalley (1984, p. 71).
Note: Unadjusted cases. Worldwide GNP in 1977 was U.S. $7.82 trillion.

standing these results, which are dramatic, a few important caveats have to be borne in mind, several noted by the authors themselves.

1. The estimates are based on CES production functions for capital and labor for each region/country, with labor reassigned according to the principle of equalization of wages in the "unadjusted" full-mobility exercise reported in table 18.2 the alternative estimates reflecting different assumptions imposed on the elasticity of substitution in the postulated CES production function. The model used therefore automatically builds into itself diminishing returns, with only single (and common-across-countries) output in an aggregated production function. Varying the substitution elasticity downward naturally produces then lower gains from labor reallocation to equalize fully or partially its marginal product across countries. It is, however, not clear at all that such an exercise, which abstracts from commodity trade and capital flows, will not exaggerate the gains from labor mobility in this grossly aggregative model. Trade theorists have recently been studying the question as to whether, for instance, commodity trade and factor mobility are complements or substitutes, and whether capital and labor mobility, in turn, are complements or substitutes: questions which are obviously trivially answered in the Heckscher-Ohlin-Samuelson model where they are all equivalent. The literature on these questions, from a positive-theoretic standpoint, is recent and growing notable among these contributions being Markusen (1983) and Wong (1983, 1984). Insofar as

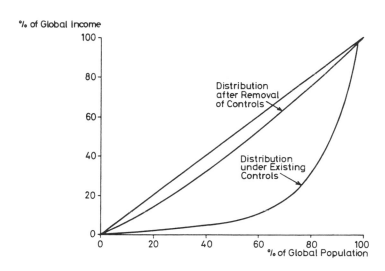

Figure 18.1

there is indeed substitution between commodity trade and capital mobility, it would appear that the Hamilton-Whalley procedure would tend to exaggerate the output gains from reallocating labor by omitting those aspects from their very model. The question remains therefore open here to further analysis.

2. Their conclusion concerning the egalitarian impact of labor mobility is yet more dramatically a consequence of the assumptions that substitution elasticities are identical across countries and that (implicitly) the migrants' income is to be considered part of the income of the country of emigration. Consider figure 18.2, therefore, which depicts their model in essence. The I and E schedules are the marginal-product schedules of the countries that will import and export labor, respectively, when immigration restrictions come off. $L_I O$ is the I-country's and $L_E O$ is the E-country's labor supply. With restrictions on migration in place, the wage is OP in I and OQ in E. With restrictions removed, a uniform wage is reached at $O'R$ and $O'O$ labor migrates from E to I. Now, the total impact on output and the impacts on different groups can be seen to be the following:

PQR $=$ total world gain,

PSR $=$ gain by the original nationals and residents of country I,

SQTR $=$ gain by migrants,

QTR $=$ loss of TLBs in country E, and hence loss of country E if migrants considered not part of E's welfare,

SQR $=$ gain of country E *if* TLB loss is combined with migrants' gain.

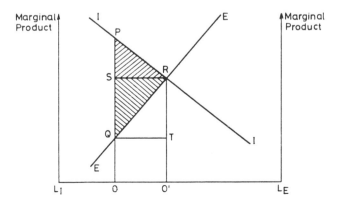

Figure 18.2

In the Hamilton-Whalley model, SQR is implicitly treated as the correct measure of the change in income of the country or region whose labor emigrates in the exercise. Therefore, the exercise assigns gain to each country from the reallocation of labor; and with the gains (PQR and SQR in figure 18.2) being relatively close to each other due to identity of the elasticity of substitution across countries everywhere whereas per capita incomes initially are far apart among them, it follows that per capita incomes by nation get closer and the Lorenz curve in figure 18.1 shows greater equality after the removal of immigration restrictions. Aside from difficulties with the parametric assumptions, I have a question: Would it really make sense to continue thinking of migrants in a world without any or substantial immigration restrictions as if they were part of the society, and hence the social welfare function, of the country of emigration?

3. Moreover, the Hamilton-Whalley exercise may tend to obscure the fact that some developing countries tend to see immigration restrictions on *skilled* migration as a blessing in disguise since they consider the out-migration of such manpower to developing countries as inflicting losses on TLBs over whom nations' welfare is implicitly defined. There is indeed a vast literature on this problem of the "brain drain."[11] But the models outnumber greatly the empirical analyses: the availability of reliable data on international migration is generally limited. The theoretical analysis, on the other hand, has been lively and instructive. For example, the "brain drain" phrase was followed by the countervailing argument that, in many cases, the migrants had no jobs and therefore the migration of unemployed labor was not a loss, that the proper phrase for the migration phenomenon was: "safety-valve" or "spillover" migration. But then, in turn, this contention was countered by the argument, formalized variously by Bhagwati and Hamada (Bhagwati, 1976, chs. 6 and 7), that the domestic unemployment was by no means exogenous to the possibility of outmigration but that the latter could, and often did, influence the demand for education and hence the supply of educated labor and hence unemployment. Similarly, the argument that developing countries lost to migration doctors, whose social marginal product was greatly in excess of their remuneration in societies where there were very few doctors, has been countered by Hla Myint (1968) with the argument that most of them happen to stay anyway in cities where they crowd each other and that statistics on per capita availability are hopelessly misleading. But then, as I have argued with Hamada, the outmigration possibility may interfere with the "internal diffusion" process: as doctors crowd in the cities, they slowly begin to move partially and sometimes fully to practice in smaller towns (Bhagwati, 1976, ch. 7).

My own judgment is that the normative impacts of the outmigration of skilled manpower are complex and can go in contrary directions. Hence, I have consistently objected to the notion, fairly popular in certain circles, that Paretian compensation principles be applied to tax migrants to compensate TLBs or to immigrant countries (a naturally far more popular idea with developing countries) towards the same end.

My own favorite idea has been to approach the question of taxation of migrants in much broader philosophical and economic terms: i.e., to raise the question whether it makes good sense to exempt one's nationals from income taxation simply because they happen to reside (prosperously) in New York whereas one taxes (the far less prosperous) nationals who happen to reside in New Delhi. The moral-philosophical issues, and the second-best issues raised by this for optimal-income-taxation theory and tax practice, have been now introduced into public-finance literature which had hitherto been marked by absence of any analytical attention to this problem.[12] I cannot help remarking cynically that, with all the recent attention addressed to "self-reliance" in Southern policymaking, the notion that one's nationals abroad should also be co-opted into the tax net, à la U.S. practice of global taxation of nationals based on citizenship rather residence, does not raise much enthusiasm even among the Southern left-wing intellectuals. After all, many of these reside abroad and most, in turn, have someone abroad from their extended families, so that it is evidently self-serving to raise uninformed objections to this egalitarian proposal and indeed much more comforting to agitate instead for more foreign aid to be paid by other countries' treasuries!

The Anatomy of Specific Restrictionist Regimes

Turning now to the less ambitious but more readily analyzable problem of how specific immigration regimes seem to work, I must note first that there is an immense diversity of practices. This is inevitable, of course, since the quota regimes inevitably reflect a variety of economic and political factors that are specific to the country in question; and, as became evident in a ten-country NBER project on exchange control regimes and their consequences directed by Krueger and myself, the economic impacts can vary interestingly with the specific features of the control regime.[13]

I will argue this theme by reference to two major immigration regimes that were being run on explicitly contrasting principles: the pre-1973 West German *gastarbeiter* system and the post-1965 U.S. immigration system. The former was set up on explicitly economic-need criteria; the latter is instead a "familial and refugee-oriented" system with no evident reference to economic motivation as its driving force. Let me then contrast them on the following dimensions: (1) quantity of immigration; (2) destination of immigrants by sector of use; (3) source of immigrants by country of origin; and (4) skill composition of immigrants.

Quantity

As described by Mehrländer (1979, 1980) the West German *gastarbeiter* system did not initially set up target quantities of immigration and then proceed to allocate them to destination, geographical or sector of use. Rather, it was a system under which specific firms could, after appropriate procedures securing the consent of labor and local government, recruit needed foreign labor abroad. The total quantity of immigration was therefore simply the inadvertent sum of these "micro" decisions under what Bhagwati et al. (1983) have called a "quasi-open-door" policy of immigration.[14] This, in turn, immediately means that the destination-of-employment pattern becomes a meaningful economic question under this regime, with answers that I discuss below.

By contrast, the U.S. immigration system works with prior quotas allocated over different categories, mostly familial and by refugee category and some in professional, technical and kindred (PTK). Except for very small numbers admitted on specific assignments (e.g., H-1 visas), the system eschews destination questions. The total (legal) annual numbers that have been admitted are substantially below what the *gastarbeiter* system has led to, and, as I have already noted, the inflow of larger numbers of illegal immigrants into the United States has been partly assigned to this difference between the two central regimes.

Yet another aspect of the quantity of immigration overall which might be mentioned here is the analytical attention which has been addressed recently by trade theorists to the interesting welfare-theoretic question: suppose that a capital-rich country could choose between two alternative policies, one of permitting capital to flow to the labor-rich country and the other of permitting instead labor to come in from the labor-rich country, which of these policies would be the better from the viewpoint of its own advantage? This question was posed long ago in a neglected paper by Ramaswami (1968) and was resurrected in my Ramaswami lecture (Bhagwati, 1979b) and has now led to a considerable body of work by Bhagwati and Srinivasan (1983), Wong (1983), Wooton and Saavedra-Rivano (1983), Srinivasan (1983), and several other writers, utilizing a variety of models of a general-equilibrium-theoretic variety, and rank-ordering policies that include optimal taxation of out-going capital and of incoming labor (including discriminatory taxation of foreign vis-à-vis domestic labor: a question that raises in turn several pertinent policy questions of feasibility).

Destination by Sector

As I have already noted, the question of destination of immigrants by sector is largely moot in the U.S. context since the immigration is largely not by recruitment and occupational and destination mobility is generally not controlled.[15] It is not particularly meaningful therefore to discuss the question of destination by sector in the U.S. context.

By contrast, the German system until 1973 worked by recruitment. Besides, there were restrictions on mobility and it seems that a good working hypothesis is that mobility in an expanding economy was generally low for immigrant labor anyway. We should expect therefore that economic analysis destination-of-sector should in principle be possible. Bhagwati et al. (1983) therefore hypothesized that differential demand factors across German industries should be able to explain the differential resort to importation of foreign labor into Germany under this system. They were successful in doing this, utilizing as explanatory variables the change in effective protection, the rate of growth of demand, and capital intensity of industries, and the rate of growth of foreign labor in the industry as the dependent variable. Where, in particular, the reduction in protection was greater, the fall in utilization of foreign labor was greater, and where output grew more rapidly, so did the utilization of foreign labor.

Source Pattern of Immigrants

As it happens, the source pattern of U.S. immigration is equally difficult to analyze as a general proposition since it largely reflects the familial and refugee considerations. However, let me make two remarks. First, embedded in the system is the provision for admission of PTKs on a virtually equal-access, open-queue basis, since the 1965 Act. This makes it possible to argue that the source composition of PTK immigrants will be much the same as if the immigration was on an internal-migration free-flow basis. This hypothesis actually does work (see Lucas, 1976, and the review in Krugman and Bhagwati, 1976). Second, while it is true that readily-economic arguments will not be seen to impact on the source composition of other immigrants into the U.S., there is the possibility of a more sophisticated, lobby-oriented argumentation to explain the final outcomes. For instance, it is conceivable that well-financed lobbies can bend the immigration regime to bias the actual working of the immigration rules in favor of their own friends abroad. I would suggest that the refugee composition into the U.S. should, if closely scrutinized, show precisely the role of such factors in an augmented-economic-style explanation.

For the West German case, however, such extra sophistication is not strictly necessary since the system really worked by explicit economic criteria as already indicated. In the Bhagwati-Schatz-Wong study (1983), for instance, the source pattern is shown to reflect relative wage rates and sizes of labor force in the different supplying countries, much as it does in internal-migration studies; and it is remarked that this similarity in a recruitment, international-immigration model is not too surprising since the probability of finding a better recruit (at the common wage German law requires to hire at from every source including German) improves with the size of the applicant pool and that pool, in turn, is likely to increase with lower wage rates and a larger work force.

Skill Composition

Finally, the two systems contrast greatly on their skill composition. The *gastarbeiter* system has drawn overwhelmingly on relatively unskilled labor. The U.S. system, based on familial and refugee considerations, has typically thrown up a significantly higher educational and skill level on the average. Partly, of course, the latter phenomenon reflects the stay-on loophole I have described and discussed; partly, it has reflected specific policy decisions; partly, it has reflected also the tremendous opportunity that the United States has presented to highly-skilled professional manpower in the postwar period.

One of the major complaints of the developing countries against the U.S. system, therefore, has been that the immigration system has been discriminatory to its own advantage; that, by drawing high skill and talent, it deprives the developing countries of valuable skills whereas by rejecting the low skill and brute manpower, while integrating the skilled manpower into the international salary structure, it puts great stress on the developing countries' income-distributional policies and even on their capacity to grow into modern, technologically mature societies. This issue gets us back somewhat to the questions that I raised earlier in regard to the impact of the "brain drain": questions that are interesting to analyze, with disturbing as well as comforting answers in principle, but with little empirical argumentation to help us decide among the different models.[16]

18.3   Concluding Remarks

In conclusion, I would like to draw attention to one aspect of the immigration restriction regimes today. This is simply that, as doubtless the reader will have inferred for himself, there is virtually no international code of conduct in regard to the question of how immigration restrictions ought to be operated. These restrictions are entirely a matter of national sovereignty, with practically no international constraints systematically sought to be imposed on national action by countries of immigration other than their own conscience, by and large. The international "governance" of the issue is also provided by fragmented attention paid to the subject matter by diverse bureaus and agencies: ILO addressing questions concerning foreign workers, the UN High Commissioner for Refugees addressing refugees, the UNESCO and UNCTAD addressing the brain drain, and so on, with varying efficacy and jurisdictional legitimacy as recognized by the member states. It is indeed remarkable that none of the architects of Bretton Woods thought that the superstructure we would provide for international economic governance in an interdependent world should extend to an agency that would oversee international migration questions (though Keynes did have the famous memorandum on an agency for international commodity stabilization that never came to pass).[17] I find it strange that, as we currently address the issues of reform in the mechanism of international economic management, there is still no concern with attempting to set up such a supra-national agency or at least a code of conduct.[18]

I think that it is time indeed for us, economists and intellectuals, to begin to fill this serious lacuna in the legacy of Bretton Woods.

Notes

Thanks are due to the German Marshall Fund for partial financial support of the research reflected in this paper.

1. The 1921 Act was preceded by several other local exclusionary laws since the end of the nineteeth century.

2. Interestingly, such restrictions were common also in the czarist period, as anyone familiar with Herzen's (1968) memoirs should know. The socialist countries also do not show any significant immigration from other countries, as far as I can tell, so that their practice concerning both internal and international (whether inward or outward) personal mobility is generally characterized by extremely restrictive outcomes. Perhaps the only exception is Yugoslavia which, of course, practices socialism of a very different kind and which is characterized by a remark-

able leniency and pragmatism in regard to its integration into the West European *gastarbeiter* system during its heyday.

3. For what appears to be an overdrawn parallel between human and animal behavior in regard to territoriality, see Ardrey (1966).

4. Of the several possible illustrations of this uneasy blend of principles and prejudice in the debates over immigration bills in the U.S. the historian Reimers (1982, p. 25) has chosen a few telling ones. Thus, a 1950 Senate, report stated: "... the subcommittee holds that the peoples who had made the greatest contribution to the development of this country were fully justified in determining that the country was no longer a field for further colonization, and henceforth *further immigration would not only be restricted but directed to admit immigrants considered to be more readily assimilable because of the similarity of their cultural background to those of the principal components of our population* (italics inserted)". Take again Senator McCarran telling the Senate: "... the cold hard truth is that in the United States today there are hard-core indigestible blocs who have not become integrated into the American way of life, but who, on the contrary, are its deadly enemy. The cold, hard fact is, too, Mr. President, that this Nation is the last hope of western civilization; and if this oasis of the world shall be overrun, perverted, contaminated, or destroyed, then the last flickering light of humanity will be extinguished. A solution of the problems of Europe and Asia, Mr. President, will not come as we transplant these problems en masse to the United States of America."

5. I am not mentioning here the prejudice factor which was obviously of great importance in the enactment of both the British and the U.S. immigration legislation at the time. In particular, the fact that the immigration in question was largely shifted from the Anglo-Saxon and Teutonic sources to Central European Jews had a great deal to do with the agitation and outcry in favor of the legislation. On the British debate at the time, see the excellent account in Gainer (1972).

6. Grossman (1982), similarly using a traditional economic framework, shows that now, from a production perspective, immigrants in the United States substitute for unskilled American workers fairly easily, are less substitutable for skilled workers, and complement capital. This evidence provides an economic reason why one observes businessmen being in favor of immigration, labor unions (especially industrial labor unions) being opposed, and professional and skilled labor being uninvolved.

7. A central problem in effective enforcement arises from at least two aspects of illegal immigration, both reflecting civil-libertarian traditions. First, the U.S. government simply will not shoot at illegals crossing the border, though (as I argue later) bribing the foreign government to shoot at its emigrants may be a possible cynical option when that government is a dictatorship and wholly devoid of civil-libertarian traditions and constraints. Ultimate sanctions are thus not possible. Second, few U.S. citizens can be expected to hand over illegal immigrants to the law, even if no selfish interest is involved, simply because one is dealing with human beings and likely to empathize with them, as is indeed the case with many

church groups which have been giving sanctuary to the incoming refugees from Central and South America.

8. The latest problems in regard to asylum have arisen in Canada (see the *Globe and Mail*, January 9, 1984, report on refugee status sought by Tamil refugees in Canada and other accounts of such claims by Tamils in Switzerland) where the immigration authorities are faced with the problem of sifting through thousands of such asylum claims.

9. See the approving *Boston Globe* (July 25, 1983) editorial on Federal Judge Woodrow Seals' judgment which argued that, by barring illegal aliens' children from an education, the proposed Texas Law (which Judge Seals declared unconstitutional) was "creating an enormous public cost, both financial and social, to be borne in the not-so-distant future."

10. I am not raising here the still further complication that the immigrant labor in the DC may be from a different LDC than the one exporting competing goods to the DC, in which case you have here even an inter-LDC income-distributional problem. See further discussion in Bhagwati (1979a).

11. The many excellent theoretical analyses, starting with the major contributions by Johnson, Grubel and Scott, have been reviewed and synthesized in Bhagwati and Rodriguez's paper in Bhagwati (1976, ch. 5).

12. See the 1982 *Journal of Public Economics Symposium* that I have noted earlier, and also Bhagwati (1979a)

13. The synthesis volume (Bhagwati, 1978) addressed this issue at length, drawing on the country volumes in the project, whereas the companion synthesis volume by Krueger (1978) addresses more the problems raised by attempts at liberalization.

14. Immigrants could not simply walk in freely as under an "open door," they could be brought in without difficulty and overall quota constraints as long as firms were recruiting them.

15. The Canadians use a "points" system where more points are awarded if you go to a backward area. It is not clear, however, whether mobility restrictions once you get in are really a serious constraint.

16. Djajic (1984) has even constructed a model with the paradoxical possibility that changing immigration laws to permit more skills to come in may reduce the average skill level of immigrants in steady state!

17. Lal Jayawardene brought this Keynes memorandum to my attention and I published it in the *Journal of International Economics* (Keynes, 1974).

18. I addressed this issue in a letter to the *New York Times*, February 13, 1983, and in an Associated Press interview, published in *New Haven Register*, March 1, 1983, and was surprised to find that there was a great deal of intellectual interest in the question.

References

Agarwal, Vinod, and D. Winkler. 1983. United States Immigration Policy and Indirect Immigration of Professionals. Mimeo.

Ardrey, Robert. 1966. *The Territorial Imperative.* New York.

Baumol, William J. 1982. The Income Distribution Frontier and Taxation of Migrants. *Journal of Public Economics* 18: 340–361.

Bhagwati, Jagdish N. (ed.). 1976. *The Brain Drain and Taxation.* Amsterdam: North Holland.

Bhagwati, Jagdish N. 1978. *Anatomy and Consequences of Exchange Control Regimes.* NBER Studies in International Economic Relations, vol. 10. Cambridge, MA.

Bhagwati, Jagdish N. 1979a. *The Economic Analysis of International Migration.* Lecture delivered to Nordisk Migrasjonsforskerseminar, Nordic Council of Ministers, Oslo. Reprinted in J. N. Bhagwati, *Essays in International Economic Theory International Factor Mobility*, vol. 2. Ed. by R. Feenstra. Cambridge: MIT Press, ch. 44.

Bhagwati, Jagdish N. 1979b. International Factor Movements and National Advantage. *Indian Economic Review* 14, 1979, No. 2: 73–100. Reprinted in J. N. Bhagwati, *Essays in International Economic Theory: International Factor Mobility*, vol. 2. Ed. by R. Feenstra. Cambridge: MIT Press, ch. 42.

Bhagwati, Jagdish N. 1982a. Directly Unproductive Profit-Seeking (DUP) Activities. *Journal of Political Economy* 90: 988–1002. Reprinted in J. N. Bhagwati, *Essays in International Economic Theory: International Factor Mobility*, vol. 2. Ed. by R. Feenstra. Cambridge: MIT Press, ch. 17.

Bhagwati, Jagdish N. (ed.). 1982b. *Import Competition and Response.* NBER, A Conference Report, Chicago.

Bhagwati, Jagdish N. 1982c. Shifting Comparative Advantage, Protectionist Demands and Policy Response. In J. N. Bhagwati (ed.), *Import Competition and Response.* NBER, A Conference Report, Chicago 1982, pp. 153–184.

Bhagwati, Jagdish N., and Koichi Hamada. 1982. Tax Policy in the Presence of Emigration. *Journal of Public Economics* 18: 291–317.

Bhagwati, Jagdish N., and Martin Partington (eds.). 1976. *Taxing the Brain Drain.* Amsterdam: North Holland.

Bhagwati, Jagdish N., and John G. Ruggie (eds.). 1984. *Power, Passions, and Purpose: Prospects for North–South Negotiations.* Cambridge: MIT Press.

Bhagwati, Jagdish N., and T. N. Srinivasan. 1977. Education in a "Job Ladder" Model and the Fairness-in-Hiring Rule. *Journal of Public Economics* 7: 1–22.

Bhagwati, Jagdish N., and T. N. Srinivasan. 1983. On the Choice Between Capital and Labour Mobility. *Journal of International Economics* 14: 209–221. Reprinted in

J. N. Bhagwati, *Essays in International Economic Theory: International Factor Mobility*, vol. 2. Ed. by R. Feenstra. Cambridge: MIT Press, ch. 43.

Bhagwati, Jagdish N., Richard Brecher, and T. N. Srinivasan. 1984. DUP Activities and Economic Theory. In David C. Colander (ed.), *Neoclassical Political Economy: The Analysis of Rent-Seeking and DUP Activities*. Cambridge; MA: Ballinger.

Bhagwati, Jagdish N., Klaus Werner Schatz, and Kar-Yiu Wong. 1983. *The West German Gastarbeiter System of Immigration*. Columbia University Discussions Paper No. 192. New York. May (Forthcoming in European Economic Review).

Djajic, Slobodan. 1984. *Skills and the Pattern of International Migration*. Queens University, Kingston, Ont., Canada. February. Mimeo.

Gainer, B. 1972. *The Alien Invasion: The Origins of the Alien Acts of 1905*. London.

Grossman, Jean Baldwin. 1982. The Substitutability of Natives and Immigrants in Production. *The Review of Economics and Statistics* 64: 596–603.

Hamilton, Bob, and John Whalley. 1984. Efficiency and Distributional Implications of Global Restrictions on Labour Mobility: Calculations and Policy Implications. *Journal of Development Economics* 14: 61–75.

Harris, John R., and Michael P. Todaro. 1970. Migration, Unemployment and Development: A Two-Sector Analysis. *The American Economic Review* 60: 126–142.

Herzen, Alexander. 1982. *My Past and Thoughts: The Memoirs of Alexander Herzen*, rev. ed. Translated into English by Constance Garnett. Berkeley: University of California Press.

Keynes, John Maynard. 1974. The International Control of Raw Materials. *Journal of International Economics* 4: 299–315.

Krueger, Anne. 1978. *Liberalization Attempts and Consequences*. NBER, Cambridge, MA.

Krugman, Paul R., and Jagdish N. Bhagwati. 1976. The Decision to Migrate: A Survey. In J. N. Bhagwati (ed.), *The Brain Drain and Taxation*. Amsterdam: North Holland, pp. 31–53.

Lucas, Robert E. 1976. The Supply-of-Immigrants Function and Taxation of Immigrants' Incomes: An Econometric Analysis. In J. N. Bhagwati (ed.), *The Brain Drain and Taxation*. Amsterdam: North Holland, pp. 63–85.

Markusen, James R. 1983. Factor Movements and Commodity Trade as Complements. *Journal of International Economics* 14: 341–356.

Mayer, Wolfgang. 1974. Short-Run and Long-Run Equilibrium for a Small Open Economy. *Journal of Political Economy* 82: 955–967.

Mehrländer, Ursula. 1979. Federal Republic of Germany. In Daniel Kubat, Ursula Mehrländer, and Ernst Gehmacher (eds.), *The Politics of Migration Policies: The First World in the 1970s*. New York: Center for Migration Studies, pp. 145–162.

Mehrländer, Ursula. 1980. The "Human Resource" Problem in Europe: Migrant Labor in the Federal Republic of Germany. In Uri Ra'anan (ed.), with the participation of John P. Roche and other contributors, *Ethnic Resurgence in Modern Democratic States: A Multidisciplinary Approach to Human Resources and Conflict*. New York: Pergamon, pp. 77–100.

Myint, Hla. 1968. The Underdeveloped Countries: A Less Alarmist View. In Walter Adams (ed.), *The Brain Drain*. New York: Macmillan.

Mirrlees, James A. 1982. Migration and Optimal Incomes Taxes. *Journal of Public Economics* 18: 319–341.

Piore, Michael J. 1979. *Birds of Passage: Migrant Labour and Industrial Societies*. Ann Arbor, MI: University Microfilms International.

Ramaswami, V. K. 1968. International Factor Movement and the National Advantage. *Economica*, N. S., 35: 309–310.

Reimers, David M. 1982. Recent Immigration Policy: An Analysis. In: Barry R. Chiswick (ed.), *The Gateway: U.S. Immigration Issues and Policies* Washington: American Enterprise Institute Symposia, pp. 13–53.

Saavedra-Rivano, Neantro, and Ian Wooton. 1983. The Choice Between International Labour and Capital Mobility in a Dynamic Model of North–South Trade. *Journal of International Economics* 14: 251–261.

Sapir, André. 1983. Foreign Competition, Immigration and Structural Adjustment. *Journal of International Economics* 14: 381–394.

Sasson-Koob, Saskia. 1984. *The Foreign Investment Connection: Rethinking Migration*. New York. Mimeo.

Srinivasan, T. N. 1983. International Factor Movements, Commodity Trade and Commercial Policy in a Specific Factor Model. *Journal of International Economics* 14: 289–312.

Weiner, Myron, and Mary Fainsod Katzenstein, with K. V. Narayana Rao. 1981. *India's Preferential Policies: Migrants, the Middle Classes and Ethnic Equality*. Chicago: University of Chicago Press.

Williamson, Jeffrey G. 1982. Immigrant-Inequality Trade-offs in the Promised Land: Income Distribution and Absorptive Capacity Prior to the Quotas. In Barry R. Chiswick (ed.), *The Gateway: U.S. Immigration Issues and Policies*. Washington: American Enterprise Institute Symposia, pp. 251–288.

Wilson, John D. 1982. Optimal Linear Income Taxation in the Presence of Emigration. *Journal of Public Economics* 18: 363–379.

Wong, Kar-Yiu. 1983. On Choosing among Trade in Goods and International Capital and Labor Mobility: A Theoretical Analysis. *Journal of International Economics* 14: 223–250.

Wong, Kar-Yiu. 1984. Are International Trade and Factor Mobility Substitutes? University of Washington, Seattle. Mimeo.

Wooton, Ian, and Neantro Saavedra-Rivano. 1983. The Choice between International Labor and Capital Mobility in a Dynamic Model of North–South Trade. *Journal of International Economics* 14: 251–261.

19

Global Interdependence and International Migration

Interdependence in the world economy is manifest to all in the areas of international trade and finance.[1] The world economy is indeed characterized by a growing integration of markets for commodities, services, and capital.

This integration reflects the inevitable interaction between market forces and governmental policies and designs. But, broadly speaking, we can distinguish two stylized scenarios: in one the governmental designs, reflected in the creation of an international infrastructure, have envisaged and stimulated the pursuit of policies that have produced the integration; in the other the process has been reversed. The phenomenal trade expansion of the postwar period is an excellent example of the former process; the unprecedented and unforeseen expansion of the private international financial markets fits the latter mold equally well.[2]

In the former case, the process was sanctioned by the international infrastructure provided by the Bretton Woods architects. The General Agreement on Tariffs and Trade (GATT) provided the umbrella under which their liberal vision of an expanding, open-trading world economy would be pursued.[3] The International Monetary Fund (IMF) was equally charged with, and played a role in, creating and maintaining the international monetary order that permitted the unprecedented trade and expansion to take place. This Bretton Woods infrastructure thus provided the mechanics for taking major strides toward a liberal international economic order, which would witness a rapid expansion of the world economy.[4]

In the latter case, however, where governments have largely followed the market forces, the design of international institutions or conventions has naturally lagged behind the market phenomena. This is true, for instance, of efforts at devising multinational codes for transnational corporations and of the growth of the Group of Five (G-5) countries and other intergovernmental groups seeking to manage, by international coordination, the economic consequences to each of a world economy characterized by increased interdependence in capital and trade flows.

International migration, defined broadly as transnational flows of people (whether "permanent" or "temporary" and no matter how motivated), falls naturally into the category where policies have followed, rather than led, the flows reflecting underlying economic and political forces.

Thus it is noteworthy that the Bretton Woods infrastructure simply did not address questions pertaining to international migration: no institutions, no codes were considered. No such infrastructure blessed the growth of international migration, nor did it seek to define the economic and social principles that should govern the process.

Rather, such conventions and institutions have emerged with a deliberate lack of speed in response to migrations that occurred willy-nilly and in substantial magnitudes in the postwar world. Thus significant refugee and illegal migrations have occurred around the world, crisscrossing poor and rich nations in a complex maze, reflecting largely political upheavals and market forces, respectively. Again, underlying economic needs of the rich countries led until the 1970s to sizable legal inflows of *gastarbeiter* and other workers into Western Europe, and during the 1970s into the member countries of the Organization of Petroleum Exporting Countries (OPEC), under strictly defined immigration policies.

Overlying the process has been the fact that the magnitude and composition of international migration have been largely governed by *autonomy of action* by the receiving countries. This reflects the fact that the economist's traditional use of the utilitarian criterion to arrive at the liberal world order—where goods and capital flow freely (with exceptions that define suitably devised interventions by benign and omnipotent governments)— does not extend to flows of people across national borders. When international migration is discussed, the philosophical criterion used to judge policies shifts inevitably to "communitarian" ideas, such as those propounded by the philosopher Michael Walzer, which legitimate the "right to exclude."[5] Revealed criteria also suggest that theories of natural rights whereby men and women may locate where they wish—theories that were fashionable in sixteenth-century Spain when the conquest of the Americas was thus legitimated and the freedom of location meant in effect the right to gain, not give, entry—are not popular.[6] Restrictions on exit are regarded as reprehensible, but symmetrical restrictions on entry are considered far less distasteful, if at all.

International migration flows therefore closely reflect deliberate policy choices by the countries of destination, though less so for refugee and illegal migrations. Unlike models of internal migration, where supply and demand (or "pull" and "push") factors play unhampered on the economic stage, analyses of international migration must therefore put the destination country's immigration control policies firmly at center stage.[7]

We will do well to remember these important asymmetries of analysis that must necessarily characterize the study of international migration. This is particularly so for the study of skilled migration, which Mark Perlman has suggested as the special focus of the present paper. Its magnitude, its composition by occupation and by source, and related issues are questions that cannot be answered except by reference to the interaction between market forces and the structure of immigration country objectives as embodied in their immigration legislation.

The paper is divided into four further sections. The first puts the phenomenon of skilled migration, popularly described as the "brain drain," in the perspective of different kinds of postwar flows of people among broad groups of countries: the rich, the poor, and the centrally planned economies. The second section focuses on the skilled flows, with primary emphasis on U.S. experience. The next section raises several policy issues, and the final section briefly suggests areas for further academic research, in light of the foregoing analysis.

19.1 Patterns of Postwar International Migration Flows

The postwar patterns of international migration flows can be broadly portrayed. Note at the outset, however, that "migration," though popularly thought of as a permanent shift of people across national boundaries, is no longer treated as such in the scientific discussions, simply because it is evident that people often go back and forth, that over a life span even apparently permanent migrants occasionally return to their source countries in retirement, and that the legal and statistical classifications that divide incoming aliens into temporary and permanent migrants on the basis of types of visas or declared intentions have little value for economic analysis.[8]

Nonetheless, such data as are available have been classified in precisely this way. Thus the most-quoted statistics relate to gross, permanent, legal immigrants as defined by the immigration legislation and practices of the major traditional countries of destination for European emigrants: the United States, Canada, Australia, and New Zealand.

Such legal, permanent immigrants have remained the major source of international migratory flows in the postwar world economy. The United

States is estimated to have received nearly 8 million such immigrants between 1960 and 1980, amounting to an estimated share in U.S. population growth of over 16 percent. During the same period Australia, Canada, and New Zealand took in roughly 5.7 million.[9] All in all, the gross legal permanent immigration during this period may well have been in the range of 15 to 17 million in the world economy.

Was it unprecedentedly huge? It probably was not. The historical data in table 19.1 show that in the nineteenth century, right up to the first enactment of national legislation on immigration in 1921, the average rates of immigration per 1,000 U.S. population were three to five times those since the 1950s. Table 19.2 suggests the same historical conclusion about shares of immigration in population growth for the United States and Canada in particular. Table 19.3 suggests the same from the opposite end, looking at the share of emigrants in the population of the countries of emigration. What are different today, however, are the enormous growth in the postwar world economy of temporary foreign worker programs (estimated to have reached as many as 13 to 15 million by 1980), the accelerated refugee movements in Asia, Africa, and Central America, and the growth of substantial illegal immigration into Europe and more dramatically into the United States.

Although these distinctions are relevant, table 19.4 presents a taxonomy that builds on two other functional distinctions with policy relevance: (1) dividing source and destination countries into poor, rich, and centrally planned economies; and (2) breaking the flows into two main categories: unskilled and skilled.[10] The major categories of postwar flows (illegal migration, refugee movements, worker programs, legal migration, and movements related to multinationals and technical assistance) are set out. The data in the field of international migration are notoriously beset by conceptual difficulties and paucity. Therefore, much of the discussion below is necessarily qualitative, while indicating broad orders of quantitative significance where possible.

From Poor to Poor Countries

At first blush, it would appear that the flows between poor countries must be confined to the unskilled and skilled refugee migrations that unfortunately crowd the television screens. Indeed, such movements have constituted an increasing fraction of total refugee flows (which appear to have been primarily European in origin during the 1940s and 1950s). Domestic upheavals and military conflicts have produced refugees in millions, fleeing,

Table 19.1
U.S. immigration, 1820–1984 (thousands)

	Number	Rate[a]		Number	Rate[a]
1820–1984	51,950	3.4	1965	297	1.5
			1966	323	1.6
1820–30[b]	152	1.2	1967	362	1.8
1831–40[c]	599	3.9	1968	454	2.3
1841–50[d]	1,713	8.4	1969	359	1.8
1851–60[d]	2,598	9.3	1970	373	1.8
1861–70[e]	2,315	6.4	1971	370	1.8
1871–80	2,812	6.2	1972	385	1.8
1881–90	5,247	9.2	1973	400	1.9
1891–1900	3,688	5.3	1974	395	1.9
1901–10	8,795	10.4	1975	386	1.8
1911–20	5,736	5.7	1976	399	1.9
1921–30	4,107	3.5	1977	462	2.1
1931–40	528	0.4	1978	601	2.8
1941–50	1,035	0.7	1979	460	2.1
1951–60	2,515	1.5	1980	531	2.3
1961–70	3,322	1.7	1981	597	2.6
1971–80[f]	4,493	2.1	1982	594	2.6
1981–84	2,294	2.5	1983	560	2.4
			1984	544	2.3

Source: U.S. Immigration and Naturalization Service, *Statistical Yearbook*, annual; and releases.
Note: Through 1976 for years ending June 30, except as noted; beginning 1977 years ending September 30. For definition of immigrants, see text. For 1820–67 alien passengers arriving; for 1868–91 and 1895–97 immigrants arriving; for 1892–94 and 1898 to the present, immigrants admitted. Rates based on Bureau of the Census estimates of resident population on July 1 through 1929 and of total population thereafter (excluding Alaska and Hawaii before 1959). See also *Historial Statistics, Colonial Times to 1970*, series C 89.
a. Annual rate per 1,000 U.S. population; ten-year rate computed by dividing sum of annual immigration totals by sum of annual U.S. population totals for same ten years.
b. October 1, 1819–September 30, 1830.
c. October 1, 1830–December 31, 1840.
d. Calendar years.
e. January 1, 1861–June 30, 1870.
f. Includes transition quarter, July 1 to September 30, 1976.

Table 19.2

Gross permanent immigration as a percentage of total population growth, 1851−1980

	United States	Canada	Australia and New Zealand	Latin America
1851−80	29.3	42.4	20.0	9.3
1881−1910	43.1	106.3[a]	80.7	22.1
1911−40	23.4	59.6	52.4	10.9
1941−60	8.0	36.2	58.0[b]	3.2[b]
1961−80	16.6	47.1	56.5	na

Source: Swamy, *Population and International Migration*, table 1.
a. Population growth less than immigration because of out-migration.
b. Immigration from Europe only, 1946−55.

Table 19.3

Permanent emigration as a percentage of increase in population of emigrants' countries, 1851−1980

	Europe	Asia[a]	Africa[a]	Latin America
1851−80	11.7	0.4	0.01	0.3
1881−1910	19.5	0.3	0.04	0.9
1911−40	1.4	0.1	0.03	1.8
1940−60	2.7[b]	0.1	0.01	1.0
1960−70	5.2	0.2	0.10	1.9
1970−80	4.0	0.5	0.30	2.5

Source: Swamy, *Population and International Migration*, table 2.
Note: Numbers are calculated from data on gross immigration in Australia, Canada, New Zealand, and the United States.
a. The periods from 1850 to 1960 pertain to emigration only to the United States.
b. Emigration only to the United States.

Table 19.4
Patterns of postwar international migration flows

Origin	Destination		
	Poor countries	Rich countries[a]	Centrally planned economies
Poor countries	Unskilled Some refugee migration (e.g., Guatemala to Mexico) Several others, legal and illegal (e.g., Bangladesh to India, Ghana to Nigeria) Skilled Some refugee migration Intergovernmental and international technical assistance programs (e.g., India to Nepal)	Unskilled Gastarbeiter programs of European countries OPEC[b] area inflows U.S. temporary worker programs Illegal immigration Legal immigration Refugees Skilled Brain drain to United States and OECD[b] countries OPEC[b] area inflows Refugees	Rare
Rich countries	Unskilled Rare Skilled Technical assistance programs MNC[b]-related outflows	Unskilled Gastarbeiter programs (Italy, Spain, Greece, to richer Western Europe) Skilled Brain drain from Europe to North America; some reverse flows MNC[b]-related flows	Rare
Centrally planned economies	Refugee outflows (e.g., Cambodia and Vietnam to Thailand, Malaysia, and Indonesia) Technical assistance programs	Refugee outflows (e.g., Soviet Union to United States)	Some (e.g., Vietnamese workers in Soviet Union; imported workers in East Germany)

Note: Only predominant patterns are listed. The entries are not exhaustive.
a. Including OPEC countries of the Middle East.
b. OPEC = Organization of Petroleum Exporting Countries; OECD = Organization for Economic Cooperation and Development; MNC = multinational corporations.

for instance, from East Pakistan into India, from Ethiopia into Somalia (over 1 million in 1980), from southern Sudan into Ethiopia, from Ruanda and Zaire into Uganda, from Uganda into Sudan and Zaire, from Burundi into Tanzania, from Equatorial Guinea into Gabon and Cameroon, from Angola and Zimbabwe into Botswana, and from Chad into Nigeria.[11] Refugees have simply fled to the first safe haven that crossing the border offered.

At the same time, however, there have been some nonrefugee flows of unskilled migrant workers between the poor countries. Such "economic" migration is usually from the poorer to the more prosperous of the poor nations. Argentina, for example, has traditionally attracted migrants from other countries of the southern cone; Venezuela has received migrants from Colombia and Ecuador; and Singapore has attracted workers from Malaysia, Thailand, Sri Lanka, and Indonesia.[12] In Africa the more prosperous and well-managed Ivory Coast has attracted migrants; so have Ghana, Senegal, and Gambia in a lesser degree.[13]

Some of this migration reflects traditional migratory patterns among tribes cutting across modern postcolonial nation-states, resulting in informal, often uncontrolled, and even illegal modern migrations. Some of it also reflects new economic realities making temporary recruitment of workers a mutual-gain transaction between the governments of the sending and receiving countries, as when Cameroon signed a bilateral agreement with Gabon in 1977 for the export of workers and Equatorial Guinea contracted for workers with the Nigerian government.

Much of this nonrefugee migration has been unskilled. But skilled migration has also occurred, chiefly through the activities of multinationals, which, whether they are of poor country or rich country origin, increasingly recruit nationals of developing countries for posting in other developing countries, and also through the many technical assistance programs of developing countries and of international agencies, which do likewise.

From Poor to Rich Countries

The most dramatic flows of people in the postwar period have occurred in the *gastarbeiter* programs of Western Europe until the mid-1970s and the imported worker programs of the OPEC countries of the Middle East during the 1970s.

West European countries drew on *gastarbeiters* until the mid-1970s when, faced with the OPEC-induced recession, they began to draw back from these programs.[14] The workers were drawn from poorer neighboring countries such as Greece, Italy, Portugal, Turkey, Spain, and Yugoslavia.

The numbers involved were substantial. The estimated number of migrant workers in the important West European countries was 6.3 million in 1975 and roughly the same in 1980, having risen steadily through the 1960s (table 19.5).[15] The total increment in the work force in the countries of destination was significant as well: by 1974 the imported workers were as much as 18 percent of the work force in Switzerland and 8 percent in Belgium, France, and Germany.[16] For Western Europe as a whole, the 6.3 million constituted nearly 15 percent of the work force. Similarly, the workers abroad were often a sizable fraction of their own countries' work forces. The best estimates available show these fractions for the sending countries for the European *gastarbeiter* system as high as 11 percent for Portugal and 4–5 percent for Turkey and Greece (table 19.6).

The importation of workers from the poor nations also increased dramatically in the OPEC region, just as the European *gastarbeiter* program went into a virtual freeze, both phenomena being the opposed outcomes (for oil producers and consumers) of the same phenomenon of a sevenfold increase in the price of oil. Table 19.6 shows for some major source countries of manpower in this region, such as Egypt, the Yemen Arab Republic, the People's Democratic Republic of Yemen, and Jordan, legal emigrant workers as percentages of their total work force at dramatically high levels, ranging from 9 percent to 40 percent in the middle and late 1970s. For the sparsely populated receiving countries too, the proportion of migrant workers to the indigenous work force has been very high. In Kuwait, Libya, Saudi Arabia, Oman, Qatar, and the United Arab Emirates, the imported workers from the Arab states and from Pakistan, Korea, Turkey, India, and Bangladesh have amounted to as much as 34 percent for Saudi Arabia and 85 percent for the United Arab Emirates in 1975.[17]

The import of "temporary" workers has also been undertaken by the United States, principally from the West Indies and Mexico, earlier under the bracero program and later under specific programs for that purpose, including the 1986 legislation.[18]

The number of "temporary" migrant workers in the world economy may well have been in the range of 13–15 million in 1980, including over 6 million *gastarbeiter* in Europe, nearly 3 million foreign workers in the Middle East, and the imported workers in South America and Africa.

None of these reflect the increasing flows of illegal immigrants. While the problem is by no means insignificant in Europe (and for migrations from poor to poor nations in Africa and South America), the most striking illegal flow from the poor to the rich nations has been on the Mexico–United States border, with estimates ranging from 2 to 10 million by the

Table 19.5
Recorded number of migrant workers, selected western European countries, 1980, and totals from the 1960s (thousands)

Country of Origin	Austria	Belgium	France[a]	West Germany	Luxembourg	Netherlands	Sweden	Switzerland	United Kingdom[b]	Total
Algeria	—	3.2	322.7	1.6	—	—	—	—	—	327.5
Finland	—	—	—	3.7	—	—	108.0	—	1.0	112.7
France	—	38.5	—	54.0	8.5	2.0	—	—	14.0	117.0
Greece	—	10.8	3.0	138.4	—	1.2	7.5	—	6.0	166.9
Italy	—	90.5	146.4	324.3	11.2	12.0	—	301.0	73.0	958.4
Morocco	—	37.3	116.1	16.6	—	33.7	—	—	—	203.7
Portugal	—	6.3	430.6	59.9	13.7	4.2	—	—	5.0	519.7
Spain	—	32.0	157.7	89.3	2.3	10.4	—	85.7	17.0	394.4
Tunisia	—	4.7	65.3	—	—	1.1	—	—	—	71.1
Turkey	28.2	23.0	20.6	623.9	—	53.2	—	20.1	4.0	773.0
Yugoslavia	115.2	3.1	32.2	367.0	0.6	6.6	24.0	62.5	5.0	616.2
Other	31.3	83.2	192.4	490.1	15.6	73.2	94.6	237.0	804.0	2,021.4
Total 1980	174.7	332.6	1,487.0	2,168.8	51.9	197.6	234.1	706.3	929.0	6,282.0
Total 1975	195.8	316.8	1,584.3	2,204.7	46.8	187.0	204.0	753.7	863.3	6,309.6
Total 1970	148.0	217.0	1,300.0	1,800.0	—	190.0	218.0	829.0	700.0	5,402.0
Total 1960	6.0	138.0	975.0	279.0	—	57.0	122.0	515.0	451.0	2,543.0

Source: W. R. Böhning, *Studies in International Labour Migration* (London: Macmillan, 1984), p. 19.
Note: No entry where no migrants recorded or estimated, magnitude less than 500, or not applicable.
a. *Enquête sur l'emploi*, which provides an underestimate by several 100,000 because small-scale employers, home-based workers, and workers living at construction sites are not or are insufficiently covered.
b. May–June 1979, estimate by the Department of Labour on the basis of the 1979 Labour Force Survey.

Table 19.6
Legal emigrant labor as a percentage of the labor force in the emigrant country, 1975–81

Country	Year	Percentage of labor force
Bangladesh	1979–80	[a]
India	1980	[a]
Pakistan	1979–80	6.0
Egypt	1980	9.0
People's Democratic Republic of Yemen	1980	34.0
Yemen Arab Republic	1981	39.0
Sudan	1975	[a]
Syria	1975	2.0[b]
Tunisia	1975	2.0[b]
Jordan	1975	40.2[b]
Botswana	1979	8.0
Lesotho	1978	40.0
Greece	1980	4.5
Italy	1980	4.0
Portugal	1980	11.0
Spain	1980	2.5
Turkey	1980	4.5
Yugoslavia	1980	6.0

Sources: Bangladesh: Ashraf Ali Syed, *Labor Migration from Bangladesh to the Middle East*, World Bank Staff Working Paper no. 454 (Washington, DC: World Bank, 1981). India and Egypt: author's estimates. Pakistan: Ijaz Gilani and Fatheen Kahn, "Labour Migration from Pakistan to the Middle East and Its Impact on the Domestic Economy," *Journal of Pakistan Institute of Development Economics*, Research Report Series, nos. 126, 127, 128 (June, July 1981), table 6. Jordan, Syria, Sudan, Tunisia: Ismail Serageldin, *Manpower and International Labor Migration in the Middle East and North Africa* (New York: Oxford University Press, 1983), table 8.2. Botswana: National Migration tudy, *Migration for Botswana: Patterns, Causes, and Consequences* (Gaborone: Central Statistics Office, Ministry of Finance and Development Planning, 1982), vol. 1, p. 30. Lesotho: World Bank and United Nations Development Program, *Balance of Payments: Lesotho* (1981), app. A. Southern Europe and Turkey: Organization for Economic Cooperation and Development, *Southern Europe and Turkey: Survey* (Paris: OECD, 1981). Swamy, *Population and International Migration*, table 3.
Note: Data on migrant workers are not every accurate—the table provides only approximate values.
a. Less than 1 percent of employed labor force.
b. Percentage of employed labor force.

early 1980s. The policy responses of countries faced with illegal inflows have varied from drastic and summary expulsions to humane grants of amnesty.[19]

Refugee flows from the poor to the rich countries are also a common and increasing feature of the world economy. Flows from Haiti, Afghanistan, and Central America to the United States and from Sri Lanka to West Germany, Switzerland, and Canada are among the most familiar illustrations of a trend that has put an increasing strain on the willingness of the countries of destination to grant asylum and immigration status to the refugees.[20] It has thus created pressures to insist on the strictest interpretation of the tortuous distinction between "economic" and "political" refugees: the former being not entitled to asylum or immigration, the latter being true refugees.[21]

Legal permanent immigration from the poor into the rich countries has been a major component of unskilled flows as well. Much of this influx reflects the "familial," as against "economic," criteria by which immigration control systems such as that of the United States are operated, eschewing strictly economic selection criteria. A respectable component of migration from poor to rich nations is in fact *skilled migration*. This phenomenon has been sharply accentuated in the United States since the 1965 Immigration Act, which eliminated country-specific preferences and made it possible for professionals of all countries to compete on an equal basis for access to U.S. immigration quotas. The next two sections of this paper are wholly devoted to a discussion of this kind of migration.

While this brain drain, or what some call the perverse or "reverse transfer of (embodied) technology," tends to be more permanent when professionals move from poor to rich nations, because of the migrants' own aspirations and the readier willingness of the destination countries to accept skilled professionals as members of society, the flow to the OPEC countries has been essentially temporary. They have sought to prevent permanent settlement, fearing alien influence, and have even sought to isolate the aliens from the host country populations. Equally, professionals view their migration to the Middle East as a means of quick and substantial financial gain rather than as a permanent shift of their location, unlike a move to the more open, advanced, and pluralistic societies of the West.

From Rich to Poor Countries

Migratory flow from rich to poor countries is like taking water uphill. It has to be random rather than systematic. It occurs predominantly only as part of government technical assistance programs or the influx of personnel in subsidiaries of multinational corporations to the poor countries.

From Rich to Rich Countries

The *gastarbeiter* programs in Western Europe drew extensively on poorer European countries such as Greece, Italy, and Spain for unskilled workers, but major flows of skilled migration have also occurred among the rich countries. In fact, the phrase "brain drain" came into vogue to describe the loss to the United States of European scientists in the 1960s, not the later emergence of this phenomenon from the underdeveloped countries to the United States, Canada, and Europe. The brain drain between rich countries soon ceased to be a source of worry and discord, as many European scientists returned home when the demands of the U.S. space programs reached a plateau in the 1970s and as the U.S. immigration system shifted in 1965 to accommodate an increasing fraction of professionals from non-European, underdeveloped countries.

From Centrally Planned Economies to Poor Countries

The centrally planned economies have generally had negligible illegal or legal out-flows of their populations to the outside world. Their willingness and ability to adopt draconian border regulation measures appear to preclude significant mobility.

The outflow of refugees has been much larger, however, from the Asian than from the European centrally planned economies. Boat refugees from Vietnam and refugees pouring out of Cambodia and Laos have reached dramatic numbers. By 1980 over 800,000 refugees from Cambodia were in Thai and other frontier camps. Laos also generated over 250,000 refugees between 1975 and 1978. Over 250,000 North Vietnamese of Chinese ethnicity fled to China in the late 1970s.

From Centrally Planned Economies to Rich Countries

The classic outflow of refugees here has been from Hungary, Czechoslovakia, and Poland to Europe and to the United States after their aborted uprisings. The Soviet emigration, largely of Jewish refugees, has been more heavily directed to the United States, the magnitudes varying with the state of U.S.-Soviet relations. The boat refugees from Vietnam have also been relocated in significant numbers in Europe, Australia, and mainly the United States.

Between Centrally Planned Economies

Contrary to the popular conception that the centrally planned economies discourage any transnational labor mobility, they do have some finite flirtation with one another's work forces. Data here are even scarcer than elsewhere on migrant workers, but foreign workers have been observed in East Germany from Bulgaria, Czechoslovakia, Poland, and Romania. There are also contractual arrangements for importing workers from the under-developed countries: Angola, Cuba, and Mozambique. Czechoslovakia is also known to receive workers from Poland and Yugoslavia.

Skilled technicians have also moved among the centrally planned economies. "Hungary has been sending some 3,000 technicians and engineers each year to work on two-to-three-year contracts in various industrial establishments in the German Democratic Republic. Hungary also receives small numbers of specialized workers from the German Democratic Republic and Romania." [22] In fact, such skilled worker movements crisscross many centrally planned economies, including Bulgaria and Romania. The number of such workers, however, appears to be minuscule.

19.2   Skilled Migration

The phenomenon of skilled migration fits neatly, but modestly, into the complex mosaic of international migratory flows. For its small size, however, it has been characterized by large concerns. These concerns have related to the loss of skilled nationals to foreign, often richer, nations, converting the *phenomenon* of skilled migration into the *problem* of the brain drain.

Interestingly, these concerns were first raised in European countries losing scientists to the United States in the 1960s. With a shift in the composition of professional immigrants to developing countries, the brain drain has had to share the stage with the rather cumbersome phrase "reverse transfer of technology."

How large are these flows? Before turning to the numbers, it is worth noting the serious difficulties with them.

1. They are gross flows, not net of return migration. This is a serious problem if we are considering the brain drain between rich countries: skilled

migrants have often returned to their home countries. It is less of a problem for the brain drain from developing countries: many fewer return, given the vast disparities of incomes and facilities between their home and destination countries.

2. The data on professional immigrants are generally categorized by class of immigration visa—in the United States by the third and sixth preference categories. But professional immigrants can and do come in under the kinship and refugee categories; we simply do not know how many.

3. Cross-country comparisons are notoriously difficult because of differences of classification.

4. We have little systematic information on the educational levels of the professional immigrants.

Yet we must cautiously use the data we have. Professional, technical, and kindred immigrants (third and sixth preference) in the United States are only about 11 to 14 percent of total immigrants (table 19.7).[23] While the U.S. immigration system has remained broadly oriented to refugees and kin, however, others have not. Canada, in particular, has deployed a skill-based point system since 1962, when it shifted from a kinship-based

Table 19.7
Immigrants to the United States by class of admission, 1979–84

Class of admission	1979	1980	1981	1982	1983	1984
Total immigrants	460,348	530,639	596,600	594,131	559,763	543,903
Numerically restricted immigrants	279,478	289,479	330,409	259,749	269,213	262,016
Third preference (including spouses and children)	13,249	18,583	18,872	26,001	27,250	24,852
Third preference ("professionals" only)	5,075	8,238	8,103	11,961	12,336	10,691
Sixth preference (including spouses and children)	24,460	25,786	25,439	25,181	28,218	24,669
Sixth preference ("needed skilled or unskilled workers" only)	11,623	12,599	11,873	12,041	12,706	11,393

Source: Immigration and Naturalization Service, *Statistical Yearbook* (Washington, DC, 1986), table IMM 1.5, p. 11.

system. As a result, Canada increased its share of professionals in immigration from an annual average of 12 percent in 1956–60 to 20 percent in 1962–71 while the corresponding share of unskilled workers declined from 36 percent to 16 percent.[24]

More compelling is the fact that the changes in immigration laws away from country ceilings and racial discrimination have shifted the source of professional and technical workers toward the poor countries, dramatically in the United States and less so in Canada. The changed legislation was passed in 1965 in the United States and in 1967 in Canada (and similarly in Australia in 1958 and 1966 and in the United Kingdom in 1962 and 1965).

The share of developing countries in total skilled immigration to the United States rose to an average of nearly four-fifths through the 1970s (table 19.8). The rise was far more modest for Canada, but Don de Voretz and Dennis Maki, using a narrower definition of professionals, have calculated that the share of professional immigrants from developing countries in total professional immigrants almost doubled, from 19.7 percent during 1962–66 to 33.3 percent during 1968–73.[25]

The size of these skilled flows is significant for both source and destination countries for some professions, such as medicine. In 1971–72 half the annual increment in the stock of physicians and surgeons in the United States was from immigrants, and in 1962–66 40 percent.

The numbers are equally compelling for source countries. For the Philippines and for Sri Lanka, for example, the emigration of doctors, engineers, and other professionals in the 1970s has been a sizable fraction of the stocks of those professionals in Sri Lanka and of the increments in that stock in the Philippines (tables 19.9 and 19.10).

It is evident that many professional immigrants are students who stay on. Table 19.11 reports on this phenomenon for the United States for 1968–69 for selected source countries. The students who stay on through visa adjustments constitute a sizable fraction of the total professional immigration, the implied fractions being particularly large for India, Iran, and Korea. F, H, and J visas, by and large, relate to such change of status by students to permanent residence. For 1984–86 such conversions were heavily skewed in favor of Asian source countries, such as India, South Korea, Taiwan, Iran, and Pakistan (table 19.12).

19.3   Policy Responses

The phenomenon of professional migration, increasingly now from the developing or less-developed countries (LDCs) into the developed coun-

Table 19.8
Skilled migration from developing countries to the United States, Canada, and the United Kingdom, 1961–76

	Skilled migrants from developing countries[a]				Share of developing countries in total skilled migration (percent)		
	United States	Canada	United Kingdom	Total	United States	Canada	United Kingdom
1961–65	14,514	6,147[b]	20,411[c]	41,072	37	20	26
1966	7,635	5,930	10,812	24,377	49	23	26
1967	8,239	8,614	8,156	25,009	52	25	21
1968	8,052	7,489	9,418	24,959	50	24	23
1969	8,419	8,286	9,932	26,637	64	28	22
1970	11,412	6,867	8,635	26.914	69	27	19
1971	16,098	6,195	7,843	30,136	85	31	18
1972	15,822	7,070	8,833	31,725	86	36	19
1973	10,602	6,180	—	16,782[d]	77	25	15
1974	8,725	7,631	—	16,356[d]	80	27	15
1975	9,298	6,362	—	15,660[d]	72	25	14
1976	—	4,842	—	4,842[e]	—	24	—
Total	118,816	81,613	84,040	284,469	61	26	22

Sources: For the United States: unpublished data supplied by the National Science Foundation, Washington, DC. For Canada: Department of Manpower and Immigration, Immigration Statistics. Peter Mandi, "The Brain Drain: A Sub-system of Centre Periphery Relationship," *Development and Peace*, vol. 2 (Spring 1981), table 1.
a. The concept of skilled migration used is wider for Canada and the United Kingdom than for the United States. The United States figures include only the "professional" categories (engineers, natural and social scientists, and doctors); figures for the United Kingdom and Canada include "professional, technical, and kindred workers."
b. Total for 1963–65 only.
c. Total for 1964–65 only.
d. Total for the United States and Canada only.
e. Total for Canada only.

Table 19.9
Emigration of professional personnel from Sri Lanka in relation to domestic stock, 1971–74

	Stock in 1971	Emigration 1971–74	Emigration as percentage of stock
Doctors	3,294	672	20.4
Engineers	1,983	370	18.7
Accountants	614	219	35.7
All categories	21,297	1,930	9.1

Source: Department of Immigration and Emigration, *Report of the Cabinet Committee Inquiring into the Problem of Technologically, Professionally, and Academically Qualified Personnel Leaving Sri Lanka*, Sessional Paper no. 10, Colombo, November 1974, p. 10, table I. From Mandi, "Brain Drain," table 3.

Table 19.10
Flow of skilled migrants from the Philippines, 1965–76

	Average annual flow of skilled emigrants (1)	Average annual increase in the domestic stock of skilled manpower (2)	Flow as percentage of increase (1)/(2)
Doctors[a]	320	1,517	21.1
Engineers[a]	677	6,142	11.0
Physical and social scientists[b]	331	3,197	10.4
Others[b]	5,953	62,614	9.5

Source: Mandi, "Brain Drain," table 2.
a. Average of the two-year period 1975–76.
b. Average of the six-year period 1965–70.

Table 19.11
Selected migration flows to the United States, July 1, 1968, through June 30, 1969

Country of origin	Total immigrants	Total professional immigrants irrespective of preference	Total indirect immigrants (all nonimmigrant visa adjustments)	Indirect professional immigrants (F, H, J visa adjustments)[a]
Australia	1,384	300	398	58
France	2,024	252	458	44
Greece	17,724	586	1,133	256
India	5,963	2,889	2,779	1,720
Iran	1,352	486	739	376
Israel	2,049	386	851	172
Italy	23,617	501	1,749	64
Japan	3,957	403	997	312
Korea (South)	6,045	1,081	1,812	959
Netherlands	1,303	222	200	35
Norway	636	134	86	14
Philippines	20,744	7,396	2,460	560
Spain	3,916	414	1,182	367
Sweden	722	153	116	13
Thailand	1,250	400	180	99
Turkey	2,058	269	531	84
United Kingdom	15,014	2,519	1,294	142

Source: All the data are from United States, Department of Justice, Immigration and Naturalization Service, *Annual Report*. Reproduced from Vinod Agarwal and Donald Winkler, "Migration of Professional Manpower to the United States," *Southern Economic Journal* (1985), table 1.

a. F visas are held by students and their spouses and children, H visas by temporary workers and trainees, and J visas by exchange visitors, their spouses and children, and the fiancés, fiancées, and children of citizens.

Table 19.12
Aliens adjusted to permanent resident status in the United States, by status at entry and region of birth, fiscal years 1984, 1985, and 1986

Region of birth	Total	F1, M1	F2, M2	H's	J1	J2
1984						
Europe	36,657	1,169	40	2,435	363	207
Asia	110,702	11,630	1,163	3,237	550	332
Africa	9,605	3,151	77	317	95	57
Oceania	1,625	138	8	137	43	25
North America	30,627	1,439	57	1,603	82	47
Central America	4,828	390	18	57	8	6
South America	10,030	1,321	59	302	62	38
All countries	199,274	18,851	1,404	8,031	1,195	706
1985						
Europe	35,356	1,319	55	2,102	430	199
Asia	112,200	13,161	1,288	3,765	597	407
Africa	11,138	3,406	109	270	93	50
Oceania	1,660	156	14	124	29	13
North America	42,710	1,551	61	1,484	97	58
Central America	4,888	385	11	46	7	6
South America	10,579	1,437	59	239	45	36
All countries	213,644	21,031	1,586	7,984	1,291	763
1986						
Europe	34,243	1,236	74	1,534	501	228
Asia	110,238	12,060	1,266	3,153	495	331
Africa	10,408	3,145	115	238	90	51
Oceania	1,582	132	10	93	31	8
North America	58,249	1,542	77	949	104	58
Central America	5,225	423	14	34	10	13
South America	10,877	1,815	78	187	58	38
All countries	225,598	19,430	1,613	6,154	1,279	714

Source: U.S. Department of Justice, Immigration and Naturalization Service, *Statistical Yearbook*, annual.

A's—foreign government officials
B1—temporary visitors for business
B2—temporary visitors for pleasure
C's—transit aliens
D1—crewmen
E's—treaty traders and investors
F1, M1—students
F2, M2—spouses and children of students
G's—international representatives
H's—temporary workers and trainees
I1—representatives of foreign information media
J1—exchange visitors
J2—spouses and children of J1's
J's—fiancés(ées) and children of citizens
L's—intracompany transferees
N1—NATO officials
PR, RE—parolees and refugees

tries, has shifted the focus of concerns and policy responses since the late 1960s away from the original 1950s and early 1960s arena of skilled migration from the European Community to the United States. The issue has simply vanished from international forums oriented to the developed countries, such as the Organization for Economic Cooperation and Development in Paris, where it used to be seriously debated, and become a subject of interest to LDC-oriented international forums, such as the United Nations Conference on Trade and Development in Geneva. Since the international agencies largely reflect rather than lead national concerns, the brain drain has been on the minds of many LDC governments, leading even the moderate among them to propose policy responses that appear at first blush to be radical in scope.

Welfare Effects

Before I consider the policy proposals, however, I must stress that "brain drain" is an emotive phrase that necessarily suggests that the outflow of skilled manpower *is* a problem. Much of the scientific literature on the brain drain during the 1960s and 1970s, however, starting from the early work of Harry G. Johnson and of Herbert Grubel and Anthony Scott, showed clearly that this was not necessarily a valid inference.[26] For one thing, if we divide the source country population into the migrants and "those left behind" (itself an emotive phrase, which also suggests that migrants are permanent rather than to-and-fro migrants), the literature notes that the question of the effect on the welfare of those left behind is fairly complex. Let me illustrate with just a few examples relating to flows of professional, technical, and kindred workers.

In place of the brain drain model, one can build a spillover model, where there is unemployment among the professionals who emigrate. In this case the outflow is a safety valve that both releases resources used by families or the state to support these professionals, who produce zero output, *and* diminishes the explosive political impact in urban areas of such unemployment. At the same time, however, as Koichi Hamada and I have argued formally, the *dynamic* effect of such an outflow may well be to raise the expected return to this class of professionals (given the substantially higher salaries in developed countries) and thus to raise the supply of them and create a larger steady-state pool of unemployed professionals in the source country.[27] In models of rural-urban migration (such as that of Seymour Harris and Michael Todaro), the unemployed are situated in the urban sector. In the international context, where immigration controls regulate entry, the unemployed must reside in the LDCs, waiting to emigrate. Thus it may be erroneous to argue that there is nothing wrong if the doctors who emigrate are "driving cabs in Manila": the possibility of emigration can increase the number of such distinguished cabdrivers. The possible fallacy of the former argument consists in assuming that there is a fixed supply of doctors.

Again, the critics of the "alarmist" brain-drain analysts have charged a fallacy of composition. There are admittedly far too few doctors in India per capita. Does that necessarily imply that the emigration of Indian doctors is harmful to India? Hla Myint has noted that the per capita figures are misleading, that doctors are to be found greatly crowded in the urban areas and the implied externality is to be found in the rural areas. He is right. But again one has to look at the dynamics of the process. There is an ongoing "internal diffusion" process: as doctors crowd into the urban areas, some begin to migrate to the surrounding quasi-urban areas, and others begin to establish one-day practices there, in a reverse urban-rural process of sorts. The brain-drain possibility then slows down this internal diffusion.[28]

While the Johnson-Grubel-Scott skepticism was necessary and clarified the nature of the argumentation required to assess the effects of professional outflows, my empirical judgment is that these outflows often create difficulties for small source countries with limited educational opportunities and substantial outflows. For large countries such as India, however, the emigration of doctors, engineers, and so on is not really a problem, although there is scope for worry about the emigration of talented, as against merely trained, professionals. Institution building in particular is likely to be adversely affected. But even here the presence of a country's distinguished nationals in prestigious foreign institutions can improve their productivity and enhance opportunities for other nationals to train abroad by exploiting the resulting networking contacts.

Thus in the former group of countries policy responses to prevent the brain drain have attracted more attention. In the latter group attention has been focused on policy responses that exploit the phenomenon to create increased advantage for the source LDCs.

The subject of both classes of policy responses is human migration, dictated by personal constraints and choices. In my view the possibility of migration should therefore not be simply *forbidden* on utilitarian grounds, citing advantage to the source countries. Rather it should be perceived as reflecting an important human right that may nonetheless be tempered by consequentialist measures falling short of absolute prohibitions.

Let me turn now to policies aimed at reducing the brain drain and to those that seek instead to accommodate to it and mitigate its consequences, and increase its possible advantages, for LDCs.

Policies to Reduce the Brain Drain

Policies to reduce the brain drain have been debated ever since the phenomenon became a public policy issue. They divide into restrictive and incentive policy suggestions.

Restrictive Policies
The restrictive policy actions are, of course, the LDC counterpart of immigration restrictions in developed countries; the latter already restrict the inflow of professionals while the proposed LDC restrictions can shift the breakdown of their total between developing and developed sources of emigration. These restrictions can take the form of denying passports to exiting professionals, requiring periods of domestic service for newly graduated professionals (as for medical graduates in many countries), or making exit more difficult in other ways (as when the holding of the American Medical Association's examination for foreign doctors is forbidden in India). Few of these restrictions can really be applied to those students who stay on abroad after their studies, although the government of Sri Lanka experimented with making the renewal of passports conditional on transmission of funds and might well have made the renewal impossible so as to attempt to force the return of the émigrés.

Typically, however, these kinds of restrictions are likely both to be nuisances that are inequitably surmountable by the powerful or the ingenious and to be resented at large by the very professionals whom they seek to hold back, with possibly adverse effects on their efficiency and commitment to their societies. Hence such restrictions are invoked only infrequently and are occasionally canceled (as in Sri Lanka) in response to effective protests by the professionals.

A policy action recently addressed to reducing the professional inflow from LDCs (though not necessarily from developed countries) was the now defunct U.S. ruling that required professional exchange visitors from LDCs to return to their home country or another LDC for a period of two years before they could reenter the United States as immigrants. A later example is U.S. legislative action making the immigration of foreign medical graduates extremely difficult, with reliance instead on expanding domestic training facilities.

A somewhat tangential U.S. policy has recently been to deny student visas in an increasing number of cases on the assumption that students stay on (as discussed with reference to table 19.8). This policy has not been motivated, as far as I can judge, by a need to halt the brain drain, although that is its indirect result. Rather it is motivated by a desire to prevent indirect immigration by students from LDCs. At a time when there are vast numbers of illegal immigrants, with a virtually open United States–Mexico border beyond effective control, the tendency has been to tighten flows through any immigration channels that can be better controlled, Haitian refugees and LDC students becoming the evident objects of such attention. Such road-blocks to students are undesirable in themselves, and a better policy aimed at controlling indirect professional immigration (if that is desired at all) would be to tighten the visa conversion process.

The existing "prior restraint" denial of visas is doubly offensive because U.S. consulates typically deny student visas to those with lesser means on the unproven but probably false hypothesis that the poorer they are, the more likely it is that they will stay on.[29] This principle of selective exclusion of the less endowed students violates the egalitarian principles that animate both U.S. society and its educational system (relative to those of European colleges, which have usually given easier access to the elite than to the meritorious from the LDCs). It is certainly a matter that universities in the United States need to look into more closely.

Incentive Policies
As for the incentive policy suggestions, these are generally designed to make emigration less atractive. Thus salary increases and improved research facilities are typically advocated. But while a number of institutional features of professional life in LDCs could be improved, the basic difficulty lies in the impossibility of significantly narrowing the gap in professional facilities when the developed and developing countries are so far apart in resources in the first place. Besides, prescriptions to raise professional salaries yet further toward international levels have inegalitarian and welfare-reducing consequences that LDCs surely cannot ignore. Thus, even if these policies were somehow to be implemented on a significant scale and were to reduce the outflow of professional manpower, they would have to be carefully weighed for their other deleterious effects on the LDCs adopting them.

I must also mention the occasional argument (which I touched on earlier from a different vantage point) that several LDCs have overexpanded their educational facilities and that their professional emigration is a direct result of such overexpansion and consequent unemployment. Certainly, reducing the scale of educational facilities in any country experiencing emigration would *ceteris paribus* (regardless of unemployment levels) tend to lower emigration to higher-wage countries by raising, under "normal" assumptions, the domestic return to education. The desirability of such a policy, however, would depend on the precise conditions in the labor market for these professionals and the social objectives of the LDC. Thus, if the *net* domestic availability (that is, domestic supply minus emigration) of professionals falls as their total output is restricted, this could well be considered a serious negative effect of the policy. Even if the labor market is characterized by a temporary "surplus," given the current sticky wage level, it is perfectly conceivable that the reduced domestic availability, including the present surplus, would inhibit the diffusion of this kind of professional into the countryside, where the social return to their professional presence is highly valued. Furthermore, it is extremely improbable that a policy of restricting educational facilities for professionals, even if considered desirable, could be politically implemented, especially when emigration possibilities have made the returns from such educational attainment even more attractive.

Policies to Mitigate the Consequences of the Brain Drain

Fundamentally, however, the proposals to prevent the brain drain are flawed. For one thing, the forces that motivate it are much too strong to make restrictive contols effective. They include the internationalization of the professional classes; the vast disparities in facilities and incomes between the developing and the developed countries; the independence in developed countries from the bureaucratic controls that are pervasive in the LDCs; the fact that the frontiers of science are mainly in the developed countries; and the associated fact that rewards come not simply from achievement but also from its recognition, which often depends on location and contacts. Few LDCs can contemplate Soviet-style restrictions on outflows, no matter how undemocratic their regimes are at times. Interestingly, the authoritarian regimes seem to prefer decimation or expulsion of their professionals to keeping them in.

Equally, the developed countries are caught in a dilemma. On the one hand, their immigration policies are increasingly designed to favor skilled over unskilled immigrants. On the other hand, because racial bias and corresponding country quotas are no longer considered defensible, we have seen that the professional immigrants come increasingly from the

LDCs. There is simply no way, therefore, that developed countries can be expected to cut back effectively on professional immigration from the LDCs. In fact, LDCs themselves would object to a return to the earlier racial quotas as an offensive affront to their rights in the community of nations. It is necessary, therefore, to change the 1950s and 1960s focus on policies to control the brain drain to policies designed to mitigate its consequences, where they are deleterious for the LDCs, and to secure for LDCs, whether harmed or otherwise, greater benefits from the skilled migration across borders.

Institutional Changes

If the professional outflows, direct or indirect, are to be treated as inevitable, how then can the source LDCs benefit from the skills of their nationals (or former nationals) working abroad?

It seems evident that the institutions in both developed and developing countries will have to permit greater flexibility in their administrative policies so that professionals from LDCs can work to the advantage of their home countries. Most universities do not permit professors to hold dual appointments. But if universities in developed countries would permit such dual appointments with LDC universities, allowing locational changes between the two campuses (say, each getting the faculty member every other year), the LDCs would gain the benefits of their émigré professionals. The problem is similar to that of making institutional changes to accommodate part-time female workers in the developed countries; it requires imaginative flexibility, admittedly at some cost to efficiency.

Developed countries could help increase the incentives for professionals to remain in the LDCs by giving them temporary access to facilities in the developed countries in a number of ways. Thus major foundations in the developed countries have initiated programs to finance recurrent and protracted visits by LDC research professionals to universities and institutes: this permits flirting to be an effective substitute for marriage. Such programs enable the professionals to retain their domicile in the LDCs, where they can proceed with institution building at the substantially lower salaries there while enjoying both an increased average income and intellectual stimulus from the foreign visits. The counterpart of these programs is the financing of visits by scientists from developed countries to the LDC institutions.[30]

The flexibility will be equally necessary at the LDC end, I should stress. Institutional changes will have to be made to accommodate such "sharing" patterns. Facilitating changes would enable their professionals to have generous leaves, permitting their use of opportunities to spend greater time abroad in stimulating environments. Faced with hesitation on the part of university administrators to adapt their conventionally tough leave policies, I once reminded my vice-chancellor in Delhi that professors could migrate if straitjacketed and that, if they did not, he should remember that the brain could drain away faster sitting in one dreary dulling place than by migrating with the body elsewhere.

Tax Policies

An alternative, but complementary, approach to the question of professional migration has come from a different direction. In the early 1970s I proposed a "brain drain tax." The idea was to have the migrants themselves contribute a fraction of their considerably enhanced earnings through an income tax to the development of LDCs. I felt that this was a measure of self-help by LDCs, with their own nationals contributing to their countries' development instead of exclusively urging the developed countries to tax their citizens to help the LDCs through foreign aid. As it happens, this idea received a considerable amount of attention at the UNCTAD, at several international conferences, and from lawyers and economists generally.[31]

An altogether different approach to taxation related to the brain drain has come from the concerned leaders of the LDCs.[32] In their view, the receiving countries ought to pay compensation to the sending LDCs. Whereas my proposal would extend income tax jurisdiction by LDCs to their professional nationals abroad, this alternative proposal would tax developed countries instead. Let me address the rationales of the two proposals carefully, taking the latter first.

Consider the following two statements:

I would also like to propose the establishment of an International Labour Commission Facility (ILCF). It could be elaborated along the lines of the Trust Fund for Compensatory Facilities of the International Monetary Fund. The proposed Facility would draw its resources principally from labour-importing countries, but in a spirit of solidarity and goodwill, other ILO members may contribute to it. The accumulated resources will be diverted to developing labour-exporting countries in proportions relative to *the estimated cost incurred due to the loss of labour.*[33]

The Commission on Development recommends that, in order to *"compensate"* for the reverse transfer of technology, resulting from such exodus, amounting to several billions of dollars for the last decade, special arrangements including the possibility of establishing special funds, should be made to provide the necessary resources for strengthening the technological capabilities of the developing countries.[34]

Prime Minister Edward Seaga of Jamaica is also said to be persuaded that compensation is owed to LDCs for the educational costs saved by developed countries by importing professionals.[35]

The problems with such compensation ideas, however, are fundamental. First, the educational costs estimated and cited by many experts do not make any adjustments for the fact that the higher education acquired by LDC professionals is often acquired not at home but in developed countries, this being obvious for the many student stay-ons but true also of many professionals migrating directly. The labor certification that is often necessary for such immigration requires networking contacts, which prior study in the country of immigration often facilitates. Second, and more important, it is simply implausible to ask developed countries for such compensation when they could readily stop the immigration of LDC professionals and shift to admitting more professionals from other developed countries, reverting to the pre-1960s practices. From the viewpoint of developed countries, admitting LDC professionals is itself a benefit extended to the LDCs, giving their nationals a chance to get into countries with greater opportunities and prosperity. The notion of compensating LDCs for what is seen as a benefit extended to them is unlikely to sit well with governments and their constituencies.

Rather than claim compensation, either for educational costs or for difficulties imposed on those left behind in small, undereducated LDCs, as a rationale for getting developed countries to make a transfer to LDCs, I have proposed an alternative approach that may justify such a transfer. I have suggested that since developed countries presumably profit from professional immigration, whether or not from LDCs, the LDCs may well suggest that part of this gain be shared with the LDCs from which the professionals come.[36] Thus, since professionals earn higher than median salaries and are therefore taxed to redistribute to the less affluent in their host countries, some of this redistributed revenue might be shared with their home LDCs to redistribute to the less affluent there as well. This is sharing, *not* compensation; it is therefore likely to be a less grating rationale to accept than Prime Minister Seaga's latest reiteration of demands on the developed countries' exchequers for compensatory funds.

I lean instead to the view that professionals abroad, indeed citizens abroad more generally, ought to be subject to income taxation by their home countries. Except for the United States and the Philippines, all countries, including LDCs, follow the schedular system of income tax jurisdiction, under which citizens are taxed by residence and hence escape home country taxation altogether. The ludicrous result is that Indians earning, net of U.S. taxes, incomes substantially higher than the most prosperous Indians at home, pay no taxes to India while enjoying the benefits of Citizenship. This is a system of "representation without taxation," standing the sentiments at the Boston Tea Party on their head.

I have therefore been arguing for the adoption by the LDCs of the global system of income tax jurisdiction, as in the United States, where citizenship, not residence, is the basis for taxation. This would enable those left behind to profit from the professional emigration. Professionals would then not escape the obligation to be taxed for social purposes such as redistribution simply by residing abroad. Since income taxation is also interpretable as a way of recovering the costs of educational expenditures, the global system would also ensure that professional emigrants would partially fulfill their obligations in this regard.[37]

Objections to this proposal have ranged from questions of human rights to tax administration. A typical objection is that such exercise of tax jurisdiction would violate human rights. An exit tax, especially of the Soviet variety, comes close in spirit to doing this, but not an income tax. Exercise of income tax jurisdiction over nationals abroad is recognized in international law as perfectly legitimate; it is in fact the practice of U.S. tax authorities. Tax administration, however, raises difficulties. To administer it effectively, the global tax system requires that information on the taxable income of migrant citizens be verifiable. The cooperation of the receiving countries in this matter becomes important, if not essential. Progress here is not impossible; increasingly exchange of information hitherto regarded as beyond jurisdiction—such as information on bank accounts abroad—is becoming available by treaty. Within the United States the states are increasingly furnishing information to the federal government. The sums that can be raised, even by adopting simple and very modest surcharge formulas (as by the Philippines, which imposes a 1, 2, 3 percent tax on net-of-foreign-tax incomes of citizens abroad), are quite sizable, given the number of citizens, including professionals, now abroad.[38]

The real bottleneck to this proposal is rather the political economy of the migration process. Few of those who influence tax legislation in the LDCs, whether intellectuals or politicians, are without some family member residing abroad. It is much easier for them to demand more taxes to be paid to help their country by Professor Perlman than by their kith and kin in Pittsburgh. The problem is even more acute for the articulate expatriate community of development experts who reside in London, Paris, and other capitals. The notion that they should pay taxes to their own countries—as a reflection of the egalitarian ability-to-pay criterion of income taxation within a society and equally as a fine example of the principle of self-reliance by developing countries—is rarely perceived by them as a pleasing one.

I have, however, been pleased to see that, in common with Senator William Proxmire, increasing numbers of Indian professionals who live and work at home under difficult conditions and high taxes have come to see the egalitarian, if not the efficiency, logic of the global tax system.[39] The idea of exercising income tax jurisdiction over nationals abroad has gained appeal, reflecting "horizontal equity" concerns between migrants and those left behind and thus beginning to change the political economy of the problem toward an acceptance of the global system of income taxation.[40]

19.4 Research Agenda

My distinguished discussants will, I am sure, draw their own conclusions about the research agenda that my analysis suggests. I might indicate, however, two salient conclusions of my own.

First, the phenomenon of international migration is sufficiently important, in a world economy and polity characterized by substantial international personal mobility, to warrant a systematic attempt at devising an international infrastructure, whether an institution like the GATT or simply a code, that addresses the resulting issues systematically and without leaving the matter to be decided by virtually autonomous actions of the receiving countries.[41]

Since the questions raised are both economic and moral, as we are dealing with humanity as the central actor in the phenomenon of migration, the institution or the code will have to be broader in scope than simply the economic-agenda-oriented institutions and codes that address issues of trade, exchange rates, and capital flows. We need to address questions such as these:

1. Should governments be allowed to expel, as Ghana did, foreign nationals, even illegal ones, except over a protracted period so as to minimize economic hardship for the migrants and the economic difficulties that would follow for the source countries?

2. How should legal migrants be treated? Should they be offered civil rights equal to those of natives, or are there specific constraints on their rights as members of the host society that are acceptable in civilized societies? For example, Sweden permits migrants to vote in all but national

elections, but the United States does not; the question bears very closely on how effectively migrants' rights can be protected in pluralistic societies.

3. Should the nature and degree of enforcement at the border be a matter entirely within the discretion of the receiving country? That is, should countries be freely allowed, to put it starkly, to shoot at people coming across the border or should the illegal immigrants across the Rio Grande just be bused back to come right across the border the next day?

There are two approaches to devising the institutions and codes on such questions. Either one can proceed from first principles, as in political theory, and define what one would like to see, quite regardless of what governments are likely to accept. Alternatively—a procedure I prefer—one can examine the evolving practices and construct a set of rules that better reflect the limits within which acceptable rules can be defined. A research agenda could thus pointedly address the experience we have had of receiving countries' practices in dealing with refugees, illegal migrants, and others (examining, for instance, the United States–Mexico, the Bangladesh-India, and other border situations, where illegal migration has been a major problem).

Second, I would certainly like to have a research program addressed to the question of devising institutional flexibility, in both developing and developed countries, to ensure that LDCs manage to share effectively in the services of their professional émigrés. I would like to see the diaspora model examined in regard to the issue of taxation. Both sets of responses to the inevitable out-migration of professionals from developing to developed countries should make it easier to accommodate to the process of such skilled migratory flows without desperate attempts at interfering with the desirable freedom of such professionals to migrate and relocate where they wish.

Notes

This paper has benefited from comments by Mark Perlman, John Dunlop, and others at the University of Pittsburgh Bicentennial Activities Symposium, March 18–19, 1987. Brian Wesol provided excellent research assistance. The World Bank does not accept responsibility for the views expressed herein, which are those of the author and should not be attributed to the World Bank or to its affiliated organizations.

1. By interdependence I simply mean linkages. Greater linkage for a country, however, does not necessarily imply greater "dependence"—that is, vulnerability

to the outside world. Thus a higher debt may imply a greater vulnerability by the creditor, not the debtor. Again, an increased trade share by a *force majeure* such as the United States may mean that it becomes more concerned with issues such as reciprocity in trade and hence problematic in its external economic relations for other trading partners than when it had a lower ratio of trade to GNP.

2. Successive tariff-cutting trade rounds under GATT auspices have brought average tariffs on semimanufactures and manufactures in the United States, the European Community, and Japan down to 4.9 percent, 6.0 percent, and 5.4 percent, respectively, since the Tokyo round in the late 1970s.

The market forces may have reflected government actions. Thus the OPEC surpluses, which greatly accentuated the growth of the world's capital market, were themselves a product of a governments-led cartel. Again, the recycling of petrodollars was not just a market phenomenon: it was a policy goal of the United States.

3. Strictly, the GATT is not a Bretton Woods institution. But, along with the International Monetary Fund and the World Bank, which are, the GATT is regarded (in view of the context and timing of its conception and birth) as part of the trinity of Bretton Woods institutions.

4. There is room for debate whether rapid growth led to rapid liberalization of trade, and vice versa. The sensible position seems to be that, in pluralistic economies, trade liberalization will *politically* proceed faster when growth is higher and prosperity eases the task of adjustment whereas *economically* more rapid growth will follow if trade is liberalized rather than hampered. The process must be regarded as interactive.

5. Michael Walzer, *Spheres of Justice: A Defence of Pluralism and Equality* (New York: Basic Books, 1983).

6. Cf. the views of Franciscus a Vittoria in his *Reflectiones Theologicae* (Spanish edition, Buenos Aires, 1946), where he wrote of the "Right of Natural Society and Communication" and argued that "it has been a custom from the beginning of the world for anyone to go into whatever country he chooses and prohibition of entrance is a violent measure not removed from war."

7. This is not to deny that these policies are influenced by market forces of supply and demand. An expansion of immigrant quotas may well reflect an increased scarcity of labor that results in pressure group lobbying to increase the quotas. But it also may not.

8. The popular terms for people who go back and forth between countries are "to-and-fro" and "yo-yo" migrants. Even the nineteenth century migration to the United States, often thought of as permanent, was characterized by a nonnegligible life cycle and other phenomena of return migration. The present sophistication has replaced the earlier practice in the scientific literature of ignoring the distinction between "gross" and "net" inflows of aliens in interpreting the customary gross

inflow figures and of discussing the consequences of phenomena such as the brain drain as once-and-for-all movements of the skilled to other nations.

9. Gurushri Swamy, *Population and International Migration*, World Bank Staff Working Paper, no. 689 (Washington, DC, 1985).

10. The categorization by these two classes is not straightforward or uniform among countries, as I will note later.

11. For details, see United Nations, *International Migration Policies and Programmes* (New York, 1982), ch. 5.

12. Swamy (*Population and International Migration*) quotes estimates putting the number of migrant workers in Argentina and Venezuela at about 2 million recently.

13. Swamy puts the figure for Ghana and Ivory Coast together at 1 million foreign workers in 1975 (ibid.).

14. The drawing back, however, did not mean that the stock of *Gastarbeiters* was reduced. Ironically, the "temporary" workers could not really be returned to the source countries in most cases, illustrating the dilemmas posed by worker programs for hard policy options. As Max Frisch, the Swiss novelist, has remarked, "We imported workers and got men instead."

15. These totals include the workers from the poorer countries of the Organization for Economic Cooperation and Development (OECD), such as Spain, Italy, and Greece.

16. Swamy, *Population and International Migration*, p. 7.

17. Ibid.

18. The bracero program lasted over two decades and imported nearly 4.5 million farm workers. It was terminated in 1964 but has been effectively replaced by the H-2 visa program, which admits similar workers.

19. The most disturbing instances of the former relate to flows between poor countries. Ghana in 1969 expelled 200,000 to 500,000 illegal aliens within two weeks by enforcing the Alien Compliance Act. The most recent example of amnesty is the U.S. legislation conferring amnesty on illegal immigrants who have resided continuously in the United States since 1982.

20. These refugees may be either skilled or unskilled. The composition is mixed and varies among countries and over time.

21. Curiously, the arbitrariness of such distinctions goes to absurd lengths from an economist's viewpoint. Thus Prime Minister Ytzhak Shamir of Israel wants to direct Soviet Jews, refugees by any definition, toward Israel. These Soviet émigrés then have a definite offer of destination in friendly Israel. But if the United States admits them nonetheless as refugees, it is manifest that the Soviets are making an

"economic" choice between Israel and the United States as their destination. But U.S. policy (which Pnme Minister Shamir would like to change to exclude Soviet refugees from the United States) admits them as "political" refugees while rejecting many others, including Salvadorans, Haitians, and Guatemalans, as "economic" refugees even when they have no other destination.

22. United Nations, *International Migration Policies and Programs*, pp. 35–36.

23. The sixth preference includes some unskilled immigrants (such as housemaids) as well. The third and sixth preference visas together constitute 20 percent of the numerically restricted preference system visas of the United States, but the spouses and children of the primary recipients of these visas are also charged to these two categories.

24. Barry Chiswick, Testimony before Subcommittee on Immigration and Refugee Policy of the Committee on the Judiciary, U.S. Senate, 97th Congress, November 23, 1981, serial no. J-97-83; and Louis Parnai, "Canada's Immigration Policy: 1962–74," *International Migration Review* (Winter 1975), pp. 469–472.

25. Don VeVoretz and Dennis Maki, "The Size and Distribution of Human Capital Transfers from LDCs to Canada: 1966–1973," *Economic Development and Cultural Change* (July 1980), table 1.

26. Harry G. Johnson, "The Economics of the 'Brain Drain': The Canadian Case," *Minerva* (1965); and Herbert Grubel and Anthony D. Scott, "The International Flow of Human Capital," *American Economic Review* (May 1966).

27. Jagdish Bhagwati and Koichi Hamada, "The Brain Drain, International Integration of Markets for Professionals, and Unemployment: A Theoretical Analysis," *Journal of Development Economics*, vol. 1, no. 1 (1974); reprinted in Jagdish Bhagwati, ed., *The Brain Drain and Taxation II: Theory and Empirical Analysis* (Amsterdam: North Holland, 1976), ch. 6.

28. Ibid.

29. There is much casual evidence on this subject but no systematic data, since the visa denial procedure is inherently free from public scrutiny and certainly not subject to due process restraints. This problem has, however, raised a substantial protest in India.

30. In both cases, of course, the results can be deleterious if the programs are ill-administered. If the LDCs manage them so that the foreign visits are controlled and allocated on a patronage basis, the programs will generate diversion of professional energy into patronage cultivation; and the use of funds to bring in low-grade but highly paid scientists may well generate resentment in the indigenous professional community.

31. The original proposal was spelled out in Jagdish Bhagwati, "The Loss of Innocence: U.S. in the Nixon Era," *Daedalus* (1972), and then in Jagdish Bhagwati and William Dellalfar, "The Brain Drain and Income Taxation," *World Develop-*

ment, vol. 1, no. 1 (1973). It has gone through extensive examination and reformation since then. Cf. Jagdish Bhagwati and Martin Partington, eds., *Taxing the Brain Drain: I. A Proposal* (Amsterdam: North Holland, 1970), and Jagdish Bhagwati and John Wilson, eds., *Income Taxation and International Mobility* (Amsterdam: North Holland, 1989).

32. The idea is also in the academic literature, although my own writings have discounted its appeal. It has recently been pushed by Crown Prince Hassan bin Talal of Jordan in 1977 and by Prime Minister Edward Seaga of Jamaica .

33. Address by Crown Prince Hassan bin Talal to the International Labor Organization (ILO), Geneva, June 1977.

34. Committee on International Economic Cooperation (Paris, 1977).

35. Cited in André Payenne, "Plugging the Brain Drain: A Third World Call for Western Reparations," *World Press Review* (August 1985), pp. 33–34.

36. Jagdish Bhagwati, "The Brain Drain: International Flow Accounting Compensation, Taxation, and Related Proposals" (Paper for the Intergovernment Group of Experts Meeting, UNCTAD, Geneva); printed in Jagdish Bhagwati, ed., *Essays in Development Economics*, vol. 1, *Dependence and Interdependence* (Oxford: Basil Blackwell, 1985), ch. 19.

37. The question has been dealt with analytically in the format of the optimal tax literature in a Symposium Issue of the *Journal of Public Economics*, vol. 18 (1962); and it is also the subject of further analysis in Bhagwati and Wilson, *Income Taxation*.

38. Bhagwati, *The Brain Drain and Taxation II*.

39. Senator Proxmire has been a driving force in ensuring that Americans abroad keep paying their share of U.S. taxes, so that the pub-crawling Americans in Paris do not get free drinks while the proletariat in Pittsburgh bears the burden of U.S. taxation. Cf. Bhagwati, "The Brain Drain."

40. The extensive analysis of this idea has explored several other objections also. Let me mention a few salient ones: Would it mean that Ugandans abroad would have to pay taxes to Idi Amin? No; they could refuse to pay. Besides, Western courts today do not enforce laws of foreign nations. If tax information were supplied to LDCs by developed countries, would Idi Amin get information on Ugandans abroad? No; such arrangements are governed by tax treaties, and these could readily accommodate suspension during well-defined political emergencies. Would it encourage change of nationality and thus hurt revenues gathered? No; for the schedular system produces no revenues at all, whereas the global system, even if some emigrants changed nationality, would produce revenues greater than zero. Besides, the optimal tax rates chosen would reflect this consideration. Further, where tax rates have been kept low, as in the Philippines, few nationality changes have been induced. Would it cut into remittances? No; few of the professionals and others who would be so taxed (while the poorer emigre citizens would benefit

from exemptions) make remittances anyway; remittances are a feature of unskilled and poorer migration.

41. There are, indeed, beginnings of such a code, such as the ILO conventions on immigrant workers' rights. But they relate to limited aspects of the many problems raised by migrations of various kinds.

20

International Migration and Income Taxation

This chapter provides an overview of recent developments in analysis of the question raised by international mobility of people of the appropriate exercise of income tax jurisdiction over them by the different nation-states between which this international mobility is defined.

20.1 Evolution of the Problem

The question itself is novel in the concerns of public finance theorists, having generally been neglected because *either*, as with the celebrated Meade Commission in the United Kingdom, it was simply assumed implicitly in the policy realm that the income tax jurisdiction must exclude nonresident nationals (this being the so-called "schedular" system in Anglo-Saxon legal jargon), as was the historically received U.K. practice, *or* the theoretical analyses of optimal income taxation were generally "closed" on the dimension of the people over whom the social welfare function was defined.[1]

Where did the problem, which has now attracted the analyticall skills of many of the best public-finance theorists and of distinguished profesors of law, and the attention of policymakers in national and international forums, then come from?

"Taxing the Brain Drain" and Thereafter

The major impetus came paradoxically from the analytical work on the "brain drain," or (less emotively) the outmigration of skilled people, that engaged the attention of theorists of international trade and development during the 1960s. In particular, the focus of this literature, especially the early writings of Johnson (1965, 1967) and Grubel and Scott (1966), was to address the policy concerns that this phenomenon was harmful to the developing countries.

The chief contribution of this literature on international personal mobility was to focus attention on the distinction between migrants and nonmigrants (or TLBs, "those left behind," a term that itself prejudged the nature of the brain drain phenomenon in a world of immigration restrictions). These authors introduced the notion that the welfare effect of outmigration on the source country must be considered in light of its effect on TLBs, rather than on indices such as overall GNP or per capita GNP. Thus, in a model with diminishing returns operative, a *finite* outflow of migrants would lose for TLBs the "surplus" that they enjoyed from the presence of the migrants: outmigration was therefore a source of loss to TLBs. But for infinitesimal changes in the size of the labor force, TLBs would be simply unaffected (though the per capita GNP would fall).[2]

The controversy was then focused exclusively on the question whether TLBs would be harmed or helped by the outmigration, and had reached rapidly diminishing returns by the late 1960s.

Refocusing Issue, New Perspective—Rationale I

I happened then to refocus the issue (Bhagwati, 1972; Bhagwati and Dellalfar, 1973) in an altogether different direction by essentially introducing a fiscal policy instrument that could be used in conjunction with free outmigration. Thus, the question was not just a welfare comparison between no-migration and outmigration. Rather, outmigration with deployment of tax policy instruments would be compared with no-migration. This was an important shift of focus because, from the viewpoint of policy, permitting outmigration must be regarded as a human right and therefore, even if it imposes costs on TLBs, emigration restrictions are not a feasible response in civilized societies. But other policy instruments may well be.

In considering therefore tax policy as such an instrument, I proposed that it would make sense to tax the outmigrants to compensate the TLBs and that, if outmigration was Pareto-better, it should be possible to compensate the TLBs and still leave the migrants better off than they were without migration.

The essential idea behind such a "tax on the brain drain," as the proposal came to be known in the literature, can be set forth with reference to figure 20.1. Assuming that there are no externalities or distortions, the *MP* (marginal product) is both *PMP* (private) and *SMP* (social), and exhibits diminishing returns for the LDC (less developed country) and the DC (developed country). The premigration supply of labor in each country is

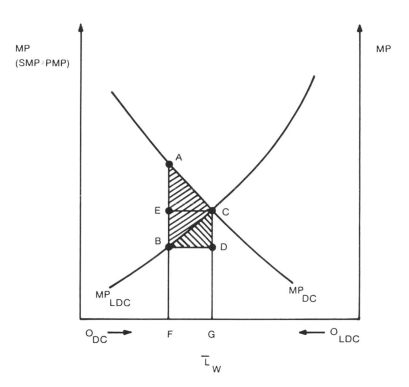

1. LDC: Migrants' *Gain* =ECDB = EBC + BCD.
2. LDC: TLBs' *Loss* = BCD.
3. LDC: Migrants + TLBs Together: *Gain* = EBC.
4. DC: Monmigrants' *Gain* = AEC.
5. WORLD *Gain* = ABC = EBC + AEC.
                  (3)   (4)

Figure 20.1

$O_{DC}F$ and $O_{LDC}F$, respectively, adding up to $O_{DC}O_{LDC}$. This leads to initial wages being AF and BF in the DC and the LDC, respectively. Hence, wage-equalizing migration will result in migration of GF labor to the DC and an equalized wage CG.

Now, it is evident that the gains and losses come out as follows:

LDC:

1. Migrants' gain = $ECDB \equiv EBC + BCD$.

2. TLBs' *loss* = BCD.

3. (Migrants + TLBs) *gain* = EBC.

DC:

4. Native nonmigrants' *gain* = AEC.

WORLD:

[LDC (migrants + TLBs) *gain* (3) + DC *gain* (4)] *gain* = ABC.

Therefore it is clear that if a tax can be levied on the LDC migrants to compensate the TLBs, the TLBs come out as well off as, and the other two groups better off than, under nonmigration, making the outcome Pareto-better *actually* (and not just in the potential-compensation sense).

Once the problem is then cast in this format, it is also immediately clear that international personal mobility, which has often been treated in traditional trade theory as symmetric to the case of international capital mobility, is really asymmetric to it in an essential way. For, if in figure 20.1, we were considering capital mobility instead of labor mobility, it *would* make sense to treat impact on LDC welfare as simply EBC. But when people move out of a society, TLBs are likely to think of national welfare as defined for themselves alone. The income-distributional problem between TLBs and the outmigrants has no real counterpart in the analysis of international capital flows.

Further Refocus and Novel Questions in Public Finance Theory—Rationale II
But, in turn, this leads one to reexamine the notion that internation mobility, and indeed tax policy in regard thereto, can be thought of exclusively in terms of a sharp focus on the welfare impact on TLBs alone, even though "national advantage" is the objective.

The Johnson-Grubel-Scott focus on TLBs is strictly relevant only if the outmigration is considered permanent; and even then, it may not be. Certainly, however, in the world of modern communications, frequent journeys back and forth between home and host countries, retention of ethnic ties, and increased tolerance for ethnic diversity in host countries such as the United States, migration is no longer thought of as removing one's population out of the set over which social welfare is defined. Especially if citizenship is retained, as a mark of one's societal affiliation to the home country, it seems perfectly appropriate to extend income taxation on the principle of "ability to pay" to citizens who reside abroad, quite regardless of the "compensatory" type of redistributive argument advanced under rationale I, above.

To put it somewhat vividly, if the early Americans thought that "taxation without representation" was not a good idea, "representation without taxation" would be equally inappropriate and would be the case if the "schedular" system of income tax jurisdiction was adopted à la the practice of European countries and their excolonies. This was the rationale, in fact, behind my original proposal to "tax the brain drain" with an income tax surcharge on what LDC migrants paid to their host countries: prosperous migrants from LDCs would make a contribution, reflecting their ability to pay, toward the revenue needs of their home countries. In the early formulations of my ideas, the citizenship nexus was implicit; the nexus became clearer as discussions with lawyers and policymakers made manifest the fact that citizenship alone would provide the basis, as it does in the United States, for income taxation of migrants by their home countries.

Rents and Rationale III

I had also suggested that, given the extensive nature of immigration restrictions, migrants typically enjoyed rents. If so, the oldest argument for taxation in economics suggested that these rents be taxed for social use such as redistribution to the LDCs for development. This is a cute idea; but, as you discover when you work on public policy issues, cuteness in economics does not translate into feasibility in politics. If the United States taxed its immigrants for such a purpose, levying, say, an income tax surcharge on Bhagwati (I hold a U.S. green card and an Indian passport) but not on Obstfeld, there would be an immediate threat of the U.S. Supreme Court declaring the practice *ultra vires* the Constitution in being discriminatory. In the United Kingdom, since immigrants are typically from the Commonwealth countries of darker pigmentation, the outcry could also invoke notions of racism.[3]

In the end, therefore, the strongest and clearest rationale for considering the exercise of income tax jurisdiction over nationals residing abroad, i.e., for adopting the so-called "global" system of income taxation, seemed to be the argument that citizenship provides the nexus for income taxation by the home country according to "ability to pay," regardless of where you reside. Thus, while the original idea of exploring the issue had come from examining the policy implications of the brain drain from LDCs to DCs, this served only as a scaffolding that was discarded, whereas the analytical problem became a more general, and specifically defined one: that of examining the question of the appropriate design of income taxation on nationals residing abroad. This also shifted attention, from the earlier examination within the context of models of brain drain, as in McCulloch and Yellen (1976), to analysis of the question within the context of the modern theory of optimal income taxation, as in Hamada (1975) and Bhagwati and Hamada (1982).

Extending Optimal Income Tax Models

While therefore the central thrust to this new branch of income tax theory was provided by these policy interests, the desire to extend the closed-economy optimal-income-tax model of Mirrlees to an open-economy context (where people can move abroad and not be taxed) appears to have motivated John Wilson in his dissertation at MIT in the late 1970s to explore independently (but not without, in the end, input down the road from the policy-induced literature, since I wound up as a member of his dissertation committee, with Peter Diamond as his principal advisor) some of the consequences of international migration for the Mirrlees conclusions on optimal income taxation.

The U.S. Policy Debate

Finally, as the policy-induced literature grew out of the original "brain-drain-taxation" format into the more general question of the appropriate exercise of income tax jurisdiction when citizens are internationally mobile, it became evident that the *actual practice* on this question was radically different between the few practitioners of the "global" system—the United States, the Philippines and, in principle, Mexico—and the many practitioners of the "schedular" system (predominantly led by the European countries). I stumbled into this discovery as, together with distinguished tax and human-rights lawyers such as Oliver Oldman, Richard Pomp, and Frank Newman, I was examining the feasibility of my taxing-the-brain-drain proposal at a conference in Bellagio (February 15–19, 1975).[4] In turn, this led to the realization that, in thc U.S. tax policy discussions, the global system of taxation had been the subject of intense lobbying and congressional debates for decades: with equity-oriented congressmen embracing it with vigor while U.S. citizens resident abroad and U.S. corporations competing for construction jobs abroad were opposing it with equal passion. Some of the issues that I discuss below in regard to the income tax jurisdiction question have emerged from reflection on this policy debate altogether different from the brain-drain policy debate—in particular, the question of the coexistence of global and schedular income tax systems in the world economy and its implications for the global system's economic efficiency.[5]

These three strands of influence, in descending order of importance, converged to provide the impetus for a substantial examination of the theory and practices of optimal income taxation for "open" economies, i.e., for economies with citizens who are internationally mobile, at a 1981 conference on the subject in New Delhi. The main theoretical papers from this conference were published in a symposium issue of the *Journal of Public Economics* (1982), the contributions being by Baumol, Bhagwati and Hamada, Mirrlees, and Wilson.

I and Wilson have also just completed editing a volume (1989) that brings together these plus several other papers on the subject, and have written a substantial "Overview" of the issues for that volume, on which I shall now draw intensively for the rest of this chapter.

20.2 Two Key Questions

In evaluating the merits and demerits of the global and the schedular income tax systems, the analysts have approached the question at two levels of analysis:[6]

1. If the schedular system is adopted, thus exempting citizens resident abroad from taxation, then we are evidently in a "second-best" situation vis-à-vis the optimal income tax solutions in, say, the Mirrlees and Atkinson models; how does the optimal choice of the tax rates, for instance, modify in this case?

2. If the global tax system is adopted, permitting taxation of citizens abroad, how should the tax rates be set on them vis-à-vis the citizens who are domestic residents?

Before reviewing the nature of the analytical contributions to these two questions, however, it is useful to consider the various criteria that different authors in the BW (Bhagwati and Wilson, 1989) volume have used to evaluate the different income tax regimes.

20.3   Social Welfare Criteria

If a government is to choose among alternative tax systems, it must have a criterion for evaluating the relative desirability of these tax systems. Two separate and well-known approaches to tax design can be used to justify the proposal that citizens living abroad continue to pay domestic income taxes.

According to the "benefit approach," each citizen's tax burden should rellect the benefts that he receives from the goods and services provided by the government. An important benefit often received by LDC citizens before they emigrate is state-subsidized educational services. Some proponents of a tax on the "brain drain" have therefore argued that such a tax could be imposed to compensate LDCs for the loss of human capital that they experience as a result of emigration. Interestingly, opponents of home-country income taxes on emigrants have also used the benefit approach partially to justify their stand. Thus, Hufbauer argues in the BW volume against such taxes by noting that "... the assertion of these taxes amounts to assertion of a quasi-property claim by the state, a claim not balanced by public goods or cultural associations offered by the state to the citizen living abroad."[7] Clearly, the difference of opinion here involves critically a matter of timing: should tax payments be received only when the benefits are received, or should we take a wider view that "lifetime benefits," appropriately discounted over time, should equal discounted lifetime payments?

A proponent of the "ability-to-pay approach," such as myself, would argue that this controversy is largely irrelevant because it ignores equity considerations. According to this approach, everyone's tax burden should in some sense reflect his ability to pay. It can then be argued that most LDC emigrants should pay taxes to the home government becausc their level of economic well-being is generally significantly higher than that of those citizens remaining in the home country.

Both approaches represent only partial guides to tax policy, however, becausc they ignore efficiency considerations. Taxes that are both administratively feasible and equitable invariably distort economic decision making, and some taxes are better than others simply because the efficiency losses that they create are less severe.

The theoretical papers in the BW volume explicitly attempt to incorporate the trade-off between efficiency and equity into the design of income tax systems for open economies. They do so by taking the "social welfare approach." This approach treats tax policy as a problem in applied welfare economics, thereby allowing the modern tools of economic theory to be brought to bear on tax policy issues.

Under the social welfare approach, the objective of a tax planner is to maximize a social welfare function that has as arguments the utilities of individuals.[8] Assumptions must be made about both the form of this function and the cardinal properties of utility functions, and these assumptions essentially represent value judgments about the relative desirability of different distributions of economic well-being.

For closed economies, a popular value judgment seems to be that all individuals should be treated equally in the measurement of social welfare. That is, any two individuals with identical utilities should count equally in the measurement of social welfare. However, once different national boundaries are admitted, the economist has two problems: (1) should nationals abroad count equally with resident nationals, and (2) should non-nationals count equally with one's own nationals? The latter question is one of "world welfare" and arises even if people never cross national boundaries; treatment of the issue divides the "cosmopolitans" from the "nationalists." The former question, on the other hand, is central even to the "nationalist" approach; and, as I have noted, the treatment of this extends from counting nationals abroad equally to attaching zero value to them (as when the focus is on nonmigrants, the TLBs, exclusively).

Most of the theorists who have recently explored the question of the appropriate exercise of income tax jurisdiction in open societies have focused on the nationalist criterion, ignoring the cosmopolitan or host-country perspective. The only exception is Wilson (1982b) who adopts a world-welfare, cosmopolitan view, maximizing social welfare which is a function of utilities of individual members of the world population, and this function is increasing in each utility.[9] Since it is unlikely that national governments will take a cosmopolitan view, especially as the world economy is not blessed with mechanisms to ensure that potential Pareto-superiority translates via transfers into actual Pareto-superiority, the economic analysts have typically taken the nationalist criterion for analyzing the problem at hand.

It is important to note, however, especially in the year of James Buchanan's Nobel award, that all economists do not share the view that governments will follow what I call the "puppeteer" model of political economy, where politicians simply pursue the objectives, with policy formulations worked out with reference thereto, that the economist defines. Thus, governments may have their own "autonomous" objectives, which may well be malign or simply different from the economists' conventional, often utilitarian objectives. Thus, for instance, Niskanen (1971) models government decision-making as the outcome of the expenditure-maximizing behavior of government bureaucrats, while Brennan and Buchanan (1980) assume that the government attempts to maximize its surplus, defined as the excess of tax revenue over public expenditures. Again, even if governments are largely concerned with the welfare of the populace, they may be greatly constrained by the "directly unproductive profit-seeking" (DUP) activities of political pressure groups (see Bhagwati, 1982).

Hufbauer's argument in the BW volume against citizenship-based tax systems clearly reflects his fear that governments will abuse the power to tax citizens abroad. Although this is certainly a legitimate concern, it may be (as I discuss below) that the possible government abuses of their ability to tax emigrants are outweighed by the potential efficiency and equity gains.

20.4   The Schedular System: Income Tax Not Extended to Citizens Abroad

In light of the foregoing discussion, consider now the problems that a schedular income tax system would create in the optimal-income-tax framework. This system amounts to saying that a country faces potential emigration but cannot tax its citizens abroad.

This may not be a problem that needs analysis simply because countries on the schedular system need to know what their choice of income tax regime entails. It may also be that a schedular tax regime may be the only *feasible* policy option.

This may be because politically it may be impossible to shift to a global regime because of DUP-theoretic lobbying by current and potential emigrants. I have found, for example, that my continued advocacy of the global tax regime in LDCs typically arouses hostility from fairly well-placed and politically influential groups, since, with current migration patterns, nearly each member of most of these groups has *someone* abroad and hence they see a stake in international migration and an immediate personal loss from the adoption of the global tax regime. Equally, the expatriate LDC community, often radical in its aspirations and vociferous in its demands for foreign aid and in its slogans of "self-reliance," finds it impossible to embrace the notion that it must make its own tax contribution to the revenues of the LDCs.

But the objection to the shift may also be because of problems with feasibility at an administrative level. Pomp, a well-known Professor of Tax

Law and formerly Director of the International Tax Program at Harvard, has examined the Filippino experience with its collection of tax revenues from citizens abroad in his contribution to the BW volume, and finds that there are serious difficulties because of the difficulty of devising suitable tax rolls and because of inadequate capacity for tax audits. Due to the current absence of bilateral tax treaties that permit sharing of tax information between the host countries and the Philippines, these difficulties cannot be obviated, even though the Filippino system is simple and consists essentially in piggybacking with surcharges of 1, 2, and 3 percent on foreign tax payments (and therefore, in principle, requires only knowing accurately the host-country tax returns of the Filippinos being assessed). If the global system is to be adopted widely, it will require entertaining reform in bilateral tax-information-sharing procedures, much as federal nations are beginning to see movement in that direction between constituent states. Of course, progress in reaching such bilateral arrangements will depend partly on the perceived desirability of the global tax system and the drawbacks of the schedular system.

Consider then the schedular tax system and how the nontaxation of citizens abroad will affect national well-being. Thus, consider the use of an income tax to raise national welfare by redistributing income between people with different productivities in work. Intuitively, the existence of a high propensity to migrate, if appropriately defined, should imply that the income tax creates a sizable distortion of migration decisions. Thus, a high propensity should significantly reduce the extent to which it is desirable to use income taxation as a tool for income redistribution. Surprisingly, a common implication of the papers in the BW volume is that this intuition is not always valid.

Thus Mirrlees (1982) constructs a simple model where the income tax distorts only migration decisions. The migration propensity of a given type of worker is defined as the elasticity of the supply of nonmigrants with respect to after-tax income in the home country. The main implication of the model is that "rather high tax rates are justifiable even if the propensity to migrate is quite large."

Bhagwati and Hamada (1982) and Wilson (1980, 1982a) take the standard closed-economy optimal income tax models, where education decisions or labor-leisure decisions are the focus, and extend them by including migration decisions. Unlike Mirrlees, they constrain the tax system to be linear, in which case the tax schedule can be completely described by two parameters, a constant marginal tax on income and a uniform poll subsidy. The particular way in which these papers characterize the impact of potential emigration on the optimal income tax is to ask how the optimal marginal tax depends on whether the home country is "open" or "closed" to migration. Intuitively, opening the country should lower the optimal marginal tax by introducing an additional cost associated with income redistribution, namely, the distortion of migration decisions. In Bhagwati and Hamada's (BH) model, where only high-income individuals are potential emigrants, the marginal migration distortion is measured by the revenue loss that occurs when these individuals emigrate in response to a rise in the marginal tax. Yet BH demonstrate that opening the borders to migration may actually raise the optimal marginal tax (see their proposition 3). Wilson (1982a) explains this possibility in terms of the "income effects" created by opening the borders, and then he shows that it depends on BH's particular definition of a "closed country." Under the alternative definition introduced by Wilson (1980), closing the country must raise the optimal marginal tax.[10] In any case, an important message of BH's result is that one cannot unambiguously state that the existence of potential emigration makes the optimal tax structure less egalitarian.

This message appears in a different form in Wilson (1980). By not restricting the innate "ability" levels possessed by potential emigrants, he is able to demonstrate that the effect of potential emigration on the optimal income tax depends on the distribution of ability levels among potential emigrants. Closing the country to migration will raise the optimal marginal tax if the people who migrate in response to a tax change possess sufficiently high or low ability levels. However, if these potential emigrants possess ability levels in some intermediate range, then closing the country will lower the optimal marginal tax. The basic argument is that these potential emigrants are individuals who bear a positive tax burden while residing in the home country, but will desire to emigrate if the marginal tax is reduced. Consequently, the marginal tax should be raised to encourage them to remain in the home country, where they pay taxes.

The issue of how *tax rates* differ between closed and open regimes should be distinguished from the issue of how *welfare* differs between these regimes. Whereas BH find that a country's marginal tax may rise or fall when the borders are opened to migration, they conclude unambiguously that national welfare, which is determined in their model by the utilities of the low-income workers remaining in the home country, must fall (see their proposition 1). The basic reasoning is that opening the borders allows high-income individuals to escape taxation and thereby worsens the trade-off between equity and efficiency as viewed by the home country.

20.5   The Global System and the Taxation of Citizens Abroad

Taxing the incomes of citizens abroad clearly provides a domestic government both efficiency and equity gains. The global system is definitely superior. But it is not clear how much of a tax burden emigrants should bear relative to residents.

Bhagwati and Hamada (1982) investigate this issue using a model where the decisions facing an individual are how much education to obtain and whether to emigrate. They prove that emigrants and residents should both be taxed nearly 100 percent, with educational expenses being subsidized nearly 100 percent. Their analysis does not indicate, however, how emigrants should be taxed relative to residents in more realistic models where (nearly) 100 percent taxation is undesirable. On the other hand, the significant contribution of Mirrlees (1982) is to investigate a model where incomes should be taxed significantly less than 100 percent because indivduals are able to engage in tax avoidance activities.

20.6   Extensions

There are several directions in which the theoretical research discussed in the previous sections could be usefully extended.

1. *Evasion.* One important extension would be to model explicitly some of the more important mechanisms, both legal and illegal, by which residents and emigrants avoid paying taxes. Doing so should provide a better understanding of the relative magnitudes of the "taxable work elasticities" that are central to the relative rates at which emigrants and residents should be taxed in the Mirrlees model.

Furthermore, it would then be possible to model the enforcement methods that the home government might use to reduce illegal tax evasion among both residents and emigrants. Presumably, such methods would be more effective at reducing tax evasion by residents rather than by emigrants.[11] If so, the implementation of an optimal enforcement program might tend to raise the optimal rates at which residents should be taxed relative to emigrants.

Even for closed economies, there has been almost no research on optimal taxation in the presence of illegal tax evasion (see Sandmo, 1981, for an exception). One problem with modeling tax evasion is that it is inherently a problem involving intertemporal decision-making. An individual's present and future probabilities of getting caught, along with the various penalties, will normally depend on his past history of tax evasion. Consequently, his present decision to evade taxes will partially depend on his expectations about future work or leisure activities; and this decision will also influence his future choices among these activities.

These intertemporal aspects are especially evident in the open-economy context, as is nicely illustrated by Pomp (1985) in his discussion of the "tax clearance system" used by the Philippines prior to 1973 to enforce its income tax on emigrant incomes. Without a "tax clearance certificate," a citizen could not leave the Philippines or, if already abroad, could be prevented from renewing his or her Philippines passport. Pomp observes that the tax clearance system was not viewed as a satisfactory device for dealing with tax delinquents. One problem is that it reduced the number of times the emigrants returned to the Philippines for visits, thereby diminishing the amount of revenue and foreign exchange generated by these visits. Furthermore, it may have induced a sizable number of emigrants to obtain DC citizenship, in which case their tax liability to the Philippines was entirely eliminatcd. To analyze appropriately the problems created by the tax clearance program, it is clear therefore that we would need a model that recognized the possibility that emigrants could return to the home country either permanently or for temporary visits.

The absence of intertemporal considerations is an important limitation of the models. The model presented by Bhagwati and Hamada (1982) does contain an intertemporal utility maximization problem where individuals must choose how many years of education to receive before they start earning income. But each individual earns all of his or her other lifetime income in only one location, at home or abroad. This limitation, which is shared by the other theoretical models in the BW volume, prevents consideration of many important legal and illegal tax avoidance methods.

One particularly important legal method by which an emigrant may avoid paying taxes to the home government is to change citizenship.[12] Presumably, the emigrant's ability and willingness to do so are positively related to the number of years spent abroad. This relation would appear to provide a pure efficiency argument for a tax system where the total tax burden faced by an emigrant declines with the number of years spent abroad.

2. *Remittances.* Another issue not addressed in existing theoretical models concerns the remittances that migrants make to friends and relatives remaining in the home country. If an emigrant's willingness to make these remittances is negatively related to his or her tax payments to the home

country, a significant "remittance elasticity" may provide a justification for taxing emigrants at relatively low rates.

Such empirical estimates as are available, however, suggest that remittances are an important characteristic of low-income rather than of high-income emigrants. If so, this may moderate in turn the remittance-led justification for taxing emigrants at relatively low rates, since most remittances may then be from emigrants who are below the tax-exemption limit and because the propensity to remit may be declining with taxable income.

20.7   Political Economy: DUP Activities and Malign Governments

A major characteristic that all the theoretical contributions here share is that they assume, with conventional economics, the assumption of a *benign* government. Such a government simply exists with a view to implementing the optimal or suboptimal tax policy whose consequences we analyze.

But a powerful new trend in economic theory rejects this view of the government and permits what are described variously as directly unproductive profit-seeking DUP (Bhagwati, 1982) activities. In this view, lobbying activities are addressed to enacting policies that improve one's income or are triggered by such policies. For example, a tariff may be enacted by tariff seeking; and the revenues from the tariff may trigger revenue seeking by lobbies. Again, the bureaucrats or politicians who are cogs in the governmental machine may act as a malign force, utilizing policies to garner rewards for themselves rather than for the populace. They may divert revenues to personal use to buy gold beds or to fatten their Swiss numbered accounts.

This latter viewpoint is expounded by Hufbauer in the BW volume. He claims that "malign states are far more commonplace than benign states." He goes on to argue that emigration may serve the important function of limiting the degree to which a government is able to exploit its citizens. To support his argument, he recalls Tiebout's (1956) famous insight that local public goods could be efficiently provided by communities within a country if people could costlessly migrate between communities until they obtained their most preferred tax-expenditure packages.

Extensive research in recent years has uncovered many reasons why decentralized decision making by local governments is likely to be inefficient, even if there are no impediments to labor mobility (see Bewley, 1981, for a survey). These negative results would seem to be applicable to the uncoordinated decision-making by national governments in the world economy. However, just as Tiebout's argument certainly contains an important grain of truth, so does the assertion that emigration opportunities between countries serve to make national governments more responsive to the preferences of the populace.

Presumably, a malign LDC government could use its ability to tax citizens working abroad to further its own objectives at the expense of the populace. Consequently, a DC government could appeal to the malign nature of most governments to justify not aiding LDCs in the collection of taxes on emigrant incomes. However, the case against taxing emigrants is far less clear-cut than it may appear at first, even if the assertion that governments are malign is accepted at face value. Thus, Bhagwati and Wilson (BW, 1989, "Overview") have constructed a model that demonstrates the utility of the global tax system even when governments are malign. The statement that governments are generally "malign" simply does not constitute a compelling argument against the global tax system.

Finally, it should be noted that under commonly accepted international law the income tax jurisdiction of the home country may be exercised by a malign government but simply cannot be enforced in the host-country courts. It is always open for citizens escaping malign countries to refuse to pay without legal harassment by the host country. The disturbing notion that somehow Picasso would have had to pay income taxes to Franco of Spain or that Idi Amin would chase Ugandans through the courts in New York is occasionally aired. But it has simply no foundation whatsoever.

20.8   Concluding Observations: The Harmonization Question

Evidently, the research reported here starts us on the road to an extension of the usual income tax theory to an open economy (where the openness implies international personal mobility). But it is only a beginning, and many problems, such as those that were already sketched above, will need to be modeled in turn.

I may conclude, however, by remarking on one further problem that is particularly important if only one country or subset of countries in the world economy proceeds to exercise tax jurisdiction on citizens abroad.

This is the problem of harmonization implied by the coexistence of different income tax systems. It is best illustrated by reference to the questions raised in the concrete case of the United States. Recall that in the United States (and the Philippines) the global income tax system that extends the income tax to citizens abroad is practiced. Other countries are on the "schedular" income tax system that does not.[13] For the United

States, this has meant a twofold problem, with consequent opposition to its global system from political lobbies preferring the schedular system.

1. Private U.S. citizens abroad, who are taxed on the basis of the global system, allege that they are unfairly taxed because nationals of other countries abroad (e.g., Frenchmen in Bangkok, alongside Americans) are not so taxed by their own governments and because nationals of the countries where they reside (e.g., Thais in Bangkok) are subject only to domestic taxes (e.g., the Thai income tax) that are equally borne by the U.S. citizens on top of such U.S. income tax as becomes applicable. Hence the intranational (*horizontal*) *equity* of the global system runs afoul of the international (*horizontal*) *equity* claims.

2. Also, once trade in goods and services is considered, the harmonization issue becomes one of otherwise distorting comparative advantage, and hence efficiency, in turn. If U.S. firms have to pay the U.S. income tax on U.S. citizens they employ abroad, whereas French firms employing Frenchmen abroad do not have to pay the French income tax, distortion of comparative advantage could easily follow. That is to say, French firms having to pay certain net-of-tax salaries for, say, Saudi construction contracts would then have a smaller real cost, ceteris paribus, than would U.S. firms competing for the same contracts. Of course, this model, unlike the models of personal income taxation in this volume, which are in the tradition of the classic papers of Mirrlees (1971) and Atkinson (1973), assumes that the incidence of the global tax system does not fall on the taxed individuals. It also assumes, in the stark version outlined above, that the French firms must hire Frenchmen and the U.S. firms must hire Americans: if the two were total substitutes, as they almost certainly are not for different reasons, the harmonization issue would disappear. This problem needs formal analysis but has certainly played a major role in the political economy of American income taxation. People such as Senator Proxmire, who accept the equity underlying the global system and argue that the café-crawling Americans in Paris ought to pay their share of American taxes instead of leaving the burden to be borne by the workers in Detroit, have traditionally been pitted against pressure groups such as corporations handling construction works abroad.[14]

Notes

This chapter was written while the author was on leave as Consultant to the World Bank during 1986–87. The World Bank does not accept responsibility for the views expressed herein, which are those of the author and should not be attributed to the World Bank or its affiliated organizations. The chapter was presented as a paper at the Tel-Aviv Conference on Public Finance, organized by Pinhas Sapir Center for Development, December 22–25, 1986. Thanks are due to John Wilson for his extensive collaboration on the substance of the latter parts of this paper. The research underlying this chapter was originally supported by a grant from the German Marshall Fund of the United States.

1. The escape of some from the income tax net, through outmigration and the use of the schedular system, was thus not modeled. "Closed" models nonetheless could have explored analytically similar issues by permitting nontaxability of a subset through evasion or avoidance. Alternatively, similar questions may arise in exploring federal models with local income tax jurisdictions.

2. For a synthesis and extension of the substantial literature on the welfare effects of (skilled) outmigration, see Bhagwati and Rodriguez (1976).

3. These and other difficulties emerged at the 1975 Bellagio Conference, where my tax proposal was discussed; cf. Bhagwati and Partington (1976).

4. The proceedings of that conference resulted in two companion volumes, one edited by me and the other jointly with a Professor of Law at the University of London, Martin Partington: Bhagwati (1976) and Bhagwati and Partington (1976). Also see the article by Oliver Oldman, the Learned Hand Professor of Law at Harvard, and Richard Pomp in the *Harvard International Law Journal* (Winter 1979) and Pomp's later article in the *Journal of International Law and Politics*, New York University (Winter 1985).

5. Eventually, as I note below, we have a "harmonization" issue here that the optimal-income-taxation type of modeling does not address.

6. The two systems are being treated here as "idealized" pure systems whereas, in practice, each tends to be compromised somewhat in the other's direction. Thus, Section 911 of the U.S. tax law now permits exemptions that constitute currently a noticeable leak from the global approach.

7. Citizenship does provide assurance of having access to these benefits at will, so that Hufbauer's argument is certainly overstated even if its premises are not challenged.

8. Utilitarianism may not be accepted, of course, as a decisive choice criterion by all. Thus, within international trade theory, since the early work of Harry Johnson (1965) and Bhagwati and Srinivasan (1969), for instance, it has long been customary to put "noneconomic" objectives alongside goods and services into the social utility function as arguments. Recently, nonutilitarian approaches have become even more fashionable, thanks to the impetus provided by Nozick's theory of rights.

9. Wilson notes, however, he means that if a country's income tax system maximizes national welfare, then it is likely to be inefficient from the viewpoint of

world welfare. By "inefficient," he means that there exists a change in the tax system, accompanied by lump sum transfers of income between countries, which raises every country's national welfare. The problem here is that it is difficult to imagine the correct international income transfers being implemented in the actual world economy.

10. Bhagwati and Hamada close the economy by allowing no individual to emigrate. Wilson (1980, 1982a), on the other hand, considers a closed economy to be formed by taking an open economy where emigration occurs freely, with its tax set optimally, and then imposing the constraint that no individual may change his residence in response to changes in the tax. This means, of course, that individuals who are emigrants (residents) in the optimal open economy remain so in the closed economy.

11. This need not be so, paradoxically, if bilateral cooperation on tax information makes evasion more difficult for emigrants while domestic tax enforcement continues for political and administrative reasons to be difficult.

12. Renunciation of citizenship and refusal to pay (thus making it extremely risky to return to one's home country in any way) are other alternatives to change of citizenship.

13. As noted earlier, these contrasts are not wholly pure. Thus, for example, the United States does not extend several exemptions (other than double-tax avoidance) to citizens abroad, and there are certainly restrictions in European systems on the definition of foreign residence that justifies exclusion from tax liability. The central thrust, and principles, of the two tax systems are very clear and different, however, in both cases.

14. For a historical review of this tussle, see Bhagwati and Wilson in the BW volume (1988, ch. 1).

References

Atkinson, A. B. 1973. How Progressive Should Income Tax Be? In M. Parkin (ed.), *Essays in Modern Economics*. London: Longmans.

Baumol, W. J. 1982. The Income Distribution Frontier and Taxation of Migrants, *Journal of Public Economics* 18: 343–362. Reprinted in Jagdish Bhagwati and John Wilson (eds.), *Income Taxation and International Mobility*. Amsterdam: North Holland, 1987.

Berry, R., and R. Soligo. 1969. Some Welfare Aspects of International Migration, *Journal of Political Economy* 77.

Bewley, T. 1981. A Critique to Tiebout's Theory of Local Public Expenditures. *Econometrica* 49: 713–740.

Bhagwati, Jagdish N. 1972. The Loss of Innocence: U.S. in the Nixon Era. *The Daedalus*. American Academy of Arts and Sciences, Cambridge, MA.

Bhagwati Jagdish N. (ed.). 1976. *The Brain Drain and Taxation II: Theory and Empirical Analysis.* Amsterdam: North Holland.

Bhagwati, Jagdish N. 1977. The Brain Drain: International Flow Accounting, Compensation, Taxation and Related Proposals," Paper for the Intergovernmental Group of Experts Meeting, UNCTAD, Geneva. Also in J. Bhagwati (ed.), *Essays in Development Economics: Dependence and Interdependence,* vol. 1. Oxford: Basil Blackwell, 1985, ch. 19.

Bhagwati, Jagdish N. 1980. North–South Dialogue: An Interview. *Third World Quarterly* (April).

Bhagwati, Jagdish N. 1982. Directly Unproductive Profit-Seeking (DUP) Activities. *Journal of Political Economy* 90: 988–1002.

Bhagwati, J., and W. Dellalfar. 1973. The Brain Drain and Income Taxation. *World Development* 1, no. 1.

Bhagwati, J., and K. Hamada. 1974. The Brain Drain, International Integration of Markets for Professionals and Unemployment: A Theoretical Analysis. *Journal of Development Economics* 1, no. 1. Reprinted in J. N. Bhagwati (ed.), *The Brain Drain and Taxation II: Theory and Empirical Analysis.* Amsterdam: North Holland, 1976.

Bhagwati, J., and K. Hamada. 1982. Tax Policy in the Presence of Emigration. *Journal of Public Economies* 18: 291–318. Reprinted in Jagdish Bhagwati and John Wilson (eds.), *Income Taxation and International Mobility.* Amsterdam: North Holland, 1987.

Bhagwati, J., and Martin Partington (eds.). 1976. *Taxing the Brain Drain: A Proposal, vol. I.* Amsterdam: North Holland.

Bhagwati, J., and Carlos Rodriguez. 1976. Welfare-Theoretical Analyses of the Brain Drain. Also in J. N. Bhagwati (ed.), *The Brain Drain and Taxation II: Theory and Empirical Analysis.* Amsterdam: North Holland, 1976, ch. 5.

Bhagwati, Jagdish, and T. N. Srinivasan. 1969. Optimal Policy Intervention to Achieve Non-economic Objectives. *Review of Economic Studies* (October).

Bhagwati, Jagdish, and John Wilson (eds.). 1989. *Income Taxation and International Mobility* Cambridge: MIT Press.

Brennan, G., and J. M. Buchanan. 1980. *The Power to Tax.* Cambridge: Cambridge University Press.

Grubel, Herbert, and A. Scott. 1966. The International Flow of Human Capital. *American Economic Review* (May).

Hamada, K. 1975. Efficiency, Equity, Income Taxation, and the Brain Drain: A Second Best Argument. *Journal of Development Economics* 2: 281–287. Argument reprinted in J. N. Bhagwati (ed.), *The Brain Drain and Taxation II: Theory and Empirical Analysis* Amsterdam: North Holland, 1976, ch. 10.

Hufbauer, G. C. 1987. The State, the Individual and the Taxation of Economic Migration. In Jagdish Bhagwati and John Wilson (eds.), *Income Taxation and International Mobility*. Cambridge: MIT Press, 1989.

Johnson, H. G. 1965. The Economics of the "Brain Drain": The Canadian Case. *Minerva*.

Johnson, H. G. 1967. Some Economic Aspects of Brain Drain. *Pakistan Development Review* 3.

McCulloch, Rachel, and Janet L. Yellen. 1976. Consequences of a Tax on the Brain Drain for Unemployment and Income Inequality in the Less Developed Countries. Also in J. N. Bhagwati (ed.), 1976, *The Brain Drain and Taxation II: Theory and Empirical Analysis*. Amsterdam: North Holland, 1976, ch. 8.

Mirrlees, J. A. 1971. An Exploration in the Theory of Optimal Income Taxation. *Review of Economic Studies* 38: 175–208.

Mirrlees, J. A. 1982. Migration and Optimal Income Taxes. *Journal of Public Economics* 18: 319–342. Reprinted in Jagdish Bhagwati and John Wilson (eds.), *Income Taxation and International Mobility*. Cambridge: MIT Press, 1989.

Niskanen, W. 1971. *Bureaucracy and Representative Government*. Chicago: Aldine-Atherton.

Oldman, Oliver, and Richard Pomp. 1975. The Brain Drain: A Tax Analysis of the Bhagwati Proposal. *World Development* 3.

Oldman, Oliver, and Richard Pomp. 1979. Tax Measures in Response to the Brain Drain. *Harvard International Law Journal* 20(1).

Pomp, Richard D. 1985. The Experience of the Philippines in Taxing Its Nonresident Citizens. *Journal of International Law and Politics* 17, 2: 245–286. Reprinted in Jagdish Bhagwati and John Wilson (eds.), *Income Taxation and International Mobility*. Cambridge: MIT Press, 1989.

Sandmo, A. 1981. Income Tax Evasion, Labor Supply, and the Equity-Efficiency Tradeoff. *Journal of Public Economics* 15: 265–288.

Tiebout, C. M. 1956. A Pure Theory of Local Expenditures. *Journal of Political Economy* 64: 416–424.

Tobin, J. 1974. Notes on the Economic Theory of Expulsion and Expropriation. *Journal of Development Economics* 1, 1.

Wilson, J. D. 1980. The Effect of Potential Emigration on the Optimal Linear Income Tax. *Journal of Public Economics* 14: 339–353.

Wilson, J. D. 1982a. Optimal Linear Income Taxation in the Presence of Emigration. *Journal of Public Economics* 18: 363–380. Reprinted in Jagdish Bhagwati and John Wilson (eds.), *Income Taxation and International Mobility*. Cambridge: MIT Press, 1989.

Wilson, J. D. 1982b. Optimal Income Taxation and Migration: A World Welfare Point of View. *Journal of Public Economic* 18: 381–398. Reprinted in Jagdish Bhagwati and John Wilson (eds.), *Income Taxation and International Mobility*. Cambridge: MIT Press, 1989.

21   The West German *Gastarbeiter* System of Immigration

with Klaus-Werner Schatz and Kar-yiu Wong

Immigration systems are control systems. Governments attempt with their aid to restrict and direct the inflow of migrants. Some systems are ostensibly run on "noneconomic principles: as in the present U.S. case where "familial" and "refugee" considerations are much the most important. But other systems, such as the German *gastarbeiter* system, have been run explicitly on "economic" lines and thus directly invite economic analysis.

This paper is addressed to an economic analysis of the West German *gastarbeiter* (i.e., "guestworker" or foreign worker) system. Section 21.1 states the main features of this immigration system, with a view to defining the key institutional aspects that must determine the manner in which we must pose our econometric hypotheses. Section 21.2 then undertakes the analysis of cross-sectional industrywise utilization of foreign workers in Germany during the period 1964–65 to 1971–72: a period which is argued to be suited to such investigation. Section 21.3 analyzes a different question: Since West Germany's *gastarbeiters* come from different sources (i.e., Yugoslavia, Turkey, Greece, Italy, Portugal, and Spain in the main), what explains the resulting composition of immigrant-inflow into Germany?

21.1   The *Gastarbeiter* System: Key Features and Consequent Hypotheses

The most important aspect to note in analyzing international, as distinct from internal, migration is that the former is generally subject to controls whereas the latter is generally not. The analyst, therefore, has to grasp clearly the behavior of the government in regard to the control of the immigration flows. In analyzing issues such as the overall inflow, the destination-by-sector composition and the source-of-origin composition of immigrants, the precise forms of the immigration system are clearly critical since they must have a decisive impact on these outcomes.

Key Features of the *Gastarbeiter* System

The German *gastarbeiter* system, in the years of its operation until 1973 when major new restrictions were adopted in light of the difficult macro-economic situation, was devised and operated during a period of virtually full employment characterized by around 0.50 percent unemployment rate. It had, in consequence, the following important features: (1) the government did not impose prior limits (like in the U.S. system for immigrants) on the number of *gastarbeiters* that would be let in annually; (2) rather, provided there was no objection from unions and the local authorities, the employers could recruit *gastarbeiters* from foreign countries, so that the annual aggregate inflow was essentially an unplanned aggregate of firm-wise decisions; (3) the importation of *gastarbeiters* by the firms was then principally *via* recruitment abroad, with the aid of official recruiting offices in the major source countries; (4) the ability of *gastarbeiters* to shift employment away from the initial-recruitment position to other industries and regions was regulated by types of permit and length of stay and was by no means symmetric with the rights of native workers in that regard; and (5) German labor law forbade, in principle, the recruitment of foreign labor except at identical wages with native German labor in identical jobs.

While several writers have described the German *gastarbeiter* system in a way supportive of the critical description above, we might cite Mehrlaender (1979, 1980) in brief support. Thus, Mehrlaender (1980, pp. 77–78) writes:

The conclusion of the [Italy-German] agreement on recruitment was preceded, however, by consultation among relevant German agencies, including the Federal Government, representatives of the Federal Employment Agency, the employers and the trade unions. The employers were interested primarily in reaching a decision in principle to encourage recruitment of foreign workers. In contrast, the trade unions foresaw the danger that (nonunion) labor might be utilized to keep wages down, and, for that reason, demanded that foreign workers should be accorded the same rights with regard to wages and social benefits as their German counterparts. The unions reached agreement on this point with the Federal Government and the employers' representatives.

Mehrlaender (1979, pp. 149–150) further writes that:

Residence permits may stipulate geographic areas and time limits. At first, a residence permit is granted for one year only and is tied to designated employment... A foreigner, who has been in Germany, legally, for at least five years and is considered to have integrated himself into the economic and social life, is eligible to receive domicile permit (*Aufenthaltsberechtigung*). Once granted, the permit allows its holder to move within the country without restriction ... Work permits are issued by the Federal Labor Office (*Bundesanstalt für Arbeit*). All aliens intending to work in Germany need a work permit. There are two classes of work permits: a general permit, issued normally for one year and geared to the labor conditions prevailing, or to special needs of certain industries; and, there is a special work permit (*besondere Arbeitserlaubnis*), issued to aliens who have a steady employment record for the preceding five years, or who have been living in Germany legally for the last eight years or more, or who are married to a German citizen. This permit may carry a geographical limitation and is normally issued for five years.

Generally following the same steps in the recruitment procedures a German employer first notifies his nearest Employment Office (*Arbeitsamt*) about his manpower needs.... When no Germans are available, the request is routed to the Federal Labor Office in Nuremberg. From there, the appropriate German commission in a sending country is notified.

Implications of These Key Features: Hypotheses

Features 1–3 imply that, as long as there were "shortages" in the German economy for labour, and there were no problems of social unrest resulting from the final magnitude of foreign labor inflow, the government effectively operated with a quasi-open door, letting private firm-level decisions (motivated by joint employer–employee interests) determine the magnitude of the entry through the door.[1]

This interpretation of the *gastarbeiter* immigration system, combined with features (4) and (5) implies immediately that the "model" that applies in the German case is one where the level and the industrywise composition of immigrant labor are determined by internal "demand" considerations rather than, as in the free-migration models, by the interaction of supply *and* demand factors.

An idealized way to see the essence of this proposition is to consider figure 21.1. The foreign-labor supply curve is depicted as S_F, indicating the availability of labor at wage W_F. The domestic supply and demand curves for labor are S_D and D_D, respectively. (The domestic supply curve might well be made sharply inelastic at higher wages than $\overline{W}$ if we hypothesize that German labor supply "dried up" at that point.) If there were free immigration, YZ amount of foreign labour would come in and the wage would be W_F. If a simple immigration quota were set at QR, the wage would be $\overline{W}$ ($> WF$) and each immigrant would earn a "rent" of

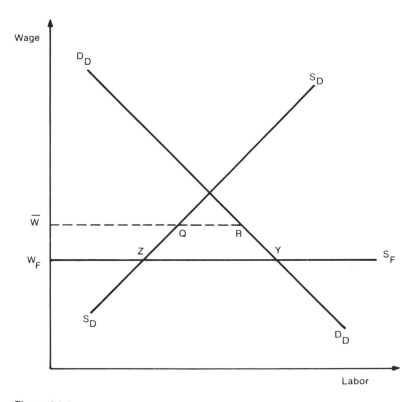

Figure 21.1

$(\overline{W} - WF)$. The German system can be taken to imply that the employers and employees settle on wage $\overline{W}$ and then recruit labor of quantity QR. Native *and* foreign labor get the same wage $\overline{W}$, as required by feature (5) of the system.[2] It is then evident that if the S_F curve moves up (but is below $\overline{W}$), it will have no effect on the level of German *gastarbeiter* recruitment and hence inflow: it will simply cut into the *gastarbeiters'* gain from entering Germany. In this precise sense, we have a "demand-determined" model of international immigration here.[3]

We thus hypothesize, in section 21.2, that cross-sectional differences among several sectors in the growth of their use of foreign relative to domestic labour during the decade l964–65 to 1971–72—a period whose choice we justify presently—reflect the cross-sectional differences in factors affecting the growth of demand for them and hence for labor.[4]

How does such a "demand-determined" immigration system work in regard to the source-composition of immigrants? Let us first note the factors why the results may diverge from those in the free-immigration models, noting next the factors that, however, lead to similar results. If all foreign workers in the German workplace must be paid the same wage, then one could argue that the employers may choose randomly, regardless of wage differences at origin. Therefore, at the plant or firm level, one may expect that, over time, the share of workers from different origins will converge toward the mean (i.e., $1/n$th if there are n sources). Correspondingly, we may expect that wage differences among alternative sources have no explanatory power; nor may we expect differences in work force size among alternative sources to be relevant if the choice of workers is truly random. In all these respects, the free-immigration models yield theoretically, as also in econometric studies (reviewed, among others, by Krugman and Bhagwati, 1976, to date), opposing conclusions. Wage (or income, current or permanent) differences at different origins do matter. Initial shares tend to diverge rather than converge: "one Turk leads to another," i.e., information and supportive networks enable those outside the immigration barriers to get inside. And larger work forces at an origin, ceteris paribus, must also imply (like lower wages) a greater inflow into a destination.

But the German model of immigration, once we allow for active recruiting by firms, could still generate results similar to the free-immigration models. Suppose that lower wage levels and larger work forces imply a relatively greater supply of potential recruits to choose from. Since labor is not homogeneous, it may well be that a better selection of recruits will be available where the pool of applicants is larger. Again, while the information network argument may not hold in the recruitment model, it is possible that firms may prefer to hire from the same source as before since the costs of managing workers primarily speaking foreign languages and with specific cultural attributes will increase with the number of sources tapped. As it happens, our results (section 21.3) support the hypothesis that the recruitment model of German immigration seems to produce, on balance, source-patterns similar to, rather than different from, those we would expect from the free-immigration models.

Choice of Period 1964–65 to 1971–72

The choice of period for analysis is usually dictated in analyses such as ours by the availability of matching data on different variables. In the present case, we have lack of necessary data on the employment of foreigners for the years 1973–76 because the Federal Office introduced a new registra-

tion system in 1973 for foreigners and adopted a new industrial classification, so that employment figures for foreign workers by industry were
published again, beginning in 1977 only, and leaving us with data only by
broad sectors for 1973–76. Effectively, therefore, we are confined to continuous industrywise data only up to 1971–72.

However, there is also good and indeed decisive reason to confine our
period to before 1973. For, in November 1973, the German *gastarbeiter*
system effectively changed in the restrictive direction. Thus, Mehrlaender
(1980, p. 79) writes:

Until 1973, the Bonn government had left employment of foreign citizens almost
entirely to regulation by market forces. The recession beginning at the end of
1973, exacerbated by the oil crisis with its accompanying mass unemployment,
caused the FRG [Federal Republic of Germany] to abandon the policy of entrusting
the recruitment of - foreign workers to the requirements of industry. A decision to
halt recruitment came into force at the end of November 1973, and this approach
has been maintained to the present. The continued unfavorable situation of the
labor market is the most obvious reason for the current policy.

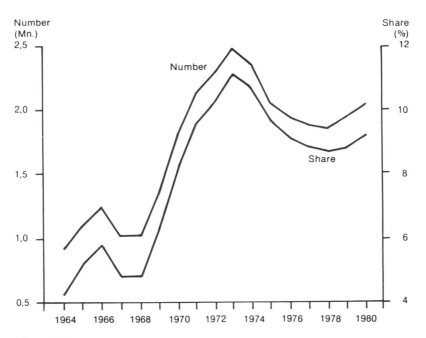

Figure 21.2a
Number and share of foreign wage earners in total wage earners in the Federal Republic
of Germany, 1964–80.

These changes are evident in figure 21.2b where, after 1973, the growth of *gastarbeiters* in Germany virtually ceases, the new (gross) *gastarbeiter* inflow reduces to a fraction, and the foreign population also stabilizes.

It follows therefore that one should expect the underlying model explaining industrywise cross-sectional utilization of *gastarbeiters* to change after 1973. With the break of such importation since 1973, changes in foreign labor utilization by different sectors would represent virtually reallocations, by and large, of a given foreign labor force rather than, as in the pre-1973 period, largely differential net imports of foreign labor. In fact, our attempts at treating the period 1964–65 to 1979–80 as one period for analysis in section 21.2 yielded no results of significance whereas separating the period into two and considering only the earlier period 1964–65 to 1971–72 yielded significant and plausible results, underlining the relevance of our foregoing argument.

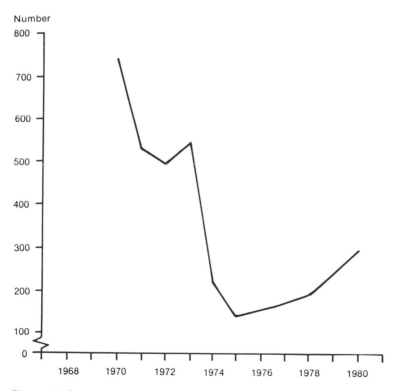

Figure 21.2b
Number of foreign workers entering the Federal Republic of Germany, 1968–80 (in thousands).

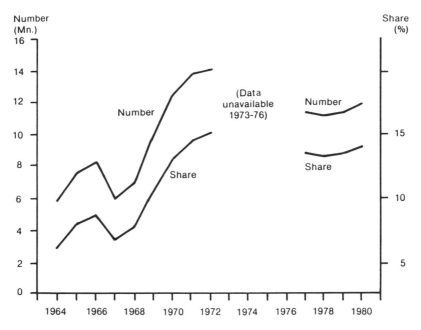

Figure 21.2c
Number and share of foreign wage earners in total wage earners in manufacturing sectors in the Federal Republic of Germany, 1964–80.

21.2 The Growth of *Gastarbeiters* in Germany: A Cross-Sectional Analysis of German Industries

The *gastarbeiter* system, as described in section 21.1, makes it plausible for us to test the hypothesis that, cross-sectionally for "industries" utilizing foreign labor, *the rate of growth* of such labor utilization would be largely determined by differential growth in their demand.

We therefore used, as our explanatory variables, the *change* in the degree of protection (both nominal and effective) and the rate of growth of value of output. The reason for including both variables, even though one might think that the output effect would fully capture the effect of the change in the degree of protection, is simply that the period is sufficiently short for the output change of protection change not to have worked itself out and the "signaling" effect of the protection change therefore provides added explanatory power: as in fact the econometric results underline. Besides, profitability of additional hiring seems to be better captured by the change in the *value* of output, rather than in real output: as again our results indicate.

We also hypothesized that the growth rate of foreign labor utilization, given the demand factors, would tend to vary inversely with the capital-intensity, especially with capital defined to include skills or human capital:[5] the search for foreign labor could be balanced in capital-intensive activities by search for capital-using and labor-saving techniques.

We used a 26-sector industry classification, set forth in column (2) of table 21.1. Of these, we had to omit sector 54–58 because protection data for it were not available. Sector 33 was also omitted as it is already included in sectors 26–27 and 34. Columns (3) and (5) give the estimated nominal rates of protection, whereas columns (4) and (6) give the estimated effective rates of protection for these sectors for 1964 and 1972, respectively. Columns (7)–(9) and columns (10)–(12) give the capital-intensity data for 1964–65 and 1971–72, respectively. Finally, columns (13) and (14) give the value-of-production data for 1964–65 and 1971–72, respectively.

Table 21.2, in turn, contains the data on foreign workers, again by our industrial classification, and on total employment within which they are embedded, as also on the source-breakdown by the principal countries of origin, for 1964–65 and 1971–72. We should add that these sectors contain virtually 60 percent of total foreign workers in Germany during 1964–72.

We present two main regression results, eqs. (1) and (2),[6]

$$\frac{\Delta F}{F} = 113.384 + 0.7901 \frac{\Delta P}{P} + 3.3599 \Delta T_n - 0.8989k,$$
$$(7.9566) \ (5.6878) \qquad (1.2467) \qquad (-4.4748)$$

$$R^2 = 0.6698, \qquad \text{adj. } R^2 = 0.6203, \qquad \text{SER} = 25.012, \tag{1}$$

$$\frac{\Delta F}{F} = 112.889 + 0.7044 \frac{\Delta P}{P} + 2.4347 \Delta T_e - 0.8307k,$$
$$(8.8853) \ (6.1163) \qquad (1.8075) \qquad (-4.3027)$$

$$R^2 = 0.6942, \qquad \text{adj. } R^2 = 0.6483, \qquad \text{SER} = 24.074, \tag{2}$$

where F is the number of foreign workers, P is the output of each industry (in 1,000 DM), T_n is the nominal tariff rate (in percent), T_e is the effective tariff rate (in percent), k is the capital (physical-plus-human)–labor ratio (in 1,000 DM per employee) and Δ represents the first difference in the relevant variable. All rates of change are expressed in percent.

Equation (1) uses the change in nominal protection, whereas eq. (2) uses the change in effective protection but otherwise they are identical. Equation (1), with an $R^2 = 0.67$, and with all estimated coefficients significant,[7]

Table 21.1
Industrywise nominal and effective rates of protection, capital-intensity and production, several years during 1964−65 and 1971−72 (− 1: missing value).

Industry (1)	(2)	Nominal and effective traiff protection			
		1964		1972	
		Nominal (3)	Effective (4)	Nominal (5)	Effective (6)
09−11	Chemical industry[b]	14.3[f]	18.7[f]	11.2[f]	14.4[f]
12−13	Plastics manufacturing[c]	17.0	18.0	11.8	8.4
14	Stone, sand, and clay industry	7.9	11.5	3.3	3.7
15	Fine ceramics	14.9	16.1	9.4	9.9
16	Glass industry	17.5	21.8	9.5	11.1
17−18	Iron and steel industry[d]	7.1	25.9	5.1	18.3
19	Foundries	11.9	19.1[g]	7.7	12.1[g]
20−22	Steel drawing, cold rolling mills, and steel forging	10.2	6.7	7.6	7.7
23−25	Constructional engineering and light metal products	7.7	5.0	4.0	1.4
26−26	Mechanical engineering	9.6	3.5	6.2	2.5
28−30	Manufacture of road vehicles[e]	15.9	12.6	8.6	5.8
31	Shipbuilding	0.8	− 13.4	0.4	− 10.1
32	Aircraft and aerospace industry	4.0	− 3.0	3.2	− 0.9
33	Office and data processing machines	− 1.0	− 1.0	− 1.0	− 1.0
34	Electrical engineering	11.5	8.0	7.2	4.5
35−36	Precision engineering, optics, clocks, and watches	11.5	6.6[i]	7.9	4.5
37	Metal products, n.e.s.	13.1	12.9	7.2	5.6
38−29	Musical instruments, toys, and jewellery	13.0	10.2	9.3	6.9
40−42	Sawmills, timber processing, and wood processing	13.4	19.8	7.3	10.5
430	Pulp, paper, and paperboard	12.6	41.3	9.4	29.6
431−433	Paper manufactures	17.0	24.8	13.2	19.9
44	Printing	8.8	8.4	6.1	5.3
45−46	Leather and letherproducts	16.3	24.1	7.5	9.9
47−51	Textiles	12.7	24.0	10.3	20.8
52−53	Clothing	16.5	22.3	14.0	20.7
54−58	Food, drink, and tobacco	− 1.0	− 1.0	− 1.0	− 1.0
09−58	Manufacturing	11.0	14.8	7.4	7.7

Sources: Columns (3)−(6): Juergen B. Donges, Gerhard Fels, Axel D. Neu, Protektion und Branchenstruktur des westdeutschen Wirtschaft Kieler Studien No. 126 (Tubingen, 1975); columns (7)−(12): Rolf Krengel et al., Produktionsvolumen und -potential, Produktionsfaktoren des Bergbaus und des Verarbeitenden Gewerbes in der Bundesrepublik Deutschland (Berlin, var. iss.); columns (13)−(14): Statistisches Bundesamt, Fachserie 4, Reihe 4.1, Beschaftigung, Umsatz u.a. der Unternehmen und Betriebe im Bergbau und Verarbeitenden Gewerbe, var. iss.—Own calculations and estimates.
a. The industry classification follows the German SYPRO classification. However, the deviations in notes b−j below must be noted.

Table 21.1 (continued)

Physical, human and total capital-intensity (DM per employee)							
1964–65			1971–72			Production (1,000 DM)	
Physical (7)	Human (8)	Total (9)	Physical (10)	Human (11)	Total (12)	1964–65 (13)	1971–72 (14)
92,871	42,263	135,134	122,682	86,625	209,307	44,524,609	01,523,709
27,161	18,706	45,867	37,916	41,061	78,977	8,090,679	18,643,630
54,147	19,679	69,826	67,455	35,595	103,050	11,568,410	21,514,808
22,824	11,123	33,947	31,286	37,672	68,958	1,890,850	2,393,930
28,674	20,753	49,467	45,714	49,843	95,557	2,970,958	5,331,522
75,996[i]	27,024[i]	103,020[i]	98,444[i]	61,217[i]	159,661[i]	26,592,498	40,417,553
35,927[g]	19,732[g]	55,659[g]	48,323	54,980	94,283	5,233,577	7,163,998
48,830	19,813	68,643	61,980	37,888	99,868	9,423,677	13,193,073
17,780	27,696	45,456	23,075	57,727	80,802	7,733,533	13,016,374
27,709	26,112	53,821	31,221	57,361	88,582	36,788,657	70,024,026
48,344	30,409	76,753	53,295	57,330	110,625	25,859,821	61,210,000
41,414	35,743	77,157	43,103	74,821	117,924	2,589,237	4,492,267
15,945	35,822	31,767	19,181	86,729	107,910	916,432	2,775,422
− 1[j]	− 1[j]	− 1[j]	38,056	80,565	118,621	− 1[j]	5,210,474
23,617	22,836	46,453	28,689	52,438	81,127	30,038,575	61,817,384
19,357	18,287	37,644	21,184	36,611	57,795	3,670,559	7,896,087
22,682	15,293	37,575	34,665	36,439	71,104	14,308,420	21,867,433
12,324	9,817	22,141	29,957	26,877	50,834	1,725,240	3,217,332
27,463	14,698	42,161	34,437	31,912	66,349	11,223,418	22,289,501
78,952	21,781	100,733	98,197	50,705	148,902	4,177,576	5,827,597
22,769	10,891	33,660	38,463	38,678	74,141	4,796,463	6,203,161
32,170	17,056	45,226	38,098	48,296	86,394	6,073,305	10,145,127
16,304	16,875	33,179	28,020	36,818	64,818	5,310,667	6,368,747
33,207	13,530	46,737	46,067	31,733	77,820	20,356,673	27,166,865
10,742	3,938	14,680	12,834	11,156	23,990	11,550,085	17,186,636
68,923	14,072	82,995	79,108	26,722	105,830	51,472,360	86,150,801
38,641	20,884	59,525	48,891	47,362	96,253	349,886,379	631,897,003

b. Including mineral oil refineries.
c. Including rubber and asbestos industry.
d. Including nonferrous metal industry.
e. Including repair.
f. Excluding mineral oil refineries.
g. Excluding nonferrous metal foundries.
h. Excluding clock industry.
i. Excluding nonferrous metal industry.
j. Included in items 26–27 and 34.

Table 21.2
Employment of foreign workers: Total and source composition, 1964–65 and 1971–72
(− 1: missing value).

Industry (1)	1964–65 Total employment (2)	Foreign employment, of which from Total (3)	Turkey (4)	Yugoslavia (5)	Italy (6)	Greece (7)	Spain (8)	Portugal (9)
09–11	626,000	30,200	1,217	− 1	8,508	7,381	5,198	162
12–13	259,500	24,086	1,737	− 1	5,356	8,053	5,006	364
14	303,000	31,683	3,661	− 1	15,543	3,521	4,182	282
15	78,000	8,996	1,013	− 1	1,730	3,250	1,977	63
16	90,500	9,666	1,003	− 1	3,989	1,463	1,310	457
17–18	570,000	23,052	4,584	− 1	3,851	4,513	4,504	484
19	166,500	20,839	3,132	− 1	7,703	3,245	4,300	270
20–22	275,500	21,279	2,809	− 1	6,557	5,744	3,837	483
23–25	226,000	15,083	2,123	− 1	3,756	1,479	2,184	185
26–27	1,117,000	75,463	8,840	− 1	17,904	12,421	14,658	538
28–30	707,000	64,247	10,590	− 1	18,437	13,474	10,436	472
31	78,500	4,344	1,561	− 1	540	170	718	318
32	32,000	1,001	154	− 1	103	88	105	6
33	73,000	− 1	− 1	− 1	− 1	− 1	− 1	− 1
34	1,099,500	72,182	5,953	− 1	15,108	20,635	11,334	296
35–36	176,500	11,074	633	− 1	2,816	2,221	2,115	65
37	395,000	61,835	3,588	− 1	19,737	16,279	13,381	489
38–39	96,000	2,712	158	− 1	839	458	552	12
40–42	446,500	27,248	2,739	− 1	10,165	4,532	4,351	279
430	82,500	5,791	236	− 1	1,839	1,925	1,070	53
431–433	146,500	10,754	550	− 1	3,415	2,770	1,821	83
44	249,000	6,505	273	− 1	1,295	1,181	921	29
45–46	206,000	13,963	806	− 1	3,718	2,765	3,277	27
47–51	612,500	64,124	5,218	− 1	19,412	17,009	10,297	951
52–53	478,500	25,346	2,190	− 1	6,409	4,287	4,090	109
54–58	806,000	37,848	1,830	− 1	8,892	6,683	9,898	211
09–58	9,324,000	669,315	66,592	− 1	187,616	145,541	121,516	6,681

Table 21.2 (continued)

1971–72

| Total employment (10) | Foreign employment, of which from | | | | | | |
	Total (11)	Turkey (12)	Yugoslavia (13)	Italy (14)	Greece (15)	Spain (16)	Portugal (17)
694,000	55,449	7,646	5,368	12,850	10,828	5,878	1,247
325,500	61,637	14,597	7,312	10,270	12,983	6,735	3,387
272,000	43,454	12,520	7,266	11,141	2,637	3,775	1,889
67,500	14,221	3,408	1,116	2,367	3,226	1,899	538
97,500	17,878	4,497	1,825	4,437	1,790	1,532	1,751
462,000	39,537	16,490	3,150	4,406	5,167	3,873	1,848
14,450	30,152	10,354	3,012	7,170	3,164	3,315	1,159
263,000	36,496	10,107	4,927	7,502	6,577	3,300	1,847
187,000	33,990	6,886	11,548	4,732	2,291	2,211	539
1,240,750	173,741	39,096	38,747	26,676	22,129	16,355	3,360
852,500	142,252	39,404	20,205	26,612	24,470	13,268	3,430
72,500	11,820	5,914	1,721	725	246	759	719
41,000	2,767	311	202	269	364	290	15
99,500	−1	−1	−1	−1	−1	−1	−1
1,220,250	182,593	37,769	39,171	25,175	36,998	12,884	1,956
191,000	25,869	3,835	6,552	5,454	3,674	2,163	523
391,000	13,584	25,801	19,328	31,933	28,851	16,257	4,121
92,000	6,554	1,239	1,262	1,610	979	546	62
406,000	55,328	13,697	12,147	11,082	5,919	5,375	1,793
71,000	12,237	1,969	1,839	2,764	3,284	1,338	403
154,000	22,726	4,594	2,759	5,132	4,726	2,277	629
264,000	16,154	2,109	2,167	3,087	3,201	1,358	163
156,500	22,987	4,171	4,420	4,517	3,391	3,052	259
516,000	117,581	31,934	14,623	23,606	19,998	9,207	8,218
419,500	55,033	12,943	9,350	12,151	7,914	3,349	1,265
821,000	81,002	15,812	15,166	12,549	10,916	12,289	2,665
9,422,500	1,397,317	327,019	235,179	258,211	225,717	133,280	43,778

shows that the rate of change of foreign workers ($\Delta F/F$) between 1964–65 and 1971–72 is positively related to the change in production ($\Delta P/P$) and (not significantly) to the change in nominal protection (ΔT_n) but inversely related to overall capital-intensity (k). Equation (2) represents even a marginally better fit, with $R^2 = 0.69$. This equation is also better since the shift to the more appropriate measure of protection, i.e., effective protection, makes the estimated coefficient (2.43) almost significant at the 5 percent level. Therefore, eqs. (2) clearly dominates, conceptually and by statistical criteria, eq. (1) and must be preferred.

The inverse relationship to overall capital-intensity may be discussed further. It presupposes that, the more capital-intensive an industry, the more it will respond to growing demand by economising on labor-use rather than by importing foreign labor, ceteris paribus, i.e., there should be a positive relationship between change in the degree of capital-intensity and capital-intensity in the data. There is, in fact, empirical support for this relationship. For our data, we estimate

$$\Delta k 17.121 + 0.3569k,$$
$$(4.2769)\ (5.5063)$$

(3a)

$$R^2 = 0.5795, \qquad \text{adj. } R^2 = 0.5604, \qquad SER = 8.5746,$$

where $k = 1000$ DM (human + physical) per employee. Other measures of capital-intensity show the same relationship:

$$\Delta k_p = 2.3976 + 0.2312k_p,$$
$$(1.2156)\ (4.7921)$$

(3b)

$$R^2 = 0.5107, \qquad \text{adj. } R^2 = 0.4885, \qquad SER = 5.037,$$

$$\Delta k_h = 7.6314 + 0.9123k_h,$$
$$(2.8052)\ (7.5466)$$

(3c)

$$R^2 = 0.7214, \qquad \text{adj. } R^2 = 0.7087, \qquad SER = 5.279,$$

where k_p is the physical capital-labor ratio and k_h is the human capital–labor ratio.

A word on what we did *not* find is in order as well. We could not find evidence that differential changes in the availability of domestic workers or their cost as measured by real wages had an impact on the demand for, and hence importation of, foreign labor. Using the real wage rate (W) obtained by deflating by the German CPI and domestic employment (D) for each sector, we obtained the best regressions as follows:

$$\frac{\Delta F}{F} = 158.072 + 0.3798 \frac{\Delta P}{P} + 1.9165\Delta T_n - 0.9628k$$
$$\phantom{\frac{\Delta F}{F} =} (3.6131) \ (1.0705) \phantom{\frac{\Delta P}{P}} (0.6218) \quad (-4.5360)$$

$$ -0.1091 \frac{\Delta w}{w} + 1.0596 \frac{\Delta D}{D},$$
$$ (-0.1313) \phantom{\frac{\Delta w}{w}} (1.3615)$$

(4a)

$$R^2 = 0.7070, \quad \text{adj. } R^2 = 0.6256, \quad \text{SER} = 24.83,$$

$$\frac{\Delta F}{F} = 149.405 + 0.4328 \frac{\Delta P}{P} + 1.5003\Delta T_e - 0.9090k$$
$$\phantom{\frac{\Delta F}{F} =} (3.4854) \ (1.1876) \phantom{\frac{\Delta P}{P}} (0.8012) \quad -4.2673)$$

$$ -0.1657\frac{\Delta w}{w} + 0.7791\frac{\Delta D}{D},$$
$$ (-0.2002) \phantom{\frac{\Delta w}{w}} (0.8390)$$

(4b)

$$R^2 = 0.7110, \quad \text{adj. } R^2 = 0.6308, \quad \text{SER} = 24.665.$$

The coefficients for the real wage rate and the domestic employment are not significant; besides, a rise in domestic employment should have been negatively related to the growth of the foreign labor force.[8]

Next, consistent with our emphasis that the German immigration system implies a "demand-determined" quota model, we could find no regressions that established a relationship between our dependent variable (or any variations therein) and the differential between the German wages and wages in the source countries of *gastarbeiter* origin. Moreover, we had been originally prepared to find, instead of the positive relationship between change in degree of protection and change in the growth of foreign labor force, a negative relationship as suggested by the hypothesis of Bhagwati (1982) and Sapir (1983) that the German government may have been more willing to let industries suffering from reduced tariff protection (under policy-dictated tariff changes as in the Kennedy Round) import more labour. Evidently, however, the government was *not* playing such a constraining role. As already indicated, the firm's decision to import labor was more or less a sufficient determinant of *gastarbeiter* inflow during the decade of our analysis, and this implied a positive, rather than a negative, relationship between the two variables.[9]

21.3   Source Composition of *Gastarbeiter* Inflow

Next, we analyzed the source composition of workers from five principal supplying countries: Turkey, Italy, Greece, Spain, and Portugal.[10] Again, the data for 24 sectors (excluding numbers 54–58) were analyzed as in eqs. (1) and (2) above. The hypothesis tested successfully was the following.

The precise variable chosen as the left-hand side variable in eq. (5), which was estimated, was θ_d which was the deviation from the mean (0.2) of the share of the incremental inflow of workers from each of the five source countries during the period 1964–65 to 1971–72.[11] Three right-hand side explanatory variables were explored: (1) θ_i, the deviation from the mean (0.2) of the share of workers from each country in the base year 1964–65; (2) θ_p, the deviation from the mean (0.2) of the share of the growth rate of population (as a proxy for the labor force) of each source country during the period 1964–65 to 1971–72; and (3) θ_w, the deviation from the mean of the wage rate in each country in 1971 (since we could not get reliable data for 1964).[12] After numerous trials, the best fit was yielded by the following equation:[13]

$$\theta_d = (0.8451\theta_p - 1.3161\theta_w,$$
$$\quad\quad (5.6035) \ (-3.7739)$$

$$\text{SER} = 0.2456.$$

(5)

The negative relationship between θ_w and θ_d, on the one hand, and the positive relationship between θ_p and θ_d, on the other hand, can be interpreted as indicating that where the relative wage is lower and the incremental size of the work force is larger in a source country, the potential pool of applicants available to recruiters of *gastarbeiters* will be higher and hence recruitment is likely to produce a better, more productive worker for the same (German) wage. However, confronted with the results of many trials, we had to discard the hypothesis that initial shares had any significant effect, positive or negative, on the source composition of *gastarbeiters*.[14] We should have liked to probe this further, at the firm level, but presently the *gastarbeiter* data are simply not available at that level.[15] At the present level of aggregation, however, this absence of any significant relationship between θ_i and θ_d does suggest a difference from the results for some free-immigration (rural–urban, internal migration) studies that indicate that initial migrant stocks from a source are positively related to new inflows owing to information networks.

Finally, we may remark that there is no inconsistency in principle between our findings that wage differences do not significantly influence the interindustrial *gastarbeiter* pattern whereas they do affect the source composition. Presumably, these are not substantial enough to make a difference in the former case and are swamped wholly by the direct demand factors such as rate of growth of output or change in protection, whereas they are substantial enough to affect the recruitment pool and thus get reflected in the statistical results for the latter case.

21.4   Concluding Observations

Our results suggest strongly that the econometric analysis of international immigration (quota) systems must reflect the institutional features that characterize them. These features vary, not merely across countries (e.g., the United States and West Germany) but also, as in the German case before and after 1972–73, within a country at different points of time. Again, this implies possible *differences* from the results expected and observed for the free-immigration studies relating to internal migration within countries, though the specific features of the quota-systems operated by international-immigration authorities can equally generate some *similarities* (as in section 21.3).

Notes

Thanks are due to German Marshall Fund Grant No. 1-34015 and the Ford Foundation for research support to Bhagwati in undertaking the analysis in this paper. Thanks are due to Joe Altonji, Andre Sapir, Jean Waelbroeck, and an anonymous referee for valuable comments and to Jungi Shiba for computational assistance.

1. The door was not fully open since immigrants could not freely walk in but had to be recruited to come into Germany.

2. A formal recruitment model is called for but is beyond the scope of the present paper. We also could formalize the possibility that, despite the law dictating feature 5, effective discrimination takes place against *gastarbeiter* job reclassification etc. For more analysis of these aspects, see Bhagwati (1982).

3. This precise and particular meaning and characterization of the concept of "demand-determined" model of international immigration, and its contrast with the usual internal models of migration, were explicitly discussed in Bhagwati (1979). The concept of demand-determined immigration has also been used by Michael Piore to imply instead a situation where firms in the country of immigration actively recruit labor.

4. Feature 4 assures, by reducing reallocative mobility within the country, that primary recruitment would tend to be somewhat correlated with the final sectoral destination of gastarbeiters over this period. But we do not have the longitudinal or other data to test this hypothesis properly.

5. Human capital has been measured, as originally suggested by Bhagwati (1964) and Kenen (1965), as the difference between an industry's actual wage and salary sum per worker and the reward for unqualified labor in the same industry.

6. As usual, the t-statistics are given in parentheses. The variance of $(\Delta F/F)$ is assumed to be dependent on $(1/F)^2$, i.e., the square of the reciprocal of the initial number of foreign workers. The heteroskedasticity in eqs. (1) and (2) is corrected by weighting the explanatory and dependent variables (including the constant term) with the initial number of foreign workers and estimating the equations with the weighted data by the ordinary least squares method. To investigate the sensitivity of eqs. (1) and (2) to the weighting procedure and the possibility of misspecification, the equations are repeated using the unweighted data. The results are reported as follows:

$$\frac{\Delta F}{F} = 121.151 + 0.5428 \frac{\Delta P}{P} + 6.8261\Delta T_n - 0.4719k,$$
$$\quad\quad (5.0831)\ (3.6724) \quad\quad (2.2494) \quad\ (-2.0883)$$

$$R^2 = 0.5301, \quad\quad \text{adj. } R^2 = 0.4596, \quad\quad \text{SER} = 28.903,$$

$$\frac{\Delta F}{F} = 103.992 + 0.4814 \frac{\Delta P}{P} + 2.8854\Delta T_e - 0.3137k,$$
$$\quad\quad (5.0394)\ (2.9858) \quad\quad (1.8741) \quad\ (-1.3793)$$

$$k^2 = 0.4991, \quad\quad \text{adj. } R^2 = 0.4240, \quad\quad \text{SER} = 29.839.$$

These equations are not significantly different from eqs. (1) and (2).

7. All estimates are significant at a 1 percent level, except that the estimated coefficient for ΔT_e in significant at 10 percent level and that for ΔT_n is not significant. The latter two were, however, included in the equation because we believe that they are important variables to explain the effects of protection on the inflow of foreign workers.

8. From a theoretical perspective, our demand-determined model suggests also that differential changes in productivity could affect the demand for all, and hence for foreign, labor. Unfortunately, we do not have the necessary estimates of total productivity change to test for this added variable's possible impact. If the variable does matter, its omission from our estimates will create bias in the estimated coefficients. However, we may argue that only the coefficient of the change in output will be biased since we hypothesize that the change in employment of foreign workers is negatively related to productivity increase and since the change in output is the only variable in eqs. (1) and (2) which is related (positively) to productivity. Furthermore, it follows that if we had indeed been able to manage to include the omitted variable in the regression equations, the coeffficients for the change in output would have been only larger, thus merely reinforcing our findings.

9. It has been suggested to us by Andrew Sapir that labor-intensive industries, exposed to external competition, could be getting both more protection *and* be importing more foreign labor. One key element of this hypothesis, however, is empirically refuted. Thus, we can find no significant relationship between labor-

intensity in an industry and change in the degree of its nominal and effective protection; the regression results can be obtained from the authors on request.

10. The data for Yugoslavia are not available for the early 1970s, so it had to be excluded from the analysis.

11. The deviations are altogether 96 in number since there are 24 sectors and five sources (of which one has to be dropped since it is not independent as the sum of all deviations must total to zero).

12. The wage data utilized were, therefore, the recorded average wage payments in *each* industry within each source country (e.g., Turkey) rather than identical (average) wages in that source country. This procedure implies, of course, that *gastarbeilers* are more likely to move internationally within the same industry—an assumption that may definitely make sense in a "recruitment" model of immigration as in the present case.

13. Estimated with a constant term, eq. (6) yielded a coefficient which was not significant and hence eqs. (6) was reestimated, dropping the constant term. Of course, all variables in the equation are in the deviation-from-the-mean form so that the summation (over all five source countries) of each variable is equal to zero and hence we should theoretically also expect the constant term to be insignificant.

14. It may be mentioned that, since 1968, Italian workers could come in freely under the EEC rules. However, it is widely believed that the bulk of the Italian inflow into Germany continued to take place subject to a job being first offered in Germany.

15. The importance of this further probing may be seen from one example. Assume that, in a two-firm industry, one firm (randomly) hires Turks initially and the other hires Greeks. Let the "Turkish firm" be bigger than the "Greek firm." Now, let each firm hire more of the same, for reasons spelled out in the text. So, the Greek firm hires more Greeks and the Turkish firm hires more Turks. But add now the assumption that all firms are on an expansion path which decelerates over time. Then, in a two-period model, a faster growth of the smaller Greek firm will suffice to lead to *converging* shares at the industry level in source-composition of *gastarbeiters*. Thus, at a (firm or plant) micro-level, the recruitment model may be working exactly like the free-immigration model but the industry-level data may suggest the opposite! Evidently, we must await micro-level data to test for this.

References

Bhagwati, J. N. 1964. The Pure Theory of International Trade: A Survey. *Economic Journal* (March). Reprinted in R. Feenstra (ed.), *International Factor Mobility: Essays in International Economic Theory*, vol. 2. Cambridge: MIT Press, ch. 59.

Bhagwati, J. N. 1979. The Economic Analysis of International Migration. Plenary lecture delivered to Nordisk Migrasjonsforskerseminar, Nordic Council of Ministers, Oslo, Norway. In R. Feenstra (ed.), *International Factor Mobility: Essays in International Economic Theory*, vol. 2. Cambridge: MIT Press.

Bhagwati, J. N. 1982. Shifting Comparative Advantage, Protectionist Demands, and Policy Response. In J. N. Bhagwati (ed.), *Import Competition and Response*. Cambridge: MIT Press, pp. 153–195.

Kenen, P. B. 1965. Nature, Capital and Trade. *Journal of Political Economy* 73, 5: 437–460.

Krugman, P., and J. N. Bhagwati. 1976. The Decision to Migrate. In J. N. Bhagwati (ed.), *The Brain Drain and Taxation*. Amsterdam: North Holland, pp. 31–51.

Mehrlaender, U. 1979. Federal Republic of Germany. In D. Kubal, U. Mehrlaender, and E. Gehmacher (eds.). *The Politics of Migration Policies*. New York: Center for Mugration Studies, pp. 145–162.

Mehrlaender, U. 1980. The "Human Resource" Problems in Europe: Migrant Labor in the Federal Republic of Germany. In U. Ra'anan (ed.), *Ethnic Resurgence in Modern Democratic States*. New York: Pergamon, pp. 77–100.

Sapir, A. 1983. Foreign Competition, Immigration and Structural Adjustment. *Journal of International Economics* 13.

22   Structural Adjustment and International Factor Mobility

In this paper, I forgo the temptation to produce a formal model. Instead, I choose to raise some pertinent theoretical and policy issues that relate to the interaction between trade in goods and international factor mobility in so far as it has bearing on the major theme of this conference: namely the question of "structural adjustment" in developed, open economies.

In section 22.1, the question of the response by such economies to the phenomenon of import competition (or, equivaiently, a shift of comparative advantage) is examined. I bring centrally into the picture the possibility of deploying changes in factor levels (through variations in controls on, and inducements to, labor immigration and direct investment). I consider how these changes, in turn, would influence the welfare, and hence the lobbying incentives, of different economic agents affected by the postulated import competition. This analysis thus brings into central focus a major aspect of the response to import competition: namely, that it is not confined by any means to tariff lobbying, as in recent formal models of political economy, but must be placed in the context of a wider menu of policy instruments available to assist the lobbying factors or industries Besides, the stress on this wider menu of instruments also suggests that there may be additional flexibility in making adjustment to import competition and that the adjustment possibilities may vary with the nature of the shift in comparative advantage.

In section 22.2, I wish to raise an altogether different kind of question, more directly policy oriented, that has come to the forefront of recent discussions on the future of the international trading system. The United States has been contending that free trade in goods, or effective and fair competition in trade and proper access to foreign markets, are not possible unless other trading countries also permit foreign investment to be freely made in their economies. The United States feels that, in the absence of a Code or GATT amendment on freer flows of direct investment, it is not able to compete freely and fairly abroad. The protectionist sentiment in the United States is therefore likely to be encouraged unless the merits of this novel argument are fully discussed and appropriate action, including the possible rejection of the U.S. contention on the basis of reasoned analysis, is taken. Such a protectionist setback would obviously compromise the "rule of law" under the GATT system that has overseen the postwar expansion of world trade, and hence further imperil the forces that have promoted structural adjustment in the trading countries in response to comparative advantage shifts.

22.1   Import Competition, International Factor Mobility, and Response

Formal Models of Response

Economists have approached the phenomenon of "structural adjustment," whether in advanced or in underdeveloped economies, from two very different viewpoints. On the one hand, there is a great deal of recent work on how governments *ought to* respond to the phenomenon of import competition. This draws upon the tradition where economists presume a benign government that is the custodian of national interest, often defined conventionally along the usual welfare-theoretic lines.[2] On the other hand, drawing on the tradition of political economy, which is aimed rather at explanation of what *will* happen, other economists have recently attempted to analyse the *actual* response of economies to the phenomenon of import competition.[3]

I find the latter approach the more useful to take here, and will concentrate therefore on delineating its principal features to date and then proceeding to extend it in the direction suggested in my introductory remarks. The general-equilibrium, trade-theoretic work in this area, which includes recent papers by Feenstra and Bhagwati (1982) and Findlay and Wellisz (1982), may be characterized in the following way.

1. Economic *agents* that will engage in lobbying are defined. In the Findlay-Wellisz model, these are the two specific factors in the two activities in the Jones-Neary model of sector-specific factors (often also christened the Ricardo-Viner model and also to be found in the work of Samuelson). The interests of those factors are in conflict since goods price changes affect them in an opposite manner. In Feenstra-Bhagwati, there is only one economic agent (that hurt by import competition) that engages in lobbying in a Heckscher-Ohlin-Samuelson (HOS) model.

2. The agents lobby to have a *policy* adopted or to oppose it. In both Findlay-Wellisz and Feenstra-Bhagwati, that policy is uniquely defined to be a *tariff*.

3. The "government," as an economic agent, is not explicit in Findlay-Wellisz. The cost-of-lobbying functions that postulate the tariff as a function of the lobbying resources spent in proposing and opposing a tariff are *implicitly* assuming a government that is subject to these opposing lobbying efforts. And whatever preferences the government has are reflected implicitly in the postulated function.[4] On the other hand, in Feenstra-Bhagwati, there is a *two-layer* government: the lobbying process interacts with one branch of government (e.g., the legislature, which in the United States reflects special interests very clearly) to enact a *lobbying tariff*. Another branch of the government (e.g., the president in the United States, who reflects more the general interest traditionally) then comes into the picture. It seeks to use the tariff revenues generated by the lobbying tariff to bribe the lobby into accepting a different, welfare-superior *efficient tariff*. This yields to the lobby, from the revenue bribe *plus* the earned income from the marketplace at the efficient tariff, the same income as from the lobbying tariff.[5]

These papers define rather well how the theoretical analysis of endogenous policymaking can be approached in the conventional manner of economic theory. By taking a simple set of political-economic assumptions, they manage to get a neat simple model working: exactly as good economic theory does. In fact, from a pedagogic viewpoint, the extension of the traditional $2 \times 2 \times 2$ HOS-type of trade theory model to an augmented $2 \times 2 \times 2 \times 2$ model, where two lobbies, plus capitalists and workers engage in tariff-seeking lobbying, would be a splendid exercise! It would imply combining, suitably and easily, elements from the Findlay-Wellisz and Feenstra-Bhagwati models.

But these models can be enriched in different directions. Of particular theoretical interest is the role of the government itself. Recall that the Feenstra-Bhagwati model postulates a rather sophisticated, and realistic, two-layer view of the government. It builds in *both* the view (taken exclusively in Findlay-Wellisz) that the government is "acted upon" by political lobbies and the tariff then becomes a function of the resources expended (presumably in financing reelection) by the respective lobbies *and* the view that the government acts so as to maximize a conventional social welfare function. Instead, one could well take, for example, the view sometimes propounded that the government will maximize its *revenue*, since that will maximize its patronage. If so, Johnson's classic analysis of maximum-revenue tariff yields, of course, in a conventional world where other economic agents are not engaged in lobbying, the politically-endogenous tariff.

More pertinent to my present theme, as also important in reality, is the necessity to extend the analysis rather on the dimension of the policy instruments for which the economic agents can lobby in response to import competition. Thus, as a supplement to tariffs, I shall consider policy instruments in regard to international factor and technological flows. Without formally incorporating them into a model that endogenously yields the equilibrium choice or policy mix of instruments in response to import competition, I shall simply focus on the *preferences* that different economic agents could have between these instruments. Such analysis can throw some light on the incentives for lobbying for the adoption of different policies by the government and hence can yield the necessary insights into why certain policy options, rather than others, emerge as actual responses to import competition.[6]

Allowing International Flows of Labor, Capital, and Technology

In defense of the following analysis, I must stress that most countries exercise immigration controls, so it is, indeed, an act of governmental policy that broadly determines labor inflows into a country. Hence, it is realistic to assume that this is a policy that can be the target of lobbying. The flow of direct investment, in turn, is controlled by many countries: Japan, Canada, and France are among the advanced countries that have fairly strict policies in this regard. Hence, I need not apologize for not making the customary "trade-theoretic" assumptions. These hypothesize *full* international factor mobility of one factor on the other in response to factor reward differentials and then solve for the effects of a shift in comparative advantage in this context; that model is not really relevant.

The Nature of Shifts in Comparative Advantage and Response Options
Drawing on recent experience in Western Europe and the United States, I further like to think of shifts in their comparative advantage as occurring primarily at two ends of the goods spectrum: (1) the traditional, *senescent* labor-intensive industries such as large parts of textiles, shoes, and footwear. There, the newly industrialized countries, NICs (or SOUTHNICs as

I call them) have acquired the more-or-less given know-how and have HOS advantages in these activities, and (2) the technologically progressive, often capital-intensive, modern *Schumpeterian* industries at the other end of the spectrum. There the shift in comparative advantage is occurring from more rapid and effective technical progress abroad: especially in Japan, whose considerable import dependence combined with relatively phenomenal growth result in a need and ability to export the products of her technologically sophisticated industries.

In case 1, it is easy to see that, aside from protection, there is the possibility of importing foreign labor to "adjust structurally" to the fact that labor-abundance (i.e., "cheap wages") abroad is the cause of shifting comparative advantage. The possibility of shifting production abroad is not particularly meaningful here since the foreign firms are more likely to have minor Hymer-like advantages, and one's own firms have instead such disadvantages, in operating abroad in such stagnant industries.[7] Nor is importation of superior foreign technology or cheaper foreign capital for investment generally a feasible option in such industries.

By contrast, in case 2, the Schumpeterian industries, the menu of response options is *substantially* greater. Indeed, it includes a variety of patterns of direct foreign investment traceable primarily to the fact that superior know-how is available elsewhere. One implication of this contrast between the senescent and the Schumpeterian industries facing shifts in comparative advantage, is that the prospect of a *protectionist* response and outcome is correspondingly greater in the senescent than in the Schumpeterian industries.

Lobbying Incentives in Senescent Industries
As I have noted already, in addition to protection, the policy option of importing foreign labor is available in this case. (This is so, except when the cost of lobbying for it on social and political grounds is sufficiently high to rule it out altogether: as in Germany where the *gastarbeiter* system has come to a virtual halt on net inflow since the mid-1970s.)

In my earlier (1982) paper, I used a number of formal models in general equilibrium to rank-order protection and labor-importation policies in terms of their impact on the welfare of workers and capitalists *and* on conventionally defined social welfare. I assumed that politically the government could be pressured into restoring the output level of the senescent industry suffering the shift in comparative advantage. I draw on some of these models and extend the argument further.

1. *Jones-Neary model.* Consider the Jones-Neary model where capital is specific but labor is mobile between the two sectors. Ask then what happens to the choice between labor importation and protection in this model, when the terms of trade shift adversely against the labor-intensive importable activity.[8]

The terms-of-trade shift causes an unambiguous fall in the rental on capital in the labor-intensive importable industry, while the return to labor (after reallocation) will rise in terms of the importable but fall in terms of the exportable good. (If the importable sector is "small," then evidently the real wage of labor is likely to fall as the weight of the exportable good in consumption will be the greater.) In this model, therefore, *both* capitalists *and* labor are likely to have an incentive to lobby for protection. But capitalists may also settle for the incremental import of labor. For, as Mayer (1974) has shown, such an increment in labor, at a constant goods price-ratio, *will* increase the rental unambiguously to capital in both sectors while the real wage falls unambiguously.

On "economic welfare" dimension, the choice is clear-cut in this model, as long as an otherwise free-trade situation, free from distortions, is considered. Thus, the protection option implies bearing the standard cost of distorted production and consumption. However, with the real wage declining as labor is imported, the importation of a finite quantity of foreign labor yields a "surplus" to the host country: labor importation is therefore welfare improving. Thus, any branch of the government that responds to economic-welfare motivation will favor labor importation as against raising a protective tariff.

This model therefore suggests a *conflict* of interest between the capitalists/employers and the workers: while both may lobby for protection, capitalists can also go along the road of labor importation. Moreover, the government will recognize that labor importation is more advantageous nationally than is protection, and that relaxing immigration quotas gives it good marks internationally, while protection does the opposite. It is therefore likely to prefer relaxation of immigration quotas, thus raising the cost of lobbying for tariff protection. The net outcome therefore may well be the importation of labor.

2. *Industry-specific foreign labor being paid a differential wage.* The preceding model considered foreign labor to be industry nonspecific and equally assumed that the return to foreign and domestic labor was equal. However, take now a different mix of assumptions. Assume that the foreign labour is imported on an industry-specific contractual basis *and* can be effectively paid a lower wage than domestic labor.

Take this model, then, in the form of a Haberler-Brecher model with Haberler (1950)-type sector-specific factors and a Brecher (1974)-type sticky real wage for labor. Let Q_1 be the initial production vector, AQ_1B being the production possibility curve given the immobility of factors. When the terms of trade shift from P_1 to P_2, turning against the importable, labor-intensive good Y, labor in Y production insists on maintaining its real wage in terms of good X. This leads to workers being laid off in industry Y until the marginal physical product of labor in Y rises sufficiently (at Q_2) to restore Y labor's real wage in terms of good X.

In this situation, suppose that the Y capitalists are allowed to import foreign labor, to restore their output to Q_1 and that the foreign labor is allowed to be imported at a lower real wage than the one local labor insists on. Then part of the incremental output of good Y (namely Q_2Q_1) will accrue to the capitalists, as demonstrated in figure 22.2. There, OS represents the real wage of domestic labor in terms of Y (at Q_2 in figure 22.1); OZ is the lower fixed real wage at which foreign labor can be

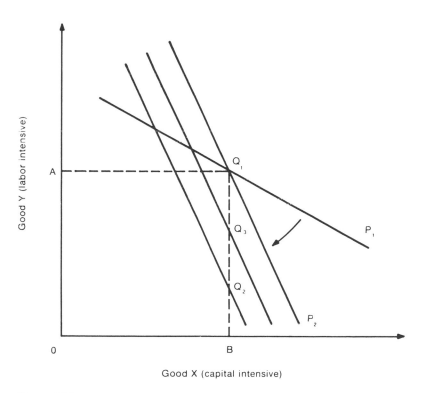

Figure 22.1

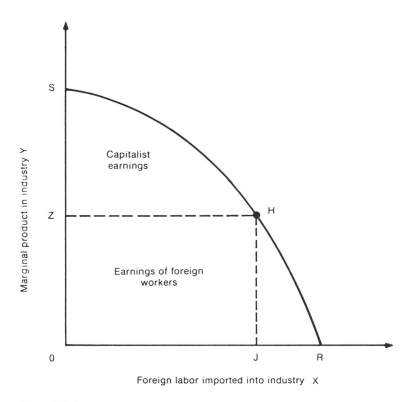

Figure 22.2

imported in an amount permitted oy the immigration quota; OJ is the immigration quota; SHR is the marginal product curve for imported labor in industry Y, given the employment of domestic capital and labour (at Q_2 in figure 22.1). The total increment in Y output that results is then $SHJO$, which is assumed to correspond to Q_2Q_1 in figure 22.1. But, of this increment, only $OZHJ$ accrues as earnings of foreign workers. The rest (SHZ) accrues to the domestic capitalists, and this division corresponds to Q_3Q_1 for foreign workers and Q_2Q_3 for domestic capital in figure 22.1. Thus, reverting to figure 22.1, national welfare is now defined, in the labor-importation option, by the availability line P_2 passing through Q_3.

By contrast, the protection option will maintain domestic labor's real wage while restoring labor employment as well. It will also increase capitalist earnings but this increase cannot be rank ordered with the increase under the labor-importation option, and economic welfare may be above or below that at Q_3 (the labor-importation option)—this because protection will mean that production will be restored to Q_1 but that there will be a consumption-distortion cost that may outweigh the production gain under the alternative labor-importation policy.

3. *Joint "exploitation" of foreign labor.* Both of the above models suggest that capitalists and workers will divide on the labor-importation option vis-à-vis the protectionist option. But it is interesting to look more closely at the German *gastarbeiter* system where foreign labor was imported massively by several industries. The remarkable aspect is that both capitalists *and* workers were enthusiastic about importing foreign labor and that the consent of *both* was necessary before an employer could proceed to apply to recruit foreign labor. One needs therefore alternative models that would fit these facts better.

My current candidate, on which I am working but have as yet no formal or econometric results to present, is the following: suppose that suitable job reclassification and promotion procedures effectively manage to yield to a native German a higher wage than to an imported, equivalent foreign worker.[9] Then a union and the employers in a firm could employ foreign workers at a wage that is equivalent to their supply price (which will certainly exceed handsomely the opportunity-cost wage in Anatolya for a Turkish worker) but is *below* the value of their marginal product in Germany. The difference could then be shared between the union and the employers. Such a model, if embedded in a Haberler-Brecher economy in terms of figure 22.2, would imply that the foreign workers were paid less than $OZHJ$, and that the "capitalist earnings," now augmented, would be divided with the unionized native workers. "Economic welfare" would be enhanced, of course, since the foreign workers would not merely generate the normal surplus but also an added element, reflecting their Joan-Robinsonian "exploitation."[10]

In conclusion of this line of analysis, let me simply say that the labor immigration regimes, the political processes governing legislation regarding protection and immigration, and the degree of unionization affecting chances of labor's successful lobbying, are suffficiently diverse across countries for us not to dismiss any particular model as unrealistic or unhelpful. Let me turn now, however, to the case where Schumpeterian industries face import competition.

Lobbying Incentives in Technically Progressive, Schumpeterian Industries
The fact that technical change is the major source of shifts in comparative advantage in the Schumpeterian industries affects critically the nature of

the lobbying responses and policy options that open up there in face of import competition.

In particular, it opens up three possibilities, which I should like to emphasize here at some length.

1. *Technology licensing response.* Since technology is superior abroad, and is indeed postulated to be the source of the differential advantage that is causing the import competition, one possibility is to try to import that technology. Dinopoulos (1983) has extended the Bhagwati-Sapir type of analysis, sketched above for the senescent industry case, to allow for the licensing of technology when the Schumpeterian industry is capital intensive. He uses both the HOS and the Jones-Neary models.[11]

2. *Mutual penetration of investment (MPI) response.* Yet another possible response is where, faced with competition in similar products that is intensified thanks to technological (or taste) shifts, the competing firms in different countries wind up investing in each other's comparative advantage in R&D. For example, European and Japanese small cars compete with American large cars, and this competition intensifies with time as the Japanese get better at the game (for example, Toyota started production only after the war). The Japanese press ahead with R&D on production of small cars, whereas the Americans get steadily better at producing the gas guzzlers. The MPI thesis then is that the response to such intensified competition could be to induce mutual investment by the competing firms in one another's R&D-induced advantages.[12]

The MPI response seems a possible outcome when the competition among similar products intensifies but results in a stand-off, with the products of neither country's firms gaining dominance through R&D breakthroughs or taste shifts (whether exogenous or advertising-induced).[13]

This then is an outcome where unions ought to be indifferent because no jobs are threatened while the entrepreneurs reduce the threat to their profits from import competition by *de facto* productwise cartelization. The government may not be unduly disturbed about the outcome (unless the result is the total elimination of competition in the industry *and* the government has an antitrust policy which it furthermore seeks to implement in this instance).

3. *Inducing foreign investment by superior competitors.* Finally, consider the case where the foreign superiority is very considerable and the foreign products are becoming increasingly competitive so that there is no comfortable way for both the foreign and domestic "similar" products in the same "industry" to survive. This is what I call the "growing dominance of the external products" type of scenario in Bhagwati (1982a).

In this case, the entrepreneurs will want protection but may settle for greater access to cheaper foreign labor to offset the loss of comparative advantage if the government so insists in view of the situation. While entrepreneurs may be indifferent between protection and greater access to foreign labor, the labor lobby's interests will generally prefer protection to labor importation, for reasons that need not be spelled out again. However, labor may be indifferent between a policy of actual protection and one where they are allowed merely to use the *threat* of protection to get the foreign firms to invest where the labor is: for both policies will equally secure their jobs. On the other hand, the entrepreneurs will prefer actual protection to the policy that merely uses protectionist threats to draw in foreign firms: for, while the Union of Automobile Workers (UAW), for example, does not care whether its members are employed by Datsun, (Nissan) or by Ford, Ford does![14]

Thus, here we have the intriguing response possibility where domestic labor tries to import foreign entrepreneurs (with superior know-how), whereas in the senescent industries we had the spectacle of domestic entrepreneurs trying to import foreign labor!

As it happens, the protectionist threat resulting from the deteriorating competitive position of the U.S. car industry is an example of the scenarios spelled out above. The American car industry, largely due to the steady erosion of the market for gas guzzlers in recent years, has been turning increasingly to producing small cars for survival. This has shifted the problem of competition from one where the Americans and the foreign small car-makers both had their own special niches in the market, with MPI (and variants thereof in the form of mutually supportive and profitable arrangements for marketing, joint production, etc.) as the relevant model. The model is now one where the competition is more fierce and is over a product type (the small car) where the foreign car-makers have always had the edge. The result has indeed been for unions to move abroad in order to threaten the foreign car-makers either to produce in the United States or to face protection. And Japanese investment by Datsun (Nissan), Honda, and Toyota has actually materialized (along with some VERs as well).

22.2   Free Trade and Free Capital Mobility

I have considered so far international flows of investment and technology as alternative responses to tariff protection when structural adjustment is called for in light of shifts in comparative advantage. I now shift my focus and consider the other interface between structural adjustment and factor mobility, mentioned in my introduction. This is the possibility that structural adjustment to shifts in comparative advantage, as dictated by free trade policies, would not occur unless free mobility of capital was also permitted across the trading countries. This contention has implications for GATT reform, i.e., specifically, for the pertinent question whether GATT should be extended to encourage and oversee freer mobility of capital among the member countries. (This is a question that certainly underlies the U.S. complaint against Canada at the GATT precisely on this issue.) But before I enter that aspect of the problem, let me first distinguish among the different aspects of the contention that free mobility of capital is essential for a free-trade world system.

First, there is the simple view that the *purely* economic case for capital mobility is identical to the case for free trade: that is, it represents a mutually rewarding transaction and, besides, it improves world efficiency. Needless to say, this argument ought to extend to free international labor mobility as well; but few liberals extend their case for the Liberal International Economic Order to permit *that*. Moreover, the utilitarian ethical premises underlying their contentions rapidly yield to other implicit ethical criteria justifying "the right to exclude" when labor immigration is discussed.

Next, and this is a recent contention, there is the view that it is possible for countries to have effective, invisible barriers to free trade in goods if the right to make "trade-related investments" is not simultaneously available.

Finally, it is also argued that interference with the free mobility of capital is often the instrument through which interference with free trade is deliberately practiced: for example, performance requirements are imposed concerning maximum permissible imports or minimum exports.

Let me consider each of these arguments, in turn.

1. Contrary to widespread belief, the theoretical case for free capital mobility, in the presence of free trade, is by no means symmetrical with the case for free trade. In the latter case, the classic papers of Samuelson et al. have long shown that free trade between free agents with given endowments will assure gain (or, more precisely, cannot bring harm) to every trading agent. In the former case, however, this is no longer true: free capital mobility, introduced when free trade already exists, can harm individual agents and there is no presumption at all that *both* agents will gain from the introduction of such capital mobility.[15] This startling proposition emerges rather pointedly from the work of Brecher and Choudhri (1982) and is also

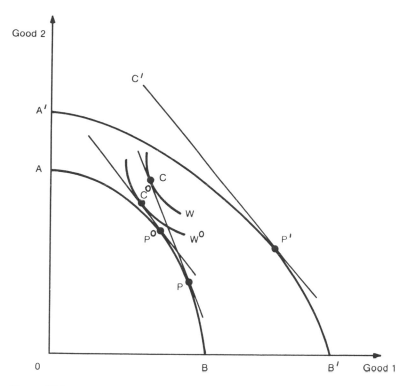

Figure 22.3

found in the steady-state analysis of Saavedra (1982) using the Findlay (1980) North–South model of a Solow-Lewis international economy. Let me take the former analysis and show, simply, why free international capital mobility may immiserise a country in the presence of free trade.

Consider figure 22.3 where AB is the production-possibility curve (PPC) of the host country receiving the foreign investment. $A'B'$ is the augmented PPC, with the foreign capital having come in. Let the terms of trade worsen in the postinflux situation from the original PC to $P'C'$. With foreign capital earning the value of its domestic marginal product, the host country's *national* budget line is, not $P'C'$ but P^0C^0. Therefore, as shown in Bhagwati and Brecher (1980), national welfare after the influx of foreign capital is at W^0. Before the influx it was at $W(> W^0)$. Therefore, the influx of capital has been immiserizing. By symmetric reasoning, the home country (exporting capital) has been enriched.[16]

On reflection, it is easy to see that this case implies that the "disexternality" of a deterioration in the terms of trade decisively makes the social marginal product of foreign capital inflow less than its private marginal product in the host country. It immediately reminds one of the Brecher–Díaz-Alejandro–Uzawa case where a capital influx in a small, tariff-distorted economy with a capital-intensive importable good turns out to be immiserizing. The parallel is interesting: in the latter case, there is a distortion in the form of a finite tariff for a small country whose optimal policy should be free trade, whereas in the former case the distortion is the presence of free trade for a large country (with variable terms of trade).

2. What then about the next argument distinguished above? The notion underlying it is that, unless the right to enter retail and distribution outlets in the country of potential importation of your goods is granted, there will be an effective trade barrier (a nontariff barrier, NTB) against your goods. This contention is based on the complaints of Western exporters to Japan: that the Japanese distribution outlets implicitly attach a "tax premium" on handling foreign goods. This acts as an implicit tariff barrier that should be added to the *visible* tariffs and NTBs imposed by the Japanese government. Hence, Western investment in such outlets is regarded as essential to entering the Japanese market effectively and at visible tariff rates that are, in fact, extremely low.

This contention is widely believed, of course, and is based on the complaints of several potential exporters to Japan. It does require that every Japanese retail organisation acts in implicit concert on this issue. This may well be the case if extra cement is provided for such implicit collusion by the prospect of MITI reprisals, somehow, for breaking ranks. There may well be something to this, though I must confess that the conditions which I have noted for the argument to be valid are not exactly easy to satisfy. That American and European businessmen (and policymakers who listen to these businessmen) buy it, however, is indisputable.

The argument, however, raises another interesting set of theoretical questions similar to the one which I raised above for the first argument. What may we presume to be the effect of such freer mobility of capital if it does indeed reduce, in some or full degree, the implicit protection that is otherwise in place? Analytically, then, we have here a particularly interesting case, where the postulated distortion, in the shape of the implicit tariff, is itself endogenous to the capital inflow. Thus, for any specified capital movement, the home country's primary gain from the outflow of capital (assuming that the foreign earnings exceed the domestic) would be added to by the gains from freer trade if the tariff reduction were welfare improving.[17] In fact, it should be possible for the capital-exporting country to

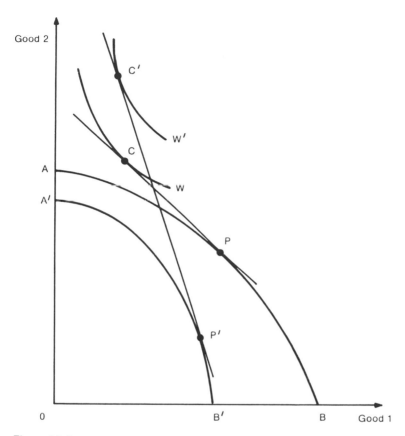

Figure 22.4

profit from such exportation, even by subsidising directly unprofitable capital exports, simply because the possible welfare gain from freer trade in goods may offset this primary loss! Thus, in figure 22.4, consider the case where the country literally throws capital abroad, at zero direct return. It thus shrinks its PPC down from *AB* to *A'B'*, but the improvement in its terms of trade due to the foreign (host) country's resulting implicit tariff reduction improves its terms of trade from *P'C'* to *PC*. The primary loss in income from the export of capital is then offset by the secondary gain from terms of trade improvement, in this instance, from the joint effect of the capital movement and the induced tariff reduction.

3. Finally, we have the question of the use of investment controls to affect trade directly. Safarian (1982) has noted several such practices, which consist mainly of so-called "performance requirements." These require-

ments typically take the form of imposing domestic-content and minimum-export clauses, before the foreign firm is allowed to invest in the host country. According to one U.S. study by the Labor-Industry Coalition for International Trade, quoted by Safarian, "all but two of the top twenty recipients of direct investments, which include many developed countries, have performance requirements which limit imports or expand exports."

In addition, regulations that close certain sectors to foreign investments altogether (or to expansion by existing foreign firms therein) have played a role in affecting the competitive access of foreign firms to domestic markets in these countries. Typically, this comes about because purchases by other governmental agencies are directed to these sectors and, until the Tokyo Round, such purchases were not subject to GATT scrutiny. Now they are, but with important exceptions: the increased and fair access provisions on governmental purchases are not merely not available, under current interpretation asserted by member countries on a most favored nation (MFN) basis. They also exclude from their purview entities in power generation, transportation and telecommunications. Again, regional and local governmental purchases are excluded from the scope of the Tokyo Round Code on governmental procurement.

Doubtless, these investment policies directly affect trade flows. The pertinent question that does arise, however, is whether the resulting trade impacts ought to be treated on a par with direct trade barriers. Here, I think that there are persuasive reasons why the two should not be treated with equal disdain.

First, as I have already noted above in regard to the case for free capital mobility, there is a presumption that an open trading system benefits each participating agent, but there is no such presumption in regard to an open investment system. Hence, even on strictly orthodox economic grounds, countries may legitimately want to worry about putting safeguards on incoming or outgoing investments, though it is always necessary to ask whether their precise actions are sensible or counterproductive.

Second, and more pertinent presently, investments raise issues of political impact (ranging from conflicts of sovereignty to destabilisation and military intervention in defence of investments), and also cultural values. Trade in goods does not quite raise such issues, in general. At least, we have learned to regard political and cultural fallouts from nearly all types of trade in goods with a certain sense of ridicule. It does not seem that nation states, which inevitably worry about these "noneconomic" aspects of foreign investment and often have regulations and restrictions designed to reflect these worries, will wind up accepting significant restrictions on their freedom of action in this regard. That, in consequence, trade flows are influenced is simply an outcome that must regrettably be accepted.

The advocacy of freedom of investment internationally is, therefore, more pointedly an ideological position. And its elevation to the agenda for GATT reform, or appeal to it at GATT (as in the U.S. complaint against Canada) for remedial action under the present rules, is likely to make little headway. (That is, except for argument 2 above, concerning *necessary investment to ensure access*, based on the Japanese example of investment in retailing being critical in ensuring open access to the Japanese market for goods.) Instead, the resulting lack of "progress" in getting freer *investment* policies adopted may gratuitously aggravate the nascent and possibly growing sense in the United States that the current *trading* rules are unfair. This will increase the probability of protectionist pressures being translated into legislated protection whenever import competition requires structural adjustment.

Perhaps it may be helpful, in this context, for the proponents of free investment flows to recall that restrictions on international labor mobility also have similar trade impacts. But it is readily agreed that such restrictions are desirable on social and political grounds, and even for economic reasons similar to those used in examining argument 1 above. It would be strange, if not self-serving, for countries such as the United States to push then for changes in rules concerning investment while turning away from analogous changes in rules concerning international labor mobility.

22.3 Concluding Remarks

In conclusion, I should draw attention to some recent policy-oriented analytical problems that are of interest, which I have not considered in the present paper but which do have some bearing on its subject matter.

In particular, I must mention the structural adjustment choice that presents itself as a choice between capital and labor mobility as policy options. Interestingly, Lenin and others who followed immediately in his footsteps do not appear to have considered the possibility of developed capitalist economies importing their proletariat rather than exporting their capital in the imperialist stage of predetermined evolution: an omission that is ironic since Lenin himself was an early *intellektuelle Gastarbeiter* in Zürich of yesteryear! Only recently has the problem of a choice between these two options, each representing an alternative approach to structural change in the world economy, been posed from the viewpoint of national and international advantage: and it has evident bearing on policy issues of concern (e.g. should the United States, which is capital-rich, encourage or induce Mexico to permit an increased inflow of U.S. capital into Mexico or should it permit more freely the immigration of Mexican labor instead).[18]

Again, it has been contended that trade liberalisation, permitting structural adjustment to comparative advantage, ought to be looked at closely because it may benefit foreign-owned factors of production to the detriment of national welfare. This argument obviously arises when factors are internationally mobile, or else there would be no foreign-owned factors of production in one's midst. It has had particular currency in Latin America. As it happens, it is entirely valid *in principle*. Thus, in a series of papers, Bhagwati and Tironi (1980), Bhagwati and Brecher (1980), and especially Brecher and Bhagwati (1981) have analyzed the implications of the presence of such foreign-owned factors of production. They have alerted the analyst to the ways in which redistributive effects between foreign-owned and domestic factors of production could reverse the beneficial effects of policies such as trade liberalization or of otherwise welfare-improving customs unions such as the Latin American Common Market.

We may turn the above problem around. It is then easy to see that, if your factors of production are located abroad, foreign protection may not harm you, simply because any loss on the gain from trade could be offset by an improvement in the earned incomes of your factors in the foreign country. The conditions for a paradoxical outcome, such that foreign protection is to your advantage taking this redistributive effect into account, can be readily established—in the case of exported labor, you would have to attach weights to quantities of labor at home and abroad. At the same time, it is easy to see that the antiprotectionist enthusiasm and eagerness of countries exporting goods that compete with foreign industries that intensively use their own labor (as is at times the case with senescent industries in Western countries) may be less than compelling! I had hoped to use German data on employment of foreign labor by sectors (which are about the best available in this area) and "runs" of the Deardorff-Stern model. My intention was to identify changes in employment brought about by changes in German tariff and NTB barriers, to make estimates of changes in Turkish, Yugoslav, Greek, Spanish, Portuguese, and Italian employment in Germany that might ensue from such liberalization, and to set these changes off against changes in domestic employment in these countries so as to put some empirical flesh on my notions. Unfortunately, some bugs remain, and I must settle for simply making the point at a theoretical level.

Notes

1. Thanks are due to the German Marshall Fund for their financial support of the research underlying this paper.

2. Interesting papers along these lines include Mussa (1982) and Neary (1982).

3. Many *empirical* papers have been written in this kind of area, by Pincus (1975), Helleiner (1977) and others. Specially notable here are also novel efforts at explaining the *differential* tariff cuts under the Kennedy Round by Cheh (1974) and Riedel (1977) for the United States and West Germany, respectively. The *theoretical* papers of note, however, were initiated by Brock and Magee (1978) and followed by trade-theoretic models developed by Findlay and Wellisz (1982) and Feenstra and Bhagwati (1982), which are discussed below.

4. Aside from endogenizing the tariff in their model, Findlay-Wellisz also consider the question of the welfare impact of such an endogenous tariff vis-à-vis the free-trade optimum position. The welfare consequences of endogenizing the tariff are discussed at length in Bhagwati (1980). It is shown that, in general, an endogenous tariff at t percent cannot be rank ordered vis-à-vis an exogenous tariff at the same rate. This has to do with the second-best nature of this comparison and the consequent possibility that negative shadow factor-prices may be present. The general question of directly unproductive profit-seeking (DUP) activities, of which tariff-seeking is one instance, and their welfare impact which may be positive when second-best considerations are inextricably present, has been discussed in Bhagwati (1982c).

5. Feenstra-Bhagwati note that the efficient tariff may, paradoxically, exceed the lobbying tariff if the shadow price of lobbying activity is negative .

6. In sketching this analysis, I draw upon recent work of Bhagwati (1982) and Sapir (1983). This considers the possibility that. in labor-intensive industries, the response to import competition may be to lobby, not just for tariff protection but also for relaxation of immigration quotas such that more foreign labor may be imported.

7. Regional movement of such industries *within* a country, to where labor is cheaper, is of course a well-known pattern: as with U.S. textiles and footwear.

8. In Bhagwati (1982b), I also consider shifts in comparative advantage coming from the *domestic*, rather than the *external*, side.

9. This is necessary to assume since German) law prohibits discrimination in pay between workers for identical jobs.

10. Exploitation is therefore *not* essential to the argument leading to both workers and capitalists wanting foreign labor. But I believe that it does operate, in fact, in the German case.

11. There are interesting contrasts between the HOS and Jones-Neary models in rank ordering the different policies in terms of their overall welfare impact. This is

because the latter model produces diminishing returns and hence the possibility of gain from welfare improvement vis-à-vis even the free-trade situation in the usual manner which is familiar from the analysis of skilled migration. See Sapir (1983) and Dinopoulos (1983) for further elaboration.

12. The MPI "model" is contrasted with Vernon's Product Cycle "model," as two alternative Hymeresque theories of direct investment, in Bhagwati (1982). The Dunlop-Pirelli example is also given to illustrate the MPI model.

13. Impure forms of the MPI phenomenon may involve one-way equity purchase in exchange for marketing facilities.

14. The UAW has an industrywide contract.

15. On the other hand, it must be stressed that, compared to autarchy in *both* goods and capital flows, free trade in goods, combined with free capital mobility, will indeed assure gain to every agent. Besides, just as the introduction of free capital mobility in the presence of free trade need not assure gain to every agent, so the introduction of free trade in the prior presence of free capital mobility also need not assure gain to every agent.

16. In this model, with diversification in both countries before and after the capital flow takes place, there is a *necessary* conflict of interest between the two countries whenever the terms of trade change as a result of the capital flow! This conclusion concerning necessary conflict can be shown to hold equally in this model if free trade is introduced when free capital mobility holds prior to the introduction of free trade. I am grateful to Richard Brecher for this observation.

17. Freer trade need not. of course, be welfare improving, though that is presumed to be the case in the discussion of this problem. The conditions for the different outcomes can be readily established.

18. While Bhagwati (1979) posed this theoretical problem in the context of the U.S.-Mexico choice noted above, it turns out that Ramaswami (1968) had already posed this problem "before its time," with resulting neglect, and had used a one-good model (with therefore no trade in goods) to study it. For recent extensions of that analysis, see Calvo and Wellisz (1983) and Bhagwati and Srinivasan (1983), and for further analysis in the context of models allowing for trade in goods, see Wong (1983) and Saavedra-Rivano and Wooton (1983).

References

Baldwin, R. E. 1982. The Political Economy of Protectionism. In J. N. Bhagwati (ed.), *Import Competition and Response*. Chicago: University of Chicago Press, pp. 263–286.

Bhagwati, J. N. 1979. International Factor Movements and National Advantage. *Indian Economic Review* 14: 73–100.

Bhagwati, J. N. 1980. Lobbying and Welfare. *Journal of Public Economics,* 14: 355–363.

Bhagwati, J. N. (ed.). 1982a. *Import Competition and Response.* Chicago: University of Chicago Press.

Bhagwati, J. N. 1982b. "Shifting Comparative Advantage, Protectionist Demands, and Policy Resppnse. In J. N. Bhagwati (ed.), *Import Compelition and Response.* Chicago: University of Chicago Press, pp. 153–184.

Bhagwati, J. N. 1982c. The Theory of Directly-Unproductive Profit-Seeking (DUP) Activities. *Journal of Political Economy* 90.

Bhagwati, J. N., and R. A. Brecher. 1980. National Welfare in an Open Economy in the Presence of Foreign-Owned Factors of Production. *Journal of International Economics* 10: 103–116.

Bhagwati, J. N., and T. N. Srinivasan. 1983. On the Choice between Capital and Labour Mobility. *Journal of International Economics* 13.

Bhagwati, J. N., and E. Tironi. 1980. Tariff Change, Foreign Capital, and Immiserization: A Theoretical Analysis. *Journal of Development Economics* February: 103–115.

Brecher, R. A. 1974. Minimum Wage Rates and the Pure Theory of International Trade. *Quarterly Journal of Economics* 88: 98–116.

Brecher, R. A., and C. Díaz-Alejandro. 1977. Tariffs, Foreign Capital and Immiserizing Growth. *Journal of International Economics* 7: 317–322.

Brecher, R. A., and J. N. Bhagwati. 1981. Foreign Ownership and the Theory of Trade and Welfare. *Journal of Political Economy* 89: 497–511.

Brecher, R. A., and E. U. Choudhri. 1982. Immiserizing Investment from Abroad: The Singer-Prebisch Thesis Reconsidered. *Quarterly Journal of Economics* 47: 181–190.

Brock, W. A., and S. P. Magee. 1978. The Economics of Special Interest Politics: The Case of Tariffs. *American Economic Review* 68: 246–250.

Calvo, G., and S. Wellisz. 1983. International Factor Mobility and National Advantage. *Journal of International Economics* 13.

Cheh, J. H. 1974. United States Concessions in the Kennedy Round and Short-Run Labor Adjustment Costs. *Journal of International Economics* 4: 323–340.

Dinopoulos, E. 1983. Import Competition and Lobbying Response: The Schumpeterian Industry Case. *Journal of International Economics* 13.

Feenstra, R. C., and J. N. Bhagwati. 1982. Tariff Seeking and the Efficient Tariff. In J. N. Bhagwati (ed.), *Import Competition and Response.* Chicago: University of Chicago Press, pp. 245–258.

Findlay, Ronald. 1980. The Terms of Trade and Equilibrium Growth in the World Economy. *American Economic Review* 70 (June): 291–299.

Findlay, R., and S. Wellisz. 1982. Endogenous Tariffs, the Political Economy of Trade Restrictions, and Welfare. In J. N. Bhagwati (ed.), *Import Competition and Response*. Chicago: University of Chicago Press, pp. 223–234.

Haberler, G. 1950. Some Problems in the Pure Theory of International Trade. *Economic Journal* 60: 223–240.

Helleiner, G. K. 1977. The Political Economy of Canada's Tariff Structure: An Alternative Model. *Canadian Journal of Economics* 4: 318–326.

Jones, R. 1971. A Three Factor Model in Theory, Trade, and History. In J. N. Bhagwati, et al. (eds.), *Trade, Balance of Payments, and Growth*. Amsterdam: North Holland.

Mayer, Wolfgang. 1974. Short-Run and Long-Run Equilibrium for a Small Open Economy. *Journal of Political Economy* 82 (July/August): 955–967.

Mussa, M. 1982. Government Policy and the Adjustment Process. In J. N. Bhagwati (ed.), *Import Competition and Response*. Chicago: University of Chicago Press, pp. 73–120.

Neary, J. P. 1978. Short-Run Capital Specificity and the Pure Theory of International Trade. *Economic Journal* 88: 488–510.

Neary, J. P. 1982. Intersectoral Capital Mobility, Wage Stickiness and the Case for Adjustment Assistence. In J. N. Bhagwati (ed.), *Import Competition and Response*. Chicago: University of Chicago Press, pp. 39–67.

Pincus, J. 1975. Pressure Groups and the Patterns of Tariffs. *Journal of Political Economy* 83: 757–778.

Ramaswami, V. K. 1968. International Factor Movements and the National Advantage. *Economica* 35: 309–310.

Riedel, J. 1977. Tariff Concessions in the Kennedy Round and the Structure of Tariff Protection in West Germany: An Econometric Assessment. *Journal of International Economics* 13.

Saavedra-Rivano, Neantro. 1982. North–South Models and Capital Mobility. Unpublished Ph.D. dissertation. Columbia University.

Safarian, A. E. 1982. Trade-Related Investment Issues. Institute for International Economics, Washington, DC. Mimeo.

Sapir, A. 1983. Foreign Competition, Immigration and Structural Adjustment. *Journal of International Economics* 13.

Wong, K. Y. 1983. Trade Flows and Factor Mobility between Two Technologically Different Countries. *Journal of International Economics* 13.

VI   Developing Countries

23

Dependence and Interdependence: Developing Countries in the World Economy

It is a great honor for me to have been asked to give this year's Sturc Memorial Lecture. I must compliment Isaiah Frank on the brilliant timing of the lecture. Although he did not arrange for it, the Wall Street crash of two weeks ago provides me with an excellent entree into the major theme of my lecture today: the need to restore clarity of vision, the ambition of purpose, and the substance of action to the management of the critical problems and challenges that the developing countries face today.

The prospect of a hanging, the English aphorism goes, clears the head beautifully. By offering an apocalyptic glimpse into the future, Wall Street has ceased to be the much-flaunted ally of the administration's record of what I am afraid must be characterized as the ideology of "fine-tuned nonintervention," where problems are permitted to propel one toward the precipice and policy action is unleashed only when considered altogether unavoidable. Wall Street has turned instead into a stern foe, shaking the administration out of its preferred mode of benign, but often unwittingly malign, neglect.

This can only be to our good. For developing countries, through an interesting evolution of the world economy and accompanying cycles in North–South relations, now constitute unmistakably a highly differentiated group. Wholly different problems afflict broad groups of developing countries, requiring clarity of analysis and vision if they are to be adequately addressed. Equally, the growing integration of the developing countries into the world economy over the last four decades, again differently defined for diverse countries, has led to a state of interdependence between them and the developed countries that creates both vulnerabilities and opportunities. If the ambition of purpose and the substance of action are missing, the vulnerabilities turn benign interdependence into malign dependence: it would be as if you had climbed into bed with a witless elephant. But the opportunities presented by the interdependence are equally profound; and action, both national and international, based on a clear view of the developing countries' new map, is called for. It presents us with a unique opportunity to create a shared success.

23.1 Historical Evolution: Toward Diversity

Let me turn at the outset to the evolution of the developing countries into their present, differentiated state. For only by examining the past can we illuminate the present and dare to hope for the future.

From the perspective of my theme today, the developing countries have gone through distinct and dramatic cycles since the end of World War II.[1] Two episodes divide the postwar period into three phases: the success of the Organization of Petroleum Exporting Countries (OPEC) by 1973 and the Volcker-Reagan recession of the early 1980s. Since the latter in turn is hard to imagine without the post-OPEC macroeconomic difficulties in the member countries of the Organization for Economic Cooperation and Development (OECD) the one compelling event in the postwar period is certainly the rise of OPEC. The analysis of the developing countries that I sketch could therefore be written in oil.

Through these years there has been a tension within the developing countries between the desire to *unite* behind shared political and economic aspirations in the international economic arena and the contrary compulsions to *pull apart*, which come from inherited and growing differences in political ideology, economic performance, and interests resulting from differential integration into the world economy.

The first phase, the pre-OPEC period, was characterized by relative harmony and unity. The centrifugal forces were nascent, and the largely shared ideology underlying Bretton Woods provided a strong cement both within the developing countries and between them and the developed countries.

The second phase, or OPEC's golden years from 1973 through 1981, began by strengthening the unity of the developing countries, prompting a political alliance behind the demands of the New International Economic Order (NIEO). It initiated, depending on your perspective, a negotiating or a confrontational posture toward the developed countries so that the phrase "North–South negotiations," symbolic of intragroup cohesion and intergroup division, came into our lexicon. The unity of the developing countries, however, proved illusory as the premise from which it was derived. That the developing countries had "commodity power" analogous to oil power was a notion founded on quicksand. The real legacy of OPEC would paradoxically turn out, therefore, to be not unity but rather its opposite, for OPEC rudely fragmented the developing countries into the lucky members of OPEC, the high-flying (principally South American) borrowers of recycled OPEC funds, and the rest.

Eventually, these divisions would endure and, in the third phase, initiated by the deep recessions of 1981 and 1982, reinforce other factors in fragmenting the developing countries yet further and more emphatically into their present state of diversity and consequent perplexity, if not paralysis, among the proponents of unity in the South. Permit me now to develop this skeletal sketch more fully.

Phase I: 1946 to 1973

The design of Bretton Woods reflected a largely Benthamite conception of the international management superstructure. It was essentially building at an international level the minimal framework of rules that would permit voluntary transactions among different economic agents to secure maximal good. Informed by the interwar experience with competitive exchange rates depreciations and the Smoot-Hawley tariff's sorry history, the architects of Bretton Woods contemplated an international regime that would preclude such mutually destructive policies. The orderly management of international monetary equilibrium would in turn lead to advantageous trade among nations, provided they dismantled their inherited trade barriers and offered binding commitments to keep them down so as to guarantee market access. But it was evident that the resulting economic efficiency was not adequate: civil society at home, no matter how efficiently organized economically, redistributes to assist the less advantaged. The international regime, therefore, needed an institution to direct capital flows to the developing countries that the imminent end of the colonial era would bring onto the world stage.

The international institutional structure that finally emerged from Bretton Woods broadly reflected these principles of a liberal international economic order. The International Monetary Fund (IMF) would provide the macroeconomic equilibrium without which the maintenance of a liberal trading system is economically less compelling and politically more unmanageable. The General Agreement on Tariffs and Trade (GATT), in turn, provided the rules, reflecting multilateralism and nondiscrimination which would then enable the contracting parties to reap the gains from trade. The World Bank was designed to channel resources to the developing nations, strengthening the liberal infrastructure which would otherwise be long on the market and short on sentiment.

It is important to recall that the United States, having emerged as the dominant world power, provided the key driving force behind the adoption of this institutional infrastructure and the critical political and ideological support for its sustenance through the next three decades. *Pax Americana* had succeeded the *Pax Britannica* of the previous century.

Doubtless, the conception was not all American; had it been, its success would have been more problematic. The design of Bretton Woods was a shared vision. The role of John Maynard Keynes was pivotal, as was the intellectual input of many of Britain's best minds. Indeed, the British view of the matter is conveyed in the ditty:

In Washington Lord Halifax
Once whispered to Lord Keynes:
It's true *they* have the money bags
But *we* have all the brains.

But the sun had set on the British empire, and the capricious hand of history had favored the United States, making ours virtually the American century.

From the perspective of today, what is remarkable perhaps is not what was constructed at Bretton Woods by these remarkable men, among whom we must count Emest Sturc, who was not merely present at the creation but splendidly dedicated his life to the efficient and enlightened functioning of its institutional legacy. Rather, it is what was left out.

Thus, many have wondered why the volatility of commodity prices was not addressed when it has subsequently emerged as a continuing concern, and acutely so with the turbulence and collapse of prices that have afflicted Africa in recent times. But one need not wonder long. Keynes indeed had worried about this to the extent of proposing a buffer stock plan, to be operated by an agency called Intemational Commodity Control, or, in brief, COMMOD, in a draft dated January 20, 1942, only to have it debated by several British official and ministerial committees and eventually shelved.[2]

What *is* remarkable, however, is the total lack of prescience concerning the question of intemational migration. No institution with responsibility for codifying the economic and political rights and obligations of migrants, the receiving and the sending countries, appears to have been conceived, let alone proposed. Literature is enriched by the immediacy of experiences, but economics is constrained by it. There was little in the interwar experience to suggest the extraordinary flows of *gastarbeiters*, skilled professionals, illegal migrants, and refugees, often originating in the developing countries, who would crisscross the globe in the postwar years. The absence of a compelling past evidently obscured the consideration of the impending future.

These omissions notwithstanding, the Bretton Woods institutions reflected a broad ideological consensus among the developed countries on the shape of a desirable international regime. During the 1950s and 1960s, the golden years of unprecedented expansion of world trade and income, as the developed countries drastically dismantled their tariffs under successive GATT rounds of negotiations, the liberal premises of the Bretton Woods regime generally acquired the legitimacy that success begets. The interesting question then is: How did the new developing nations perceive their role and interests in this regime?

A benign attitude toward the regime initially obtained among the developing countries simply because they too prospered during these decades. Their growth rates generally exceeded not merely their own prewar performance as colonies but those of present-day developed countries during their own transition in the nineteenth and twentieth centuries. Better still, they exceeded many of the most optimistic estimates of experts as they contemplated and masterminded the developmental programs of the developing countries in the late 1940s and early 1950s.

The pre-Industrial Revolution growth rates had reflected mainly capital accumulation. The Industrial Revolution had accelerated growth by unleashing the more powerful forces of technical change. In David Landes' memorable phrase, Prometheus had been unbound. The developing countries in general could not but do better by both mobilizing internal savings and external aid to increase investment rates to unprecedented levels and by absorbing a substantial backlog of technology.

A liberal international regime that offered the developing countries the advantages of access to trade, technology, and aid was thus seen as largely beneficial. But this view was tempered by the belief that their underdeveloped status as unequal partners justified asymmetrical rules exempting the developing countries from fully reciprocal obligations under the liberal regime. The doctrine of Special and Differential Treatment in trade, such as that which would be enacted in Part IV of GATT for their benefit, was thus an important part of the developing countries' concerted agenda for accommodation before regime acceptance. And the demand was conceded, not because the developing countries were strong but paradoxically because they were weak. Their share in world trade was so miniscule, but their number was so large, that the demands for asymmetry of obligations by the developing countries could be accommodated, fraying the liberal trading regime only at the margin while securing a large and growing membership of the institution that embodied the principles of the liberal order. Again, the relative economic significance of the developing countries in world trade implied that the "cost" to the developed countries of their escape from symmetric obligations of market access was small enough to warrant neglect and invite indulgence.

The overall result was then a relative unity within the South and, in turn, a degree of harmony with the North. It was frankly not arduous for the developing countries, often sharing a psychopolitical affinity owing to a common and immediate colonial history, to forge alliances in urging aid targets and seeking special and differential treatment in trade, platforms that implied "take," not "give," in the political lexicon. Nor were the developed countries inclined, as I have argued, to refuse substantial accommodation to these platforms in the larger interest of preserving the liberal regime's general acceptability.

But if the forces of unity and harmony were dominant during this period, the factors that could introduce centrifugal tendencies and discord were beginning to surface. The *ideological* dominance of the liberal approach to international regime making was beginning to be challenged, and the developing countries, differently affected by the new winds of ideological diversity, were also beginning to be differentiated by their *interests* as conditioned by their economic performance and by their varying integration into the world economy.

Thus, the liberal international regime had been premised on the belief that, given the structure of rules, interactions among all nations, developed and developing, would be mutually beneficial. There was now increasing intellectual skepticism of this non-zero-sum game ideology and affirmation instead of the contrary possibilities, even probability, of zero-sum outcomes to the detriment of the developing countries. Integration into the world economy, in this view, would invite disintegration of the national economy, not its prosperity.

Nowhere was this ideological schism more manifest than in the fluid perceptions of foreign-aid programs, multilateral and bilateral. While aid flows had certainly increased owing to the cold war being fought with economic weapons in the Third World, the ideological justification for such assistance remained the liberal view that it aided development and, in turn, would aid all good things like peace and democracy. But increasingly there was skepticism. The Right claimed malign impact on development, charging that by dovetailing aid into governmental budgets and plans, aid donors strengthened the state and weakened the private sector, under-mining rather than promoting development. The Left charged that aid assisted the rich and bypassed and even further impoverished the poor, thus negating the essential objective of redistribution from the rich in the developed countries to the poor of the developing countries. The broadly shared concern underlying these extreme assertions is conveyed, with comic relief, by the account of the meeting of three distinguished aid-seeking civil servants from Sri Lanka, all of Volckeresque dimensions, with their Whitehall counterparts. Asked wittily by their hosts whether they represented the starving masses of Sri Lanka, their Cambridge-educated leader is reputed to have risen to the occasion by retorting, "No, but we represent their aspirations!"

The ideological dissonance was equally manifest in other areas of inter-actions, between the developing and the developed countries. Thus, in-ternational migration of the skilled from the developing countries accel-erated significantly after legislations such as the 1965 U.S. immigration reform, which eliminated racial quotas and thus opened up more equal and hence greater access to immigration to the North from the South. This, in turn, led to a shift from the conventional open-door attitude of the affected developing countries to concern with the possibly deleterious effects of the "brain drain." Equally, the growth of foreign investment, certainly seen in a benign light in the Bretton Woods conception, would soon elicit eco-nomic reservations and political worries, ranging from fear as captured so well in Raymond Vernon's classic title, *Sovereignty at Bay*, to the radical certainty that it constituted continuation of colonialism by other means.

Developing countries chose differently from this menu of competing ideologies. In large part, present politics and past history conditioned this choice. But it is also fair to say that those countries that managed to do remarkably well and pulled ahead of the pack were among those that remained wedded to the Bretton Woods order. On the other hand, those that managed to lag behind tended to become skeptical of the international regime, their concerns varying with the nature of their integration in the world economy and corresponding perception of vulnerability.

Among the former group were the East Asian economies, the Gang of Four, the Four Tigers (South Korea, Taiwan, Hong Kong, and Singapore), which chalked up a remarkable growth performance during these years. Interestingly, in the 1950s, when all eyes were focused on the two Asian giants, China and India, and when the one compelling question was how democratic India would fare relative to the communist China, none thought that the economic success stories would transpire instead in these obscure countries of the Pacific. By contrast, the economic performance of both China and India turned out to be almost undistinguished, to the point where the sheer force of compound arithmetic would push the Four Tigers and their standards of living, both average and for the poor, soaring above those of these two giants.

Success has many fathers. And many economists have seen in these success stories the vindication of their conflicting pet theories. But it is indisputable that the Four Tigers rode to prosperity mainly on the back of an energetic commitment to an outward-oriented trade strategy, which enabled them to reap massive gains from trade in a world that offered expanding markets, thanks to the liberal international regime. Their prosperity then owed much to this regime. Quite regardless, therefore, of other factors such as closer political affinity to the United States, these nations could not be among those that would entertain skeptical thoughts on the advantages of this regime. Their loyalty to it was assured.

Painting again with a broad brush, one can argue that many developing countries, even when they accepted the economic tenets of the international regime, had reservations about their voice in its institutions. The politically conscious among the G-77 group of developing nations thus increasingly sought a greater presence and role in the Bretton Woods institutions while simultaneously seeking institutional diversification in their interest, as with the creation of the United Nations Conference on Trade and Development (UNCTAD) in 1964. The intensity and tenaciousness of these efforts varied with the political consciousness and leadership aspirations of these developing countries. Again, the economically triumphant Pacific nations seemed to prefer a low political profile; political voice seemed less important to them than the appropriateness of the liberal regime that had brought them economic largesse. Differential economic performance, despite general prosperity, evidently implied, therefore, different interests and tradeoffs, making the task of arriving at unified platforms by the developing countries that much more difficult.

Phase II: 1973 to 1981

The forces of both unity and diversity were, however, paradoxically reinforced simultaneously, if only temporarily, by the spectacular success of OPEC in 1973.

OPEC provided a dramatic role model where *unilateral* action by producers of a commodity had managed to raise prices and thus wrest for them a substantially higher share of world income. This suggested to developing countries, despite the distress among the importers of oil, that what was done with oil could be done with other commodities as well. The concept of "commodity power" was thus born. Whereas many had lamented for years that specialization by developing countries on producing and exporting primary commodities was a sign of *weakness*, paradoxically it was now interpreted as a measure of *strength*. Cartelization would harness *economic* power to raise prices; embargos could deploy *political* power to extract regime changes.

In retrospect, it seems really odd that anyone should have believed that OPEC could be cloned for bauxite and bananas. And yet, hold your breath. Henry Kissinger, the great master of *realpolitik*, was among those who feared such spread of *Riyadhekonomik*. Even my good friend, Fred Bergsten, announced the arrival of the new era of commodity power in no uncertain terms. The euphoria of the developing countries was not just their own affliction; it possessed many, among them the most perspicacious and circumspect.

Nonetheless, its premise was false, and its promise would prove to be illusory. But it did provide a powerful unifying impulse to the developing countries during the period of its credibility. Until OPEC, the developing countries had been in a mode of seeking and receiving within a liberal regime that broadly commanded consensus despite emerging diversity of ideology and interests. They had received because of their weakness; and little of what they had received challenged the main tenets of the liberal international regime. In no sense had the periphery *negotiated* with the center. Negotiations presuppose strength, an approximate parity of passions and power among the parties, and the developing countries had little of it.

The new perception of commodity power changed that. The leaders among the G-77 saw in it the capacity to transmit from "receiving" to "taking." "Accommodation" would yield to "concessions." The time for a new international economic order had arrived.

The euphoria over commodity power produced the unifying sentiment. A platform that threw everyone's demands onto the agenda of the NIEO provided the necessary cement. Even had these manifold demands been made with diplomatic concern for the sensibilities of the North, they would have been perceived with less than equanimity. But they were not, for these were dizzying times for the developing countries. The ideological rhetoric of the NIEO at the United Nations, a certain militancy of manner, were perhaps inevitable. But their legacy would be not an enduring unity of the South but rather a reactive ideological militancy of the United States later, with the arrival of the present administration.

It was not long before OPEC-inspired commodity power was seen to be a mirage. The *unifying* forces it had released, coalescing behind the drive for NIEO, were therefore short lived. Not so, however, were the *fragmenting* effects of OPEC.

For, OPEC had irretrievably thrown the developing countries into a new configuration that accentuated their different circumstances rather than their common destiny. The oil-rich nations, among them Mexico and Nigeria, were set apart by their newfound largesse. The Third World had splintered to yield a Fourth. But the flip side of the coin was the recycling of OPEC funds through the Western banks, principally to the not-so-poor nations of South America. This changed the landscape yet more dramatically, ushering in the era of massive portfolio capital flows and setting the stage for the debt crisis of this particular group of developing countries. But for the time being these nations became the admired few, registering high debt-led growth rates. The distress caused by oil-price increases among many of the remaining, and indeed poorer, developing countries equally set them apart, often inviting proposals for official debt relief, while the outward-oriented East Asian economies adjusted well to the distress, continuing to outperform the rest of the developing world. Diversity of circumstance and interests was clearly beginning to occupy center stage.

Phase III: 1981 to 1987

But the kaleidoscope would turn again with the sharp recession of 1981 and 1982, rearranging the winners and the losers.

The recession destroyed the invincibility of OPEC. Milton Friedman had long predicted this inevitable event but had been smart enough not to specify when! The bonanza of OPEC surpluses for South America was over; oil power had joined the ranks of commodity power. Equally, the curious policy mix in the United States, combining an expansionary fiscal and a contractionary monetary policy, had produced high interest rates in the midst of recession. The debtor countries were thus caught in a triple bind that included the drying up of the net influx of portfolio funds they had been addicted to since the mid-1970s, the income effect of foreign recession on their exports, and the increased interest burden on their current stock of debt.

Much has been written on the question of whether the debtors were profligate or the lenders imprudent. The truth is somewhere in between.

Mr. Walter Wriston's emissaries did blandish money everywhere, encouraging borrowers indiscriminately during the 1970s. But South America exuberantly embraced them whereas the countries of Asia generally did not. Even casual cross-sectional empiricism tells us, therefore, to be skeptical of the one-sided critiques that exonerate the big debtors from any role in their present predicament. What one *can* say in their defense is that the combination of recession and high interest rates was unique in the history of the business cycle and that prudent borrowers could have expected lower interest rates to offset the adverse impact of falling foreign demand during a recession, whereas higher interest rates reinforced it.

The collapse of primary commodity prices that the recession precipitated, and that has continued since, accentuated the difficulties in South America but devastated many economies in Africa. Dollar indices of current export commodity prices constructed by UNCTAD (thirty-nine products, excluding petroleum) and by the World Bank (thirty-three products, excluding petroleum) show that they fell by nearly 40 percent during 1980–82 alone.[3] After a mild recovery in 1983, as the economic upturn began, they fell again and have continued doing so since.

The African situation has been further compounded by drought and famine in much of sub-Saharan Africa. With the drastic slump in commodity prices and famine, it has also become evident that the continent has generally been crippled by civil wars and strife and, unlike the countries of Asia for instance, has generally regressed into a situation where social and economic infrastructure, skills and absorptive capacity have become matters of central concern. It is simply unthinkable, for instance, that today's developing countries in Asia would lack their own organizational resources and would have to turn to Peace Corps volunteers and foreign agencies to distribute food aid in a famine; and yet that is precisely what happened in Africa recently. The problems here evidently are elemental and, in fact, a throwback to the considerations that preoccupied development economists at the *start* of the postwar period!

At the same time, the threat of protectionism has become worrisome in the OECD countries in the 1980s, halting and even reversing with voluntary export restraints and administered protection the liberalizing trend set by successive GATT rounds of tariff reductions. While this protectionism was fueled by the recession and owes much to the subsequent overvaluation of the dollar that squeezed the traded sector, it has also been aided by structural changes in the world economy.

In particular, the OECD countries have faced a double squeeze. Japan and the advanced nonindustrial countries (NICs) have been pressuring the high-tech industries, whereas the developing countries have been competing successfully with the labor-intensive industries at the lower end of the spectrum. This has thus not merely resulted in added adjustment problems for the affected industries. It has also caused many in Europe and the United States to fear that "deindustrialization" may follow, with both sunrise and sunset industries in peril.[4]

Yet again, in the United States, the protectionist drive has been aided by what I have called the "diminished giant" syndrome.[5] The relative decline of the U.S. economy, though it continues to be a *force majeure*, and the sudden rise of the Pacific nations in world income and trade, have produced demands in the United States today for "fair trade" and reciprocity vis-à-vis foreigners allegedly engaging in unfair trade, similar to those that a diminishing Britain witnessed at the end of the nineteenth century.

For the East Asian countries that profited from open and expanding world markets through their outward-oriented policies, this protectionist threat (rather than access to finance, official or private) is the most critical problem. It is also a matter of some, if lesser, concern for the countries seeking export earnings to service their debts and for the late converts to the advantages of outward-oriented trade strategy.

23.2   The Map Today

The developing countries then are in strikingly different situations of vulnerability today.

Now, each country is unique. Raul Prebisch, who came from Argentina, used to regale his friends with the witticism: "There are developed countries, developing countries, Japan and Argentina." But we can nonetheless usefully think of the developing countries today in terms of broad groups, each characterized by a different but common set of afflictions. In my view four such broad groups can be meaningfully defined.

1. *South America*. Debts to *private* lenders are evidently important here, crying for a solution that needs international action. The region has many fragile democracies in recent transition from a long tradition of authoritarian regimes. Per capita incomes are among the highest in developing countries.

The region has a tradition of appalling macroeconomics, with multiple-digit inflations a persistent problem and stabilization a perennial objective. I might remark in passing that this tradition is evidently what gave us the legacy of the monetarist prescription for clients seeking IMF assistance.

Presented in the 1950s and early 1960s with countries that persistently and extravagantly inflated, printing money and spending it through the budget, and that reluctantly adjusted their exchange rates in the face of such inflation, what could the Fund's theoreticians, such as Jacques Polak, have done except to say: Stop printing money, reduce budget deficits, and adjust your exchange rates to realistic levels?[6] The macroeconomic excesses of South America have been so great, and in such striking contrast to the outcomes in Asian countries, that I have been tempted to assert that macroeconomics reflects culture and must be of one piece with literature. The extravagant macroeconomics of multiple-digit inflations by the ebullient policymakers of South America reminds one of the exuberant, almost surrealistic portrayals in Gabriel Garcia Marquez, whereas the macroeconomics of one-digit inflations in India recalls the tranquility of Malgudi village in R. K. Narayan.

2. *Africa.* Debts to *official*, rather than private, lenders are important here. Commodity prices are central to well-being and have currently collapsed, making debt relief critical. Microeconomics has often been poor. Infrastructure and skills have lagged abominably, hurting often from internal and external strife as well.

3. *The NICs.* Both macroeconomics and microeconomics are fine here. Debts are manageable and managed. Their only concern is with the continuation of open markets abroad. The containment of OECD protectionism is their major hope.

4. *India and China.* Both have had excellent macroeconomics but disappointing microeconomics. While this is inevitable in traditional communist regimes, India's surrender to stifling controls and inward-looking trade policies has meant that the excellent macroeconomic performance that I contrasted with South America's earlier has not been exploited successfully to date. Both countries are now set on unshackling their economies, a course of action that requires more internal resolve and political skills than external assistance. Low-cost aid, such as the International Development Association (IDA) provides, remains important, given the enormous populations and poverty that afflict both India and China. High-cost commercial borrowing, which both nations have prudently minimized, is unwise until internal productivity of resource use improves and successful outward orientation is implemented.

In each instance then, the nature of required internal effort varies and the role of discipline remains paramount. But it is manifest that international and often multilateral action tailored to the *differential* needs of each group is equally important. It is equally obvious that the pressure to "capture" the multilateral institutions such as the World Bank to devote principal attention to just one problem, e.g, the debt crisis, is to be deplored.

23.3 The United States: Ideological Militancy and Fine-tuned Nonintervention

Unfortunately, however, such clarity of vision has been slow to emerge. Nor, I must confess, has the key actor on the stage, the Reagan administration, given us much hope that, even had the vision been clear, forceful, and effective, action would have been forthcoming. I am afraid that, in matters of international economic management, its record has been one of a curious mix of ideological militancy and fine-tuned nonintervention.

The ideological militancy, of a conservative hue, was particularly manifest in the first term. It was largely reactive to the confrontational days of the NIEO but probably would have surfaced anyway.

The early militancy was directed at the multilateral agencies, including the Fund and the Bank, to purge them of practices that were viewed as ideologically liberal and hence supportive of statism and destructive of market forces. The complacent Oblomovism, by contrast, was directed at the management of the world economy in key matters requiring instead critical attention: in particular, the macromanagement of exchange rates and the coordination of the fiscal-monetary mixes of the key surplus and deficit countries, and the debt crisis.

The ideological activism was manifest in the general disdain for the United Nations. The United Nations had been the forum for the demands for NIEO during the 1970s. It was therefore a surefire lightning rod for conservatives.[7]

But the militancy extended also to other United Nations agencies, principally the UNCTAD. UNCTAD increasingly came to be viewed in the administration as an institution that favored politics over economics and one that was partisan and could not be trusted to be an honest broker on developmental problems and solutions. UNCTAD, therefore, came to be regarded, I have remarked, as if it was UNWASHED and UNKEMPT instead. The irony is that, as Raul Prebisch often reminded us, the UNCTAD *was* meant to be partisan, to provide a secretariat that *would* reflect developing-country viewpoints and concerns; the developed countries after all had the OECD, for instance. And UNCTAD did play the role of a catalyst on many issues that would subsequently claim legitimate attention on our intellectual and policy agenda. I can underline this no better than by recalling that services such as shipping and insurance had been discussed at the UNCTAD long before they entered the GATT agenda of today, with an amusing sequel told me by Dr. Giarini of the International Insurance Association's prestigious thinktank. On being informed by Dr. Giarini that the Tenth Annual Geneva Lecture would be delivered by me on the subject of trade in services since it was an issue before the GATT, an eminent man of British insurance and peer of the realm who serves on his Council asked him, "Hmmm! GATT. What *is* it? Is it some sort of UNCTAD?"[8]

But if the administration preferred the Bretton Woods agencies to the United Nations, these too had to be reshaped in a conservative image. Thus, the U.S. representatives generally reversed positions on a number of the initiatives of the earlier administrations. For instance, at the Fund, the administration became lukewarm about the use of the Extended Fund facility, which had been set up in 1974 to provide longer-term finance to facilitate "structural adjustment." It also opposed single-handedly the use of this facility by India on the ground that, despite the sorry situation developing in South America, India should utilize private borrowing before turning to the Fund. Again, there was successful pressure from the United States to restrict the utility of the Compensatory Financing Facility, the low conditionality window at the Fund, through added conditionalities and reduced automaticity, which by 1983 had drastically restricted its soft-conditionality character. At the Bank, there was unabashed dragging of feet on IDA replenishment.

In fact, this ideological assertiveness implied that even bilateral aid programs would increasingly be reflective of criteria other than those of redistribution according to need. There thus followed a distinct shift in the composition of aid in favor of recipients successfully invoking security objectives, Egypt and Israel being among the principal beneficiaries. Indeed, while in 1980 economic and humanitarian assistance had been two-thirds of security assistance in the foreign-aid spending, by 1986 it had fallen to less than half. The United States was rebuilding its aid programs in the Soviet image; quid pro quo bilateralism was becoming a driving force.[9] The energetic pursuit of such quid pro quos, unmindful of necessary nuances, has also been manifest in the occasional retribution visited upon aid recipients who step out of line. A striking example of such a punishment disproportionate to the crime is provided by the suspension of aid to Zimbabwe over a cabinet minister's anguished and undiplomatic criticism of the administration's South Africa foreign policy at a July 4 celebration in the U.S. Embassy, reminding one of Samuel Johnson's protest when his

Oxford tutor fined him for cutting a class: "Sir, you have sconced me two-pence for non-attendance at a lecture not worth a penny."[10]

The ideological militancy in support of market approaches has been manifest also in the astonishing decisions it has inspired in other important areas of international concern and concerted action. Thus, the administration withdrew support from the carefully negotiated Law of the Sea Treaty because of its "statist" provisions concerning an international seabed authority. Again, it was the only nation that refused to sign the international convention adopted at the United Nations with guidelines for marketing baby-food formula. Moreover, at the 1984 Mexico conference on population, the administration insisted on the doctrine that population growth would necessarily be benign in that it would automatically generate the income required to maintain itself. I call this a doctrinal shift from the hand-and-mouth theory of population in the poor countries to the hand-to-mouth theory! Again, it was a celebration of the doctrine that laissez-faire is ideal: it would produce not merely babies, but also the formula, Pampers, and cribs to take care of them.

The exaggerated commitment with which the administration pursued the case for markets and against government has led me to describe this period as the Age of Certainty. It would have invited mere ridicule had it been of no consequence. But, coming from the powerful United States, it had teeth and provoked dread and anger. The supreme confidence in going from abstract economic principles to concrete policymaking in the developing countries reminds me of the moral certitude that characterized the typically well-meaning but misguided British official in early nineteenth-century India, as described by a perceptive commentary of the time:

Every man writes as much as he can, and quotes Montesquieu, and Hume, and Adam Smith. Most of their papers might have been written by men who were never out of England, and their projects are nearly as applicable to that country, as to India ... [There is none to be dreaded] half so much as an able Calcutta civilian, whose travels are limited to two or three hundred miles, with a hookah in his mouth, some good but abstract maxims in his head, the Regulations in his right hand, the Company's Charter in his left, and a quire of wirewoven foolscap before him.[11]

Perhaps this is what Prime Minister Indira Gandhi wished to convey at the Cancun Summit when, in a jovial riposte to President Reagan's observation that developing countries should lift themselves up by their own bootstraps, she remarked that many in these countries could not afford the boots in the first place.

A good case can be ruined by a bad advocate. The case for more markets was indeed mauled by the ideological fervor. There is little doubt that the invisible hand is seen too infrequently in many developing countries. Indeed, I have myself been a proponent of reduced controls, increased incentives, greater outward orientation in trade, and similar reforms in many developing countries since the mid-1960s. But to imply that governments should self-destruct, as in the models of Milton Friedman and Mikhail Bakunin, is to lose all sense of proportion. It is also plain wrong, for governments have indeed much to do in the developing countries. The key question is not *whether* governments ought to intervene, but *how*.

A trend toward occasionally simplistic and often strong conditionality has been alleged to be the consequence and has certainly been a source of unhappiness in several developing countries with the Fund and the Bank. Since the same pressures afflict both institutions, and in turn their clients, the unhappiness extends also to the new issue of "crossconditionality," i.e., the coordination and homogenization of conditionality by both institutions, leaving little scope to dissenting client states to breathe by changing patrons. This concern is a recurrent one, surfacing whenever conditionality becomes suffocating. Development economists of goodwill have suggested exotic measures such as arbitration procedures to settle irreconcileable differences between donors and recipients[11] or the romantic, recent proposal[12] (put forth, of course, by economists from the "middle powers") that conditionality be brokered by panels that include the "honestly neutral" economists from these middle powers such as Canada! The easier answer is to introduce common sense and a proper appreciation of the limits of economic science and the constraints of political realities into the operation of conditionality while maintaining a pragmatic and broad support for market-oriented reform where appropriate.

Paradoxically, the militant activism in propagating the conservative ideology that I have just sketched has gone hand in hand with a laidback, hands-off style in the management of international macroeconomic equilibrium, with indirect consequences for the developing nations, and in the debt crisis whose impact on the affected developing nations is direct and immediate.

The neglect of international macroeconomics, more specifically the managed float system, hardly needs emphasis from me. If you had thought that former Treasury Secretary John Connally's famous remark, "The dollar is our currency and your problem," could not be bettered, you were wrong. Chairman Beryl Sprinkel is credited with the priceless observation: "Let the Europeans look after their exchange rates; we will look after ours." The continuing imbalances in the world economy, calling for a coordination of monetary and fiscal policies dovetailed into relatively stable and sustainable exchange rates, have finally caught up with us rather dramatically, underlining the superiority in this instance of the ancient adage that "a stitch in time saves nine" over its latter-day antithesis that "if it ain't broke, don't fix it."

But the tendency to avoid action until altogether necessary, which is reminiscent of St. Augustine's prayer that Eric Roll recalled in his Sturc Lecture two years ago: "Oh Lord, grant me continence and chastity, but not just yet," has been equally manifest in the refusal to come to terms with the debt crisis with the aid of any one of innumerable proposals for debt relief. The administration has moved, only as necessary in face of imminent disaster, from one game plan to another, each distinguished by desperate hope but not effective action. The early embrace of the notion that the market would sort out the good from the bad debtors and seek its own solutions, was replaced by resort to the Fund as the guarantor of a "deflate-and-adjust" strategy to restore the debtors' creditworthiness. When that became unsustainable, there was another quickstep to the World Bank, hitherto the target of scorn in this game, and the propagation of the Baker Plan to "grow and adjust," restore creditworthiness, and induce new flows. The next turn of the screw, which surely must come as others have in the past on the schedule some of us predicted long ago, should push the administration finally into a realistic adoption of the debt-relief scenario that is long overdue. Hopefully, this too will transpire before a financial cataclysm overtakes us from the debtor nations.

23.4   The Developing Countries: Opportunities in Interdependence

But I would be remiss if I urged the United States to start minding its responsibilities, chiefly those that arise from the increased *vulnerabilities* that interdependence creates, and did not remind the developing countries of the *opportunities* that increased integration into the world economy offers for their own fruitful action. Let me illustrate with a telling example from international migration. There, as elsewhere, developing countries have need and scope for flexible adaptation in a manner that can turn constraints into opportunities.

Take skilled migration or "brain drain." For the developing countries with high skills, this has been a substantive phenomenon; it has also been considered a significant problem. Measures to contain it have been debated endlessly, raising a disturbing trade-off between economics and ethics. The former suggests restrictions on emigration and the latter finds them reprehensible.

But the trade-off is largely artificial. The fact of such outmigration also presents overwhelming advantages if only the developing countries will change their attitudes, policies, and institutions to consider those who migrate abroad as part of a diaspora, rather than regarding them fearfully and disapprovingly as citizens who have moved away to the detriment of those left behind.

I should like to underline this by developing a rather novel argument that arises, curiously enough, in the context of the current concerns of Brazil, India, and other large developing countries over the proposed extension of GATT-type rules to trade in services.[13] These developing countries have resisted such efforts, among their major objectives being to protect locally produced computer hardware in the information sectors. This has not merely produced a confrontation with the United States and, to a lesser extent, other developed countries at the Uruguay Round. It has also been a particularly expensive way for these countries to build up technological know-how through "learning by doing." For, the effect of this policy has been to spread computer illiteracy in the population (through scarcity and high prices of computers due to the protection) and to impose high costs on user-producers who must make do without lower-cost and freer access to modern information technology.

But this is exactly where the emigration of the skilled opens up a new approach. A country such as India has the possibility of using outmigration as an alternative policy instrument to achieve the desired mastery of know-how without these costs. Remember that the know-how is embodied in one's citizens. If one then looks at the national-origin composition of scientists in only the artificial intelligence, robotics, and computer science labs and institutes in the United States, it is possible to find numerous Indian mathematicians and scientists, even in leadership positions. These Indians embody know-how in these fields at the very cutting edge of technology, know-how that could not have been often acquired except under advantageous foreign conditions.

Since the sociology of international migration of professional classes increasingly permits immigrants to retain ethnic ties to their countries of origin, and therefore the diaspora model has increasingly come into its own, the Indian government has the option of utilizing this U.S.-based resource any time it wishes to do so. Going the protectionist route will yield a lower level of embodied technology in resident nationals (who may leave anyway) and will sacrifice computer literacy and efficiency in production. Permitting inexpensive imports at world prices avoids these costs, and free outmigration of scientists permits the best know-how to be embodied in one's nationals.

To put it differently, the two objectives of (1) spreading computer literacy and encouraging adoption of efficient production processes, and (2) building up technical know-how among one's nationals are impossible to achieve with one policy instrument, namely, protection. They are achievable, and are in effect dominated in outcome, by the use of two policy instruments: world-price imports of computers and related technology and an open-door policy on emigration.

If there is a further objective of utilizing domestically this know-how embodied in nationals abroad, evidently you need a further set of policy instruments. Chief among them are institutional changes and flexibility. For instance, universities and research institutes can be persuaded to relax rules, permitting institutionalized sharing of faculties between the developed countries of destination and the developing countries of origin, so that the latter can have at least partial access to their talent abroad, profiting from promiscuity where marriage is impossible!

The skilled outmigration that has traditionally been judged to be a worrisome problem, a vulnerability, a source of disintegrating integration into the center by the periphery, in fact presents, a helpful policy option, an opportunity. But seizing that opportunity requires not merely an adaptive change in conceptualizing the phenomenon of skilled emigration. It also requires attention to appropriate policies to turn a potential advantage into a true dividend.

Such flexibility of attitudes and policies, as well as a determination to put one's economic house in order in matters where the nature of required reform is manifest to all, will have to be on the developing countries' internal agenda. It provides the necessary counterpart to the agenda for the developed countries and the Bretton Woods agencies to provide the external conditions appropriate to the developmental tasks at hand.

A drowning man must grab the lifeline if he is to make it. But we must not forget the lifeline either. I am reminded of the story of the stiff-upper-lipped Englishman on the bridge as a man is drowning below, crying frantically, "Help, help! I cannot swim!" Nonchalantly, the Englishman puffs on his pipe and responds, "I cannot swim either; but I would not make such a fuss about it." I remain optimistic, and I am sure Ernest Sturc would have shared the optimism that the developed countries and the multilateral institutions will not follow in the Englishman's footsteps.

Notes

1. I draw here, but from the altogether different perspective of the thesis of increasing diversity among developing countries, on a historical analysis that I have sketched broadly in Bhagwati (1984, 1986).

2. Keynes' draft memorandum was published by me in the *Journal of International Economics* (1974), having been brought to my attention by Lal Jayawardene. A brief but splendid account of its origin and demise is provided by Nicholas Kaldor (1987). It is important to remember that Keynes' concerns were more with the impact of volatile commodity prices on the stability of the world economy than the effect on the developing countries' economic well-being, his arguments being more in line with the subsequent writings of Kaldor.

3. Cf. Avramovic (1987) for further details.

4. I have dealt with this issue in more detail in the 1987 Ohlin Lectures on Protectionism: Bhagwati (1988).

5. Cf. Bhagwati and Irwin (1987).

6. The problem has rather been that this prescription has tended to be applied to the regions whose adjustment problems arose from exogenous causes such as terms-of-trade deterioration or harvest failure. If the Fund is to be faulted, it is for its rather surprising failure to date in evolving a clear, suitable taxonomy of disturbance sources and structural economic characteristics (e.g., whether the country is debt ridden) and corresponding sets of suitable policy instruments appropriate to each class of cases so distinguished.

7. I have dealt with this issue in greater depth in my 1985 Bernard Fain Lecture (Bhagwati, 1986).

8. There *is* evidence, I am afraid, of a certain deterioration in the quality of professional work at UNCTAD in recent years. But this is as much a consequence of abandonment by the United States of its interest, loyalty, and voice as its cause.

9. I borrow this phrase from Padma Desai's (1984) apt characterization of Soviet aid programs.

10. Cf. Bate (1975, p. 95).

11. Cf. Rosenstein-Rodan (1968).

12. Cf. The Commonwealth Secretariat Report (1986) on this subject.

13. Cf. Bhagwati (1987) for further details.

References

Avramovic, D. 1987. Commodity Problem: What Next? *World Development* 15 (5): 645–656.

Bates, W. Jackson. 1975. *Samuel Johnson*. New York: Harcourt, Brace Jovanovich.

Bhagwati, Jagdish. 1984. Rethinking Global Negotiations. In J. Bhagwati and John Ruggie (eds.), *Power, Passions, and Purpose: Prospects for North-South Negotiations*. Cambridge: MIT Press.

Bhagwati, Jagdish. 1986. Ideology and North-South Relations," 1985 Bernard Fain Lecture, *World Development* 14(6), pp. 767–774.

Bhagwati, Jagdish. 1987. Trade in Services and the Multilateral Trade Negotiations. *World Bank Economic Review* 1(4): 549–569.

Bhagwati, Jagdish. 1988. *Protectionism: Ideology, Interests and Institutions*. 1987 Ohlin Lectures, Cambridge, MA: MIT Press.

Bhagwati, Jagdish, and Douglas Irwin. 1987. The Return of the Reciprocitarians—US Trade Policy Today. *World Economy* 10(2): 109–130.

Commonwealth Secretariat. 1986. *Cross-Conditionality*. London.

Desai, Padma. 1984. The Soviet Union and the Third World: A Faltering Partnership? In Jagdish Bhagwati and John Ruggie (eds.), *Power, Passions, and Purpose: Prospects for North–South Negotiations*. Cambridge: MIT Press. Reprinted in Padma Desai. *The Soviet Economy: Problems and Prospects*. Oxford: Basil Blackwell, 1987.

Kaldor, Nicholas. 1987. The Role of Commodity Prices in Economic Recovery. *World Development* 15(5): 551–558.

Keynes, John Maynard, 1974. The International Control of Raw Materials. *Journal of International Economics* 4(3): 299–316.

Rosenstein-Rodan Paul. 1968. The Consortia Technique. *International Organization* 223–230.

Vernon, Raymond. 1971. *Sovereignty at Bay*. New York: Basic Books.

24   Export-Promoting Trade Strategy: Issues and Evidence

The question of the wisdom of adopting an export-promoting trade strategy has recurred in the history of the developing countries. Development economics was born in an atmosphere of export pessimism at the end of the World War II. By the late 1960s, however, the remarkable success of the few economies that pursued "export-promoting" (EP) rather than "import-substituting" (IS) policies swung the weight of academic opinion behind the EP strategy. Aiding this process were numerous academic findings from research projects around the world, which investigated both these EP successes and the failures of the IS countries.[1]

The debt crisis of the 1980s, the sluggish world economy, and the continuing depression of primary product prices have revived export pessimism afresh. It is time again, therefore, to examine the old and new arguments that question the wisdom of the EP strategy.

The early postwar arguments in support of export pessimism are briefly reviewed below, before the precise content of an EP strategy is stated. The article then considers a few salient lessons that have emerged in the studies on the advantages of the EP strategy and examines several new sources of skepticism concerning export-promoting trade policies. The contrasts between the old (postwar) pessimism and the new pessimism prevalent today are then exploited briefly to draw a central policy lesson for the developing countries, especially in regard to the multilateral trade negotiations (MTN).[2]

24.1   The First Export Pessimism

It is well known that export pessimism characterized the thinking of most influential development economists and policymakers in the developing countries after World War II. The most articulate proponents of the pessimist school of thought were the two great pioneers of development economics: Raul Prebisch (see Prebisch 1952, 1984) and Ragnar Nurkse (see Nurkse 1959). Their diagnoses, however, had significant differences.

Prebisch considered the terms of trade of primary products, then the chief exports of developing countries, to be declining regardless of the policies of the developing countries. Left to themselves, producers in the developing countries would have responded to this secular price shift by industrializing, which would make (trade tariff) protection or (domestic subsidy) promotion unnecessary and unjustified.[3] By contrast, Nurkse's export pessimism arose from the notion that foreign markets simply could not accommodate imports on a sufficient scale as developing countries accelerated their development. Therefore, export pessimism explicitly meant "elasticity" pessimism, and the case for government intervention then follows.[4] Nurkse, therefore, advocated what he called a policy of "balanced growth."

Paradoxically, however, Nurkse was mindful of the costs of indiscriminate protectionism, as he had also written about the collapse of the world trading system during the 1930s (Nurkse 1953). "Balanced growth" could only mean government incentives to assist industrialization, a prescription that appears to have combined uneasily with the caveats that Nurkse expressed about protection. By contrast, Prebisch's brand of pessimism did not justify protectionism but was nevertheless widely used by his followers to do so in Latin America.

The export pessimism of these influential economists was cast in the mold of natural forces and phenomena that the developing countries faced. Nurkse, for instance, wrote about increasing economy in the use of raw materials and a shift further from natural to synthetic materials, both dampening the demand for developing countries' exports over time. Developing countries could do nothing to change these conditions at the source, just as one cannot do anything about bad weather. But their policies had to adjust to these conditions, just as one can buy an umbrella against the rain. (By contrast, as I note below, the second export pessimism of the 1980s is rooted in protectionist threats, which can be addressed at the source and hence have critically different implications for developing country policies.)

The export pessimism following World War II was to prove unjustified by the unfolding reality. World trade did not merely grow rapidly during the 1950s and 1960s, it grew even faster than world income. The growth rates in both output and trade were unprecedented for such sustained periods (see table 24.1). Furthermore, the economies that shifted quickly to an EP strategy experienced substantial improvements in their export performance. This was particularly the case for four Far Eastern economies—

Table 24.1
Postwar growth rates of world output and trade (average annual percentage change)

Period	World output	World trade
1953–63	4.3	6.1
1963–73	5.1	8.9
1973–83	2.5	2.8

Source: Hufbauer and Schott (1985), table A-1, p. 97.

Hong Kong, Singapore, the Republic of Korea, and Taiwan—but it was by no means confined to them. The dramatic rise in these economies' share of trade in GDP over this period placed them well above the regression lines for trade–GDP ratios and per capita incomes. These regressions would suggest that trade–GDP ratios fall as per capita income rises, whereas these successful exporters showed a spectacular rise in their trade shares as their per capita incomes grew rapidly.[5] Clearly, history has sided with economists such as Cairncross (1962) and Krueger (1961) who had been among the foremost critics of export pessimism.

Although the evidence of successful trade expansion decisively refuted the validity of export pessimism, the economic analysis in support of such pessimism was also to prove enlightening and has a bearing on the dissection of the resurgent, second export pessimism prevalent today. Nurkse, for instance, had embraced Robertson's classic phrase: trade as "an engine of growth," which established a rather strong and direct link in the export pessimists' minds between external conditions and internal expansion. In a classic throwback to this form of argumentation, Lewis (1980) argued more recently in a much-quoted passage:[6]

The growth rate of world trade in primary products over the period of 1873 to 1913 was 0.87 times the growth rate of industrial production in the developed countries; and just about the same relationship, about 0.87, also ruled in the two decades to 1973 ... We need no elaborate statistical proof that trade depends on prosperity in the industrial countries (p. 556).

But, it is evident from several analyses,[7] the latest being by Riedel (1984), that such stable relationships (which suggest the exclusive dominance of demand in determining trade performance) simply cannot be extracted from the export experience of developing countries in the postwar period. The export performance of these and other countries must be explained by domestic incentives (or supply) more than by external (or demand) conditions. It is worth restating the two main arguments supporting this conclusion.

First, although Lewis addresses the linkage between industrial country incomes and developing country exports of primary products, Riedel (1984, table 4) shows that even this aggregate developing country relationship is not stable. The stability, in turn, obviously cannot be maintained for individual developing countries.

Second, it is important to note again that the postwar period has seen a dramatic shift in the export composition of developing countries toward manufactures. Developing country exports of manufactures grew threefold in the 1955–78 period and represented one-fourth of overall exports. Manufactures are now close in magnitude to the other nonfuel exports such as food, minerals, and agricultural raw materials. Of course, the successful exporters of the postwar period dominate this shift. But their experience, based on domestic policies, proves that one cannot assess trade potential through mechanical linkages to industrial country income expansion.

The most compelling aggregate statistics show that during the prosperous 1960s, developing countries' exports of manufactures grew nearly twice as fast as the industrial countries' incomes. The expansion of developing countries' trade over the 1950s and 1960s occurred as protection in the industrial countries was diminishing sharply as a consequence of first the elimination of quotas and then the reduction in tariffs. Even during the troubled 1970s, developing countries' exports of manufactures grew more than four times as rapidly as the industrial countries' income.[8]

The only key question that has remained at issue, therefore, is what has been called the "fallacy of composition": Can all, or most, developing countries become successful exporters simultaneously? Or, focusing on the successful Asian exporters, the question may be put: Can the Asian export model be successfully exported to all? The suspicion still lingers that the success of a few was built on the failure of the many and that, if all had shifted to the EP strategy, none would have fared well.

There are two distinct sources of this worry. The first presumes that markets would not be able to absorb all of the exports that would materialize if developing countries shifted to an EP strategy. The second argues that while the markets could be found, they would be closed by protectionist measures, provoked by the import penetration and outcries of market disruption. The second source is the major cause of export pessimism today, while the first source was the one that afflicted the earlier wave of export pessimism. I now examine the former argument and defer discussion of the latter.

First, as I shall argue more fully below, the fear that world trade would have to grow by leaps and bounds if most developing countries pursued an EP strategy is unwarranted. This fear follows from trying to put all countries on the curve estimated in Cline (1982) for the Asian exporters with very high ratios of trade to national income. The pursuit of an EP strategy simply amounts to the adoption of a structure of incentives which does not discriminate against exports in favor of the home market. This does not imply that the resulting increases in trade—income ratios will be necessarily as dramatic as in the Far Eastern case.

Second, the share of developing countries in the markets for manu-factures in most industrial countries has been, and continues to be, rela-tively small. In the aggregate, the share of manufactured exports from developing countries in the consumption of manufactures in the industrial countries runs at a little over 2 percent. "Absorptive capacity" purely in the market sense, therefore, is not prima facie a plausible source of worry.

Third, a chief lesson of the postwar experience is that policymakers who seek to forecast exports typically understate export potential by under-stating the absorptive capacity of import markets. This comes largely from having to focus on known exports and partly from downward estimation biases when price elasticities for such exports are econometrically mea-sured. Experience underlines the enormous capacity of wholly unforeseen markets to develop when incentives exist to make profits; "miscellaneous exports" often represent the source of spectacular gains when the bias against exports, typical of IS regimes, is removed.

Fourth, trade economists have increasingly appreciated the potential for intraindustry specialization as trade opportunities open. The progressive dismantling of trade barriers within the European Communities (EC), for instance, led to increased mutual trade in similar products rather than to massive reductions in the scale of output in industry groups within in-dustrial member states.[9] There is no reason to doubt that such intraindustry trade in manufactures among developing countries and between them and the industrial countries can also develop significantly.

Finally, if we reckon with the potential for trade between developing countries where policies can change to permit its increase, and the pos-sibility of opening new sectors such as agriculture and services to freer trade, then the export possibilities are even more abundant than the pre-ceding arguments indicate.[10]

Therefore, although the postwar export pessimism was unjustified, it provided a rationale for the adoption of inward-looking trade policies in many developing countries. In addition, trade restrictions were adopted to protect the industries that had grown up fortuitously in Latin America because World War II had provided artificial inducement to set up domestic capacities to produce interrupted supplies from traditional, competitive suppliers abroad.[11] Often, chiefly in Latin America, there was also a reluctance to devalue. Combined with high rates of inflation, this caused continuously overvalued exchange rates that amounted to a de facto IS trade policy (see the appendix).[12]

24.2   What Is an Export-Promoting Trade Strategy?

What exactly is meant by an export-promoting trade strategy? Clarification of the question is important, especially as the everyday usage of this phrase evokes many unrelated notions.

The definitions of EP and IS that are most widely accepted, and are used by economists who have long studied these matters, relate to incentives. The IS strategy is defined as the adoption of an effective exchange rate for the country's exports (EER_x) which is less than that for imports (EER_m). EER_x would include, for a peso currency country, not just the pesos earned at parity from a unit dollar's worth of export, but also any export subsidy, tax credits, and special credits. (It would also include, say, for tractor export the subsidy on the input of steel that is used in the exported tractor, so that there is no distinction between EER comparisons defined on value added or gross value, for the purpose at hand.) Similarly EER_m would add to the parity any import duty, import premiums resulting from quantitative restrictions (QRs), and other charges. If a dollar's worth of exports fetches altogether 100 pesos, whereas a dollar's worth of imports fetches 130 pesos, the incentive structure implies $EER_x < EER_m$. This constitutes a "bias against exports," a concept that seems to have come independently into use in Bhagwati (1968), Little, Scitovsky, and Scott (1970), and Balassa (1971). This is also the hallmark of the IS strategy: it creates a net incentive to import-substitute relative to what international prices dictate.

Suppose, however, that EER_m yields 100 pesos per dollar's worth of imports, while EER_x is also 100 pesos. Then, the home market sales will give a producer as much as exporting will: the incentive structure then implies $EER_x = EER_m$. Thus bias against exports will have been eliminated. This is defined as the EP strategy.

These definitions of EP and IS strategies are now in common usage. But they do raise a question: how do we christen the case where there is a significant excess of EER_x over EER_m? Where the effective exchange rate is more favorable for exports than for imports, should we not call that EP instead of the one where $EER_x \approx EER_m$ as the above definitions do, and instead call the case with $EER_x \approx EER_m$ simply the trade-neutral or bias-free strategy? Perhaps that might have been the ideal way to do it. But the EP strategy came to be defined in the academic literature as the one with bias-free incentives simply because the empirical studies of the four Far Eastern economies, particularly in the NBER project, strongly suggested that these successful outward-oriented developers were closer to neutrality than to a substantial positive bias in favor of exports.[13] Furthermore, countries that went from an IS strategy to a neutral strategy, which eliminated the bias against exports and improved their export performance, prompted researchers to define EP strategy in terms of neutrality. Given the now common usage of these terms, therefore, I have suggested recently the following terminology that does least violence to what has been the practice to date:[14]

IS strategy: $EER_x < EER_m$

EP strategy: $EER_x \approx EER_m$

Ultra-EP strategy: $EER_x > EER_m$

Nonetheless, it is not uncommon, especially among policymakers, to find references to EP (or outward-oriented) trade strategy as including both the neutral and the pro-export bias strategies.[15] The reader must be alert to see what exactly is the implicit definition being used in a particular context.

These definitions clearly relate to average incentives. Nonetheless, it is obvious that, within EP for instance, some activities may be import-substituting in the sense that their EER_m exceeds the average EER_x. Thus, the pursuit of either the EP or the ultra-EP strategy does not preclude import-substituting in selected sectors. This is true for most of the successful Far Eastern developers. Nor does this fact render meaningless the distinction among the different trade strategies, as is sometimes contended. As I have argued elsewhere (Bhagwati 1986c):

We also need to remember always that the average EER_x and EER_m can and do conceal very substantial variations among different exports and among different imports. In view of this fact, I have long emphasized the need to distinguish between the questions of the degree of import substitution and the pattern of import substitution. Thus, within the broad aggregates of an EP country case, there may well be activities that are being import-substituted (i.e., their EER_m exceeds the average EER_x). Indeed there often are. But one should not jump to the erroneous conclusion that there is therefore no way to think of EP versus IS and that the distinction is an artificial one—any more than one would refuse to acknowledge that the Sahara is a desert, whereas Sri Lanka is not, simply because there are some oases (p. 93).

Nor should one equate the EP strategy with the absence of government intervention, as is often done by proponents of the IS strategy and sometimes by advocates of the EP strategy as well. It is true that a laissez-faire policy would satisfy the requirement that $EER_x = EER_m$. This is not a necessary condition for this outcome, however. The Far Eastern economies (with the exception of Hong Kong) and others that have come close to the EP strategy have been characterized by considerable government activity in the economic system. In my judgment, such intervention can be of great value, and almost certainly has been so, in making the EP strategy work successfully. By publicly supporting the outward-oriented strategy, by even bending in some cases toward ultraexport promotion, and by gearing the credit institutions to supporting export activities in an overt fashion, governments in these countries appear to have established the necessary confidence that their commitment to the EP strategy is serious, thus inducing firms to undertake costly investments and programs to take advantage of the EP strategy.

The laissez-faire model does not quite capture this aspect of the problem since governments, except in the models of Friedman and Bakunin, fail to abstain or self-destruct; they will invariably find something, indeed much, to do. Therefore, explicit commitment to an activist, supportive role in pursuit of the EP strategy, providing the assurance that it will be protected from inroads in pursuit of numerous other objectives in the near future, would appear to constitute a definite advantage in reaping the benefits of this strategy.

Some other caveats are also in order.

Development economists such as Chenery and his many associates have used the terminology of IS and EP in a wholly different fashion. They have typically used identities to decompose observed growth of output in an industry or the economy into components attributable to export promotion, import substitution, and other categories.[16] Quite aside from the fact that such decompositions are, except under singular circumstances, statistical descriptions without analytical significance, they also have no relationship to the incentives-related definitions of trade strategy that have been set out here. Unfortunately, this distinction occasionally gets confused in popular discussions, especially as economists sometimes deploy both usages simultaneously (that is, using the incentives-based definition to group countries into alternative categories and the Chenery-type terminology to explain their economic performance, as in Balassa 1983).

The incentives-defined EP strategy also has to be distinguished from the traditional concept of "export-led" growth, in which a country's exports generate income expansion attributable to direct gains from trade and indirect beneficial effects. The notion of export-led growth is closer to Nurkse's and Lewis's export pessimism that was dissected earlier. The incentives-related EP definition has literally nothing to do with such beneficial external phenomena. Whether the success of an EP strategy, defined in terms of freedom from bias against exports, requires the presence of a beneficial external environment is a separate issue that will be treated again in a later section that focuses on the revived export pessimism.

Finally, it is worth stressing that the concept of EP or outward orientation relates to trade incentives (direct trade policies or domestic or exchange rate policies that affect trade) but does not imply that the EP strategy countries must be equally outward-oriented in regard to their policies concerning foreign investment. Hong Kong and Singapore have been more favorable in their treatment of foreign investors than the great majority of the IS countries, but the historic growth of Japan, presumably as an EP country, was characterized by extremely selective control on the entry of foreign investment. Logically and empirically, the two types of outward orientation, in trade and in foreign investment, are distinct phenomena, though whether one can exist efficiently without the other is an important question that has been raised in the literature and is surrounded by far more controversy than the question of the desirability of an EP strategy in trade.

24.3   Why Does an Export-Promoting Strategy Aid Development?

With the EP strategy defined in terms of the incentive structure, the substantive conclusion that has emerged from the major research projects listed earlier is that the economic performance of the EP countries has been remarkably strong, although they had no one rooting for their success when development efforts were being initiated in the early 1950s. Here, as elsewhere, history has turned up surprises.

In evaluating this outcome, we have to distinguish between two questions: Why should the EP strategy have been helpful in accelerating economic development? Could the acceleration have been caused by factors other than the EP strategy?

The Evidence

The serious evidence on the successful impact of the EP strategy on economic performance, as measured by an improved growth rate, has to be found in the country studies of the research projects on trade and development (listed earlier). Among these, the most compelling evidence is in the analyses in the NBER project where the EP strategy was carefully defined and transitions to it from an IS strategy by various phases were systematically investigated.[17]

There is also much cited evidence that relates largely to associations between growth rates of exports and growth rates of income, as in the work of Michaely (1977) who used data for 1950–73 for forty-one countries, and the further extension of this type of work by Balassa (1978) and Feder (1983).[18] Complementing this approach is the altogether different statistical formulation in Michalopoulos and Jay (1973). This study takes a very different approach to the problem by using exports as an argument in estimating an economywide production function from aggregate output and factor use data. Using data for thirty-nine countries this study argued that exports are an independent input into national income.[19]

Neither the Michaely-Balassa-Feder nor the Michalopoulos-Jay findings, however, bear directly on the question whether the EP strategy is productive of more growth, because the incentive-related EP strategy is not the one used to examine the question of income or growth performance. It is necessary to identify whether the superior export growth rates (or higher export magnitudes) belong to the EP countries.

This is particularly worrisome since high growth rates of exports may have been caused by high growth rates of output (which, in turn, may have resulted from other exogenous factors such as a higher savings effort), rather than the other way around. Thus, if IS does not parametrically reduce trade greatly, it is conceivable that this reverse causation could lead the rapidly expanding countries, whether EP or IS, to show higher export growth rates than less rapidly expanding economies.

Hence, while these cross-country regressions are certainly interesting, valuable and suggestive, they cannot be considered compelling on the issue in question, especially as they (and conclusions based on them) are likely to be critically dependent on the period, sample of countries, and variables chosen. By contrast, the detailed country studies are methodologically superior and more persuasive. And, as noted already, they do indicate the superiority of the EP strategy.

The Reasons

Economists have been preoccupied with the reasons why the IS strategy has been generally dominated by the EP strategy, and why the countries that rapidly made the transition from the former to the latter have done better. The following hypotheses have been advanced, based on the usual mix of analytical insights, casual empiricism, and econometric evidence.[20]

Resource Allocation Efficiency
The first set of reasons for the success of the EP strategy relies on the fact that it brings incentives for domestic resource allocation closer to international opportunity costs and hence closer to what will generally produce efficient outcomes. This is true, not merely in the sense that there is no bias against exports and in favor of the home market (that is, $EER_x \approx EER_m$) under the EP strategy, but also in the sense that the IS countries seem to have generally had a chaotic dispersion of EERs among the different activities within export and import-competing activities as well. That is, the degree of IS goes far and the pattern of IS reflects widely divergent incentives. By contrast, the EP strategy does better both on degree (since $EER_x \approx EER_m$) and on pattern.

Why is the degree of bias so large and the pattern wrong under IS? The answer seems to lie in the way in which IS is often practiced and in the constraints that surround EP. Thus IS could, in principle, be contained to modest excess of EER_m over EER_x. But typically IS arises in the context of overvalued exchange rates and associated exchange controls. So there is no way in which the excess of domestic over foreign prices is being tracked by government agencies in most cases, and the excesses of EER_m over EER_x simply go unnoticed. The nontransparency is fatal. By contrast, EP typically tends to constrain itself to rough equality, and ultra-EP also seems to be moderate in practice, because policy-induced excesses of EER_x over EER_m often require subsidization that is constrained by budgetary problems.

In the same way, the pattern of EER_m can be terribly chaotic because exchange controls and QRs on trade will typically generate differential premiums and hence differential degrees of implied protection of thousands of import-competing activities. By contrast, the EP strategy will typically unify exchange rates, which avoids these problems and, when it relies on export subsidization, will be handled both with necessary transparency and with budgetary constraints that would then prevent wide dispersions in EERs.

The chaotic nature of differential incentives among diverse activities in IS regimes has been documented by estimates of effective rates of protection (ERPs), though these estimates can be misleading in quantitative restrictions regimes where the import premiums may reflect effects of investment controls, indicating therefore resource denial rather than resource attraction to the high-premium and therefore, other things being equal, the high-ERP activities. The estimates of cross-sectional domestic resource costs (DRCs), which provide instead a guide to differential social returns to different activities, have also underlined these lessons. The conceptual and measurement analyses of several distinguished economists, including Michael Bruno, Max Corden, Harry Johnson, and Anne Krueger, have contributed greatly to this literature.

Directly Unproductive Profit-Seeking and Rent-Seeking Activities

Yet another important aspect of the difference between EP and IS strategies is that IS regimes are more likely to trigger what economic theorists now call directly unproductive profit-seeking (DUP) activities (Bhagwati 1982b). These activities divert resources from productive use into unproductive but profitable lobbying to change policies or to evade them or to seek the revenue and rents they generate.[21] Rent-seeking activities (Krueger 1974), where lobbies chase rents attached to import licenses and other quantitative restrictions, are an important subset of such DUP activities. The diversion of entrepreneurial energies and real resources into such DUP activities tends to add to the conventionally measured losses from the high degree and chaotic pattern of IS.[22]

It must be admitted that, although economists have now begun to make attempts at estimating these costs, they are nowhere near arriving at plausible estimates simply because it is not yet possible to estimate realistically the production functions for returns to different kinds of lobbying. But, as Harrod once remarked, arguments that cannot be quantified are not necessarily unimportant in economics, and the losses arising from DUP and rent-seeking activities seem presently to illustrate his observation.[23]

Foreign Investment

If IS regimes have tended to use domestic resources inefficiently in the ways that were just outlined, the same applies to the use of foreign resources. This is perhaps self-evident, but substantial theoretical work by Bhagwati (1973), Brecher and Diaz-Alejandro (1977), Uzawa (1969), Hamada (1974), and others has established that foreign investment that comes in over QRs and tariffs—the so-called tariff-jumping investment— is capable of immiserizing the recipient country under conditions that seem uncannily close to the conditions in the IS countries in the postwar decades. These conditions require capital flows into capital-intensive sectors in the protected activities. It is thus plausible that, if these inflows were not actually harmful, the social returns on them were at least low compared with what they would be in the EP countries where the inflows were not tariff-jumping but rather aimed at world markets, in line with the EP strategy of the recipient countries.

In addition, I have hypothesized (Bhagwati 1978, 1986a) that, other things being equal, foreign investments into IS countries will be self-limiting in the long run because they are aimed at the home market and therefore constrained by it. If so, and there seems to be some preliminary evidence in support of this hypothesis in ongoing econometric analysis,[24] then IS countries would have been handicapped also by the lower amount of foreign investment flows and not just by their lower social productivity compared with the EP countries.

Gray Area Dynamic Effects

Although the arguments so far provide ample satisfaction to those who seek to understand why the EP strategy does so well, dissatisfaction has continued to be expressed that these are arguments of static efficiency and that dynamic factors such as savings and innovations may well be favorable under an import-substituting trade strategy.

Of course, if what we are seeking to explain is the relative success of the EP countries with growth, this counterargumentation makes little sense since, even if it were true, the favorable effects from these "gray area" sources of dynamic efficiency would have been outweighed in practice by the static efficiency aspects. But the counterargumentation is not compelling anyway. Overall, it is not possible to claim that IS regimes enable a country to save more or less than EP regimes: the evidence in the NBER project, for instance, went both ways. Nor does it seem possible to maintain that EP or IS regimes are necessarily more innovative. It is possible to argue that EP regimes may lead to more competition and less-sheltered markets and hence more innovation. But equally, Schumpeterian arguments suggest that the opposite might also be true.[25]

The few recent studies that have appeared do suggest that the EP strategy may encourage greater innovation. Krueger and Tuncer (1980) examined eighteen Turkish manufacturing industries during the 1963–76 period. They found that periods of low productivity growth roughly occurred during periods when foreign exchange controls were particularly restrictive and hence the IS strategy was being accentuated. The overall rate of productivity growth was also low throughout the period during which Turkey pursued an IS strategy. In an analysis of productivity change in Japan, Korea, Turkey, and Yugoslavia, Nishimizu and Robinson (1984) argue that if growth is decomposed into that due to "domestic demand expansion," "export expansion," and "import substitution," the interindustrial variation in factor productivity growth reflects (except for Japan) the relative roles of export expansion and import substitution, the former causing a positive impact and the latter a negative one. However, as the authors recognize, export expansion may have been caused by productivity change rather than the other way around, the regressions begging the issue of causality.

What is the influence of economies of scale in EP and IS regimes? Theoretically, the EP success should be increased because world markets are certainly larger than home markets. But, systematic evidence is not yet available on this question. For instance, evidence is lacking to indicate whether firms that turn to export markets are characterized by greater scale of output than those firms that do not. Experience in the case of the EC suggests that trade may lead not to changes in the level of output so much as to product specialization.

Suppose however that we do assume that economies of scale will be exploited when trade expands. The cost of protection, or the gains from trade, will then rise significantly. Harris (1986) has calculated for Canada that a 3.6 percent rise in GNP could follow from the unilateral elimination of Canadian tariffs, if the economies of scale are fully exploited.

Finally, in the matter of X efficiency, it is again plausible that firms under IS regimes should find themselves more frequently in sheltered and monopolistic environments than those under EP regimes; a great deal of such evidence is available from the country studies in the several research projects discussed. X efficiency therefore ought to be greater under the EP regime. However, as is well known, this is a notoriously gray area where measurement has often turned out to be elusive.

Although the arguments for the success of the EP strategy based on economies of scale and X efficiency are plausible, empirical support for them is not available. The arguments on savings and innovation provide a less than compelling case for showing that EP is necessarily better on their account than IS.

Growth and Other Objectives

A final word is necessary on the superior economic performance of the EP strategy. Much like the die-hard monetarists who keep shifting their definitions of money as necessary in order to keep their faith, the proponents of IS have tended to shift their objections as required by the state of the art.

When it became evident that the EP strategy yielded higher growth and that the static versus dynamic efficiency arguments were not persuasive and probably went in favor of the EP strategy, the IS proponents shifted ground. They took to arguing that the objective of development was not growth but the alleviation of poverty or unemployment and that EP might be better for growth but was worse for these other objectives. This was part of a larger argument that became fashionable during the 1970s in certain development circles: that growth had been the objective of development to date; that the objective was wrong; that the true objective of poverty amelioration was ill served by development efforts directed at growth; and that growth even harmed (in certain formulations of such critics) the poor.

The evidence does not support the views that growth was desired in itself, that poverty elimination was not a stated objective which was pursued by the acceleration of growth rates to "pull up" the poor into gainful employment, and that growth on a sustained basis has not helped the poor. These orthodoxies are no longer regarded as plausible, as I have argued at length elsewhere.[26]

In regard to the narrower question at hand, that is, whether the EP strategy procures efficiency and growth but adversely affects poverty and employment, evidence has now been gathered extensively in a sequel NBER project, directed by Krueger (1982). Essentially, she and her associates document how investment allocation under EP requires the expansion of labor-intensive activities, because developing country exports are typically labor-intensive. Therefore, EP strategies tend to encourage the use of labor and hence the growth of employment and the alleviation of poverty in countries that typically have underemployed labor.

Moreover, after more than two decades of successful growth in the EP regimes, especially in the four Far Eastern economies, it has become easier for economists to contemplate and comprehend the effects of compound rates and the advantages of being on rapid escalators. Even if it had been true that the EP strategy yielded currently lower employment or lower real wages, the rapid growth rates would overwhelm these disadvantages in the time of simply one generation. It would appear therefore that both the employment-intensive nature of EP growth in developing countries and the higher growth rates in the EP countries have provided a substantial antidote to the poverty and underemployment that afflicted these countries at the start of their development process.

24.4   The Second Export Pessimism

These lessons were important. Many developing countries learned them the hard way: by following IS policies too long and seeing the fortunate few pursuing the EP strategy do much better. Perhaps learning by others' doing and one's own undoing is the most common form of education!

But just as these lessons were widely accepted, and a "new orthodoxy" in their favor was established, a new wave of export pessimism arrived on the scene. This second export pessimism, which is paradoxically both more serious and more tractable in principle, tends to undermine the desired shift to the EP strategy in the developing countries.

There are two sets of factors generating this pessimism: (1) objective events such as the slowing down of the world economy since the 1970s and the resurgence of powerful protectionist sentiments in the industrial countries, and (2) new intellectual and academic arguments in support of inward-looking trade policies in the developing countries. The two are not entirely unrelated since theory, especially international trade theory, does not grow in a vacuum. But they can be dealt with sequentially nonetheless.

In essence, the second export pessimism rests on the view that, whatever the market-defined absorptive capacity for the exports of the developing countries, the politics of protectionism in the industrial countries (which still constitute the chief markets of developing country exports) is such that the exports from developing countries face serious and crippling constraints that make the pursuit of an EP strategy (with $EER_x \approx EER_m$) inefficient, if not positively foolish.

If this assessment is correct, then the EP strategy's premise that foreign markets are available at prices largely independent of one's own exports is certainly not valid. But this must be correctly understood. If Brazil successfully exports footwear, for example, and the importing countries invoke market-disruption-related QRs, or frivolous countervailing duty (CVD) retaliation, then Brazil faces a less than perfectly elastic market for footwear, and an optimal tariff (that is, a shift to IS strategy) *in this sector* is called for. This should justify only selective protection, carefully devised and administered, not a general IS strategy. If, however, this response is feared no matter what is exported, that is, the fear of protectionism is nearly universal in scope, a generalized shift to IS strategy unfortunately would be appropriate.

The second pessimism, like the first, takes the latter, vastly more fearsome form, extending to exports generally. The resulting case for a general shift to the IS strategy then collapses only if the protectionist threat can be shown to be less serious than it appears or if the threat, even though serious, can be contained by multilateral efforts or other policy options that ought to be undertaken along with the EP strategy. As it happens, a case can be made in support of both these responses.

24.5 How Serious Is the Protectionist Threat?

In assessing the extent to which the protectionist threat must be taken seriously, one may first make the prudential statement that it should never be regarded lightly. Sectional interests have always provided the political momentum through congresses and parliaments to protectionist responses to import competition. The postwar history of trade barriers also shows, however, the important role that executive branches have played in upholding the national interest, broadly served by freer trade and specialization. The real question is: has the threat become sufficiently more serious so that the developing countries ought to turn away from embracing the EP strategy?

First, a few facts need to be noted. As table 24.1 briefly indicates, trade expansion has certainly slowed considerably since the 1970s. But even so, world trade has grown faster than world income during the 1970–83 period. More compelling is the fact that the developing countries' exports of manufactures to the industrial countries have grown almost twice as fast as the exports of these countries to one another, showing even during the 1970s a growth rate of more than 8 percent annually. This has happened during a period when nontariff barriers (NTBs), such as voluntary export restraints (VERs), began to proliferate and when the OECD countries showed sluggish growth rates and increased unemployment.

That exports from the developing countries continued to grow in this fashion was first highlighted by Hughes and Krueger (1984) who thought that it was a puzzle since a large amount of actual protection seemed to have already been adopted. This puzzle has stimulated Baldwin (1982, 1985) into developing an interesting thesis: that protection is far less effective than one thinks simply because there are many ways in which exporting countries can get around it in continuing to increase their export earnings. Thus, Baldwin has written:

Consider the response of exporting firms to the imposition of tighter foreign restrictions on imports of a particular product. One immediate response will be to try to ship the product in a form which is not covered by the restriction ... One case involves coats with removable sleeves. By importing sleeves unattached, the rest of the coat comes in as a vest, thereby qualifying for more favorable tariff treatment ...

The use of substitute components is another common way of getting around import restrictions. The quotas on imports of sugar into the United States only apply to pure sugar, defined as 100 percent sucrose. Foreign exporters are avoiding the quotas by shipping sugar products consisting mainly of sucrose, but also containing a sugar substitute, for example, dextrose ... At one time, exporters of running shoes to the United States avoided the high tariff on rubber footwear by using leather for most of the upper portion of the shoes, thereby qualifying for duty treatment as leather shoes" (1985, p. 110).

Yoffie (1983) has also recently examined the VERs on footwear and textiles from a political scientist's perspective and found that the dynamic exporting economies such as Korea and Taiwan have embraced them with considerable ingenuity, much like what Baldwin has documented, to continue expanding their exports significantly.

There is also a more subtle factor at play here which relates to why VERs may have provided the mechanism by which the executive branches of government interested in maintaining freer trade may have succeeded in keeping trade expanding. VERs are, in that view, a "porous" form of protection that is deliberately preferred because of this nontransparent porousness. I have argued recently (Bhagwati 1986b) that in industries such as footwear, two characteristics seem to hold that lend support to this porous protection model as an explanation for why protection is ineffective: (1) undifferentiated products (that is, cheaper varieties of garments and footwear) make it easy to "transship," that is, to cheat on rules of origin, passing off products of a country restricted by VERs as products of countries not covered by VERs; and (2) low start-up costs and therefore small recoupment horizons apply in shifting investment and hence products to adjacent third countries that are not covered by VERs, so that an exporting country can get around (admittedly at some cost) the VERs by "investment-shunting" to sources unafflicted by VERs. This strategy allows the exporter to recover his investment costs, since it is usually some time before the VERs get around to covering these alternative sources, or VERs are eliminated as the political pressure subsides (as was the case with U.S. footwear).[27]

In both ways, therefore, VERs in these types of industries can yield a "close-to-free-trade" solution for the exporting countries. These countries can continue to profit from their comparative advantage by effectively exploiting, legally (through investment-shunting) and illegally (through transshipments), the fact that VERs leave third countries out whereas importing country tariffs and quotas do not.[28]

But the question then arises: why would the protecting importing countries prefer this porous protection? Does it not imply that the market-disrupted industry fails to be protected as it would under a corresponding import trade restraint? Indeed it does. But that is precisely its attractiveness.

If executive branches want free trade in the national interest whereas legislatures respond to the sectoral interests—definitely the stylized description of the "two-headed" democracies in the United States and the United Kingdom—then it can be argued that executives will prefer to use a porous form of protection which, while ensuring freer market access, will nonetheless manage to appear as a concession to the political demands for protection from the legislature or from their constituencies. Undoubtedly, these protectionist groups and their congressional spokesmen will eventually complain about continuing imports. But then the executive branch can always cite its VER actions, promise to look into complaints and perhaps bring other countries into the VER net, and continue to obfuscate and buy time without effectively protecting.[29]

If the foregoing arguments suggest that executives have been clever enough, both in exporting and importing countries, in keeping markets much more open than the casual reading of the newspapers would suggest, there are also additional forces in favor of freer trade that have now emerged in the world economy which need to be considered in making a reasonable assessment of the prospects for increased protectionist measures. I believe that the international political economy has changed dramatically in the last two decades to generate new and influential actors that are supportive of freer world trade.

A fairly common complaint on the part of analysts of the political economy has been the asymmetry of pressure groups in the tariff-making process. The beneficiaries of protection are often concentrated, whereas its victims tend to be either diffused (as is the case with final consumers) or unable to recognize the losses they incur (as when protection indirectly affects exports and hence hurts those engaged in producing exportables).[30]

Direct foreign investment (DFI) and the growing maze of globalized production have changed this equation perceptibly. When DFI is undertaken, not for tariff-jumping in locally sheltered markets, but for exports to the home country or to third markets, as is increasingly the case, protectionism threatens the investments so made and tends to galvanize these influential multinationals into lobbying to keep markets open. For example, it was noticeable that when the U.S. semiconductor suppliers recently gathered to discuss antidumping legal action against Japanese producers of memory microchips known as EPROMs (or erasable programmable read-only memories), noticeably absent were Motorola Inc. and Texas Instruments Inc. who produce semiconductors in Japan and expect to be shipping some back to the United States.[31]

Almost certainly a main reason why U.S. protectionism has not translated into a disastrous Smoot-Hawley scenario, despite high unemployment levels and the seriously overvalued dollar (in the Dutch Disease sense), is that far fewer congressmen today have constituencies where DFI has not created such protrade, antiprotectionist presence, muddying waters where protectionists would have otherwise sailed with great ease. The "spiderweb" phenomenon resulting from DFI that criss-crosses the world economy has thus been a stablilizing force in favor of holding the protectionists at bay.

It is not just the DFI in place that provides these trade-reinforcing political pressures.[32] The reaction against import competition has been diluted by the possibility of using international factor mobility as a policy response. Thus, the possibility of undertaking DFI when faced with import competition also provides an alternative to a protectionist response. Since this is the capitalist response, rather than a response of labor to "losing jobs abroad," the defusion of the protectionist threat that is implied here works by breaking the customary alliance between capital and labor within an industry in their protectionist lobbying, a relationship with which Magee has made us long familiar.

Labor today seems also to have caught on to this game and is not averse to using threats of protection to induce DFI from foreign competitors instead. The United Auto Workers labor union in the United States appears to have helped to induce Japanese investments in the car industry. This is quite a generic phenomenon where DFI is undertaken by the Japanese exporting firms to buy off the local pressure groups of firms or unions that threaten legislative pressures for tariffs to close the import markets. This type of induced DFI has been christened "quid pro quo DFI" (Bhagwati 1985c) and appears to be a growing phenomenon (certainly on the part of Japanese firms), representing a new and alternative form of response to import competition than provided by old-fashioned tariff-making.[33]

In short, both actual DFI (through the spiderweb effect) and potential DFI (outward by domestic capital and quid pro quo inward by foreign capital) are powerful forces that are influencing the political economy of tariff-making in favor of an open economy. They surely provide some counterweight to the gloom that the protectionist noises generate today.

But all these arguments could collapse under the weight of the contention that if many countries were indeed to shift to the EP strategy, whether through conversion to the view or through conditionality such as that envisaged under the plan put forth by U.S. Treasury Secretary James Baker III in 1985, the pressures to close markets would multiply owing to the magnitude of the absorption of exports that this would imply for the industrial countries.

This takes us back partly to the Cline (1982) estimates and the several refutations of the pessimism engendered by them that were set out earlier.[34] But it remains true that, even if the estimates in Cline are not to be taken seriously, the addition of any kind of trade pressure in a significant degree could touch off a wider range of sectoral, safeguard moves in the industrial countries in the present climate. It is indeed possible to argue that (1) Cline-type estimates are not plausible and exaggerate what would happen, (2) there is a great deal of absorptive capacity in the market sense in the world economy which can readily handle improved export performance resulting from the shift of many developing countries to the EP mode of organizing trade, and (3) there are powerful new forces in the international political economy that may make the protectionist bark worse than the protectionist bite. Nonetheless, the danger of protectionism does remain acute, especially in the present macroeconomic situation of sluggish growth and the continuing trade deficit in the United States. The capacity of the U.S. executive branch to hold the line against protectionism has been significantly eroded by the neglect of fiscal deficits and the upsurge in congressional support for protection and fair trade. The fragility of the situation requires serious attention to other policy instruments such as the multinational trade negotiations (MTN), as discussed below.

An important consequence of the second wave of export pessimism, which is based on this protectionist threat rather than on the belief in market-determined forces that limit export prospects, is that developing countries can join in the process of trying to contain this threat and thereby change the very prospects for their trade. This suggests that they join hands with the industrial countries in efforts such as the MTN to contain the threat to the world trading system and to keep markets open to expanding trade levels. Shifting to the IS strategy, therefore, based on export pessimism reflecting protectionist sentiments simply makes no sense from an economic viewpoint unless the developing countries are convinced that protectionism is here to stay and will be translated into actuality no matter what is done—an assumption that seems to be wholly unwarranted in light of the discussion earlier in this section. A far more sensible policy approach seems rather to be to join with the executives of countries that support freer trade initiatives, among them certainly the United States, in containing the protectionist sentiments through strategies such as entering into trade negotiations.

24.6   New Arguments for the IS Strategy

It may be useful to address some new intellectual defenses of the IS strategy that have recently emerged in the academic literature.[35]

Labor Market Imperfections

In recent articles, especially Fields (1984), it has been argued that the EP strategy is not appropriate when there are excessively high wages in the economy and that EP countries such as Jamaica have done badly by ignoring this caveat. Now, the theoretical literature on market imperfections and optimal policy that emerged in the postwar period, with the independent contributions by Meade (1951) and Bhagwati and Ramaswami (1963) setting off the spectacular growth of the subject during the 1960s, has shown that factor market imperfections are best addressed by domestic, rather than trade, taxes and subsidies.[36] It is true, however, that the second-best policy measures in such a case could be trade tariffs and subsidies.

There are two other problems with Fields's argument. First, he does not establish that countries such as Jamaica have been following the EP strategy in the incentive-related sense that is relevant. As it happens, Jamaica certainly has not and has for long periods been in the IS mode instead. This confusion of concepts and hence conclusions is not confined to Fields's analysis, but afflicts even the proponents of EP strategy in some cases. Second, it is not at all clear from Fields that the high wages constitute a market imperfection in the sense required for departure from unified exchange rates in the form of the IS strategy.

In my view, wages are relevant in a different sense that is macro-theoretic, rather than microtheoretic as Fields suggests. If overall wages are "too high," that can only mean that somehow they, and therefore the price level as well, are out of line with the exchange rate. That is, the country is suffering from overvaluation. In short, if that is so, we have already seen that the country is pursuing an IS strategy, whether it intends to or not. Therefore, a country simply cannot hold on to any EP strategy if it continues to experience excessive wages. The sustained pursuit of EP, so that investors respond to the incentives that EP defines, thus requires a sound macro policy as its foundation. Sound macro policies may then also bring, in turn, their own other rewards that supplement those that follow from the export-promoting strategy.

Satisficing Theory of IS

An interesting thesis has been proposed by the political scientist Ruggie (1983), which seems to argue that the advantage of an EP strategy cannot be enjoyed by many developing countries because they simply do not possess the flexibility of resource movements and the necessary political capacities to manage such flexibility that the pursuit of EP requires. I would call this therefore the "satisficing" theory of the IS strategy: developing countries in this predicament must make do without the gains from trade and efficiency improvements that EP strategy brings.

This is a difficult argument to judge since, even if it were valid within its premises, I do not find it compelling if such political constraints are equated with the fact of being less developed economically. In fact, given the lack of democratic structures with pressure group politics and attendant constraints on economic action by the government, it is doubtful whether developing countries are not the ones at advantage in this matter!

Again, is it clear that tensions and distributional conflicts are necessarily more difficult under an EP strategy? An IS strategy while insulating the economy relatively from external disturbances, may create yet more tensions and conflicts if the resulting stultification of income expansion accentuates the zero-sum nature of other policy options in the system. The correct statement of the Ruggie thesis would then seem to be that, in the pursuit of any development strategy, the compatibility of it with the political structure and resilience of the country needs to be considered. And this caveat needs to be addressed not only to the EP proponents.

Coping with External Instability

A similar economic concern has been that, while EP may be better under steady-state conditions, it exposes the economy to the downside in the world economy and makes it more vulnerable to instability.

Of course, the downside effects have to be set off against the upside effects. When this is done, it is not evident that countries pursuing EP strategies are necessarily worse off. As it happens, even the downside experience of EP strategy countries during the years after the oil shock seems to have been more favorable than the experience of the IS strategy countries, according to statistical analysis by Balassa (1983 and 1984). The reason seems to have been their greater capacity to deal with external adversity by using export expansion more successfully to adapt to the world slowdown and thus avoiding import contraction.

25.7   Conclusion

Export promotion policies emerge with success from the detailed scrutiny offered in this article. Equally important is the fact that their successful adoption will require collaborative and intense efforts to ensure that the protectionist threat, recently escalating, is not allowed to break out into actual protection on a massive scale.

The multilateral trade negotiations offer the only reasonable prospect for maintaining a momentum in favor of a freer world trading system. Failure to pursue them successfully, in a spirit of accommodation and mutual understanding of constraints and needs, will only undermine what seems like the best mechanism for containing the protectionist threat.

Appendix: Theoretical Clarification of Key Concepts

Definitions

Figure 24.1 illustrates, in the two-good model, the definitions of the export-promoting (EP), import-substituting (IS), and ultraexport-promoting (ultra-EP) trade strategies.

AB is the country's production possibility curve. With given international prices P^*S, equilibrium production would be reached at P^* under unified exchange rates which ensure that the relative goods prices domestically are equal to P^*S. Therefore, at P^*, we have $EER_x = EER_m$, where EER refers to the effective exchange rate. This is defined as the EP strategy.

When the incentive to produce the import-competing good exceeds that to produce the exportable good, because of a tariff or overvalued exchange rates, for example (as shown below), production shifts to P_m. Here, $EER_x < EER_m$. This is the IS strategy.

If the biased incentive goes in the other direction, the relative incentives imply $EER_x > EER_m$ and production shifts to the right of P^*, to say P_x. This is defined as the ultra-EP strategy.

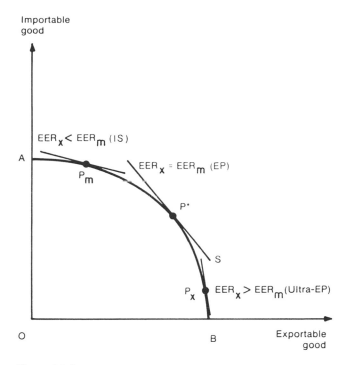

Figure 24.1

Overvalued Exchange Rates and IS Strategy

An overvalued exchange rate will imply the pursuit of the IS strategy. Figure 24.2 demonstrates this with the standard supply and demand diagram for foreign exchange.

If the exchange rate is adjusted to clear the market, at S, then $EER_x = EER_m$ because an identical parity applies to both export and import transactions. But consider now an overvalued exchange rate with exchange controls in place. Under these circumstances the overvalued exchange rate γ_m leads to OW foreign exchange being earned, corresponding to R on the SS curve. This foreign exchange will then be rationed to users, fetching a market-determined price which exceeds γ_x. That price is determined by Q on the DD curve, with γ_m representing then the price corresponding to quantity OW. Evidently then, $(\gamma_m - \gamma_x)/\gamma_x$ represents the rate of premium that scarce foreign exchange commands in this overvalued exchange rate system.

It is also evident that $\gamma_x = EER_x$ and $\gamma_m = EER_m$ and therefore $EER_x < EER_m$ by the magnitude of the premium on rationed foreign

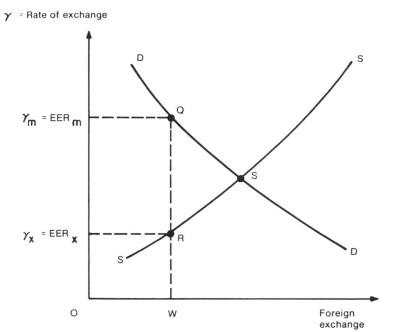

Figure 24.2

exchange. The overvalued exchange rate therefore implies the pursuit of an IS strategy, whether it is intended or not.

The Cost of Protection with Tariff-Seeking

The new theory of directly unproductive profit-seeking (DUP) and rent-seeking activities, which incorporates lobbying and related policy-triggered and policy-influencing activities into formal economic theorizing, is illustrated in figure 24.3 by reference to the phenomenon of tariff-seeking lobbying.

AB is the production possibility curve if there is no tariff-seeking activity. If, as in conventional analysis, we assume an exogenously specified tariff, equilibrium production shifts to *P* (where, of course, $EER_x < EER_m$).

Suppose now that this very tariff is instead arrived at by lobbying which uses up real resources, diverting these resources from being productively employed in producing the two goods. Then, the resources that are available to produce the two goods in this endogenous tariff, or equivalently tariff-seeking, equilibrium can be hypothetically seen to result in a "net-of-tariff-seeking" production possibility curve $A_1 B_1$ and production at P_1.

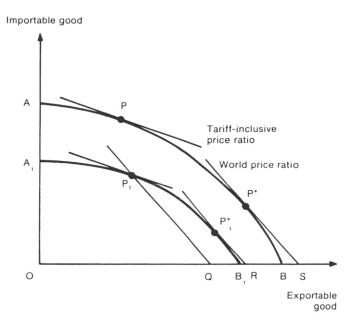

Figure 24.3

The total cost of protection is QS, measured in the conventional equivalent variation fashion. By putting the given world price ratio tangent to $A_1 B_1$ at P_1^*, we can then decompose this total cost of protection as follows: $QS = QR + RS$ where QR is the conventional cost of protection (but measured along the net curve $A_1 B_1$) and RS is the additional cost of tariff-seeking (representing the cost of diverting resources from productive use to tariff-seeking lobbying).[37]

Notes

Thanks are due to Armeane Choksi, Martin Wolf, Constantine Michalopoulos, Sarath Rajapatirana, Swaminathan Aiyar, Mohsin Khan, Vittorio Corbo, Adrian Wood, and Bela Balassa for helpful comments and to Sunil Gulati, Susan Hume, Douglas Irwin, and David Laster for research assistance.

1. The chief studies were directed by Little, Scitovsky, and Scott (1970) at the Organization for Economic Cooperation and Development (OECD), Balassa (1971) at the World Bank, Bhagwati (1978) and Krueger (1978) at the National Bureau of Economic Research (NBER) in the United States, and Donges (1976) at the Kiel Institute in Germany. Complementing and overlapping each other, these studies represent a comprehensive analysis of the central question that has preoccupied development economists from the very beginning of the discipline.

2. Among other reviews that complement this article, the reader may consult Behrman (1984) Bhagwati and Srinivasan (1979) Findlay (1984) and Srinivasan (1986a, 1986b).

3. Prebisch may have subsequently embraced the Nurkse view that primary product markets were also price inelastic, according to Balassa. I refer here to the main Prebisch thesis as originally propounded and widely attributed to him.

4. In technical jargon, we have here the classic case for an optimal tariff since the terms of trade vary with the level of trade.

5. This is an example of the dangers of using such regressions, with little underlying rationale, for predictive purposes. I have considered this issue at great length (Bhagwati 1985a, p. 2).

6. Compare Goldstein and Khan (1982) and Riedel (1984), who analyze this argument fully in two splendid and independent articles. Also of importance is the classic examination of the issue by Kravis (1970).

7. See again the results cited in the synthesis volumes of the research projects listed in note 1. The Goldstein-Khan (1982) analysis also bears directly on this issue.

8. Compare Riedel's (1984) discussion of this finding in table 4.

9. There is a substantial empirical literature on this subject, with important contributions by Balassa, Grubel, and Lloyd. In addition, recent theoretical work by Dixit, Lancaster, Krugman, Helpman, and others has provided the analytical explanation for such intraindustry trade.

10. All these arguments are effectively a rebuttal of Dornbusch's (1986) restatement of the limited absorptive capacity thesis for developing country exports, which asserts that substantial terms of trade losses would follow from the simultaneous resort to EP strategy by many developing countries.

11. I am indebted to Vittorio Corbo for pointing this out to me.

12. Compare the comment on Prebisch in Bhagwati (1985a).

13. The estimated excess of EER_x over EER_m appeared to be below 10 percent at maximum in the few careful cross-section estimates we had. This is reconfirmed for Korea in a more recent analysis by Nam (1986).

14. The strategies have been illustrated in the simplified two-goods model of traditional trade theory in figure 24.1 in the appendix.

15. See also Krueger's (1980) informal usage of the phrase in this fashion.

16. Compare Chenery, Shishido, and Watanabe (1962) for one such decomposition. For an analytical synthesis and evaluation of alternative measures of import substitution, see Desai (1979).

17. See, in particular, the synthesis volumes by Bhagwati (1978) and Krueger (1978).

18. Krueger's (1978) synthesis volume also contains similar cross-country regressions for the ten semi-industrialized countries in the NBER project. See the extensive review in Lal and Rajapatirana (1987).

19. Balassa's (1978) reestimation of Michaely-type regressions also incorporates the Michalopoulos-Jay approach, thus combining the two different methodologies under one rubric.

20. It is well known, of course, that factors that lead to improved efficiency and hence to income improvement need not necessarily lead to sustained higher growth rates. Thus, in the Harrod-Domar model, where labor supply is slack, a once-for-all improvement in efficiency will indeed translate into a permanent higher growth rate of income, but not so in the steady state in the Solow model, where the growth rate is determined by the growth rate of labor and the rate of technical change. In the text, however, we are explaining growth rates over a period of two or three decades, which makes these subtleties not particularly relevant, in my judgment. Moreover, it is important to note that, for any given growth rate, a more efficient economic regime will require less savings (and hence less blood, sweat, and tears) to sustain it than a less efficient economic regime.

21. See Bhagwati and Srinivasan (1983, p. 30) for a taxonomy of such lobbying activities.

22. The appendix to this article explains the manner in which the conventional cost of distorted production decisions resulting from protection is augmented by the cost of tariff-seeking lobbying when the protective tariff is the result of such lobbying. Costs of other kinds of lobbying, including the effects of DUP activities such as illegal trade (that is, tariff evasion), can be similarly illustrated. If the EP strategy relies not on exchange rate flexibility but simply on selective export subsidies to eliminate the bias against exports (as in phase II, delineated in the Bhagwati-Krueger NBER project), the DUP activities can be expected to arise extensively in that regime as well.

23. Krueger's (1974) classic article contains estimates of rent-seeking costs, that is, resources spent in chasing premiums or rents on quantitative restrictions. These high estimates, up to 15 percent of GNP, are based on the assumption that rents result in an equivalent loss of resources in equilibrium (the so-called one-on-one postulate in rent-seeking theory). Recently, computable general equilibrium models have begun to incorporate such DUP and rent-seeking activities, so that progress can be expected in assessing the magnitude of such costs. Compare Dervis, de Melo, and Robinson (1981) and Grais, de Melo, and Urata (1986).

24. See the discussion in Balasubramanian (1984) and in Bhagwati (1986a). In private communication, Balasubramanian has provided further results in support of this hypothesis.

25. See Bhagwati (1978), where some chapters summarize and evaluate these arguments with evidence from the ten country studies.

26. See Bhagwati (1985d) where I review the arguments and the evidence on these issues, drawing also on the valuable contributions of Surjit Bhalla, Pranab Bardhan, Paul Isenman, Ian Little, Irma Adelman, Montek Ahluwalia, Keith Griffen, Paul Streeten, and T. N. Srinivasan, among others.

27. The investment shunting need occur only insofar as it is necessary to meet value-added rules of origin, of course, making the cost of profiting from this porousness even less than otherwise.

28. Of course, the VERs in this instance represent only a partial and suboptimal approximation to the free trade solution, which remains the desirable but infeasible alternative. Moreover, not all exporting countries are capable of the flexible and shrewd response that underlies the model of porous protection sketched above.

29. This "two-headed" version of governments is what underlies the Feenstra-Bhagwati (1982) model of the efficient tariff. There, the model postulates that one branch of the government (pursuing special interests) interacts with a protectionist lobby to enact a political economy tariff. Then, another branch of the government (pursuing the national interest) uses the revenue generated by this tariff to bribe the lobby into accepting a less harmful tariff that nonetheless leaves it as well off as under the political economy tariff. When this model was presented to a scientific conference in 1978, the general reaction was that the model had a "schizophrenic" two-headed government! Traditional trade theory is so often modelled in terms of a monolithic government that what was obviously a realistic innovation was regarded as a bizarre feature of the model.

30. See, for example, Olson (1971), Finger (1982), and Mayer (1984).

31. See the report by Miller (1985).

32. Helleiner (1977) and most recently Lavergne and Helleiner (1985) have argued that multinationals have become active agents exercising political pressure in favor of free trade. The structure of trade barriers has been related to patterns of DFI by Helleiner but the later work by Lavergne finds this relationship to be fairly weak. This hypothesis and research do not extend to the *potential* DFI effects in favor of freer trade (which would occur if DFI becomes an alternative response to import competition), which is discussed in Bhagwati (1982b, 1986a) and in the text.

33. In fact, the Ministry of International Trade and Industry of Japan has recently completed a survey of Japanese DFI abroad and found that a large fraction of the respondents cited reasons of the quid pro quo variety to explain their investment decisions. I am indebted to Professor Shishido of the International University of Japan for this reference. See also the theoretical modeling of such quid pro quo DFI in Bhagwati, Brecher, Dinopoulos, and Srinivasan (1987) and in Bhagwati and Dinopoulos (1986), the former using perfectly competitive structure and the latter using monopoly and duopoly structures instead.

34. See also the critique offered by Ranis (1985). Cline (1985) basically defends his position by arguing that the high ratios of trade to GNP typical of Far Eastern economies are likely to trigger difficulties and that he should not have been read

to mean that the EP strategy would necessarily lead to such phenomenally high trade growth rates and trade ratios.

35. In the following, I select for treatment only the most important such arguments, given the central theme of this paper. For a more comprehensive review of recent arguments for protection, including those applying to industrial countries—as in Kaldor's (1966) argument for protection to prevent British deindustrialization or Seabury's (1983) advocacy of protection to prevent American deindustrialization for defense reasons—see my analyses in Bhagwati (1985c, 1985e, 1986c). For a different emphasis, more skeptical of antiprotectist arguments and EP strategy, see Streeten (1982).

36. The theory has been synthesized in Bhagwati (1971), and there is also a splendid short treatment by Srinivasan (1987) in his entry on distortions for *The New Palgrave*.

37. For the original analysis of this problem, see Bhagwati (1980). Further discussion of the question can be found in Bhagwati, Brecher, and Srinivasan (1984).

References

Balassa, Bela. 1971. *The Structure of Protection in Developing Countries*. Baltimore: Johns Hopkins University Press.

Balassa, Bela. 1978. Exports and Economic Growth: Further Evidence. *Journal of Development Economics* (June): 181–189.

Balassa, Bela. 1983. External Shocks and Adjustment Policies in Twelve Less-Developed Countries: 1974–76 and 1979–81. Paper presented to the annual meeting of the American Economic Association, San Francisco, December.

Balassa, Bela. 1984. Adjustment to External Shocks in Developing Economics. World Bank Staff Working Paper 472. Washington, DC.

Balassa, Bela, and Carol Balassa. 1984. Industrial Protection in the Developed Countries. *World Economy* (June): 179–196.

Balasubramanian, V. N. 1984. Incentives and Disincentives for Foreign Direct Investment in Less Developed Countries. *Weltwirtschaftliches Archiv*: 720–735.

Baldwin, Robert. 1982. *The Inefficacy of Trade Policy*. Frank D. Graham Memorial Lecture, Essays in International Finance 150. Princeton, N.J.: Princeton University, Department of Economics.

Baldwin, Robert. 1985. Ineffectiveness of Protection in Promoting Social Goals. *World Economy* (June): 109–118.

Behrman, Jere. 1984. Rethinking Global Negotiations: Trade. In J. Bhagwati and J. Ruggie, (eds.), *Power, Passions, and Purpose*. Cambridge, Mass.: MIT Press.

Bhagwati, Jagdish. 1968. The Theory and Practice of Commercial Policy. Frank D. Graham Memorial Lecture, Essays in International Finance 8. Princeton, NJ: Princeton University, Department of Economics.

Bhagwati, Jagdish. 1971. The Generalized Theory of Distortions and Welfare. In J. Bhagwati et al. (eds.), *Trade, Balance of Payments and Growth: Essays in Honor of C. P. Kindleberger*. Amsterdam: North Holland.

Bhagwati, Jagdish. 1973. The Theory of Immiserizing Growth: Further Applications. In M. Connolly and A. Swoboda (eds.), *International Trade and Money*. Toronto: University of Toronto Press.

Bhagwati, Jagdish. 1978. *Anatomy and Consequences of Exchange Control Regimes*. Cambridge, MA: Ballinger for National Bureau of Economic Research.

Bhagwati, Jagdish. 1980. Lobbying and Welfare. *Journal of Public Economics* (December): 355–363.

Bhagwati, Jagdish. 1982a. Shifting Comparative Advantage, Protectionist Demands, and Policy Response. In J. Bhagwati (ed.), *Import Competition and Response*. Chicago: University of Chicago Press.

Bhagwati, Jagdish. 1982b. Directly-Unproductive, Profit-Seeking (DUP) Activities. *Journal of Political Economy* (October): 988–1002.

Bhagwati, Jagdish. 1985a. *Wealth and Poverty: Essays in Development Economics*, vol. 1. Ed. by Gene Grossman. Cambridge: MIT Press.

Bhagwati, Jagdish. 1985b. *Dependence and Interdependence: Essays in Development Economics*, vol. 2. Ed. by Gene Grossman. Cambridge: MIT Press.

Bhagwati, Jagdish. 1985c. Protectionism: Old Wine in New Bottles. *Journal of Policy Modeling* (Spring): 23–33.

Bhagwati, Jagdish. 1985d. Growth and Poverty. Michigan State University Center for Advanced Study of International Development Occasional Paper 5. East Lansing.

Bhagwati, Jagdish. 1985e. Export Promotion as a Development Strategy. In T. Shishido and R. Sato (eds.), *Essays in Honor of Saburo Okita*. Boston: Auburn House.

Bhagwati, Jagdish. 1986a. *Investing Abroad*. Esmee Fairbairn Lecture. Lancaster, England: University of Lancaster.

Bhagwati, Jagdish. 1986b. "VERs, Trade and Foreign Investment." Paper presented to the Western Economic Association Conference, San Francisco, July.

Bhagwati, Jagdish. 1986c. Rethinking Trade Strategy. In J. Lewis and V. Kallab (eds.), *Development Strategies Reconsidered*. Washington, DC: Overseas Development Council.

Bhagwati, Jagdish, R. Brecher, and T. N. Srinivasan. 1984. DUP Activities and Economic Theory. *European Economic Review* (April): 291–307.

Bhagwati, Jagdish, R. Brecher, E. Dinopoulos, and T. N. Srinivasan. 1987. *Quid pro quo* Investment and Policy Intervention: A Political-Economy-Theoretic Analysis. *Journal of Development Economics*, forthcoming.

Bhagwati, Jagdish, and E. Dinopoulos. 1986. *Quid pro quo* Investment and Market Structure. Paper presented to the Western Economic Association Conference, San Francisco, July.

Bhagwati, Jagdish, and V. K. Ramaswami. 1963. Domestic Distortions, Tariffs and the Theory of Optimum Subsidy. *Journal of Political Economy* (February): 44–50.

Bhagwati, Jagdish, and T. N. Srinivasan. 1979. Trade Policy and Development. In R. Dornbusch and J. Frenkel (eds.), *International Economic Policy: Theory and Evidence*. Baltimore: Johns Hopkins University Press.

Bhagwati, Jagdish. 1983. *Lectures on International Trade*. Cambridge: MIT Press.

Brecher, R., and C. Díaz-Alejandro. 1977. Tariffs, Foreign Capital and Immiserizing Growth. *Journal of International Economics* (November): 317–322.

Cairncross, A. 1962. *Factors in Economic Development*. London: Allen and Unwin.

Chenery, H., S. Shishido, and T. Watanabe. 1962. The Pattern of Japanese Growth, 1914–1954. *Econometrica* (January): 98–139.

Cline, W. 1982. Can the East Asian Model of Development Be Generalized? *World Development* (February): 81–90.

Cline, W. 1985. Reply. *World Development* (April).

Dervis, K., J. de Melo, and S. Robinson. 1981. A General Equilibrium Analysis of Foreign Exchange Shortages in a Developing Economy. *Economic Journal* (December): 891–906.

Desai, P. 1979. Alternative Measures of Import Substitution. *Oxford Economic Papers* (November): 312–324.

Donges, J. 1976. A Comparative Study of Industrialization Policies in Fifteen Semi-Industrial Countries. *Weltwirtschaftliches Archiv*, 626–659.

Dornbusch, R. 1986. Impacts on Debtor Countries of World Economic Conditions. Paper presented at a Seminar on External Debt, Saving and Growth in Latin America, International Monetary Fund, Washington, DC, October 13–16.

Feder, G. 1983. On Exports and Economic Growth. *Journal of Development Economics* (April): 59–73.

Feenstra, R., and J. Bhagwati. Tariff Seeking and the Efficient Tariff. In J. Bhagwati, (ed.) *Import Competition and Response*. Chicago: University of Chicago Press.

Fields, G. 1984. Employment, Income Distribution and Economic Growth in Seven Small Open Economies. *Economic Journal* (March): 74–83.

Findlay, R. 1984. Trade and Development: Theory and Asian Experience. *Asian Development Review*: 23–42.

Finger, J. M. 1982. Incorporating the Gains from Trade into Policy. *World Economy* (December): 367–377.

Goldstein, M., and M. S. Khan. 1982. Effects of Slowdown in Industrial Countries on Growth in Non-oil Developing Countries. International Monetary Fund Occasional Paper 12. Washington, D.C.

Grais, W., J. de Melo, and S. Urata. 1986. A General Equilibrium Estimate of the Effects of Reductions in Tariffs and Quantitative Restrictions in Turkey in 1978. In T. N. Srinivasan and J. Whalley (eds.), *General Equilibrium Trade Policy Modelling*. Cambridge: MIT Press.

Hamada, K. 1974. An Economic Analysis of the Duty-Free Zone. *Journal of International Economics* (August): 225–241.

Harris, R. 1986. Market Structure and Trade Liberalization: A General Equilibrium Assessment. In T. N. Srinivasan and J. Whalley (eds.), *General Equilibrium Trade Policy Modelling*. Cambridge: MIT Press.

Harrod, R. 1951. *The Life of John Maynard Keynes*. New York: Harcourt and Brace.

Helleiner, G. K. 1977. Transnational Enterprises and the New Political Economy of United States Trade Policy. *Oxford Economic Papers* (March): 102–116.

Hufbauer, G., and J. Schott. 1985. *Trading for Growth: The Next Round of Trade Negotiations*. Washington, DC: Institute for International Economics.

Hughes, H., and A. Krueger. 1984. Effects of Protection in Developed Countries on Developing Countries. In R. Baldwin and A. Krueger (eds.), *The Structure and Evolution of Recent U.S. Trade Policy*. Chicago: University of Chicago Press for National Bureau of Economic Research.

Kaldor, N. 1966. *Causes of the Slow Economic Growth of the United Kingdom*. Cambridge: Cambridge University Press.

Kravis, I. 1970. Trade as a Handmaiden of Growth: Similarities between the Nineteenth and Twentieth Centuries. *Economic Journal* 8 (December): 50–72.

Krueger, Anne. 1961. Export Prospects and Economic Growth: India: A Comment. *Economic Journal* (June): 436–442.

Krueger, Anne. 1974. The Political Economy of the Rent-Seeking Society. *American Economic Review* (June): 291–303.

Krueger, Anne. 1978. *Foreign Trade Regimes and Economic Development: Liberalization Attempts and Consequences*. Cambridge, MA: Ballinger for National Bureau of Economic Research.

Krueger, Anne. 1980. Trade Policy as an Input to Development. *American Economic Review* (May): 288–292.

Krueger, Anne. 1982. *Trade and Employment in Developing Countries: Synthesis and Conclusions.* Chicago: University of Chicago Press.

Krueger, Anne, and B. Tuncer. 1980. Estimating Total Factor Productivity Growth in a Developing Country. World Bank Staff Working Paper 422. Washington, DC.

Lal, D., and S. Rajapatirana. 1987. Trade Regimes and Economic Growth in Developing Countries. *World Bank Research Observer* 2, 2 (July): 189–217.

Lavergne, R., and G. K. Helleiner. 1985. United States Transnational Corporations and the Structure of United States Trade Barriers: An Empirical Investigation. United Nations, New York.

Lewis, W. A. 1980. The Slowing Down of the Engine of Growth. *American Economic Review* (September): 555–564.

Little, I., T. Scitovsky, and M. Scott. 1970. *Industry and Trade in Some Developing Countries.* Oxford: Oxford University Press.

Mayer, W. 1984. Endogenous Tariff Formation. *American Economic Review* 74, 5 (December): 970–985.

Meade, J. 1951. *Trade and Welfare: The Theory of International Economic Policy,* vol. 2. Oxford: Oxford University Press.

Michaely, M. 1977. Exports and Growth: An Empirical Investigation. *Journal of Development Economics* (March): 49–53.

Michalopoulos, C., and K. Jay. 1973. Growth of Exports and Income in the Developing World: A Neoclassical View. Agency for International Development Discussion Paper 28. Washington, D.C.

Miller, M. 1985. Big U.S. Semiconductor Makers Expected to Sue over "Dumping" of Japanese Chips. *Wall Street Journal,* October 1.

Nam, Chong-Hyun. 1986. Trade Policy and Economic Development in Korea. International Economics Research Division, Development Research Department, World Bank.

Nishimizu, M., and S. Robinson. 1984. Trade Policies and Productivity Change in Semi-industrialized Countries. *Journal of Development Economics* (October): 177–206.

Nurkse, R. 1953. *Problems of Capital Formation in Underdeveloped Countries.* Oxford: Basil Blackwell.

Nurkse, R. 1959. *Patterns of Trade and Development.* Wicksell Lectures. Stockholm: Almquist and Wicksell.

Olson, M. 1971. *The Logic of Collective Action: Public Goods and the Theory of Groups.* Cambridge: Harvard University Press.

Prebisch, R. 1952. Problemas Teóricos y Prácticos del Crecimiento Económico. United Nations, Economic Commission for Latin America.

Prebisch, R. 1984. Five Stages in My Thinking about Development. In P. Bauer, G. Meier, and D. Seers (eds.), *Pioneers in Development*. Oxford: Oxford University Press.

Ranis, G. 1985. Can the East Asian Model of Development be Generalized? *World Development* (April): 543–545.

Riedel, J. 1984. Trade as the Engine of Growth in Developing Countries, Revisited. *Economic Journal* (March): 56–73.

Ruggie, J. (ed.). 1983. *The Antinomies of Interdependence: National Welfare and the International Division of Labor*. New York: Columbia University Press.

Seabury, P. 1983. Industrial Policy and National Defense. *Journal of Contemporary Studies*: 5–15.

Srinivasan, T. N. 1986a. Development Strategy: Is the Success of Outward Orientation at an End? In S. Guhan and M. Shroff (eds.), *Essays on Economic Progress and Welfare*. Oxford: Oxford University Press.

Srinivasan, T. N. 1986b. International Trade for Developing Countries in the Nineteen Eighties: Problems and Prospects. In J. Dunning and M. Usui (eds.), *Economic Independence*. London: Macmillan.

Srinivasan, T. N. 1987. Distortions. In *The New Palgrave*. London: Macmillan.

Streeten, P. 1982. A Cool Look at "Outward-Looking" Strategies for Development. *World Economy* (September): 159–169.

Uzawa, H. 1969. Shihon Jiyuka to Kokumin Keizai (Liberalization of Foreign Investments and the National Economy). *Economisuto*, pp. 106–122 (in Japanese).

Yoffie, D. 1983. *Power and Protectionism*. New York: Columbia University Press.

25   Poverty and
         Public Policy

The problem of poverty is particularly acute in India. With 14 percent of the world's population, we have the misfortune of having almost twice as large a share of the world's poor. Indeed, as I shall presently underline, the question of poverty and its amelioration has been at the center of our concerns from the beginning of our planning efforts almost four decades ago. Little therefore can be said on it that some distinguished Indian economist has not already said. In some ways, therefore, to talk on the design of public policy for poverty to an Indian audience is to carry coal to Newcastle or, as the old saying goes, to teach your grandmother how to suck eggs. Nonetheless, I hope to provide a fresh perspective by putting the problem into an explicit analytical framework that permits alternative policy designs to be sharply defined and contrasted. I also intend to draw on international experience to put our efforts and problems into both historical and comparative perspectives.

25.1   Alternative Policy Designs: Indirect versus Direct Routes

It is possible, and perhaps even interesting, to speculate whether poverty would increase or diminish if governments followed a regime of *laissez faire*, letting poverty and all else take a natural course. Few will dispute however the proposition that, except in singular circumstances, public policy should assist in accelerating the amelioration of poverty.[1] The key question relates rather to the appropriate design of such public policy.

Economics trains us to think of ends and means, of targets and policy instruments. With the amelioration of poverty as the target, the policy instruments designed to achieve that target can be divided into two main classes: (1) the *indirect* route, i.e., the use of resources to accelerate growth and thereby impact on the incomes and hence the living standards of the poor, and (2) the *direct* route, i.e., the public provision of minimum-needs-oriented education, housing, nutritional supplements and health, and transfers to finance private expenditures on these and other components of the living standards of the poor.

The primary distinction between the two approaches is between creating income (and hence consumption) and providing consumption (in kind or through doles). The latter necessarily involves redistribution between different groups unless the financing comes from external resources; the former need have no such component, though complementary policies to bias the creation of income toward the poor, which I discuss below, will often involve redistributive elements. Indeed, within both approaches, the direct and the indirect, we can consider the question of "biasing" or "targeting" the policies in favor of the poor. Thus, the indirect growth-oriented route may be supplemented by policies facilitating borrowing and investment by the poor or by redistributive land reform, whereas the direct route may be explicitly targeted towards the poor via means tests or choice of health and nutritional programs that overwhelmingly benefit the poor.[2]

The optimal policy design should generally involve a mix of these two approaches unless the "productivity" of either in achieving the target substantially dominates that of the other. Thus, for instance, if growth will concentrate increased incomes entirely among the nonpoor and there is no upward mobility either, the relevant rate of return to the indirect route is zero. Indeed, if growth can be shown to be immiserizing to the poor, this return would be negative! In this event, the case for exclusive reliance on the direct route becomes overwhelming, with two critical and compelling provisos: first, that it should be shown that the factors, both economic and political, that constrain the effectiveness of the growth process in indirectly reducing poverty do not simultaneously and equally afflict the direct route and prevent it as well from effectively providing benefits to the poor, and second, that the neglect of the growth process, even if its indirect impact on poverty through increased incomes for the poor is negligible or harmful, would impair in the long run the ability of the state to sustain the expenditures required to finance the more productive direct route, especially in an economy with a growing population.

In economic thinking and in economic policy, the pendulum can swing with astonishing regularity. In the 1950s and 1960s the growth-based indirect route to attacking poverty was the more fashionable, though the direct route was both recognized and far from neglected. By the 1970s however, one could hear nothing but a gloomy refrain that the indirect route of growth was ineffective and, worse still, harmful to the poor, and only the direct route in the shape of a Basic Needs strategy was the answer.

By the 1980s, the indirect route was restored to grace and seen in a more favorable light, the alarmist assertions of experience with it were being discredited, and the matching difficulties that attend on traveling the direct route were being increasingly appreciated.

Before I proceed to an analysis of the lessons that we have learnt in consequence of this extensive debate, and what they suggest for Indian public policy on poverty, let me turn to two fallacies that have plagued this debate, making it captive to fractious and misplaced ideological confrontations.

Growth: Target or Instrument?

The first fallacy asserts that growth was a rival target to poverty rather than an instrument to ameliorate it. Indeed, in the 1970s it was commonplace to claim that we had been preoccupied in the 1950s and 1960s with growth, rather than the alleviation of poverty, as our objective. This was the central theme of writings on developmental economics, originating with varying degrees of explicitness from international agencies such as the International Labor Organization (ILO).

Let me confess that this contention may be both true and false. I say this, not in the frolic spirit of my good friend, the philosopher Sidney Morgenbesser. On being asked by one of his radical students during the Cultural Revolution whether he thought that Chairman Mao was right in arguing that a proposition could be both true and false, he instantly replied: I do and I don't. Rather, I wish to enter the *caveat* that developing countries form such a mosaic ranging from city states such as Hong Kong to subcontinents such as China, or from democracies such as India to dictatorships such as today's Chile and yesterday's Argentina, that almost everything is valid somewhere and almost nothing is true everywhere. I must confess that the enormity of this problem was brought home to me when I, coming from India with its population of over 750 million, recently visited Barbados with a population of 250,000. Asked to talk at the Central Bank, I found myself in the governor's office on the top floor, only to realize that you could practically look out over the island. There was evidently no sensible distinction here between partial- and general-equilibrium analysis! So, to shield myself, I reminded my audience of the famous Mao-Nasser story. On a visit to Peking, Nasser looked unhappy. Concerned, Mao inquired what was wrong. Nasser answered: I am having trouble with my neighbors, the Israelis. How many are there, asked

Mao. About two million, Nasser replied. Oh, said Mao, which hotel are they staying at?

I have no doubt that *somewhere* growth became an objective in itself during the early postwar years. Indeed, it may well have in countries where elites identified GNP, and associated size of the national economy, with respectability and strength in the world economy and polity. But, in influential developmental planning circles,[3] GNP was simply regarded as an *instrumental* variable, which would enable one to impact on the ultimate and *central objective* of reducing poverty.

In fact, in India, which was the focus of intellectual attention during the 1950s for several reasons, reduction of poverty was explicitly discussed during the late 1950s and early 1960s as the object of our planning efforts. In the Planning Commission, where the great Indian planner Pitambar Pant headed the Perspective Planning Division, work was begun at this time on this precise issue. How could we provide "minimum incomes" for meeting the basic needs of all?

The objective being to provide such minimum incomes, or to ameliorate poverty, rapid growth was decided upon as the principal instrumentality through which this objective could be implemented. Let me explain why we came to focus on growth as the central weapon in our assault on poverty.

I can speak to the issue, as it happens, from the immediacy of personal experience. I returned to India during 1961, to join the Indian Statistical Institute which had a small think tank attached to Pant's Division in the Planning Commission. Having been brought in by Pant to work as his main economist, I turned immediately to the question of strategy for minimum incomes. I assembled such income distribution data as were then available for countries around the world, both functional and personal, to see if anything striking could be inferred about the relationship between the economic and political system and policies and the share of the bottom three or four deciles. You can imagine the quality of these data then, by looking at their quality now almost a quarter of a century later. Nor did we have then anything systematic on income distribution in the Soviet Union. And we had admittedly nothing on China which was an exotic reality, about to make its historical rendezvous with the Cultural Revolution, but already suggesting to the careful scholar that its economic claims were not to be taken at face value.

The scanning of, and reflection on, the income distribution data suggested that there was no dramatic alternative for raising the poor to minimum incomes except to increase the overall size of the pie. The intercountry differences in the share of the bottom deciles, where poverty was manifestly rampant, just did not seem substantial enough to suggest any alternative path. The strategy of rapid growth was therefore decided upon, in consequence of these considerations, as providing the only reliable way of making a *sustained*, rather than a one-shot, impact on poverty.

I will presently discuss this strategy and its success or failure in some depth.[4] However, let me return to stress the theme that growth therefore was indisputably conceived to be an instrumental variable, not as an objective per se. It is not surprising therefore that the strange assertions to the contrary by institutions and intellectuals who belatedly turned to questions of poverty in the 1970s have provoked many of us who were "present at the creation" to take the backward glance and then to turn again to stare coldly and with scorn at these nonsensical claims.

Gilbert Etienne, the well-known sociologist-cum-economist, whose heretical and brilliant work on India's Green Revolution I shall soon cite, has exclaimed: "The claim that development strategies in the 1950s and 1960s overemphasized growth and increases of the GNP at the cost of social progress is a surprising one! ... Equally peculiar is the so-called discovery of the problem of poverty" (1982, pp. 194, 195). T. N. Srinivasan and B. S. Minhas, both of whom have worked with great distinction on questions of poverty and who followed me to join Pant's think tank, have been even more critical. I am afraid that I have also been moved to write (1984) in a personal vein: "... on hearing the claim that poverty had only recently been discovered and elevated as a target of development, I fully expected to find that chapter 1 of my 1966 volume on *The Economics of Underdeveloped Countries* would be titled Growth; behold my surprise when it turned out to be Poverty and Income Distribution!"

Growth and Ideology: Pull-up versus Trickle-down

The more egregious fallacy, however, has been for several economists and ideologues to assume that the growth-oriented indirect route must necessarily be a conservative option. The more liberal and radical among them have therefore tended to rush to their computers and their pens each time any evidence suggests that the indirect route may be productive of results, seeking to discount and destroy any such inference.

I have never quite understood this phenomenon, for the growth strategy was conceived by us at the start of our planned assault on poverty as an *activist*, interventionist strategy. The government was to be critically involved in raising internal and external savings, in guiding if not allocating investment, in growing faster so that we could bring gainful employment and increased incomes to more of the poor. Whether the policy framework we worked with in India to use the indirect growth-based approach was an appropriate one, and whether therefore this route was efficiently exploited, is a different but critical issue which I will presently address.

Since, therefore, the growth strategy was an activist strategy for impacting on poverty, I have always preferred to call it the *pull-up*, rather than the *trickle-down*, strategy. The trickle-down phrase is reminiscent of "benign neglect," and its use in the first Reagan administration to accompany efforts at dismantling elements of the welfare state has imparted yet other conservative connotations to it. The pull-up phrase, on the other hand, correctly conveys a more *radical* interventionist image and the intellectual context in which it emerged was defined by the ethically-attractive objective of helping the poor.

Lest you think that words do not matter, remember your Orwell or the endless battle for the dominant ground between euphemisms and calling a spade a spade. My favorite example from economics is the business schools' preferred use of the word "multinationals," nudging your subconscious in the direction of multilateralism and hence evoking the image of a benign institution, and the radicals' insistence on calling these international corporations "transnationals," strongly suggesting transgression.

25.2   The Indirect, Growth-Based Route: Experience and Lessons

Let me then turn to the experience with the indirect, growth-based route.

Immiserizing Growth?

It should be conceded immediately that it is easy enough for economists to construct cases where growth will bypass or will even harm the poor. The pious know that affluence can impoverish one's soul; the economist need not be surprised that it can impoverish one's neighbors too. In fact, in my early scientific work in the late 1950s, I developed a theory of immiserizing growth which established the conditions which yielded a yet stronger possibility: growth would immiserize oneself.[5] The precise demonstration concerned an economy where increased productivity led to a sufficiently large deterioration in the terms of trade whose adverse effect outweighed the primary gain from growth. Thus, imagine that extension work leads to farmers raising grain production but this, in turn, lowers the grain price so much that the farmers' income falls instead of rising.

As it happens, the paradox that affluence can immiserize oneself is possible to demonstrate even if the affluence comes from transfer payments. Thus international trade theorists have examined conditions under which the recipient of aid may be immiserized rather than enriched, so that a gift horse turns out to be a Trojan horse instead.[6]

Such self-immiserizing possibilities naturally require more stringent conditions than the possibility that *your* affluence causes *my* misery (even when envy is wholly absent). Thus, consider the scenario where the more affluent farmers adopt the new seeds, grain prices fall and the marginal farmers who have not adopted the new techniques find their stagnant output yielding less income in consequence. In such a situation, the green revolution immiserizes the poor and, the radicals would hope, may usher in the red revolution.

It is not true that we were unaware of such possibilities, that growth could be a disturbingly uneven process. But the key question was: What should this awareness imply for *policy*? Evidently, you would first need to assess both how such unacceptable outcomes would arise in your specific circumstances and the probability of their arising in practice. Next, the policy set would have to be augmented to include, in addition to growth, further suitable instruments to prevent these unpleasant outcomes. The former requires judgment, based on empirical assessment; the latter, the possibility of finding suitable and feasible policy instruments.

Let me illustrate by reference to the possibility of immiserizing growth that I cited earlier. In the international context, my 1958 model of immiserizing growth was widely considered relevant, including by the distinguished Ragnar Nurkse in his 1959 *Wicksell Lectures*, because of the generally shared empirical assessment that the export markets of the developing countries were extremely tight, implying that the terms of trade would deteriorate sharply as a consequence of growth in the developing countries. But this assessment, not validated by subsequent analysis and events, did *not* imply that growth policy had to be abandoned. Rather the growth policy had to be supplemented by an appropriate policy of import substitution, so that we would have what Nurkse called "balanced growth."[7]

At least in the Indian context, the view taken was that, in the *long haul*, such adverse possibilities could not be the probable, central result of expanding incomes for any sizable group of the poor, but that rather the process would pull up increasing numbers into gainful work.

While, as I have remarked, the limited and sketchy income distribution data revealed little of any consequence on how to improve this pull-up process, there was awareness that the pull-up effect on poverty would improve, ceteris paribus, if institutional mechanisms such as special credit facilities for the poor were developed, necessary land reforms were implemented, and the access of the scheduled and backward classes (which have disproportionate numbers among the poor) to the opportunities provided by a growing economy were enhanced through preferential schemes. *Policy-induced pro-poor bias* was thus to be introduced into the growth process, to offset and outweigh any bias in the opposite direction that the market, interacting with inherited political and social forces, may imply.[8] The concern, therefore, was not with sustained immiserizing outcomes and how to cope with them but rather with the devising of policy instruments to bias the growth process towards greater efficacy of the pull-up effects.

There was also a distinct component, in the strategy, of the *direct* route, in the public provision of services such as clean water, sanitation, health services, and education. The primary thrust of the Indian strategy, however, was to rely on the indirect route. This decision reflected the constraints imposed by the appalling dimensions of India's poverty, and the democratic politics of the country, on our ability to finance a significant reliance instead on the direct route over a sustained period. Noting the former constraint on our planning and fiscal efforts, the famous Polish economist, Michal Kalecki, whose left-wing credentials were never in doubt, had remarked during his visit to India in the early 1960s: "the trouble with India is that there are too few exploiters and too many exploited."

The efficacy of the Growth Strategy

India was the focus of interest and attention in the 1950s; distinguished economists and intellectuals descended on it the way they do on China today. Our ideas were influential and came to be shared widely in the efforts by many developing countries to accelerate their growth rates. I have argued elsewhere (1984) that there was a definite optimism during the 1950s and 1960s both that growth could be rapid and that it would indeed impact on poverty. But by the early 1970s and later, there were increasing claims that called the efficacy of this strategy into doubt. The criticisms took two different forms:

1. Growth was irrelevant and proverty had increased regardless. A 1977 ILO study (quoted by Etienne, 1982, p. 198) asserted that "The number of

rural poor in Asia has increased and in many instances their standard of living has tended to fall. Perhaps, surprisingly, this has occurred irrespective of whether growth has been rapid or slow or agriculture has expanded swiftly or sluggishly."

2. Growth had in fact accentuated poverty: it made the rich richer and the poor poorer. Ghose and Griffin argued in 1979 that "it is not lack of growth but its very occurrence that led to deterioration in the conditions of the rural poor" (quoted by Etienne, 1982, p. 198).

In assessing these claims of increasing immiserization, or mere stagnation in living standards, of the poor, it is necessary to examine not just the evidence and its plausibility, but also whether there was indeed satisfactory growth for the pullup strategy to work where it is alleged to have failed. I am persuaded that the evidence is far less alarming than what is claimed, that where growth has been rapid it has impacted on poverty, that in the Indian case the growth strategy has produced inadequate results because the policy framework for producing growth has produced inadequate growth in the first place, and hence that the Indian experience suggests lessons in favor of superior growth-producing policies rather than lessons against using the growth-based indirect route to affecting poverty.

International Experience

Let me first stress that countries such as South Korea and Taiwan which have grown much faster than us in the postwar period to date, have had a substantial impact on their living standards. To see the force of the argument, that India's poor growth performance has affected its prospects for raising living standards, it is useful to understand the force of compound interest. "Had India's GDP grown as rapidly from 1960 to 1980 as South Korea's, it would stand at $531 billion today rather than $150 billion— surpassing that of the UK, equal to that of France, and more than twice that of China. India's per capita income would have been $740 instead of $260; even with the benefits of growth inequitably distributed, it is not unreasonable to believe that most of the poor would have been substantially better off." [9] I shall, therefore, return to the question of our policy framework for promoting growth, especially as the moves toward a New Economic Policy were designed to remedy the deficiencies which afflicted that framework.

Indian Experience

But, even with the relatively dismal growth rate we have had, the evidence is more compelling that some dent has been made on poverty than the doom-and-gloom analysts have often suggested.

The evidence of the National Sample Surveys of consumption is an important source of information here. So are household income and other surveys. Before I sketch what these imply, it is pertinent to remark that many noneconomist observers have been skeptical of the reliability of this type of evidence. Distinguished social and economic anthropologists such as M. N. Srinivas, Louis Dumont, and Polly Hill have remarked, with varying degrees of candidness, on the quality of Indian data on the subject, and, mind you, these are generally regarded as possibly the best statistics in the developing world. The concepts are inadequate; the implementation yet poorer. Polly Hill (1984, p. 495) has written in frustration and with evident exaggeration that, India's pride, "the All-India National Sample survey is perhaps the most remarkable example of wasted statistical effort in the entire world!" Srinivas has complained of the brilliant mathematical statisticians who devise and direct the massive questionnaires to be filled out by field investigators that "this kind of study cannot be left to the hit and run method of an inferior class of investigators who commute from the cities to nearby villages." It is not entirely unreasonable therefore to rely, at least for an alternative view of the matter, on the results from the "naked eye" anthropological-cum-longitudinal approach to make the required inferences.

Here, I must confess that I have been much impressed by the analysis of Gilbert Etienne (1982), who has argued convincingly from firsthand evidence from extended stays in a number of Indian villages, which he surveyed earlier, that poverty has indeed been impacted on, and that too where agricultural growth has occurred. Etienne's technique is to do what I call "doing in India what you do in China," i.e., disregard the numbers (which in any case are not available in a reliable fashion for China which has only recently opened itself to a measured degree of external and internal scrutiny and independent analysis) and carefully assess what you see. He has gone back over time to several villages that he had looked at intensively, often more than a decade earlier. And he observes, asks, examines, and records: much like Jan Myrdal (1966) in his celebrated Report from Liu Ling, but with more anthropological, sociological, and economic discipline and less poetry. The results are what we did expect: growth has indeed pushed several of the poor on in life. Doubtless, some poor have been left behind; others have been impoverished even further. But then, as Arthur Lewis has wisely remarked, it is inherent in the developmental process that some see the opportunities and seize them, leaving others behind until they wish to and can follow. Politics and economics can both constrain the capacity of the laggards to follow. Thus, for instance, the green revolution in some instances may well have polarized the distribution of property in the countryside, enriching the farmers with access to credit, fertilizers, and irrigation and immiserizing those who did not. But, if Etienne is correct, this has not happened in anything like a significant degree in his cross section of villages in India. Of course, what Etienne observes may be true only for "his villages." But his unscientific sample is compensated in some degree by the closer scrutiny and care that the scientific surveys evidently do not possess. What do the latter show?

As it happens, even the statistical evidence from these surveys is corroborative, if not wholly conclusive, of the fact that the proportion of the poor below an accepted poverty line has diminished and strongly suggestive of the hypothesis that growth has been a proximate cause of the reduction in poverty.

The recently published estimates of a team headed by B. S. Minhas, who has distinguished himself for pioneering work on estimating poverty along with other noted economists such as Dandekar and Rath (1971), are perhaps the most carefully constructed sets of poverty statistics on the subject.[10] They utilize new consumer prices for updating the base-year poverty lines and reexamine the recent calculations of the Planning Commission which had suggested a dramatic decrease in the proportion of the poor in the last decade.[11] It is noteworthy that, while their calculations reduce the degree of improvement estimated by the Planning Commission, they conclude that "the incidence of poverty in 1983 in terms of proportion of people below the poverty line was substantially lower than the corresponding estimates for the 1970s" (Minhas et al., 1987, p. 47), though there is no evidence of a fall in the absolute *numbers* below the poverty line and, if anything, there may be a small rise in these numbers, reflecting of course the dual pressure and double squeeze of a low growth rate and a rising population.

Again, I must note that Minhas's early work (1970, 1971) had drawn attention to the fact that the incidence of poverty goes down in years of good harvests and up in years of bad harvests. This phenomenon is reconfirmed in his recent estimates (Minhas et al., 1987).

My distinguished former student, K. Sundaram of the Delhi School of Economics, who has done notable work with Suresh Tendulkar (1983a, 1983b, 1983c) on the poverty problem, has correctly reminded us (1986) that this relationship requires us to be cautious in inferring any trend in decline of the poverty ratio from the two observations for 1977–78 and 1983 on whose basis we have had to work as far as the estimates based on the NSS Consumer Expenditure Surveys are concerned.[12] The poverty ratio has fluctuated sharply with agricultural production and the time-series evidence suggests that no trend should be inferred unless more data points are available: the two pleasant observations may simply be reflective of good harvests rather than a better trend.

But this very critique or cautious reminder implies that indeed, as Minhas had noted, there *is* some evidence for the favorable impact of growth on poverty, at least in the rural sector where 80 percent of the poor are to be found.

In fact, Montek Ahluwalia's classic 1978 paper on rural poverty and agricultural performance had analyzed all-India time-series data to underline this precise link. This work has also provoked controversy, with the radical response being provided by Saith (1981) who has drawn the opposite conclusions while working with the same data set. Careful analysis of the two papers by Subodh Mathur (1985), examining both the econometrics and the economics of the issue, reaches the conclusion that "aggregate all-India data support Ahluwalia's contention that agricultural growth reduces poverty."

However, Srinivasan (1985), who has raised several compelling objections to the econometric procedures and inferences in Saith's analysis, also cautions that Ahluwalia's results, which are only confirmed by inclusion of additional data which have become available since 1978 (Ahluwalia, 1985), should not be treated as a decisive test of the pull-up hypothesis. For, the data show that "there was no upward trend in net domestic product of agriculture per head of rural population—there was very little to trickle-down at the all-India level." Discussing also the related work by Bardhan (1982), utilizing some state-level data of still less reliability, Srinivasan has concluded that meaningful tests with more and better longitudinal data than have been available are necessary, by regions or areas differentiated by high and low growth rates, before firm conclusions can be drawn on the issue. But the existing analyses do favor the presumption, for the present, that the effect of growth is to reduce, rather than to bypass or exacerbate, poverty.

Other sources of evidence also suggest that, while poverty remains appalling in its dimensions, it has diminished at least as a proportion of the population. Thus, a careful examination of the estimates of income distribution for India by Bhalla and Vashishtha (1985) concludes that household income surveys (as distinct from NSS-surveys-based estimates discussed above) indicate that if households are ranked by per capita incomes, neither the bottom 20 percent nor the bottom 40 percent exhibit any significant change in their share of income between 1964–65 and 1975–76. At the same time, of course, per capita income had increased, so that a constant share would imply a higher absolute level, indicating a decline in poverty. Again, however, these surveys suffer from serious difficulties of comparability, arising from differences in definitions and coverage. Comparable data sets relate only to 1970–71 and 1975–76 for the large rural sector, and these indicate favorable conclusions again.

Furthermore, the two recent NCAER longitudinal, nationwide surveys of identical households for 1970–71 and 1981–82 have suggested that, even in the lowest three deciles, there has been a significant rise of households across the poverty line. The proportions who did so are as high as 46, 41, and 54 percent for the lowest, the second-lowest, and the next deciles. The results are indeed remarkable, suggesting both that poverty can be impacted and that it has been. Again, however, trends cannot be inferred from two observations, and there are problems, noted by Dr Sundaram (1986, pp. 21–28), with the sample size relating to the poor households and with the fact that there is no way one can infer whether the households changed their fortunes due to increased productivity and income or due to demographic factors. But, when all this is noted, the fact remains that these surveys yield results that do not provide support for the hypothesis of stagnation or immiserization in the living standards of the poor.

Growth and the New Economic Policy
If then much of this evidence, with all warts duly registered, suggests some success in assaulting poverty, and this too with only our limited success in enhancing growth, the key question rather becomes: Why has our growth been so disappointing?

Our record of growth is admittedly one of acceleration over the pre-Independence period and compares well with that of countries in the nineteenth century. But we need to remember that this is the case with most of the developing countries in the postwar period and that, compared to *them*, we appear as unfortunate laggards.

In fact, most of us were pleasantly surprised, despite our optimism, at the remarkable growth rates turned up by the developing countries after World War II. The reasons are probably self-evident. Whereas the pre-Industrial Revolution growth rates were dependent largely on capital accumulation, they increased in the post-Industrial Revolution period because of unprecedented technical change. The developing countries, by contrast, could combine increasing rates of external and internal savings with influx of off-the-shelf technology and thus grow very rapidly. Many did.

The productivity of the increased rates of investment has, however, varied, depending on the policy framework within which the economy operated. There is sufficient evidence, in my judgment, that our policy framework degenerated by the early 1960s on critical fronts, confining us to a trend growth rate of roughly 3.5 percent per annum or about 1.5 percent per capita growth rate annually.[13]

Despite an almost three-quarters increase in our fixed investment rate over the period 1950–84, we had little improvement in the growth rate. If we break the period into 1951 to 1965 (coinciding roughly with the Nehru and pre-wheat-revolution era) and 1968 to 1984 (omitting the two severe drought years of 1965–66 and 1966–67), the trend growth rate is 3.88 percent in the former period and 3.75 percent in the latter, there being no statistically significant difference between the two rates (Bhagwati and Srinivasan, 1984). The decadal average growth rate of the 1950s (3.59 percent), 1960s (3.13 percent), and 1970s (3.62 percent) are also similar. Evidently, we got our policy framework wrong.

Economic analysis is often unable to detect unique causes of the phenomena being explained. In this instance as well, the contributory factors are by no means the only two I shall cite, but they are certainly among the most important.[14] The first relates to the excessive and explosive growth of controls over industry and foreign trade until the most recent changes; the second concerns the failure to exploit the advantage of foreign trade.

The growth of controls turned our governmental intervention, so necessary in a developing country, into a counterproductive one. A government of "don'ts" will stifle initiative; it will also divert entrepreneurial energies into a number of wasteful rent-seeking and other directly unproductive profit-seeking (DUP) activities. By contrast, a government of "do's," such as the one which the successful countries of the Far East have had, is likely to harness its people's energies more productively, even if its prescriptions are mistaken from time to time. It is an increasing appreciation of these questions, and the sense that our Kafkaesque maze of controls could not possibly be sensible, that led me and others during the late 1960s, and recently many others still, to call for a progressive dismantling of this monstrous constraint on our economic efforts. I may remind you in particular that I. G. Patel, who oversaw our economic policy with distinction for much of this period, recently took the occasion of the Kingsley Martin Memorial Lecture to join us in our corner and ask dramatically for a "bonfire" of the industrial licensing system.[15]

As for the inability we have exhibited in exploiting the gains from trade in a world economy that grew at unprecedented rates in the 1950s and

1960s and which still continues to absorb rapidly expanding exports from the developing countries, the explanation lies in what social scientists call the "self-fulfilling prophecy." Despite all evidence to the contrary, our planning and policy framework was continually based on what economists call "export pessimism." The failure to use the exchange rate actively to encourage exports as in other countries, the inflexibilities (introduced by the pervasive controls) which must handicap the ability to penetrate and hold fiercely competitive foreign markets, the protection and hence attractiveness of the home market: these policies produced a dismal export performance, while other successful countries expanded their exports rapidly and gained in economic growth greatly.[16] How dismal our export performance has been can, in fact, be understood readily by noting that our share in world exports was only 0.41 percent by 1981, having fallen almost continually since 1948 when it was 2.4 percent. This certainly affected even our industrial sector's growth. Other countries which began with a much smaller industrial base are not only exporting more manufactures than India but, what is more striking, catching up with India in the absolute size of their manufacturing sector. The size of Korea's manufacturing sector, for example, was less that 25 percent of India's in 1970 (measured as value added). By 1981, it was already up to 60 percent. Korea's manufactured exports, negligible in 1962, amounted by 1980 to nearly four times those of India's![17] Simply put, we missed the bus.

I agree that we could not have grown as fast as the Far Eastern economies, the Gang of Four (as I christened them with success many years ago) or the Four Tigers, because we had a much larger agricultural base. Our agriculture, I agree again with Professors Dantwala (1970) and Srinivasan (1982) among others, grew about as fast as could be expected and charges of its neglect are seriously exaggerated.[18] But to infer from this that India could not have grown much faster than it did is to forget again the force of compound arithmetic: nonagricultural growth, in an economy geared to rapidly expanding trade and nonagricultural production, would have provided a growing impetus to the economy, steadily overwhelming the agricultural sector's importance in both value added and employment.

Growth Patterns
How would such a shift to an export-promoting strategy have affected the pull-up process of creating more gainful employment? The proponents of the import-substituting strategy, on which we continued to place total reliance instead, have suggested that the export-promoting strategy would have been less productive of employment, even if it may have produced

more efficiency. Quite aside from the fact that the empirical evidence suggests that the export promoting strategy implies in practice faster growth and impact on poverty, there is yet further evidence that, even in the short run, export promotion has been associated with more labor-intensive investment and production. I refer here to the important findings of Professor Anne Krueger (1983) and her associates in her major three-volume study of this subject. The export-promoting strategy has not merely led to more rapid income growth but also produced greater increase in demand for labor, ceteris paribus. A major reason is the labor intensive-ness of export industries in the export-strategy-led countries.

Growth and political Economy Constraints

Why did these serious deficiencies afflict our planning efforts? The question belongs to the new field of political economy. In particular, my theory of the causes and consequences of proliferation controls is that initially they were the product of ideas and ideology, then they led to the growth of interests, and now as the ideas and ideology have shifted these interests pose a critical obstacle to the desired shift of strategy.

At the outset, few of us realized that controls could proliferate in the way they did. In the early 1950s industrial controls appeared to be sensible instruments, to allocate resources in directions worked out in the Planning Commission. Industrial licensing would eliminate excess capacity by reg-ulating entry; scarce resources would be channeled in optimal directions. Pretty soon, however, the promotional agencies such as the DGTD had largely turned into restrictive and regulatory agencies instead; and in no time we were operating in a regime where one could not even exceed licensed capacity or diversify production lines in any way without retribu-tion. A straitjacket had evolved from what seemed like a reasonable econo-mic approach to investment allocation.

This economic regime spawned its own interests. The rentier society it yielded, with entrepreneurs enjoying squatters' rights, created a business class that wanted liberalization in the sense of less hassle, not genuine competition. The bureaucrats, however idealistic at the outset, could not but have noticed that this regime gave them the enormous power that the ability to confer rents generates. The politics of corruption also followed as politicians became addicted to the use of licensing to generate illegal funds for elections, and then for themselves. The iron triangle of businessmen, bureaucrats and politicians was born around the regime that economists and likeminded ideologues had unwittingly espoused.

As ideas have now changed, through the process of "learning by undoing," these interests now stand in the way of rapid, if any, change. While the erstwhile partnership of the Prime Minister Rajiv Gandhi and the then Finance Minister Vishwanath Pratap Singh was apparently determined to take the necessary steps to start on a program of removing the straitjacket on the Indian economy, and their leadership was evidently of great importance in defining sharply a promise of new policies, the hesitations and obstacles from both the intellectuals of the older vintage and the interests of the iron triangle have been manifest, raising acutely the question whether the early momentum for change can be politically maintained.[19]

Pro-Poor-Bias Policies and Political Economy Constraints
I am afraid that the pro-poor-bias policies have equally run into difficulties, arising from unequal asset distribution and hence unequal political power at the grassroots level. The degree of success of policies aimed at improving the pull-up effects of the growth process is evidently a function of the extent to which "countervailing power" is available to the poor through the presence of social action groups and politically viable proposition parties.[20]

Here again, however, I should like to emphasize that, in the longer run, substantial growth itself is a factor generating the necessary countervailing power through the marketplace, by raising the demand for labor and increasing its opportunity cost. I hypothesize that the relative success of tenancy reform in Gujerat must have also some relationship to the fact that many of those who "lost their lands" to it had little incentive to fight and evade the reform in view of the fact that they already had shifted to urban careers and the transaction costs of the efforts at evasion were in consequence just too high.

Radical Restructuring: Why Not?
Let me add some remarks about radical restructuring of the asset structure and transition to fuller socialism à la China and Cuba as possible alternatives to our policies for creating a sustained impact on poverty.

I am afraid that the skepticism that marked the enthusiasm for the Chinese experiment appears to have only been reinforced by later developments. In the 1950s it was often thought that, if only a Chinese revolution could be ushered into the developing countries, its triumphs in eliminating poverty could be replicated. The skepticism lingered because systematic scrutiny of the Chinese claims was not possible; and one legitimately wondered whether absolute poverty had truly been reduced and also whether growth could be sustained within the new framework raising questions about the sustainability of the immediate impact on poverty. Now, after the window has steadily opened wider in the aftermath of the Cultural Revolution and the failures of the Great Leap Forward, we are not sure at all.

We know now that the barefoot doctors generally wore shoes, that their professional competence occasionally exceeded only marginally that of the average grandmother, and that doctors have dragged their feet almost as successfully as elsewhere when assigned to go to the countryside, indeed to the point where Liu-shao-chi's major crimes were declared by the Red Guards and official pronouncements to include sabotage of the campaign to carry doctors to the rural areas. We are further told that the Chinese concept of equality was intracommune, *not* between communes: the rich communes did not generally share their affluence with the destitute ones. And we are now told by the new regime that more than 10 percent of the Chinese population may be below a rather austere poverty line.

These tantalizing glimpses into China's assault on poverty will almost certainly not be allowed to develop into a fuller picture as in other developing countries, since careful and unfettered scholarly scrutiny is unlikely to be possible in the degree necessary. I am afraid therefore that we shall have to reconcile ourselves to the uncomfortable situation where we do not know for certain the extent to which China's ex ante egalitarian methods failed ex post, and whether the failures were due to discordance between their announced and their true objectives or rather due to the limitations of the methods used to achieve the announced objectives.

Equitable Asset Distribution
On the other hand, the proposition that a more equitable distribution of assets at the start of the growth process will generally imply that the new incomes will, in turn, be distributed better is of course quite plausible. In the end, over a longer period, the forces that generate inequality will tend to unequalize the outcomes. But over a generation or two, the net outcomes would be more equal than if we were to start with unequal distribution of assets. The experience of South Korea and Taiwan, where Japanese occupation is largely credited with having brought about the initial asset-ownership equalization, underlines this near-truism well. Also the experience in India, where several micro-level studies have shown the link between asset-ownership and new-income distribution to be a significant factor in a fair number of cases, only underlines the wisdom of supplementing the

growth-oriented approach with policy measures that counter this bias (Tendulkar, 1983).

A policy of "redistribution with growth," where the redistribution of assets *precedes* the growth that is designed to impact on poverty, has therefore been advocated by several distinguished economists.[21] If such redistribution can be undertaken politically, and its implementation is not disruptive economically (as was the case with Soviet collectivization),[22] we can only rejoice.

From Income to Consumption

We also face, even when incomes have reached the poor, a final set of dilemmas.

First, as the sociologists of poverty have long known, the poor may spend their incomes on frills rather than on food. As the Japanese proverb goes: each worm to his taste; some prefer nettles. Perhaps you have heard of the seamen's folklore that recounts the story of the sailor who inherited a fortune, spent a third on women, a third on gin, and "frittered away" the rest.

In fact, there is now considerable econometric evidence, reviewed splendidly by Behrman and Deolalikar (1987c), that supports the common sense view that increases in income do not automatically result in nutritional improvement even for very poor and malnourished populations.[23] Their high income elasticities of expenditure on food reflect a strong demand for the nonnutritive attributes of food (such as taste, aroma, status, and variety), suggesting strongly that income generation will not automatically translate into better nutrition.

For those of us who feel that certain basic needs ought to be satisfied, this tragic assertion of what economists have come to call rather extravagantly "consumer sovereignty" leaves us confronting a familiar moral-philosophical issue. Should we actively intervene so that the poor are seduced into better fulfillment of what we regard as their basic needs? I do. In fact, I see great virtue in quasi-paternalistic moves to induce, by supply and taste-shifting policy measures, more nutrient food intake, greater use of clean water, among other things, by the poor. In thus compromising the principle of unimpeded and uninfluenced choice, for the poor and not for others, evidently I adopt the moral-philosophical position that I do not care if the rich are malnourished from feeding on too many cakes but do if the poor are malnourished from buying too little bread, when their incomes can buy them both proper nourishment if only they were to choose to do so. In this, I am in the ethical company of Sofya (Sonia) Marmeladova in Dostoevsky's *Crime and Punishment* who, in turning to prostitution to support her destitute mother, sacrifices virtue for a greater good.

Whose Consumption: Gender

Next, in addition to the first, is the other dilemma that even when households have consumed what is desirable and adequate on a per capita basis, its distribution within the household may be such as to deprive the weaker members, such as females, of an adequate access to the consumption basket. In the 1970s I was somewhat isolated (Bhagwati, 1973) as an economist in being seriously interested in the sex-bias that was visible in the statistics on educational enrollments, literacy, infant mortality, and nutritional levels, much of the evidence coming from anthropological findings and other surveys.[24]

Now, almost a decade later, many others have followed and are actively analyzing the problem so that we now know more, though not enough, about this key component of our problems in improving living standards. Among the important findings, I should note the Behrman and Deolalikar (1987b) result that the intrahousehold discrimination may not merely be in the form of lower quantities of food/nutrients allocated to weaker members such as females but may also occur in the form of greater fluctuations in the quantities allocated to them in response to adverse food price changes.

Additional policy instruments are evidently necessary to offset this bias if the elimination of poverty is to occur more rapidly and equitably. The task here is clearly harder than simply generating more income, and progress in the matter may have to depend on the spread of education in the first place.

25.3 The Direct Route: Experience and Lessons

What then have we learned about the direct route, its efficacy, and productivity?

It is important to enter the *caveat* immediately that the key issue is not whether this route produces results but rather its productivity relative to that of the indirect route. It would be astonishing indeed if greater public health expenditures or direct income transfers did not produce some improvement in the living standards of the poor, even though it is not beyond the ingenuity of economists to produce paradoxes of immiserization in this area as well.[25]

Eating Your Cake and Having It Too

At the outset, it is worth noting that there are significant externalities for growth itself from expenditures on publicly provided services. Many of us have been surprised, though pleasantly this time, by the realization that we had exaggerated our early fears about the trade-off between "consumption" expenditures (such as financing education and health) and investment expenditures aimed at growth and hence ultimate impact on poverty. It is difficult today to appreciate the widespread notion in the 1950s that primary education was simply a "natural right," whose implementation reflected the availability of resources. That it was possibly an important means for raising productivity and hence growth and therefore reducing poverty, and that it could therefore be justified also on consequentialist ethics, was a later phenomenon. This holds equally for health expenditures which were viewed with inhibited enthusiasm also for fear that they would exacerbate population growth. Only later were they considered to have a possible productivity-enchancing effect on populations that could otherwise be working at impaired efficiency or even to lead to a lowering of the birth rates if, by reducing infant mortality and increasing survival rates, they enabled parents to produce fewer babies to wind up with their target family size in a steady state.

Much of the currently available indirect or "macro" evidence on this issue has recently been ably reviewed by Bela Balassa (1983). Thus, for instance, Correa (1970) has argued that improvements in health (proxied by reductions in death rates and in work days lost) and nutrition (measured as increases in calorie intake) added 0.12 to 0.93 percentage points, and improvements in education (measured as the average level of education of the working force) added 0.05 to 0.53 percentage points to the rate of economic growth in nine Latin American countries during 1950–62. Again, Norman Hicks (1980) has estimated that a ten-year increase in life expectancy raises per capita GDP growth rates by 1.1 percentage points and a 10 percentage point increase in literacy rates by 0.3 percentage points.

But, of course, health and education expenditures affect growth *and* the other way around. Simple regressions therefore can be misleading and simultaneous estimation is necessary. David Wheeler (1980) and Robin Marris (1982) have done precisely this, the former for 88 developing countries for 1960–73 and 1970–73 as well as pooled data for the whole period, the latter for 37 middle-income and 29 low-income countries for 1965–73 and for 1973–78. Wheeler's findings indicate significant impact on growth rates from increases in calorie intake and in literacy rates. Marris's study found that primary education enrollments had a favorable effect on growth rates of per capita income whereas increased life expectancy and family planning helped through reductions in the rate of growth of population (Balassa, 1983, pp. 10–11).

But more compelling is the direct, "micro" evidence linking health, in particular, to productivity. I should note here the recent econometric work on Indian data by Deolalikar (1988), though there is by now a substantial literature that analyzes the issue both theoretically and econometrically.

More is known now, therefore, to wean us away from the fear that such educational and health expenditures are *necessarily* at the expense of growth. What is equally pleasurable is the fact that many of these arguments apply with yet greater force when the expenditures are addressed to the poorer segments of the population. The case for undertaking more such expenditures, with focus on the poor, consistent with being engrossed in the growth strategy, is therefore now seen to be stronger than ever before.[26] I think we have learnt that, within reasonable margins, we may then be able to eat our cake and have it too. Social expenditures could improve the welfare of the poor directly and also indirectly through growth which in turn would impact on poverty. But beyond these margins, the trade-off remains an issue.

Political Economy Constraints

At the same time, as Lakdawala (1986) has recently emphasized, income expansion itself can be a precondition for utilization of the publicly-provided services. For, such income can "take care of the incidental expenditure incurred in using these facilities" (p. 392).[27]

In fact, this observation underlines the fact that the political economy factors that have prompted and also constrained the measures to offset the antipoor biases in the growth-based indirect route are unlikely to disappear when we turn to the direct route. Thus, nutrition programs through schools go to those who attend schools and therefore will not seriously impact on the poor whose children do not get to school: a phenomenon already noted by researchers in the 1970s. The successful impartation of a pro-poor bias in direct expenditures for living standards improvement is, in our experience, likely therefore to face difficulties somewhat parallel to those faced in the pursuit of the pro-poor-bias policies in the indirect, growth-based route.[28] In the 1970s, when the indirect growth-based route's productivity was being significantly understated in the international discussions, as I have already argued, the productivity of the direct route was being overstated by ignoring the political-economy constraints that afflict the latter as well.

Overstated Productivity?

The productivity of the direct route may have been overstated also through an overoptimistic inference from two allegedly outstanding success stories widely cited in this literature: Sri Lanka and Costa Rica.

As it happens, however, a brilliant analysis of Sri Lanka by Bhalla (1985a, 1985b) and then by Bhalla and Glewwe (1985, 1986) has called this story into question. Apparently Sri Lanka's claim to attention consisted in substantial direct expenditures and also splendid performance on indices such as literacy, life expectancy, and infant mortality rates which were then assumed to be a result of these direct expenditures. But these indicators were already remarkably high by 1948 itself: a fact that was not allowed for in the argumentation which relied astonishingly on single-time-period cross-country comparisons.[29] When *changes* in these indices are considered for 1960–78, it turns out that Sri Lanka's performance on these criteria shrinks into mediocrity. Of six indicators analyzed, for only two—life expectancy and the death rate—does Sri Lanka do better than average, and, if a strict statistical test is used, only the death rate survives to fit this bill.

With this reversal of conclusions based on changes in, rather than on levels of, the performance indicator,[30] the question arises whether the *low* performance of Sri Lanka in this recent postwar period reflects low growth rates, reinforcing exactly the opposite conclusion to what is presumably being contended! As it happens, estimates of Sri Lanka's per capita income growth show that, during 1960–78, Sri Lanka had a negative annual growth rate of − 1.2 percent along with only five other countries including Burundi, Benin and Angola! Can it be that the diversion of expenditures away from growth to ("social") direct expenditures affected growth adversely and hence impacted on the poor more than the direct expenditures helped them? Or were economic policies so bad that growth was affected adversely and impacted on the poor, and increased direct expenditures had to be undertaken to offset the adversity for the poor? In short, the mediocrity of Sri Lanka's recent performance on the living standards of the poor may be explainable by hypotheses that only sustain the advisability of assigning primacy to the growth-oriented route to ameliorating poverty.

Of course we can still speculate as to what made Sri Lanka in 1948 such an impressive performer on living standards. Was it high growth rates or high social expenditures? Was the productivity of the latter high due to specific, manageable problems such as malaria which could be eradicated relatively easily with public-health anti-malaria programs and therefore has little value in inferring general prescriptions? Only detailed historical analysis, carefully sifting among different hypotheses, can throw light on the issue at hand. In the meantime, the ready overoptimism that the early writings on Sri Lanka's postwar experience reflected and spread must be suspended.

25.4   Concluding Observations

In the end, therefore, I see no quick fix to our immense poverty problem. We can debate whether resources can be moved further at the margin from the indirect, growth-based route to the direct, minimum needs route. But the most important lesson seems to be that, *within* each route, we can and must get significantly more returns than we have to date.

Within the indirect route, the New Economic Policy initiatives point in the right direction and, if successfully brought to fruition, promise a significantly greater impact on poverty in the next two decades than we have had with our inappropriate policy framework and dismal economic performance. Within the direct route, there is continual improvement being sought of course and an economist has little expertise to offer. Efforts such as integrated, block-level development programs and the introduction of the village community health workers, etc., are the fruit of ongoing processes of learning by experience: they ought to yield results over time.[31]

I have two further thoughts to conclude my lecture. That our low growth rate seems to have reduced our poverty ratio but left the absolute numbers of the poor at an appalling level of over 300 million, suggests not merely that we must pursue doggedly the New Economic Policy initiatives. It also underlines the critical role of a successful population control program. Derailed by the draconian measures during the emergency, this program needs to be pushed vigorously if the fruits of growth are not to be squandered on supporting increasing numbers rather than improving the well-being of fewer people.

At the same time, the political economy constraints on both the indirect and direct routes' ability to reach the poor more effectively, despite governmental attempts at offsetting these biases, underline the overreaching importance of the role of voluntary agencies and social action groups. The ex ante intention of the enlightened sectors of our governments will not effectively translate in many instances into ex post outcomes in our assault on poverty without the active association of such agencies.

These social action groups do not merely aid the poor directly but also by acting as watchdogs that assist the poor in securing effective access to the programs designed by the government for their benefit. This is the lesson, for example, of the Legal Aid Programme in India where the coopting of such agencies has turned out to be an essential ingredient in making the program more productive.

Indeed, private and public altruism have, therefore, a critically complementary role in creating a shared success in the assault on poverty.

Notes

This is the text of the 12th Vikram Sarabhai Memorial Lecture, delivered in Ahmedabad on August 28, 1987. I have profited greatly from conversation with and comments from Surjit Bhalla, Anil Deolalikar, Atul Kohli, Paul Streeten, T. N. Srinivasan, K. Subbarao, K. Sundaram, Raaj Sah, and Suresh Tendulkar. I have taken the opportunity to draw extensively on an earlier treatment of some of these issues in my Michigan State University Distinguished Speakers Series Lecture (Bhagwati, 1985b) on "Growth and Poverty," sharpening and extending, however, the analysis presented there and drawing more extensively on Indian experience.

1. Such a singular circumstance could be a Myrdal-type "soft" state or a predatory state; the former would preclude effective action whereas the latter would guarantee malign intervention.

2. There are two main "antipoverty" programs in India, the Integrated Rural Development Programme (IRDP) and the National Rural Employment Programme (NREP). Both of these are targeted at the poor and would classify as part of the indirect, growth-based strategy in my typology since they are intended to bias the creation of assets and income in favor of the poor. Thus, for instance, the IRDP aims at targeting the poor in the growth process by providing them with opportunities, in terms of transfer of assets, training etc., for income expansion. The NREP, on the other hand, creates rural employment to build assets such as roads and therefore can be seen as an attempt at biasing the income-expansion process in favor of the poor by promoting labor-intensive technologies and activities and also, insofar as the assets in turn create income differentially in favor of the poor, via the resulting capital formation as well. In practice, however, the asset formation, such as road building, may be negligible as when the new roads are immediately washed away, reducing therefore the result in this instance to what it would have been under a transfer payment to the poor as in my *direct* route. There is, therefore, an extensive debate in India whether the operation of the IRDP and NREP programs, while intended as part of the pro-poor-bias indirect (growth) strategy, are not de facto reducing to the pro-poor-bias direct (transfer) strategy. On this issue, see the interesting articles by Rath (1985) and Sundaram and

Tendulkar (1985). I am indebted to Sundaram and Tendulkar for drawing my attention to these questions.

3. Here, I refer to economists such as myself, B. S. Minhas, K. N. Raj, and T. N. Srinivasan who were actively involved in planning efforts within institutions such as the Indian Planning Commission, and to planners such as Pitambar Pant. That some of the purely academic development economists were preoccupied with models that addressed growth per se, and would discover poverty as an explicit target and as an issue for analysis many years later, is an observation compatible with the fact that some of us at the center of planning efforts were not so afflicted.

4. I have dealt with the growth strategy at much greater length in my 7th Sir Purshotam Thakurdas Memorial Lecture (Bhagwati, 1987) which should therefore be read as a companion piece to the present lecture.

5. See Bhagwati (1958). The model used was developed earlier by Johnson (1955) to examine the interactions between growth and trade.

6. Such a paradox may be described as implying an Invisible Shakedown (by the donor). See Bhagwati, Brecher and Hatta (1984).

7. In economic jargon, one has a case for an optimum tariff here. Again, later developments in the theory of immiserizing growth show how it can be ruled out if optimum tariffs are imposed; see Bhagwati (1968, 1986c).

8. On Indian policies with regard to biasing credit facilities towards the poor, see Tendulkar's (1983) excellent review.

9. This graphic comparison and scenario come from Myron Weiner's (1986) interesting analysis of the political economy of India's appallingly slow growth rate, with much of which I am in agreement. I should stress that, in using South Korea's growth rate to make this comparison compelling, I do not mean to imply that we could have improved our economic performance quite that much!

10. Minhas, Jain, Kansal, and Saluja (1987).

11. These estimates continue to use the definition of poverty line adopted by the Indian Planning Commission in the mid-1970s.

12. These surveys are available on an annual basis almost continually up to 1973–74 but only for 1977–78 and 1983 thereafter.

13. Many statistical tests have cast continuing doubt on the question whether our growth rate has finally accelerated.in the last decade. All plausible ways of splitting the period 1950 to 1984 turn up conclusions that suggest unchanged trends. See Bhagwati and Srinivasan (1984) and Joshi and Little (1986), among other analyses of these trends.

14. 1 have discussed these and other explanations at greater length in the 7th Sir Purshotam Thakurdas Memorial Lecture (Bhagwati, 1987).

15. See Patel (1986). He is fully aware, of course, that the elimination of this system is a *goal* whereas the *process* will require extremely careful management. Whether the growth of interests, supportive of this system, over its existence in the past three decades will pose insuperable obstacles to its removal is an issue in political economy that I discuss at greater length elsewhere: Bhagwati (1986a, 1986d, 1987).

16. This is not the place to report yet again on the numerous research projects that showed in the 1960s and 1970s how export pessimism had been unjustified but had led to dismal export, and in turn to dismal economic, performance in many countries. Useful reviews of this research are now available; see Bhagwati (1986b) and Balassa (1986).

17. See Bhagwati and Srinivasan (1984).

18. Ibid.

19. That the interests followed the ideology and now constrain a shift in the ideology is a thesis different from that of Professor Pranab Bardhan (1985) who differs from me both in starting from the interests and also in relating them wholly to public sector losses and therewith to slow growth. I have discussed the role of public sector savings in India's slow growth at some length in the Sir P.T. Memorial Lecture, again emphasizing the early role of ideas and the *subsequent* role of interests.

20. Evidence on the relationship of party politics to the successful implementation of antipoverty programs have been ably analyzed recently by the Princeton political scientist Atul Kohli (1987).

21. See Adleman and Morris (1973) and Chenery et al. (1974). In this generic class of strategies, I would also include an altogether different kind of proposal that I made for Indian planners to consider in 1973 in the Lal Bahadur Shastri lectures. I argued for a fractional nationalization of land in each village (or similar unit), which could be set apart to form a Chinese-style commune. Those destitute who wished to follow the slow and protracted route offered by the Indian strategy of predominantly relying on growth to impact on poverty, would take their chances there; but those who wished to gain employment and some income right away would have immediate access to the commune à la China. The combination of both strategies, and access to either *by choice*, would mean that the destitute were not forced into the Indian option of freedom but slow poverty alleviation *or* into the Chinese option of freedom through forced removal to the communes but more rapid and, one hoped, sustained removal of abject poverty.

22. These are hazards that do not seem to have afflicted China since the elimination of the kulaks seems to have occurred principally during the long civil war itself; see Desai (1975).

23. For a fine review of India's experience with interventions to fill nutritional gaps at the household level, see Subbarao (1987).

24. See, for instance, Sundaram (1973), Rosenzweig and Schultz (1982), Sen (1984) and Kakwani (1986).

25. A successful antitmalaria program, for example, may increase population pressure, reduce real wages, affect nutritional intake of the poor, and disproportionately depress their living standards inclusive of their own life expectancy. Economists who like immiserization paradoxes on the indirect route should look out for them on the direct route as well.

26. On the other hand, the difficulties of directing the expenditures on primary education and health effectively to the poorer classes when the elites control the political system need to be recalled again. Questions such as the relative priority attached to primary and higher education in state spending and its relationship to the class nature of the state have been discussed at length by economists such as Samuel Bowles and myself. See the extended analysis in my "Education, Class Structure and Income Equality" (1973a).

27. This observation is also corroborated by the careful study of the regional variations in the impact of India's antipoverty programs by Subbarao (1985).

28. This is evident also from the important in-depth analysis of the working of the NREP program in Gujarat State by Indira Hirway (1986a, 1986b).

29. This argument was advanced by Isenman (1980) and Sen (1981), among others.

30. The lack of availability of data on changes in levels of direct expenditures prevents us from drawing more compelling inferences here, as noted by Bhalla (1985) himself. Also, such evidence as is available on changes in educational expenditures does not help the critics of Bhalla either; see Bhalla and Glewwe (1986) and the later animated comments by Pyatt (1987) and Isenman (1987) and the riposte by Glewwe and Bhalla (1987).

31. See the excellent review of these problems and their possible solutions in Lakdawala (1985), based on his tenure as Deputy Chairman of the Planning Commission.

References

Adelman, Irma, and Cynthia Taft Morris. 1973. *Economic Growth and Social Equity in Developing Countries* Stanford, CA: Stanford University Press.

Ahluwalia, Montek S. 1976. Inequality, Poverty and Development. *Journal of Development Economics* 3.

Ahluwalia, Montek S. 1978. Rural Poverty and Agricultural Performance in India. *Journal of Development Studies* 14.

Ahluwalia, Montek S. 1985. Rural Poverty, Agricultural Production and Prices: A Re-examination. In John Mellor and Gunvant Desai (eds.), *Agricultural Change and Rural Poverty: Variations on a Theme by Dharam Narain*. Baltimore: Johns Hopkins University Press.

Ahluwalia, Montek S., Nicholas G. Carter, and Hollis B. Chenery. 1979. Growth and poverty in developing countries. *Journal of Development Economics 6*.

Balassa, Bela. 1983. Public Finance and Social Policy—Explanation of Trends and Developments. The Case of Developing Countries. DRDERS, World Bank Report No. DRD 65 Washington, DC: World Bank, November.

Balassa, Bela. 1986. The importance of trade for developing countries. Paper presented to the IBRD-TDRI Conference on "The MTN and Developing Country Interests," Bangkok, Thailand. October–November.

Bardhan, Pranab. 1982. Poverty and the "Trickle-down" in Rural India: A Quantitative Analysis. Berkeley University of California. Mimeo.

Bardhan, Pranab. 1986. *The Political Economy of Development in India*. Oxford: Basil Blackwell.

Behrman, Jere R., and Anil B. Deolalikar. 1987a. Health and Nutrition. In Hollis B. Chenery and T. N. Srinivasan (eds.), *Handbook on Economic Development*, vol. 1. Amsterdam: North Holland, 15.

Behrman, Jere R., and Anil B. Deolalikar. 1987b. How Do Food Prices Affect Individual Nutritional and Health Status? A Latent Variable Fixed-Effects Analysis. Mimeo.

Behrman, Jere R., and Anil B. Deolalikar. 1987c. Will Developing Country Nutrition Improve with Income? A Case Study for Rural South India. *Journal of Political Economy 95*, 3.

Bhagwati, Jagdish N. 1958. Immiserizing Growth: A Geometrical Note. *Review of Economic Studies* (June). Reprinted in Robert Feenstra (ed.), *Essays in International Economic Theory: The Theory of Commercial Policy*, vol. 1. Cambridge: MIT Press, 1983.

Bhagwati, Jagdish N. 1966. *The Economics of Developing Countries*. World University Library Series. London: Weidenfeld and Nicolson.

Bhagwati, Jagdish N. 1968. Distortions and Immiserizing Growth: A Generalization. *Review of Economic Studies 35*, 104 (October).

Bhagwati, Jagdish N. 1973a. Education, Class Structure and Income Inequality. *World Development 1*, 5.

Bhagwati, Jagdish N. 1973b. India in the International Economy. Lal Bahadur Shastri Lectures. Hyderabad, India. Reprinted in J. N. Bhagwati, *Essays in Development Economics: Wealth and Poverty*, vol. 1. Oxford: Basil Blackwell, 1985, 2.

Bhagwati, Jagdish N. Development Economics: What Have We Learned? *Asian Development Review 2*, 1.

Bhagwati, Jagdish N. 1985a. Gandhi's Break with the Past: Is India's Economic Miracle at Hand? *The New York Times*, June 9.

Bhagwati, Jagdish N. 1985b. Growth and Poverty. Michigan State University Center for Advanced Study of International Development. Occasional Paper No. 5. East Lansing, MI.

Bhagwati, Jagdish N. 1986a. Controls Must Be Liberalized: An interview with Jagdish Bhagwati. *Frontline* (May–June).

Bhagwati, Jagdish N. 1986b. Export-Promoting Trade Strategy: Issues and Evidence. World Bank Policy Issues Paper, VPERS. Washington, DC: World Bank. Forthcoming in *World Bank Research Observer* (1988).

Bhagwati, Jagdish N. 1986c. Immiserzing Growth. *The New Palgrave*. London: Macmillan.

Bhagwati, Jagdish N. 1986d. New Economic Policy: Plea for Faster Domestic Liberalization. Interview by P. K. Roy in *The Economic Times*, September 16.

Bhagwati, Jagdish N. 1987. Indian Economic Performance and Policy Design. 7th Sir Purshotam Thakurdar Memorial Lecture. Bombay: Indian Institute of Bankers, December 21.

Bhagwati, Jagdish N., Richard Brecher, and Tatsuo Hatta. 1984. The generalized Theory of Transfers and Welfare: Bilateral Transfers in a Multilateral World. *American Economic Review* 73, 4 (September).

Bhagwati, Jagdish N., and T. N. Srinivasan. 1984. Indian Growth Strategy: Some Comments. *Economic and Political Weekly* (December).

Bhalla, Surjit S. 1985a. Is Sri Lanka an Exception: A Comparative Study of Living Standards. In T. N. Srinivasan and Pranab Bardhan (eds.), *Rural Poverty in South Asia*. New York: Columbia University Press.

Bhalla, Surjit S. 1985b. Sri Lankan Achievements: Facts and Fancy. In T. N. Srinivasan and Pranab Bardhan (eds.), *Rural Poverty in South Asia*. New York: Columbia University Press.

Bhalla, Surjit S., and Paul Glewwe. 1985. Living, Standards in Sri Lanka in the Seventies: Mirage and Reality. Washington, DC: World Bank Development Research Department.

Bhalla, Surjit S., and Paul Glewwe. 1986. Growth and Equity in Developing Countries: A Reinterpretation of the Sri Lankan Experience. *World Bank Economic Review* 1, 1 (September).

Bhalla, Surjit S., and P. Vashistha. 1985. Income Distribution in India—A Reexamination. In T. N. Srinivasan and Pranab Bardhan (eds.), *Rural Poverty in South Asia*. New York: Columbia University Press.

Chenery, Hollis B., Montek S. Ahluwalia, C. L. G. Bell, John Duloy, and Richard Jolly. 1974. *Redistribution with Growth.* Oxford: Oxford University Press.

Correa, H. 1970. Sources of economic growth in Latin America. *Southern Economic Journal* 37.

Dandekar, V. M., and N. Rath. 1971. *Poverty in India* Bombay: Indian School of Political Economy.

Dantwala, M. L. 1970. From Stagnation to Growth. *Indian Economic Journal* 28, 2.

Deolalikar, Anil B. 1988. Does Nutrition Determine Labor Productivity in Agriculture? Wage Equation and Farm Production Function Estimates for Rural South India. *Review of Economics and Statistics* 70, 2 (May).

Desai, Padma. 1975. China and India: Development during the Last 25 Years. *The American Economic Review* 65, 2.

Dhar, P. N. 1986. Indian Economy: Past Performance and Current Issues. Paper presented to the Conference on the Indian Economy, Boston University, Boston, MA.

Dhar, P. N. 1987. The Political Economy of Development in India. *Indian Economic Review* 32, 1.

Etienne, Gilbert. 1982. *India's Changing Rural Scene, 1963–1979.* Oxford: Oxford University Press.

Glewwe, Paul, and Surjit S. Bhalla. 1987. A Response to Comments by Graham Pyatt and Paul Isenman. *World Bank Economic Review* 1, 3.

Hicks, Norman. 1980. Economic Growth and Human Resources. *World Bank Staff Working Paper*, No. 408. Washington, DC: World Bank.

Hill, Polly. 1984. The Poor Quality of Official Socio-economic Statistic Relating to the Rural Tropical World: With Special Reference to South India. *Modern Asian Studies* 18, 3.

Hirway, Indira. 1986a. *Abolition of Poverty in India.* New Delhi: Vikas.

Hirway, Indira. 1986b. *Wage Employment Programmes in Rural Development.* New Delhi: Oxford and IBH Publishing House.

Isenman, P. 1980. Basic Needs: The Case of Sri Lanka. *World Development* 8, 3.

Isenman, P. 1987. A Comment on "Growth and Equity in Developing Countries: A Reinterpretation of the Sri Lankan Experience" by Bhalla and Glewwe. *World Bank Economic Review* 1, 3.

Johnson, Harry G. 1955. Economic Expansion and International Trade. *The Manchester School* 23 (May).

Joshi, Vijay, and I. M. D. Little. 1986. Indian Macroeconomic Policies. Nuffield College, Oxford University. Mimeo.

Kakwani, Nanak. 1986. Is Sex Bias Significant? *World Institute for Development Economics Research.* Helsinki. December.

Kohli, Atul. 1987. Politics of Economic Liberalization in India. Department of Political Science, Princeton University. Mimeo.

Kreuger, Anne O. 1983. *Trade and Employment in Developing Countries: Synthesis and Conclusions.* Chicago: University of Chicago Press.

Lakdawala, D. T. 1986. Planning for Minimum Needs. Indulal Yagnik Memorial Lecture. In T. N. Srinivasan and Pranab Bardhan (eds.), *Rural Poverty in South Asia.* New York: Columbia University Press, 12.

Marris, Robin. 1982. Economic Growth in Cross Section: Experiments with Real Product Data, Social Indicators, Model Selection Procedures, and Policy Benefit/ Cost Analysis. Washington, DC: World Bank, Mimeo.

Mathur, Subodh C. 1985. Rural Poverty and Agricultural Performance in India: A Comment. *Journal of Development Studies.*

Minhas, Bagicha S. 1970. Rural Poverty, Land Distribution and Development Strategy. *Indian Economic Review* 5, new series: 97–126.

Minhas, Bagicha S. 1971. Rural Poverty and Minimal Level of Living: A Reply. *Indian Economic Review* 6, new series: 69–77.

Minhas, B. S. L. R. Jain, S. M. Kansal, and M. R. Saluja. 1987. On the Appropriate Choice of Consumer Price Indices and Data Sets for Estimating the Incidence of Poverty in India. *Indian Economic Review* 22, 1.

Myrdal, Jan. 1966. *Report from a Chinese Village.* New York: Signet Books.

Nurkse, Ragnar. 1959. *Patterns of Trade and Development.* Wicksell Lectures. Stockholm: Almquist and Wicksell.

Patel, I. G. 1986. On Taking India into the Twenty-First Century (New Economic Policy in India). Kingsley Martin Memorial Lecture. *Modern Asian Studies* 21, 2.

Pyatt, Graham. 1987. A Comment on "Growth and Equity in Developing Countries: A Reinterpretation of the Sri Lankan Experience" by Bhalla and Glewwe. *World Bank Economic Review* 1, 3.

Rath, N. 1989. Garibi Hatao. *Economic and Political Weekly,* February, 9.

Rosenzweig, Mark, and Paul Schultz. 1982. Market Opportunities, Genetic Endowments and Intra-family Resource Distribution: Child Survival in Rural India. *American Economic Review* 72, 4 (September).

Saith, A. 1981. Production, Poverty and Prices in Rural India. *Journal of Development Studies* 17.

Sen, A. K. 1981. Public Action and the Quality of Life in Developing Countries. *Oxford Bulletin of Economics and Statistics* (November).

Sen, A. K. 1984. Family and Food: Sex Bias in Poverty. In *Resources, Values and Development*. Oxford: Basil Blackwell.

Srinivasan, T. N. 1979. Trends in Agriculture in India: 1949–50 to 1977–78. *Economic and Political Weekly* 15 (30, 31, 32, special number, August).

Srinivasan, T. N. 1982. Was Agriculture Neglected in Planning. Paper presented to the Golden Jubilee Seminar of the Indian Statistical Institute. Calcutta. December. Revised March 1982.

Srinivasan, T. N. 1985. Agricultural Production, Relative Prices, Entitlements and Poverty. In John Mellor and Gunvant Desai (eds.), *Agricultural Change and Rural Poverty: Variations on a Theme by Dharam Narain*. Baltimore: Johns Hopkins University Press.

Streeten, Paul. 1981. *First Things First: Meeting the Basic Human Needs in Developing Countries*. Oxford: Oxford University Press.

Subbarao, K. 1985. Regional Variations in Impact of Anti-poverty Programmes: A Review of Evidence. *Economic and Political Weekly* 20, 43 (October 26).

Subbarao, K. 1987. Interventions to Fulfill Nutrition Gaps at the Household Level: A Review of India's Experience. Paper prepared for a Workshop on Poverty in India, Queen Elizabeth House, Oxford University.

Sundaram, K. 1973. Education, Class Structure and Income Inequality: Further Evidence. *World Development*, 1, 6.

Sundaram, K. 1986. Growth, Inequality and Poverty: The Indian Experience. New Delhi: Centre for Policy Research, Chanakyapuri.

Sundaram, K., and S. D. Tendulkar. 1983a. Poverty Reduction and Redistribution in Sixth Plan: Population Factor and Rural-Urban Equity. *Economic and Political Weekly* 18, 38 (September 17).

Sundaram, K., and S. D. Tendulkar. 1983b. Poverty in the Mid-term Appraisal. *Economic and Political Weekly* 18 (November 5–12).

Sundaram, K., and S. D. Tendulkar. 1983c. Towards an explanation of Inter-regional Variations in Poverty and Unemployment in Rural India. In T. N. Srinivasan and Pranab Bardhan (eds.), *Rural Poverty in South Asia*. New York: Columbia University Press.

Sundaram, K., and S. D. Tendulkar. 1985. Integrated Rural Development Programme in India: A Case Study of a Poverty Eradication Programme. In S. Mukhopadhyay (ed.). *Case Studies on Poverty Programmes in Asia*. Kuala Lumpur, Malaysia: APDC.

Tendulkar, Suresh D. 1983. Rural Institutional Credit and Rural Development: A Review Article. *Indian Economic Review* 18, 1.

Weiner, Myron. 1986. The Political Economy of Growth in India. *World Politics* 38, 4.

Wheeler, David. 1980. Human Resource Development and Economic Growth in Developing Countries: A Simultaneous Model. World Bank Staff Working Paper, No. 407. Washington, DC: World Bank. July.

Name Index

Subject Index